PLINY

NATURAL HISTORY

VII

LCL 393

PLINY

NATURAL HISTORY

BOOKS XXIV–XXVII

WITH AN ENGLISH TRANSLATION BY

W. H. S. JONES

SECOND EDITION

HARVARD UNIVERSITY PRESS
CAMBRIDGE, MASSACHUSETTS
LONDON, ENGLAND

First published 1956
Reprinted 1966
Revised 1980
Reprinted 1992

ISBN 0-674-99432-9

Printed in Great Britain by St Edmundsbury Press Ltd,
Bury St Edmunds, Suffolk, on acid-free paper.
Bound by Hunter & Foulis Ltd, Edinburgh, Scotland.

CONTENTS

PREFACE

I WISH to thank Professor A. C. Andrews of the
University of Miami for the great help he has been
in the preparation of this volume. I sometimes refer
to him as A.C.A. Expert botanical knowledge is
essential for the solution of many problems that have
arisen, especially in the compilation of the *Index of
Plants*. My rough draft of this he revised, making
many additions: these amount to several pages.
For the errors that inevitably remain in my work I
alone am responsible.

My thanks are also due to the staff of the Cambridge School of Botany and to Professor C. O. Brink
of the same University.

PREFACE TO SECOND EDITION

PROFESSOR A. C. Andrews, to whose expert assistance
this volume owes so much, maintained a cumulative
list of corrections and improvements to the Index of
Plants in Pliny: all these are now incorporated, as
also is his acceptance of Fournier's contention, *Rev.
Phil.* 26 (1952) 187, that *populus* in XVI 73, 206, and
231 should be emended to *opulus*. An additional
note by him on XXVII 92 is to be found on p. 483.

May, 1980   G.P.G.

INTRODUCTION

THE MANUSCRIPTS OF THESE BOOKS
(CHIEFLY FROM MAYHOFF)

N Nonantulanus (Sessorianus) 5th or 6th century,
a palimpsest, now in Rome, once in a
Benedictine Monastery at Nonantula, near
Modena.

LATER MANUSCRIPTS

1st family

V Leidensis Vossianus, 11th century or earlier.
R codex Florentinus Riccardianus, about 1100
A.D.
d codex Parisinus latinus, 6797, 13th century.
F codex Leidensis, 11th century.
T codex Toletanus, 13th century.
x the better parts of X, *ex exemplari prioris
familiae* (Mayhoff).

2nd family

E codex Parisinus latinus 6795, 10th or 11th
century.
r corrections from an unknown MS. noted in R.
a codex Vindobonensis CCXXXIV.
X codex Luxemburgensis, the parts not included
in x.

" *Codd.*" in the *apparatus criticus* is usually the same
as Mayhoff's *ll.*, *i.e.*, a *consensus* of VR(r)dE, some-

times only a *consensus* of several MSS. of the more reliable kind. *Vulg.* = the *textus receptus* of the early editions. Of FTx Mayhoff says : " *lectiones ita tantum adnotatae sunt, ut e silentio nihil concludendum sit.*"

The edition of Dalecamp (1587) has in the margin : (1) readings of a lost MS. ; (2) readings of a lost edition or conjectures of an unknown scholar.

In the critical notes (1) is called " cod. Dal." and (2) " vet. Dal."

As to the value of these MSS., I have generally followed Mayhoff. The method adopted in fixing the text has been to accept as correct the parts where Detlefsen and Mayhoff agree, except in a few places where internal evidence or the text of Dioscorides pointed to another reading. Where these two editors differ I have tried to choose the likelier of the two readings. If I felt that neither alternative could be accepted, I have sometimes ventured on an emendation suggested by a friend or thought out by myself, but never, I hope, where a reasonable reading is found in at least one MS. of fair authority. Such a method as this would be unsafe were it not for the fact that Mayhoff's *apparatus criticus* is both full and trustworthy.

Although one who has not collated, or at least personally examined, the MSS. in Mayhoff's *apparatus*, cannot claim to appreciate fully their relative importance, yet he must acquire, as he studies their various readings, some conception of the weight to be attached to them. Such a critic, however, should exercise even greater caution than the critic fully equipped for his task. For his judgment, however great his knowledge is of Plinian usage, of the parallel passages in Theophrastus and Dioscorides,

INTRODUCTION

and of the principles of textual criticism, is certain to
be influenced unduly by the subjective element in
his reasoning. A translator, however, although he
would prefer to spend all his time and care on his
proper task of translating, is sometimes compelled to
defend a new reading or suggest an emendation,
because in his opinion such a course is required by the
sense of the passage. But the extra caution necessary in these cases has made me refrain from mention-
ing some emendations of my own that I thought
possible or even likely. It is, moreover, often forgotten that an ancient author—and this perhaps
applies especially to Pliny—may himself have made
mistakes, even bad ones, that escaped the notice
of his *corrector*, if he had one.

Some Difficult Words in Pliny.

THE ADJECTIVE *PINGUIS* APPLIED TO LEAVES

There are in Pliny few words more perplexing than
pinguis when applied to leaves. Forcellini says
" pinguia folia: crassa et veluti carnosa." Pliny,
however, uses it to translate λιπαρός, which is very
common in Dioscorides, and is rendered by Hort
" glossy " (leaves) in his edition of Theophrastus.

It is therefore tempting to use " glossy " to translate Pliny's *pinguis* (and the λιπαρός of Dioscorides)
on all occasions, but there are difficulties. The latter
has (IV 170): κλῶνας λιπαρούς, and " glossy twigs "
seems unlikely; while Pliny in XXV § 124 speaks of
radicibus pinguibus, which is surely " juicy roots." It
would appear that " juicy " is at least a possible
translation of *pinguis*, especially as Pliny often speaks
of leaves having a *sucus*. Examples are: *sucus*

xi

foliorum (XXIV §§ 47 and 131); *foliis exprimitur sucus* (XXIV § 70); *fit et foliis sucus* (XXIV § 109); *sucus e fronde* (XXV § 68).

The claims of " fleshy " have to be considered. On the face of it, perhaps, it is a more natural epithet for leaves than either " glossy " or " juicy," and it is the only meaning given by Forcellini. Against the rendering must be put the frequent use of σαρκώδης by our Greek authorities in this sense, often in close conjunction with λιπαρός.

In Pliny XXV § 161 occurs a phrase which seems at first sight to settle the matter. He speaks of *folia . . . carnosa, pinguia,*[1] *larga suco.* Does this mean " fleshy, glossy, juicy leaves " ? The last two epithets, however, may be connected, which would give the sense: " rich with copious juice." This is perhaps unlikely, but cannot be ruled out as impossible. The parallel passage in Dioscorides (IV 88, 89) does not help in deciding the question.

Hort may be right in translating λιπαρός by " glossy," but what did Pliny take it to mean when applied to leaves ? A consideration of all the pertinent passages suggests a combination of " glossy " and " fleshy," i.e., not necessarily large, but " sleek and plump." Perhaps, if a single word must be chosen to render *pinguis* whenever it occurs, " rich " gets as near to Pliny's idea of the meaning as the English language will permit. But unfortunately modern botanists are opposed to this rendering.

It may seem that the best course would be to identify the leaf referred to, and to vary the translation to suit the actual facts. Botanists, however,

[1] Littré translates *pinguia* (into the French) "grasses"; Bostock and Riley "unctuous."

point out (1) that identification is often uncertain; (2) that we may know the genus, but not the species of the plant mentioned, and (3) that a leaf is often both fleshy and glossy.

On the whole, perhaps " fleshy " is the best translation, except in cases where another rendering is obviously desirable.

Words signifying colours are very troublesome in the botanical parts of Pliny; *niger, candidus, albus, purpureus*, bewilder the translator nearly every time they occur.

I have used " black " and " white " unless there is something in the context that makes " dark " and " light " more appropriate; the comparative *nigrior*, for instance, is more likely to be " darker " than " blacker " when applied to leaves or stalks.

Pliny has quite a long section (IX, 124–141) dealing with *purpura*. It is plain from this that the colour referred to was usually a deep red tinged with more or less blue, our " purple " in fact, the most esteemed variety being like clotted blood. There were many shades of it, a common one being bright red.

The word *purpureus* covered a very wide range of meanings; Pliny applies it to the violet (XXI, 64), to plums (XX, 41), to figs (XV, 69) and to lettuce (probably a form of headed lettuce) (XIX, 126). The last suggests our " brown cos " and " continuity." In books XX–XXVII Pliny is mostly translating Greek, and πορφύρεος seems to be a somewhat wider term than *purpureus*, which is Pliny's equivalent. To these elements of uncertainty must be added the possibility that flowers may have varied their shades in the last two thousand

years, so that modern plants are not an infallible guide.

On the whole it seems best to keep " purple " (Littré has regularly " pourpre ") unless the context shows that such a rendering is impossible or absurd.

Vero in Pliny is often neither intensive nor adversative, neither " indeed " nor " however," but almost a mere connective particle equivalent to *item*. Sometimes, but by no means always, it introduces a climax. Usually, however, a slight, generally a very slight, adversative force remains, and I have always tried " however " and " indeed " before falling back on a purely connective word.

Oleum, translated " oil," was usually, perhaps always, olive oil. When another kind of oil is indicated an epithet is added.

The Latin names of plants have been kept unless to do so would be absurd; I write for instance *sideritis* and *ageraton*, but " rose " and " plantain." In other words, English names are used only when they are familiar and also correct identifications. The *Index of Plants* should clear up most of the difficulties that may occur.

PLINY:
NATURAL HISTORY
BOOK XXIV

PLINII NATURALIS HISTORIAE

LIBER XXIV

I. Ne silvae quidem horridiorque naturae facies medicinis carent, sacra illa parente rerum omnium nusquam non remedia disponente homini, ut medicina[1] fieret etiam solitudo ipsa, ad[2] singula[3] illius discordiae atque concordiae miraculis occursantibus. quercus et olea tam pertinaci odio dissident ut altera in alterius scrobe depacta emoriantur, quercus vero et iuxta nucem iuglandem. pernicialia et brassicae cum vite odia, ipsum olus quo vitis fugatur adversum 2 cyclamino et origano arescit. quin et annosas iam et quae sternantur arbores difficilius caedi, celerius marcescere tradunt, si prius manu quam ferro attingantur. pomorum onera iumenta statim sentire[4]

---

[1] medicina Vdx, *Mayhoff*: medicinae *Detlefsen*.
[2] ipsa, ad *ego*: ipsa, et ad *Mayhoff*: ipsa, sed ad *multi codd. Fortasse* sed *per dittographiam est ortum.*
[3] singula *Detlefsen, Mayhoff*: singulas, *cod.* a: stgula V[1]: est gula V[2]. *Num latet* singulariis *vel* singularibus *sine* ad?
[4] iumenta statim sentire *cod.* a, *Detlefsen*: a iumentis statim sentiri Vdx, *Mayhoff*.

---

[a] The tense of *fieret* shows that the participle *disponente* is imperfect, referring to the time of the actual creation. The *ut* might be final: " for the very desert to become a drug store."

2

PLINY: NATURAL HISTORY

BOOK XXIV

I. Nor even the woods and the wilder face of *The sym-*
Nature are without medicines, for there is no place *pathies and*
where that holy Mother of all things did [a] not *Nature.*
distribute remedies for the healing of mankind, so
that even the very desert was made a drug store,[b] at
every point occurring wonderful examples of that
well-known antipathy and sympathy. The oak and
the olive are parted by such inveterate hatred that,
if the one be planted in the hole from which the other
has been dug out, they die, the oak indeed also dying
if planted near the walnut. Deadly too is the
hatred between the cabbage and the vine; the very
vegetable that keeps the vine at a distance itself
withers away when planted opposite cyclamen or
wild marjoram. Moreover, trees, it is said, that are
now old and being felled are more difficult to cut
down, and decay more quickly, if man's hand touch
them before the axe. There is a belief that beasts of

[b] I think that *medicina* here means the shop or booth
(*officina*) where the physician prescribed and sold his medicines.
Cf. Pliny XXIX. § 12 : *Cassius Hemina . . . auctor est primum
e medicis venisse Romam . . . Archagathum . . . eique . . .
tabernam in compito Acilio emptam.* This sense occurs in
Plautus, and Pliny, in a rather poetic passage, may well have
so used it metaphorically.

ac, nisi prius ostendantur his, quamvis pauca portent,
sudare ilico. ferulae asinis gratissimo sunt in pabulo,
ceteris vero iumentis praesentaneo veneno, qua de
causa id animal Libero patri adsignatur, cui et
3 ferula. surdis etiam rerum sua cuique sunt venena ac
minimis quoque. philyra coci et polline nimium
salem cibis eximunt, praedulcium fastidium sal
temperat. nitrosae aut amarae aquae polenta
addita mitigantur, ut intra duas horas bibi possint,
qua de causa in saccos vinarios additur polenta.
similis vis Rhodiae cretae et argillae nostrati. con-
cordia valent, cum pix oleo extrahitur, quando
utrumque pinguis naturae est. oleum solum calci
miscetur, quando utrumque aquas odit. cummis
aceto facilius eluitur, atramentum aqua, innumera
praeterea alia quae suis locis dicentur adsidue.

4   Hinc nata medicina. haec sola naturae placuerat
esse remedia parata vulgo, inventu facilia ac sine
inpendio et quibus vivimus. postea fraudes hominum
et ingeniorum capturae officinas invenere istas in
quibus sua cuique homini venalis promittitur vita.
statim compositiones et mixturae inexplicabiles de-
5 cantantur, Arabia atque India remedia [1] aestimantur,
ulcerique parvo medicina a Rubro mari inputatur,[2]
cum remedia vera cotidie pauperrimus quisque

---

[1] remedia *Mayhoff*: in media *plerique codd.*: in medio *cod.*
a, *Detlefsen* vel Media *coni. Mayhoff*.
[2] inputatur *codd., Mayhoff*: inportatur *Detlefsen*.

---

[a] *Creta* was perhaps fuller's earth.
[b] The sentence in form is similar to § 1 : *ut medicina fieret
etiam solitudo ipsa*. With Mayhoff's ingenious emendation :
" Arabia, India or Media are highly commended."
[c] With the reading *inportatur :* " for a tiny sore a medicine
is imported from the Red Sea " (Arabian and Persian Gulfs).

burden know at once when their load consists of fruit,
and unless it is first shown to them straightway begin
to sweat, however small their load may be. Fennel-
giant makes very agreeable fodder for the ass; to other
beasts of burden, however, it is a quick poison. For
this reason the animal is sacred to Father Liber, as is
also fennel-giant. Lifeless things also, even the most
insignificant, have each their own special poisons.
By means of linden bark and fine flour cooks extract
excessive salt from food; salt reduces the sickli-
ness of over-sweet things; water that is nitrous or
bitter is sweetened by the addition of pearl barley,
so that within two hours it is drinkable, and for this
reason pearl barley is put into linen wine-strainers.
The chalk ^a of Rhodes and the potter's earth of our own
country possess a similar property. Affinities show
their power when pitch is taken out by oil, both being
of a greasy nature. Oil alone mixes with lime, both
hating water. Gum is more easily removed by
vinegar, ink by water, and countless other examples
besides will be carefully given in their proper
place.

Hence sprang the art of medicine. Such things *The origin of*
alone had Nature decreed should be our remedies, pro- *medicine.*
vided everywhere, easy to discover and costing nothing—the things in fact that support our life. Later
on the deceit of men and cunning profiteering led to
the invention of the quack laboratories, in which each
customer is promised a new lease of his own life at a
price. At once compound prescriptions and mysteri-
ous mixtures are glibly repeated, Arabia and India ^b
are judged to be storehouses of remedies, and a small
sore is charged ^c with the cost of a medicine from the
Red Sea, although the genuine remedies form the

5

PLINY : NATURAL HISTORY

cenet. nam si ex horto petantur, aut herba vel
frutex quaeratur, nulla artium vilior fiat. ita est
profecto, magnitudine populi R. periit ritus, vin-
cendoque victi sumus. paremus externis, et una
artium imperatoribus quoque imperaverunt. verum
de his alias plura.

6 II. Loton herbam itemque Aegyptiam eodem
nomine alias et Syrticam arborem diximus suis locis.
haec lotos, quae faba Graeca appellatur a nostris,
alvum bacis sistit, ramenta ligni decocta in vino
prosunt dysintericis, menstruis, vertigini, comitialibus, cohibent et capillum. mirum his ramentis
nihil esse amarius fructuque dulcius. fit et e scobe
eius medicamentum ex aqua myrti decocta, subacta
et divisa in pastillos, dysintericis utilissimum pondere
victoriati cum aquae cyathis tribus.

7 III. Glans intrita duritias quas cacoethe vocant
cum salsa axungia sanat. vehementiores ilignae[1] et
in omnibus cortex ipse corticique tunica subiecta.
haec decocta iuvat coeliacos. dysintericis et inlinitur

[1] ilignae *Detlefsen* : iligna *Sillig, Mayhoff* : ligna *aut*
lichenas *codd.*

---

[a] The ordinary meaning of *nam* would make good sense, but
the Plinian usage fits better the logic of the passage.
[b] See XXI. § 103 and XIII. §§ 104 ff. Perhaps *Syriacam*,
referring to the *faba Syriaca*, should be read for *Syrticam*.
[c] This weight and coin is first mentioned by Pliny in XX.
§ 264. It was half a denarius, that is, half a drachma.
[d] This chapter is difficult to translate, or even to understand, because Pliny, after beginning with the medicinal uses of
glans, proceeds, without telling the reader that he has passed
on to the oak, to talk of *folia et bacae*. Accordingly, it is
uncertain whether *cortex* means the peel of the acorn or the
bark of the tree. Dioscorides is quite clear. Under δρῦς he
says (I. 106, Wellmann) : μάλιστα δὲ αὐτῆς στύφει τὸ μεταξὺ
τοῦ φλοιοῦ καὶ τοῦ πρέμνου ὑμενοειδές, ὁμοίως καὶ τὸ περὶ τῇ

daily dinner of even the very poorest. But[a] if remedies were to be sought in the kitchen-garden, or a plant or a shrub were to be procured thence, none of the arts would become cheaper than medicine. It is perfectly true that owing to their greatness the Roman people have lost their usages, and through conquering we have been conquered. We are the subjects of foreigners, and in one of the arts they have mastered even their masters. But of this more elsewhere.

II. In their proper places I have already spoken of the plant called lotus,[b] and also of the Egyptian plant called by the same name, sometimes known also as the tree of the Syrtes. The berries of this lotus, which by our countrymen is called the Greek bean, check looseness of the bowels. Shavings of the wood, boiled down in wine, are good for dysentery, irregular menstruation, giddiness and epilepsy. They also prevent the hair from falling out. It is strange that nothing is more bitter than these shavings or sweeter than lotus fruit. From the sawdust also of the wood a medicine is prepared by boiling it down in myrtle water; it is then kneaded and cut into lozenges, which make a very useful medicine for dysentery, the dose being one victoriatus [c] to three cyathi of water. *The lotus.*

III. Pounded acorns with salted axle-grease cure the indurations that are called malignant. More potent are those of the holm-oak, and in all acorns [d] the more potent parts are the peel itself and the skin just under it. A decoction of the latter is good for coeliac affections. In cases of dysentery also even *Acorns.*

βαλάνῳ ὑπὸ τὸ κέλυφος. Under αἱ βάλανοι: ἁρμόζουσι δὲ πρὸς τὰ ἰοβόλα ἐσθιόμεναι, καὶ τὸ ἀφέψημα δὲ αὐτῶν καὶ τοῦ φλοιοῦ βοηθεῖ τοξικῷ μετὰ γάλακτος βοείου πινόμενον. . . . ἰσχυρότεραι δὲ τῶν δρυΐνων αἱ πρίνιναι τῇ δυνάμει εἰσί. There is no confusion here between the acorn and the oak.

vel ipsa glans. eadem resistit serpentium ictibus.
rheumatismis, suppurationibus. folia et bacae vel
cortex vel sucus decocti prosunt contra toxica.
cortex inlinitur decoctus lacte vaccino serpentis
plagae, datur et ex vino dysintericis. eadem et ilici
vis.

8   IV. Coccum ilicis vulneribus recentibus ex aceto
inponitur, epiphoris ex aqua, oculis subfusis sanguine
instillatum.[1] est autem genus ex eo in Africa fere et
Asia nascens celerrime in vermiculum [2] se mutans,
quod ideo scolecium vocant inprobantque. princi-
palia eius genera diximus.

9   V. Nec pauciora gallae genera fecimus, solidam
perforatam, item albam nigram, maiorem minorem.
vis omnium similis, optima Commagena. excrescentia in corpore tollunt, prosunt gingivis, uvae, oris
exulcerationi. crematae et vino extinctae [3] coeliacis,
dysintericis inlinuntur, paronychiis ex melle, et
unguibus scabris, pterygiis, ulceribus manantibus,
condylomatis, ulceribus [4] quae phagedaenica vocantur.
in vino autem decoctae auribus instillantur, oculis

---

[1] instillatum *codd.* : instillatur *vulg., Mayhoff.*
[2] vermiculum EX *vulg.* : vermiculum id *Mayhoff* : vermis
subtilis *Sillig, Detlefsen* : vermis ultimis *aliquot codd.*
[3] *Post* extinctae *lacunam indicat Mayhoff, qui coll. Dioscoride* (I. 107) sanguinem sistunt; ex aqua aut vino tritae
excidisse putat.
[4] ulceribus *cod. Dal., Sillig, Mayhoff*: vulneribus *Detlefsen, codd.*

---

[a] Or :—" It is used in an application for cases of dysentery,
or the acorn itself is so used."
[b] See note *d* on p. 6. The " berries " may be the galls
caused by the gall-fly *Neuroterus baccarum.*
[c] Either poisons generally or those used to poison arrows
(τόξα) and other weapons. See also note *a* on p. 20.

the acorn itself is applied.[a] The same decoction is a
remedy for snake bites, fluxes and suppurations. The
leaves[b] and berries, or the bark,[b] or the liquid of a
decoction, counteract poisons.[c] A decoction of the
bark[b] in cows' milk is applied to snake bites, and
the bark in wine is given for dysentery. The holm-
oak has the same properties.

IV. The scarlet berry[d] of the holm oak is applied to   Holm-oak
fresh wounds in vinegar and to fluxes of the eyes in   "berry."
water; it is dropped into eyes that are blood-shot.
There is also a kindred berry, found commonly in
Africa and Asia, quickly turning into a little worm;
for this reason it is called scolecium,[e] and is in low
esteem. The main varieties of it I have already[f]
given.

V. We have classified[f] just as many varieties of   Gall-nuts.
gall-nut—the solid and the perforated, the white and
the dark, the larger and the less. The properties
of all are alike, although the best kind comes from
Commagene. They remove excrescences of flesh,
and are good for the gums, the uvula, and an ulcerated mouth. Burnt and then extinguished with wine
they are applied[g] for coeliac affections and dysentery,
in honey to whitlows, scabrous nails, hangnails,
running sores, condylomata, and the sores called
"phagedaenic." A decoction moreover in wine is
dropped into the ears and also used as an application

---

[d] The kermes insect of the *Quercus coccifera*.
[e] "Worm berry."
[f] Book XVI. §§ 32 and 26.
[g] Mayhoff thinks that there is a lacuna here, because of
certain words in Dioscorides I. 107. But Pliny by no means
corresponds to Dioscorides closely in this chapter, and has left
out much that is found in the Greek. Accordingly it is unsafe
to postulate a lacuna in any particular passage.

inlinuntur, adversus eruptiones, panos cum aceto.
10 nucleus commanducatus dentium dolorem sedat, item
intertrigines et ambusta. inmaturae ex his ex
aceto potae lienem consumunt. eaedem crematae
et aceto salso extinctae menses sistunt vulvasque
procidentes fotu. omnis capillos denigrat.[1]
11   VI. Viscum e robore praecipuum diximus haberi,
et quo conficeretur modo. quidam contusum in aqua
decocunt,[2] donec nihil innatet. quidam comman-
ducantes acinos expuunt cortices. optimum quod
sine cortice quodque levissimum, extra fulvum, intus
porraceum. nihil est glutinosius. emollit, discutit
tumores, siccat strumas. cum resina et cera panos
12 mitigat omnis generis. quidam et galbanum adiciunt
pari pondere singulorum, eoque modo et ad vulnera
utuntur. unguium scabritias expolit, si septenis
diebus solvantur [3] nitroque conluantur. quidam id
religione efficacius fieri putant prima luna collectum
e robore sine ferro, si terram non attigerit, comitialibus

[1] denigrat VEX, *Mayhoff* : denigrant dT *vulg.*, *Detlefsen*.
[2] *Num* decocunt *post* innatet *transponendum*?
[3] solvantur *codd.*: illinantur *coni. Mayhoff, qui confert Dioscor.* III. 89 *et Plin.* XX. §§ 39, 93, 101, 103, XXI. § 142.

---

[a] See XVI. §§ 30 and 245–248. *Viscum* is used of the plant,
of the berries, and also of the birdlime made from these. See
XVI. § 248, *viscum fit ex acinis.*
[b] Dioscorides III. 89 : κόπτεται δὲ ὁ καρπός, εἶτα πλύνεται,
εἶτα ἕψεται ἐν ὕδατι· ἔνιοι δὲ μασώμενοι αὐτὸν ἐργάζονται, " the
fruit is crushed, then washed, then boiled in water; some work
it up by chewing." This is clear sense, but Pliny's text scarcely agrees with it. There is nothing in Pliny to correspond to
πλύνεται or ἐργάζονται, and nothing in Dioscorides to correspond
to *donec nihil innatet* and *expuunt cortices.* It is possible that
donec nihil innatet should be transposed : " crushed in water

for the eyes; with vinegar it is used for eruptions and superficial abscesses. The inner part of the nut when chewed relieves toothache, and also chafing of the skin and burns. Taken unripe in vinegar gall-nuts reduce a swollen spleen; then again, burnt and extinguished in salt and vinegar, they check excessive menstruation and prolapse of the uterus if used as a fomentation. All kinds of gall-nut blacken the hair.

VI. I have already said [a] that the choicest mistle- *Mistletoe.* toe is thought to come from the hard-wood oak, and I have given the way of preparing it. Some crush it and boil in water until none of it floats on the surface; others chew the berries and spit out the skins.[b] The best birdlime from mistletoe is without any skin, and very smooth,[c] yellow on the outside and leek-green within. Nothing is more sticky than this birdlime. It is emollient, disperses tumours, and dries up scrofulous sores; with resin and wax it softens superficial abscesses of every sort. Some add galbanum also, equal in weight to each of the other ingredients, and this mixture they use also for the treatment of wounds. The lime smooths scabrous nails, but the application must be taken off [d] every seven days and the nails washed with a solution of soda.[e] Some superstitiously believe that the mistletoe proves more efficacious if it be gathered from the hard-wood oak at the new moon without the use of iron, and without its touching

until nothing floats on the surface," crushing and washing being thus combined. More probably Pliny is translating, not the passage as it appears in Dioscorides, but one closely related to it.

[c] Dioscorides has λεῖος.

[d] With Mayhoff's conjecture, " applied (again)."

[e] *Nitrum* was sodium carbonate mixed with chlorides and calcium carbonate. It was brought from pools N.-W. of Cairo.

mederi, conceptum feminarum adiuvare, si omnino
secum habeant, ulcera commanducato inpositoque
efficacissime sanari.

13   VII. Roboris pilulae ex adipe ursino[1] alopecias
capillo replent. cerri folia et cortex et glans siccat
collectiones suppurationesque, fluctiones sistit.
torpentes membrorum partes conroborat decoctum
eius fotu, cui et insidere expedit siccandis adstrin-
gendisque partibus. radix cerri adversatur scorpionibus.

    VIII. Suberis cortex tritus ex aqua calida potus
sanguinem fluentem ex utralibet parte sistit.
eiusdem cinis ex vino calido sanguinem excreantibus
magnopere laudatur.

14   IX. Fagi folia manducantur in gingivarum lab-
rorumque vitiis. calculis glandis fagineae cinis
inlinitur, item cum melle alopeciis.

15   X. Cupressi folia trita recentibus vulneribus[2]
inponuntur, et capiti cum polenta, si a sole doleat,
item ramici, qua de causa et bibuntur. testium
quoque tumori cum cera inlinuntur, capillum deni-

---

[1] ursino *vulg. Mayhoff*: vere ursino *Detlefsen, Strackium
secutus* : vero ursino *codd. Vide notam (b).*
[2] recentibus vulneribus *ex Plinio iun.* 74, 7 *coni. Mayhoff;
ego quoque ipse ex Dioscoride ita suspicatus sum* : serpentibus
ulceribus *Mayhoff in textu* : serpentium ictibus *Detlefsen* :
serpentibus *aut* serpentis *aut* serpentium *codd. Cf. Dioscorides* I. 74 τὰ δὲ φύλλα λεῖα καταπλαττόμενα τραύματα κολλᾷ.

---

[a] For this use of *omnino* see IX. § 185, XVI. § 149, XXII.
§ 60, XXIV. § 95, XXV. § 101, XXVI. § 98, XXVIII. §§ 79, 80,
83, 85, XXXII. § 8.
[b] The emendation of Strack (*vere*—"real bear's grease"—
for *vero*) is very ingenious. Perhaps a lacuna after *pilulae*,
with *vero* an adverb.
[c] For *alopecia* see list of diseases.

the ground; that so it cures epilepsy, helps women to conceive if they merely [a] carry it on their persons; that chewed and applied to sores it heals them most effectively.

VII. The globules growing on the hard-wood oak *Hard-wood* mixed with [b] bear's grease restore hair lost through *oak globules.* mange.[c] The leaves, bark and acorns of the Turkey *Turkey Oak.* oak dry up gatherings and suppurations, and check fluxes. Paralysed parts of limbs are strengthened by fomenting with a decoction of it, which as a sitz bath is useful for drying and bracing these parts. The root of this tree counteracts the poison of scorpions.

VIII. The bark of the cork-tree, pounded and taken *Cork.* in hot water, arrests haemorrhage from either part [d] of the body, and the ashes of the same taken in heated wine are highly praised as a cure for spitting of blood.

IX. Beech leaves are chewed for affections of the *Beech leaves.* gums and of the lips. The ashes of the beech nut make a liniment for stone in the bladder, and with honey for mange.

X. The pounded leaves of the cypress are applied *Cypress* to fresh [e] wounds, and with pearl barley to the head *leaves.* in cases of sunstroke;[f] they make an application also for hernia, for which too they are taken in drink. With wax they make an ointment also for swollen

---

[d] Usually taken to be mouth and nose. In view of the fact that *pars* often means " side," perhaps mouth and nose make one *pars,* and the anus (piles, etc.) the other.

[e] *Recentibus vulneribus* seems the most likely restoration of the MSS. *serpentibus.* It is supported by Dioscorides I. 74, and if *vulneribus* were omitted (haplography), *serpentibus* might naturally be written for the now meaningless *recentibus.* Cf. § 8 of this book.

[f] " Headache after exposure to the sun," perhaps.

grant ex aceto. eadem trita cum duabus partibus
panis mollis e vino Ammineo subacta pedum ac
nervorum dolores sedant. pilulae adversus serpentium ictus bibuntur, aut si eiciatur sanguis, collectionibus inlinuntur. ramici quoque tenerae tusae cum
axungia et lomento prosunt. bibuntur ex eadem
causa. parotidi et strumae cum farina inponuntur.
16 exprimitur sucus tusis cum semine [1] qui mixtus oleo
caliginem oculorum aufert. item victoriati pondere
in vino potus inlitusque [2] cum fico sicca pingui,
exemptis granis, vitia testium sanat, tumores discutit
et cum fermento strumas. radix cum foliis trita
pota vesicae et stranguriae medetur, et contra
phalangia. ramenta pota menses cient, scorpionum
ictibus adversantur.

17   XI. Cedrus magna, quam cedrelaten vocant, dat
picem quae cedria vocatur, dentium doloribus
utilissimam. frangit enim eos et extrahit, dolores
sedat. cedri sucus ex ea quomodo fieret diximus,
magni ad volumina [3] usus, ni capiti dolorem in-

---

[1] *Post* semine *punctum Mayhoff.*
[2] inlitusque *codd.* : inlitusve *e Plinio iun. Mayhoff.*
[3] volumina *plerique codd., Sillig, Mayhoff* : collyria *Detlefsen* :
duo lumina X : lumina *vulg.*

---

[a] Perhaps merely " darken," though *denigro* is a strong
word. See § 10.
[b] See XX. § 153, XXII. § 119, XXVI. § 49, XXVIII. § 177,
XXX. § 71, XXXIV. § 103.
[c] "Cedar-fir." The ordinary *cedrus* was the prickly juniper
(*Juniperus oxycedrus*), not cedar of Lebanon. But the "big
cedar" was *Juniperus excelsa.* What is the subject of *vocant* ?
Presumably the Greek botanists.
[d] See XVI. § 52. But in this chapter the method is described
of extracting resin from pitch-pine (*taeda*). Pliny says there
that this resin is called *cedrium* in Syria, adding that the
Egyptians use it for embalming corpses.

testicles; applied in vinegar they turn the hair black.[a]
The same, pounded with twice the quantity of soft
bread and kneaded in Amminean [b] wine, soothe
pains in the feet and sinews. The globules on this
tree are taken in drink for snake bites or for the
bringing up of blood, and used as an application for
gatherings. Gathered while soft, and pounded with
axle-grease and bean meal, they are also good for
hernia. For the same purpose they are taken in
drink. Mixed with meal they are applied to parotid
tumours and to scrofulous sores. Pounded with the
seed these globules yield a juice, which mixed with
oil takes away films on the eyes. Taken too in doses
of one victoriatus in wine and used as an ointment
with a rich dried fig, from which the seeds have been
removed, it cures affections of the testicles, disperses
tumours, and with leaven heals scrofulous sores.
Cypress root, pounded with the leaves and taken in
drink, cures affections of the bladder and strangury,
and counteracts the poison of spiders. The shavings
taken in drink act as an emmenagogue, and neutralize the stings of scorpions.

XI. The big cedrus, which they call cedrelate,[c] *The big cedrus.*
yields a pitch which is called cedria, very useful for
toothache; for it breaks the teeth and brings them
out, easing the pain. I have already described [d] how
cedrus juice is extracted from the wood, of great use
for book-rolls [e] were it not for the headache it causes.

[e] The reading (*volumina*) of the great majority of the MSS.
is slightly confirmed by Pliny's speaking in the context of the
preserving qualities of cedar resin. The headache apparently
is that said to be given to those using the rolls for writing or
reading. Detlefsen's *collyria* would be more attractive were
cedria among the ingredients of Celsus' prescriptions (VI. vi.
M 2 ff) for eye salves. *Lumina* (tapers, torches) is possible.

ferret. defuncta corpora incorrupta aevis servat,[a]
viventia corrumpit, mira differentia, cum vitam
18 auferat spirantibus defunctisque pro vita sit. vestes
quoque corrumpit et animalia necat. ob haec non
censeam in anginis hoc remedio utendum neque in
cruditatibus,[1] quod suasere aliqui, gustatu.[b] dentes
quoque conluere ex aceto in dolore timuerim vel
gravitati aut vermibus aurium instillare. portentum
est quod tradunt abortivum fieri in venere ante perfusa virilitate. phthiriasis perunguere eo non dubita-
verim, item porrigines. suadent et contra venenum
19 leporis marini[c] bibere in passo. facilius in elephantiasi
inlinant.[2] et ulcera sordida et excrescentia in his
auctores quidam et oculorum albugines caliginesque
inunxere eo et contra pulmonis ulcera cyathum eius
sorberi iusserunt, item adversus taenias. fit ex eo et
oleum quod pisselaeon vocant,[d] vehementioris ad
omnia eadem usus. cedri[e] scobe serpentes fugari
certum est, item bacis tritis cum oleo si qui perun-
guantur.

¹ cruditatibus *codd., edd.*: raucitatibus *coll. Dioscoride
coni. Mayhoff*; *nescio an recte.*
² inlinant V¹ *Sillig, Mayhoff*: inlinunt *Brotier, Detlefsen*:
varia codd.

[a] An instrumental ablative, although Pliny uses this case
to express duration. Pliny also has *in aevum* XXXV. § 4.
[b] Though there are no signs of variants in the MSS., it is
likely enough that the conjecture *raucitatibus* (sore throat) of
Mayhoff is correct, for Dioscorides has παρισθμίων φλεγμοναῖς.
Corresponding to *gustatu*, however, is περίχριστος.
[c] A mollusc, *Aplysia vulgaris*. Above, *phthiriasis* is
(Greek φθειριάσεις) acc. pl.
[d] " Pitch oil."
[e] The mention of berries makes some commentators think
that Pliny is here confusing cedar and juniper. But the
" cedars " of this chapter *are* junipers.

It preserves dead bodies uncorrupted by time,[a] but causes living ones to decay—a strange inconsistency, to rob the living of their life and to give a quasi-life to the dead! It also makes clothes decay and kills animal life. For this reason I should not think it ought to be used as a remedy for quinsy, or for indigestion,[b] as some have recommended, taken by the mouth. I should also be afraid to rinse the teeth with it in vinegar, when they ache, or to drop it into the ears for hardness of hearing or worms. Gossip records a miracle : that to rub it all over the male part before coition prevents conception. I should not hesitate to use it as an ointment for phthiriasis or for scurf. It is also recommended to take it in raisin wine to counteract the poison of the sea hare,[c] but more readily it might be used as liniment for leprosy. For foul sores and excrescences in them, and for spots and films on the eyes, certain authorities have prescribed it as an ointment, and have directed that a cyathus of it be drunk for sores on the lung, as well as for tapeworm. There is prepared from it an oil also, which they call pisselaeon,[d] used for all the same purposes, but of greater potency. It is well ascertained that snakes are kept away by the sawdust of cedrus, and that to rub the body with the crushed berries [e] mixed with oil has the same result.[f]

[f] There is a great similarity between this chapter and Dioscorides I. 77 (Wellmann). A few sentences may be quoted : σηπτικὴν μὲν τῶν ἐμψύχων, φυλακτικὴν δὲ τῶν νεκρῶν σωμάτων. . . . σὺν ὄξει δὲ ἐγκλυζομένη σκώληκας τοὺς ἐν ὡσὶ κτείνει. . . . εἴς τε ἐμβρώματα ὀδόντος ἐνσταγεῖσα θραύει μὲν τὸν ὀδόντα, παύει δὲ τὴν ἀλγηδόνα . . . περιχρισθεῖσα δὲ αἰδοίῳ πρὸ τῆς συνουσίας ἀτόκιόν ἐστι, συναγχικῶν τε περίχριστός ἐστι καὶ παρισθμίων φλεγμοναῖς βοηθεῖ . . . πρός τε λαγωοῦ θαλασσίου

17

20 XII. Cedrides, hoc est fructus cedri, tussim sanant, urinam cient, alvum sistunt, utiles ruptis, convulsis, spasticis, stranguriae, vulvis, ad antidota contra[1] lepores marinos eademque quae supra, collectionibus inflammationibusque.

21 XIII. De galbano diximus. neque umidum neque aridum probatur, et quale docuimus. per se bibitur ad tussim veterem, suspiria, rupta, convulsa. inponitur ischiadicis, lateris doloribus, panis, furunculis, corpori ab ossibus recedenti, strumis, articulorum nodis, dentium quoque doloribus. inlinitur et cum melle capitis ulceribus. purulentis infunditur auribus cum rosaceo aut nardo. odore comitialibus subvenit, et vulva strangulante vel in stomachi defectu. abortus non exeuntes trahit adpositu vel suffitu, item

22 ramo hellibori circumlitum atque subiectum. serpentes nidore urentium fugari diximus. fugiunt et perunctos galbano. medetur et ab scorpione percussis.

---

[1] ad antidota contra *Ianus* : contra aculeata *Detlefsen* : contra aconita *Mayhoff* : admoti contra *vulg.*: contra admota *codd.*

πόσις σὺν γλυκεῖ λαμβανομένη βοηθεῖ. ὠφελεῖ καὶ ἐλεφαντιῶντας . . . καθαίρει καὶ τὰ ἐν πνεύμονι ἕλκη καὶ ἰᾶται ταῦτα ὅσον κύαθος ῥοφουμένη. The statements that Pliny records doubtfully appear in the Greek; but the great difficulty is, not to explain the similarities, but to account for the differences.

[a] No restoration of this *locus corruptus* is really satisfactory. The vulgate, if *admoti* be changed to *admotae* (since *cedris* is feminine), is possible, but *vulvis admotae* sounds odd after a list of datives depending upon *utiles*. If the order of *contra admota* be sound, then *admota* has replaced some substantive, to recover which is next to impossible, as in chapter XII there is but a general resemblance to the end of Dioscorides I. 77, where we read ἔμμηνα ἄγουσι μετὰ πεπέρεως λεῖαι πινόμεναι, καὶ πρὸς λαγωοῦ θαλασσίου κ.τ.λ. This, translated into Latin, would be nothing like Pliny's corrupt text. At the end of chap. 77,

XII. Cedrides, that is the fruit of the cedrus, cure *Fruit of the* *cedrus.*
a cough, are diuretic, arrest looseness of the bowels,
and are useful for ruptures, sprains, spasms, strangury
and uterine affections, forming an ingredient of antidotes [a] for the poison of sea hares and those poisons
mentioned above,[b] and being used for gatherings
and inflammations.

XIII. About galbanum I have already spoken.[c] *Galbanum.*
The best kind is considered to be that which is neither
moist nor dry, and such as I have indicated. It is
taken in drink by itself for chronic cough, asthma,
ruptures and sprains; it is used as an application for
sciatica, pains in the sides, superficial abscesses, boils,
separation of flesh from bones, scrofulous sores, knotty
lumps at the joints, and tooth-ache. With honey too
it makes an ointment for sores on the head. With
rose oil or nard it is injected for pus in the ears. Its
smell is beneficial for epilepsy, choking of the uterus,
and for weakness [d] of the stomach. A pessary or
fumigation brings away the foetus when there is a
miscarriage, and so will a branch of hellebore smeared
with it and laid under the woman. I have said that
snakes are kept off by the fumes caused by burning
it; [e] they do not come either near persons rubbed
with galbanum. It heals also scorpion stings. A

however, Dioscorides has μείγνυνται δὲ καὶ ἀντιδότοις, which
makes Jan's restoration slightly the most preferable.

[b] The phrase *eadem quae supra* is vague, and it seems hope-
less to try to identify *eadem.*

[c] See XII. § 126.

[d] Cf. XIX. § 92, *defectus praecipue stomachi excitat.* A
favourite word of Pliny, *defectus* seems to mean the failure to
function of any organ.

[e] The active *urentium* is odd, but the meaning is certain,
for XII. § 126 has *sincerum si uratur fugat nidore serpentes.*

bibitur et in difficili partu fabae magnitudine in cyatho vini, vulvasque conversas corrigit, cum murra autem et vino mortuos partus extrahit. adversatur et venenis, maxime toxicis,^{a} cum murra et vino. serpentes oleo et spondylio mixto tactu necat. nocere urinae existimatur.

23   XIV. Similis hammoniaci natura atque lacrimae, probandae ut diximus.^{b} mollit, calefacit, discutit, dissolvit. claritati visus in collyriis convenit, pruritum, cicatrices, albugines oculorum tollit, dentium dolores sedat, efficacius accensum.^{c} prodest dyspnoicis, pleuriticis, pulmonibus, vesicis, urinae cruentae, lieni, ischiadicis potum—sic et alvum solvit—articulis et podagrae cum pari pondere picis aut cerae et rosaceo coctum. maturat panos, extrahit clavos cum melle—sic et duritias emollit—lieni cum aceto et cera Cypria vel rosaceo efficacissime inponitur.^{d} lassitudines perungui cum aceto et oleo exiguoque nitro utile.

24   XV. Et styracis naturam in peregrinis arboribus exposuimus. placet praeter illa quae diximus maxime pinguis, purus, albicantibus fragmentis. medetur tussi, faucibus, pectoris vitiis, vulvae

---

^{a} *Toxicum* can be a mere synonym of *venenum*, but here it obviously refers to a special kind of poison. Cf. XVI. § 51, *sunt qui et taxica hinc appellata dicant venena—quae nunc toxica dicimus—quibus sagittae tinguantur.* See p. 8 note c.

^{b} Book XII. § 107.

^{c} The older editions punctuate so as to limit *efficacius* to *sedat*. This is probably right, for *accensum* must mean " alight," not " burnt," (as Bostock and Riley). So the meaning is, that a piece of the gum ammoniac is set alight and applied to the aching tooth. This is strange, not to say heroic treatment, and one wonders whether the text is corrupt, but there are no variants.

^{d} Mayhoff suggests *inlitum*, " applied."

piece the size of a bean is taken in a cyathus of wine for difficult deliveries, and it reduces a displaced uterus; while with myrrh and wine it brings away a dead foetus. With myrrh and wine it also counteracts poisons, particularly those used on arrows.[a] Mixed with oil and spondylium it kills snakes if it but touches them. It is supposed to make urination difficult.

XIV. Similar is the nature of ammoniacum and of its tear, which should be tested in the way I mentioned.[b] It softens, warms, disperses, and dissolves. In eye salves it promotes clearness of vision. It removes itch, scars, and white spots on the eyes, and relieves tooth-ache, more effectively when it has been set alight.[c] It is good for difficulty of breathing, pleurisy, affections of the lungs and bladder, blood in the urine, diseases of the spleen, and sciatica, if it be taken in drink—thus administered it also loosens the bowels—and, boiled[d] with an equal weight of pitch or wax and with rose oil, it makes a good ointment for diseases of the joints and for gouty pains. It brings superficial abscesses to a head, and extracts corns, when mixed with honey—so applied it also softens indurations—and combined with vinegar and Cyprian wax or rose oil it makes a very effective application for diseases of the spleen. A rubbing with ointment made up of this gum, with vinegar, oil and a little soda, is a good remedy for fatigue.

XV. The nature of storax also I have spoken of in[e] my account of foreign trees. In addition to the qualities there mentioned, the most esteemed kind is very rich, unadulterated, and breaks up into white fragments. It cures coughs, affections of the throat,

Ammoniacum.

Storax.

[e] See XII. § 124.

praeclusae duritieve laboranti, ciet menses potu
adposituque, alvum mollit. invenio potu modico
tristitiam animi resolvi, largiore contrahi, sonitus
aurium emendare infusum, strumas illitum nervo-
rumque nodos. adversatur venenis quae frigore
nocent,[1] ideo et cicutae.

25   XVI. Spondylium una demonstratum infunditur
capitibus phreneticorum et lethargicorum, item
capitis doloribus longis cum oleo vetere ;[2] bibitur
et in iocinerum vitiis, morbo regio, comitialibus,
orthopnoicis, vulvarum strangulatione, quibus et
suffitu prodest. alvum mollit. illinitur ulceribus
26 quae serpunt cum ruta. flos auribus purulentis
efficaciter infunditur, sed sucus, cum exprimitur,
integendus est, quoniam mire adpetitur a muscis et
similibus.   radix derasa et in fistulas coniecta callum
earum erodit.   auribus quoque instillatur cum suco.
datur et ipsa contra morbum regium et in iocineris
vitio et vulvarum.   capillos crispos facit peruncto
capite.

---

[1] nocent *codd.*, *Detlefsen* : necent *Mayhoff.*
[2] *Sic dist. Mayhoff, Dioscoridem secutus:* longis. cum oleo
vetere bibitur *ceteri edd.*

---

[a] *Contrahere* is an unfortunate word to use in this context,
as it can mean both (1) to cause, bring about, and (2) to cut
short, lessen.

[b] Mayhoff's conjecture *necent* (for *nocent* of the MSS.) would
mean " kill."

[c] See XII. § 128.

[d] I think that the antecedent of *quibus* may be, not all the
preceding nouns, but *vulvarum*, for Dioscorides has ὑποθυ-
μιώμενος δὲ ἀνακαλεῖται τοὺς καταφερομένους immediately after
ὑστερικὴν πνίγα.

chest diseases, and obstructions or indurations of the uterus; by the mouth or as a pessary it acts as an emmenagogue; it loosens the bowels. I find in my authorities that a moderate dose dispels melancholy, but that a larger one causes[a] it; that an injection cures singing in the ears, a local application scrofulous sores and knotty lumps on the sinews. It counteracts poisons that harm[b] by chilling, and therefore, among others, hemlock.

XVI. Spondylium, which I described at the same time,[c] is with old oil poured on the heads of sufferers from phrenitis, lethargus and headache of long standing. It is also taken in drink for affections of the liver, for jaundice, epilepsy, asthma, and choking of the uterus; for these[d] fumigation is also beneficial. It loosens the bowels. With rue it is used as a liniment for spreading sores. The blossom[e] is injected with good results into purulent ears, but the juice, when it is[f] being extracted, must be covered over, since it has a wonderful attraction for flies and such-like insects. The shavings of the root inserted into fistulas eat away their callosities. They are also dropped with the juice into the ears. The root also itself is given for jaundice and for affections of the liver and of the uterus. If the head is rubbed with it,[g] the hair becomes curly.

Spondylium.

---

[e] By "blossom" Pliny means the juice of the flowers, as we see from Dioscorides III. 76 (Wellmann): τοῦ δὲ ἄνθους χλώρου ὁ χυλὸς πρὸς ἡλκωμένα ὦτα καὶ πυορροῦντα ἁρμόζει. Here once more Pliny and Dioscorides are very alike for a whole chapter, and the one can be safely checked by the other.

[f] By using the present (*exprimitur*) Pliny implies that the juice must be at once covered up.

[g] Again juice is meant, as is shown by *peruncto*.

23

27 XVII. Sphagnos sive sphacos sive bryon et in
Gallia, ut indicavimus, nascitur, vulvis insidentium
utilis, item genibus et feminum tumoribus mixtus
nasturtio et aquae salsae tritus. cum vino autem et
resina sicca potus urinam pellit celerrime. hydropicos inanit cum vino et iuniperis tritus ac potus.

XVIII. Terebinthi folia et radix collectionibus
inponuntur. decoctum eorum stomachum firmat.
semen in capitis dolore bibitur in vino et contra
difficultatem urinae, ventrem leniter emollit, venerem
excitat.

28 XIX. Piceae et laricis folia trita et in aceto decocta
dentium dolori prosunt, prodest[1] cinis corticum
intertrigini et ambustis. potus alvum sistit, urinam
movet, suffitu vulvas corrigit. piceae folia privatim
iocineri utilia sunt drachmae pondere in aqua mulsa
pota. silvas eas dumtaxat quae picis resinaeque
gratia radantur utilissimas esse phthisicis aut qui
longa aegritudine non recolligant vires satis constat,
et illum caeli aera plus ita quam navigationem
Aegyptiam proficere, plus quam lactis herbidos per
montium aestiva potus.

29 XX. Chamaepitys Latine abiga vocatur propter
abortus, ab aliis tus terrae, cubitalibus ramis, flore
pinus et odore. altera brevior et incurva, ⟨foliis

---

[1] prosunt, prodest *Detlefsen* : prodest *codd.* : prosunt *vulg.*
Post trita *lacunam indic. Dioscoridem secuti Ian., Mayhoff,
sic fere explendam* : inflammationibus medentur, **trita**. *Sed hoc
loco non ita similes sunt Plinius et Dioscorides.*

---

[a] See XII. § 108.
[b] *Privatim* is a difficult word in Pliny. Usually rendered
"especially," it often suggests that the other things are
excluded.

XVII. Sphagnos, or sphacos, or bryon, grows also, *Sphagnos.* as I have [a] pointed out, in Gaul. It is useful in the sitz bath for uterine affections, and beaten up, and mixed with cress and salt water, it is also good for the knees and for swellings on the thighs. Taken in drink moreover, with wine and dry resin, it very quickly acts as a diuretic. Beaten up and drunk with wine and juniper berries, it drains off the water in dropsy.

XVIII. The leaves and root of the turpentine-tree *Turpentine tree (terebinth).* are applied locally to gatherings; a decoction of them strengthens the stomach. The seed is taken in wine for headache and strangury; it is a gentle aperient and an aphrodisiac.

XIX. The leaves of pitch-pine and of the larch *Pitch pine and larch.* crushed and boiled down in vinegar are good for toothache, and the ash of their bark for chafing and burns. Taken in drink it checks looseness of the bowels, is diuretic, and as a fumigation reduces a displaced uterus. The leaves of pitch-pine are specific [b] for affections of the liver, the dose being a drachma by weight taken in hydromel. It is well known that woods consisting only of those trees from which pitch and resin are scraped off are very beneficial to consumptives, or to those who cannot convalesce after a long illness, and that the air in districts so planted is more health-giving than a sea-voyage to Egypt, or than draughts of milk from cattle that have grazed along summer pastures in the mountains.

XX. The ground-pine, the Latin name of which is *The ground-pine.* abiga, because it causes abortion, and to some known as "earth-incense," has branches a cubit in length, with the flowers and the smell of the pine. A second species is shorter and bent, with leaves like those of

aizoo⟩[1] similis. tertia eodem odore et ideo nomine
quoque, parvula, cauliculo digitali, foliis scabris,
exilibus, albis, in petris nascens, omnes herbae, sed
propter cognationem nominis non differendae. prosunt adversus scorpionum ictus, item iocineri inlitae
cum palmis aut cotoneis ; renibus et vesicae decoctum
30 earum cum farina hordeacea. morbo quoque regio
et urinae difficultatibus ex aqua decoctae bibuntur.
novissima contra serpentes valet cum melle, sic et
adpositu vulvas purgat. sanguinem densatum extrahit pota. sudores facit perunctis ea, peculiariter
renibus utilis. fiunt ex ea et hydropicis pilulae cum
fico alvum trahentes. lumborum dolorem victoriati
pondere in vino finit et tussim recentem. mortuos
partus ex aceto cocta et pota eicere protinus dicitur.

31 XXI. Cum honore et pityusa simili de causa
dicetur, quam quidam in tithymali genere numerant.
frutex est similis piceae, flore parvo purpureo. bilem
et pituitam per alvum detrahit radix decocti[2] hemina
aut seminis lingula in balanis. folia in aceto decocta
furfures cutis emendant, mammas quoque mixto
rutae decocto et tormina et serpentium ictus et in
totum collectiones incipientes.

---

[1] incurva, ⟨foliis aizoo⟩ *ex Dioscoride coni. Mayhoff, sed in
extu lacunam indicat*: incurvae E(?) *vulg.* : incurva VdX.
[2] decoctā *vel* decoctā *vel* radicis decoctae *coni. Warmington.*

---

[a] The correction of Mayhoff makes good sense, and corresponds to Dioscorides III. 158 (Wellmann): φύλλα δὲ ἔχει ὅμοια
ἀειζώῳ. But it is very conjectural. The vulgate *incurvae* has
little MS. support, and *incurvae similis* ("like one bent ") is
an odd phrase.

[b] All three are *plants*, with a name derived from the *tree*
πίτυς.

[c] "*Sive conglobatum . . . quod in praecipitatis potissimum
evenit.*" (Didot edition from Hardouin.)

aizoüm.[a] A third variety has the same smell, and
therefore also the same name; it is rather small,
with a stem as thick as a finger, and with rough, slender, pale leaves, growing on rocky soils. All three
are [b] plants, not trees, but should be considered here
because their names are derived from that of the pine.
They are good for the stings of scorpions, and also for
the liver when applied with dates or quinces, as is a
decoction of them with barley meal for the kidneys
and bladder. Decoctions of them in water are taken
also for jaundice and for strangury. The last mentioned kind mixed with honey counteracts the poison
of serpents, and in this form too purges the uterus
when used as a pessary. Taken as drink it draws away
extravasated blood.[c] Rubbing with it promotes perspiration, and it is particularly good for the kidneys.
It is also made up into pills with figs for dropsy;
these purge the bowels.[d] In doses of one victoriatus
by weight in wine it ends lumbago, and also coughs
if taken in good time. A decoction in vinegar taken
as a drink is said to expel at once the dead foetus.

XXI. For a like reason honourable mention shall *Pityusa.*
be made of pityusa also, which some include in the
same class as tithymalus. It is a shrub like the pitch-
pine, with a small, purple [e] flower. Bile and phlegm
are carried off in the stools by a decoction of the root,
the dose being one hemina, and by suppositories made
of a spoonful of the seed. A decoction of the leaves
in vinegar removes scaly eruptions on the skin and,
mixed with a decoction of rue, is good for affections
of the breasts, for griping pains, for snake bites and
for gatherings in general in their early stages.

[d] Or, "pills, which with fig purge etc." It is implied that
this relieves the dropsy.   [e] A mistake.

32 XXII. Resinam e supra dictis arboribus gigni
docuimus et genera eius et nationes in ratione vini,
ac postea in arboribus. summae species duae, sicca
et liquida. sicca e pinu et picea fit, liquida tere-
bintho, larice, lentisco, cupresso. nam et hae ferunt
33 in Asia et Syria. falluntur qui eandem putant esse e
picea atque larice. picea enim pinguem et turis
modo sucosam fundit, larix gracilem ac mellei coloris,
virus redolentem. medici liquida raro utuntur et in
ovo fere e larice propter tussim ulceraque viscerum
34 —nec pinea magnopere in usu—ceteris non nisi
coctis. et coquendi genera satis demonstravimus.
arborum differentia placet terebinthina odoratis-
sima atque levissima, nationum Cypria et Syriaca,
utraque mellis Attici colore, sed Cypria carnosior
crassiorque. in sicco genere quaerunt ut sit candida,
pura, perlucida, in omni autem ut montana potius
quam campestris, item aquilonia potius quam ab alio
vento. resolvitur resina ad vulnerum usus et malag-
35 mata oleo, in potiones [1] amygdalis amaris. natura
in medendo contrahere vulnera, purgare, discutere
collectiones; item pectoris vitia terebinthina.[2]
inlinitur eadem calida membrorum doloribus spatia-

[1] *Fortasse excidit* cum *ante* amygdalis.
[2] item pectoris vitia terebinthina] *dist. ego* : item pectoris
vitia. terebinthina *Detlefsen* : lenit pectoris vitia terebinthina; *Mayhoff.*

---

[a] See XIV. § 122.
[b] See XVI. § 38.
[c] To which does *hae* refer ?
[d] See XVI. § 54.
[e] The bare ablative appears strange. Perhaps the juice of
the almonds has, or was supposed to have, a softening
effect. Perhaps almond oil is meant. See XXV § 118.

XXII. That resin is derived from the trees men- Resin.
tioned above, with its various kinds and native regions,
I have stated in my account of wine,[a] and afterwards [b]
when dealing with trees. The most general classes
are two—the dry resin and the liquid. Dry resin
comes from the pine and the pitch-pine, the liquid
from the terebinth, larch, lentisk and cypress. For
in Asia and Syria these last [c] also produce it. They
are mistaken who think that the same resin comes
from the pitch-pine as comes from the larch. For
the pitch-pine exudes a resin that is rich, and like
frankincense in consistency, while the larch produces
a thin resin with the colour of honey and a very
offensive odour. Medical men use liquid resin only
occasionally, generally that from the larch and
administered in egg, for coughs and ulcerated bowels,
nor is that from the pine much used; the others are
only employed after boiling. The various ways of boiling I have fully explained.[d] Of the various trees producing resin, the favourite is the terebinth, which yields
one highly scented and very light; of the regions,
Cyprus and Syria are most favoured; both resins are
of the colour of Attic honey, but the Cyprian is thicker,
with more body in it. In the dry kind the qualities
looked for are whiteness, purity and transparency;
in every kind, however, that from a mountain soil is
preferred to that from the plains, and a north-east
aspect produces more highly esteemed resin than any
other. Resin is dissolved in oil for the treatment
of wounds and for poultices; by means of [e] bitter
almonds when used for draughts. Its medical properties are to close wounds, to act as a detergent, and
to disperse gatherings; terebinth resin is also good for
chest complaints. The last when warmed is used as

tisque[1] in sole avellitur,[2] et totis corporibus man-
gonum maxime[3] cura ad gracilitatem emendandam,
spatiis ita laxantium cutem per singula membra,
36 capacioraque ciborum facienda corpora. proximum
locum optinet e lentisco. inest ei vis adstringendi,
movet at ante ceteras urinam. reliquae ventrem
molliunt, cruda concocunt, tussim veterem sedant,
vulvae onera extrahunt etiam suffitae. privatim
adversantur visco, panos et similia cum sebo taurino
et melle sanant. palpebras lentiscina commodissime
replicat, fractis quoque utilissima et auribus purulentis, item in pruritu genitalium. pinea capitis
vulneribus optime medetur.

37   XXIII. Pix quoque unde et quibus conficeretur
modis indicavimus, et eius duo genera, spissum
liquidumque. spissarum utilissima medicinae
Bruttia, quoniam pinguissima et resinosissima utras-
que praebet utilitates, ob id magis rutila quam
ceterae. id enim quod in hoc adiciunt, ex mascula
arbore meliorem esse, non arbitror posse intellegi.
38 picis natura excalfacit, explet. adversatur privatim
cerastae morsibus cum polenta, item anginae cum

---

[1] spatiatisque] spasticisque *Mayhoff*; *sed vide infra* spatiis.
[2] avellitur *plures codd.*, *Detlefsen* : abluitur *Mayhoff*, *qui*
in sole abluitur *in parenthesi ponit.*
[3] maxime] *An* maxima ?

---

[a] Mayhoff's text : " and for cramps—it is washed off in the
sun—."
[b] For *privatim* see note b XXIV. 28, p. 24.
[c] See XIV. § 127 foll., and XVI. § 52 foll.
[d] That is, of resin and of pitch.

an ointment for pains in the limbs; it is removed after a walk has been taken [a] in the sun. Slave-dealers especially are anxious to use this ointment for rubbing over the whole bodies of their slaves, with the object of correcting thinness; by walks afterwards they loosen the skin of every limb, and they have the further object of making possible the assimilation of a greater quantity of food. Next in popularity after terebinth resin comes that from the lentisk, which has an astringent quality and is more diuretic than the others. The rest of the resins loosen the bowels, cure indigestion, relieve chronic coughs, and also, when used as a fumigation, remove obstructions in the uterus. These are specific [b] for the poison of mistletoe, and with beef suet and honey they heal superficial abscesses and similar affections. Lentisk resin is a most excellent remedy for turning outwards ingrowing eye-lashes, and is also very useful for fractures and for pus in the ears, and also for irritation of the genitals. Pine resin is a very good remedy for wounds in the head.

XXIII. Pitch too, its source and the methods of preparing it, I have already [c] mentioned, as well as its two kinds, the thick and the thin. Of the thick pitches the most useful in medicine is the Bruttian, because being both very rich and very resinous it combines the useful properties of both,[d] the yellow-red kind being of higher value than any other because of this combination. For the further opinion about pitch, that the male tree produces a better kind, cannot I think be entertained. The nature of pitch is to warm, and to fill out the flesh. Mixed with pearl barley it is a specific antidote for the bite of the horned viper, and with

Pitch.

melle, destillationibus et sternutamentis a pituita.
auribus infunditur cum rosaceo, inlinitur cum cera.[1]
sanat lichenas, alvum solvit, excreationes pectoris
adiuvat ecligmate aut inlitis tonsillis cum melle.
sic et ulcera purgat, explet. cum uva passa et
axungia carbunculos purgat et putrescentia ulcera,
quae vero serpunt cum pineo cortice aut sulpure.

39 phthisicis cyathi mensura quidam dederunt et contra
veterem tussim. rhagadas sedis et pedum panosque
et ungues scabros emendat, vulvae duritias et con-
versiones, odore item lethargicos.[2] strumas cum
farina hordeacea et pueri inpubis urina decocta ad
suppurationem perducit. et ad alopecias sicca pice
utuntur, ad mulierum mammas Bruttia ex vino
subfervefacta cum polline farraceo quam calidissimis[3]
inpositis.

40 XXIV. Liquida pix oleumque quod pisselaeon
vocant quemadmodum fieret diximus. quidam
iterum decocunt et vocant palimpissam. liquida
anginae perunguntur intus. iuvat[4] aurium dolores,
claritatem oculorum, oris circumlitiones, suspiriosos,[5]
vulvas, tussim veterem et crebras exscreationes

---

[1] inlinitur cum cera.] *Haec verba post* pituita *ponenda esse putat Mayhoff, fortasse recte.*

[2] lethargicos.] *Ita dist. Urlichs.*

[3] calidissimis] *hic* linteis *add. Mayhoff.*

[4] iuvat aurium *Detlefsen*: et uva, ⟨oleum iuvat⟩ aurium *coni. Mayhoff.*

[5] suspiriosos *Alexander Benedictus* (1507), *Mayhoff*: suspiriosas *multi codd.*

---

[a] Mayhoff would transpose the second part of this sentence to the end of the preceding.

honey a good remedy for quinsy, catarrhs and sneezing caused by phlegm. Mixed with rose oil it is
poured into the ears, and with wax it is compounded
into an ointment.[a] It heals lichen and relaxes the
bowels; expectoration it eases if used as an electuary
or applied to the tonsils in combination with honey.
So used it also cleanses sores and fills them out.
With raisins and axle-grease it cleanses carbuncles
and festering sores; for creeping sores, however, it
is combined with pine bark or sulphur. Some
authorities have prescribed it in doses of one cyathus
for consumption and chronic cough. It cures chaps
in the seat, and on the feet, superficial abscesses,
scabrous nails, indurations and displacements of the
uterus, and lethargus by inhalation.[b] Scrofulous
sores it causes to suppurate if boiled with barley meal
and the urine of a child not yet adolescent. Dry pitch
is also used for mange; Bruttian pitch heated in wine,
with wheat meal, is applied to the breasts of women,
the applications being as hot as can be borne.[c]

XXIV. How liquid pitch and the oil called *Liquid pitch.*
pisselaeon [d] are made has been described already.[e]
Some boil it down twice and call it palimpissa.[f] Liquid
pitch is employed for painting quinsy internally. It
is good for ear-ache, for promoting clearness of vision,
for use as a lip-salve, for asthmatics, the uterus,
chronic cough, frequent expectoration, cramp, ner-

[b] Perhaps the comma should be transferred from *conver-
siones* to *odore*, thus making " by inhalation " apply to
uterine troubles.
[c] Mayhoff's *linteis* means linen swabs used for the applications.
[d] *I.e.* " pitch oil."
[e] See XVI. § 52.
[f] *I.e.* " pitch (boiled) twice."

pectoris, spasmos, tremores, opisthotonos, paralysis, nervorum dolores, praestantissimum ad canum et iumentorum scabiem.

41 XXV. Est et pissasphaltos mixta bitumini pice naturaliter ex Apolloniatarum agro. quidam ipsi miscent. praecipuum ad scabiem pecorum remedium aut si fetus mammas laeserit matrum.[1] optimum ex eo quod cum fervet innatat.

XXVI. Zopissam eradi navibus diximus cera marino sale macerata. optima haec a tirocinio navium. additur autem in malagmata ad discutiendas collectiones.

XXVII. Taeda decocta[2] in aceto dentium dolores efficaciter conluunt.

42 XXVIII. Lentisci ex arbore[3] et semen et cortex et lacrima urinam cient, alvum sistunt. decoctum eorum ulcera quae serpunt fotu. inlinitur umidis[4] et igni sacro, gingivas conluit. folia dentibus in dolore[5] atteruntur, mobiles decocto conluuntur, capillum tinguit.[6] lacrima sedis vitiis prodest, cum quid siccari excalfierive opus sit. decoctum et e lacrima[7] stomacho utile, ructum et urinam movens,

---

[1] matrum *veterem lectionem secuti Sillig, Detlefsen* : nativum *Mayhoff, qui punctum post* laeserit *ponit* : maturum *codd.*

[2] taeda decocta *Detlefsen* : taedae . . . . . decoctae *Mayhoff, qui ex Plinio iuniore lacunam sic explet,* in astulas concisae : *varia codd.*

[3] lentisci ex arbore *Detlefsen* : lentisci arboris *Mayhoff* : lentiscis EX : arbores EV *vulg.*

[4] umidis *Warmington* : in umidis *codd.*

[5] in dolore *vulg., Mayhoff* : dolore *codd., Detlefsen.*

[6] tinguit *codd., Detlefsen* : tingunt *vulg., Mayhoff.*

[7] e lacrima *codd.* : *in uncis Mayhoff* : et delere vult *Sillig.*

---

[a] See Dioscorides I. 73 § 1 (Wellmann) : ἐν Ἀπολλωνίᾳ τῇ πρὸς Ἐπιδάμνῳ.

[b] With Mayhoff's reading : " The best natural kind is that which, etc."

vous tremors, opisthotonic tetanus, paralysis, pains in the sinews, and most effectively for itch-scab in dogs and beasts of burden.

XXV. There is also pissasphaltos, that is pitch combined with bitumen, found in a natural state in the territory of Apollonia ;[a] it is sometimes made artificially. It is a specific for itch-scab in cattle and for the sores caused by the young on the teats of their mothers. The best part [b] of it is that which floats on the surface when it is boiled. *Pissasphaltos.*

XXVI. Zopissa, as I have said,[c] is scraped off ships, wax being soaked in sea brine. The best is taken from ships after their maiden voyage. It is also added to poultices to disperse gatherings. *Zopissa.*

XXVII. A decoction in vinegar of pitch pine [d] makes an efficacious wash for aching teeth.

XXVIII. Of the lentisk tree the seed, bark and gum-drops are diuretic, and astringent to the bowels. A decoction of them is a useful fomentation for creeping sores. It makes a liniment for moist sores and also for erysipelas, and it rinses the gums. The leaves are rubbed on the teeth when [e] they ache ; loose teeth are rinsed with the decoction, which also dyes the hair. The gum-drops are good for troubles of the seat, when there is a call for a drying and warming remedy. The decoction too of the gum is useful for the stomach, being carminative and diuretic, and is *The lentisk tree.*

[c] See XVI. § 56. Has *pice cum* been lost before *cera* ? See *ibid.* : zopissam vocari derasam navibus maritimis picem cum cera.

[d] Mayhoff from Pliny Junior : " Pitch pine cut into shavings and boiled in vinegar."

[e] In the MSS. the preposition *in* is found before *umidis*, where it is not wanted, and omitted before *dolore*, where it is. Perhaps it got misplaced in the archetype.

quod et capitis doloribus cum polenta illinitur.
43 folia tenera oculis inflammatis illinuntur. mastiche lentisci replicandis palpebris et ad extend-
endam cutem in facie et zmegmata adhibetur, et
sanguinem reicientibus, tussi veteri, et ad omnia
quae acaciae vis.[1] medetur et attritis partibus sive
oleo e semine eius facto ceraeque mixto, sive foliis ex
oleo decoctis, sive cum aqua ita[2] foveantur. scio
Democratem medicum in valitudine Considiae M.
Servili consularis filiae omnem curationem austeram
recusantis diu efficaciter usum lacte caprarum quas
lentisco pascebat.

44 XXIX. Platani adversantur vespertilionibus,
pilulae earum in vino potae denariorum iiii pondere omnibus serpentium et scorpionum venenis,
item ambustis. tunsae autem cum aceto acri
magisque scillite sanguinem omnem sistunt et lenti-
ginem et carcinomata malandriasque veteres addito
45 melle emendant. folia autem et cortex inlinuntur
collectionibus et suppurationibus, et decoctum eorum,
corticis autem in aceto dentium remedium est,
foliorum tenerrima in vino albo decocta oculorum.
lanugo florum[3] et auribus et oculis inutilis. cinis
pilularum sanat ambusta igni vel frigore. cortex e
vino scorpionum ictus restinguit.

[1] quae acaciae vis *ex Dioscoride Sillig, Detlefsen, Mayhoff*:
quaevis, qua eius, quae eis, que vis *codd.* : quae hammoniaci
vis *vulg.*
[2] ita *Mayhoff*: ut ita VdT: utilia X : virilia *Hermolaus Barbarus. Mayhoff ita emendat* : si hae cum aqua ita foveantur.
[3] florum *coni. Warmington* : foliorum *codd.*

also applied with pearl barley for headache. The tender leaves are applied to inflamed eyes. The mastic of the lentisk is applied for bending back the eye-lashes, for filling out and smoothing the skin of the face, being also useful for spitting of blood, chronic cough, and in all cases where the medical properties of gum acacia are called for. Abrasions are treated by applying the oil made from the seed of lentisk mixed with wax, or a decoction of the leaves in oil; or they may be fomented with these preparations and water. I know for a fact that when the illness of Considia, daughter of Marcus Servilius, a consular, long [a] resisted all rigorous treatment, it was cured by the physician Democrites, who used the milk of goats which he fed on the lentisk.

XXIX. The plane tree neutralizes the poison of the *The plane.* bat; its seed-globules taken in wine in a dose of four denarii act similarly on all poisons of serpents and scorpions, besides healing burns. Pounded moreover with strong vinegar, especially squill-seasoned vinegar, it checks all bleeding, and with the addition of honey removes freckles, cancerous sores and chronic pustules on the neck. The leaves moreover and bark make ointment for gatherings and suppurations, and so does a decoction of them; a decoction of the bark in vinegar is a remedy for sore teeth, but for the eyes a decoction of the most tender leaves in white wine must be made. The down of the flowers is harmful both to the ears and to the eyes. The ashes of the burnt globules heal burns and frost-bites. The bark in wine allays the stings of scorpions.

---

[a] Littré takes *diu* with *usum.* Query: "who refused rigorous treatment."

46   XXX. Fraxinus quam vim adversus serpentes
haberet indicavimus. semen foliis eius inest, quae [1]
medentur iocineris, laterum doloribus in vino, aquam
quae subit cutem extrahunt. corpus obesum levant
onere sensim ad maciem reducentia,[2] isdem foliis cum
vino tritis ad virium portionem, ita ut puero quinque
folia tribus cyathis diluantur,[3] robustioribus septem
folia quinis vini. non omittendum ramenta eius et
scobem a quibusdam cavenda praedici.

XXXI. Aceris radix contunsa e vino iocineris
doloribus efficacissime inponitur.

47   XXXII. Populi albae uvarum in unguentis usum
exposuimus. cortex potus ischiadicis et stranguriae
prodest, foliorum sucus calidus aurium dolori.
virgam populi in manu tenentibus intertrigo non
metuatur.[4] populus nigra efficacissima habetur quae
in Creta nascitur. comitialibus semen ex aceto
utile.[5] fundit illa et resinam exiguam, qua utuntur
ad malagmata. folia podagris in aceto decocta
inponuntur. umor e cavis populi nigrae effluens et [6]

[1] quae *cum duobus codd., vulg., Sillig, Detlefsen* : quo *cum
duobus Mayhoff.*

[2] reducentia *codd.* : reducentibus *Mayhoff.*

[3] diluantur *cum duobus codd. Detlefsen* : dirivantur E :
dentur *vulg.* : diribeantur *Mayhoff qui confert* XI. § 44 *et*
XXXVI. § 118.

[4] metuatur *aut* metuitur *codd.*

[5] utile *Mayhoff* : inditur *Detlefsen* : in *codd.*

[6] et attritu odoratus] *post* papulasque (*sed cum vv. ll.*)
codd.; *transposuit Urlichs*; est attritu odoratus *in parenthesi
Mayhoff.*

---

[a] See XVI. § 64.
[b] I.e. the "wings," in each of which a seed lies.
[c] I.e. winged seeds.
[d] Book XII. § 132. *Uvarum* seems to refer to *catkins.*
[e] Dioscorides I. 83 (Wellmann) says : τὸ ἐξ αὐτῶν δάκρυον

XXX. The power of the ash-tree to neutralize the *The ash.* poison of snakes I have already mentioned.[a] The seed lies between its leaves,[b] which in wine are used for pains in the liver and sides, and draw off the subcutaneous water of dropsy. They lessen corpulence, gradually reducing the body to leanness. These leaves [c] are also beaten up with wine in proportion to the strength of the body; for a child five leaves are soaked in three cyathi of wine, for stronger patients seven leaves in five cyathi. I must not forget the warning of some authorities, who declare that the shavings and sawdust of the ash are to be avoided.

XXXI. The root of the maple crushed in wine *The maple.* makes a very efficacious application for pains of the liver.

XXXII. The clusters of the white poplar, as I have *The white* already described,[d] are used in making unguents. A *poplar.* draught made from the bark is good for sciatica and strangury, and the juice of the leaves, warmed, for ear-ache. Those who hold in their hand a twig of poplar need not fear chafing between the legs. The *The black* black poplar that grows in Crete is considered the *poplar.* most efficacious; the seed in vinegar is good for epilepsy. It also discharges a small quantity of resin, which is used for poultices. A decoction of the leaves in vinegar is applied locally for gout. The moisture exuding from the hollows of the black poplar, and giving out an odour [e] when applied with rubbing,

. . . καταχεόμενον πήγνυσθαι καὶ γίνεσθαι τὸ καλούμενον ἤλεκτρον . . . εὐῶδες ἐν τῇ παρατρίψει. This points to a lacuna in the text of Pliny (or possibly to a mistake or omission on the part of Pliny himself), for though ἤλεκτρον could easily be rubbed, an *umor* could only be used in rubbing something else. Yet Pliny's *attritu odoratus* is obviously a translation of something like εὐῶδες ἐν τῇ παρατρίψει.

attritu odoratus verrucas papulasque tollit. populi
ferunt et in foliis guttam ex qua apes propolim
faciunt. gutta quoque ad quae propolis ex aqua
efficax.

48   XXXIII. Ulmi et folia et cortex et rami vim habent
spissandi et volnera contrahendi. corticis utique
interior tilia lepras sedat et folia ex aceto inlita.
corticis denarii pondus potum in hemina aquae
frigidae alvum purgat pituitasque et aquas privatim
trahit. inponitur et collectionibus lacrima et volneribus et ambustis quae decocto fovere prodest.
49 umor in folliculis arboris huius nascens cuti nitorem
inducit faciemque gratiorem praestat. cauliculi
foliorum primi vino decocti tumores sanant extrahuntque per fistulas.   idem praestant et tiliae corticis.
multi corticem commanducatum volneribus utilissimum putant, folia trita aqua adspersa pedum
tumori. umor quoque e medulla, uti diximus,
castratae arboris effluens capillum reddit capiti
inlitus defluentesque continet.

50   XXXIV. Arbor tilia lenius ad eadem fere utilis
est atque [1] oleaster. folia autem tantum in usu et ad
infantium ulcera et in ore, et commanducata et
decocta urinam cient, menses sistunt inlita, sanguinem
pota detrahunt.

---

[1] atque *cum codd. fere omnibus Detlefsen* : ad quae *cum* X
Mayhoff, qui atque *contra Plinii usum esse dicit.*

---

[a] This seems to be the meaning of *spissare* here because of *volnera contrahendi* immediately following. *Spissare*
is a common word in Pliny, usually without an expressed object, but in XXVI. § 46 *ad spissanda corpora* seems to mean
" to give tone to (harden ?) the body," as in Celsus II. i. § 10.

removes warts and pimples. Poplars also produce on their leaves drops from which bees make bee-glue. With water these drops also have the same healing properties as bee-glue.

XXXIII. The leaves, bark and branches of the elm *The elm.* are styptic,[a] and have the property of closing wounds. The inner bark in particular relieves leprous sores, as also does a local application of the leaves soaked in vinegar. One denarius of the bark, taken in a hemina of cold water, purges the bowels, being specific for carrying off phlegms and watery humours. Its tear is also applied locally to gatherings, wounds and burns, which it is good to foment with a decoction. The moisture forming in the pods of this tree brings a brightness to the skin and makes the looks more pleasing. The tips of the little stalks of the leaves boiled down in wine cure tumours and draw out the pus through fistulas. The same property is shown by the inner barks. Many hold that the bark when chewed is very good for wounds, and that the leaves, pounded and sprinkled with water, are so for swollen feet. An application of the moisture too, that exudes, as I have said,[b] from the pith of the tree when lopped, restores hair to the scalp and prevents it from falling out.

XXXIV. The linden tree is good for practically *The linden.* the same purposes as the wild olive, but its action is milder. Only its leaves, however, are used both for babies' sores and for those in the mouth; they may be chewed or a decoction may be made of them; they are diuretic. Applied locally they check menstruation; taken in drink they draw off extravasated blood.

[b] Book XVI. § 192.

51 **XXXV.** Sabucus habet alterum genus magis silvestre quod Graeci chamaeacten, alii helion[1] vocant, multo brevius. utriusque decoctum in vino veteri, foliorum vel seminis vel radicis, ad cyathos binos potum stomacho inutile est,[2] alvo detrahens aquam. refrigerat etiam inflammationem, maxime recentis ambusti,[3] et canis morsum cum polenta mollissimis foliorum inlitis. sucus cerebri collectiones privatimque membranae quae circa cerebrum

52 est lenit infusus. acini eius infirmiores quam reliqua ; tingunt capillum, poti acetabuli mensura urinam movent. foliorum mollissima ex oleo et sale eduntur ad pituitam bilemque detrahendam. ad omnia efficacior quae minor. radicis eius decoctae in vino duo cyathi poti hydropicos exinaniunt, volvas emolliunt, has et foliorum decocta[4] insidentium. caules teneri mitioris[5] sabuci in patinis cocti alvum solvunt, resistunt folia et serpentium ictibus in

53 vino pota. podagricis cum sebo hircino vehementer prosunt cauliculi inliti ; iidem in aqua macerantur ut sparsa ea pulices necentur. foliorum decocto si locus spargatur, muscae necantur. boa appellatur morbus papularum, cum rubent corpora; sabuci ramo verberatur. cortex interior tritus ex vino albo potus alvum solvit.

[1] helion] *add.* acten *e Dioscoride* (ἔλειος ἀκτή) H. Haffter.
[2] est *cum codd. Detlefsen* : set *ex Dioscoride* (μέντοι) *coni.* Mayhoff. *Pro* inutile *fortasse* utile, *quod in* X *invenitur.*
[3] recentis ambusti *codd.* : recentia ambusta *Mayhoff.*
[4] decocta *codd.* : decoctum *Mayhoff.*
[5] minoris *coni. Warmington coll.* § 51 : mitioris *codd.*

---

[a] *Infundo* is used of administering food and drink generally or of medicine in particular. Sometimes, but not as often as might be expected, it is used of injections. Here it seems to be used, not of injections into the skull, but of anointing.

XXXV. The elder has a second, a much smaller *The elder.*
pecies, growing wilder and called by the Greeks
chamaeacte, by others helion. A decoction in old
wine of the leaves, seed, or root, of either species,
taken as drink up to two cyathi for a dose, is bad for
the stomach, though carrying off watery humours
from the bowels. It also reduces inflammation,
especially that of a recent burn, and a dog-bite is
relieved by a poultice of its most tender leaves with
pearl barley. An application *a* of the juice softens
gatherings on the brain, being specific when these are
on the membrane that surrounds it. Its berries have
weaker properties than the other parts. They dye
the hair. A dose of one acetabulum taken in drink is
diuretic. The softest of the leaves are eaten with oil
and salt to bring away phlegm and bile. For all
purposes the smaller kind is the more efficacious. A
decoction of the root in wine, taken in doses of two
cyathi, draws off the water of dropsy; it also softens
the uterus, as does also sitting in baths of a decoction
of the leaves. The tender stalks of the cultivated
elder boiled in a saucepan relax the bowels; the leaves
taken in wine also counteract the bites of snakes.
An application of young shoots with goat-suet is very
good for gout; these are also steeped in water to kill
fleas by sprinkling. If a place is sprinkled with a
decoction of the leaves flies are killed. Boa *b* is the
name given to a disease when the body is red with
pimples; beating with a branch of elder is administered as a remedy. The inner bark pounded and
taken in white wine relaxes the bowels.

b Hardouin was wrong in supposing it to be measles, because
that disease was probably not known until the time of Rhazes.
See list of diseases.

54 XXXVI. Iunipirus vel ante cetera omnia excalfacit, extenuat, cedro alias similis. et huius duo genera, altera minor altera. utraque accensa serpentes fugat. semen stomachi, pectoris, lateris doloribus utile. inflationes algoresque discutit, tusses, con-
55 coquit duritias. inlitum tumores sistit, item alvum bacis ex nigro vino potis, item ventris tumores inlitis. miscetur et antidotis, oxyporis; urinas ciet. inlinitur et oculis in epiphoris. datur convolsis, ruptis, torminibus, volvis, ischiadicis cum vino albo potum pilulis quaternis aut decoctis viginti in vino. sunt qui et perunguant corpus [1] e semine eius in serpentium ictus.[2]

56 XXXVII. Salicis fructus ante maturitatem in araneam abit, sed, si prius colligatur, sanguinem reicientibus prodest. corticis e ramis primis cinis clavum et callum aqua mixta sanat. vitia cutis in facie emen-
57 dat, magis admixto suco suo. est autem hic trium generum : unum arbor ipsa exsudat cummium modo, altero manat in plaga, cum floret, exciso cortice trium digitorum magnitudine. hic [3] ad expurganda quae obstent oculis, item ad spissanda quae opus sunt ciendamque urinam et ad omnes collectiones intus extrahendas. tertius sucus est detruncatione ramo-

---

[1] *Post* corpus *excidisse* suco *putat Mayhoff.*
[2] ictus VT f, *Detlefsen* : metu *vulg., Mayhoff* : metus EX.
[3] hic *codd.* : vis *Mayhoff.*

---

[a] Hard swellings or abscesses.
[b] Galen uses ὀξύπορον (or ὀξυπόριον) of a carminative, a sense that suits very well XX. § 65 and § 256. Mayhoff is surely right in putting a comma after *antidotis*, avoiding in this way the awkwardness of taking *oxyporus* as an adjective (" quick-acting "). Cf. Dioscorides III. 57 : μειγνύμενον ταῖς ἀντιδότοις καὶ ὀξυπόροις χρησίμως.
[c] Mayhoff's *vis* would mean : " Its property is to clear away, etc."

XXXVI. The juniper, even above all other remedies, *The juniper.* is warming and alleviates symptoms; for the rest, it resembles the cedrus. Of it there are two species, one smaller than the other. Either kind when set on fire keeps off snakes. The seed is beneficial for pains in the stomach, chest and side, dispels flatulence and the feeling of chill, relieves coughs and matures indurations.[a] Applied locally it checks tumours; the berries taken in dark wine bind the bowels, and a local application reduces tumours of the belly. The fruit is also an ingredient of antidotes and of digestive remedies,[b] and is diuretic. It is also applied locally to the eyes for fluxes, and it is used for sprains, ruptures, colic, uterine disorders and sciatica, either in doses of four berries with white wine, or a decoction of twenty in wine. There are also some who smear the body with an extract of the seed as a protection against snake-bite.

XXXVII. The fruit of the willow before maturity *The willow.* develops a kind of cobweb, but if it be gathered earlier it is good for the spitting of blood. Mixed with water, the ash from the burnt bark of the tips of the branches cures corns and callosities. It removes spots on the face, more thoroughly when mixed with willow juice. This juice, however, is of three kinds: one exudes like gum from the tree itself; the second flows from an incision, three fingers wide, made in the bark while the tree is in blossom. This sort[c] is useful for clearing away humours that obstruct the eyes, also for thickening[d] where that is necessary, for promoting urine and for draining outwards all gatherings. The third kind of juice is obtained by lopping

[a] The word *spissare* is difficult. See note on XXIV § 48.

rum a falce distillans. ex his ergo aliquis cum rosaceo
in calyce punici calfactus auribus infunditur vel folia
58 cocta et cum cera trita imponuntur.[1] item podagricis cortice et foliis in vino decoctis foveri nervos
utilissimum. flos tritus cum foliis furfures purgat in
facie. folia contrita et pota intemperantiam libidinis
coercent atque in totum auferunt usum saepius
sumpta. Amerinae nigrae semen cum spuma argenti
pari pondere a balneo[a] inlitum psilotrum est.

59   XXXVIII. Non multum a salice vitilium usu distat
vitex, foliorum quoque adspectu, nisi odore gratior
esset. Graeci lygon vocant, alias agnon, quoniam
matronae Thesmophoriis Atheniensium castitatem
custodientes his foliis cubitus sibi sternunt. duo
genera eius : maior in arborem salicis modo adsurgit,
minor ramosa, foliis candidioribus, lanuginosis.
prima album florem mittit cum purpureo, quae et
candida vocatur, nigra quae tantum purpureum.
60 nascuntur in palustribus campis. semen potum vini
quendam saporem habet et dicitur febres solvere et,
cum unguantur oleo admixto, sudorem facere, sicut
lassitudinem dissolvere. urinam cient et menses.
caput temptant vini modo—nam et odor similis
est [2]—inflationes pellunt in inferiora, alvum sistunt,
61 hydropicis et lienibus perquam utiles. lactis ubertatem faciunt,[b] adversantur venenis serpentium,

---

[1] *Ita dist. Mayhoff, Dioscoridem et Serenum secutus. Comma
post* imponuntur, *punctum post* podagricis *Detlefsen.*
[2] est *cum tribus codd. Detlefsen* : et *cum duobus Sillig* : set
Mayhoff.

---

[a] Or, " from " or "after using." Cf. *a balneo* § 58.
[b] The plural verb seems to imply that either kind of agnus
may be used.

off the branches, when it drips under *a* the sickle.
One, then, of these juices warmed in a pomegranate
rind with rose oil is poured into the ears, or a local
application is made of the boiled leaves beaten up with
wax. For gout too it is most useful to foment the
sinews with a decoction of the bark and leaves in wine.
The blossom beaten up with the leaves removes scurf
on the face. The leaves thoroughly pounded and
taken in drink check over-lustful desire; too many
doses produce absolute impotence. The seed of the
black willow of Ameria with an equal weight of
litharge, applied after the bath, acts as a depilatory.

XXXVIII. The agnus castus is not very different *The agnus*
from the willow, either for its use in wickerwork or in *castus.*
the appearance of its leaves, but it has a more pleasant
smell. The Greeks call it lygos, sometimes agnos,
because the Athenian matrons, preserving their
chastity at the Thesmophoria, strew their beds with
its leaves. There are two kinds of it. The larger
grows up to be a tree like the willow; the smaller is
branchy, with paler, downy leaves. The first bears
pale blossom with some purple in it, and is called the
white agnus; the other, which bears only purple
blossom, is called the dark agnus. They grow on
marshy plains. The seed taken in drink has a taste
somewhat like wine; it is said to reduce fevers, to
stimulate perspiration when applied as embrocation
with oil, and also to dispel lassitude. The trees *b*
furnish medicines that promote urine and menstruation. They go to the head like wine—for the smell
too is similar—drive flatulence into the lower bowels,
check diarrhoea, and greatly benefit dropsy and
splenic diseases. They *b* encourage abundant rich
milk, and neutralize the poisons of serpents, especially

47

maxime quae frigus inferunt, minor efficacior ad
serpentes, bibitur seminis drachma in vino vel posca
aut duabus foliorum tenerrimorum. et inlinuntur
utraque adversus araneorum morsus; vel perunctis
tantum, suffitu quoque aut substratu fugant venenata.

62 ad venerem impetus inhibent, eoque maxime
phalangiis adversantur, quorum morsus genitale
excitat. capitis dolorem ex ebrietate sedant cum
rosaceo flos tenerique cauliculi. seminis decoctum
vehementiorem capitis dolorem dissolvit fotu, et
vulvam etiam suffitu vel adposito purgat, alvum cum
puleio et melle potum. vomicas et panos difficile

63 concoquentes[1] cum farina hordeacea mollit. lichenas
et lentigines cum aphronitro et aceto semen sanat, et
oris ulcera et eruptionum[2] cum melle, testium cum
butyro et foliis vitium, rhagadas sedis cum aqua
illitum, luxata[3] cum sale et nitro et cera. cum[4]
semine et folium[5] additur in malagmata[6] . . . . . .
nervorum et podagras. semen instillatur in oleo
decoctum capiti in lethargia et phrenesi. virgam
qui in manu habeant aut in cinctu negantur inter-
triginem sentire.

[1] concoquentes *excepto* X *codd.* : concoquent tusi X :
concoquens *Mayhoff*.

[2] eruptionum] eruptiones ulcerum *vel* eorum *coni. Mayhoff*.

[3] luxata E, *Detlefsen* : luxatis *cum multis codd. Mayhoff, qui
ita emendat* : cum sale et nitro et cera et semine ⟨utilissimae⟩
et folio. additur in malagmata ⟨ad vitia⟩ nervorum etc.

[4] cum *ego* ; et *codd. et edd.*

[5] folium E : folio *ceteri codd.*

[6] *Excidit hic aliquid,* ad dolorem *vel* ad vitium.

---

[a] Forcellini *s.v.* concoquo supplies *collectum pus.* If the
reading be correct this will be the right explanation, as *concoquo*
seems never to be used intransitively. The MS. X has *facile*

48

those that bring on chill. The smaller kind makes the more effective remedies for the bite of serpents; one drachma of the seed, or two of the most tender leaves, is taken in wine, or in vinegar and water. Either kind makes a liniment for the bites of spiders; mere smearing drives away poisonous creatures, as does fumigation also, or placing some of the plant under the bed. They check violent sexual desire, and for this reason in particular they act as antidotes to the venomous spider, the bite of which excites the genitals. The blossom and tender shoots mixed with rose oil clear away headache due to intoxication. The seed takes away by fomentation with a decoction the more severe type of headache, purges the uterus also by fumigation or a pessary, and the bowels if drunk with pennyroyal and honey. Boils and superficial abscesses that refuse to come to a head [a] are softened by an application of it with barley meal. With saltpetre and vinegar the seed cures lichens and freckles, with honey sores of the mouth and of eruptions,[b] those of the testes with butter and vine leaves, chaps in the seat when applied with water, dislocations when applied with salt, soda and wax. With the seed the leaves too are added to plasters ⟨for the relief of painful⟩ sinews and of gout. A decoction of the seed in oil is poured in drops on the head of sufferers from lethargus or phrenitis. It is said that those who keep a twig in their hand or in their girdle do not suffer from chafing between the thighs.

concoquent tusi, showing that some scribes felt the difficulty. With Mayhoff's conjecture translate : " With barley meal it softens, though it matures them with difficulty, boils, etc."

[b] Mayhoff's conjecture would give : " sores in the mouth and eruptions of them." He compares XXII § 54 ulcerum eruptiones.

64 XXXIX. Ericen Graeci vocant fruticem non multum a vitice[1] differentem, colore roris marini et paene folio. hoc adversari serpentibus tradunt.

65 XL. Genista quoque vinculi usum praestat, floris apibus gratissimi. dubito an haec sit quam Graeci auctores sparton appellavere, cum ex ea lina piscatoria apud eos factitari docuerim, et numquid hanc designaverit Homerus, cum dixit navium sparta dissoluta. nondum enim fuisse Hispanum Africanumve spartum in usu certum est, et cum fierent sutiles naves, lino tamen, non sparto umquam sutas. semen eius, quod Graeci eodem nomine appellant in folliculis passiolorum modo nascens purgat hellebori vice drachma et dimidia pota in aquae mulsae cyathis

66 quattuor ieiunis. rami simul et frondes[2] aceto macerati pluribus diebus et tunsi sucum dant ischiadicis utilem cyathi unius potu. quidam marina aqua macerare malunt et infundere clystere. perunguntur eodem suco ischiadici addito oleo. quidam et ad stranguriam utuntur semine. genista tunsa cum axungia genua dolentia sanat.

[1] a vitice § 67 collato Mayhoff : a myrice E, Detlefsen.
[2] simul et frondes ego ex Mayhoffii coniecturis : similiter frondei Ianus, Detlefsen : similiter fronde codd.

[a] With the reading myrice, " tamarisk."
[b] Book XIX. § 15.
[c] See Iliad II. 135, σπάρτα λέλυνται. Pliny, as Varro in

XXXIX. The Greeks call erice (heath) a shrub *Erice.*
differing only a little from the agnus castus ; [a] it has
the same colour and very nearly the same leaf as
rosemary. Report says that it counteracts the
poison of serpents.

XL. Genista also is used for cords, and has a flower *Greenweed.*
of which bees are very fond. I wonder whether this
is the plant that Greek writers have called sparton,
because, as I have mentioned,[b] from it the Greeks
are wont to make their fishing lines, and whether
Homer had it in mind when he said that " the ships'
cords [c] (*sparta*) were loosed." It is certain that
the Spanish or African esparto grass was not yet in
use, and though ships were made with sewed seams,
yet it was with flax that they were sewed and never
with esparto. The seed of this plant, which the
Greeks call by the same name, grows in pods like
those of the cowpea, and purges instead of hellebore if a drachma and a half with four cyathi of
hydromel are drunk on an empty stomach. The
branches, together with the leaves, soaked in vinegar
for several days and then beaten up, yield a juice
beneficial for sciatica in doses of one cyathus. Some
prefer to soak them in sea-water and inject as an
enema.[d] The same juice with the addition of oil is
used as an embrocation for sciatica. Some too use
the seed for strangury. Pounded genista with axle-
grease cures painful knees.

Aulus Gellius XVII. 3, takes σπάρτα to be the cords with which
the planks of a ship were bound together, and not the
rigging.
    [d] See Dioscorides *Euporista* I. 231 (238): σπάρτον θαλάσσῃ
βρέξας ἐφ' ἱκανὰς ἡμέρας εἶτα ἐγκόψας καὶ χυλίσας ἔνες. This
shows that *pluribus diebus* means " for several days." With
the reading of Jan, " The leafy branches likewise."

67 XLI. Myricen[1] ericam vocat Lenaeus similem
scopis Amerinis; sanari dicit ea carcinomata in vino
decocta tritaque cum melle inlita. eandem esse
arbitrantur quidam tamaricen. sed ad lienem
praecipua est,[2] si sucus eius expressus in vino bibatur.
adeoque mirabilem eius antipathian contra solum
hoc viscerum faciunt, ut adfirment, si ex ea alveis
68 factis bibant sues sine liene inveniri. et ideo homini
quoque splenico cibum potumque dant in vasis ex ea
factis. gravis autem auctor in medicina virgam ex
ea defractam, ut neque terram neque ferrum attin-
geret, sedare ventris dolores adseveravit inpositam
ita ut tunica cinctuque corporis adprimeretur. volgus
infelicem arborem eam appellat, ut diximus, quoniam
nihil ferat nec seratur umquam.

69 XLII. Corinthus et quae circa est Graecia bryan
vocat eiusque duo genera facit, silvestrem plane
sterilem, alteram mitiorem. haec fert in Aegypto
Syriaque etiam abundanter lignosum fructum
maiorem galla, asperum gustu, quo medici utuntur
vice gallae in compositionibus quas antheras vocant.
et lignum autem et flos et folia et cortex in eosdem
70 usus adhibentur, quamquam remissiora. datur
sanguinem reicientibus cortex tritus et contra profluvia feminarum, coeliacis quoque. idem tunsus

---

[1] Myricen ericam *Mayhoff*: Myricen iam ericam *Ianus,
Detlefsen*: muricen eam ericam *codd.*
[2] sed ad lienem praecipua est] *ita Detlefsen cum codd.*: et
ad lienem praecipuam *Mayhoff, qui post* tamaricen *punctum
tollit.*

---

[a] See XVI. § 108. Perhaps, "never grows from seed."
[b] For *coeliacus morbus* see Celsus IV. 19 § 1. W. G. Spencer
in his last note on that passage says that Celsus appears to

XLI. Lenaeus calls the myrice (tamarisk) erica *Tamarisk.* (heath), comparing it to the brooms of Ameria. He says that boiled in wine, beaten up with honey, and applied to cancerous sores it heals them. Some authorities consider it to be the same as tamarice. But it is specific for splenic trouble if its juice is extracted and drunk in wine; so wonderful do they make out its antipathy to be to this internal organ, and to this only, that they affirm that if pigs drink out of troughs made of this wood they are found to be without a spleen. And for that reason they give to a man also, if he has an enlarged spleen, food and drink in vessels made of tamarisk. A respected medical authority, moreover, has asserted that a twig, broken off from it without its touching the ground or iron, relieves belly-ache, if it be so applied as to be pressed to the body by the tunic and the girdle. The common people, as I have said, call this tree unlucky, because it bears no fruit and never is planted.[a]

XLII. Corinth and the part of Greece around it call *Brya.* brya a tree of which they distinguish two kinds: the wild, which is absolutely barren, and the cultivated. The latter in Egypt and Syria bears, and that abundantly, large-stoned fruit bigger than a gall-nut and bitter to the taste, which physicians use instead of gall-nuts in the medical mixtures which they call *antherae.* The wood also, and the blossom, leaves and bark, are used for the same purposes, although they are less potent. The pounded bark is given for the spitting of blood and for excessive menstruation, also to sufferers from coeliac disease.[b] An application of

describe pyloric spasm and intestinal atony, referring also to Aretaeus II. 7 περὶ κοιλιακῆς διαθέσιος. See list of diseases.

inpositusque collectiones omnes inhibet. foliis exprimitur sucus ad haec eadem. et in vino decocuntur,[1] ipsa vero adiecto melle gangraenis inlinuntur.
decoctum eorum in vino potum vel ipsa[2] imposita
71 cum rosaceo et cera[3] sedant. sic et epinyctidas
sanant, dentium dolori et aurium decoctum eorum
salutare est, radix ad eadem similiter. folia hoc
amplius ad ea quae serpunt inponuntur cum polenta.
semen drachmae pondere adversus phalangia et
araneos bibitur, cum altilium vero pingui furunculis
inponitur. efficax et contra serpentium ictus praeter-
72 quam aspidum. nec non morbo regio, phthiriasi,
lendibus decoctum infusum prodest abundantiamque
mulierum sistit. cinis arboris ad omnia eadem prodest. aiunt, si bovis castrati urinae immisceatur vel
in potu vel in cibo, venerem finiri. carbo ex eo
genere urina ea restinctus in umbra conditur. idem
cum libeat accendere † resolvitur †.[4] Magi id et spa-
donis urina fieri tradiderunt.

[1] decocuntur: decoquitur *coni. Mayhoff puncto post* eadem
deleto.
[2] ipsa *add. Sillig*: *lacunam indicat Mayhoff* Ianum *secutus.*
[3] cera *codd.*: ceria *Detlefsen. Fortasse* ulcera *pro* et cera.
[4] resolvitur *codd.*: restituitur *Mayhoff*: igni *add. Io. Müller.
Vossius coni.* carbo extincta venere urina ea restinctus in
umbra conditur, idem, si libeat accendere rursum, uritur.

---

[a] *Sedant* here is apparently without a direct object. Detlefsen has *ceria*, for which follicular abscesses see Celsus V. 28
§ 13. Mayhoff, recording this conjecture, adds *non conveniens*
sedandi *verbo*. But Pliny has *tumorem* and *scabiem* as direct
objects of *sedare*. Perhaps we should read *ulcera* for et cera.
[b] Either " night rash from flea bites " or an eye disease. See
list of diseases.
[c] Two views have been taken of this sentence. One is that
it gives the method of preparing the mixture to be used as an
antaphrodisiac. This is the only meaning, I think, to be

54

the same bark pounded checks all kinds of gatherings.
From the leaves is extracted a juice employed for the
same purposes. The leaves are also decocted in
wine; but by themselves with honey added they
are applied to gangrenous sores. A decoction of
them taken in wine or the leaves themselves applied
locally with rose oil and wax are soothing.[a] So used
they also cure epinyctis;[b] a decoction of them is healing to tooth-ache and ear-ache; the root is similarly
used for the same purposes. The leaves furthermore
are applied with pearl barley to spreading ulcers. A
drachma by weight of the seed is taken in drink for
the poison of phalangia and other spiders; it is
applied however with chicken fat to boils. It is an
antidote also to the poison of serpents except that of
the asp. It is also good for jaundice, phthiriasis and
nits, if a decoction is used as a liniment, and this
too checks excessive menstruation. The ash from the
tree is good for all the same purposes. They say that if
it is mixed with the urine of a castrated ox and taken
in either drink or food it is antaphrodisiac. A burning
coal of this wood is quenched with the urine mentioned
and kept in the shade. This, when you want to light
it, crumbles to powder.[c] The Magi have recorded
that the urine of a eunuch also has the same effect.

extracted from the reading of the MSS. Mayhoff's *restituitur*
requires *venerem* as the understood direct object of *accendere*:
in other words, the sentence gives, not a method of preparing
the mixture, but one of counteracting it. The conjectures of
Voss put this view far more clearly. " A burning coal, when
desire is quenched, is put out by such urine and stored in a
shady place; if the wish to kindle desire comes back, the
same coal is burned." The rekindling of the coal rekindles
sexual desire by imitative magic. This interpretation com-
mends itself to students of folk-lore, but is based on bold
and dubious conjecture.

73 XLIII. Nec virga sanguinea felicior habetur.
cortex eius interior cicatrices quae praesanuere
aperit.

XLIV. Sileris folia inlita fronti capitis dolores
sedant. eiusdem semen contritum in oleo phthiriasis coercet. serpentes et hunc fruticem fugiunt
baculumque rustici ob id ex eo gerunt.

74 XLV. Ligustrum si eadem arbor est quae in
oriente cypros, suos in Europa usus habet. sucus
eius nervos, articulos, algores, folia ubique veteri
ulceri, cum salis mica et oris exulcerationibus prosunt,
acini contra phthiriasim, item contra intertrigines vel
folia. sanant et gallinaceorum pituitas acini.

XLVI. Folia alni ex ferventi aqua remedio sunt
tumoris.

75 XLVII. Hederae genera viginti demonstravimus.
natura omnium in medicina anceps. mentem turbat
et caput purgat largius pota, nervis intus nocet,
iisdem nervis adhibita foris prodest. eadem natura,
quae aceto est, omnia genera eius refrigerant.
urinam cient potu, capitis dolorem sedant, praecipue
cerebro continentique cerebrum membranae utiliter

ᵃ *Inlinere* is nearly always used of liniments and ointments,
which can be smeared on the parts affected. Here apparently
it is used of leaves just placed on the forehead, the word
used in such cases being generally *imponere* (see also § 76
below). Perhaps, however, the leaves are to be applied in
some liquid or oily base.

ᵇ *Phthiriasis* (plural) in the Latin is a transliteration of the
Greek φθειριάσεις.

ᶜ Some verb seems to have fallen out here. Mayhoff conjectures *discutit*, which suits *algores* but not *nervos* or *articulos*.
Curat would suit all three nouns; but, although *curare* ("to
treat") is used several times in Celsus with the meaning "to
treat successfully," it is apparently not so found in Pliny.
Brakman would supply *sanat*. See *Mnemosyne* 1930.

XLIII. Nor is the red-twigged tree considered *Cornel.*
more lucky. Its inner bark opens scars which have
healed too soon.

XLIV. The leaves of siler applied [a] to the fore- *Siler.*
head relieve headache. The seed of it too crushed
in oil checks phthiriasis.[b] Serpents keep away from
this shrub also, and for this reason rustics carry a
walking stick made of it.

XLV. Privet, if it is the same tree as the cypros of *Privet.*
the East, has its own uses in Europe. Its juice
benefits [c] sinews, joints and chills; its leaves everywhere are used to treat chronic ulcer and, with a
sprinkling of salt, sores in the mouth; the berries are
employed for phthiriasis, and the berries or the leaves
for chafing between the thighs. The berries also
cure the pip in chickens.

XLVI. The leaves of the alder in very hot water *The alder.*
are a remedy for tumours.

XLVII. I have pointed out [d] twenty kinds of ivy. *Ivy.*
The medicinal properties of all are twofold in action.
Ivy deranges the mind and also clears the head when
taken too copiously in drink; [e] taken internally it injures sinews, while an external application does
them good. All kinds of ivy, being of the same character as vinegar, are of a cooling nature. They are diuretic when taken in drink; they relieve headache;
especially beneficial to the brain and to the membrane

---

[d] Book XVI. § 141 ff.

[e] The word *anceps* in the preceding sentence, and the contrasted *nocet . . . prodest* in the second clause of this, indicate
that there is also a contrast in the first clause. The translation
given above suggests that a strong dose is mentally harmful but
physically beneficial, but it must be admitted that in the Latin
the contrast would be plainer if for *et* were to be read *at* or *sed*
(Mayhoff often reads *set*). But the MSS. show no variants.

mollibus inpositis foliis cum aceto et rosaceo tritis et
76 decoctis, addito postea rosaceo oleo. inlinuntur
autem fronti, et decocto eorum fovetur os caputque
perunguitur. lieni et pota et inlita prosunt. decocuntur et contra horrores febrium eruptionesque
pituitae aut in vino teruntur. corymbi quoque poti
vel inliti lienem sanant, iocinera autem inliti. trahunt et menses adpositi. sucus hederae taedia
narium graveolentiamque emendat, praecipue albae
77 sativae. idem infusus naribus caput purgat, efficacius addito nitro. infunditur etiam purulentis
auribus aut dolentibus cum oleo. cicatricibus quoque
decorem facit. ad lienes efficacior albae ferro calefactus. satis est acinos sex in vini cyathis duobus
sumi. acini ex eadem alba terni in aceto mulso poti
taenias pellunt, in qua curatione ventri quoque
inposuisse eos utile est. hedera quam chrysocarpon
appellavimus[a] bacis aurei coloris viginti in vini sextario
tritis, ita ut terni cyathi potentur, aquam quae cutem
subierit urina educit. Erasistratus eiusdem acinos
quinque tritos in rosaceo oleo calefactosque in cortice
punici instillavit dentium dolori a contraria aure.
78 acini qui croci sucum habent praesumpti potu a
crapula tutos praestant, item sanguinem excreantes

---

enclosing it is an application of soft leaves pounded
and boiled with vinegar and rose oil, more rose oil
being added afterwards. They are also applied to the
forehead, and a decoction of them is used to foment
the mouth and to rub the head. They are good for
the spleen whether taken in drink or used as liniment.
They are also boiled or beaten up in wine for the
shivers of ague and for outbursts of phlegm. Clusters
also of ivy berries cure splenic trouble, either taken
in drink or applied locally; for liver trouble, however,
they must be applied. Pessaries of berries promote
menstruation. Ivy juice, especially that of the white
cultivated ivy, cures complaints and offensive smell
of the nostrils. The same poured into the nostrils
clears the head, more thoroughly if soda is added. It
is also poured with oil into purulent or painful ears.
It furthermore removes the ugly marks of scars.
For troubles of the spleen the juice of the white kind
warmed with hot iron is more efficacious. A sufficient
dose is six berries taken in two cyathi of wine. Berries
of white ivy taken three at a time in oxymel expel
tapeworms, and in this treatment it is also beneficial
to apply the berries to the belly. The ivy that I have
called golden-berried [a] draws off in the urine the subcutaneous water of dropsy, if twenty of the golden
berries are beaten up in a sextarius of wine and the
mixture is drunk in doses of three cyathi. Erasistratus prescribed five berries of the same ivy, pounded
in rose oil and warmed in the rind of a pomegranate,
for tooth-ache, the injection to be made drop by drop
into the ear opposite to the pain. If the berries that
have a saffron juice are taken in drink beforehand,
they keep off the headache that follows drinking; they
are likewise good for the spitting of blood and for

PLINY : NATURAL HISTORY

aut torminibus laborantes. hederae nigrae candidiores corymbi poti steriles etiam viros faciunt. inlinitur decocta quaecumque in vino omni[1]
79 ulcerum generi, etiamsi cacoethe sint. lacrima hederae psilotrum est phthiriasimque tollit. flos cuiuscumque generis trium digitorum captu dysintericos et alvum citam emendat in vino austero bis die potus. et ambustis inlinitur utiliter cum cera. denigrant capillum corymbi. radicis sucus in aceto potus contra phalangia prodest. huius quoque ligni
80 vaso splenicos bibentes sanari invenio. et acinos terunt moxque comburunt et ita inlinunt ambusta prius perfusa aqua calida. sunt et qui incidant suci gratia eoque utantur ad dentes erosos, frangique tradunt, proximis cera munitis ne laedantur. gummi etiam in hedera quaerunt, quam ex aceto utilissimam dentibus promittunt.
81 XLVIII. Graeci vicino vocabulo cisthon appellant fruticem maiorem thymo, foliis ocimi. duo eius genera : flos masculo rosaceus, feminae albus. ambo prosunt dysintericis et solutionibus ventris in vino austero ternis digitis flore capto et similiter bis die poto, ulceribus veteribus et ambustis cum cera et per se oris ulceribus. sub his maxime nascitur hypocisthis, quam inter herbas dicemus.

---

[1] omni *Mayhoff* (Appendix): omnium *codd.*

---

^a See XXVI. § 49.

colic. The whiter clusters of the dark ivy taken in drink make even men sterile. A decoction in wine of any kind of ivy is applied locally to every kind of ulcer, even if it is malignant. The tears of the ivy act as a depilatory and remove phthiriasis. The blossom of any sort of ivy, taken in dry wine twice a day, a three-finger pinch at a time, corrects dysentery and looseness of the bowels. With wax it is useful as an ointment for burns. The clusters turn the hair black. The juice of the root, taken in vinegar, is good for the bite of poisonous spiders. I find also that patients with diseases of the spleen are cured if they drink from a vessel made of this wood. They crush too the berries, then burn them, and in this way apply them to burns that have previously been bathed with warm water. There are also some who make incisions in ivy for the sake of the juice, which they use for decayed teeth; they say that the teeth break off, those nearest being protected by wax lest they should be injured. They obtain also a gum from ivy, which in vinegar is recommended as very useful for the teeth.

XLVIII. The Greeks give the name cisthos, which *Cisthos.* is very like cissos (ivy), to a shrub larger than thyme and with leaves like those of ocimum. There are two kinds of it; the flower of the male is rose-coloured, of the female, white. Both are good for dysentery and looseness of the bowels, the dose being as much of the blossom as can be taken in three fingers, this quantity to be swallowed in a dry wine twice a day; for chronic ulcers and for burns the blossom is applied with wax, and by itself for ulcers in the mouth. It is especially under these shrubs that there grows the hypocisthis, which I shall describe [a] when I treat of herbs.

82 XLIX. Cissos erythranos ab iisdem appellatur
similis hederae, coxendicibus utilis e vino potus, item
lumbis, tanta vi acini ut sanguinem urina detrahat.
item chamaecisson appellant hederam non attol-
lentem se a terra. et haec contusa in vino acetabuli
mensura lieni medetur, folia ambustis cum axungia.
milax quoque, quae[1] anthophoros cognominatur,
similitudinem hederae habet, tenuioribus foliis.
coronam ex ea[2] factam inpari foliorum numero aiunt
83 capitis doloribus mederi.   quidam duo genera milacis
dixere: alterum[3] inmortalitati proximum[3] in con-
vallibus opacis, scandentem arbores,[4] comantibus
acinorum corymbis, contra venenata omnia efficacissimum in tantum ut acinorum suco infantibus saepe
instillato nulla sint[5] postea venena nocitura.   alterum
genus culta amare et in his gigni, nullius effectus.
illam esse milacem priorem cuius lignum ad aures
84 sonare diximus. similem huic aliqui clematida
appellaverunt, repentem per arbores, geniculatam
et ipsam. folia eius lepras purgant; semen alvum
solvit acetabuli mensura in aquae hemina aut aqua
mulsa. datur ex eadem causa et decoctum eius.

[1] quae *Mayhoff* : qui *aut* quia *aut* qui et *codd.*
[2] ea *Mayhoff* : eo *codd.*
[3] alterum . . . . . proximum] alteram . . . . . proximam
Mayhoff.
[4] arbores *Hermolaus Barbarus* : arborum *codd.* : arborem
coni. Mayhoff.   Inter arborum *et* comantibus *lacunam statuit
Urlichs, quem sequitur Detlefsen.*
[5] efficacissimum in tantum ut . . . . nulla sint *etc.
ego conicio* : efficacissimi *sine* ut *et* sint *cum codd., Detlefsen* : ut *et* (*post* nocitura) sint *vulg.* : efficacissime iuvantem
Mayhoff, qui post suco *dist. et* quippe *pro* saepe *coni.*

XLIX. The plant called cissos erythranos by the Plants like ivy.
Greeks is like ivy. Taken in wine it is good for
sciatica and lumbago; so strong is the property
of the berry that it brings away blood in the urine.
Chamaecissos again is the name they give to an ivy
that never rises from the ground. This too crushed
in wine and taken in doses of an acetabulum cures
splenic trouble; the leaves with axle-grease are
applied to burns. The milax also, which has the
further name of anthophoros (flower-bearer), has a
likeness to the ivy, though the leaves are more slender.
A chaplet of it made with an odd number of leaves is
said to be a cure for headache. Some authorities have
declared that there are two kinds of milax. One is
very nearly everlasting, grows in shaded valleys, is a
climber of trees, bears berries in luxuriant clusters, and
is most efficacious against all poisonous things to such
a degree that, if the juice of the berries is repeatedly
administered [a] in drops to babies, no poison will here-
after do them any harm. The other kind is said to be
fond of cultivated ground and to grow there, having
no medicinal value. The former milax they state to
be the one the wood of which, we said,[b] gives out a
sound when placed close to the ear. Like it is the
plant that some have called clematis,[c] which climbs
along trees and is itself jointed. Its leaves cleanse
leprous sores; its seed loosens the bowels if an
acetabulum of it is taken in a hemina of water or in
hydromel. A decoction of it is administered for the
same purpose.

[a] *Instillato* is difficult. The verb is often used of dropping
into the ears, and that may be the meaning here, but *auribus*
would be expected. Perhaps Pliny wrote *infantium auribus*,
which might easily be " telescoped " into *infantibus*.
[b] See XVI. § 155.   [c] See *Index of Plants*.

85 L. Harundinis genera xxviii demonstravimus, non
aliter evidentiore illa naturae vi quam continuis
his voluminibus tractamus, siquidem harundinis
radix contrita inposita filicis stirpem corpore extrahit,
item harundinem filicis radix. et quo plura genera
faciamus,[1] illa quae in Iudaea[2] Syriaque nascitur
odorum unguentorumque causa. urinam movet cum
gramine aut apii semine decocta, ciet et menstrua
86 admota. medetur convulsis duobus obolis pota,
iocineri, renibus, hydropi, tussi etiam suffitu magisque
cum resina, furfuribus ulcerumque manantibus cum
murra decocta. excipitur et sucus eius fitque elaterio
similis. efficacissima in omni harundine quae proxima radici,[3] efficaciora genicula. harundo Cypria,
quae donax vocatur, corticis cinere alopecias emen-
87 dat, item putrescentia ulcera. foliis eius ad extra-
hendos aculeos utuntur, efficacibus et contra ignes
sacros collectionesque omnes. vulgaris harundo
extractoriam vim habet[4] recens tusa, non in radice
tantum, multi[5] enim et ipsam harundinem tradunt.
medetur et luxatis et spinae doloribus radix in aceto
inlita, eadem recens trita et in vino pota venerem
concitat. harundinum lanugo inlata auribus obtun-
dit auditum.

[1] faciamus *Detlefsen* : facimus *aut* fecimus *codd.*
[2] Iudaea *Mayhoff, Detlefsen, cum codd.* : India *Hermolaus Barbarus.*
[3] radici *aut* radice *codd.* : a radice *Detlefsen.*
[4] *Hic in codd. et scriptum est.*
[5] multi *Detlefsen* : in mulso *Mayhoff, qui Cels. V. 26, 35 confert* : multū *codd.*

L. I have pointed out [a] twenty-eight kinds of reed, *Reeds.*
and nowhere is more obvious that force of Nature
which I describe in these books one after another, if indeed the root of the reed, crushed
and applied, draws a fern stem out of the flesh,
while the root of the fern does the same to a splinter
of reed. To increase the number of the various
reeds there is that which grows in Judaea and Syria and
is used for scents and unguents; boiled down with grass
or celery seed this is diuretic, and when made into
a pessary acts as an emmenagogue. A cure for
sprains, for troubles of the liver and of the kidneys, and for dropsy, is two oboli taken in drink;
for a cough also inhalation is used, the addition of
resin being an improvement; for scurf and running
sores is used a decoction with myrrh. Its juice also
is collected and made into a drug like elaterium.
Of all reeds the parts nearest the root are the
most efficacious, and the joints are more efficacious [b]
than other parts. The Cyprian reed, called donax,
has a bark which, reduced to ash, is a remedy for
mange and also for festering sores. Its leaves are
used for extracting splinters, and are also good for
erysipelas and for all gatherings. The common reed
has the power to extract if freshly pounded, and not
the root only, for many hold that the reed itself
too has this property. The root applied in vinegar
cures dislocations and pains of the spine; the same
ground fresh and taken in wine is aphrodisiac. The
down on reeds placed in the ears deadens the
hearing.

[a] See XVI. § 156 ff.
[b] Another possible rendering is " the parts nearest the root
are very efficacious and the joints are more efficacious still."

88   LI. Cognata in Aegypto res est harundini papy-
rum,[1] praecipuae utilitatis, cum inaruit, ad laxandas
siccandasque fistulas et intumescendo ad introitum
medicamentorum aperiendas. charta quae fit ex eo
cremata inter caustica est. cinis eius ex vino potus
somnum facit, ipsa ex aqua inposita callum sanat.

89   LII. Ne in Aegypto quidem nascitur hebenus, ut
docuimus, nec tractamus in medicina alienos orbes,
non omittetur tamen propter miraculum. scobem
eius oculis unice mederi dicunt, lignoque ad cotem
trito cum passo caliginem discuti, ex aqua vero radice
albugines oculorum, item tussim pari modo dracunculi radicis adiecto cum melle. hebenum medici et
inter erodentia adsumunt.

90   LIII. Rhododendros ne nomen quidem apud nos
invenit Latinum, rhododaphnen vocant aut nerium.
mirum folia eius quadripedum venenum esse, homini
vero contra serpentes praesidium ruta addita e vino
pota. pecus etiam et caprae, si aquam biberint in
qua folia ea maduerint, mori dicuntur.

91   LIV. Nec rhus Latinum nomen habet, cum in
usum pluribus modis veniat. nam et herba est
silvestris, foliis myrti, cauliculis brevibus, quae taenias

---

[1] *Nonnulli* papyrus *malint.*

---

[a] Both Littré and the Bohn translators understand *herba*
with *ipsa*, translating as in the text. But the sudden change
of gender from neuter to feminine is startling, and perhaps
with *ipsa* is to be understood *charta*.
[b] See XII. § 17.
[c] These are all Greek words : ῥοδόδενδρος or ῥοδόδενδρον
(rose tree), ῥοδοδάφνη (rose bay) and νήριον. The shrub is

LI. Akin to the reed is a plant growing in Egypt, *Papyrus.* the papyrus, which, when it has been dried, is especially useful for expanding and drying fistulas, and, by swelling, for opening them to admit medicaments. The paper made from it is, when burnt, one of the caustic remedies. Its ash taken in wine induces sleep. The plant[a] itself applied with water cures callosities.

LII. Not even in Egypt does the ebony-tree grow, *Ebony.* as I have stated,[b] and in my medical research I omit foreign regions; yet I must not pass it by, as it is a great marvel. Its sawdust is said to be a sovereign remedy for the eyes; its wood, ground on the whetstone and mixed with raisin wine, to dispel dimness of vision; its root, applied however in water, to disperse white specks on the eyes; cough too to be cleared away if an equal measure of dracunculus root is added along with honey. Physicians include ebony among erosive remedies.

LIII. The rhododendros[c] has not even found a *Oleander.* Latin name among the Romans, names for it being rhododaphne[c] or nerium.[c] It is a strange fact that, while its leaves are poisonous to quadrupeds, to man on the other hand, if rue is added and the mixture taken in wine, they are a protection against the poison of snakes. Sheep too and goats, if they drink water in which these leaves have been steeped, are said to be killed by it.

LIV. Neither has rhus received a Latin name, *Rhus.* although many uses are made of it. For it is both a wild plant with myrtle-like leaves and short stems, which expels tapeworms, and also the shrub called

described by Dioscorides (IV. 81, Wellmann). See *Index of Plants.*

pellit, et frutex coriarius appellatur, subrutilus, cubitalis, crassitudine digitali, cuius aridis foliis ut
92 malicorio coria perficiuntur. medici autem rhoicis utuntur ad contusa, item coeliacos et sedis ulcera aut quae phagedaenas vocant. trita cum melle et inlita cum aceto * * * decoctum eorum instillatur auribus purulentis. fit et stomatice decoctis ramis ad eadem quae ex moris, sed efficacior admixto alumine. inlinitur eadem hydropicorum tumori.
93 LV. Rhus qui erythros appellatur semen est huius fruticis. vim habet adstringendi refrigerandique. adspergitur pro sale obsoniis alvo soluta, omnesque carnes cum silphio suaviores facit. medetur ulceribus manantibus cum melle, asperitati linguae, percussis lividis, desquamatis; eodem modo capitis vulnera ad cicatricem celerrime perducit, feminarum abundantiam sistit cibo.
94 LVI. Alia res erythrodanum, quam aliqui ereuthodanum vocant, nos rubiam, qua tinguntur lanae pellesque perficiuntur. in medicina urinam ciet, morbum regium sanat ex aqua mulsa, et lichenas ex aceto inlita, ischiadicos, paralyticos ita ut bibentes laventur cotidie. radix semenque trahunt menses, alvum sistunt et collectiones discutiunt. contra

---

a Dioscorides (I. 108, Wellmann) has πτερύγιά τε καὶ φαγεδαίνας ἐπέχει καταπλασσόμενα τὰ φύλλα μετ' ὄξους ἢ μέλιτος. This suggests pterygia sistunt or sanant as part of the lost words.

b The corresponding sentence in Dioscorides (I. 108, Wellmann) is interesting. καὶ ὁ καρπὸς δὲ τὰ αὐτὰ ποιεῖ, ἁρμόζων ἐν προσοψήμασι κοιλιακοῖς καὶ δυσεντερικοῖς, ἀφλέγμαντά τε τηρεῖ σὺν μέλιτι καταπλασθεὶς θλάσματα, ἀποσύρματα, πελιώματα, γλώττης τε τραχύτητας σμήχει σὺν μέλιτι καὶ λευκὸν ῥοῦν ἵστησιν.

" the tanner's ", of a reddish colour, a cubit high, and of the thickness of a finger, the leaves of which when dried are used as is pomegranate rind in the tanning of leather. Physicians moreover use the leaves of rhus for bruises, likewise for coeliac trouble, sores in the seat and for what they call eating (phagedaenic) ulcers. Pounded with honey and applied with vinegar . . .ᵃ a decoction of them is dropped into suppurating ears. A decoction of the branches makes a mouth-wash, which is used for the same purposes as that made from mulberries, but it is more efficacious when mixed with alum. This is also applied to dropsical swellings.

LV. What is called rhus erythros (red sumach) is the seed of this shrub. It has astringent and cooling properties. It is sprinkled on viands instead of salt when the bowels have been relaxed, and with silphium added makes all meat sweeter. With honey it cures running sores, roughness of the tongue, and livid or excoriated bruises; applied in the same way it very quickly causes wounds on the head to cicatrize.ᵇ Taken as food it checks excessive menstruation. *Rhus erythros.*

LVI. A different plant is erythrodanum, called by some ereuthodanum, and rubia by the Romans, which is used to dye wool and to tan leather. As a medicine it is diuretic, and taken in hydromel cures jaundice (lichen too if applied with vinegar), sciatica and paralysis if the patient bathes daily while taking the draught.ᶜ The root and the seed are emmenagogues, check diarrhoea and disperse gatherings. The *Erythrodanum.*

ᶜ The qualifying clause may be taken with *paralyticos* only or with it and *ischiadicos*. From *et* to *inlita* is a parenthesis, and is marked as such by Mayhoff.

serpentes rami cum foliis inponuntur. folia et
capillum inficiunt. invenio apud quosdam morbum
regium sanari hoc frutice etiam si alligatus spectetur
tantum.

95 LVII. Distat ab eo qui alysson vocatur foliis
tantum et ramis minoribus ; nomen accepit quod a
cane morsos rabiem sentire non patitur ex aceto potus
adalligatusque ; mirum est quod additur, saniem
conspecto omnino frutice eo siccari.

96 LVIII. Tinguentibus et radicula lanas praeparat
quam struthion a Graecis vocari diximus. medetur
morbo regio et ipsa pota[1] et decoctum eius, item
pectoris vitiis ; urinam ciet, alvum solvit, vulvas
purgat, quamobrem aureum potorium medici vocant. ea et ex melle prodest[1] magnifice ad tussim,
orthopnoeae coclearis mensura, cum polenta vero et
97 aceto lepras tollit. eadem cum panace et capparis
radice calculos frangit pellitque, panos discutit cum
farina hordeacia et vino decocta. miscetur et malag-
matis et collyriis claritatis causa, sternutamento

---

[1] pota et decoctum eius, item pectoris vitiis ; urinam ciet,
alvum solvit, vulvas purgat, quamobrem aureum potorium
medici vocant. ea et ex melle prodest *ego* : et decoctum eius
potu, item pectoris vitiis. urinam ciet, alvum solvit. et
vulvas purgat, quam ob rem aureum πεσσὸν medici vocant ex
ea. e melle prodest *Mayhoff* : decocto eius poto, item pectoris
vitiis. urinam ciet, alvum solvit et vulvas purgat, quamobrem
aureum poterion medici vocant. ea et ex melle prodest
Detlefsen : ipsa *aut* ipsam *sine* et *ante* decoctum ; decocta ;
potu *aut* poto *aut* pota ; pecion *aut* pectori *aut* petition ; ex
ea et *codd. Cf.* XXXIII. § 136 mille convivas totidem aureis
potoriis.

---

[a] *Sanies* is said by Celsus (V. 26, 20) to be thinner than blood,
varying both in thickness and colour, while *pus* is the thickest
and whitest of the three, more sticky than either *sanies* or
blood. Pliny is thinking of the discharge from a dog-bite.

branches with the leaves are applied for snake-bites.
The leaves also dye the hair. I find in some authorities that jaundice is cured if this shrub is merely
looked at while worn as an amulet.

LVII. The plant called alysson differs from the last *Alysson.*
only in having smaller leaves and branches. It has
received its name because it prevents persons bitten
by a dog from going mad if they take it in vinegar
and wear it as an amulet. The authorities add the
wonderful marvel that the mere sight of this shrub
dries up sanies.[a]

LVIII. Radicula too prepares wools for the dyers; *Radicula.*
I have said[b] that it is called struthion by the Greeks.
It cures jaundice both when taken by itself in drink
and in the form of a decoction, and likewise chest
troubles; it promotes urine, loosens the bowels and
purges the uterus, for which reason physicians call it
" golden goblet ".[c] With honey too it is a splendid
remedy for a cough, and in doses of a spoonful for
orthopnoea; but with pearl barley and vinegar
it removes leprous sores. Again, with panaces[d]
and caper root it breaks up and expels stone in the
bladder, and a decoction with barley meal and wine
disperses superficial abscesses. It is used as an ingredient of poultices, and of eye-salves to improve

[b] See XIX. § 48.
[c] The text has suffered in this sentence through probably
the sleepiness of a scribe. I have tried to restore the sense
and the grammar while retaining as many words of the
MSS. as possible. I suggest *potorium* because of XXXIII.
§ 136; otherwise *poterion* (Sillig and Detlefsen) or *poculum* (the
vulgate reading) would suit the passage. The objection to
Mayhoff's ingenious πεσσὸν is that it would apply only to *vulvas
purgat.*
[d] See *Index of Plants.*

utilis inter pauca, lieni quoque ac iocineri. eadem
pota denarii unius pondere ex aqua mulsa suspiriosos
sanat, sic et pleuriticos et omnes lateris dolores.

98   Apocyni semen ex aqua—frutex est folio hederae,
molliore tamen, et minus longis viticulis, semine
acuto, diviso, lanuginoso, gravi odore—canes et
omnes quadripedes necat in cibo datum.

99   LIX. Dictum[1] rosmarinum est. duo genera eius:
alterum sterile, alterum cui et caulis et semen
resinaceum, quod cachrys vocatur. foliis odor turis.
radix vulnera sanat viridis inposita et sedis proci-
dentia, condylomata, haemorrhoidas, sucus et fruticis
et radicis morbum regium et ea quae repurganda
100   sunt. oculorum aciem exacuit. semen ad vetera
pectoris vitia datur potui et ad vulvas cum vino et
pipere, menses adiuvat, podagris inlinitur cum aerina
farina, purgat etiam lentigines et quae excalfacienda
sint, aut cum sudor quaerendus, inlitum, item convulsis. auget et lacte in vino potum, item radix.
ipsa herba strumis cum aceto inlinitur, ad tussim
cum melle prodest.

101   LX. Cachrys multa genera habet, ut diximus.
sed haec quae ex rore supra dicto nascitur, si frice-
tur, resinosa est. adversatur venenis et venenatis
praeterquam anguibus. sudores movet, tormina
discutit, lactis ubertatem facit.

---

[1] dictum *add. Urlichs* : *post* rosmarinum *trans. Mayhoff.*

---

[a] See XIX. § 187.
[b] See Celsus VI. 18, 8.
[c] See XVI. § 30, where the cachrys is said to be the *pilula* of
the oak, fir, larch, pitch pine, linden, nut (chestnut ?) and plane.
Pliny also uses the word for the capsule of rosemary. Theophrastus IX. xi. 10 calls κάχρυ (neuter) the fruit of the *libanotis.*

the vision; it is especially useful for making the patient sneeze, and also for troubles of the spleen and liver. The same plant taken in hydromel in doses of one denarius by weight cures asthma and pleurisy and all pains in the side.

Dog's-bane is a shrub having a leaf like that of ivy *Dog's-bane*. but softer; the tendrils are shorter, and the seed is pointed, grooved, downy, and strong smelling. If given in their food this seed in water kills dogs and all other quadrupeds.

LIX. Rosemary has been mentioned already.[a] *Rosemary*. There are two kinds of it; one is barren, and the other has a stalk and a resinous seed called cachrys. The leaves have the smell of frankincense. A local application of the fresh root heals wounds, prolapsus of the anus, condylomata,[b] and haemorrhoids. The juice both of the shrub and of the root cures jaundice and such conditions as call for cleansing. It sharpens the eyesight. The seed is given in drink for chronic complaints of the chest and with wine and pepper for uterine trouble; it is an emmenagogue, and with darnel meal is applied locally for gout; an application also clears away freckles, and is used when a calorific or sudorific is called for, also for sprains; milk is increased when it, and when the root, is taken in wine. The herb itself is applied with vinegar to scrofulous sores, and with honey is good for a cough.

LX. There are, as I have said, many kinds of *Cachrys*. cachrys.[c] But the one growing on rosemary, the plant just described, is resinous if rubbed. It neutralizes poisons, and the venom of all creatures except snakes. It promotes perspiration, dispels colic, and produces a rich supply of milk.

73

102 LXI. Herba Sabina brathy appellata a Graecis
duorum generum est, altera tamarici folio similis,
altera cupressi. quare quidam Creticam cupressum
dixerunt. a multis in suffitus pro ture adsumitur, in
medicamentis vero duplicato pondere eosdem effectus habere quos cinnamum traditur. collectiones
minuit et nomas conpescit, inlita ulcera purgat,
partus emortuos adposita extrahit et suffita. inlinitur igni sacro et carbunculis cum melle[1]; ex
vino pota regio morbo medetur. gallinacii generis
pituitas fumo eius herbae sanari tradunt.

103 LXII. Similis herbae huic Sabinae est selago
appellata. legitur sine ferro dextra manu per
tunicam qua[2] sinistra exuitur[3] velut a furante,
candida veste vestito pureque lautis nudis pedibus,
sacro facto prius quam legatur pane vinoque. fertur
in mappa nova. hanc contra perniciem omnem
habendam prodidere Druidae Gallorum et contra
omnia oculorum vitia fumum eius prodesse.

104 LXIII. Idem samolum herbam nominavere nascentem in umidis, et hanc sinistra manu legi a ieiunis

[1] *Ita dist. Val. Rose et Mayhoff:* ex *codd.*: carbunculis, cum
melle et vino *vulg., Detlefsen.*
[2] qua *plerique codd., Detlefsen:* operta *Mayhoff:* *fortasse*
quieta.
[3] exuitur *codd., Detlefsen:* eruitur *vulg., Mayhoff:* exeritur
C. F. W. Müller, fortasse recte.

---

[a] I do not think that there is any need to depart from the
MSS., except, perhaps, to alter *exuitur* to *exeritur* with C. F. W.
Müller. The reason for the proposed changes is to make
sinistra ablative, some old editions and the MS. X actually
adding *manu*. It is true that the left hand is usually the one
used in this kind of magic (XXI. § 176, XXVII. §§ 36, 117), but

74

LXI. Sabine herb, called brathy by the Greeks, is of *Savin.*
two kinds. One has a leaf like that of the tamarisk,
the other like that of the cypress, for which reason
some have called it the Cretan cypress. Many use it
instead of frankincense for fumigations; in medicines
moreover a double dose is said to be equivalent in
strength to a single dose of cinnamon. It reduces
gatherings and checks corroding sores; an application
cleanses ulcers, and used as a pessary or for fumigation
it brings away the dead foetus. With honey it is used
as an ointment for erysipelas and carbuncles; taken
in wine it cures jaundice. By fumigation sabine herb
is said to cure the pip in chickens.

LXII. Like this sabine herb is the plant called selago *Selago.*
It is gathered without iron with the right hand, thrust
under the tunic through the left arm-hole, as though
the gatherer were thieving.[a] He should be clad in
white, and have bare feet washed clean; before
gathering he should make a sacrificial offering of
bread and wine. The plant is carried in a new napkin.
The Druids of Gaul have recorded that it should be
kept on the person to ward off all fatalities, and that
the smoke of it is good for all diseases of the eyes.

LXIII. The same authorities have called samolus *Samolus.*
(brook-weed) a plant growing in moist regions,[b]
which (they say) is to be gathered with the left hand

here the right hand pretends to be the left and deceives the
plant, taking it by surprise before its virtue can slip away.
Such deception of *e.g.* rice is still common in the East.
Mayhoff's text gives: "the right hand being covered by the
tunic, it is torn off by the left hand etc."

[b] I think that *et* before *hanc* is "and" not "also." The
latter meaning would make necessary a radical reconstruction
of § 103. But there seem to be contrasts between the two cases,
dextra)(*sinistra* and *sacro facto pane vinoque*)(*a ieiunis.* One is
tempted to suggest *at* for *et.*

contra morbos suum boumque, nec respicere legentem, neque alibi quam in canali deponere, ibi conterere poturis.

105 LXIV. Cummium genera diximus. in his maiores effectus melioris cuiusque erunt. dentibus inutiles sunt, sanguinem coagulant et ideo reicientibus sanguinem prosunt, item ambustis, arteriae vitiis inutiles, urinam cient, amaritudines hebetant.[1] adstrictis ceteris, quae ex amygdala amara est spissandisque visceribus efficacior, habet excalfac-

106 torias vires. postponuntur[2] prunorum autem et cerasorum ac vitium. siccant inlitae et adstringunt, ex aceto vero infantium lichenes sanant, prosunt et tussi veteri quattuor obolis in musto[3] potis. creduntur et colorem gratiorem facere ciborumque adpeten-

---

[1] Sic dist. Mayhoff. hebetant, adstrictis ceteris. quae ex amygdala amara est, spissandique (sic multi codd.) viribus efficacior vulg.: adstrictis ceteris visceribus, quae ex amygdala amara est, spissandique efficacior Detlefsen (Urlichs secutus): hebetant. adstrictoriis ceteris, quae ex amygdala amara est spissandisque visceribus efficacior Mayhoff.

[2] postponuntur Detlefsen coll. XIII. § 66 : deterior ex amygdalis amaris et ceraso, pessima e prunis : proponuntur codd., Mayhoff.

[3] musto Sillig, Ianus, vet. Dal.: mixto codd., Mayhoff.

---

[a] Book XIII. §§ 66 ff.

[b] If with Mayhoff we put a full stop at hebetant and a comma at ceteris we can make sense of this passage without emendation. As is pointed out in Forcellini, adstrictus sometimes means " astringens, acerbus, στρυφνός." Cf. XXVII § 121, gustu adstricto. If the full stop is put at ceteris, some word meaning " properties ", e.g. viribus, must be understood with it : " gums deaden bitterness, and their properties generally are astringent." The other punctuation seems better. Possibly there is a lacuna after amara. Dioscorides I 123, τὸ δὲ κόμμι αὐτῆς (sc. ἀμυγδάλης πικρᾶς) στύφει καὶ

by fasting persons to keep off the diseases of swine and oxen. As one gathers it one must not look at it, nor place the plant anywhere except in the trough, where it should be crushed for the animals to drink.

LXIV. I have mentioned [a] the different kinds of gums. The better the sort of each kind the more potent its effect. Gums are injurious to the teeth, coagulate blood and therefore benefit those who spit blood; they are also good for burns though bad for affections of the trachea; they promote urine and lessen the bitter taste in things. Gums generally are acrid,[b] but the gum that comes from bitter almonds, and is more efficacious for giving astringency to the internal organs, possesses heating properties. The gums from plums, cherries and vines are less esteemed. An application of gum has drying and astringent properties, in vinegar moreover it cures lichens on babies, and four oboli taken in must [c] are good for a chronic cough. Gums are believed to improve the complexion and also the appetite; they

Gums.

θερμαίνει, shows that the bitter almond is referred to, but the run of the sentence makes us expect a nominative adjective to be joined to *efficacior.* Perhaps—it is only a guess—the sentence should run : *adstrictis ceteris, quae ex amygdala amara ⟨excipitur amara⟩ est spissandisque visceribus efficacior ; habet excalfactorias vires.* The logic of the passage would be that other gums lessen bitter tastes, but gum from bitter almonds is itself bitter.

[c] It is difficult to make sense here of *in mixto,* " in a mixture." Moreover, *in* is not the usual preposition in such phrases, but *ex* or *cum.* This objection, of course, applies to *musto* as much as to *mixto.* *Musto,* however, is probably right, although *immixtarum,* " four oboli of mixed gums " would suit the sense of the passage and avoid the difficulty of *in.* But were *immixtarū* the original reading, it is hard to understand why it was altered to *in mixto.*

PLINY : NATURAL HISTORY

tiam, et calculosis prodesse cum passo potae. oculorum et vulnerum utilitatibus maxime conveniunt.

107   LXV. Spina Arabica—spinae Aegyptiae [1] laudes in odorum loco diximus—et ipsa stringit spissatque destillationes omnes et sanguinis excreationes mensumque abundantiam, etiamnum radice valentior.

108   LXVI. Spinae albae semen contra scorpiones auxiliatur. corona ex ea inposita capitis dolores minuit. est huic similis quam Graeci acanthion vocant, minoribus multo foliis, aculeatis per extremitates et araneosa lanugine obductis, qua collecta etiam vestes quaedam bombycinis similes fiunt in oriente. ipsa folia vel radices ad remedia opisthotoni bibuntur.

109   LXVII. Et acacia e [2] spina fit in Aegypto alba nigraque arbore, item viridi,[3] sed longe meliore [4] prioribus. fit et in Galatia deterrima spinosiore arbore. semen

---

[1] Spina Arabica—spinae Aegyptiae *Mayhoff*: spinae Arabicae *Urlichs, Detlefsen*: spina (-ae) aegyptia(-ae) spinae arabicae *codd.*

[2] acacia e *Hard., Mayhoff*: acaciae *plerique codd., Detlefsen.*

[3] viridi EX *vulg., Mayhoff*: viridis *reliqui codd., Detlefsen.*

[4] meliore *Urlichs, Mayhoff*: melior ē *aliquot codd., Sillig*: melior *Detlefsen.*

---

[a] Book XIII. § 63, where, however, Pliny makes no mention of the Arabian thorn. The text in § 107 is obviously corrupt in the MSS. ; Mayhoff (Appendix p. 484) calls it a *locus desperatus.* Either Pliny spoke of both thorns or he mentioned only the Arabian, forgetting what he had said in XIII. 63. A scribe was likely enough, if Pliny made this mistake, to add a mention of the Egyptian thorn; but if Pliny had spoken only of the Egyptian a scribe would not be likely to add the Arabian. So we can either try to harmonize what is said of the two thorns, with Mayhoff, or omit all reference to the Egyptian thorn, with Urlichs and Detlefsen. That Pliny is thinking of the *spina Arabica* is shown by Dioscorides III. 13 : στύφουσα, καὶ πρὸς

78

are good for stone when taken with raisin wine. They
are especially useful for the eyes and for wounds.

LXV. The Arabian thorn—I have mentioned[a] the *Arabian thorn.*
merits of the Egyptian thorn in my section on scents
—even by itself by its thickening nature checks all
fluxes, spitting of blood and excessive menstruation,
and there is even more potency in its root.

LXVI. The seed of the white thorn is a help *White thorn.*
against the stings of scorpions, and a crown of it
when worn lessens headache. Like it is the plant
called acanthion by the Greeks, but this has much
smaller leaves, which have prickly points and are
covered with down like cobweb. In the East this is
even gathered to make a silk-like cloth.[b] The
leaves by themselves,[c] or the roots, are taken in
drink as a cure for opisthotonic tetanus.

LXVII. A gum also is produced in Egypt from the *Acacias.*
acacia-thorn, from a pale tree and a dark, and likewise from a green tree, which is far better than the
former two.[d] Gum is also produced in Galatia; it is
very inferior, and comes from a more thorny tree than

ῥοῦν γυναικεῖον καὶ πρὸς ἀναγωγὴν αἵματος καὶ πρὸς ἄλλους ῥευ-
ματισμοὺς ἡ ῥίζα παραπλησίως εὐθετεῖ (of the ἄκανθα Ἀραβική).
For *spina* see *Index of Plants.*

[b] Not real silk, but obtained from the caterpillar of *Lasio-campa otus,* from which *vestes Coae* were made.

[c] *Ipsa* seems here, as often in Pliny, to mean that no other
ingredient is added to the remedy. It is uncertain, however,
whether the leaves are to be swallowed, perhaps beaten up, in
water or wine, or whether an infusion is to be made of leaves
or root. The latter way of preparing the medicine would be
more natural, but the usual verb for it is *decoquere.*

[d] The text seems to be corrupt here beyond reconstruction.
I print Mayhoff's text. Detlefsen's would give : " An acacia
thorn grows in Egypt, both with a pale and with a dark tree :
and also a green one, which is far superior to the others."
Acacia can mean either the tree or the gum from it.

omnium lenticulae simile, minore tantum et grano
et folliculo. colligitur autumno, ante collectum
nimio validius spissat. sucus ex folliculis aqua caelesti
perfusis, mox in pila tusis exprimitur organis, tunc
densatur in sole mortariis in pastillos. fit et[1]
foliis minus efficax. ad coria perficienda semine pro
110 galla utuntur. foliorum sucus et Galaticae acaciae
nigerrimus inprobatur, item qui valde rufus. purpurea aut leucophaea et quae facillime diluitur—vis[2]
summa ad spissandum refrigerandumque est—
oculorum medicamentis ante alia utiles[3]. lavantur in
eos usus pastilli, ab aliis torrentur, ab aliis perur-
untur. capillum tingunt, sanant ignem sacrum,
ulcera quae serpunt et umida vitia corporis, collectiones, articulos contusos, perniones, pterygia.
abundantiam mensum in feminis sistunt vulvamque et
sedem procidentes, item oculos, oris ulcera et
genitalium.

111 LXVIII. Vulgaris quoque haec spina ex qua
aenae fulloniae inplentur radicis[4] usus habet. per
Hispanias quidem multi et inter odores et ad unguenta utuntur illa aspalathum vocantes. est sine

[1] et *codd. et edd.*; *an* ex ? *Post* mortariis *add.* et digeritur
Warmington.
[2] vis *cum aliquot codd. Mayhoff, qui dist. ut in textu.
Fortasse*: vi . . . refrigerandum sunt, *ut ipse Mayhoff coni.*
[3] utiles *codd., Mayhoff* : utilis *Sillig, Detlefsen.*
[4] radicis] *an* radiculae *legendum? Sed vide XII. § 110*
radix (*sc.* aspalathi) unguentis expetitur.

---

[a] Perhaps *mortariis* should be deleted as a gloss on either
pila or *organis.*

the others. The seed of all the trees is like the lentil, only both grain and pod are smaller. It is gathered in autumn; if gathered earlier, its tonic properties are too powerful. The pods are steeped in rain-water and then pounded in a mortar. The juice is then extracted from them by presses, and finally thickened into lozenges by exposure to the sun in basins.*a* A juice is also extracted from the leaves, but it is less efficacious. For tanning leather they use the seed instead of gall-nuts. The juice of the leaves and of the Galatian acacia is very dark, and considered of little value, as is also the juice of the deep-red kind. The purple gum, the dun-coloured, and that which dissolves most easily— these have the highest tonic and cooling qualities *b*—are particularly useful for eye-salves. For these purposes the lozenges are washed by some, roasted by others and by others thoroughly burnt. They dye the hair, and cure erysipelas, creeping ulcers, moist complaints of the body,*c* gatherings, bruised joints, chilblains and hangnails.*d* They check excessive menstruation in women and are good for prolapsus of the uterus and anus, also for the eyes and for sores of the mouth and of the genitals.

LXVIII. Our common thorn also, from which the *Other thorns.* fullers' coppers are filled, has a root with uses. Throughout the Spains, many use it as a scent and as an ingredient of ointments, calling it aspalathus.

---

b Mayhoff's conjecture, *sunt* for *est*, with *vi* of the MSS. retained, is perhaps simpler. The sense, however, is not altered.

c Perhaps excessive or offensive perspiration.

d The eye-complaint may be referred to here.

dubio hoc nomine spina silvestris in oriente, ut
diximus, candida, magnitudine et arboris iustae,
112 (LXIX) sed et frutex humilior, aeque spinosus, in
Nisyro[1] et Rhodiorum insulis, quem alii erysisceptrum,
alii sphagnon,[2] Syri diaxylon vocant. optimus qui
minime ferulaceus, rubens aut in purpuram vergens
113 detracto cortice. nascitur pluribus locis, sed non
ubique odoratus. quam vim haberet caelesti arcu
in eum innixo diximus. sanat taetra oris ulcera et
ozaenas, genitalia exulcerata aut carbunculantia,
item rhagadia, inflationes potu discutit et strangurias.
cortex sanguinem reddentibus medetur. decoctum
eius alvum sistit. similia praestare silvestrem quoque
putant.

114   LXX. Spina est appendix appellata, quoniam
bacae puniceo colore in ea appendices vocantur.
hae crudae per se et aridae in vino decoctae alvum
citam ac tormina conpescunt. pyracanthae bacae
contra serpentium ictus bibuntur.

115   LXXI. Paliurus quoque spinae genus est. semen
eius Afri zuram vocant, contra scorpiones efficacissimum, item calculosis et tussi. folia adstrictoriam vim

---

[1] Hic coll. Diosc. Syria add. Warmington.
[2] sphagnon] phasganon Pintianus, Mayhoff.

---

    [a] See Book XII. § 110.   Dioscorides (I. 20, Wellmann) has :
ἀσπάλαθος, οἱ δὲ ἐρυσίσκηπτρον, οἱ δὲ σφάγνον, Σύροι δὲ διάξυλον
καλοῦσι.   θάμνος ἐστὶ . . . γεννώμενος ἐν Νισύρῳ καὶ Συρίᾳ καὶ
τῇ Ῥοδίᾳ, ᾧ χρῶνται οἱ μυρεψοὶ εἰς τὰς τῶν μύρων στύψεις.
There is a well attested reading φάσγανον (sword) : hence
Mayhoff's phasganon.   Dioscorides speaks also of κύπερος· οἱ δὲ
ἀσπάλαθον καλοῦσιν (I. 4).
    [b] See XII. § 110 in eodem tractu aspalathus nascitur, spina

There is without doubt, as I have said,[a] a wild thorn of this name in the East, white, and as big as an ordinary tree, (LXIX) but it is also the name of a shrub, lower in height but equally thorny, that grows in the islands Nisyrus and Rhodes, called by some erysisceptrum, by others sphagnos, and by the Syrians diaxylon. The best is that least like fennel-giant, of a red colour or inclining to purple when the bark has been removed. It grows in several regions, but not everywhere has it a perfume. I have described[b] its powerful scent when the rainbow rests extended over the shrub. It cures foul ulcers in the mouth, polypus, ulcerated genitals and those with carbuncles, and also chaps; taken in drink it clears away flatulence and strangury. The bark is good for those who bring up blood, and a decoction of it checks looseness of the bowels. The wild shrub also is thought to have similar properties.

LXX. There is also a thorn with the name of appendix, because the bright red berries hanging from it are called appendixes. These, either raw by themselves or dried and boiled down in wine, check looseness of the bowels and colic. The berries of pyracantha are taken in drink for the bites of serpents.

LXXI. Paliurus too is a species of thorn. Its seed the Africans call zura; it is very efficacious for scorpion sting, and likewise for stone and cough. The leaves have an astringent quality. The root dis-

---

candida magnitudine arboris modicae, flore rosae. radix unguentis expetitur, tradunt in quocumque frutice curvetur arcus caelestis, eandem quae sit aspalathi suavitatem odoris exsistere ; sed si in aspalatho, inenarrabilem quandam. quam quidam erysisceptrum vocant, alii sceptrum. See *Index of Plants, s.v.* Aspalathus.

83

habent. radix discutit panos, collectiones, vomicas, urinas trahit pota. decoctum eius in vino alvum sistit, serpentibus adversatur. radix praecipue datur in vino.

116 LXXII. Aquifoliae folia[1] contusa addito sale articulorum morbis prosunt, bacae purgationi feminarum, coeliacis, dysintericis, cholericis. in vino potae sistunt alvum. radix decocta et inlita extrahit infixa corpori, utilissima et luxatis tumoribusque. aquifolia arbor in domo aut villa sata veneficia arcet. flore eius aquam glaciari Pythagoras tradit, item baculum ex ea factum in quodvis animal emissum, etiamsi citra ceciderit defectu mittentis, ipsum per sese cupito[2] propius adlabi, tam praecipuam naturam inesse arbori. taxi arboris fumus necat mures.

117 LXXIII. Nec rubos ad maleficia tantum genuit natura, ideoque et mora his, hoc est vel hominibus cibos, dedit. vim habent siccandi, adstringendi, gingivis, tonsillis, genitalibus accommodatissimi. adversantur serpentium sceleratissimis, haemorrhoidi et presteri, flos aut mora scorpionibus, vulnera sine collectionum periculo iungunt, urinas eorum caules 118 cient. teneri[3] tunduntur exprimiturque sucus, mox sole cogitur in crassitudinem mellis, singulari remedio

---

[1] aquifoliae folia *Mayhoff* : aquifolia *Detlefsen* : aliqui folia *aut* folia aliqui *codd.*

[2] cupito *Detlefsen* : cubito *Mayhoff* : cubito, cubitu, recubitu *codd.*

[3] eorum caules cient. teneri *Detlefsen* : cient. caules eorum teneri *Mayhoff* : *varia codd.*

---

[a] The vulgate *recubitu* is explained by Forcellini as *subsultus ille quem faciunt corpora in solum durum incidentia.* Some have even thought that there is an allusion to the boomerang. This does not suit *adlabi*, and in the context *propius* must be nearer the mark, not nearer the thrower. *Recubitu* arose from wrong division of *sese cubitu.* As a cubit is not far for a missile

perses superficial abscesses, gatherings and boils; taken in drink it is diuretic. A decoction of it in wine checks looseness of the bowels and neutralizes the poison of serpents. The root especially is given in wine.

LXXII. The leaves of the holly, crushed and *Holly.* with the addition of salt, are good for diseases of the joints, while the berries are good for menstruation, coeliac trouble, dysentery and cholera. Taken in wine they check looseness of the bowels. An application of the decocted root extracts objects embedded in the flesh, and is very useful for dislocations and swellings. A holly tree planted in a town house or country house keeps off magic influences. Pythagoras has recorded that by its blossom water is solidified, and that a holly stick, cast at any animal, even if through want of strength in the thrower it falls short of the quarry, of its own accord rolls nearer the mark,[a] so powerful is the nature of this tree. The smoke of the yew tree kills rats and mice.

LXXIII. Not even brambles did Nature create *Brambles.* for harmful purposes only, and so she has given them their blackberries, that are food even for men. They have a drying and astringent property, being very good for gums, tonsils and genitals. They counteract the venom of the most vicious serpents, such as the haemorrhois and prester ; the bloom or the berry counteracts that of scorpions. They close wounds without any danger of gatherings. Their stalks are diuretic, being pounded when young and the juice extracted, which is then condensed in the sun to the

to ricochet I have preferred (doubtfully) Detlefsen's *cupito* to Mayhoff's *cubito*. Warmington would read *cubitu*: the holly stick, lying down as it were, moves towards the mark.

contra mala oris oculorumque, sanguinem exscreantes, anginas, vulvas, sedes, coeliacos intellegitur potus aut inlitus. oris quidem vitiis etiam folia commanducata prosunt, et ulceribus manantibus aut quibuscumque in capite inlinuntur. cardiacis vel sic per se inponuntur a mamma sinistra, item stomacho in

119 doloribus oculisque procidentibus. instillatur sucus eorum et auribus. sanat condylomata cum rosaceo cerato. cauliculorum ex vino decoctum uvae praesentaneum remedium est. idem per se in cibo sumpti cymae modo aut decocti in vino austero labantes dentes firmant. alvum sistunt et profluvia sanguinis, dysintericis prosunt, siccantur in umbra, ut cinis crematorum uvam reprimat. folia quoque arefacta et contusa iumentorum ulceribus utilia traduntur.

120 mora quae in his nascuntur vel efficaciorem stomaticen praebuerint quam sativa morus. eadem compositione vel cum hypocisthide tantum et melle bibuntur in cholera et a cardiacis et contra araneos. inter medicamenta quae styptica vocant nihil efficacius rubi mora ferentis radice decocta in vino ad tertias partes, ut coluantur eo oris ulcera et sedis foveanturque[1]; tanta vis est ut spongeae ipsae lapidescant.

[1] foveanturque *tres codd., Detlefsen*: foveantur, quae *duo codd., Mayhoff.*

---

[a] Perhaps " on."

[b] For *cardiacus morbus* see Celsus III. 19 with Spencer's note. The Romans seem to have confused certain forms of indigestion and heart trouble. Perhaps the latter is alluded to here.

[c] See Celsus VI. 6, 8 for πρόπτωσις of the eyes.

thickness of honey, and is considered to be, whether taken by the mouth or used as ointment, a specific for affections of the mouth or eyes, for spitting of blood, quinsy, troubles of the uterus or anus, and for coeliac affections. For affections of the mouth, indeed, even the chewed leaves are efficacious, and they are used as ointment for running sores, or for any kind of sore on the head. Even prepared thus without other ingredient they are applied near *a* the left breast for heart-burn,*b* also to the stomach for stomach-ache, and to the eyes for procidence.*c* The juice of them is also dropped into the ears. Added to rose wax-salve it heals condylomata. A decoction in wine of its tender shoots is a quick remedy for affections of the uvula. The same shoots, eaten by themselves like cabbage sprouts, or a decoction of them in a dry wine, strengthen loose teeth. They check looseness of the bowels and discharges of blood, and are good for dysentery. They are dried in the shade and then burnt so that the ash may reduce a relaxed uvula. The leaves also dried and crushed are said to be useful for sores on draught animals. The blackberries which grow on them can furnish a better mouth-medicine than even the cultivated mulberry. Made up on the same prescription or with hypocisthis and honey only, they are taken in drink for cholera, for heart-burn, and for the stings of spiders. Among the medicines that are called styptics, there is none more effective than the root of a bramble bearing blackberries boiled down in wine to one third, so that sores in the mouth and the anus may be rinsed with the decoction and fomented; so powerful is it that the very sponges used become hard as stone.

121 LXXIV. Alterum genus rubi in quo rosa nascitur gignit pululam castaneae similem, calculosis praecipuo remedio. alia est cynorrhoda quam proximo dicemus volumine. cynosbaton alii cynapanxin, alii neurospaston vocant. folium habet vestigio hominis simile. fert et uvam nigram, in cuius acino nervum habet, unde neurospastos dicitur tota, alia quam cappari quod medici cynosbaton appellarunt. huius thyrsus ad remedia splenis et inflationes conditus ex aceto manditur. nervus eius cum mastiche Chia com-
122 manducatus os purgat. ruborum rosa alopecias cum axungia emendat, mora capillum tingunt cum omphacino oleo. flos mori messe colligitur. candidus pleureticis praecipuus ex vino potus, item coeliacis. radix ad tertias decocta alvum sistit et sanguinem. item dentes collutos decocto. eodem suco foventur sedis atque genitalium ulcera. cinis e radice reprimit uvam.
123 LXXV. Idaeus rubus appellatus est, quoniam in Ida non alius nascitur. est autem tenerior ac minor, rarioribus calamis innocentioribusque, sub arborum umbra nascens. huius flos cum melle epiphoris inlinitur et ignibus sacris, stomachicisque ex aqua bibendus datur, cetera eadem praestat quae supra dicta.

---

[a] Book XXV. § 17. The round growth is the spiny gall caused by the gall-fly *Rhoditas rosarum*, not the gall of XXV. 18.

[b] The identification of this neurospastos is difficult, because Pliny has possibly confused here different shrubs. See *Index of Plants*, and Dioscorides I 94 and II 173.

[c] It is very doubtful what *thyrsus* means here. In XXI. § 87 it is distinguished from *caulis*. If the black currant be the plant referred to in the present passage, the *thyrsus* may be the cluster of stalks on which the currants form.

[d] Or, " with diseases of the oesophagus."

LXXIV. A second kind of bramble, on which a rose grows, produces a little round growth like a chestnut, an excellent remedy for the stone. It is different from the dog-rose, about which I shall speak [a] in the next book.

The cynosbatos is called by some cynapanxis, by others neurospastos. It has a leaf like a man's foot-print. It also bears a black cluster, in the berry of which it has a string, whence the whole shrub is called neurospastos.[b] It is different from the caper that the physicians have called cynosbatos. The stalk [c] of this, pickled in vinegar, is chewed as a remedy for affections of the spleen and for flatulence. The string of it chewed up with Chian mastic cleanses the mouth. The rose-blossom of brambles with axle-grease clears away mange; the berries mixed with oil of unripe grapes dye the hair. The blossom of the blackberry is gathered at harvest-time. The white blossom taken in wine is excellent for pleurisy and also for coeliac affections. The root, boiled down to one-third, checks looseness of the bowels and haemorrhage; the decoction also makes a wash that strengthens the teeth. With the same juice are fomented sores of the anus and of the genitals. The ash from the root replaces a relaxed uvula.

LXXV. The Idaean bramble was so called because no other grows on Mount Ida. It is, however, more delicate than other brambles and smaller, with the canes farther apart and less prickly; it grows under the shade of trees. The blossom of it with honey is applied to fluxes of the eyes and to erysipelas, and in water it is given as a drink to patients with disordered stomachs [d]; its other properties are the same as those mentioned above.

124   LXXVI. Inter genera ruborum rhamnos appellatur
a Graecis candidior, fruticosior et[1] ramos spargens
rectis aculeis, non ut ceteri aduncis, foliis maioribus.
alterum genus eius silvestre, nigrius et quadamtenus
rubens, fert veluti folliculos. huius radice decocta in
aqua fit medicamentum quod vocatur lycium.
semen secundas trahit. ille autem candidior adstringit magis, refrigerat, collectionibus et vulneribus adcommodatior. folia utriusque et cruda et
decocta inlinuntur cum oleo.

125   LXXVII. Lycium praestantius spina fieri tradunt
quam et pyxacanthon chironian[a] vocant, qualem in
Indicis arboribus diximus,[b] quoniam longe praestantissimum existimatur Indicum. coquuntur in aqua
tusi rami radicesque summae amaritudinis aereo vase
per triduum, iterumque exempto ligno, donec mellis
crassitudo fiat. adulteratur amaris sucis, etiam
126 amurca et felle bubulo. spuma eius ac flos quidam
oculorum medicamentis additur. reliquo suco
faciem purgat et psoras sanat, erosos angulos oculorum veteresque fluctiones, aures purulentas, tonsillas,
gingivas, tussim, sanguinis excreationes fabae magnitudine devoratum aut, si ex vulneribus fluat, inlitum,
rhagadia, genitalium ulcera, adtritus, ulcera recentia
et serpentia ac putrescentia, in naribus clavos,
suppurationes. bibitur et mulieribus in lacte contra

---

[1] fruticosior et *plures codd.*, *Mayhoff*: frutex is floret X :
et fruticosior, is floret *Detlefsen, vulg.*

---

[a] From Chiron, the centaur who was credited with great
medical knowledge.
[b] See XII. § 31.

LXXVI. Among the different kinds of brambles is
one called rhamnos by the Greeks, paler, more bushy,
throwing out branches with straight thorns, not hooked
like those of other brambles, and with larger leaves.
The other kind of it is wild, darker and inclining to
red, bearing a sort of pod. A decoction of the root
of this in water makes a drug called lycium. *Lycium, etc.*
The seed of it brings away the after-birth. The other,
the paler kind, is more astringent, cooling, and more
suitable for the treatment of gatherings and wounds.
The leaves of either kind, raw or boiled, are made up
into an ointment with oil.

LXXVII. A superior lycium is said to be made from
the thorn which is also called chironian [a] boxthorn,
the characteristics of which I have described [b] among
Indian trees, for Indian lycium is considered by far
the best. The pounded branches and roots, which
are of extreme bitterness, are boiled in water in a
copper vessel for three days; the woody pieces are
then taken away and the rest boiled again until it is of
the consistency of honey. It is adulterated with bitter
juices, even with lees of olive oil and with ox gall.
The froth, which may be called the flower of the
decoction, is an ingredient of remedies for the eyes.
The rest of the juice is used for clearing spots from
the face and for the cure of itch, chronic fluxes
of the eyes and corroding sores in their corners, pus
in the ears, sore tonsils and gums, cough and spitting
of blood. For these a piece the size of a bean is
swallowed, or if there is discharge from wounds it is
applied locally, as it is to chaps, ulcers of the genitals,
excoriations, fresh, spreading and also festering
ulcers, excrescences in the nostrils and suppurations.
It is also taken in milk by women for excessive men-

127 profluvia. Indici differentia glaebis extrinsecus
nigris, intus rufis, cum fregeris, cito nigrescentibus.
adstringit vehementer cum amaritudine, ad eadem
omnia utile, sed praecipue ad genitalia.

128 LXXVIII. Sunt qui et sarcocollam spinae lacri-
mam putent, pollini turis similem, cum quadam
acrimonia dulcem, cumminosam.[1] sistit fluctiones,
inlinitur infantibus maxime. vetustate et haec
nigrescit, melior quo candidior.

129 LXXIX. Unum etiamnum arborum medicinis
debetur nobile medicamentum quod oporicen vocant.
fit ad dysintericos stomachique vitia in congio musti
albi lento vapore decoctis malis cotoneis quinque cum
suis seminibus, punicis totidem, sorborum sextario,
et pari mensura eius quod rhun Syriacam vocant,
croci semuncia. coquitur usque ad crassitudinem
mellis.

LXXX. His subtexemus ea quae Graeci com-
municatione nominum in ambiguo fecere anne arborum essent.

130 Chamaedrys herba est quae Latine trixago dicitur.
aliqui eam chamaeropem, alii Teucriam appellavere.
folia habet magnitudine mentae, colore et divisura

---

[1] cumminosam *Detlefsen, Mayhoff*: gummosam. cum vino
tusa *vulg.*

---

[a] Sarcocolla is a Greek word (σαρκοκόλλα) meaning " the
fastener of (cut) flesh." Dioscorides (III. 85, Wellmann)
gives an account similar to Pliny's, but adds that it came from
Persia : ἔστι δάκρυον δένδρου γεννωμένου ἐν τῇ Περσίδι, ἐοικὸς
λιβανωτῷ λεπτῷ, ὑπόκιρρον, ἔμπικρον τῇ γεύσει. δύναμιν δὲ
ἔχει κολλητικὴν τραυμάτων καὶ ἐφεκτικὴν τῶν ἐν ὀφθαλμοῖς
ῥευμάτων.
[b] The Greek ὀπωρική, " fruit conserve."

struation. The Indian variety is distinguished by the lumps being black outside and red inside, quickly turning black when they have been broken. This kind is very astringent, and bitter. It is useful for all the same purposes as are the other kinds, but especially for treating the genitals.

LXXVIII. Some think that sarcocolla [a] is the tear-like drop of a thorn. It is like powdered frankincense, sweet with a touch of harshness, and gummy. It checks fluxes, and is used especially as an ointment for babies. It too grows black with age, and the whiter it is the better its quality. *Sarcocolla.*

LXXIX. There is still one famous remedy, called oporice, [b] to be included among the medicines that are obtained from trees. Used for dysentery and stomach troubles, it is made in the following way. In a congius [c] of white grape-juice are boiled down over a slow heat five quinces, seeds and all, five pomegranates, one sextarius of sorb-apples, an equal quantity of what is called Syrian sumach, and half an ounce of saffron. The boiling continues until the consistency is that of honey. *Oporice.*

LXXX. To these remedies I will add those which, because the Greeks have given the same name to different objects, we might be led to suppose came from trees. [d]

The chamaedrys (" ground oak ") is a plant whose Latin name is trixago. Some have called it chamaerops, and others the Trojan plant. It has leaves of the same size as mint leaves, coloured and indented as are those of the oak. Some have called it " saw- *" Ground " trees.*

---

[c] A *congius* was a liquid measure containing six *sextarii*, or nearly six English pints.

[d] The plants that follow are all ground " trees."

quercus. alii serratam et ab ea serram inventam esse
dixerunt, flore paene purpureo. carpitur praegnans
suco in petrosis, adversus serpentium venena potu
inlituque efficacissima, item stomacho, tussi vetustae,
pituitae in gula cohaerescenti, ruptis, convulsis,
131 lateris doloribus. lienem consumit, urinam et
menses ciet, ob id incipientibus hydropicis efficax,
manualibus scopis eius in tribus heminis aquae
decoctis usque ad tertias. faciunt et pastillos terentes eam ex aqua ad supra dicta. sanat et vomicas et vetera ulcera vel sordida cum melle. fit et
vinum ex ea pectoris vitiis. foliorum sucus cum oleo
caliginem oculorum discutit, ad splenem ex aceto
sumitur, excalfacit et perunctione.

132   LXXXI. Chamaedaphne unico ramulo est, cubitali
ferme; folia tenuiora lauro; semen rubens adnexum
foliis. inlinitur capitis doloribus recens, ardores
refrigerat, ad tormina cum vino bibitur. menses
sucus eius et urinam ciet potu partusque difficiles in
lana adpositus.

133   LXXXII. Chamelaea similitudinem foliorum oleae
habet—sunt autem amara, odorata [1]—in petrosis
palmum altitudine non excedente. alvum purgat,
detrahit pituitam, bilem, foliis in duabus absinthii
partibus decoctis, suco eo cum melle poto. foliis

[1] *Sic dist. Mayhoff.*

---

[a] Or : " It also heals abscesses and chronic sores, and even
foul ones if honey is added."

[b] Perhaps " inflammation." See note on XXVI § 32.

[c] The method of preparing the medicine may apply only if
it be taken for the cure of bile. The Latin would allow of this
interpretation, but it seems more natural, and equally good
Latin, for the method to apply to all the three purposes
mentioned.

shaped," saying that it gave rise to the invention
of the saw; its blossom is almost purple. It is
cropped in rocky localities and is full of juice, being a
very efficacious remedy, either by the mouth or as an
ointment, for the poison of serpents, and also for disordered stomach, chronic cough, phlegm collected in
the throat, ruptures, sprains and pain in the side.
It reduces the spleen, promotes menstruation, and is
diuretic, being for this reason efficacious in incipient
dropsy, a handful of its sprays being boiled down to
one-third in a sextarius and a half of water. It is
ground in water to make lozenges for the purposes
mentioned above. With honey it also heals abscesses
and chronic sores, even when foul.[a] There is also
made from it a wine, which is useful for troubles of
the chest. The juice of the leaves with oil clears
away dimness of vision; for the spleen it is taken in
vinegar. Used also as embrocation it is warming.

LXXXI. The chamaedaphne (" ground bay ") *Chamae-*
consists of a single small stem, about a cubit high; *daphne.*
the leaves are more slender than those of the bay;
the seed, of a red colour, is attached to the leaves. It
is applied fresh to the head for headache, it cools
feverishness,[b] and for colic it is taken with wine. Its
juice when taken by the mouth promotes menstruation and urine, and applied as a pessary in wool it
makes easier difficult child-birth.

LXXXII. The chamelaea (" ground olive ") has *Chamelaea.*
leaves which resemble those of the olive—they are
bitter, however, and scented—growing in rocky
places and not exceeding a span in height. It purges
the bowels, and draws away phlegm and bile; a decoction is made of the leaves with twice the quantity[c]
of wormwood, this juice being drunk with honey.

impositis et ulcera purgantur. aiunt, si quis ante solis
ortum eam capiat dicatque ad albugines oculorum
se capere, adalligata discuti id vitium, quoquo modo
vero collectam iumentorum pecorumque oculis
salutarem esse.

134 LXXXIII. Chamaesyce lentis folia habet nihil se
adtollentia, in aridis, petrosis, claritati oculorum et
contra subfusiones utilissima [1] et cicatrices, caligines,
nubeculas inuncta.[1] vulvae dolores sedat adposita in
linteolo. tollit et verrucas omnium generum inlita.
prodest et orthopnoicis.

135 LXXXIV. Chamaecissos spicata est tritici modo,
ramulis quinis fere, foliosa [2]—cum floret, existimari
potest alba viola—radice tenui. bibunt ischiadici
folia tribus obolis in vini cyathis duobus septem [3]
diebus, admodum amara potione.

LXXXV. Chamaeleucen apud nos farfarum sive
farfugium vocant. nascitur secundum fluvios, folio
populi, sed ampliore. radix eius inponitur carbonibus
cupressi, atque is nidor per infundibulum bibitur
inveteratae tussi.

[1] utilissima et cicatrices, caligines, ⟨muriculas,⟩ nubeculas
inuncta *vulg.* in vino cocta *ante* inuncta *addito*: utilissimum
[*cum lacunae signo*]—inunctus *Ianus, Detlefsen*: utilis suco ad
cicatrices, caligines, nubeculas inuncto *Mayhoff*: utilissimum
et . . . inuncto *aut* inuncta *aut* iniunctus *codd.*

[2] *Sic dist. Mayhoff.*

[3] septem *Detlefsen, codd.*: septenis *Mayhoff.*

[a] The text of this sentence is most uncertain, Perhaps
Pliny wrote hurriedly or carelessly; *in aridis, petrosis,* a loose
ablative with nothing to depend on, suggests that he did so.
The text of Detlefsen is impossible to translate without filling

An application of the leaves also cleanses ulcers. It is said that if anyone before sunrise says while plucking it that he does so " to cure white spots in the eyes," it disperses this affection if worn as an amulet; but that, in whatever way it is gathered, it is beneficial for the eyes of beasts of burden and of cattle.

LXXXIII. The chamaesyce (" ground fig ") has leaves like those of the lentil, and not rising above the ground. It is found in dry and rocky localities. Very useful [a] for clearness of vision and for arresting cataract, an ointment prepared from it is also used most beneficially for scars, dimness of sight and films over the eyes. Applied as a pessary on a bit of linen it soothes pains of the uterus. Warts too of every kind are removed by an ointment made from it. It is also beneficial for orthopnoea. *Chamaesyce.*

LXXXIV. The chamaecissos (" ground ivy ") is a plant with ears like those of wheat, with about five little branches and many leaves. When in blossom it might be taken for the white violet. The root is slender. For sciatica three oboli of the leaves are taken in two cyathi of wine for seven days, but it is a very bitter draught. *Chamaecissos.*

LXXXV. The chamaeleuce (" ground poplar ") is called by us Romans farfarum or farfugium. It grows by the side of rivers, and has leaves like those of the poplar, but larger. Its root is placed on live coals of cypress wood, and the fumes of it inhaled through a funnel for chronic cough. *Chamaeleuce.*

up the lacuna; that of Mayhoff, " with a juice used as an ointment for scars, etc.," is clever, but still leaves the Latin odd. The general sense is quite plain. *Utilissima* and *utilissimum* (spelt -*mū*) might easily be confused.

136   LXXXVI. Chamaepeuce laricis folio similis lumborum et spinae doloribus propria est. Chamaecyparissos herba ex vino pota contra venena serpentium omnium scorpionumque pollet. Ampeloprason in vinetis nascitur, foliis porri, ructu gravis, contra serpentium ictus efficax. urinam et menses ciet, eruptiones sanguinis per genitale inhibet potum inpositumque. datur et a partu mulieribus et contra canis morsus. ea quoque quae stachys vocatur porri similitudinem habet, longioribus foliis pluribusque et odoris iucundi colorisque in luteum inclinati. pellit menstrua.

137   LXXXVII. Clinopodium alii cleopiceton, alii zopyrontion, alii ocimoides appellant, serpyllo similem, surculosam, palmi altitudine, in petrosis, orbiculato florum[1] ambitu speciem lecti pedum praebente. bibitur ad convulsa, rupta, strangurias, serpentium ictus, item decoctae[2] sucus.

138   LXXXVIII. Nunc subtexemus herbas mirabiles quidem, sed minus claras, nobilibus in sequentia volumina dilatis.

Centunculum vocant nostri, foliis ad similitudinem capitis paenularum, iacentem in arvis, Graeci clematidem, egregii effectus ad sistendam alvum in vino austero. idem sanguinem sistit tritus

---

[1] florum *Warmington* : foliorum *codd.*
[2] decoctae sucus *duo codd. et Mayhoff, qui et* ius *pro* sucus *coni., fortasse recte* : decocta et sucus *ceteri codd., Detlefsen.*

---

[a] Dioscorides III. 95 (Wellmann) : (ἔχον) ἄνθη ὅμοια κλίνης ποσὶν ἐκ διαστημάτων, "having flowers like the feet of a couch at intervals." This is a good description of wild basil; it is the flowers, not the leaves, that are arranged in a circle at intervals. Unless Pliny has made a mistake, we must read, as in the Latin text, *florum* for *foliorum* of the MSS.

LXXXVI. The chamaepeuce ("ground larch") has *Chamae-*
a leaf resembling that of the larch and is specific for *peuce.*
lumbago and pains in the spine.   The chamaecyparis- *Chamaecy-*
sos ("ground cypress") taken in wine is a powerful *parissos.*
antidote to the poisons of all serpents and scorpions.
The ampeloprason ("vine leek") grows in vineyards, *Ampelo-*
has the leaves of a leek, causes violent belching, but *prason.*
is an antidote for the bites of serpents.   It promotes
urine   and   menstruation.   Taken   in   drink   and
applied externally it checks discharges of blood from
the genital organ.   It is also administered to women
after child-birth and for the bites of dogs.   That plant
also which is called stachys bears a resemblance
to the leek, but has longer and more numerous
leaves, a pleasant smell and a colour verging on
saffron yellow.   It is a powerful emmenagogue.
    LXXXVII.   Clinopodium also called cleopiceton, *Clinopodi-*
zopyrontion or ocimoides, is like wild thyme, ligneous, *um.*
a span high, and found on rocky soils; the flowers
are arranged in a round circuit,[a] giving the appearance of the feet of a couch.   It is taken in drink for
sprains,   ruptures,   strangury   and   the   bites   of
serpents;   the juice of a decoction is likewise employed.
    LXXXVIII.   I shall now append some plants,
wonderful indeed but not so well known, postponing
more famous ones for succeeding books.
    Roman authorities give the name centunculus to a *Species of*
plant with leaves resembling the hood of a mantle, *"clematis."*
found lying on the ground in cultivated fields, and
called by the Greeks clematis.[b]   Taken in a dry
wine it is very good for arresting looseness of the
bowels.   Bleeding too is arrested by this plant

    [b] Not our clematis.   See *Index of Plants.*

oxymelitis aut aquae calidae cyathis quinque denarii
unius pondere, sic et ad secundas mulierum efficax.

139 LXXXIX. Sed Graeci clematidas et alias habent,
unam quam aliqui aetiten vocant, alii laginen, nonnulli tenuem scamoniam. ramos habet bipedales,[1]
foliosos, non dissimiles scamoniae, nisi quod nigriora
minoraque sunt folia. invenitur in vineis arvisque.
estur ut olus cum oleo ac sale, alvum ciet. eadem dysintericis cum lini semine ex vino austero sorbetur.

140 folia epiphoris inponuntur cum polenta subposito udo
linteolo. strumas inposita ad suppurationem per-
ducunt, deinde axungia adiecta percurant, item
haemorrhoida cum oleo viridi, phthisicos iuvant cum
melle. lactis quoque ubertatem faciunt in cibis, et
infantibus inlita capillum alunt, ex aceto edentium
venerem stimulant.

141 XC. Est alia clematis Aegyptia cognomine, quae
ab aliis daphnoides, ab aliis polygonoides vocatur,
folio lauri, longa tenuisque, adversus serpentes et
privatim aspidas ex aceto pota efficax.

142 XCI. Aegyptus hanc maxime gignit, quae et
aron, de qua inter bulbos diximus, magnae cum
dracontio litis. quidam enim eandem esse dixere.
Glaucias satu discrevit, dracontium silvestrem arum

---

[1] bipedales *Hard.* : pedales *multi codd., Mayhoff.*

---

[a] See XIX. § 96. The translation might be : " known also
as aron," but there is no other evidence that clematis was
called aron.

[b] Littré has : " par le lieu de leur croissance," and so
Bostock and Riley.

pounded and taken in doses of one denarius by weight to five cyathi of oxymel or warm water; this prescription also helps the after-birth.

LXXXIX. But the Greeks have also other kinds of clematis, one of which some call aetites, others lagine, and others the " slender scammony." It has branches two feet long, leafy, and not unlike those of scammony, except that the leaves are darker and smaller. It is found in vineyards and cultivated fields, is eaten as salad with oil and salt, and relaxes the bowels. With linseed it is also drunk in a dry wine by sufferers from dysentery. The leaves with pearl barley are applied to fluxes from the eyes, a damp rag being first placed underneath. An application draws scrofulous sores to suppuration, and then a further application with axle-grease completes the cure. With green oil also they are beneficial for haemorrhoids, and with honey for consumptives. Taken as a food they also promote an abundant supply of human milk, applied to the heads of babies they stimulate the growth of hair, and eaten with vinegar they act as an aphrodisiac.

XC. There is another clematis, called also the Egyptian, by some daphnoides and by others polygonoides, with a leaf like that of the bay; it is long and slender, and taken in vinegar is efficacious against the bite of serpents, being specific for that of asps.

XCI. It is Egypt especially that produces this clematis, and also the aron, which I have mentioned [a] in my section on bulbs; about it and dracontium there has been sharp controversy, for some have asserted that the two are the same. Glaucias distinguished them by their mode of reproduction,[b] declaring that dracontium is wild aron. Some have

Aron, dracontium, and dracunculus.

pronuntiando. aliqui radicem arum appellarunt. caulem vero dracontium, in totum alium, si modo hic est qui apud nos dracunculus vocatur. namque aros radicem nigram in latitudinem rotundam habet multoque maiorem et [1] qua manus inpleatur, dracunculus subrutilam et draconis convoluti modo, unde et nomen.

143 XCII. Quin et ipsi Graeci inmensam posuere differentiam : semen dracunculi fervens tradendo, tantumque ei virus ut olfactum gravidis abortum inferret, aron miris laudibus tulere, primum in cibis, feminam praeferentes, quoniam mas durior esset et in coquendo lentior. pectoris vitia purgare, aridum potioni inspersum aut ecligmate urinam et

144 menses ciere, sic et in oxymelite potum. stomacho interaneisque exulceratis ex lacte ovillo bibendum, ad tussim in cinere coctum dedere ex oleo. alii coxere in lacte ut decoctum biberetur. epiphoris

145 elixum inposuere, item suggillatis, tonsillis. Glaucias [2] ex oleo haemorrhoidum vitio infudit,[3] lentigines ex melle inlinens.[4] laudavit et pro antidoto contra venena, pleureticis, peripleumonicis quo tussientibus

---

[1] et codd. et Mayhoff: ut Detlefsen.
[2] tonsillis. Glaucias Mayhoff: tonsillis, Detlefsen: tonsillas fere omnes codd.
[3] infudit V, Mayhoff : infudit dX, Sillig: infudere vulg., Detlefsen: effudit Cleophantus Ianus.
[4] illinens codd.: illinentes vulg., Detlefsen.

---

[a] With the reading of Detlefsen : "much too large merely to fill the hand."
[b] Draco, from which "dracunculus" is derived. Dioscorides says (II. 166) that it is the καυλός (stem) which is ὀφιοειδής (" like a snake ").
[c] Or, with no comma at cibis and primum = priorem, "preferring the female as a food etc."

called the root aron, but the stem dracontium, though
the latter is a totally different plant, if at least it is
the same as that called by the Romans dracunculus.
For the aron has a black root, broad and round, and
much larger, large[a] enough to fill the hand, but
dracunculus a reddish one like a coiled snake,[b] from
which its name is derived.

XCII. The Greeks themselves moreover have put
a wide difference between the two plants. They
describe the seed of dracunculus as hot, with so
foul a stench that the smell causes pregnant women
to miscarry; aron they have lauded to the skies
as an excellent food,[c] preferring however the female
plant, on the ground that the male is harder, and
slower to cook,[d] adding that it clears the chest of
disorders, and that dried and sprinkled in drink or
made into an electuary it is diuretic and an emmenagogue, as it is also when drunk in oxymel.
They prescribed it to be drunk in sheep's milk for
ulcerated stomach and bowels; cooked on hot ash
and taken in oil they gave it for a cough. Others
boiled it in milk for the decoction to be drunk.
Thoroughly boiled it was applied by them to fluxes
from the eyes, and likewise to bruises and to affected
tonsils. Glaucias[e] injected it in oil for troublesome
piles, using it with honey as an ointment for freckles.
He recommended it also as an antidote against
poisons, and, prepared as for coughs, for pleurisy and

---

[d] Or, " slower to digest," if *coquo* ever = *concoquo.*
[e] The emendation of Mayhoff (*tonsillis Glaucias* copied as
tonsillas) is confirmed by the reading *tonsillas,* and by the
mention of the physician Glaucias three sections earlier. Both
Sillig and Jan thought that a name had been lost as a subject to
infudit.

modo. semen intritum cum oleo aut rosaceo infunditur aurium dolori. Dieuches tussientibus et suspiriosis et orthopnoicis et pura excreantibus farinae permixtum pane cocto dedit. Diodotus phthisicis e melle ecligmate et pulmonis vitiis, ossibus etiam fractit

146 inposuit. partus omnium animalium extrahit naturae circumlitum. sucus radicis cum melle Attico oculorum caligines, stomachi vitia discutit, tussim decocti ius cum melle. ulcera omnium generum, sive phagedaenae sint sive carcinomata, sive serpant, sive polypi

147 in naribus, sucus mire sanat. folia ambustis prosuns et vino et oleo cocta. alvum inaniunt ex sale et aceto sumpta, et luxatis cum melle cocta prosunt, item articulis podagricis cum sale recentia vel sicca. Hippocrates utralibet ad collectiones cum melle inposuit. ad menses trahendos seminis vel radicis drachmae duae in vini cyathis duobus sufficiunt. eadem potio, si a

148 partu non purgentur, et secundas trahit. Hippocrates et radicem ipsam adposuit. dicunt et in pestilentia salutarem esse in cibis. ebrietatem discutit. serpentes nidore, cum crematur, privatimque aspidas fugat aut inebriat ita ut torpentes inveniantur. perunctos quoque aro e laureo oleo fugiunt. ideo et

---

[a] Dieuches was a " Dogmatic " of the fourth century B.C.

[b] This, i.e., " bread crumbs," must, I think, be the sense of *farinae pane cocto*. But one would expect *panis cocti*. Perhaps *farinae* is a gloss that has crept into the text.

[c] Diodotus was a physician of the first or second century B.C.

[d] *Ius* seems to denote a more liquid form of juice than *sucus*.

104

pneumonia. The seed pounded up with olive oil or
rose oil is injected for ear-ache. Dieuches [a] administered it, thoroughly mixed with the powder from a
loaf,[b] for coughs, asthma, orthopnoea, and the spitting
of pus. Diodotus [c] gave it in the form of an honey
electuary for consumption and complaints of the
lungs, and even used it as an application for broken
bones. Applied round the sexual parts it helps
delivery of all animals. Dimness of vision and disorders of the stomach are removed by the juice of
the root with Attic honey, and cough by the broth [d]
of a decoction with the addition of honey. The
juice is a wonderful remedy for ulcers of all kinds,
whether corroding, cancerous, spreading, or polypus in the nostrils. The leaves, boiled in wine and
oil, are good for burns. Taken in salt and vinegar
they are a strong purge, boiled with honey they are
good for dislocations, and also fresh or dried, with
salt added, for gouty joints. Hippocrates [e] applied
them, fresh or dried, with honey locally to boils. As an
emmenagogue two drachmae of the seed or root in
two cyathi of wine are sufficient, and the same
draught, if cleansing after delivery is not effected, also
brings away the after-birth. Hippocrates also used
the root by itself as a pessary. It is said too that
in times of plague it is healthful to take it in one's
food. It dissipates the effects of drunkenness. The
fumes arising from it when it burns keep away serpents, especially asps, or make them so tipsy that
they are found in a state of torpor. Serpents are also
kept off if the body is thoroughly rubbed with aron
in oil of bay. For this reason it is also considered

[e] As I can find no reference to aron in the Hippocratic *Corpus*, Pliny is alluding to some work now lost.

contra ictus dari potu in vino nigro putant utile. in foliis ari caseus optime servari traditur.

149 XCIII. Dracunculus quem dixi hordeo maturescente effoditur luna crescente. omnino habentem serpentes fugiunt. adeo [1] percussis prodesse potum aiunt; maiorem vim esse,[2] si ferro non attingatur. sucus eius et aurium dolori prodest.

150 Id autem quod Graeci dracontium vocant triplici effigie demonstratum mihi est : foliis betae, non sine thyrso, flore purpureo ; hoc est simile aro. alii radice longa veluti signata articulosaque monstravere, tribus omnino cauliculis, folia eius [3] decoqui ex aceto contra serpentium ictus iubentes. tertia demonstratio fuit folio maiore quam cornus, radice harundinea, totidem, ut adfirmabant, geniculata [4] nodis quot haberet annos, totidemque esse folia. hi ex vino vel aqua contra serpentes dabant.

151 XCIV. Est et aris quae in eadem Aegypto nascitur, similis aro, minor tantum minoribusque foliis et [5] utique radice, quae tamen olivae grandis magnitudinem inpleat, alba geminum caulem, altera unum tantum emittens. medetur utraque ulceribus manantibus, item ambustis ac fistulis collyrio inmisso.

---

[1] adeo] in aceto *coni. Mayhoff*: ideo X, *vulg.*

[2] vim esse *coni. Detlefsen, quem sequitur Mayhoff*: ut menses (*aut* messes) *codd.*

[3] folia eius X, *vulg.*: foliisque *Detlefsen*: foliis *codd., Sillig, Mayhoff, qui etiam* cauliculi foliis *coni.*

[4] harundinea . . . geniculata *Detlefsen*: harundineae . . . geniculatae *Mayhoff*: *utraque lectio in codd. invenitur.*

[5] et *delere vult Warmington.*

---

[a] What we call " red " wine.

[b] In parts of this chapter, Pliny appears to confuse two different plants.

beneficial for snake-bites if one takes aron in a draught of dark *a* wine. It is said that cheese keeps very well if wrapped in leaves of aron.*b*

XCIII. The dracunculus I have referred to is dug up when the barley is ripening and the moon is crescent. Merely to have it on the person keeps away serpents. All the more beneficial a draught is it said to be to those who have been bitten; and its potency to be greater if iron does not touch the plant. Ear-ache too is relieved by its juice.

That plant, however, which the Greeks call dracon- *Dracontium.* tium has been pointed out to me in three illustra-tions; the first *c* has leaves like those of beet, a thyrsus and a purple flower; this is like the aron. Others have pointed out a kind with a long root, which is as it were stamped and knotted, and with three stems in all, prescribing a decoction of its leaves in vinegar for the bite of serpents. The third plant pointed out had a leaf larger than that of the cornel and a root like that of a reed, the knots on it being, they said, as many as the plant is years old, the leaves too being also equal in number. They prescribed this plant in wine or water for snake-bite.

XCIV. There is also a plant called the aris, which *Aris and* too is a native of Egypt. It is similar to the aron, *other plants.* only itself and its leaves are smaller, as is also the root in particular, though it is as big as a full-sized olive. The white kind puts out twin stems, the other kind one only. Either is good for running sores as well as for burns, and for fistula also if a suppository made

---

c For the identifications see *Index of Plants.* Pliny in XXV § 8 refers to painted *effigies* of plants in herbals. He implies here that he had never actually seen *dracontium*, but only such coloured drawings.

nomas sistunt decocta folia earum [1] in aqua et postea [2] trita rosaceo addito. sed unum miraculum ingens ; contacto genitali cuiusque feminini sexus animal in perniciem agi.

152   XCV. Myriophyllon, quod nostri milifolium vocant, caulis est teneri, similis feniculo, plurimis foliis, unde et nomen accepit. nascitur in palustribus, magnifici usus ad vulnera cum aceto. bibitur ad difficultates urinae et vesicae aut suspiria praecipitatisque ex alto. eadem efficacissima ad dentium dolores. Etruria hoc nomine appellat herbam in pratis tenuem, a lateribus capillamenti modo foliosam, eximii usus ad vulnera, boum nervos abscisos vomere solidari ea rursusque iungi addita axungia adfirmans.

153   XCVI. Pseudobunion napi folia habet, fruticans palmi altitudine, laudatissima in Creta. contra tormina, stranguriam laterum praecordiorumque dolores bibuntur rami eius quini senive.

154   XCVII. Myrris, quam alii myrrizan, alii myrran vocant, simillima est cicutae caule foliisque et .flore, minor tantum et exilior, cibo non insuavis. ciet menstrua et partus cum vino. aiunt eandem potam in pestilentia salutarem esse. subvenit et phthisicis in sorbitione data. aviditatem cibi facit, phalangiorum morsus restinguit. ulcera quoque in

---

[1] decocta folia earum *Sillig, vet. lect. Dal.*: decocto earum *Detlefsen*: inlitu decoctarum *ex Dioscoride Mayhoff.*

[2] postea trita] posca tritarum *Detlefsen*: postea tritarum *Mayhoff.*

---

[a] This chapter is like Dioscorides II 168, where however ἀρίσαρον is the name of the plant discussed. One sentence is very informative : φθείρει δὲ καὶ αἰδοῖον παντὸς ζῴου ἐντεθεῖσα ἡ ῥίζα.

of it be inserted. Corroding ulcers are arrested by an application of their leaves boiled in water and then beaten up with the addition of rose oil. But there is one great marvel connected with this plant: if it touches the sexual organs of any female animal she is driven to destruction.[a]

XCV. The myriophyllon, which our people call millefolium, has a tender stem like that of fennel, *Millefolium.* with abundance of leaves, which have also given the plant its name.[b] It is found in marshy districts, and with vinegar makes a splendid treatment for wounds. In drink it is taken for strangury, affections of the bladder, asthma, and falls from a height. It is also very efficacious for tooth-ache. In Etruria the name is given to a slim meadow-plant, with many leaves at the sides like hair, and extremely beneficial for wounds; the people declare that applied with axle-grease it unites the tendons of oxen when cut by the plough-share and closes the wound.

XCVI. The pseudobunion has the leaves of the *Pseudo-*navew; it grows into a bush about a span in height, *bunion.* the most esteemed being found in Crete. For colic, strangury and pains in the sides or hypochondria doses of five or six sprays are taken in drink.

XCVII. The myrris, also called myrriza or myrra, *Myrris.* is very like hemlock in stem, leaves and flower, but smaller and more slender, and not unpleasant as a food. With wine it promotes menstruation and facilitates delivery. It is said that it is also healthful to take it in drink in time of plague. Given in broth it helps consumptives. It sharpens the appetite and allays the bite of poisonous spiders. Sores too on the

[b] Myriophyllon means " plant with ten thousand leaves," and millefolium " plant with a thousand leaves."

facie aut capite sucus eius in aqua triduo maceratae
sanat.

155 XCVIII. Oenobreches folia lentis habet, longiora
paulo, florem rubentem, radicem exiguam et gracilem. nascitur circa fontes. siccata in farinae
modum et inspersa vino albo strangurias finit, alvum
sistit. sucus eius perunctis cum oleo sudores movet.

156 XCIX. In promisso herbarum mirabilium occurrit
aliqua dicere et de magicis. quae enim mirabiliores?
primi eas in nostro orbe celebravere Pythagoras
atque Democritus, consectati Magos. coracesia
et calicia Pythagoras aquam glaciari tradit, quarum
mentionem apud alios non reperio, nec apud eum
alia de his.

157 C. Idem minyada appellat et nomine alio corin-
thiam, cuius decocto in aqua suco protinus sanari
ictus serpentium, si foveantur, dicit. eundem
effusum[1] in herbam qui vestigio contigerint aut forte
respersos insanabili leto perire, monstrifica prorsus
natura veneni praeterquam contra venena.

158 CI. Ab eodem Pythagora aproxis appellatur herba
cuius radix e longinquo concipiát ignes ut naphtha, de
qua in terrae miraculis diximus. idem tradit, qui

---

[1] eundem effusum *vulg., Mayhoff*: eandem effusam *codd.,
Detlefsen. Difficilior haec lectio non potior.*

---

[a] These, perhaps " girls' plant " and " beauty plant," have
not been identified with any certainty. It is said that
Cissampelos pareira gives a kind of consistency to water without impairing its transparency. It is difficult, if not impossible,
to identify the plants mentioned in this section of Pliny with
their scanty descriptions, fanciful names, and "magical"
properties.

[b] Is it unreasonable to suppose that the names *minyas* and
corinthia are not unconnected with the legend of the sorceress

face or head are cured by its juice obtained by
steeping the plant in water for three days.

XCVIII. The oenobreches has leaves like those of *Oenobreches.*
the lentil, but a little longer, a red flower and a small,
slender root. It grows round springs. Dried till it
is like flour, and sprinkled in white wine, it stops
strangury and checks looseness of the bowels.
Rubbing with its juice mixed with oil causes perspiration.

XCIX. My proposed task of discussing wonderful
plants suggests that I also say a few words about
those that are magical. For what plants are more *Magical*
wonderful than they? These were first brought to *plants.*
the notice of our part of the world by Pythagoras and
Democritus, who followed as their authority the
Magi. Pythagoras declares that water is congealed
by the plants coracesia and calicia;[a] but I find no
mention of them in other authorities, nor does
Pythagoras tell us anything else about them.

C. The same authority gives the name of minyas,
or corinthia,[b] to a plant of which, he says, the decocted
juice, used as a fomentation, immediately heals the
bites of serpents. He adds that if it is poured on
the grass and a person happens to tread on it, or if
by chance it is sprinkled on the body, inevitable
death ensues; so absolutely devilish is the poison of
this plant, except that it counteracts other poisons.

CI. The same Pythagoras calls aproxis a plant *Aproxis.*
whose root catches fire at a distance like naphtha;
I have spoken about it in my section on the marvels
of the earth.[c] He also informs us that the symptoms

Medea? The Minyae were the companions of Jason; Corinth
was the scene of Euripides' *Medea.*
   [c] See Book II. § 235.

morbi humano corpori inciderint florente brassica,[1]
quamvis sanatos admonitionem eorum sentire, quotiens
ea herba floreat, qui [2] florente acciderint aut frumento
159 aut cicuta aut viola similem conditionem habere. nec
me fallit hoc volumen eius a quibusdam Cleemporo
medico adscribi, verum Pythagorae pertinax fama an-
tiquitasque vindicant. et id ipsum auctoritatem volu-
minum adfert, si quis alius curae suae opus illo viro
dignum iudicavit, quod fecisse Cleemporum, cum alia
suo et nomine ederet, quis credat?

160 CII. Democriti certe chirocmeta esse constat. at [3]
in his ille post Pythagoram Magorum studiosissimus
quanto portentosiora tradit! aglaophotim [4] herbam,
quae admiratione hominum propter eximium colorem
acceperit nomen, in marmoribus Arabiae nascentem
Persico latere, qua de causa et marmaritim vocari.
hac Magos uti, cum velint deos evocare.

161 Achaemenida colore electri sine folio nasci in [5]
Taradastilis Indiae, qua [6] pota in vino noxii per
cruciatus confiteantur omnia per varias numinum

[1] brassica *Detlefsen, Mayhoff, codd.*: aproxi *vulg.*
[2] quotiens ea herba floreat, qui *Detlefsen*: quotiens floreat;
item si *Mayhoff*: quotiens *solum codd.*
[3] at *om.* d, *fortasse recte.*
[4] *Ante* aglaophotim *add.* ut *Mayhoff.*
[5] nasci in *Detlefsen*: nascentem *Mayhoff*: nascens in *codd.*
[6] qua *Detlefsen, Mayhoff*: quae *codd.*: cuius radice in
pastillos digesta in dieque *vulg.*

---

[a] The vulgate reading *aproxi* has no MS. authority, although
X has *approxica*, but I feel that *aproxi* makes the better sense,
and that *brassica* is a blunder.

of diseases which have attacked the human body when the cabbage [a] is in blossom, even though the patient has been cured, are felt to recur every time this plant [b] blossoms; he speaks of a similar peculiarity following diseases which have attacked when wheat, hemlock or the violet is in flower. I am aware that this book of his is ascribed by some to the physician Cleemporus, but an ancient and unbroken tradition assigns it to Pythagoras. Were the author anyone else, the mere fact that he has considered the result of his labour worthy of that great thinker enhances the authority of a book; but who would believe that Cleemporus acted so, since he published other works, and that under his own name?

CII. That Democritus was the author of the book called *Chirocmeta* is a well-attested tradition; yet [c] in it this famous scientist, the keenest student next to Pythagoras of the Magi, has told us of far more marvellous phenomena. For example, the plant aglaophotis, [d] which received its name from men's *Aglaophotis.* wonder at its magnificent colour, being native, he says, to the marble quarries of Arabia on the Persian side, is therefore also called marmaritis. The Magi use it, he tells us, when they wish to call up gods.

The achaemenis, he reports, is of an amber colour, *Achaemenis.* leafless and found among the Taradastili of India; criminals, according to him, if they drink it in wine, confess all their misdeeds because they suffer tor-

[b] It is difficult to decide whether this refers to *brassica* or to the *aproxis*. If to the former, this sentence has nothing whatever to do with the *aproxis*; if to the latter, the reason for the introduction of *brassica* is very obscure.

[c] The *at* of nearly all MSS. mars the logic of this passage, and may be an instance of dittography from *constat*.

[d] " Bright light," perhaps peony (*Paeonia officinalis*).

imaginationes, eandem hippophobada appellat, quoniam equae praecipue caveant eam.

162   Theombrotion xxx schoenis a Choaspe nasci, pavonum[1] picturis similem, odore eximio. hanc a regibus Persarum bibi contra omnia corporum incommoda instabilitatemque mentis et iustitiae,[2] eandem semnion a potentiae maiestate appellari.

Aliam deinde adamantida Armeniae Cappadociaeque alumnam. hac admota leones resupinari cum hiatu lasso. nominis causam esse quod conteri nequeat.

Arianida in Arianis gigni igneam colore, colligi, cum sol in leone sit. huius tactu peruncta oleo ligna accendi.

163   Therionarca in Cappadocia et Mysia nascente omnes feras torpescere nec nisi hyaenae urina adspersa recreari.

Aethiopida in Meroe nasci, ob id et meroida appellari, folio lactucae, hydropicis utilissimam e mulso potam.

[1] pavonum *Sillig, Detlefsen* : pavonis *cum aliquot codd. Mayhoff.*

[2] instabilitatemque mentis et iustitiae] inmota stabilitate mentis et iustitiae *Detlefsen* : incommoda; a stabilitate mentis et iustitiae *Mayhoff, qui* mentis et iustitiae *uncis seclusit* : instabilitatemque mentis *vulg.* : *fortasse* ad stabilitatem mentis et iustitiae : *varia codd.*

---

[a] I take the " tortures " to be those caused by the haunting phantoms, as is suggested by the repeated *per* of *per cruciatus* and *per varias numinum imaginationes*, though the phrases are separated. But by *per cruciatus* Pliny may simply mean : " while they are being tortured as part of their punishment." So Mayhoff (Appendix): *noxii inter cruciatus.*

[b] " Food for the gods."

[c] The *schoenus* was a measure of forty stades in length, about five miles.

tures[a] from divers phantoms of spirits that haunt them; he also called it hippophobas, because mares have an intense aversion to it.

The theombrotion[b] grows, says Democritus, thirty schoeni[c] from the Choaspes, being like a peacock in its colourings and of a very fine scent. He goes on to state that the kings of Persia take it in drink for all bodily disorders and for instability of intellect and of the sense of justice,[d] and that it is also called semnion[e] from the majesty of its power.

Theombrotion.

Democritus goes on to mention another plant, the adamantis,[f] a native of Armenia and Cappadocia; if it be placed, he says, near lions they lie on their backs and wearily yawn. The reason for the name is because the plant cannot be crushed.

Adamantis and other plants.

Ariana is given as the home of the arianis, a plant of the colour of fire. It is gathered, he says, when the sun is in Leo, and pieces of wood soaked in oil catch fire at its touch.

Democritus says that the therionarca,[g] growing in Cappadocia and Mysia, makes all wild beasts become torpid, and that they cannot be revived unless sprinkled with the urine of a hyaena.

He tells us that the aethiopis grows in Meroë, that therefore its other name is the meroïs, that it has the leaf of the lettuce and that it is very beneficial for dropsy if taken in honey wine.

---

[d] The text here is uncertain. Detlefsen's conjecture, yielding a good sense, would mean: " to keep unshaken their intellectual powers and sense of justice "; Mayhoff's: " bodily disorders; from its reliability, and from the majesty, etc."

[e] The word *semnion* means " the august plant."

[f] " Unbreakable."

[g] " That benumbs beasts."

Ophiusam in Elephantine eiusdem Aethiopiae, lividam difficilemque aspectu, qua pota terrorem minasque serpentium obversari ita ut mortem sibi eo metu consciscant, ob id cogi sacrilegos illam bibere, adversari ei palmeum vinum.

164 Thalassaeglen circa Indum amnem inveniri, quae ob id nomine alio potamaugis appellatur, hac pota lymphari homines obversantibus miraculis.

Theangelida in Libano Syriae, Dicte Cretae montibus et Babylone et Susis Persidis nasci, qua pota Magi divinent.

Gelotophyllida in Bactris et circa Borysthenen. haec si bibatur cum murra et vino, varias obversari species ridendique finem non fieri nisi potis nucleis pineae nucis cum pipere et melle in vino palmeo.

165 Hestiaterida a convictu nominari in Perside, quoniam hilarentur illa, eandem protomediam, qua primatum apud reges obtineant, casigneten quoniam secum ipsa nascatur, nec cum aliis ullis herbis, eandem dionysonymphadem, quoniam vino mire conveniat.

Helianthes vocat in Themiscyrena regione et Ciliciae montibus maritimis, folio myrti. hac cum adipe leonino decocta, addito croco et palmeo vino,

---

^a " Snake plant."
^b " Sea brightness."
^c " River gleam."
^d " Messenger from god "(?).
^e " Leaves of laughter."
^f " Plant of the family hearth."
^g " Headship of the Medes."
^h " Sister plant." Authorities differ here; some take all four names to refer to the same plant, others think that there are two, the second being the *casignete*.
ⁱ " Bride of Dionysus."

The ophiusa [a] he speaks of as growing in Elephan- *Ophiusa.*
tine, which also belongs to Ethiopia, a plant livid
in colour and revolting to look at, to take which in
drink causes such terrible visions of threatening
serpents that fear of them causes suicide; wherefore
those guilty of sacrilege are forced to drink it. An
antidote is palm wine.

The thalassaegle [b] we are told is found along the *Thalassaegle.*
river Indus, and is therefore also called potamaugis,[c]
to drink which causes men to rave, while weird
visions beset their minds.

The theangelis,[d] Democritus says, grows on Mount *Theangelis.*
Lebanon in Syria, on Mount Dicte in Crete, and in
Babylon and Susa in Persia; the Magi take it in
drink to gain power to divine.

The gelotophyllis [e] grows in Bactria and along the *Gelotophyllis.*
Borysthenes. If this be taken in myrrh and wine
all kinds of phantoms beset the mind, causing laughter
which persists until the kernels of pine-nuts are taken
with pepper and honey in palm wine.

According to the same authority the hestiateris [f] *Hestiateris.*
is a Persian plant, so named from its promotion of
good fellowship, because it makes the company gay;
it is also called protomedia,[g] from its use to gain the
highest position at Court; casignete,[h] because it
grows only in company with its own species, and not
with any other plants; also dionysonymphas,[i] because
it goes wonderfully well with wine.

Helianthes [j] is the name given to a plant with *Helianthes.*
leaves like those of the myrtle, growing in the district
of Themiscyra and on the mountains along the coasts
of Cilicia. A decoction of it in lion's fat, with saffron
and palm wine added, is used, he says, as an ointment

[j] " Sun flower."

perungui Magos et Persarum reges ut fiat corpus
aspectu iucundum, ideo eandem heliocallida nominari.

166 Hermesias ab eodem vocatur ad liberos generandos
pulchros bonosque, non herba sed conpositio e nucleis
pineae nucis tritis cum melle, murra, croco, vino
palmeo, postea admixto theombrotio et lacte. bibere
generaturos iubet et a conceptu et [1] puerperas partum
nutrientes, ita fieri † excellentes animo et forma atque
bonos.†[2] atque harum omnium magica quoque voca-
bula ponit.

167 Adiecit his Apollodorus adsectator eius herbam
aeschynomenen, quoniam adpropinquante manu folia
contraheret, aliam crocida, cuius tactu phalangia
morerentur, Crateuas onothurin,[3] cuius aspersu e
vino feritas omnium animalium mitigaretur, ana-
campserotem celeber arte grammatica paulo ante,
cuius omnino tactu redirent amores vel cum odio
depositi. et abunde sit hactenus attigisse insignia
Magorum in herbis alia de his aptiore dicturis loco.

---

[1] et *coni. Dal.* : *om. Detlefsen, Mayhoff, codd.*
[2] excellentes animo et forma atque bonos X, *vulg. ante
Sillig* : excellentes animi et formae bonis *Detlefsen, Mayhoff* :
excellentis d *Sillig* : *an* excellentis animi et formae bonos ?
[3] onothurin *coni. Ianus collato Dioscoride IV. 117 (Wellmann)* :
oenotherin *Detlefsen* : oenotheridem *vulg.* : *varia codd.*

---

[a] " Beauty of the Sun."
[b] The text is very uncertain. Perhaps the original was
excellentis animi et formae, bonos or *bonis* being added by some
scribe who remembered the opening words of this section. See
Additional Notes, p. 483.
[c] The " shy " plant.
[d] Probably Apion (*circa* A.D. 38).
[e] " Restorer of lost love."

by the Magi and the Persian kings to give to the body a pleasing appearance, and therefore it is also called heliocallis.[a]

The same authority gives the name hermesias to *Hermesias.* a means of procreating children who shall be handsome and good. It is not a plant, but a compound of ground kernels of pine nuts with honey, myrrh, saffron and palm wine, with the later addition of theombrotion and milk. He prescribes a draught of it to those who are about to become parents, after conception, and to nursing mothers. This, he says, results in children exceeding fair in mind and body, as well as good.[b] Of all these plants he adds also the magical names.

Apollodorus, a follower of Democritus, added *Aeschyno-* to these plants one that he called aeschynomene,[c] *mene.* because on the approach of a hand it contracts its leaves, and another called crocis, whose touch, he declares, kills poisonous spiders; Crateuas added the onothuris, by the sprinkling of which in wine he asserted that the fierceness of all animals is calmed; and a little while ago a well-known grammarian [d] added anacampseros,[e] by the mere touch of which, he said, love was restored, even though the lovers parted in hatred. These few remarks are quite enough to have been said for the present about the wonderful powers ascribed to plants by the Magi, as I shall speak of them again on a more fitting occasion.[f]

---

[f] In this chapter Pliny uses indirect speech, as if to disclaim responsibility for the truth of the account he is giving. It is awkward for a translator to represent this in a modern language, and it might have been better to prefix to the chapter a sentence to the effect that what follows is given on the authority of others.

168   CIII. Eriphiam multi prodidere. scarabaeum haec
in avena habet sursum deorsum decurrentem cum
sono haedi, unde et nomen accepit. hac ad vocem
nihil praestantius esse tradunt.

CIV. Herba lanaria ovibus ieiunis data lactis
abundantiam facit. aeque nota lactoris vulgo est,
plena lactis quod degustatum vomitiones concitat.
eandem hanc aliqui esse dicunt, alii similem illi quam
militarem vocant, quoniam vulnus ferro factum
nullum non intra dies quinque sanat ex oleo
inposita.

169   CV. Celebratur autem et a Graecis stratiotes, sed
ea in Aegypto tantum et inundatione Nili nascitur,
aizoo similis, ni maiora haberet folia. refrigerat
mire et vulnera sanat ex aceto inlita, item ignes
sacros et suppurationes. sanguinem quoque qui
defluit a renibus pota cum ture masculo mirifice
sistit.

170   CVI. Herba in capite statuae nata collecta in
vestis alicuius pannum et inligata lino [1] rufo capitis
dolores adposita confestim sedare traditur.

CVII. Herba quaecumque e rivis aut fluminibus
ante solis ortum collecta ita ut nemo colligentem
videat adalligata laevo bracchio ita ut aeger quid sit
illud ignoret tertianas arcere traditur.

CVIII. Lingua herba nascitur circa fontes. radix
eius conbusta et trita cum adipe suis—adiciunt ut

---

[1] lino *Sillig, Mayhoff*: in lino *codd.*

CIII. Many have described the eriphia. It has a *The eriphia.*
beetle running up and down inside its stem, making a
noise like that of a kid; hence also comes its name.[a]
It is said that nothing is better than this plant for
improving the voice.

CIV. The wool-plant given to fasting sheep pro- *The wool-plant and lactoris.*
duces an abundance of milk. Equally well known
generally is the lactoris, a plant full of milk a taste of
which produces vomitings. Some say that this is
the same plant (others say one like it) as that called
the military plant, because there is no wound made
by iron which is not cured within five days by an
application of it in oil.

CV. Another plant highly popular among the *The stratiotes.*
Greeks is the stratiotes, but it grows only in Egypt
when the Nile is in flood; it is like the aizoüm, only
its leaves are larger. It is wonderfully cooling, and
applied in vinegar heals wounds, as well as erysipelas
and suppurations. It also arrests haemorrhage of
the kidneys in a marvellous way if taken in drink
with male frankincense.

CVI. A plant that grows on the head of a statue, *Various plants.*
gathered into a piece taken from some garment and
tied on with red thread, is said to relieve headache
immediately on being applied.

CVII. Any plant whatsoever, gathered before
sun-rise out of streams or rivers, provided that
nobody sees the gatherer, if it is tied as an
amulet to the left arm, is said to keep away tertian
agues, provided that the patient does not know
what is going on.

CVIII. The plant called " tongue " grows around *" Tongue."*
springs. Its root, burnt and pounded with pig's

a The " kid-plant."

121

nigra sit et sterilis—alopecias emendat unguentium
in sole.

171　CIX. Cribro in limite abiecto herbae intus extantes
decerptae adalligataeque gravidis partus adcelerant.

CX. Herba quae gignitur super fimeta ruris contra
anginas efficacissime pollet ex aqua pota.

CXI. Herba iuxta quam canes urinam fundunt
evulsa ne ferro attingatur luxatis celerrime medetur.

172　CXII. Rumpotinum arborem demonstravimus
inter arbusta.　iuxta hanc viduam vite nascitur herba
quam Galli rodarum vocant.　caulem habet virgae
ficulneae modo geniculatum, folia urticae in medio
exalbida, eadem procedente tempore tota rubentia,
florem argenteum, praecipua contra tumores fervor-
esque et collectiones cum axungia vetere tusa ita ut
ferro non attingatur.　qui perunctus est despuit ad
suam dexteram terna.　efficacius remedium esse
aiunt, si tres trium nationum homines perungant
dextrorsus.

173　CXIII. Herba impia vocatur incana, rorismarini
aspectu, thyrsi modo vestita atque capitata.　inde
alii ramuli exsurgunt sua capitula gerentes, ob id
impiam appellavere, quoniam liberi super parentem
excellant.　alii potius ita appellatam, quoniam
174　nullum animal eam attingat, existimavere.　haec

ᵃ Book XIV, § 12.

fat—they add that the pig should be black and barren—cures mange if the patients use it as embrocation in the sunshine.

CIX. If the plants that sprout up inside a sieve thrown away on a cross-path are plucked and used as an amulet, they hasten the delivery of lying-in women.

CX. A plant growing on the top of country dung-heaps is, if taken in water, a very efficacious remedy for quinsies.

CXI. A plant near which dogs make water, if uprooted without the touch of iron, is a very quick remedy for dislocations.

CXII. In my account of vine-supporting trees the tree called rumpotinus received a notice.[a] When it does not support a vine there grows near it a plant called by the Gauls rodarum. It has a stem with knots, like a twig of a fig-tree; the leaves are those of a nettle, whitish in the centre, but in course of time becoming red all over; the blossom is silvery. If the leaves are beaten up with old axle-grease, without being touched by iron, they are a sovereign remedy for tumours, inflammations and gatherings. After being rubbed with it the patient spits to his right three times. They say that the remedy is more efficacious if three persons of different nationalities do the rubbing from left to right.

CXIII. What is called the unfilial plant is of a hoary white, in appearance like rosemary, clothed with leaves like a thyrsus and terminating in a head, from which sprout up little branches that also terminate each in a little head of its own. This is why the plant has been called unfilial, because the children out-top their parent. Others have thought that it has been so named rather because no animal *The unfilial plant.*

123

inter duos lapides trita fervet praecipuo adversus
anginas suco, lacte et vino admíxto. mirum traditur
numquam eo morbo temptari qui gustaverint. itaque et subus dari, quaeque medicamentum id
noluerint haurire eo morbo interimi. sunt qui
avium nidis inseri aliquid ex ea putent atque ita non
strangulari pullos avidius devorantes.

175   CXIV. Veneris pectinem appellant a similitudine
pectinum, cuius radix cum malva tusa omnia corpori
infixa extrahit.

CXV. Veterno liberat quae exedum vocatur.
notia herba coriariorum officinis familiaris [1] est aliis
aliisve nominibus, efficacissimamque adversus scorpionem esse potam e vino aut posca reperio.

176   CXVI. Philanthropon herbam Graeci appellant
nasute, quoniam vestibus adhaerescat. ex hac
corona inposita capitis dolores sedat. nam quae
canaria appellatur lappa, cum plantagine et milifolio
trita ex vino carcinomata sanat, ternis diebus [2] soluta.
medetur et subus effossa sine ferro addita in colluviem
poturis vel ex lacte ac vino. quidam adiciunt
effodientem dicere oportere : haec est herba argemon
quam Minerva repperit subus remedium quae de illa
gustaverint.

177   CXVII. Tordylon alii semen silis [3] esse dixerunt,
alii herbam per se, quam et syreon vocaverunt.

---

[1] familiaris *Ian., Detlefsen, Mayhoff* : eam hilaris *aut* ea
villaris *codd.*
[2] *Mayhoff* (Appendix) non *add. vel a ante* ternis.
[3] silis *tres codd., Mayhoff* : sesilis *Detlefsen*.

---

[a] *Impius* has also the meaning "impious."
[b] " Lover of man."
[c] Or " sesilis " (Detlefsen).

touches it.[a] Crushed between two stones this plant gives out an effervescing juice, which added to milk and wine is a sovereign remedy for quinsies. Attributed to it is this wonderful property; that they who have tasted it are never attacked by quinsy. Accordingly, they say, it is also given to pigs, and those refusing to swallow the medicine are cut off by that complaint. There are some who think that a little of it is woven into birds' nests, and that this is why chicks are not choked by gulping their food too greedily.

CXIV. Venus' comb is so named from its resemblance to combs; its root pounded with mallows extracts all foreign bodies lodged in the flesh. *Venus' comb.*

CXV. The plant called exedum dispels lethargy. The plant notia is well known under various names in the curriers' work-shops; I find that taken in wine or vinegar and water it is most efficacious for the sting of scorpions. *Exedum and notia.*

CXVI. Philanthropos [b] is a name which the Greeks in witty sarcasm give to a plant because it sticks to the clothes. A chaplet made out of it and placed on the head relieves headaches. But what is called dog-bur, if beaten up in wine with plantain and millefolium, heals cancerous sores, the plaster being taken off every third day. It also cures pigs, if dug up without iron; it is added to their swill before they go to feed, or else given them in milk and wine. Some add that as he is getting it up the digger should say: "This is the plant argemon, which Minerva discovered to be a remedy for the pigs that shall taste of it." *Philanthropos.* *Dog-bur.*

CXVII. Some have said that tordylon is the seed of sili,[c] others that it is itself a plant, which they have also called syreon. I find nothing recorded of *Tordylon.*

neque aliud de ea proditum invenio quam in montibus
nasci, conbustam potu ciere menses et pectoris
excreationes, efficaciore etiamnum radice, suco eius
ternis obolis hausto renes sanari, addi radicem eius
et in malagmata.

178   CXVIII. Gramen ipsum inter herbas vulgatis-
simum geniculatis serpit internodiis crebroque ab his
et ex cacumine novas radices spargit. folia eius in
reliquo orbe in exilitatem fastigantur, in Parnaso
tantum hederacia specie densius quam usquam
fruticant, flore odorato candidoque. iumentis herba
non alia gratior, sive viridis sive in fenum [1] siccata,[2]
179 cum detur adspersa aqua, sucumque eius in Parnaso
excipi tradunt propter ubertatem. dulcis hic est.
in vicem eius in reliqua parte terrarum succedit
decoctum ad vulnera conglutinanda, quod et ipsa
herba tusa praestat tueturque ab inflammationibus
plagas.[3] adicitur decocto vinum ac mel, ab aliquis et
turis, piperis, murrae tertiae portiones, rursusque
coquitur in aereo vase ad dentium dolores, epiphoras.
180 radix decocta in vino torminibus medetur et urinae
difficultatibus ulceribusque vesicae, calculos frangit.
semen vehementius urinam inpellit, alvum vomition-
esque sistit. privatim autem draconum morsibus
auxiliatur. sunt qui genicula novem vel unius vel e
duabus tribusve herbis ad hunc articulorum numerum
involvi lana sucida nigra iubeant ad remedia strumae

    [1] fenum *coni. ego et Dalec.* : feno *codd. et editores plerique.*
    [2] siccata *duo codd., Detlefsen* : siccatae *duo codd.* : siccata
et coni. Mayhoff.
    [3] plagas E(?) *Ian., Detlefsen, Mayhoff* : praeligata *Sillig* :
placat *aut* pacat *ceteri codd.*

---

    [a] For this intensifying *ipse*, cf. § 188 *ipsa claritas*, " the
peculiar glory."

it except that it grows on mountains, that burnt and taken in drink it promotes menstruation and expectoration, the root being even more efficacious, that its juice, swallowed in doses of three oboli, cures disorders of the kidneys, and that its root is also an ingredient of emollient plasters.

CXVIII. Grass, itself[a] the very commonest of plants, trails its knotted blades along the ground, and from them and out of the head sprout many new roots. Its leaves in the rest of the world grow to a fine point, and only on Mount Parnassus sprout leaves thicker together than anywhere else, of the appearance of ivy, and with a white, scented flower. To draught-cattle no other plant is more attractive, whether fresh, or dried into hay and sprinkled with water when it is given them to eat. Its juice too, which is sweet, is said to be collected on Parnassus because of its richness. Over the rest of the world a decoction is used in its place to close cuts; the crushed plant by itself has the same effect and also prevents wounds from becoming inflamed. To the decoction are added wine and honey, by some, equal parts also of frankincense, pepper and myrrh, and the whole is again boiled in a bronze vessel to make a remedy for tooth-ache and eye-fluxes. A decoction of the root in wine cures colic, strangury and sores of the bladder, breaking up stone. The seed causes a stronger flow of urine, and checks looseness of the bowels and vomiting. It is also specific for the bites of the draco.[b] Some prescribe nine knots either from one plant or from two or three to make up that number of joints, rolled up in black wool with the grease still in it, as a remedy for scrofulous sores and

Grass and its various kinds.

[b] Probably any serpent of a large size.

181 panorumve. ieiunum esse debere qui colligat, sic
abire[1] in domum absentis cui medeatur super-
venientique ter dicere ieiuno ieiunum medicamentum
dare, atque ita adalligare triduoque id facere. quod
e graminum genere septem internodia habet
efficacissime capiti contra dolores adalligatur. quidam propter vesicae cruciatus decoctum ex vino gramen ad dimidias a balineis bibi iubent.

182 CXIX. Sunt qui et aculeatum gramen vocent
trium generum. cum in cacumine aculei sunt
plurimum quini, dactylon appellant. hos convolutos
naribus inserunt extrahuntque sanguinis ciendi
gratia. altero, quod est aizoo simile, ad paronychia
et pterygia unguium et, cum caro unguibus increvit,
utuntur cum axungia, ideo dactylon appellantes, quia
183 digitis medeatur. tertium genus dactyli, sed tenuis,
nascitur in parietinis aut tegulis. huic caustica vis
est. sistit ulcera quae serpunt. gramen capiti
circumdatum sanguinis e naribus fluctiones sistit.
camelos necare traditur in Babylonis regione id quod
iuxta vias nascitur.

184 CXX. Nec feno Graeco minor auctoritas, quod
telin vocant, alii carphos, aliqui buceras, alii aegoceras,
quoniam corniculis semen est simile, nos siliciam.
quomodo sereretur docuimus suo loco. vis eius
siccare, mollire, dissolvere. sucus decocti feminarum pluribus malis subvenit, sive duritia sive

---

[1] sic abire *Detlefsen* : ita ire *cum uno cod. Mayhoff* : *varia
codd.*

---

[a] " Ox horn."   [b] " Goat's horn."
[c] See XVIII. § 140.

superficial abscesses. The person gathering it, they add, ought to be fasting, and in this state he should proceed to the house of the patient while he is away, and on his appearance say three times: " Fasting I give a cure to a fasting patient," and so fasten the nine joints as an amulet. This is to be done on three days running. The kind of grass that has seven spaces between knots makes a very effective amulet for headache. For severe pains in the bladder some authorities prescribe a decoction of grass in wine, boiled down to one half, to be drunk after the bath.

CXIX. There are some who speak of three kinds of pointed grass. When on each head there are at most five points they call it "finger grass." These points plaited together they insert into the nostrils and draw them out again to cause bleeding. The second kind, which is like the aizoüm, they use with axle-grease for whitlows, hangnails, and when flesh has grown over the nails, calling it "finger grass," because it heals the fingers. There is a third kind of finger grass, but it is slender, growing on ruins or tiles. Its properties are caustic, and it checks creeping ulcers. Grass put round the head checks copious bleeding at the nose. It is said that in the district of Babylon camels are killed by the grass that grows by the side of the roads.

CXX. Held in no less honour is fenugreek, which is *Fenugreek.* also called telis, carphos, buceras,[a] and aegoceras,[b] because its seed is shaped like small horns; the Roman name for it is silicia. The method of sowing it we have described in its proper place.[c] Its properties are to dry, to soften and to dissolve. The juice of the decoction is of help in several ailments of women: whether it is hardness, swelling or con-

tumor sive contractio sit vulvae, foventur, insidunt. infusum quoque prodest. furfures in facie extenuat.
185 spleni addito nitro decoctum et inpositum medetur, item ex aceto. sic et iocineri decoctum. Diocles difficile parientibus semen eius dedit acetabuli mensura tritum in novem cyathis sapae ut tertias partes biberent, dein calida lavarentur, et in balineo sudantibus dimidium ex relicto iterum dedit, mox a
186 balineo relicum, pro summo auxilio. farinam feni cum hordeo aut lini semine decoctam aqua mulsa contra vulvae cruciatus obiecit idem inposuitque imo ventri. lepras, lentigines sulpuris pari portione mixta farinae curavit, nitro ante praeparata cute, saepius die inlinens perunguique prohibens. Theodorus feno miscuit quartam partem purgati nasturtii
187 acerrimo aceto ad lepras. Timon semen feni acetabuli dimidii mensura cum sapae et aquae novem cyathis ad menses ciendos dedit potu, nec dubitatur quin decoctum eius utilissimum sit vulvis interaneisque exulceratis, sicuti semen articulis atque praecordiis. si vero cum malva decoquatur postea addito mulso, potus ante cetera vulvis interaneisque
130

traction of the uterus, the treatment is fomentation and the sitz bath. Injections are also of value. It checks scaly eruptions on the face. Splenic troubles are cured by a local application of a decoction to which soda has been added; the decoction may also be made with vinegar. Such a decoction is also good for the liver. In cases of difficult child-birth Diocles prescribed an acetabulum of its crushed seed in nine cyathi of concentrated must; three-quarters were to be drunk, then the patients were to bathe in hot water, next, as they were sweating in the bath, he gave further half of what remained, and then the rest after the bath. In this way the maximum benefit was obtained. A decoction in hydromel of fenugreek meal with barley or linseed was used by the same physician to make a pessary for violent pains in the uterus; he combined this treatment with a plaster at the base of the abdomen. He treated leprous sores and freckles with equal parts of sulphur and fenugreek meal, the skin having been prepared beforehand with soda, applying the mixture several times a day and not allowing the patient to be rubbed with it. Theodorus treated leprous sores with fenugreek and one-fourth part of cleaned cress steeped in the strongest vinegar. Timon prescribed as an emmenagogue a draught of half an acetabulum of fenugreek seed with nine cyathi of concentrated must and water, and there is no doubt that a decoction of it is very good for ulcerated uterus and intestines, as the seed is for the joints and hypochondria. If, however, it is boiled down with mallows, and honey wine be afterwards added, a draught is praised as a pre-eminent remedy for troubles of the uterus and

laudatur, quippe cum vapor quoque decocti plurimum
prosit, alarumque etiam graviolentiam decoctum feni[1]
emendat. farina porrigines capitis furfuresque eum
188 vino et nitro celeriter tollit. in hydromelite autem
decocta addita axungia genitalibus medetur, item
pano, parotidi, podagrae, chiragrae, articulis carni-
busque quae recedunt ab ossibus, aceto vero subacta
luxatis. inlinitur et lieni decocta in aceto et melle
tantum. carcinomata subacta ex vino purgat, mox
addito melle persanat. sumitur et sorbitio ex farina
ad pectus exulceratum longamque tussim. diu[2]
decoquitur donec amaritudo desinat, postea mel
additur. Nunc ipsa claritas herbarum dicetur.

[1] *Hic* semen VEX *Mayhoff*: *om.* d T *Hard., Detlefsen.*
[2] *Om.* diu *Mayhoff.*

intestines, seeing that the steam also from the decoction is of the highest value; a decoction of fenugreek, too, removes offensive smells of the armpits. The meal with wine and soda quickly removes scurf and dandruff on the head. A decoction too of the meal in hydromel, mixed with axle-grease, cures complaints of the genitals, likewise superficial abscesses, parotid tumours, gouty affections of feet or hands, affections of the joints and the receding of flesh from the bones; but the meal is kneaded in vinegar for dislocations. A decoction of the meal in vinegar and honey only is used as a liniment for splenic trouble. Kneaded in wine it cleanses cancerous sores; if honey is afterwards added a complete cure is effected. A gruel also of this meal is taken for ulceration of the chest and for chronic cough. It is boiled down for a long time until the bitterness disappears; afterwards honey is added. I shall now proceed to the peculiar glory of plants.

BOOK XXV

LIBER XXV

I. Ipsa quae nunc dicetur herbarum claritas,
medicinae tantum gignente eas Tellure, in admirationem curae priscorum diligentiaeque animum
agit. nihil ergo intemptatum inexpertumque illis
fuit, nihil deinde occultatum quodque non prodesse
posteris vellent. at nos elaborata his abscondere ac
2 supprimere cupimus et fraudare vitam etiam alienis
bonis. ita certe recondunt qui pauca aliqua novere
invidentes aliis, et neminem docere in auctoritatem
scientiae est. tantum ab excogitandis novis ac
iuvanda vita mores absunt, summumque opus ingeniorum diu iam hoc fuit ut intra unumquemque
recte facta veterum perirent. at, Hercules, singula
quosdam inventa deorum numero addidere, quorum [1]
utique vitam clariorem fecere cognominibus herbarum, tam benigne gratiam memoria referente.
3 non aeque haec cura eorum mira est [2] in his quae satu
blandiuntur aut cibo invitant, culmina quoque
montium invia et solitudines abditas omnesque terrae

---

[1] quorum *ego* : hominum *Detlefsen cum Pintiano* : omnium
Mayhoff cum fere omnibus codd.
[2] mira est *Mayhoff* : mira, si *Detlefsen, codd.* : mira esset
vulg.

BOOK XXV

I. This peculiar glory of plants which I am now going to speak of, Mother Earth producing them sometimes for medicinal purposes only, rouses in one's mind admiration for the care and industry of the men of old; there was nothing left untried or unattempted by them, and furthermore nothing kept secret, nothing which they wished to be of no benefit to posterity. But we moderns desire to hide and suppress the discoveries worked out by these investigators, and to cheat human life even of the good things that have been won by others. Yes indeed, those who have gained a little knowledge keep it in a grudging spirit secret to themselves, and to teach nobody else increases the prestige of their learning. So far has custom departed from fresh research and assistance to life; the supreme task of our great minds has long been to keep within individual memory the successes of the ancients, so allowing them to be forgotten. But, heaven knows, there are some whom a single discovery has added to the number of the gods, whose life on earth at any rate has been made more glorious by their names being given to plants, so kind the thanks of a mindful posterity. This careful research of theirs is less wonderful when rewarded by plants of fascinating growth or attractive as food; but they have scoured also trackless mountain heights, unexplored deserts and all the bowels of the earth, finding out the power

Of plants used specially for medicine.

137

fibras scrutati invenere quid quaeque radix polleret,
ad quos usus herbarum fila pertinerent, etiam quadripedum pabulo intacta ad salutis usus vertentes.

4 II. Minus hoc quam par erat nostri celebravere
omnium utilitatium et virtutum rapacissimi, primus-
que et diu solus idem ille M. Cato, omnium bonarum
artium magister, paucis dumtaxat attigit, boum etiam
medicina non omissa. post eum unus inlustrium
temptavit Gaius Valgius eruditione spectatus inper-
fecto volumine ad divum Augustum, inchoata etiam
praefatione religiosa ut omnibus malis humanis illius
potissimum principis semper mederetur maiestas.

5 III. Antea condiderat solus apud nos, quod equidem inveniam, Pompeius Lenaeus Magni libertus,
quo primum tempore hanc scientiam ad nostros
pervenisse animo adverto. namque Mithridates,
maximus sua aetate regum quem debellavit Pompeius, omnium ante se genitorum diligentissimus
vitae fuisse argumentis praeterquam fama intellegi-
6 tur. uni ei excogitatum cotidie venenum bibere
praesumptis remediis ut consuetudine ipsa innoxium
fieret; primo inventa genera antidoti ex quibus unum
etiam nomen eius retinet; illius inventum sanguinem
anatum Ponticarum miscere antidotis, quoniam

---

a Perhaps, " biology." But see *vita* again in §§ 7 and 22.
b *Primo* dat. of the agent.

of every root and the uses to which can be put mere slim threads of vegetation, and turning to healthful purposes that which the very beasts refuse to touch as food.

II. This subject was less popular with our country- *Roman* men than it should have been considering their vast *writers on* appetite for all things useful and good; the first *the subject.* student of it, and for a long time the only one, being that same Marcus Cato, the master of all excellent crafts, who merely touched briefly the subject, without neglecting even veterinary medicine. After him one only of our distinguished men has tried his hand at the subject, Gaius Valgius, an author of approved scholarship, who left unfinished a work dedicated to the late emperor Augustus, beginning also his preface with a devout prayer that his Imperial Highness should always, and above all others, be the healer of every human ill.

III. Before Valgius the only Roman who had written on this subject, as far as I can discover, was Pompeius Lenaeus, a freedman of Pompeius Magnus, in whose day, I find, scientific treatment of it first found a home among Roman students. For it was Mithridates, the greatest king of his time, whom *Mithridates.* Pompeius vanquished, that was, we know by evidence as well as by report, a more attentive investigator of life's problems [a] than any of those born before him. By his unaided efforts he thought out the plan of drinking poison daily, after first taking remedies, in order that sheer custom might render it harmless; he was the first [b] to discover the various antidotes, one of which is even known by his name; he also discovered the mixing with antidotes of the blood of Pontic ducks, because

veneno viverent; ad illum Asclepiadis medendi arte
clari volumina composita extant, cum sollicitatus ex
urbe Roma praecepta pro se mitteret; illum solum
mortalium certum est XXII linguis locutum, nec e
subiectis gentibus ullum hominem per interpretem
7 appellatum ab eo annis LVI quibus regnavit. is ergo
in reliqua ingenii magnitudine medicinae peculiariter
curiosus et ab omnibus subiectis, qui fuere magna pars
terrarum, singula exquirens scrinium commenta-
tionum harum et exemplaria effectusque in arcanis
suis reliquit, Pompeius autem omni praeda regia
potitus transferre ea sermone nostro libertum suum
Lenaeum grammaticae artis iussit, vitaeque ita
profuit non minus quam reipublicae victoria illa.
8   IV. Praeter hos Graeci auctores prodidere quos
suis locis diximus, ex his Crateuas, Dionysius,
Metrodorus ratione blandissima sed qua nihil paene
aliud quam difficultas rei intellegatur. pinxere
namque effigies herbarum atque ita subscripsere
effectus. verum et pictura fallax est coloribus tam
numerosis, praesertim in aemulationem naturae,
multumque degenerat transcribentium fors varia.[1]
praeterea parum est singulas earum aetates pingi,
cum quadripertitis varietatibus anni faciem mutent.

---

[1] fors varia *codd., Detlefsen* : socordia *Mayhoff* : sollertia
C. F. W. Müller.

---

[a] Mayhoff's *socordia* would give : " owing to the carelessness of the copyists " ; Müller's *sollertia* : " owing to the (misplaced, ill-timed) ingenuity of the copyists."   But surely the
reading of the MSS. gives a good sense, and accords perfectly
with Pliny's " journalese " style of writing.

they lived on poison; addressed to him were treatises, still extant, written by the famous physician Asclepiades, who when urgently invited to come from Rome sent instructions instead; Mithridates alone of men is definitely known to have spoken twenty-two languages, and no man of his subject peoples was ever addressed by him through an interpreter during all the fifty-six years of his reign. He then, with his brilliant intellect and wide interests, was an especially diligent student of medicine, and collected detailed knowledge from all his subjects, who comprised a great part of the world, leaving among his private possessions a bookcase of these treatises with specimens and the properties of each. Pompeius however on getting possession of all the royal booty ordered his freedman Lenaeus, a man of letters, to translate these into Latin. This great victory therefore was as beneficent to life as it was to the State.

IV. Besides these the subject has been treated *Greek writers on this subject.* by Greek writers, whom we have mentioned in their proper places; of these, Crateuas, Dionysius and Metrodorus adopted a most attractive method, though one which makes clear little else except the difficulty of employing it. For they painted likenesses of the plants and then wrote under them their properties. But not only is a picture misleading when the colours are so many, particularly as the aim is to copy Nature, but besides this, much imperfection arises from the manifold hazards in the accuracy [a] of copyists. In addition, it is not enough for each plant to be painted at one period only of its life, since it alters its appearance with the fourfold changes of the year.

9 V. Quare ceteri sermone eas tradidere, aliqui ne
effigie quidem indicata et nudis plerumque nominibus
defuncti, quoniam satis videbatur potestates vimque
demonstrare quaerere volentibus. nec est difficilis
cognitio : nobis certe, exceptis admodum paucis,
contigit reliquas contemplari scientia Antoni Castoris,
cui summa auctoritas erat in ea arte nostro aevo,
visendo hortulo eius in quo plurimas alebat centesi-
mum annum aetatis excedens, nullum corporis malum
expertus, ac ne aetate quidem memoria aut vigore
concussis. neque aliud mirata magis antiquitas
10 reperietur. inventa iampridem ratio est praenun-
tians horas, non modo dies ac noctes, solis lunaeque
defectuum. durat tamen tradita persuasio in magna
parte vulgi veneficiis et herbis id cogi eamque unam
feminarum scientiam praevalere. certe quid non
repleverunt fabulis Colchis Medea aliaeque, in primis
11 Itala Circe dis etiam adscripta? unde arbitror
natum ut Aeschylus e vetustissimis in poetica re-
fertam Italiam herbarum potentia proderet, multique
Circeios, ubi habitavit illa, magno argumento etiamnunc durante in Marsis, a filio eius orta gente, quoniam
esse domitores serpentium constat. Homerus qui-

---

[a] I think that there is some reason for the diminutive
hortulo. It can hardly mean in the context " little garden,"
but seems to suggest that the *hortulus* was Castor's favourite
hobby (" affectionate diminutive ").

[b] It is generally supposed that Pliny is referring to the
pentameter quoted by Theophrastus *H.P.* IX 15, 1 : Τυρρηνὸν
γενεάν, φαρμακοποιὸν ἔθνος. In this passage Theophrastus
mentions both Circe and Helen, as well as the wealth of Egypt
in drugs.

V. For this reason the other writers have given
verbal accounts only; some have not even given
the shape of the plants, and for the most part have
been content with bare names, since they thought it
sufficient to point out the properties and nature
of a plant to those willing to look for it. To gain
this knowledge is no difficult matter; I at least
have enjoyed the good fortune to examine all but
a very few plants through the devotion to science
of Antonius Castor, the highest botanical authority
of our time; I used to visit his special *a* garden, in
which he would rear a great number of specimens
even when he passed his hundredth year, having
suffered no bodily ailment and, in spite of his
age, no loss of memory or physical vigour. Nothing
else will be found that aroused greater wonder
among the ancients than botany. Long ago was *Ancient study of*
discovered a method of predicting eclipses of the *botany.*
sun and moon—not the day or night merely but the
very hour. Yet there still exists among a great number of the common people an established conviction
that these phenomena are due to the compelling power
of charms and magic herbs, and that the science
of them is the one outstanding province of women.
At any rate tales everywhere are widely cur-
rent about Medea of Colchis and other sorceresses,
especially Circe of Italy, who has even been enrolled
as a divinity. This is the reason, I think, why
Aeschylus, one of the earliest poets, declared *b* that
Italy abounds in potent herbs, and many have said the
same of Circeii, where she lived. Strong confirmatory
evidence exists even today in the fact that the Marsi,
a tribe descended from Circe's son, are well-known
snake-charmers. Homer indeed, the first ancestor

dem primus doctrinarum et antiquitatis parens,
multus alias in admiratione Circae, gloriam herbarum
Aegypto tribuit, cum etiam tum quae rigatur [1]
Aegyptus illa non esset, postea fluminis limo invecta.
12 herbas certe Aegyptias a regis uxore traditas Helenae
suae plurimas narrat ac nobile illud nepenthes
oblivionem tristitiae veniamque adferens et ab
Helena utique omnibus mortalibus propinandum.
primus autem omnium quos memoria novit Orpheus
de herbis curiosius aliqua prodidit, post eum Musaeus
et Hesiodus polium herbam in quantum mirati sint
diximus, Orpheus et Hesiodus suffitiones commen-
davere. Homerus et alias nominatim herbas cele-
13 brat, quas suis locis dicemus. ab eo Pythagoras
clarus sapientia primus volumen de effectu earum
composuit, Apollini, Aesculapio et in totum dis
immortalibus inventione et origine adsignata ; composuit et Democritus, ambo peragratis Persidis,
Arabiae, Aethiopiae, Aegypti Magis, adeoque ad
haec attonita antiquitas fuit ut adfirmaverit etiam
14 incredibilia dictu. Xanthus historiarum auctor in
prima earum tradit occisum draconis catulum re-
vocatum ad vitam a parente herba quam balim
nominat, eademque Tylonem quem draco occiderat
restitutum saluti. et Iuba in Arabia herba revoca-
tum ad vitam hominem tradit. dixit Democritus,
credidit Theophrastus esse herbam cuius contactu

---

[1] tum quae rigatur *codd. et Mayhoff* : nunc quae dicatur
coni. Detlefsen.

---

[a] See *Odyssey*, IV. 219–234.
[b] *Veniam* is translated by Littré : " et de leur cause," by
Bostock and Riley : " forgetfulness of the past."
[c] See XXI. §§ 44 and 145.
[d] Relying on these books.

of ancient learning, while expressing in several passages great admiration for Circe, gives the prize for herbs to Egypt, even though at that time the irrigated Egypt of today did not yet exist, for it was formed afterwards by the alluvial mud of the river. At any rate he says[a] that Egyptian herbs in great number were given by the wife of the king to the Helen of his tale, including that celebrated nepenthes, which brought forgetfulness and remission of sorrow,[b] to be administered especially by Helen to all mortals. But the first of all those known to tradition to publish anything about botany carefully was Orpheus; after him Musaeus and Hesiod, as we have said,[c] expressed great admiration for the plant called polium; Orpheus and Hesiod recommended fumigations. Homer mentions by name other plants also, which I shall speak of in their appropriate places. After him the celebrated philosopher Pythagoras was the first to compose a book on the properties of plants, assigning their original discovery to Apollo, Aesculapius and the immortal gods generally; Democritus also composed a similar work. Both of them visited the Magi of Persia, Arabia, Ethiopia and Egypt, and so amazed were the ancients at these books that they positively asserted[d] even unbelievable statements. Xanthus, who wrote books on history, relates in the first of them that a young snake, which had been killed, was restored to life by his father, who used a plant called by Xanthus balis, and that the same plant brought back to life one Tylo, whom the snake had killed. Juba too records that a man in Arabia was restored to life by means of a plant. Democritus said, and Theophrastus believed him, that there was a plant which, carried by

inlatae ab alite quam[1] retulimus exiliret cuneus a
pastoribus arbori adactus. quae etiamsi fide carent,
admirationem tamen implent coguntque confiteri
15 multum esse veri[2] quod supersit. inde et plerosque
ita video existimare nihil non herbarum vi effici posse,
sed plurimarum vires esse incognitas, quorum in
numero fuit Herophilus clarus medicina, a quo ferunt
dictum quasdam fortassis etiam calcatas prodesse.
observatum certe est inflammari[3] vulnera ac morbos
superventu eorum qui pedibus iter confecerint.
16 VI. Haec erat antiqua medicina quae tota migrabat
in Graeciae linguas. sed quare non plures noscantur
causa est quod eas agrestes litterarumque ignari
experiuntur, ut qui soli inter illas vivant, praeterea
securitas quaerendi obvia[4] medicorum turba. multis
etiam inventis desunt nomina, sicut illi quam retulimus in frugum cura scimusque defossam in angulis
segetis praestare ne qua ales intret. turpissima

---

[1] quam *vulg., Mayhoff* : qua *Detlefsen* : *fortasse* de qua.
[2] veri quod *ego* : quod vero *codd. et edd.*
[3] inflammari : *codd. et edd.* : vel sanari *coni. Mayhoff* :
iam sanari *vel* minus inflammari *coni. Warmington.*
[4] obvia *Mayhoff* : obvia in *Detlefsen* : obviam V.

---

[a] See X. § 40.
[b] It has been observed (e.g. by Mayhoff, who says *contra
argumenti rationem, ut videtur*) that this sentence does not fit
in with its context. After *prodesse* a sentence is expected to
the effect that a patient has become better after treading on a
certain plant (or plants). Instead of this we get a statement
that a patient has grown worse on the arrival of visitors who
have travelled on foot. As it may be just another example of
Pliny's slipshod way of reasoning, the sentence has been left
as it is in the MSS., but there is much to be said for Mayhoff's
"even cured." What perhaps Pliny ought to have said is
minus inflammari superventu vulnera : " on arrival the wounds
or illnesses are better of those who have made a journey on

the bird I have mentioned,[a] forced out by its touch a
wedge driven into a tree by shepherds. Although
these tales are incredible, yet they fill us with
wonder, and force us to admit that there is still
much truth in them. Hence too I find that most
authorities hold that there is nothing which cannot
be achieved by the power of plants, but that the
properties of most are still unknown. Among these
thinkers was Herophilus, famous in medicine, who
is reported to have said that certain plants are
perhaps beneficial even when merely trodden on. It
has been observed at any rate that wounds and
diseases get worse [b] on the arrival of people who
have made a journey on foot.

VI. Such was the condition of medicine in the *Medicinal
herbs in
modern
times.* old days, all of it finding its way into the dialects [c] of
Greece. But the reason why more herbs are not
familiar is because experience of them is confined to
illiterate country-folk, who form the only class living
among them ; moreover nobody cares to look for them
when crowds of medical men are to be met everywhere. Many simples also, though their properties
have been discovered, still lack names, for instance,
the plant I mentioned when dealing with the cultiva-
tion of crops,[d] which we know keeps all birds away if
buried at the corners of the cornfield. The most

foot." There is nothing unusual in the zeugma of taking
both *vulnera* and *morbus* with *inflammari*. Possibly *superventu*
has been misplaced by a scribe.

[c] It is difficult to see why Pliny has used the plural. In the
first place there is no point in referring to dialects, and in the
second it is a misleading, if not inaccurate, remark. Most
Greek medical works, at least down to the beginning of the
Alexandrine era, were written in an artificial variety of Ionic.
After 300 B.C., the κοινή was commonly used.

[d] See XVIII. § 160.

causa raritatis quod etiam qui sciunt demonstrare
nolunt, tamquam ipsis periturum sit quod tradi-
derint aliis. accedit ratio inventionis anceps, quippe
etiam in repertis alias invenit casus, alias, ut vere
17 dixerim, deus. insanabile ad hosce annos fuit rabidi
canis morsus pavorem aquae potusque omnis adferens odium. nuper cuiusdam militantis in prae-
torio mater vidit in quiete ut radicem silvestris rosae
quam cynorrhodon vocant blanditam sibi aspectu
pridie in fruteto mitteret filio bibendam. in Lacetania[1] res gerebatur, Hispaniae proxima parte, casu-
que accidit ut milite a morsu canis incipiente ex-
pavescere aquas superveniret epistula orantis ut
pareret religioni, servatusque est ex insperato et
18 postea quisquis auxilium simile temptavit. alias
apud auctores cynorrhodi una medicina erat spon-
giolae, quae in mediis spinis eius nascitur, cinere cum
melle alopecias capitis expleri. in eadem provincia
cognovi in agro hospitis nuper ibi repertum dracuncu-
lum appellatum caulem pollicari crassitudine, versicoloribus[2] viperarum maculis, quem ferebant contra
omnium morsus esse remedio, alium quam quos in
priore volumine eiusdem nominis diximus, sed huic

[1] Lacetania *aliquot codd., Detlefsen* : Laeetania *Hübner, Mayhoff.*
[2] versicoloribus] a versicoloribus *unus cod.* (N) : a versico-loribus viperarum maculis *post* appellatum *ponere velit Mayhoff.*

---

[a] This is taking *mitteret* to be the verb of a dependent question. It might be jussive : " how she was to send."
[b] The gall called " robin's pin-cushion."
[c] See XXIV. § 143.

disgraceful reason for this scanty knowledge is that
even those who possess it refuse to teach it, just as
though they would themselves lose what they have
imparted to others. To this must be added that
there is no sure method of discovery; for even of
those we already know chance has sometimes been the
finder; at other times, to speak the truth, the discoverer was a god. Down to recent years there has
been no cure for the bite of a mad dog, a symptom of
which is dread of water and aversion to drink of any
kind. Recently the mother of a man serving in the
praetorian guard saw in a dream how she sent [a] to
her son to be taken in drink the root of the wild rose,
called cynorrhodon, which by its appearance had *Cynorrhodon*
attracted her the day before in a shrubbery. Opera- *and hydro-*
tions were going on in Lacetania, the part of Spain *phobia.*
nearest to Italy, and by chance it happened that the
soldier, after being bitten by a dog, was beginning to
show a horror of water, when a letter arrived from the
mother, who begged him to obey the heavenly
warning. So his life was unexpectedly saved, as
was that of all who afterwards tried a similar remedy.
Elsewhere among our authorities the only medicinal
use of cynorrhodon to be found is that the ash of
the spongy substance [b] that forms in the middle of its
thorns was mixed with honey to make hair grow on
the head where mange had left it bare. In the
same province, on the land of my host, I learned
of a recent discovery there, a stalk called dra- *Dracunculus.*
cunculus, of the thickness of a thumb, with spots
of many colours like those of a viper, which people
said was a remedy for the bites of all creatures, a different plant from those I have called dracunculus
in the preceding [c] book. This one has a different

19 alia figura, aliud miraculum exerenti se terra ad
primas serpentium vernationes bipedali fere altitudine, rursusque cum isdem in terram condenti, nec
omnino occultato eo apparet serpens, vel hoc per
se satis officioso naturae munere, si tantum prae-
moneret tempusque formidinis demonstraret.

20   Nec bestiarum solum ad nocendum scelera sunt,
sed interim aquarum quoque ac locorum. In
Germania trans Rhenum castris a Germanico Caesare
promotis maritimo tractu fons erat aquae dulcis solus,
qua pota intra biennium dentes deciderent com-
pagesque in genibus solverentur. stomacacen medici
vocabant et scelotyrben ea mala. reperta auxilio est
herba quae appellatur britannica, non nervis modo
et oris malis salutaris, sed contra anginas quoque et
contra serpentes. folia habet oblonga nigra, radicem

21 nigram. sucus eius exprimitur et e radice. florem
vibones vocant, qui collectus prius quam tonitrum
audiatur et devoratus securos in totum annum a metu
anginae praestat. Frisi gens tum fida, in qua castra
erant, monstravere illam, mirorque nominis causam,
nisi forte confines oceano Britanniae veluti propinquae [1] dicavere. non enim inde appellatam, quoniam
ibi plurima nasceretur, certum est etiamtum Britan-
nia libera.

---

[1] veluti propinquae *cum multis codd. et vulg. Mayhoff* :
velut e propinquo *Detlefsen, qui Urlichs sequitur.*

---

[a] A Greek word, στομακάκη, meaning scurvy of the gums.
[b] Another Greek word, σκελοτύρβη, meaning disorder or
paralysis of the legs.
[c] Possibly, " oblong."
[d] Or : " bordering on the ocean, they dedicated the plant to
Britain, as it were to a neighbour." I once took *Britanniae*
to be the subject, having in agreement with it both

shape, and is an amazing plant in other ways; for
when snakes begin to cast their slough it springs up
to the height of about two feet, and then buries itself
in the ground when snakes do so, and while it is con-
cealed no snake at all is anywhere to be seen. This
by itself would be a kindly service of Nature, if it
only warned us and pointed out the time of danger.

Nor is it beasts alone that are guilty of causing
injury; at times waters also and regions do the *Diseases
caused by
waters and
regions.*
same. When Germanicus Caesar had moved for-
ward his camp across the Rhine, in a maritime district of Germany there was only one source of fresh
water. To drink it caused within two years the
teeth to fall out and the use of the knee-joints to
fail. Physicians used to call these maladies stomacace [a] and scelotyrbe.[b] A remedy was found in the
plant called britannica, which is good not only for
the sinews and for diseases of the mouth, but also
for the relief of quinsy and snake-bite. It has dark,
rather long [c] leaves, and a dark root. Its juice is
extracted even from the root. The blossom is called
vibones; gathered before thunder is heard, and
swallowed, it keeps away the fear of quinsy for a
whole year. It was pointed out to our men by the
Frisians, at that time a loyal tribe, in whose territory our camp lay. Why the plant was so called I
greatly wonder, unless perhaps, living on the shore of
the British ocean, they have so named the britannica
because it is, as it were, a near neighbour of Britain.[d]
It is certain that the plant was not so named because
it grew abundantly in that island: Britain was at
that time an independent state.

confines oceano and *propinquae* (" being as it were a
neighbour ").

22   VII. Fuit quidem et hic quondam ambitus nominibus suis eas adoptandi, ut docebimus fecisse reges.
tanta res videbatur herbam invenire, vitam iuvare,
nunc fortassis aliquis curam hanc nostram frivolam
quoque existimaturis; adeo deliciis sordent etiam
quae ad salutem pertinent. auctores tamen quarum
inveniuntur in primis celebrari par est effectu earum
23 digesto in genera morborum. qua quidem in repu-
tatione misereri sortis humanae subit, praeter fortuita
casusque et quae nova omnis hora excogitat, milia
morborum singulis mortalium timenda. qui gravissimi ex his sint discernere stultitiae prope videri
possit, cum suus cuique ac praesens quisque atro-
cissimus videatur. et de hoc tamen iudicavere aevi
experimenta, asperrimi cruciatus esse calculorum a
stillicidio vesicae, proximum stomachi, tertium
eorum quae in capite doleant, non ob alios fere morte
conscita.
24   A Graecis et noxias herbas demonstratas miror
equidem, nec venenorum tantum, quoniam ea con-
ditio vitae est ut mori plerumque etiam optimis
portus sit, tradatque M. Varro Servium Clodium
equitem Romanum magnitudine doloris in podagra
coactum veneno crura perunxisse et postea caruisse

ᵃ A common phrase in Pliny is *nomine adoptare*, " to give a
name to a thing."
ᵇ See §§ 70 foll. of this Book.

VII. It was one of the ambitions of the past to give one's name *a* to a plant, as we shall point out *b* was done by kings. It was thought a great honour to discover a plant and be of assistance to human life, although now perhaps some will think that these researches of mine are just idle trifling. So paltry in the eyes of Luxury are even the things that conduce to our health. It is but right, however, to mention in the first place the plants whose discoverers can be found, with their properties classified according to the kinds of disease for which they are a remedy. To reflect indeed on this makes one pity the lot of man; besides chances and changes and the strange happenings that every hour brings, there are thousands of diseases that every mortal has to dread. To distinguish which are the most grievous of them might be considered almost an act of folly, since every man considers that the particular disease from which he is suffering at the moment is the most awful. On this point, however, the experience of time has concluded that the disease causing the sharpest agony is strangury from stone in the bladder; next comes disease of the stomach, and after that pains produced by diseases of the head; these being about the only diseases that are responsible for suicides.

I myself am amazed that the Greeks have described even harmful plants, and not the poisonous ones only, since the state of human life is such that death is frequently a harbour of refuge even for the most excellent of men, Marcus Varro relating that the Roman knight Servius Clodius, owing to the severe pain of gout, was forced to rub his legs all over with a poison, after which that part of his body was as free

Plants named after persons.

The most painful diseases.

Harmful plants.

sensu omni aeque quam dolore in ea parte corporis.
25 sed quae fuit venia monstrandi qua mentes solverentur, partus eliderentur, multaque similia? ego nec
abortiva dico ac ne amatoria quidem, memor Lucul-
lum imperatorem clarissimum amatorio perisse, nec
alia magica portenta, nisi ubi cavenda sunt aut
coarguenda, in primis fide eorum damnata. satis
operae fuerit abundeque praestatum, vitae salutares
dixisse [1] ac pro ea inventas.

26 VIII. Clarissima herbarum est Homero teste quam
vocari a dis putat moly et inventionem eius Mercurio
adsignat contraque summa veneficia demonstra-
tionem. nasci eam hodie circa Pheneum et in
Cyllene Arcadiae tradunt specie illa Homerica, radice
rotunda nigraque, magnitudine cepae, folio scillae,
27 effodi autem haud [2] difficulter. Graeci auctores
florem eius luteum pinxere, cum Homerus candidum
scripserit. inveni e peritis herbarum medicis qui et in
Italia nasci eam diceret, adferrique e Campania mihi [3]
aliquot diebus ⟨posse [4]⟩ effossam inter difficultates

---

[1] dixisse] *hic lacunam indicat Ianus, quem sequitur Mayhoff*:
" *excidisse videntur* a dis priscive ": *non* pro ea *sed* postea
codd.

[2] autem haud *ego*: haud *Sillig*: autem *Detlefsen*: autem
non (*i.e.* autē ñ) *Mayhoff.* Cf. *Theophrasti H. P. IX*, 15, § 7
οὐ μὴν ὀρύττειν γ᾽ εἶναι χαλεπόν.

[3] mihi *codd.*: memini *Ianus, Detlefsen*: autumni *Mayhoff.*

[4] posse *ego addidi.*

---

[a] The negative is added because of the words of Theophrastus given in the critical note.   Homer's description is:

ῥίζῃ μὲν μέλαν ἔσκε, γάλακτι δὲ εἴκελον ἄνθος·
μῶλυ δέ μιν καλέουσι θεοί.   χαλεπὸν δέ τ᾽ ὀρύσσειν
ἀνδράσι γε θνητοῖσι· θεοὶ δέ τε πάντα ἴσασιν.

Odyssey X 304–306.

[b] The difficulties of this sentence seem to me to be lessened,
but not fully solved, by emending *mihi* to *memini* or *autumni*.

from sensation as it was from pain.   But what excuse
was there to point out the means of deranging the
mind, of causing abortion, and of many similar crimes?
I personally do not mention abortives, nor even love-
philtres, remembering as I do that the famous
general Lucullus was killed by a love-philtre, nor
yet any other unholy magic, unless it be by way of
warning or denunciation, especially as I have utterly
condemned all faith in such practices.   Enough
pains, and more than enough, will have been taken
if I point out plants healthful to life and discovered
in order to preserve it.

VIII. The most renowned of plants is, according
to Homer, the one that he thinks is called by the gods
moly, assigning to Mercury its discovery and the *Moly.*
teaching of its power over the most potent sorceries.
Report says it grows today in Arcadia round
Pheneus and on Cyllene; it is said to be like the
description in Homer, with a round, dark root, of the
size of an onion and with the leaves of a squill, and
not *a* difficult to dig up.   Greek authorities have
painted its blossom yellow, though Homer describes
it as white.   I have met a herbalist physician who
said that the plant was also to be found in Italy,
and that one could *b* be brought for me from Campania
within a few days, as it had been dug out there in
spite of the difficulties of rocky ground, with a root

These make the present tense of *adferri* easier to understand,
but leave untouched the main difficulty—that in the first
clause of the sentence a general statement is made, while in
the second the reference is to a particular specimen.   So I
propose to keep *mihi*, but to add *posse* before *effossam*: it
might easily be omitted.   Perhaps the sentence could be
construed (without any emendation): "and that one was being
brought for me from Campania etc."   But a root of 30 feet!

saxeas radicis xxx pedes longae ac ne sic quidem
solidae, sed abruptae.

28　IX. Ab ea maxima auctoritas herbae est quam
dodecatheon vocant omnium deorum maiestatem
commendantes. in aqua potam omnibus morbis
mederi tradunt. folia eius septem lactucis simillima
exeunt a lutea radice.

29　X. Vetustissima inventu paeonia est, nomenque
auctoris retinet, quam quidam pentorobon appellant,
alii glycysidem. nam haec quoque difficultas est
quod eadem aliter alibi nuncupatur. nascitur opacis
montibus caule inter folia digitorum quattuor ferente
in cacumine veluti Graecas nuces quattuor aut
quinque. inest his semen copiosum, rubrum ni-
grumque. haec medetur et Faunorum in quiete
ludibriis. praecipiunt eruere noctu, quoniam si picus
Martius videat tuendo[1] in oculos impetum faciat.

30　XI. Panaces ipso nomine omnium morborum
remedia promittit, numerosum et dis inventoribus
adscriptum. unum quippe asclepion cognominatur,
a quo is filiam Panaciam appellavit. sucus est
coactus ferulae qualem diximus, radice multi corticis
et salsi. hac evolsa scrobem repleri vario genere
31　frugum religio est ac terrae piamentum. ubi et
quonam fieret modo ac quale maxime probaretur

---

[1] tuendo codd., Mayhoff : volando coni. Sillig : eruentem
Detlefsen. Mayhoff etiam coni. vel ad tuendum (tuendū) vel
interdiu.

---

[a] Mayhoff's maiestate would give : " investing it with the
grandeur etc." Dodecatheon means " plant of the twelve
(greater) gods."
[b] volando will mean " by flying at them "; eruentem, "the
person uprooting it."
[c] See XII. § 127.

thirty feet long, and even that not entire, but broken off short.

IX. After moly the plant with the highest repu- *The dodeca-theon.* tation they call the dodecatheon, as a compliment to the grandeur *a* of all the twelve gods. It is said that taken in water it cures all diseases. Its leaves are seven, very like those of lettuce and sprouting from a yellow root.

X. The first plant to be discovered was the peony, *The peony.* which still retains the name of the discoverer; it is called by some pentorobon, by others glycyside, for an added difficulty in botany is the variety of names given to the same plant in different districts. It grows on shaded mountains, having a stem among the leaves about four fingers high, which bears on its top four or five growths like almonds, in them being a large amount of seed, red and black. This plant also prevents the mocking delusions that the Fauns bring on us in our sleep. They recommend us to uproot it at night-time, because the woodpecker of Mars, should he see the act, will attack the eyes in its defence.*b*

XI. The plant panaces by its very name promises *Panaces.* to be a cure for every disease; it has many varieties, and to the gods have been ascribed the discovery of its properties. One variety in fact has the additional name of asclepion, after which Asclepius called his daughter Panacia. The juice of this plant when curdled is like that, already described,*c* of fennel-giant, coming from a root with a thick and salty skin. When it has been pulled up it is a pious duty to fill in the hole with various cereals as an atonement to the earth. Where the juice is prepared, and how, and the most esteemed kind, I have already

inter peregrina docuimus. id quod e Macedonia adfertur bucolicon vocant armentariis sponte erumpentem sucum excipientibus; hoc celerrime evanescit. et in aliis autem generibus inprobatur maxime nigrum ac molle. id enim argumento est cera adulterati.

32 XII. Alterum genus heracleon vocant et ab Hercule inventum tradunt, alii origanum heracleoticum aut silvestre, quoniam est origano simile, radice inutili; de quo origano diximus.[1]

XIII. Tertium panaces chironium cognominatur ab inventore. folium eius simile lapatho, maius tamen et hirsutius, flos aureus, radix parva. nascitur pinguibus locis. huius flos efficacissimus, eoque amplius quam supra dicta prodest.

33 XIV. Quartum genus,[2] panaces ab eodem Chirone repertum centaurion cognominatur, sed et pharnaceon in controversia inventionis a Pharnace rege deductum. seritur hoc, longioribus quam cetera foliis et serratis. radix odorata in umbra siccatur

---

[1] simile de quo diximus, radice inutili. *coni. Warmington.*
[2] genus] *in uncis ponit Mayhoff:* servat Brakman.

---

[a] See the whole of XII. §§ 127, 128, especially the latter part of § 127 : *semine muscariis dependente ut ferulae. excipitur sucus inciso caule messibus, radice autumno. laudatur*

described[a] in my account of exotic plants. The kind imported out of Macedonia they call buco-licon,[b] because herdsmen collect the sap as it exudes of its own accord; this evaporates very rapidly. As to the other kinds, the least popular is the dark and soft, for these qualities are signs of adulteration with wax.

XII. A second kind they call heracleon, and say *Heracleon.* that it was discovered by Hercules; others call it Heracleotic or wild origanum, because it is like the origanum I have already described;[c] the root is of no value.[d]

XIII. A third kind of panaces has the surname *Chironium.* chironium from Chiron the centaur who discovered it. Its leaf is like that of lapathum, but larger and more hairy. The blossom is golden and the root small. It grows in rich soils. The blossom of this kind is very efficacious, and therefore has a wider range of usefulness than that of the kinds mentioned above.

XIV. The fourth kind is the panaces discovered by *Centaurion.* the same Chiron and surnamed centaurion, but also pharnaceon, a name derived from king Pharnaces, as there is a controversy whether he was, or was not, the discoverer. This kind is grown from seed, having longer leaves than the other kinds, and with serrated edges. Its scented root is dried in the

candor eius coacti ; sequens pallido statera, niger colos inpro-batur.
   [b] " Bucolic," " pastoral," " pertaining to oxen."
   [c] See XX. § 170.
   [d] I think that a semicolon should be put at *inutili.* If with Detlefsen and Mayhoff we put a comma only, we get the sense : " the origanum I have already described, whose root is of no value."

vinoque gratiam adicit. eius genera duo fecere alia
aliqui, alterum lato folio, alterum tenui.[1]

34 XV. Heracleon siderion et ipsum ab Hercule inventum est, caule tenui digitorum quattuor altitudine, flore puniceo, foliis coriandri. iuxta lacus et
amnes invenitur omniaque vulnera ferro inlata
efficacissime sanat.

XVI. Est Chironis inventum ampelos quae vocatur
chironia, de qua diximus inter vites, sicuti de herba
cuius inventio adsignatur Minervae.

35 XVII. Herculi eam quoque adscribunt quae apollinaris apud alios, apud nos[2] altercum,[3] apud Graecos
vero hyoscyamos appellatur. plura eius genera:
unum nigro semine, floribus paene purpureis, spinoso

[1] eius genera duo fecere alia aliqui, alterum lato folio,
alterum tenui *ego* : eius genera duo fecere aliqui, levis folii,
alterum tenuius *Detlefsen* : alia eius genera etc. *Mayhoff* : alia
omittunt codd., in quibus non eius *sed* huius *scriptum est.
Sunt aliae lectiones, sed parvi momenti. Cf.* ἄλλα δὲ πανάκη
τὸ μὲν λεπτόφυλλον τὸ δὲ οὔ. *Theophr. H.P. IX. 11, 4.*
[2] apud alios, apud nos *Urlichs* : aut *Mayhoff* : apud *aut*
aput *codd.* : *del. Detlefsen.*
[3] *Hic (ante* altercum*) a rabulis Urlichs* : ab alis *Detlefsen* :
a rabie aliis *Mayhoff*: arabilis *aut* arbilis *aut* arabas *codd.*:
ego delevi : apud Arabas altercum sive altercangenum *vulg.*

---

[a] The corresponding passage in Theophrastus implies a
reference to two other sorts of panaces; the ordinary text
of Pliny refers to two sorts of " this " kind, that is, of centaurion. Either Pliny has muddled once more, or his text
must be emended. I have adopted the second alternative,
thinking with Mayhoff that *alia* has dropped out, although

shade, and adds a pleasing taste to wine. Some hold that there are two other kinds of panaces, one with a broad, the other with a slender, leaf.[a]

XV. Heracleon siderion ("ironwort") is yet another discovery of Hercules. It has a slender stem about four fingers high, a flower of a deep red and leaves like those of coriander. It is found near ponds and rivers, and heals very thoroughly all wounds inflicted by iron.[b] *Heracleon siderion.*

XVI. A discovery of Chiron's was the vine called chironia, which I have mentioned in my section on the vines;[c] I have also mentioned a plant, the discovery of which is attributed to Minerva.[d]

XVII. To Hercules too they ascribe the plant which is called apollinaris by some, altercum by us Romans,[e] but by the Greeks hyoscyamos ("pig's bean"). There are several kinds of it: one has black seed, with flowers that are almost purple, and a *Apollinaris.*

I would insert it before *aliqui* and not after *adicit*, and agree with Detlefsen that *huius* should be changed to *eius* or *panacis.* My other emendations are based on *folio*, the reading of the MSS. V and R, and on the λεπτόφυλλον of Theophrastus.

[b] Hence the name siderion, derived from the Greek σίδηρος, iron.

[c] See XXIII. § 27.

[d] See XXII. § 43.

[e] I have adopted here the emendation of Urlichs, omitting, however, his *a rabulis.* Pseudo-Dioscorides, IV. RV 68 (Wellmann), has twenty names for hyoscyamos, including ἐμμανές, Ἀπολλινάρις and ἰνσάνα. A copyist or commentator might be tempted to add a few of these, and perhaps the vulgate text arose in this way. To see in the corrupt *arabilis* or *arbilis* of three MSS. a reference to the madness supposed to be caused by hyoscyamos is natural; hence the *a rabie* of Mayhoff. But the variations in the MSS. have the appearance of corrupt glosses. The curious *a rabulis* of Urlichs supposes a connection between *altercum* and *altercor.*

PLINY : NATURAL HISTORY

calyce;[1] nascitur in Galatia. vulgare autem candidius est et fruticosius, altius papavere. tertii semen irionis semini simile, sed omnia insaniam gignentia
36 capitisque vertigines. quartum genus molle, lanuginosum, pinguius ceteris, candidi seminis, in maritimis nascens. hoc recepere medici, item rufi seminis. nonnumquam autem candidum rufescit, si non ematuruit, inprobaturque, et alioqui nullum nisi cum inaruit legitur. natura vini ideoque mentem caputque infestans. usus seminis et per se et suco expresso. exprimitur separatim et caulibus foliisque. utuntur et radice, temeraria in totum, ut arbi-
37 tror, medicina. quippe etiam foliis constat mentem corrumpi, si plura quam quattuor bibant; bibebant[2] etiam antiqui in vino febrim depelli arbitrantes. oleum fit ex semine, ut diximus, quod ipsum auribus infusum temptat mentem, mireque ut contra venenum remedia prodidere iis qui id bibissent et ipsum pro remediis, adeo nullo omnia experiendi fine ut cogerent[3] etiam venena prodesse.

[1] spinoso calyce *ego* : spinosum calice *Mayhoff* : spinosum —talis *etc. Detlefsen* : spinosum talis *aut* tale *codd.*
[2] bibebant *ego addidi* : *lacunam indicat Ianus, quem sequitur Mayhoff, qui* tot bibi iubebant *supplere malit. Brakman quoque (Mnemosyne 1930)* bibebant *coni.*
[3] cogerent *Ianus* : cogant *Mayhoff* : cogerentur *vulg.* : cogeret *codd.*

---

[a] Mayhoff's emendation was suggested by Dioscorides IV. 68 : ὁ μὲν γὰρ . . . φέρει . . . τοὺς κυτίνους σκληροὺς καὶ ἀκανθώδεις. I have, however, slightly altered the emendation and the construction.
[b] In pseudo-Dioscorides ἰνσάνα is given as the Roman name for hyoscyamos. This is the reason why I am doubtful about the text of § 35 *in initio*.
[c] *Etiam* : " even though it is so dangerous."

thorny calyx,[a] growing in Galatia. The common kind, however, is whiter and more bushy; it is taller than the poppy. The seed of the third kind is like the seed of irio; but all kinds cause insanity [b] and giddiness. A fourth kind is soft, downy, richer in juice than the others, with a white seed, and growing in places near the sea. This is a kind that medical men have adopted, as they have that with a red seed. Sometimes, however, the white seed turns red if gathered before getting ripe, and then it is rejected; and generally no kind is ever gathered before it has become dry. It has the character of wine, and therefore injures the head and brain. Use is made of the seed as it is or when the juice has been extracted from it. The juice is extracted separately also from the stems and leaves. They also use the root, but the drug is, in my opinion, a dangerous medicine in any form. In fact, it is well known that even the leaves affect the brain if more than four are taken in drink; yet [c] the ancients used to take them in wine under the impression that fever was so brought down. An oil is made from the seed, as I have said,[d] which by itself if poured into the ears deranges the brain. It is a wonderful thing that they have prescribed remedies for those who have taken the drink, which implies that it is a poison, and yet have included it among remedies; so unwearied have been researches in making every possible experiment, even to compelling [e] poisons to be helpful remedies.

[d] See XV. § 30 and XXIII. § 94.
[e] It makes very little difference whether we read *cogerent* with Jan or *cogant* with Mayhoff. The first takes its sequence from the idea of *past* time, the second from the idea of *present* time, both implicit in *nullo fine*.

38   XVIII. Linozostis sive parthenion Mercurii inventum est. ideo apud Graecos Hermu poan multi
vocant eam, apud nos omnes mercurialem. duo eius
genera: masculus et femina, quae efficacior. caule
est [1] cubitali, interdum ramoso in cacumine, ocimo
angustioribus foliis, geniculis densis, alarum cavis
multis, semine in geniculis dependente feminae
copioso, mari iuxta genicula stante rariore ac brevi
39 contortoque, feminae soluto et candido. folia
maribus nigriora, feminis candidiora, radix supervacua, praetenuis. nascuntur in campestribus cultis.
mirumque est quod de utroque eorum genere proditur: ut mares gignantur hunc facere, ut feminae
illam. hoc contingere, si a conceptu protinus bibatur
sucus in passo edanturve folia decocta ex oleo et sale,
vel cruda ex aceto. quidam decocunt eam in novo
fictili cum heliotropio et duabus vel tribus spicis,
40 donec cogatur. decoctum dari iubent et herbam
ipsam in cibo altero die purgationis mulieribus per
triduum, quarto die a balineo coire eas. Hippocrates
miris laudibus in mulierum usum praedicavit has;

[1] est *Detlefsen* : et *unus cod. et Mayhoff, qui aliter dist. et
lacunam post* geniculis *indicat. Ego Detlefsen sequor. Desunt*
§§ 38–41 *in codd.* VRdT.

ᵃ Dioscorides has (IV. 189): ἔχει δὲ φύλλον ὅμοιον ὠκίμῳ
πρὸς τὸ τῆς ἐλξίνης, ἔλαττον δέ, κλωνία διγόνατα, μασχάλας
πολλάς, πυκνὰς ἔχοντα· τὸν δὲ καρπὸν ἡ μὲν θήλεια βοτρυοειδῆ
καὶ πολὺν ἡ δὲ ἄρρην πρὸς τοῖς πετάλοις μικρόν, στρογγύλον,
ὥσπερ ὀρχίδια κατὰ δύο προσκείμενα. This is so unlike the
Pliny passage in details, although parts are very similar
(particularly *densis, alarum cavis multis* and μασχάλας πολλάς,

XVIII. Linozostis or parthenion was discovered *Linozostis or* by Mercury, and so many among the Greeks call *parthenion.* it "Hermes' grass", but all we Romans agree in calling it mercurialis. There are two kinds of it, the male and the female, the latter having the more powerful properties. It has a stem which is a cubit high and sometimes branchy at the top, leaves narrower than those of ocimum, joints close together and many hollow axils. The seed of the female hangs down in great quantity at the joints; while that of the male stands up near the joints, less plentiful, short and twisted; the female seed is loose and white.[a] The leaves of the male plant are darker, those of the female lighter; the root is quite useless and very slender. It grows in flat, cultivated country. A remarkable thing is recorded of both kinds: that the male plant causes the generation of males and the female plant the generation of females. This is effected if immediately after conceiving the woman drinks the juice in raisin wine, or eats the leaves decocted in oil and salt, or raw in vinegar. Some again decoct it in a new earthen vessel with heliotropium and two or three ears of corn until the contents become thick. They recommend the decoction to be given to women in food, with the plant itself, on the second day of menstruation for three successive days; on the fourth day after a bath intercourse is to take place. Hippocrates [b] has bestowed very high praise on these plants for the diseases of women; no medical man

πυκνάς), that I hesitate to emend Pliny so as to harmonize his account with Dioscorides.
    [b] See Littré's vol. X. pp. 690, 691 for references to the herb mercury in the Hippocratic *Corpus.*

ad [1] hunc modum medicorum nemo novit. ille eas volvae cum melle vel rosaceo vel irino vel lilino admovit, item ad ciendos menses secundasque. idem praestare potu fotuque dixit. instillavit auribus olidis [2] sucum. suco [3] inunxit cum vino vetere

41 alvum.[4] folia inposuit epiphoris. stranguriae et vesicis decoctum eius dedit cum murra et ture. alvo quidem solvendae vel in febri decoquatur [5] quantum manus capiat in duobus sextariis aquae ad dimidias. bibitur sale et melle admixto nec non cum ungula suis aut gallinaceo decocta [6] salubrius. purgationis causa putavere aliqui utramque dandam per se sive [7] cum malva decoctam.[8] thoracem purgant, bilem detrahunt, sed stomachum laedunt. reliquos usus dicemus suis locis.

[1] ad E *cod.* a, *vulg., Detlefsen* : at *vet. Dal., Mayhoff.*
[2] olidis *Gelen., Detlefsen, Mayhoff* : solidis E a : surdis *vulg.*
[3] sucum. suco *ego* : suco *duo codd., Detlefsen* : sucum *vulg., Mayhoff.*
[4] alvum (alvū) *ego* : alvo *aut* albo *codd.*
[5] decoquatur E a, *vulg., Detlefsen* : decoquitur *Basileensis editio, Mayhoff.*
[6] decocta *vet. Dal., Sillig, Mayhoff* : decoctae E : decoctum *vulg.* : mixtum *cod.* a, *Detlefsen.*
[7] per se sive *vet. Dal.* : sive *codd., vulg., edd.* : in cibo *coni. Mayhoff.*
[8] decoctam *vet. Dal., Mayhoff* : decocta a, *Detlefsen* : decoctum E *vulg.*

***

a With the reading *at* : " but no medical man recognises now this method of treatment."

recognises its virtues after this fashion.[a] He used them as pessaries for uterine troubles, adding thereto honey, or oil of roses or of iris or of lilies, also as an emmenagogue and to bring away the after-birth. The same effects, he said, resulted from taking them in drink and from using them for fomentations. He dropped the juice into foul-smelling ears, and with the juice and old wine made an embrocation for the abdomen. The leaves he applied to fluxes from the eyes. A decoction of it with myrrh and frankincense he prescribed for strangury and bladder troubles. For loosening the bowels, however, or for fever, a handful of the plant should be boiled down to one half in two sextarii of water. This is drunk with the addition of salt and honey, and if the decoction has been made with a pig's foot or a chicken added, the draught is all the more beneficial. Some have thought that as a purge both kinds should be administered, either by themselves or with mallows added to the decoction.[b] They purge the abdomen [c] and bring away bile, but they are injurious to the stomach. Their other uses we shall give in the appropriate places.[d]

[b] With Mayhoff's conjecture *in cibo*: "both kinds should be given in food, boiled down with mallows."

[c] This seems to be the meaning here of *thorax*, as it is of θώραξ very often in Greek. Cf. Festugière on [Hippocrates] *Ancient Medicine* XXII, who quotes many passages proving that θώραξ meant the entire cavity of the torso.

[d] Throughout this chapter the translator misses the four good MSS. VRdT. In many places the reading is uncertain, and I have by emendations and changes of punctuation tried to produce a better text than either Detlefsen or Mayhoff, with an uneasy feeling that I have made no improvement, or perhaps even made bad worse.

42   XIX. Invenit [1] et Achilles discipulus Chironis qua
volneribus mederetur. quae ob id achilleos vocatur.
hac sanasse Telephum dicitur. alii primum aeru-
ginem invenisse utilissimam emplastris, ideoque
pingitur ex cuspide decutiens eam gladio in volnus
Telephi, alii utroque usum medicamento volunt.
aliqui et hanc panacem Heracliam, alii sideriten et
apud nos millefoliam vocant, cubitali scapo, ramosam,
minutioribus quam feniculi foliis vestitam ab imo.

43 alii fatentur quidem illam vulneribus utilem, sed
veram achilleon esse scapo caeruleo pedali, sine
ramis, ex omni parte singulis foliis rotundis eleganter
vestitam; alii quadrato caule, capitulis marrubii,
foliis quercus, hac etiam praecisos nervos glutinari.[2]
faciunt alii et [3] sideritim in maceriis nascentem, cum

44 teratur, foedi odoris, etiamnum aliam similem huic
sed candidioribus foliis et pinguioribus, teneriorem
cauliculis, in vineis nascentem; aliam [4] vero binum
cubitorum, ramulis exilibus, triangulis, folio filicis,
pediculo longo, betae semine; omnes volneribus
praecipuas. nostri eam quae est latissimo folio
scopas regias vocant. medetur anginis suum.

45   XX. Invenit et Teucer eadem aetate teucrion,
quam quidam hemionion vocant, spargentem iuncos

---

[1] invenit *vulg.*, *Detlefsen* : invenisse *coni. Mayhoff, qui et*
ac *non* hac *postea scribit et* quae . . . vocatur *in parenthesi
ponit.*

[2] glutinari *Urlichs, Detlefsen, Mayhoff, qui et* glutinant *coni.* :
glutinare *codd.*

[3] alii et *Mayhoff* : et *Detlefsen cum* VR d : alia (ali et ?) E :
alii *vulg.*

[4] aliam *vulg.*, *Detlefsen* : aliqui *Mayhoff* : alioqui *aut*
alioque *codd.*

XIX. Achilles too, the pupil of Chiron, discovered *a* *Achilleos.*
a plant to heal wounds, which is therefore called
achilleos, and by it he is said to have cured Telephus.
Some have it that he was the first to find out that
copper-rust is a most useful ingredient of plasters, for
which reason he is represented in paintings as
scraping it with his sword from his spear on to the
wound of Telephus, while others hold that he used
both remedies. This plant is also called by some
Heraclean panaces, by others siderites, and by us
millefolia; the stalk is a cubit high, and the plant
branchy, covered from the bottom with leaves smaller
than those of fennel. Others admit that this plant is
good for wounds, but say that the real achilleos has a
blue stalk a foot long and without branches, grace-
fully covered all over with separate, rounded leaves.
Others describe achilleos as having a square stem,
heads like those of horehound, and leaves like those
of the oak; they claim that it even unites severed
sinews. Some give the name sideritis to another
plant, which grows on boundary walls and has a foul
smell when crushed, and also to yet another, like
this but with paler and more fleshy leaves, and with
more tender stalks, growing in vineyards; finally to
a third, two cubits high, with thin, triangular twigs,
leaves like those of the fern, a long foot-stalk and
seed like that of beet. All are said to be excellent
for wounds. Roman authorities call the one with
the broadest leaf royal broom; it cures quinsy in
pigs.

XX. Teucer too in the same age discovered *Teucrion.*
teucrion, called by some hemionion; it spreads out

a By " discovering " a plant Pliny seems to mean discovering
its value in medicine.

tenues, folia parva, asperis locis, austero sapore,
numquam florentem, nec quae[1] semen gignit.
medetur lienibus, constatque sic inventam : cum
exta super eam proiecta essent, adhaesisse lieni
eumque exinanisse. ob id a quibusdam splenion
46 vocatur. narrant sues qui radicem eius edint sine
splene inveniri. quidam ramis hysopi surculosam,
folio fabae, eodem nomine appellant et colligi cum
floreat iubent—adeo florere non dubitant—maxime-
que ex Ciliciae et Pisidiae montibus laudant.

47 XXI. Melampodis fama divinationis artibus nota
est. ab hoc appellatur unum hellebori genus
melampodion. aliqui pastorem eodem nomine invenisse tradunt, capras purgari pasto illo animadver-
tentem, datoque lacte earum sanasse Proetidas
furentes.[2] quamobrem de omnibus eius generibus
48 dici simul convenit. prima duo sunt, candidum ac
nigrum. hoc radicibus tantum intellegi tradunt
plerique, alii folia nigri platano similia sed minora
nigrioraque et pluribus divisuris scissa, albi betae
incipientis, haec quoque nigriora et canalium dorso

---

[1] florentem, nec quae *Detlefsen cum uno cod.* : florem
neque *Mayhoff.*
[2] furentes] *Hic lacunam indicat Mayhoff.*

---

[a] See note on § 42.
[b] Mayhoff supposes that there is a lacuna here with the
following sense : " our authorities are not agreed about the
differences between the various kinds of hellebore."

thin, rush-like twigs with small leaves, grows on rough localities, has a harsh taste, never flowers and never produces seed. It is a cure for splenic troubles, a property discovered,[a] as is well known, in the following way; they say that when sacrificial entrails had been thrown on the plant, this stuck to the spleen and consumed it. On account of this the plant is called by some splenion. It is said that pigs which eat its root are found to be without a spleen. There are some who call by the same name a ligneous plant with branches like those of hyssop and leaves like those of the bean, and recommend it to be gathered when it is in flower—so these certainly hold that the plant has a flower—and they praise most highly the sort that comes from the mountains of Cilicia and Pisidia.

XXI. Melampus is well known for his skill in the arts of divination. From him one kind of hellebore is called melampodion. Some hold that the discovery is due to a shepherd called Melampus, who noticed that his she-goats were purged after browsing upon the plant, and by administering the milk of these goats cured the daughters of Proetus of their madness.[b] Wherefore it is well to give here together an account of every kind of hellebore. *Melampodion.*

The chief kinds are two, the white and the black. This difference, most authorities say, applies only to the roots, others say that the leaves of black hellebore are like those of the plane but smaller, darker and with more indentations; that the leaves of white hellebore are like those of sprouting beet, but also darker and turning to red on the under side of its grooves, and that both have a stem a span high, resembling that of fennel-giant, wrapped up in skins *Kinds of hellebore.*

rubescentia, utraque caule palmeo [1] ferulaceo, bulborum tunicis convoluto, radice fimbriata ceparum modo. nigro equi, boves, sues necantur, itaque cavent id, cum candido vescantur. tempestivum
49 esse tradunt messibus. plurimum autem nascitur in Oete monte, et optimum uno eius loco circa Pyram. nigrum ubique provenit, sed melius in Helicone, qui mons et aliis laudatur herbis. candidum probatur secundum Oetaeum Ponticum, tertio loco Eleaticum quod in vitibus nasci ferunt, quarto Parnasium quod adulteratur Aetolico ex vicino. nigrum ex his melampodium vocant, quo et domus suffiunt purgantque, spargentes et pecora, cum precatione
50 sollemni. hoc et religiosius colligitur, primum enim gladio circumscribitur, dein qui succisurus est ortum spectat et precatur ut id liceat sibi concedentibus diis facere, observatque aquilae volatus, fere enim secantibus interest et, si prope advolavit, moriturum illo anno qui succidat augurium est. nec album facile colligitur, caput adgravans maxime, nisi praesumatur alium et subinde vinum sorbeatur celeriterque
51 fodiatur. nigrum alii ectomon [2] vocant, alii polyrrhizon. purgat per inferna, candidum autem vomitione, causasque morborum extrahit, quondam terribile, postea tam promiscuum ut plerique studio-

---

[1] palmeo *coni. Mayhoff* XXVI. § 95 *coll.* : palmari *Urlichs, Detlefsen* : palmi *codd. et Mayhoff.*

[2] ectomon *Hard. ex Theophrasto et Dioscoride* : encymon *plures codd., Detlefsen, Mayhoff* : euchymon *vulg.*

---

[a] Cf. Theophrastus *H.P. IX. 10* § 4 καθαίρουσι δὲ καὶ οἰκίας αὐτῷ καὶ πρόβατα συνεπάδοντές τινα ἐπῳδήν.

[b] See Theophrastus IX. 10 § 4 : καλοῦσι δὲ τὸν μελανά τινες ἕκτομον Μελαμπόδιον, ὡς ἐκείνου πρῶτον τεμόντος καὶ ἀνευρόντος. Dioscorides IV. 162: ἐλλέβορος μέλας· οἱ δὲ Μελαμπόδιον, οἱ δὲ ἕκτομον, οἱ δὲ πολύρριζον καλοῦσι.

like those of bulbs, and with a root fringed like that of
onions. The black hellebore kills horses, oxen and
pigs; so they avoid it, although they eat the white
kind. The latter is said to be ripe at harvest, and it
grows abundantly on Mount Oeta, and the best on one
part of it, around the place called Pyra. The black
kind is to be found everywhere, but the better sort
grows on Helicon, a mountain celebrated also for
other plants. Next after the white hellebore of Oeta
that of Pontus is most approved; the third place is
taken by that of Elea, which is said to grow among
vines, and the fourth by hellebore of Parnassus,
which is adulterated by hellebore from the neigh-
bouring country of Aetolia. Of these the black
kind they call melampodium; with it they fumigate
and cleanse houses, sprinkling it on sheep, and
adding a formal prayer.[a] This kind is gathered
with even greater formalities. First a circle is
drawn round it with a sword; then the man who is
going to cut it looks at the East with a prayer
that the gods will grant him permission to do so.
He also keeps on the look-out for a flying eagle—for
generally one is present when men cut—and if an
eagle flies near, it is a sign that the gatherer will die
in that year. The white too is not easy to gather:
it is very oppressive to the head unless garlic is
eaten beforehand, wine swallowed every now and
then and the plant dug up quickly. Some call the
black kind ectomon,[b] others polyrrhizon.[c] This
purges by stool, but the white kind does so by
vomiting, and carries away what might cause diseases;
once regarded with horror it afterwards became so

[c] "With many roots," and ἔκτομον means "cut out," or
perhaps "cut short," cf. decurtatae § 53.

rum gratia ad pervidenda acrius quae commenta-
52 bantur saepius sumptitaverint. Carneaden respon-
surum Zenonis libris * * ,[1] Drusum quoque apud nos,
tribunorum popularium clarissimum, cui ante omnis [2]
plebs astans plausit, optimates vero bellum Marsi-
cum‧inputavere, constat hoc medicamento liberatum
comitiali morbo in Anticyra insula. ibi enim tutis-
sime sumitur, quoniam, ut diximus, sesamoides
admiscent. Italia veratrum vocat. farina eorum
per se et mixta radiculae qua lanas diximus lavari
53 sternumentum facit, amboque somnum. leguntur
autem tenuissimae radices brevesque ac velut decurtatae et imae. nam summa, quae est crassissima,
cepis similis, canibus tantum datur purgationis causa.
antiqui radicem cortice quam carnosissimo seligebant,
quod [3] tenuior eximeretur medulla — hanc umidis
spongeis opertam turgescentemque acu in longi-
tudinem findebant, dein fila in umbra siccabant his
utentes — nunc ramulos ipsos ab radice quam
gravissimi [4] corticis ita dant.[5] optimum quod acre

[1] Post libris *excidisse* se eo purgavisse *putat Mayhoff.*
[2] omnis V, *Sillig, Detlefsen, Mayhoff* : omnes *ceteri codd. et vulg.*
[3] quod VR *Detlefsen* : quo d *vulg. Mayhoff.*
[4] gravissimi *codd., vulg., Detlefsen* : grandissimi *C. F. W. Müller* : crassissimi *Mayhoff.*
[5] dant *Gelenius, Mayhoff* : dantes *codd., vulg., Detlefsen.*

---

[a] Marcus Livius Drusus, tribune of the people 91 B.C.
[b] There is much to be said for the reading *omnes* : " the commons greeted with unprecedented applause." It has strong MS. support and makes excellent sense ; on the other hand a scribe would find the temptation very strong to write *omnes* by mistake for *omnis* after *ante.*

popular that most scholars took it regularly to
sharpen their brains for their studies. It is well
known that Carneades, when preparing to reply to
the works of Zeno, ⟨purged himself with hellebore⟩,
and that Drusus [a] among us, most illustrious of our
tribunes of the people, who was cheered by all the
commons standing before him [b] but charged by the
aristocrats with causing the Marsic War, was on the
island of Anticyra cured of epilepsy by means of
this medicine. For there it is very safe to take the
drug because they add to it sesamoides, as I have
already said.[c] In Italy it is called veratrum.

Both hellebores when ground to powder, either by
themselves or combined with that of radicula, with
which I said [d] wool is washed, cause sneezing, and
both cause sleep. But the roots selected are the
thinnest, short, and as it were cut off; only the
bottom is used, for the top, which is very thick and
like an onion, is given as a purge only to dogs. The
old physicians used to choose the root with the most
fleshy skin, thinking that the pithy part they obtained from such was more delicate. This they used
to cover with moist sponges, and when it swelled
they would split it lengthwise with a needle; then
they would dry the thin strips in the shade, and so
use them. Today they administer the shoots themselves, just as they are, that grow from roots with the
heaviest [e] skin. The best hellebore has a sharp, hot

---

[c] See XXII. § 133. Anticyra is a peninsula.
[d] See XIX. § 4 and XXIV. § 9.
[e] There seems no need to change *gravissimi* to *grandissimi*
or *crassissimi*. " Heaviest " may well be " thickest." The
reading *dantes*, I think, has arisen from *utentes* just above.
The whole sentence, however, is in any case very clumsy,
with a loose, almost formless, structure.

gustu fervensque in frangendo pulverem emittit.
durare vim xxx annis ferunt.

54   XXII. Nigrum medetur paralyticis, insanientibus,
hydropicis, dum citra febrim, podagris veteribus,
articulariis morbis; trahit ex alvo bilem, pituitas,
aquas.   datur ad leniter molliendam alvum plurimum
drachma una, modice quattuor obolis. miscuere
aliqui et scamonium, sed tutius salem. in dulcibus
datum copiosius periculum infert, oculorum cali-
55 ginem fotu discutit.   ob id quidam et inunxere trito.
strumas, suppurata, duritias concoquit et purgat,
item fistulas tertio die exemptum. verrucas tollit
cum squama aeris et sandaraca. hydropicorum
ventri inponitur cum farina hordeacia et vino.
pecorum et iumentorum pituitas sanat surculo per
aurem traiecto et postero die eadem hora exempto,
scabiem quadripedum cum ture, cera ac pice vel cum
pisselaeo.

56   XXIII. Album optimum, quod celerrime movet
sternumenta, sed multum terribilius nigro, praecipue
si quis apparatum poturorum apud antiquos legat
contra horrores, strangulatus, intempestivas somni
vires, singultus infinitos aut sternumenta, stomachi
dissolutiones, tardiores vomitus aut longiores, exiguos
aut nimios.   quippe alia dare soliti quae concitarent
vomitiones ipsumque helleborum extrahere medicamentis aut clysteribus, saepius etiam sanguine venis
57 emisso.   iam vero et cum prospere cedat, terribili

---

^a Black or impure oxide of copper.
^b Disulphide of arsenic.
^c See XXIV. § 19.
^d Or possibly : " very often."

taste, and gives out dust when broken. It keeps, it is said, its efficacy for thirty years.

XXII. Black hellebore is a cure for paralysis, *Black hellebore.* madness, dropsy without fever, chronic gout and diseases of the joints; it draws from the belly bile, phlegms and morbid fluids. For gently moving the bowels the maximum dose is one drachma; a moderate one is four oboli. Some have mixed scammony also with it, but to add salt is safer. A larger dose given in sweet substances is dangerous; used as a fomentation it disperses films over the eyes. Therefore some have also pounded it and made an eye salve. It matures and clears up scrofulous sores, suppurations and indurations; fistulas also if it be taken off on the third day. With copper scales [a] and sandarach [b] it removes warts. With barley meal and wine it is applied to the abdomen for dropsy. It cures phlegms in cattle and draught animals if a spray be passed across the ear and taken out at the same hour on the next day; with frankincense, wax and pitch, or with pisselaeon [c] it cures itch in quadrupeds.

XXIII. The best white hellebore is that which *White hellebore.* most quickly causes sneezing. It is, however, far more terrifying than the black sort, especially if one reads in our old authorities of the elaborate precautions, taken by those about to drink it, against shivering, choking, overpowering and unseasonable sleep, prolonged hiccough or sneezing, fluxes of the stomach, vomiting, too slow or too long, scanty or too excessive. In fact they usually gave other things to promote vomiting, and drove out the hellebore itself by medicine or enema, or more often [d] they used even bleeding. Furthermore, even when the hellebore

177

visu,[1] variis coloribus vomitionum et post vomitiones
observatione alvi, balinearum dispensatione, totius
corporis cura, antecedente omnia haec magno terrore
famae, namque tradunt absumi carnem,[2] si coquatur
una. sed antiquorum vitium erat quod propter hos
metus parcius dabant, cum celerius erumpat quo
58 largius sumitur. Themison binas non amplius
drachmas datavit, sequentes et quaternas dedere
claro Herophili praeconio, qui helleborum fortissimi
ducis similitudini aequabat. concitatis enim intus
omnibus ipsum in primis exire. praeterea mirum
inventum est quod incisum forficulis, ut diximus,
cribrant, cortex remanet, hoc inaniunt, medulla
cadit, haec in nimia purgatione data vomitiones
sistit.

59 XXIV. Cavendum est felici quoque cura ne nubilo
die detur, inpetibiles quippe cruciatus existunt.
nam aestate potius quam hieme dandum non est in
dubio. corpus septem diebus ante praeparandum
cibis acribus, abstinentia vini, quarto et tertio die
vomitionibus, pridie cenae abstinentia. album et in

---

[1] terribili visu E *Detlefsen* : terribilius *Mayhoff* : terribilis
visu *multi codd.*
[2] carnem E, *vulg.*, *Detlefsen* : carnes *quinque codd. et
Mayhoff, qui* XXIII. §§ 126, 127, 150 *confert. Sed hic* caro
verbi coquatur *esse subiectum videtur.*

---

[a] Mayhoff's conjecture *terribilius* (*sc. helleborum est*) makes
the grammar simpler, the ablatives being causal and depend-

proves successful, the various colours [a] of the vomits are terrifying to see, and after the vomits comes the worry of watching the stools, regulating the bath, of attention to the whole body, all these troubles being preceded by the great terror caused by its reputation, for it is said that meat, if boiled with it, is consumed. It was a fault of the ancient physicians that because of these fears they used to administer this hellebore in smallish doses, since the larger the dose the quicker it is eliminated. Themison gave doses of not more than two drachmae; his successors actually increased the amount to four, because of the fine testimonial given to hellebore by Herophilus, who compared it to a truly courageous general; having aroused all within, it itself marches out in the van. Moreover, a wonderful discovery has been made; hellebore cut with scissors, as we have described, is passed through a sieve; the skin—with which they empty the stomach —remains behind, while the soft part passes through, and is given to stop the vomiting when the purging is too violent.

XXIV. Care must be taken, even with happy treatment, not to administer hellebore on a cloudy day; for to do so is followed by unbearable torture. Indeed, there is no doubt that summer is a better season to give it than winter. For seven days previously the body must be prepared by acid [b] foods and by abstinence from wine; on the fourth and third days before, an emetic must be taken, and on the preceding day there should be abstinence

How to use hellebore.

ing on the adjective. The reading in the text is harder, for the ablatives modify *cedit* understood from *cedat*.

[b] *Acribus* may mean " sharp tasted " or " pungent."

dulci datur, aptissime vero in lente and pulte. nuper invenere dissectis raphanis inserere helleborum rursusque conprimere raphanos, ut transeat vis, atque lenimento dare. reddi post quattuor fere horas
60 incipit. totum opus septenis peragitur horis. medetur ita morbis comitialibus, ut diximus, vertigini, melancholicis, insanientibus, lymphatis, elephantiasi albae, lepris, tetano, tremulis, podagricis, hydropicis incipientibusque tympanicis, stomachicis, spasticis cynicis, ischiadicis, quartanis, quae aliter non desinant, tussi veteri, inflationibus, torminibus redeuntibus.

61   XXV. Vetant dari senibus, pueris, item mollis ac feminei corporis animive, exilibus aut teneris, et feminis minus quam viris, item timidis, aut si exulcerata sint praecordia vel tumeant, minime sanguinem excreantibus causariisve latere, faucibus. medetur extra corporis eruptionibus pituitae cum axungia salsa inlitum,[1] item suppurationi veteri. mures polentae admixtum necat. Galli sagittas in venatu helleboro tingunt circumcisoque vulnere teneriorem sentiri carnem adfirmant. muscae quo-

---

[1] A latere *usque ad* inlitum *ita distinguere et emendare vult Mayhoff*: latere. faucibus medetur extra corpori inpositum, eruptionibus pituitae cum axungia salsa inlitum.

---

[a] In § 54 it is said that black hellebore is dangerous if given *copiosius in dulcibus*, so *et* is here probably not postponed, but " even."

[b] Perhaps " in sweet wine," but the plural (*dulcibus*) in § 54 is against this.

[c] See Celsus III. 21 and list of diseases.   See also note *d* on p. 88.

[d] Mayhoff's emendations and punctuation are attractive, and ease the structure of the next sentence considerably. The meaning would be : " If applied externally to the neck

from dinner. White hellebore is given even[a] in a sweet medium,[b] although most suitably in lentils or pottage. Recently the method has been discovered of splitting radishes, inserting hellebore, and then pressing the radishes together again, so that the property of the purge penetrates them; the hellebore is thus administered in a modified form. Vomiting begins after about four hours, and the whole business is over in seven. Thus given hellebore is curative of epilepsy, as has been said, giddiness, melancholia, insanity, wild distraction, white leprosy, leprous sores, tetanus, palsy, gouty affections, dropsy and incipient tympanitis,[c] stomachic affections, spasmodic grins, sciatica, quartan fever that yields to no other treatment, chronic cough, flatulence and recurrent gripings.

XXV. Hellebore is never prescribed for old people or children, or for those who are soft and effeminate in body or mind, or for the thin or delicate; for women it is less suited than for men, unsuitable too for the nervous or when the hypochondria are ulcerated or swollen, very bad when there is spitting of blood, pain in the side, or sore throat.[d] Applied externally with salted axle-grease it cures pituitous eruptions[e] on the body and also suppurations of long standing. Mixed with pearl barley it kills rats and mice. The Gauls when hunting dip their arrows in hellebore, and say that the meat when the flesh round the wound has been cut away tastes more tender. Flies too die if pounded white hellebore

it is a cure for sore throats, and an embrocation of hellebore with salted axle-grease, etc." But the falling out of *in-positum* seems too unlikely for the restoration to be adopted with confidence.

[e] See list of diseases.

que necantur albo trito et cum lacte sparso. eodem
et phthiriasis emendatur.

62 XXVI. Ipsi Mithridati Crateuas adscripsit unam,
mithridatiam vocatam (huic folia duo a radice
acantho similia, caulis inter utraque sustinens
63 roseum florem). XXVII. alteram Lenaeus, scordo-
tim sive scordion, ipsius manu descriptam,[1] magnitudine cubitali, quadriangulo caule, ramosam, querna
similitudine foliis lanuginosis. reperitur in Ponto,
campis pinguibus umidisque, gustus amari. est et
alterius generis, latioribus foliis, mentastro similis,
plurimosque utraque ad usus per se et inter alia in
antidotis.

64 XXVIII. Polemoniam alii philetaeriam ab certamine regum inventionis appellant, Cappadoces
autem chiliodynamiam, radice crassa, exilibus ramis
quibus in summis corymbi dependent, nigro semine,
cetero rutae similis, nascitur in montosis.

65 XXIX. Eupatoria quoque regiam auctoritatem
habet, caulis lignosi, nigricantis, hirsuti, cubitalis et
aliquando amplioris, foliis per intervalla quinquefolii aut cannabis per extremitates incisis quinque-
pertito, nigris et ipsis plumosisque, radice super-

---

[1] descriptam *Caesarii editio et Basileensis editio* : adscriptam *codd.*, *edd.*

---

[a] The old reading *descriptam*, although found in no MS.
and in no modern edition, is probably right; *adscriptam*
might easily have been written by a scribe who had just
written *adscripsit*, although the mistake may have been made
by Pliny's amanuensis. Another possible solution is that
adscriptam has displaced an entirely different word, such as
depictam or *collectam*.

[b] Polemon, King of Pontus, and Philetaerus, King of
Cappadocia.

and milk are sprinkled about. Phthiriasis too is cured by the same preparation.

XXVI. To Mithridates himself Crateuas ascribed *Mithridatia.* one plant, called mithridatia. It has two leaves, like those of the acanthus, springing from the root, with a stem between them which supports a rose-pink flower. XXVII. A second plant was attributed to him by Lenaeus, scordotis or scordion, a description [a] of it being in the hand of the King himself; it is one cubit high; its stem is quadrangular, its form is branchy, and the leaves, which are downy, are like oak leaves. It is found in Pontus on rich, moist plains, and is of a bitter taste. There is also another kind of it, with broader leaves and like wild mint, both kinds being useful for very many purposes, both by themselves and also with other ingredients to make antidotes.

XXVIII. Two kings [b] have claimed to be the *Polemonia.* discoverer of polemonia; accordingly some call it by that name and some philetaeria, while the Cappadocians call it chiliodynamia.[c] It has a thick root, thin branches with clusters hanging from the ends, and black seed. In other respects it is like rue, and it grows in mountainous districts.

XXIX. Eupatoria [d] too enjoys the prestige of a *Eupatoria.* royal discoverer. It has a ligneous stem, dark, hairy, and a cubit or sometimes more in height; the leaves, arranged at intervals, are like those of cinquefoil or hemp, and have five indentations along the edge; they too are dark and feathery. The root is

[c] " The plant with a thousand powers."
[d] Eupator was a surname of Mithridates VI, King of Pontus. See § 62 and XXXIII. § 151.

vacua. semen dysintericis in vino potum auxiliatur unice.

66 XXX. Centaurio curatus dicitur Chiron, cum Herculis excepti hospitio pertractanti arma sagitta excidisset ei in pedem, quare aliqui chironion vocant. folia sunt lata et oblonga, serrato ambitu, densi [1] ab radice caules ternum cubitorum geniculati. in his capita ceu papaverum. radix vasta, rubescens, tenera fragilisque, ad bina cubita, madida suco, amara cum quadam dulcedine. nascitur in collibus
67 pingui solo, laudatissima in Arcadia, Elide, Messenia, Pholoe, Lycaeo, et in Alpibus vero plurimisque aliis locis. in Lycia quidem et ex ea lycium faciunt. vis in vulneribus tanta est ut cohaerescere etiam carnes tradant, si coquantur simul. in usu radix, tantum duabus drachmis bibenda quibus dicetur. si febris sit, in aqua trita, ceteris in vino medetur. et ovium [2] morbis decoctae sucus.

68 XXXI. Est alterum centaurium cognomine lepton, minutis foliis, quod aliqui libadion vocant, quoniam

---

[1] densi e *Dioscoride, Mayhoff* : densa *codd. et Detlefsen.*
[2] ovium *vulg.* : obvius d T *Detlefsen* : febrium *Mayhoff, qui* VIII § 119, XXIII 48 *confert* : omnium *Barbarus* : iisdem *Hard.* : volvarum *Ianus* : obvium VRE.

---

[a] For the meaning of *curare* and its cognates see XXIV. § 74 note *c*.
[b] See XXIII. § 109 note *d*. Here a juice that served the same purpose as lycium proper, which was an astringent. See W. G. Spencer's *Celsus*, vol. II, pp. xl and xli.
[c] A very difficult sentence because of the uncertainty of the reading. Three of the chief MSS. give *obvium* and two *obvius*. If *ovium* was changed to *obvium* the further change to *obvius* would be inevitable because of *sucus*. Detlefsen retains *obvius*, but I can find no clear instance of its use with

useless, but the seed taken in wine is a sovereign remedy in cases of dysentery.

XXX. Centaury is said to have been the treat- *Centaury.* ment [a] given to Chiron when an arrow fell on his foot as he was handling the arms of Hercules, who was his guest; for which reason some call it chironion. Its leaves are broad and longish, serrated all round the edge; thickly from the root grow jointed stems three cubits high. On these are heads like those of poppies. The root is enormous and reddish, soft and easily broken, up to two cubits in size, streaming with juice and bitter with something of sweetness in it. It grows on hills with a rich soil, the most esteemed in Arcadia, Elis, Messenia, Pholoe and on mount Lycaeus; on the Alps too and in very many other places. In Lycia indeed they also make a lycium [b] from it. Its power to cure wounds is so strong that even pieces of meat, they say, coalesce if they are boiled with it. The part used is the root, the dose being for the patients for whom it will be prescribed two drachmae only. It should be pounded and taken in water if fever be present; those without fever should take it pounded but in wine. The juice of the decoction cures also the diseases of sheep.[c]

XXXI. There is a second centaury, surnamed *Another* lepton,[d] a plant with small leaves; some call it *centaury.* libadion,[e] because it grows along the side of springs.

---

remedies in the sense of " preventive," although *obviam* and *obviare* are used to make up phrases containing the idea of " preventing," the indirect objects being *infecunditati, timori, dedecori* and *vermibus.* See Serenus VII. *cura obvia morbis.*

[d] Greek λεπτός = small, fine.

[e] Greek λιβάς = spring, fount.

PLINY : NATURAL HISTORY

secundum fontes nascitur, origano simile, angustioribus et longioribus foliis, anguloso caule palmum alto, fruticante,[1] flore lychnidis, radice tenui et supervacua, suco efficax. ipsa herba autumno legitur, sucus e fronde. quidam caules concisos madefaciunt diebus XVIII atque ita exprimunt. hoc centaurium nostri fel terrae vocant propter amaritudinem summam, Galli exacum, quoniam omnia mala medicamenta potum e corpore exigat per alvum.

69   XXXII. Tertia est centauris cognomine triorchis. qui eam secat rarum est ut non vulneret sese. haec sucum sanguineum mittit. Theophrastus defendi eam inpugnarique colligentes tradit a triorche accipitrum genere, unde et nomen accepit. inperiti confundunt haec omnia et primo generi adsignant.

70   XXXIII. Clymenus a rege herba appellata est, hederae foliis, ramosa, caule inani articulis praecincto,[2] odore gravi et semine hederae, silvestribus et montuosis nascens. quibus morbis pota medeatur dicemus, sed hic indicandum est, dum medeatur, sterilitatem pota etiam viris fieri. Graeci plantagini similem esse dixerunt, caule quadrato, folliculis cum semine inter se inplexis veluti[3] polyporum cirris. et sucus autem in usu, vi summa in refrigerando.

[1] fruticante *Gelenii editio Basileensis, Detlefsen* : fruticanti *vulg.* : fruticosum *Mayhoff* : fruticum *aut* fruticantu *codd.*
[2] praecincto *coni. Mayhoff* : praecincta *codd. et edd.*
[3] veluti *vet. Dal., Sillig, Mayhoff* : velut in *codd., vulg., Ianus, Detlefsen.*

<hr>

[a] Theophrastus *H.P. IX. 8, 7.*

It is like origanum but with narrower and longer leaves; it has an angular, bushy stem a span high, a flower like that of lychnis, a slight root of no use in medicine, but with healing qualities in its juice. The plant itself is gathered in autumn, and the juice is extracted from the leaves. Some cut up and soak the stems, extracting the juice at the end of eighteen days. This centaury the Romans call the " gall of earth " on account of its extreme bitterness, while the Gauls call it exacum, because a draught of it evacuates from the body by stool all harmful drugs.

XXXII. There is a third, centauris surnamed *Triorchis.* triorchis. Those who cut it nearly always wound themselves. The juice it gives out is of the colour of blood. Theophrastus [a] relates that it is defended by a species of hawk called triorchis, which attacks those who gather it. From this too it has received its name. The uninformed confuse these characteristics [b] and assign them all to the first kind of centaury.

XXXIII. Clymenus is a plant called after the *Clymenus.* king of that name. It has leaves like those of ivy, many branches, a hollow stem girded with joints, a strong smell, and seed like that of ivy; it grows in wooded, hilly districts. I shall say later what diseases it cures if taken in drink; but at the moment I must point out that, while it cures, even men are made sterile by the draught. The Greeks have said that it is like the plantain, with a square stem and seed-bags intertwined like the tentacles of the polypus. The juice too is used in medicine, as it has very great powers of cooling.

[b] What are *haec omnia*. The sentence apparently means that some people recognised only one kind of centaury.

71 XXXIV. Gentianam invenit Gentius rex Illyriorum, ubique nascentem, in Illyrico tamen praestantissimam, folio fraxini, sed magnitudine lactucae, caule tenero pollicis crassitudine, cavo et inani, ex intervallis foliato, trium aliquando cubitorum, radice lenta, subnigra, sine odore, aquosis montibus subalpinis plurima. usus in radice et suco. radicis natura est excalfactoria, sed praegnantibus non bibenda.

72 XXXV. Invenit et Lysimachus quae ab eo nomen retinet, celebrata Erasistrato. folia habet ut salicis viridia, florem purpureum, fruticosa, ramulis erectis, odore acri. gignitur in aquosis. vis eius tanta est ut iumentis discordantibus iugo inposita asperitatem cohibeat.

73 XXXVI. Mulieres quoque hanc gloriam adfectavere, in quibus Artemisia uxor Mausoli adoptata herba quae antea parthenis vocabatur. sunt qui ab Artemide Ilithyia cognominatam putent, quoniam privatim medeatur feminarum malis. est autem absinthii modo fruticosa, maioribus foliis pinguibusque. ipsius

74 duo genera: altera [1] altior latioribus foliis, altera

---

[1] altera altior *ego* : altera *vulg.* : altior *codd.* : valdior *coni.* Mayhoff : ἡ μέν τίς ἐστιν αὐτῆς εὐερνής Dioscorides III. 113 (*Wellmann*). *Fortasse* valida.

---

[a] Pliny has apparently forgotten that he should have written *plurimam*, partly because of the influence of *radice*.

[b] The parallel passage in Dioscorides III. 113 (ἀρτεμισία) is : ἡ μέν τίς ἐστιν αὐτῆς εὐερνής, πλατύτερα ἔχουσα τὰ φύλλα καὶ τὰς ῥάβδους, ἡ δὲ λεπτοτέρα (? λεπτότερα), ἄνθη μικρά, λεπτά, βαρύοσμα. The reading in the text implies that Pliny translated εὐερνής by *altior* and that *altera* has been lost before *altior*. Mayhoff suggests *valdior* for *altior*, and perhaps Pliny

XXXIV. It was a king of the Illyrians named *Gentian.*
Gentius who discovered gentian, which, though it
grows everywhere, is most excellent when it grows
in Illyria. The leaf is like that of the ash but of the
size of a lettuce leaf; the stem is tender and of the
thickness of a thumb, hollow and empty, with leaves
at intervals, sometimes three cubits in height,
and growing from a pliant root, which is darkish and
without smell. It grows abundantly *a* on watery
slopes near the foot of the Alps. The parts used
are the root and the juice. The nature of the root is
warming, but it should not be taken in drink by
women with child.

XXXV. Lysimachus too discovered a plant, still *Lysimachia.*
named after him, the praises of which have been sung
by Erasistratus. It has green leaves like those of
the willow, a purple flower, being bushy, with
small upright branches and a pungent smell. It
grows in watery districts. Its power is so great that,
if placed on the yoke when the beasts of burden are
quarrelsome, it checks their bad temper.

XXXVI. Women too have been ambitious to *Artemisia.*
gain this distinction, among them Artemisia, the
wife of Mausolus, who gave her name to a plant
which before was called parthenis. There are some
who think that the surname is derived from Arte-
mis Ilithyia, because the plant is specific for the
troubles of women. It is also bushy, resembling
wormwood, but with larger and fleshy leaves. Of the
plant itself there are two kinds: one higher *b* and
with broader leaves, the other soft and with more

wrote *altera valida* contrasted with *altera tenera.* This is
perhaps what he ought to have written, but the steps by
which *altera valida* could become *altior* are conjectural.

PLINY : NATURAL HISTORY

tenera tenuioribus, et non nisi in maritimis nascens.
sunt qui in mediterraneis eodem nomine appellent,
simplici caule, minimis foliis, floris copiosi erumpentis
cum uva maturescit, odore non iniucundo. quam [1]
quidam botryn, alii ambrosiam vocant, talis in
Cappadocia nascitur.

75   XXXVII. Nymphaea nata traditur nympha zelo-
typia erga Herculem mortua — quare heracleon
vocant aliqui, alii rhopalon a radice clavae simili —
ideoque eos qui biberint eam XII diebus coitu
genituraque privari. laudatissima in Orchomenia
76 et Marathone. Boeoti mallon vocant et semen
edunt. nascitur in aquosis, foliis magnis in summa
aqua et aliis ex radice, flore lilio simili et, cum
defloruit, capite papaveris, levi [2] caule. secatur
autumno radix nigra, in sole siccatur. adversatur
lieni.[3] est et alia nymphaea in Thessalia, amne
Penio, radice alba, capite luteo, rosae magnitudine.

---

[1] quam *vulg.*, *Mayhoff* : quem *plerique codd.*, *Detlefsen.*
[2] levi e *Dioscoride Mayhoff* : in *codd.*, *vulg.*, *Detlefsen.*
[3] lieni *ego* : ita lieni *Mayhoff* : ea alvi malis *Ianus*, *Detlefsen* :
et alium d E *vulg.* : *ceteri codd. omittunt.*

---

[a] Dioscorides III. 114 : ἀμβροσία, ἣν ἔνιοι βότρυν, οἱ δὲ
ἀρτεμισίαν καλοῦσι . . . καταπλέκεται δὲ ἐν Καππαδοκίᾳ
στεφάνοις.

[b] Dioscorides (III. 132 Wellmann) has : ἀτονίαν τε ἐργά-
ζεται αἰδοίου πρὸς ὀλίγας ἡμέρας, εἴ τις ἐνδελεχῶς πίνοι. If
this is the kind of Greek that Pliny was translating, his
words should mean, not what I have written in the translation, but "are incapable of intercourse and procreation for
twelve days." But a passage in XXVI. § 94 shows that Pliny

slender leaves, growing only near the sea-side. There are some who in inland districts call by the same name a plant with a single stem, very small leaves, abundant blossom bursting out when the grapes are ripening, and with a not unpleasant smell. The sort that some call botrys, and others ambrosia, grows in Cappadocia.[a]

XXXVII. According to tradition nymphaea was *Nymphaea.* born of a nymph who died of jealousy about Hercules —for this reason some call it heracleon, others rhopalon because its root is like a club—and therefore those who have taken it in drink for twelve days are incapable of intercourse and procreation.[b] The most valued kind grows in the district of Orchomenos and at Marathon. The Boeotians call it mallon,[c] and eat the seed. It grows in watery places, with large leaves on the top of the water and others growing out of the root; the flowers are like the lily, and when the blossom is finished a head forms like that of the poppy; the stem is smooth.[d] In autumn is cut the root, which is dark, and is dried in the sun. It reduces the spleen. There is another kind of nymphaea growing in the River Penius [e] in Thessaly. It has a white root, and a yellow head of the size of a rose.

thought that permanent impotence followed several doses, for he adds that a single dose produces it for forty days.

[c] Hermolaus Barbarus conjectured *madon* from Theophrastus IX. 13, 1.

[d] If we read *in caule* the translation will be " a head like a poppy's forms on the stem." Hardouin adopted an old conjecture *tenui* : " the stem is slender."

[e] The Penius is a river of Colchis : the Thessalian river is the Peneus. Probably the mistake is Pliny's, but one MS. (d) reads *Peneo*.

PLINY : NATURAL HISTORY

77   XXXVIII. Invenit et patrum nostrorum aetate rex Iuba quam appellavit euphorbeam medici sui nomine. frater is fuit Musae a quo divum Augustum conservatum indicavimus. iidem fratres instituere a balineis frigida multa corpora adstringere. antea non erat mos nisi calida tantum lavari, sicut apud

78 Homerum etiam invenimus. sed Iubae volumen quoque extat de ea herba et clarum praeconium. invenit eam in monte Atlante, specie thyrsi, foliis acanthinis. vis tanta est ut [1] e longinquo sucus excipiatur incisa conto; subitur excipulis ventriculo haedino. umor lactis videtur defluens;[2] siccatus cum coiit, turis effigiem habet. qui colligunt clarius vident. contra serpentes medetur, quacumque parte percussa vertice inciso et medicamento addito ibi.

79 Gaetuli qui legunt taedio lacte adulterant, sed discernitur igni, id enim quod sincerum non est fastidiendum odorem habet. multum infra hunc sucum est qui in Gallia fit ex herba chamelaea granum cocci ferente. fractus hammoniaco similis est, etiam levi gustu os accensum diu detinens et magis ex intervallo, donec fauces quoque siccet.

[1] ut e longinquo *Mayhoff*: vel e longinquo *codd. et Detlefsen,* qui *postea* excipitur *cum* V *scribit.*
[2] defluens *Salmasius, Mayhoff*: defluere *codd.*

a Juba is probably the son of the Juba who committed suicide after Thapsus. He was brought to Rome by Caesar and carefully educated.
b See note on § 42 of this book.

XXXVIII. In the age too of our fathers King *Euphorbea.*
Juba [a] discovered [b] a plant to which he gave the
name euphorbea, calling it after his own physician
Euphorbus. This man was the brother of the Musa
we have mentioned [c] as the saviour of the life of the
late Emperor Augustus. It was these brothers who
first adopted the plan of bracing the body by copious
douches of cold water after the bath. Before this
the custom was to bathe in hot water only, as we
find that it is also in Homer. But the treatise also of
Juba on this plant is still extant, and it makes a
splendid testimonial. He discovered it on Mount
Atlas: it has the appearance of a thyrsus and the
leaves of the acanthus. Its potency is so great that
the juice, obtained by incision with a pole, is gathered
from a distance; it is caught in receivers made of
kids' stomachs placed underneath. Fluid and like
milk as it drops down, when it has dried and congealed it has all the features of frankincense. The
collectors find their vision improved. It is employed as treatment for snake-bite. In whatever
part of the body the bite may be, an incision is made
in the top of the skull and the medicament inserted there. The Gaetulians who gather the juice
adulterate it out of weary disgust by adding milk,
but fire is a test of genuineness, for that which is
adulterated emits a nauseating smell. Far inferior
to the Atlas juice is that which in Gaul comes from
the ground-olive, which bears a red berry like kermes.
Broken it resembles hammoniacum, and even a
slight taste leaves for a long time a burning sensation
in the mouth; after a while this increases until it
dries up even the throat.

[c] See XIX. § 128.

80 XXXIX. Celebravit et Themiso medicus vulgarem herbam plantaginem tamquam inventor volumine de ea edito. duo eius genera: minor angustioribus foliis et nigrioribus, linguae pecorum similis, caule anguloso in terram inclinato, in pratis nascens. altera maior, foliis laterum modo inclusa, quae quia septena sunt, quidam eam heptapleuron vocavere. huius et caulis cubitalis est; quae[1] in umidis nascitur multo efficacior. mira vis in siccando densandoque corpore, cauterii vicem optinens. nulla res aeque sistit fluctiones quas Graeci rheumatismos vocant.

81 XL. Iungitur huic buglossos boum linguae similis, cui praecipuum quod in vinum deiecta animi voluptates auget, et vocatur euphrosynum.

XLI. Iungitur et cynoglossos caninam linguam imitata, topiariis operibus gratissima. aiunt quae tres thyrsos seminis mittat eius radicem potam ex aqua ad tertianas prodesse, quae quattuor ad quartanas. est et alia similis ei quae fert lappas minutas. eius radix pota ex aqua ranis et serpentibus adversatur.

82 XLII. Est et buphthalmus similis boum oculis, folio feniculi, circa oppida nascens, fruticosa, ...[2]

[1] est; quae in *ego* : est et uva api. in *Detlefsen* : est. et ipsa in *Mayhoff, qui lacunam* et radices crassitudine digitali *esse coniecit* : est et vapi in *codd. Pro* vapi *coni.* napi *Ianus* (napi similis *vulg.*).

[2] *Post* fruticosa *lacunam esse puto* : *post* caulibus *Mayhoff.*

[a] As Mayhoff says, this sentence cannot be restored with any certainty. The reading of the MSS., *vapi*, is a *vox nihili*. Of the many emendations proposed that of Detlefsen is the nearest to it, and next comes that of Jan. Mayhoff's text is but a stop-gap, and the same must be said of my *quae*, which is fairly near to the MSS., but is most unlikely to have been changed by a scribe to *et vapi*. Pliny took *heptapleuron* to mean " with seven sides," but the greater plantain has seven *ribs* on the leaf. See also Mayhoff's Appendix.

XXXIX. The physician Themiso too has spread *The* the fame of a common plant, the plantain, having *plantain.* published a treatise about it as though he were the discoverer. There are two kinds of it: the smaller, with narrower and darker leaves, resembles the tongue of a sheep; the stem is angular and bends downward. It grows in meadows. The other kind is larger and enclosed with leaves as it were with sides. Since these leaves are seven in number the plant is sometimes called heptapleuron. The stem too of this is a cubit high; when *[a]* it grows on wet soils it is much more efficacious. It has a wonderful power to dry and brace the body, having a cauterizing property. There is nothing that checks so well the fluxes called by the Greeks rheumatismoi, that is, catarrhs.

XL. Akin to the plantain is buglossos, which is *Buglossos.* like the tongue of an ox. The most conspicuous quality of this is that thrown into wine it increases the exhilarating effect, and so it is also called euphrosynum, the plant that cheers.

XLI. Akin too is cynoglossos, which is like a dog's *Cynoglossos.* tongue, and a most attractive addition to ornamental gardens. It is said that the root of the kind with three seed-bearing stems, if taken in water, is good for tertians, and that with four for quartans. There is also another plant like this which bears tiny burs. Its root taken in water neutralizes the poison of frogs *[b]* and snakes.

XLII. Another plant is buphthalmus, which is like *Buphthal-* the eyes of oxen, having leaves like those of fennel, *mus.* a bushy plant growing around towns, with *[c]* . . .

[b] *Ranae* includes toads.
[c] Mayhoff suggests *mollibus*, " tender ", as the missing word.

caulibus qui et manduntur decocti. quidam calchan[1]
vocant. haec cum cera steatomata discutit.

XLIII. Invenere herbas et universae gentes,
Scythia primam eam quae scythice vocatur, circa
Maeotim nascens, praedulcem alias utilissimamque
ad ea quae asthmata vocant. magna et ea com-
mendatio, quod in ore eam habentes sitim famem-
que non sentiunt.

83   XLIV. Idem praestat apud eosdem hippace, dis-
tincta, quod in equis quoque eundem effectum
habeat, traduntque his duabus herbis Scythas etiam
in duodenos dies durare in fame sitique.

XLV. Ischaemonem Thracia invenit, qua ferunt
sanguinem sisti non aperta modo vena sed etiam
praecisa. serpit in[2] terra milio similis, foliis asperis
et lanuginosis. farcita[3] in nares quae in Italia
nascitur, et eadem adalligata, sanguinem[4] sistit.

84   XLVI. Vettones in Hispania eam quae vettonica
dicitur in Gallia, in Italia autem serratula, a Graecis
cestros aut psychrotrophon, ante cunctas laudatissima. exit anguloso caule cubitorum duum e radice
spargens folia fere lapathi, serrata, semine purpureo.
folia siccantur in farinam plurimos ad usus. fit
vinum ex ea et acetum stomacho et claritati ocu-

____

[1] calchan *multi codd., Detlefsen*: chalcan E. *Mayhoff*: cach-
lam *Hermolaus Barbarus ex Dioscoride.*

[2] in *Mayhoff*: e *aut* et *codd.*

[3] farcita (e parcita) *ego*: farcitur E: parcitum R: par-
citam V[1]: parcituram V[2].

[4] *Ante* eadem *in codd.* sanguinem; *ego transposui. Inter*
et *et* sanguinem *supplet* ciet *Mayhoff. Distinxi ego.*

____

[a] The editors suggest that Pliny has wrongly thought that
ἱππάκη, mare's-milk cheese, was a plant. The cheese is
mentioned by Hippocrates, *Airs, Waters, Places,* ch. XVIII,
but there may have been a plant of the same name.

stems that are boiled and eaten. Some call it calchas.
This plant with wax added disperses fatty tumours.

XLIII. Whole tribes too have discovered plants. *Scythice.*
Scythia first found out about the one called scythice,
which grows round Lake Maeotis. One of its
qualities is great sweetness, and it is very beneficial
for the complaint called asthma. Another great
merit of it is the freedom from hunger and thirst
enjoyed by those who keep it in their mouths.

XLIV. The same people find the same property in
their hippace,[a] which has the unique quality of
affecting horses in the same way. It is said that on
these two plants the Scythians can fast from food and
drink even for as long as twelve days at a time.

XLV. Thrace found out about ischaemon, which is *Ischaemon.*
said to stanch bleeding when a vein has not merely been
cut but even severed. It creeps along the ground
as does millet; the leaves are rough and downy.
The kind that grows in Italy, stuffed into the nostrils,
and also when used as an amulet, stanches bleeding.[b]

XLVI. The Vettones in Spain discovered the plant *Vettonica.*
called vettonica in Gaul, serratula[c] in Italy, and
cestros or psychrotrophon by the Greeks, a plant
more highly valued than any other. It springs up
with an angular stem of two cubits, spreading out
from the root leaves rather like those of lapathum, serrated, and with a purple fruiting-head. Its leaves are
dried into a powder and used for very many purposes.
From it[d] are made a wine and a vinegar, good for the

[b] Mayhoff's reading means : " stuffed into the nostrils it
causes bleeding; used as an amulet it stanches it." *Farcitus*
is a very late form, but Pliny may have used it.

[c] " The plant with leaves like a saw."

[d] *Ea* may refer to the plant or to the powder made from
the leaves, probably to the latter.

lorum, tantumque gloriae habet ut domus in qua sata
sit tuta existimetur a periculis [1] omnibus.

85   XLVII. In eadem Hispania inventa est cantabrica
per divi Augusti tempora a Cantabris reperta.
nascitur ubique caule iunceo pedali, in quo sunt
flosculi oblongi veluti calathi, in his semen perquam
minutum. nec alias defuere Hispaniae herbis ex-
quirendis, ut in quibus etiamnunc hodie in more sit
laetiore convictu potionem e centum herbis mulso
additis credere saluberrimam suavissimamque. nec
quisquam genera earum iam novit aut multitudinem,
numerus tamen constat in nomine.

86   XLVIII. Nostra aetas meminit herbam in Marsis
repertam. nascitur et in Aequicolis circa vicum
Nervesiae, vocatur consiligo. prodest, ut demon-
strabimus suo loco, deploratis in phthisi.

87   XLIX. Invenit nuper et Servilius Democrates e
primis medentium quam appellavit hiberida, quamquam ficto nomini inventione [2] eius adsignata carmine.
nascitur maxime circa vetera monumenta parietinas-
que et inculta itinerum. floret semper, folio nasturtii,
caule cubitali, semine vix ut aspici possit. radici
odor nasturtii. usus aestate efficacior et recenti

---

[1] periculis V[2] *Detlefsen* : piaculis *Mayhoff* : piculis V[1].
[2] inventione *Salmasius, Sillig* : inventioni *codd.* : *aliae
lectiones* nomine (*coni.* homini *Mayhoff*) *et* assignato.

---

[a] Mayhoff's reading (*piaculis*) is attractive because difficult,
and is different from V[1] by one letter only. It would mean
" crime " or " sin ".

[b] The *calathus* was trumpet-shaped, and so *oblongus* cannot
here mean " oblong ".

[c] I.e., the potion is called the " hundred-plant drink ".

[d] See XXVI. § 38.

[e] An obscurely expressed sentence, which led some scribes

stomach and the eyesight. So great is its fame that
the home in which it has been planted is considered
to be safe from all dangers.[a]

XLVII. In Spain too was discovered cantabrica, *Cantabrica.*
found by the Cantabri in the period of the late
Emperor Augustus. It grows everywhere, having
a rush-like stem a foot in length, on which are small,
longish [b] flowers, shaped like a work-basket, in
which are very tiny seeds. Nor have the Spains
been backward in other search after plants; for
example, even now today it is the custom at the more
festive gatherings, to mix a drink, the " hundred-
plant potion ", by adding to honey wine a hundred
plants, in the belief that such is both very healthful
and very pleasant. Nobody, however, now knows
the kinds of plants used and their exact number,
although a definite number is given in the name.[c]

XLVIII. Our own generation remembers the *Consiligo.*
discovery of a plant among the Marsi. It grows also
among the Aequicoli around the village of Nervesia,
and is called consiligo. It is beneficial, as we shall
point out in its own place,[d] in desperate cases of
consumption.

XLIX. Servilius Democrates also, one of our fore- *Hiberis.*
most physicians, recently discovered the value of
what he called hiberis, although in the verses he
wrote on its discovery he assigned this to an imaginary
person.[e] It grows chiefly near old monuments, ruins,
and the waste land beside highways. It is an evergreen, with leaves like cress, a stem a cubit high, and
with seed [f] that can scarcely be seen. The root has the
smell of cress. It is used more efficaciously in sum-

to think that the meaning is: " dedicating a poem to its discovery under a fictitious name ". [f] Or " fruiting-head".

88 tantum. tunditur difficulter. coxendicibus et articulis omnibus cum axungia modica utilissima, viris
plurimum quaternis horis, feminis minus dimidio
adalligata, ut deinde in balineis descendatur in cali-
dam et postea oleo ac vino perunguatur corpus, die-
busque vicenis interpositis idem fiat, si qua ad-
monitio doloris supersit. hoc modo rheumatismos
omnes sanat occultos. inponitur non in ipsa inflam-
matione, sed inminuta.

89 L. Animalia quoque invenere herbas, in primisque
chelidoniam. hac enim hirundines oculis [1] pullorum
in nido ⟨medentur⟩ restituuntque [2] visum, ut quidam
volunt, etiam erutis oculis. genera eius duo : maior
fruticosa, folio pastinacae erraticae ampliore, ipsa
altitudine duum cubitorum, colos albicans, flos luteus.
minori folia hederae rotundiora, minus candida.

90 sucus croci mordax, semen papaveris. florent ad-
ventu hirundinum, discessu marcescunt.[3] sucus
florentibus exprimitur, et in aereo vase cum melle
Attico leniter cinere ferventi decoquitur, singulari
remedio contra caligines oculorum. utuntur et per
se suco et in collyriis quae chelidonia appellantur
ab ea.

[1] oculis *Mayhoff* : ocules V[2] : oculos *Detlefsen*.

[2] restituuntque E, *Mayhoff*, *qui lacunam post* nido *indicat
et* medentur *coni. Ego supplementum addo Dioscoridem
secutus* : restituunt dantque V[2], *Detlefsen*. *Non* medentur
sed prosunt *supplet Brakman*.

[3] marcescunt R E *vulg.*, *Mayhoff* : inarescunt *Detlefsen* :
arescunt d T.

---

[a] I have adopted the suggestion of Mayhoff, which he does
not print in his text, because of Dioscorides II 180 : τινὲς δὲ
προσιστόρησαν ὅτι, ἐάν τις τυφλωθῇ τῶν τῆς χελιδόνος νεοσσῶν,
αἱ μητέρες προσφέρουσαι τὴν πόαν ἰῶνται τὴν πήρωσιν αὐτοῦ.
Pliny took πήρωσιν to mean that the eyes were actually gouged

mer, and only when freshly gathered will it serve.
There is difficulty in pounding it. For sciatica and all
complaints of the joints it is, with a little axle-grease
added, very beneficial. The longest application is
four hours for men and half as long for women; then
the patient must go down to the hot water of the
baths, and afterwards must be rubbed all over the
body with wine and oil. The treatment should be
repeated at intervals of twenty days, if any hint of
pain persists. This treatment cures all hidden fluxes.
The application is not made when inflammation is
acute, but only when it has gone down.

L. Animals too have discovered plants, and among *Chelidonia.*
the chief is the chelidonia. For by means of it
swallows cure the eyes of the chicks in the nest, and
restore the sight, as some hold, even when the eyes
have been torn out.[a] There are two kinds of it.
The larger kind is bushy, and its leaf is like that of
the wild carrot, but bigger, the plant itself being
two cubits high, the colour light and the blossom
yellow. The smaller has leaves like those of ivy,
rounder and less pale.[b] The juice is like saffron
juice and pungent; the seed resembles that of the
poppy. Both plants blossom when the swallow
arrives and wither when he departs. The juice is
extracted while the plants are flowering, and is gently
boiled down with Attic honey in a copper vessel over
hot ashes, being a sovereign remedy for dimness of
vision. The juice is used both by itself and in the
eye-salves called chelidonia after the plant.

out, whereas it merely means " blindness ", as can be seen
from τυφλωθῇ. The reading *ocules* of V² probably arose from
the ending of *hirundines,* the word immediately before it.
    [b] I.e., than the larger plant.

91   LI. Invenerunt et canes qua fastidium vincunt eamque in nostro conspectu mandunt, sed ita ut numquam intellegatur quae sit. etenim depasta cernitur. notata est haec animalis eius malignitas in alia herba maior. percussus enim a serpente mederi sibi quadam dicitur, sed illam homine spectante non decerpit.

92   LII. Simplicius cervae monstravere elaphoboscon, de qua diximus, item seselin [1] a partu et tamnum,[2] (LIII.) ostendere, ut indicavimus, et [3] dictamnum [4] vulneratae pastu statim telis decidentibus. non est alibi quam in Creta, ramis praetenue, puleio simile, fervens et acre gustu. foliis tantum utuntur, flos nullus aut semen aut caulis, radix tenuis ac supervacua. et in Creta autem non spatiosa nascitur, mire-

93 que capris expetitur. pro eo est et pseudodictamnum multis in terris nascens, folio simile, ramulis minoribus, a quibusdam chondris vocatum. minoris

---

[1] seselin *coni. Mayhoff* : seseli enixae *Hermolaus Barbarus* : helxinen *Mayhoff in textu et Detlefsen* : helxine *aut* helsine *codd.*

[2] et tamnum *coni. Mayhoff VIII.* § 112 *collato* : dictamnum *Hermolaus Barbarus* : dictam *Mayhoff in textu, Detlefsen, codd.*

[3] et *ego addidi.*

[4] dictamnum *del. Hermolaus Barbarus.*

---

[a] See XXII. § 79.

[b] VIII. § 112.

[c] VIII. § 97. The reading of the MSS. is very corrupt in this sentence, and the means of an approximate restoration are to be found in the following passages : XXII. § 41 : unde et helxinen dictam volunt; VIII. § 112 : a partu duas, quae tamnus et seselis appellantur, pastae redeunt ad fetum ; VIII. § 97 : dictamnum herbam extrahendis sagittis cervi monstra-

LI. Dogs too have found a plant by which they *Plants found* cure loss of appetite, and eat it in our sight, but in *by dogs.* such a way that it can never be identified, for it is seen only when chewed up. This animal shows yet greater spitefulness in its secrecy about another plant; for there is one by which it is said to cure itself when bitten by a snake, but it does not crop it when a human being is looking on.

LII. With greater frankness deer have shown us *Plants found* elaphoboscon, about which we have written,[a] and *by deer.* after yeaning have made known seselis and the black bryony, as we have pointed out [b]; (LIII.) dittany also by feeding on it when wounded, the weapons at once falling out.[c] The latter grows nowhere except in Crete, with branches very slender; it resembles pennyroyal and is burning and harsh to the taste. Only the leaves are employed; it has no flower, no seed and no stem; its root is slender and without medicinal value. Even in Crete it does not grow widely, and the goats are wonderfully eager to hunt it out. A substitute for it is false dittany, which grows in many lands, like true dittany in leaf but with smaller branches, and called by some chondris.

vere percussi eo telo pastuque herbae eius eiecto. A scribe with an aural memory of XXII. § 41 may have had it suggested to him by the similarity of *dictam* to *et tamnum* with *dictamnum* following a little later. *Seselin* is sufficiently like *helxinen* to the eye to set in motion latent aural memory, and the other change, the omission of a connecting particle before *dictamnum*, would follow naturally. Hermolaus Barbarus in 1492 saw that some restoration of the text was necessary, and would delete *dictamnum* before *vulneratae* and emend *dictam* to *dictamnum*. Whatever the details of the correct emendation may be, the corruption took place very early, before the archetype of our existing MSS. was written, as none of them has any sign that *helxine(n)* and *dictam* are wrong.

effectus statim intellegitur. dictamnum enim minima potione accendit os. qui legere eas in ferula aut
harundine condunt praeligantque ne potentia evanes-
cat. sunt qui dicant utramque nasci multifariam,
sed deteriores in agris pinguibus, veram quidem dic-
94 tamnum [1] non nisi in asperis. est et tertium genus
dictamnum vocatum, sed neque facie neque effectu
simile, folio sisymbri, ramis maioribus, praecedente
persuasione illa quicquid in Creta nascatur infinito
praestare ceteris eiusdem generis alibi genitis,
proxime quod in Parnaso. alioqui herbiferum esse
et Pelium montem in Thessalia et Telethrium in
Euboea et totam Arcadiam ac Laconicam tradunt,
Arcades quidem non medicaminibus uti sed lacte
circa ver, quoniam tum maxime sucis herbae turgeant
medicenturque ubera pascuis. bibunt autem vacci-
num, quoniam boves omnivori fere sunt in herbis.
potentia earum per quadripedes etiamnum duobus
claris exemplis manifesta fit. circa Abderam et
limitem qui Diomedis vocatur equi pasti inflam-
mantur rabie, circa Potnias vero et asini.
95 LIV. Inter nobilissimas aristolochiae nomen dedisse
gravidae videntur, quoniam esset ἀρίστη λεχούσαις.
nostri malum terrae vocant et quattuor genera eius

---

[1] dictamnum *glossema esse putat Mayhoff.*

---

[a] Or, if *etiamnum* goes with *duobus*, " by two further
examples."

It is recognised at once, as its properties are less potent, for the smallest quantity of true dittany, taken in drink, burns the mouth. Those who gather them store them in a piece of fennel-giant or reed, which they tie up at the ends, to prevent their losing efficacy. There are some who say that both plants grow in many places, but that while the inferior kinds are found on rich soils, true dittany is only seen on rough ground. There is also a third plant called dittany, unlike the others in appearance and properties; the leaves are those of sisymbrium and the branches are larger, but there is the established conviction that whatever simple grows in Crete is infinitely superior to any of the same kind to be found elsewhere, and that the next best herbs are those to be found on Mount Parnassus. Report says that simples grow besides on Mount Pelion in Thessaly, on Mount Telethrius in Euboea, and throughout Arcadia and Laconia, and that the Arcadians indeed use, not medicines, but milk in the spring season, because it is at this time chiefly that herbs are swollen with juices which, when the beasts graze, medicate their udders. But the milk they drink is cow's milk, since kine will feed on almost any kind of plant. The potency of plants becomes clear from two striking examples of their action even[a] on quadrupeds: horses that have grazed around Abdera and what is called " the bounds of Diomedes " go raving mad, as do also the asses that graze around Potniae.

LIV. Among the most celebrated plants aristo- *Aristolochia.* lochia received its name, as is clear, from women with child, because they considered it to be ἀρίστη λεχούσαις, that is, " excellent for women in child-bed." Latin writers call it " earth apple," dis-

PLINY : NATURAL HISTORY

servant: unum tuberibus radicis rotundis, foliis
inter malvam et hederam, nigrioribus mollioribusque,
alterum masculae, radice longa, quattuor digitorum
longitudine, baculi crassitudine, tertium longissimae,
tenuitate vitis novellae, cuius sit praecipua vis, quae
96 et clematitis¹ vocatur, ab aliis cretica. omnes
colore buxeo, caulibus parvis, flore purpureo. ferunt
baculas parvas ut cappari. valent radice tantum.
est et quae plistolochia vocatur, quarti generis,
tenuior quam proxime dicta, densis radicis capillamentis, iunci plenioris crassitudine. hanc quidam
97 polyrrhizon cognominant. odor omnium medicatus,
sed oblongae radici tenuiorique gratior, carnosi enim
est corticis, unguentis quoque nardinis conveniens.
nascuntur pinguibus locis et campestribus. effodere
eas messibus tempestivum, desquamato² terreno servantur. maxime tamen laudatur Pontica et in quocumque genere ponderosissima quaeque, medicinis
aptior rotunda, contra serpentes oblonga, in summa

¹ clematitis (ex Dioscoride) Hard., vulg., Mayhoff : clematis
codd. et Detlefsen.
² desquamato Detlefsen : in desquamato Mayhoff : ita
desquamato vulg. : ita e squama plerique codd.

ᵃ Masculae and longissimae agree with aristolochiae understood. Perhaps radicis has fallen out before longissimae.
ᵇ Or " oblong " (so Littré), but this rendering seems unsuitable in view of § 95. Dioscorides (III 4. § 3) has : ἥτις
καὶ κληματῖτις καλεῖται - - - ἔχουσα - - - - - - ῥίζας μακροτάτας,
λεπτάς, φλοιὸν ἐχούσας παχὺν καὶ ἀρωματίζοντα, ἰδίως
χρησιμευούσας μυρεψαῖς εἰς τὰς τῶν μύρων στύψεις. So Pliny's
oblongae radici tenuiorique should refer to clematitis, but it is

tinguishing four kinds of it: one with round tubers
on the root, and with leaves partly like those of the
mallow and partly like those of ivy, but darker and
softer: the second is the male plant,[a] with a long root
of four fingers' length, thick as a walking-stick; the
third is very long and as slender as a young vine,
with especially strong properties, and is called by
some clematitis and by other cretica. All kinds of
this plant are of the colour of boxwood, and have
small stems and purple blossom. They bear small
berries like caper berries. Only the root has medicinal value. There is also a fourth kind, called
plistolochia, more slender than the one last mentioned,
with dense, hair-like masses for a root, and of the
thickness of a stoutish rush, which some surname
polyrrhizos. All kinds have a drug-like smell, but
that of the rather long [b] and slender root is more
agreeable; its fleshy outer skin in fact is even
suitable for nard ointments. These plants grow
on plains with a rich soil. The time to dig them up
is at harvest; the earth is scraped off them before
they are stored away.[c] The most valued root, however, comes from Pontus, and in every case the
heaviest specimens are preferred; for medicines the
round is more suitable, for snake bites the longer

hard to reconcile the phrase just quoted with Pliny's description of *clematitis* in § 95.
  [c] Mayhoff's emendation would mean: " they are stored
away in earth scraped off them ". He says in a note on
XIX. § 115 (vol. III p. 495) that *in* is generally used with
servare in this sense. If this restoration is correct, the im-
plication is that the roots keep better in the earth in which
they are grown. On the whole I prefer to follow Detlefsen.
To clean the roots might help to keep pure the *odor medicatus.*

tamen gloria est, si ¹ modo a conceptu admota vulvis
98 in carne bubula mares figurat, ut traditur. piscatores
Campaniae radicem eam quae rotunda est venenum
terrae vocant, coramque nobis contusam mixta calce
in mare sparsere. advolant pisces cupiditate mira
statimque exanimati fluitant. quae polyrrhizos
cognominatur convulsis, contusis, ex alto praecipitatis radice pota ex aqua utilissima esse traditur,
semine pleuriticis et nervis, confirmare, excalfacere,
eadem satyrion esse.
99 LV. Verum et effectus ususque dicendi sunt ordien-
dumque a malorum omnium pessimo est, serpentium
ictu. medentur ergo britannica herba, panacis
omnium generum radix e vino, chironii et flos et
semen potum inlitumve ex vino et oleo, privatim quae
cunila bubula appellatur, polemonia vel philetaeris
radicis drachmis quattuor in mero, teucria, sideritis,
100 scordotis ex vino, privatim ad angues, pota et inlita
sive suco sive folio sive decocto, centaurii maioris
radix drachma in vini albi cyathis tribus, gentiana
praecipue adversus angues duabus drachmis cum

¹ si *Detlefsen* : ea (*vel* haec) si *Mayhoff* : et si *fere omnes
codd.* (*num* et *ex* est *ortum* ?).

ᵃ See note *b* on p. 206, with the μακροτάτας of Dioscorides.
ᵇ The emendation of Mayhoff makes it a little clearer that
the conditional clause applies to the *radix oblonga* and not to
the *rotunda*.
ᶜ A contradiction of *valent radice tantum* (§ 96). Throughout this chapter Pliny seems to be at his worst. It is a
mystery why he uses *oblonga* twice, when he must refer to the
plant called *longissima*, whereas in Dioscorides the corresponding Greek word applies to the root only, as does *oblonga*
in § 97.

kind,[a] but its greatest fame is that, if [b] only it is applied to the uterus in beef after conception, it forms according to report male offspring. The fishermen of Campania call the root that is round " poison of the earth ", and I have seen them scatter it over the sea, crushed and mixed with lime. The fish rush to it with wonderful greed, forthwith die, and float on the surface. The kind called polyrrhizos is reported to be very beneficial for sprains, bruises, and falls from a height, if the root is taken in water, for pleurisy and the sinews if the seed [c] is used, and to be tonic and warming ; it is reported to be the same plant as satyrion.

LV. But we must mention also the properties and uses of these plants, and begin with snake bite, the worst ill of all. Cures then are : the plant britannica ; the root of all kinds of panaces taken in wine ; both flower and seed of chironium taken in drink or applied in wine and oil ; what is called ox cunila, which is specific ; polemonia or philetaeris, the dose being four drachmae of the root in neat wine ; teucria, sideritis, and scordotis in wine, specific remedies for snake [d] wounds, the juice or leaves or a decoction being taken in drink [e] or [f] applied ; the root of the greater centaury in doses of one drachma in three cyathi of white wine ; gentian, particularly good, whether fresh or dried, for snake bites in doses of two drachmae

Cures of snake bite.

---

[a] The Latin of Pliny certainly seems to imply that he distinguished *angues* from other *serpentes,* but the only discoverable difference between the two words is that the former has a rather more poetic flavour. See too XXIX. § 71.

[e] *Pota* refers to *ex vino* above.

[f] Perhaps " and ". In such a collocation of words *et* is often ambiguous.

209

pipere et ruta, vini cyathis sex, sive viridis sive sicca.
101 et lysimachiae odorem fugiunt. datur ex vino percussis chelidonia, morsibus inponitur vettonica praecipue, cui vis tanta perhibetur ut inclusae circulo eius
serpentes ipsae sese interimant flagellando. datur ad
ictus semen eius denarii pondere cum tribus cyathis
vini vel farina drachmis tribus sextario [1] aquae—
farina et inponitur [2]—cantabrica, dictamnum, aristolochia radicis drachma in vini hemina, sed saepius
bibenda. prodest et inlita ex aceto, similiter
plistolochia, quin omnino suspensa supra focum fugat
102 e domibus serpentes.   LVI. argemonia quoque radice
eius [3] denarii pondere in vini cyathis tribus pota.
plura de ea convenit dici ceterisque, quando [4] primum
nominabuntur, in eo autem genere medendi primum
nominari quamque in quo maxime valebit. folia
habet qualia anemone, divisa apii modo, caput in
cauliculo papaveris silvestris, item [5] radicem, sucum
croci colore acrem et acutum. nascitur in arvis. apud
nos tria genera eius faciunt et id demum probant
cuius radix tus redoleat.

---

[1] sextario] ex *vel* in *anteponere velit Mayhoff*.
[2] inponitur *Detlefsen et Mayhoff* : reponitur *Ianus*, § 115
coll. : ponitur *codd. De hac sententia " locus nondum sanatus "
scribit Mayhoff*.
[3] radice eius *codd.* radicis *Mayhoff*.
[4] quando *Detlefsen* : qua *Mayhoff* : quo *aut* qm *aut* quoniam
codd.
[5] item *Detlefsen, Mayhoff, codd. Mayhoff coni. (ex Dioscoride)* teretem.

taken with pepper and rue in six cyathi of wine.
The smell too of lysimachia keeps snakes away.
Those who have been bitten are given chelidonia in
wine, and to the bites is applied in particular betony,
the power of which is said to be so great that snakes
enclosed in a circle of it lash themselves to death.
For the bites is given its seed, the dose being a
denarius with three cyathi of wine, or else it is
ground and three drachmae of the powder are given
in a sextarius of water; the powder is also applied
locally. Cantabrica too is used, and dittany, and
aristolochia, a drachma of the root in a hemina of
wine, but the dose must be repeated several times.
Aristolochia in vinegar also makes a useful application, and so does plistolochia, in fact the mere hanging
of this above the hearth makes all snakes hurry
from the house. LVI. Argemonia too is good, a
denarius of its root being taken in three cyathi of
wine.   It is proper for more details to be given about
this plant, and about the others, when the first
mention is made of them, and the first mention of
each should be when I deal with that medical treatment where its use will prove most effective.   It has
leaves like those of the anemone, divided like those
of celery, a head like that of the wild poppy upon a
small stalk, the root also *a* being like that of this
poppy, and saffron-coloured juice that is pungent and
sharp.   It grows in cultivated fields.   We Romans
distinguish three kinds of it, and the one esteemed
is that the root of which smells like frankincense.

---

a There is much to be said for Mayhoff's conjecture
teretem; see Dioscorides II. 176 ῥιζία λεπτὰ καὶ πλείω.   But
item just makes sense, and there is no variation in the
MSS.

103   LVII. Agaricum ut fungus nascitur arboribus
circa Bosporum colore candido.   dantur oboli quattuor
contriti cum binis cyathis aceti mulsi.   id quod in
Gallia [1] nascitur infirmius habetur, praeterea mas
spissior amariorque [2]—hic et capitis dolores facit—
femina solutior, initio gustus dulcis mox in amaritudinem transit.

104   LVIII. Echios utriusque generis [3] puleio similis,
foliis coronat [4]; datur drachmis duabus ex vini cyathis
quattuor.[5]   item altera, quae lanugine distinguitur
spinosa, cui et capitula viperae similia sunt, haec
ex vino et aceto.   quidam echion personatam vocant
cuius folio nullum est latius, grandes lappas ferentem.
huius radicem decoctam ex aceto dant potui.   hyos-

    [1] Gallia *Detlefsen, Mayhoff, codd.*: Galatia *ex Dioscoride
Sillig.*
    [2] spissior amariorque *Detlefsen, Mayhoff, d.*: spissiora
maiorque V : maiorque spissiorque E.
    [3] *Post* generis *lacunam statuit Ianus, nescio an recte.*
    [4] coronat; datur *coni. Mayhoff, qui XXI.* 52, 54 *confert*:
coronaria *Detlefsen* : coronata (corinata V) *codd.*
    [5] quattuor *codd. et editores recentes* : quattuor datur *vulg.*

    [a] Dioscorides has Galatia, the Greek for Gaul.
    [b] *Praeterea* is unexpected, and no emendation suggests
itself.   Dioscorides does not help, because he and Pliny
differ here so widely.   The *propterea* of V seems a mere
error.
    [c] Dioscorides says this of both " sexes " : γεύσει δὲ
ἀμφότερα ὅμοια, κατ' ἀρχὰς μὲν γλυκάζοντα, εἶτα ἐξ ἀναδόσεως
ἔμπικρα (III. 1).   The two authorities might be made to agree
by putting a full stop at *solutior,* but then *amarior* conflicts
with *dulcis.*   This difficulty might be avoided by reading
maiorque spissiorque with E, but these words seem a scribe's
correction of *spissiora maiorque* (V.), which however is surely
a wrong division of *spissior amariorque,* the reading in the
text.

LVII. An agaric grows as a white fungus on trees *Agaric.*
around the Bosporus. A dose is four oboli crushed
and two cyathi of oxymel. The kind that grows in
Gaul [a] is considered of inferior strength; further,[b]
the male is firmer and more bitter—this kind
causes headaches—but the female is softer, and at
first its taste is sweet, but afterwards turns bitter.[c]

LVIII. Echios of either kind is like pennyroyal [d]; *Echios.*
its foliage is used for chaplets. The dose is two
drachmae in four cyathi of wine; likewise [e] with the
second kind, which is marked by a prickly down, and
also has little heads like a viper's; this is taken in
wine and vinegar. Some give the name echios to
personata ("masked plant") whose leaf is broader
than that of any kind,[f] and which bears large burs.
A decoction of the root of this is given with vinegar as a

---

[d] The MSS. give no variant, and only Jan among the
editors thinks that something is wrong, or missing, here.
So I have done my best to make sense of Mayhoff's text, but
I suspect, with Jan, that there is a lacuna after *generis*. The
missing words would be something giving the sense of:
contra serpentes (*aspidas?*) *utilis. altera,* "is good for the
poison of snakes (asps?). The first kind is like etc." Perhaps
a sleepy scribe was led astray by the like endings of *utilis*
and *similis.* An *altera* to correspond to the *item altera* of the
next sentence is required, and some versions, including
Littré's, assume its presence.

[e] The translators, so far as I have seen, omit *item*. I
think that it refers to the dosage, and means that the dose
of the second kind is two drachmae of the herb to four cyathi
of liquid; only the latter, as we see from the end of the sentence,
is wine and vinegar, not wine only.

[f] Apparently "of any other kind of echios". The Latin,
however, in any other context, would surely mean, "than any
other leaf (of any plant)," which is absurd. Perhaps there is
another lacuna here. The text of this whole chapter is odd,
and the last sentence, about henbane, seems out of place.

cyamum contusum cum foliis ex vino datur peculiariter contra aspidas.

105   LIX. Nulla tamen Romanae nobilitatis plus habet
quam hiera botane.   aliqui aristereon, nostri verbenacam vocant.   haec est quam legatos ferre ad hostes
indicavimus.   hac Iovis   mensa   verritur,   domus
purgantur lustranturque.   genera eius duo sunt:
foliosa quam feminam putant, mas rarioribus foliis.

106 ramuli utriusque plures, tenues, cubitales, angulosi,
folia minora quam quercus angustioraque, divisuris
maioribus, flos glaucus, radix longa, tenuis.   nascitur
ubique in planis aquosis.   quidam non distinguunt et
unum omnino genus faciunt, quoniam utraque eosdem
effectus habeat.   utraque sortiuntur Galli et prae-
cinunt responsa, sed Magi utique circa hanc in-
saniunt; hac perunctos inpetrare quae velint, febres
abigere, amicitias conciliare nullique non morbo

107 mederi.   colligi debere circa canis ortum ita ne
luna aut sol conspiciat, favis ante et melle terrae ad
piamentum datis, circumscriptam ferro effodi sinistra
manu et in sublime tolli, siccari in umbra separatim
folia, caulem, radicem.   aiunt, si aqua spargatur

---

^a See XXII. § 5.
^b Namely on the feasts of Jupiter.
^c Bostock and Riley translate as though *hanc* were under-
stood before *febres*, but surely there is no *insania* in saying

draught. Henbane crushed with the leaves on is given in wine, especially for the poison of asps.

LIX. No plant however is so renowned among the *Hiera botane.* Romans as hiera botane (" sacred plant "). Some call it asistereon, and Latin writers verbenaca. This is the plant which I mentioned as carried to the enemy by envoys.[a] With this the table of Jupiter is swept,[b] and homes are cleansed and purified. There are two kinds of it; one has many leaves and is thought to be female, the other, the male, has fewer leaves. Each kind has several sprigs that are slender, a cubit long and angular; the leaves are smaller and narrower than those of the oak; the indentations too are deeper, the blossom is grey, and the root long and slender. It grows everywhere in flat, moist localities. Some authorities do not distinguish these two kinds but make of them one only, since both have the same properties. Both kinds are used by the people of Gaul in fortune-telling and in uttering prophecies, but the Magi especially make the maddest statements about the plant : that people who have been rubbed with it obtain their wishes, banish fevers,[c] win friends and cure all diseases without exception. They add that it must be gathered about the rising of the Dog-star without the action being seen by moon or sun; that beforehand atonement must be made to Earth by an offering of honey-comb and honey; that a circle must be drawn with iron round the plant and then it should be pulled up with the left hand and raised aloft; that leaves, stem and root must be dried separately in the shade. They say too that if a dining-couch is sprinkled with water in which

that a plant cures fevers. The madness lies in believing that anointed persons have magical powers.

triclinium qua [1] maduerit, laetiores convictus fieri. adversus serpentes conteritur ex vino.

108 LX. Est similis verbasco herba quae saepe fallit pro ea capta, foliis minus candidis, cauliculis pluribus, flore luteo. haec abiecta blattas in se contrahit ideoque Romae blattaria vocatur.

LXI. Molemonium sucum lacteum mittit concrescentem gummis modo, umidis locis. datur denarii pondus in vino.

109 LXII. Quinquefolium nulli ignotum est, cum etiam fraga gignendo commendetur, Graeci pentapetes aut pentaphyllon aut chamaezelon vocant. cum effoditur, rubram habet radicem. haec inarescens nigrescit et angulosa fit. nomen a numero foliorum. et ipsa herba incipit et desinit cum vite. adhibetur et purgandis domibus.

LXIII. Adversus serpentes bibitur et eius radix quae sparganion vocatur ex vino albo.[a]

110 LXIV. Dauci genera quattuor fecit Petronius Diodotus, quae persequi nihil attinet, cum sint differentiae duae, probatissimi in Creta, mox in Achaia et ubicumque in siccis nati, feniculi similitudine, candidioribus foliis et minoribus hirsutisque, caule pedali recto, radice suavissimi gustus et odoris.

111 hoc in saxosis nascitur meridianis. reliqua genera ubique nascuntur terrenis collibus limitibusque, nec

---

[1] *Ante* qua *add.* in *Mayhoff, qui XXIII.* § 140, *XXIV.* § 90, *XXVI.* § 29 *confert.*

---

[a] This is a strange sentence, for *eius* should naturally refer to cinquefoil, described in the last Chapter. Jan in his Index actually has : " *sparganion* quinquefolii radix 25 109." But sparganion is a plant, bur-weed, of which Dioscorides gives an account. The last sentence of this runs : δίδοται δὲ ἡ ῥίζα καὶ ὁ καρπὸς σὺν οἴνῳ θηριοδήκτοις, IV. 21. The sentence in Pliny seems to be a typical piece of carelessness.

this plant has been soaked the entertainment becomes merrier. As a remedy for snake bites it is crushed in wine.

LX. There is a plant like verbascum which is *Blattaria.* often taken for it in error, but the leaves are less pale, the stems are more numerous, and the blossom is yellow. When thrown away it attracts moths to itself, and for this reason at Rome it is called blattaria, or moth verbascum.

LXI. Molemonium exudes a milky juice which *Molemon-ium.* thickens like gum. It grows in moist localities, the dose being one denarius given in wine.

LXII. Cinquefoil is known to everyone, being *Cinquefoil.* popular for its actually producing strawberries. The Greeks call it pentapetes, pentaphyllon, or chamaezelon. When it is dug up it has a red root, which as it dries becomes black and angular. The name is derived from the number of the leaves. The plant itself buds and sheds its leaves with the vine. It is also used in purifying houses.

LXIII. For snake bite is also given in white wine *Sparganion.* the root of the plant that is called sparganion.[a]

LXIV. Four kinds of daucus [b] were distinguished *Daucus: four kinds.* by Petronius Diodotus. There is no point in giving the details of these, as there are but two species. The most highly valued grows in Crete, the next in Achaia and everywhere in dry districts; it resembles fennel, but has paler, smaller and hairy leaves, a straight stem a foot high, and a root with a very pleasant taste and smell. This kind grows on rocky soils that face the south. The other kinds grow everywhere on earthy hills and cross-paths, but

[b] See *Index of Plants.*

PLINY: NATURAL HISTORY

nisi pingui solo,[1] foliis coriandri, caule cubitali, capitibus rotundis, saepe pluribus quam ternis, radice
lignosa et, cum inaruit, supervacua. semen huius
cumino simile, prioris milio, album, acre, odoratum
omnibus et fervens. secundum priore vehementius
112 est, ideoque parce sumi debet. si iam maxime tertium genus facere libeat, est simile staphylino, quod
pastinacam erraticam appellant, semine oblongo,
radice dulci. omnia haec et hieme et aestate sunt
intacta quadripedi nisi post abortus. ex aliis usus
seminis, ex Cretico radicis est, magis ad serpentes.
bibitur e vino drachma una, datur et quadripedibus
percussis.
113   LXV. Therionarca alia quam magica et in nostro
orbe nascitur fruticosa foliis subviridibus, flore roseo,
serpentes necat. cuicumque admota ferae et haec
torporem adfert.
    LXVI. Persolata,[2] quam nemo ignorat, Graeci
arcion vocant, folia habet maiora etiam cucurbitis et
hirsutiora nigrioraque et crassiora, radicem albam et
grandem. haec ex vino bibitur denariorum duum
114 pondere.   LXVII. item cyclamini radix contra serpentes omnes. folia habet minora quam hedera,

---

[1] *Post* solo *lacunam indicat Mayhoff, qui* est unum ex his
vel est genus *supplet.*

[2] persolata E, *vulg., Detlefsen* : persollata *Ianus et Mayhoff,
qui* § 104 *coll.* personatam *conicit.*

---

[a] Here we have the singular *huius*, but in the preceding
sentence *reliqua genera.* Mayhoff supposes that a phrase
meaning " one of them " has fallen out after *solo.* But
Pliny recognises only two kinds, the second of which, summing
up the *reliqua genera,* may well be referred to by *huius.*
In this chapter Pliny is more than usually slipshod; Fée
compares it unfavourably with the corresponding passage in
Dioscorides.

only if the soil is rich; they have leaves like those of coriander, a stem a cubit high, round heads, often more than three, and a wood-like root, which when dry is worthless. Its [a] seed is like that of cummin, while that of the first kind is like millet, white, sharp, and scented and hot in all kinds. The seed of the second kind is more powerful than that of the first, and for this reason should be used sparingly. If one really desires to add a third kind, there is one like staphylinus, called wild carrot, with longish [b] seed and a sweet root. A quadruped, summer and winter, refuses to touch any of these plants except after miscarriage. Of the Cretan kind the root is used, chiefly for snake bites, of the other kinds the seed. The dose is one drachma taken in wine; it is given also to quadrupeds that have been bitten.

LXV. There is a therionarca, different from the magical plant,[c] that grows in our part of the world, a bushy plant with greenish leaves, a rose-coloured flower, and fatal to serpents. This plant too [d] benumbs any kind of wild creature it touches.

Therionarca.

LXVI. Persolata, a plant everybody knows, is called by the Greeks arcion; it has leaves larger, more hairy, darker and thicker even than those of a gourd, and a white, large root. This is taken in wine, the dose being two denarii by weight. LXVII. The root of cyclamen also is beneficial for the bites of any kind of snake. The plant has smaller, darker and thinner leaves than those of ivy, with no corners but

Persolata, or arcion.

Cyclamen.

---

[b] Or " oblong."
[c] Mentioned in XXIV. § 163 as growing in Cappadocia and Mysia.
[d] As well as the one mentioned in the other passage.

nigrioraque et tenuiora, sine angulis, in quibus albicant maculae, caule exiguo, inani, floribus purpureis, radice lata ut rapum videri possit, cortice
115 nigro. nascitur in umbrosis, a nostris tuber terrae vocatur, in omnibus serenda domibus, si verum est ubi sata sit nihil nocere mala medicamenta. amuletum vocant, narrantque et ebrietatem repraesentari addita in vinum. radix et siccata, scillae modo concisa reponitur. decoquitur eadem ad crassitudinem mellis; suum tamen venenum ei est, traduntque, si praegnas radicem eam transgrediatur, abortum fieri.

116 LXVIII. Est et altera cyclaminos cognomine cissanthemos, geniculatis caulibus supervacuis a priore distans, circa arbores se volvens, acinis hederae, sed mollibus, flore candido, specioso, radice supervacua. acini tantum in usu, gustu acres et lenti. siccantur in umbra tusique dividuntur in pastillos.

LXIX. Mihi et tertia cyclaminos demonstrata est cognomine chamaecissos, uno omnino folio, radice ramosa, qua pisces necantur.

117 LXX. Sed inter prima celebratur peucedanum, laudatissimum in Arcadia, mox Samothrace. caulis ei tenuis, longus, feniculo similis, iuxta terram foliosus, radice nigra, crassa, gravi odore, sucosa. gignitur in montibus opacis, foditur exitu autumni. placent tenerrimae et altissimae radices. hae conciduntur in quaternos digitos osseis cultellis fundunt-

---

^a That is, " earth truffle."
^b That is, " ivy-flowered."
^c That is, " ground ivy."

with white spots; the stem is short and hollow, the blossom purple, the root so broad that it might be taken for that of the turnip, and having a dark skin. It grows in shaded spots, is called by our country-men tuber terrae,[a] and ought to be grown in every home if it is true that wherever it grows no evil spells do any harm. They call it "amulet", and say that if it is added to wine intoxication comes at once. The root is also dried, cut up fine as is done with the squill, and then stored away. This is boiled down to the consistency of honey. It has however a poisonous quality of its own, and it is said that if a woman with child steps over this root she miscarries.

LXVIII. There is also another cyclamen with the surname of cissanthemos,[b] differing from the pre-ceding one in that it has jointed stems of no value, winds itself round trees, and bears berries like those of ivy, only soft, and a handsome, white flower; the root is of no value. The berries only are used ; these are sharp to the taste and sticky. They are dried in the shade, crushed, and cut up into lozenges.

LXIX. A third kind of cyclamen has been pointed out to me with the surname of chamaecissos,[c] which has only one leaf, and a branchy root fatal to fishes.

LXX. Among the most popular of plants is *Peucedanum.* peucedanum, the most esteemed kind of which grows in Arcadia; next to this comes the one growing in Samothrace. Its stem is slender, long, like fennel, and leafy near the ground; the root is dark, thick, juicy, and with a strong smell. It grows on shaded mountains and is dug up at the close of autumn. The tenderest and deepest roots are the favourites. These are cut up with bone knives into strips four

que sucum in umbra, capite prius et naribus rosaceo
118 perunctis, ne vertigo sentiatur. et alius sucus invenitur caulibus adhaerens incisisque manans.[1]
probatur crassitudine mellea, colore rufo, odore
suaviter gravi, fervens gustu. hic in usu contra
serpentes[2] et radix et decoctum eius plurimis medicamentis, suco tamen efficacissimo, qui resolvitur
amaris amygdalis aut ruta, bibiturque[3] et ex oleo
perunctos tuetur.
119 LXXI. Ebuli quoque, quam nemo ignorat, fumo
fugantur serpentes.
LXXII. Privatim adversatur scorpionibus polemoniae radix, vel adalligata tantum, item phalangio
ac ceteris minoribus venenatis, scorpionibus aristolochia, agaricum obolis quattuor in vini mixti cyathis
totidem, verbenaca et phalangio cum vino aut posca,
item quinquefolium, daucum.
120 LXXIII. Verbascum Graeci phlomon vocant. genera habet prima duo : album in quo mas intellegitur.
alterum nigrum in quo femina. tertium genus non
nisi in silvis invenitur. sunt folia brassicae latiora,

[1] incisisque manans *Detlefsen* : incisi quoque manant
Mayhoff : incisique manans *aut* manat *codd.*
[2] contra serpentes *omittunt plerique codd.* : *post* ruta *cum* a
Detlefsen.
[3] *In cod.* a *scriptum est* uriturque.

<hr>

[a] Grammatically a clumsy passage, the confusion being
increased by the accidental omission of *contra serpentes,* its
insertion in the margin, and re-insertion afterwards in the
wrong place. *Plurimis medicamentis* seems to be dative and
suco efficacissimo ablative of description.

fingers long and pour out their juice in the shade, the
cutters first rubbing their head and nostrils with rose
oil lest they should feel vertigo.   Another juice also
is found sticking to the stems and dripping from incisions in it.   It is considered good when it is of the
consistency of honey, of a red colour, with a strong
but pleasant smell, and hot to the taste.   This is used
for snake bite, as well as the root and a decoction
of it, to make many remedies,[a] the juice however
being the most efficacious; it is made thinner [b] by
bitter almonds or rue and is taken in drink, while
rubbing over the body with it and oil protects
people from snakes.

LXXI. The smoke of ebulum also,[c] a plant known *Ebulum.*
to everybody, drives snakes away.

LXXII. The root of polemonia, even when merely *Polemonia.*
attached as an amulet, is specific against scorpions,
and also against poisonous spiders and the other
smaller venomous creatures; aristolochia against
scorpions, or four-oboli doses of agaric in four
cyathi of wine stirred up with it,[d] vervain too with
wine, or vinegar and water, against poisonous spiders,
so also cinquefoil or daucum.

LXXIII. Verbascum is called phlomos by the *Verbascum*
Greeks.   There are two primary kinds of it: the *(phlomos).*
pale, which is thought to be male; the other is dark
and is regarded as female.   There is a third kind,
that is found only in woods.   The leaves of verbascum

---

[b] See note (e) on XXIV. § 34.
[c] The *quoque* suggests that the *uritur* of a in § 118 may be
right.   But it is perhaps as likely that a scribe was induced to
write *uritur* because his eye had gone on to *quoque.*
[d] This apparently is the meaning of *mixti vini*, not " mixed
wine."   The dosage perhaps applies also to aristolochia.

pilosa, caulis erectus, cubitali amplior. semen nigrum inutile, radix una, crassitudine digiti. nascuntur et in campestribus. silvestri folia elelisphaci,
121 alta, ramis lignosis. LXXIV. sunt et phlomides duae hirsutae, rotundis foliis, humiles. tertia lychnitis vocatur, ab aliis thryallis, foliis ternis aut cum plurimum quaternis crassis pinguibusque, ad lucernarum lumina aptis. aiunt in foliis eius quam feminam diximus ficus omnino non putrescere. distingui genera haec paene supervacuum est, cum sint omnia eiusdem effectus. contra scorpiones bibitur radix cum ruta ex aqua, magna amaritudine sed effectu pari.[1]

122 LXXV. Thelyphonon herba ab aliis scorpion vocatur propter similitudinem radicis. cuius tactu moriuntur scorpiones. itaque contra eorum ictus bibitur. scorpionem mortuum si quis helleboro candido linat, revivescere aiunt. thelyphonon omnem quadripedem necat inposita verendis radice, folio quidem intra eundem diem, quod est simile cyclamino. ipsa geniculata nascitur in opacis. scorpionibus adversatur et vettonicae sucus ac plantaginis.

123 LXXVI. Sunt et ranis venena, rubetis maxime, vidimusque Psyllos in certamen e [2] patinis cande-

---

[1] sed effectu pari *Mayhoff cum plerisque codd.* est effectu pari *puncto post* amaritudine *posito* Detlefsen.
[2] certamen e *Mayhoff* : certamine *codd.*

---

[a] The " lamp plant."
[b] The " wick plant."
[c] It seems impossible to decide whether " or " or " and " is the right word here.
[d] An obscure sentence. The Psylli were a north-African tribe, snake-charmers, and supposed to be immune to poisons. The hot pans were to irritate the toads. The reading *candefactas* perhaps is due to the need of an object to *admittentes*.

are broader than those of cabbage, and hairy; the
stem is upright, and more than a cubit high. The
seed is black and of no use. The root is single, and of
the thickness of a finger. The plants also grow in
flat country. Wild verbascum has leaves like
those of elelisphacus and tall, while the branches are
of a woody texture. LXXIV. There are also two *Phlomis.*
sorts of phlomis, both shaggy and with round leaves,
growing near the ground. A third is called
lychnitis,[a] by some thryallis [b]; it has three or at
most four leaves, which are thick and fleshy, and
suitable for lamp wicks. It is said that, placed in
the leaves of the kind we have called female, a fig does
not even begin to go bad. It is almost superfluous
to distinguish these various kinds, because they all
have the same properties. A draught for the sting
of scorpions is made from the root and rue in water,
which is as efficacious as it is bitter.

LXXV. Thelyphonon is a plant called scorpion *Thelypho-*
by some because its root has the shape of one. A *non.*
mere touch of it kills scorpions, and so it is taken in
drink for their stings. It is said that a dead scorpion,
if smeared with white hellebore, comes to life again.
Thelyphonon kills every kind of quadruped if its
root be applied to the genitals, the leaf indeed, which
is like that of cyclamen, does so before the end of the
same day. The plant itself is jointed, and grows in
shaded places. Good for scorpion bite is the juice of
betony or [c] plantain.

LXXVI. Frogs too have their poisons, bramble- *Remedies for*
toads a virulent one, and I have seen Psylli putting *poisons of*
them to a contest loosed from heated pans,[d] and *frogs and*
toads.

My addition of *eas* implies that *candefactis eas* has been
" telescoped " by a scribe into *candefactas.*

factis [1] eas [2] admittentes, ociore etiam quam [3] aspidum pernicie. auxiliatur phrynion in vino pota. aliqui neurada appellant, alii poterion,[4] floribus parvis, radicibus multis, nervosis, bene olentibus. LXXVII.

124 item alisma,[5] quam alii damasonion, alii lyron appellant. folia erant plantaginis, nisi angustiora essent et magis laciniosa convexaque in terram, alias etiam venosa similiter, caule simplici, tenui, cubitali, capite thyrsi, radicibus densis, tenuibus ut veratri nigri, acribus, odoratis, pinguibus. nascitur in

125 aquosis. alterum genus eiusdem in silvis,[6] nigrius, maioribus foliis. in usu radices utriusque adversus ranas et lepores marinos drachmae pondere in vini potu. lepori marino adversatur et cyclaminos. veneni vim canis quoque rabidi morsus habent, contra quos erit cynorrhodum, de quo diximus, plantago, et ad omnes bestiarum morsus, pota atque inlita, vettonica ex mero vetere.

126 LXXVIII. Peristereos vocatur caule alto foliato, cacumine in alios caules se spargens, columbis admodum familiaris, unde et nomen. hanc habentes negant latrari a canibus.

127 LXXIX. Proxima ab his malis venena sunt quae sibimet ipsis homines excogitant. contra haec

---

[1] candefactis V², *Mayhoff*: candefactas V¹Rd *vulg., Detlefsen.*

[2] eas *ego add.*: *omittunt codd.*

[3] quam *add. Warmington.*

[4] poterion *Hermolaus Barbarus ex Dioscoride*: potireton V R *Detlefsen* ²; polyrrhizon *vulg., Detlefsen.*

[5] alisma *Hermolaus Barbarus ex Dioscoride*: alcima *codd., vulg., Mayhoff.*   [6] ulvis *Fournier.*

that though their bite brings speedier death than
the bite of asps. A helpful remedy is phrynion
taken in wine, a plant that some call neuras, and
others poterion, having small flowers and many
fibrous roots with a pleasant scent. LXXVII. Likewise alisma, which some call damasonion, others
lyron. The leaves would be like those of the plantain
were they not narrower, more jagged, and bent
downwards; in other respects the two are alike, even
in their many veins. It has a single, slender stem, a
cubit high and like a thyrsus at the top, with many
close-set roots, slender like those of black hellebore,
acrid, scented and juicy. It grows in watery places.
The other kind of the same plant is found in woods;
it is darker, and has larger leaves. The roots of
both kinds are used for the poison of frogs and of the
sea-hare, the dose being a drachma by weight taken
in wine. Cyclamen is another remedy for the
poison of sea-hares. The bites of a mad dog also have
a highly venomous character, a remedy for which will
be found in cynorrhodum, of which I have spoken
already,[a] in the plantain, and for all bites of wild
beasts in betony with old neat wine, taken as drink or
applied locally.

LXXVIII. Peristereos is the name of a plant with *Peristereos.*
a tall stem covered with leaves and sprouting out
other stems at the top. It is a great favourite with
doves, whence too comes its name.[b] It is said that
dogs never bark at those who have this plant about
them.

LXXIX. Next after these plagues come the *Remedies for*
poisons that men devise for themselves. Remedies *various poisons.*

---

[a] See § 17 of this book.
[b] The name means " dove plant."

omnia magicasque artes erit primum illud Homericum
moly, dein Mithridatia ac scordotis.[1] et centaurium
potu omnia mala medicamenta exigit per alvum,
vettonicae semen in mulso aut passo, vel farina
drachma in vini veteris cyathis quattuor; vomere
128 cogendi atque iterum bibere. iis qui cotidie gustent
eam nulla nocitura mala medicamenta tradunt. poto
veneno aristolochia subvenit eadem mensura qua contra serpentes, quinquefolii sucus, agaricum, postquam
vomuerint, denarii pondere ex aquae mulsae cyathis
tribus.

129   LXXX. Antirrinum vocatur sive pararinon [2] lychnis
agria simile lino, radice nulla, flore hyacinthi, semine
vituli narium. et [3] hoc perunctos venustiores fieri nec
ullo malo medicamento laedi posse, aut si quis id in
130 bracchiali habeat, arbitrantur Magi. LXXXI. similiter ea quam eupliam vocant traduntque ea perunctos
commendatioris esse famae. artemisiam quoque
secum habentibus negant nocere mala medicamenta
aut bestiam ullam, ne solem quidem. bibitur et
haec ex vino adversus opium. alga [4] privatim potens
traditur, potatur et adversus ranas.

131   LXXXII. Pericarpum bulbi genus est. duac
eius species: cortice rubro alterum, alterum nigro
papaveri simile, sed vis maior quam priori, utrique

---

[1] *Sic dist. Mayhoff.*

[2] pararinon a, *Detlefsen* : anarrinon *Sillig post Hermolaum
Barbarum, Mayhoff* : paranarrhinon *Ianus* : *varia codd. sed*
anarrinon *Index Plinianus.*

[3] et *Mayhoff post Caesarium* : ex *codd.*

[4] alga *Detlefsen* : alcima *Mayhoff* : alligata *vulg.* : algam *codd.*

---

[a] See *Odyssey* X. 305.

[b] See § 6 of this book. The reference may be to the plant
mithridatia of § 62.

for all these and for sorceries will be found in the famous moly *a* of Homer, which is the best, next the antidotes of Mithridates,*b* and also scordotis. Centaury too taken in drink evacuates by stool all poisonous drugs, as does the seed of betony taken in honey wine or in raisin wine, or drachma doses of the powder may be taken in four cyathi of old wine; but the patients must be made to vomit and take a second draught. It is said that those who take this powder every day will not be hurt by any noxious drugs. When poison has been drunk help is given by aristolochia, the dose being the same as for snake bites, by the juice of cinquefoil, and by agaric taken after previous vomiting, the dose being a denarius by weight in three cyathi of hydromel.

LXXX. Antirrinum or pararinon is the name given to wild lychnis, a plant like flax, having no root, a flower like that of the hyacinthus, and seed like the muzzle of a calf. The Magi hold that those rubbed with it improve in beauty and can be hurt by no noxious drug; likewise if anyone wear it on the arm as an amulet. LXXXI. They say the same of the plant they call euplia, and maintain that those rubbed with it win a finer reputation. They also say that those carrying artemisia about them are not hurt by noxious drugs, or by any wild beast, and not even by the sun. This plant is also taken in wine to counteract the effects of opium. Seaweed is said to be a specific, and it is also taken in drink for the poison of frogs.

LXXXII. Pericarpum is a kind of bulb. There are two species of it; one has a red outer skin, the other is like the dark poppy, but its properties are stronger than those of the former; both however

229

autem excalfaciendo.[1] ideo contra cicutam datur,
contra quam et tus et panaces, chironium praecipue.
hoc et contra fungos.

132 LXXXIII. Verum et generatim membratimque
singulis corporum morbis remedia subtexemus orsi a
capite. alopecias emendat nymphaeae Heracliae [2]
radix, sive cum pice sive una [3] ea trita [4] inlinantur.
polythrix distat a callitriche quod iuncos albos habet
et folia plura maioraque. frutice quoque maior est,
133 defluentem capillum confirmat et densat. LXXXIV.
item lingulaca circa fontes nascens, cuius radix ad-
mixta combusta teritur cum adipe suis nigrae, id
quoque excipitur, ut eius suis quae numquam peperit;
sol deinde plurimum confert inlitae. similis usus
est cyclamini radicis. porriginem veratri radix tollit
134 in oleo decocta vel in aqua. capitis dolori medetur
panacis omnium generum radix in oleo contrita,
aristolochia, hiberis adalligata hora vel diutius, si pati
possit, comitante balinei usu. medetur et daucum.
purgat autem et cyclaminos cum melle in nares addita, et ulcera capitis sanat inlita. medetur et
peristereos.

135 LXXXV. Cacalia [5] sive leontice vocatur semen
margaritis minutis simile dependens inter folia
grandia, in montibus fere. huius grana xv in oleo

---

[1] excalfaciendo *codd.*, *Detlefsen*: in excalfaciendo *C. F. W. Müller, Mayhoff.*
[2] Heracliae *Sillig, Mayhoff*: e lacte *Detlefsen*: et cicutae *vulg.*: lacitae *aut* lacite *aut* ea cute *codd.*
[3] sive cum pice sive una *ego*: sive una (*cum lacuna*) *Mayhoff, qui* cum pice sive *per se* ex Dioscoride *supplet*: siveva *plerique codd.*
[4] trita *Ianus, Detlefsen, Mayhoff*: tritae (trite) *codd.*
[5] cacaliae *coni. Mayhoff: fortasse omissum* cui *ante* semen.

are warming. For this reason the plant is administered to counteract hemlock, as is also frankincense and panaces, and chironium in particular. The last is also used for poisoning by fungi.

LXXXIII. But we will go on to add also the various kinds of remedies for each disease attacking the various parts of the body, beginning with the head. *Remedies for diseases attacking the various parts of the body: the head.* Mange is cured by the root of the Heraclian water-lily, ground up and applied, either with pitch or by itself. Polythrix differs from callithrix in having pale, rush-like shoots and more numerous and larger leaves. The main stem too is larger. It strengthens and makes to grow more thickly hair that tends to fall out. LXXXIV. Lingulaca too may be used, that grows around springs, the root of which, reduced to ashes, is beaten up mixed with the lard of a black sow, care being taken that it is one which has never farrowed; and then it is a great advantage if the application is made in the sunshine. The root of cyclamen is used in a similar way. Dandruff is removed by the root of hellebore boiled down in oil or in water. Headache is cured by the root of any kind of panaces crushed *Other remedies for the head.* in oil, by aristolochia, by hiberis attached for an hour, or longer if the patient can stand it, a bath being taken at the same time. Daucum also is a cure. Cyclamen too with honey, if pushed into the nostrils, clears the head, sores on which are healed by the same used as ointment. Peristereos also is effective treatment.

LXXXV. Cacalia or leontice is the name of a plant with seeds like tiny pearls hanging down among large leaves, and mostly found on mountains. Fifteen grains of it are steeped in oil, and with

macerantur atque ita adversus capillos [1] caput
inungitur.

LXXXVI. Fit et ex callitriche sternumentum.
folia sunt lenticulae, caules iunci tenuissimi radice
minima. nascitur opacis et umidis, gustatu fervens.

136 LXXXVII. Hysopum in oleo contritum phthiriasi
resistit et prurigini in capite. est autem optimum
Cilicium e Tauro monte, dein Pamphylium ac
Zmyrnaeum. stomacho contrarium purgat cum fico
sumptum per inferna, cum melle vomitionibus.
putant et serpentium ictibus adversari tritum cum
melle et sale et cumino.

137 LXXXVIII. Lonchitis non, ut plerique existima-
verunt, eadem est quae xiphion aut phasganion,
quamquam cuspidi similis semine : habet enim folia
porri rubentia ad radicem et plura quam in caule,
capitula personis comicis similia, parvam exserentibus
linguam, radicibus praelongis. nascitur in sitientibus.

138 LXXXIX. e diverso xiphion et phasganion in umidis.
cum primum exit, gladii praebet speciem caule
duum cubitorum, radice ad nucis abellanae figuram
fimbriata, quam effodi ante messes oportet, siccari in
umbra. superior pars eius cum ture trita, aequo pondere admixto vino, ossa fracta capite [2] extrahit aut
quicquid in corpore suppurat, vel si calcata sint ossa
139 serpentis ; eadem contra venena efficax. caput in

[1] adversus capillos a, *Detlefsen* : adverso capillo *ceteri
codd.*, *Mayhoff.*
[2] *Mayhoff* (Appendix) e *add.*

[a] I have translated Mayhoff's text without any confidence
that it is correct, nor is Detlefsen's, with a comma before, not
after, *serpentis*, any more attractive, for Pliny's usual phrase is
contra serpentes. But cf. XXIV 61. The position of
serpentis and the plural *venena* are other objections. Now
ossa serpentis is odd. My friend Mr. John Chadwick tells me

this the head is rubbed in the contrary way to the hair.

LXXXVI. From callithrix also is made a snuff. This plant has the leaves of the lentil; the stems are very slender rushes and the root is very small. It grows in shady, moist places, and has a hot taste.

LXXXVII. Hyssop crushed in oil is good for phthiriasis and itch on the scalp. The best comes from Mount Taurus in Cilicia, the next best from Pamphylia and Smyrna. Upsetting the stomach, it purges by stool if taken with figs, by vomitings if taken with honey. Pounded with honey, salt, and cummin it is also supposed to counteract the poison of snake bites.

LXXXVIII. Lonchitis is not, as most people have thought, the same plant as xiphion or phasganion, although the seed is like a spear point; for it has leaves like those of the leek, reddish near the root and more numerous than on the stem, little heads like the masks of comedy, which put out a small tongue, and very long roots. It grows in thirsty soils. (LXXXIX.) Xiphion or phasganion on the other hand grows in moist soils. When it first leaves the ground it presents the appearance of a sword, has a stem two cubits high, and a fringed root like a filbert, which must be dug up before harvest and dried in the shade. The upper part of it, beaten up with frankincense and mixed with an equal quantity by weight of wine, extracts bone splinters from the head and all suppurating matter in the body, or any snake bones that have been trodden on; the plant also counteracts poisons.[a] Headache is relieved by

that a snake's skeleton would make a nasty wound if trodden on. That may be so, but would a person wearing sandals

dolore veratro in oleo vel rosaceo decocto tritoque
ungui convenit, peucedano ex oleo vel rosaceo et
aceto. tepidum hoc prodest et doloribus qui plerumque ex dimidia parte capitis sentiuntur et vertigini.
perungunt et radice eius sudoris causa eliciendi,
quoniam caustica vis ei est.

140 XC. Psyllion alii cynoides, alii crystallion, alii
sicelicon, alii cynomyiam appellant, radice tenui
supervacua, sarmentosum, fabae granis in cacuminibus, foliis canino capiti non dissimilibus, semine
autem pulici, unde et nomen. hoc in bacis, ipsa herba
in vineis invenitur. vis ad refrigerandum et dis-
cutiendum ingens. semen in usu. fronti inponitur
in dolore et temporibus ex aceto et rosaceo aut posca.

141 ad cetera inlinitur. acetabuli mensura sextarium
aquae densat ac contrahit; tunc terere oportet et
crassitudinem inlinere cuicumque dolori et collectioni
inflammationique. vulneribus capitis medetur aristolochia, fracta extrahens ossa et in alia quidem parte
corporis sed maxime capite, similiter plistolochia.
thryselinum est non dissimile apio. huius radix
commanducata purgat capitis pituitas.

142 XCI. Oculorum aciem centaurio maiore putant
adiuvari si addita aqua foveantur, suco vero
minoris cum melle culices, nubeculas, obscuritates

often cut himself on a snake's skeleton ? He might however
easily run a thorn into his foot during a cross-country walk.
The corresponding passage in Dioscorides (IV 20) has ἀκίδας
καὶ σκόλοπας ἐπισπᾶσθαι. It is conjectural, but just possible,
that *serpentis* has replaced an original *spina* because the *ossa*
of the first clause of this sentence was repeated a little later on
unconsciously by a careless scribe. Then the sense would be
" if a thorn has been trodden on."
    All this is so conjectural that I do not feel justified in
changing the text.

rubbing with hellebore beaten up and boiled down in oil or rose oil, or by peucedanum in oil or rose oil and vinegar. The latter made lukewarm is good for the pains generally felt on one side of the head, and also for giddiness. The body is rubbed over with the root to promote perspiration, for it has heating properties.

XC. Psyllion is called by some cynoides, by others chrystallion, by others sicelicon, and by others cynomyia; it has a slender root of no use in medicine, numerous twigs with grains like beans *a* at the point, leaves not unlike a dog's head and seed not unlike a flea: hence too its name. The seed is in berries, and the plant itself is to be found in vineyards. Its cooling and dispersing properties are very strong. The part used is the seed. For headache it is applied to the forehead and temples in vinegar and rose oil or in vinegar and water. For other purposes it is used as liniment. An acetabulum thickens and coagulates a sextarius of water; then it should be beaten up and the paste applied as liniment to any pain, gathering or inflammation. Wounds in the head are healed by aristolochia, which also brings away fragments of bone in other parts of the body, but especially in the head; the same with plistolochia. Thryselinum is not unlike celery. The root of it chewed clears away catarrhs of the head.

XCI. It is supposed that the sight is improved by the greater centaury if the eyes are fomented by an infusion of it in water; while by the juice of the lesser centaury with the addition of honey gnats are

Remedies for the eyes.

---

a This is a very strange phrase, and Fée calls the description absurd.

discuti, cicatrices extenuari, albugines quidem etiam
iumentorum sideritide. nam chelidonia supra dictis
omnibus mire medetur. panacis radicem cum polenta
epiphoris inponunt. hyoscyami semen et bibunt
obolo, tantundem meconii adicientes vinumque ad
epiphoras inhibendas. inungunt et gentianae sucum
quem collyriis quoque acrioribus pro meconio
143 miscent. facit claritatem et euphorbeum inunctis.
instillatur plantaginis sucus lippitudini. caligines
aristolochia discutit, hiberis adalligata capiti, quinquefolium. epiphoras et si qua in oculis vitia sunt
emendat verbascum. epiphoris inponitur peristereos
ex rosaceo vel aceto. ad hypochysis et caliginem
cyclamini¹ pastillos diluunt, peucedani sucum, ut
diximus, ad claritatem et caligines cum meconio et
rosaceo. psyllion inlitum fronti epiphoras suspendit.
144 XCII. Anagallida aliqui acoron² vocant. duo
genera eius : mas flore phoeniceo, femina caeruleo,
non altiores palmo, frutice tenero, foliis pusillis
rotundis, in terra iacentibus. nascuntur in hortis et
aquosis. prior floret caerulea. utriusque sucus
oculorum caliginem discutit cum melle et ex ictu

¹ cyclamini d T, *Mayhoff* : cyclameni V R : cyclamen in E,
Detlefsen.
² acoron E *vulg., Detlefsen, Mayhoff* : corchoron *Hermolaus
Barbarus e Dioscoride.*

ᵃ The Plinian use of *nam = sed.*
ᵇ In this part of the text the punctuation of Mayhoff has
been adopted.
ᶜ *Hypochysis* is a Greek accusative plural.
ᵈ A verb seems to be missing here. Mayhoff suggests *et
inlinunt.*

removed, cloudiness and films are dispersed, and scars smoothed out; also that albugo even of draught animals is made better by sideritis. But [a] chelidonia is a wonderful cure for all the above-mentioned eye troubles. The root of panaces with pearl barley is applied to the eyes for fluxes. For checking such fluxes the seed of henbane is taken in wine in doses of an obolus with the same amount of poppy juice. Juice of gentian too is used as ointment, and it is also used instead of poppy juice as an ingredient of the more pungent eye salves. Euphorbeum too improves the vision of those whose eyes are anointed with it. The juice of the plantain is dropped into the eyes for ophthalmia. Films are dispersed by aristolochia, by hiberis attached to the head, and by cinquefoil.[b] Fluxes and eye-diseases generally are made better by verbascum. To fluxes is applied peristereos in rose oil or vinegar. For cataract [c] and film lozenges of cyclamen are dissolved ⟨and applied⟩ [d]; the juice of peucedanum, as we have said, poppy juice and rose oil being added, is good for improving the vision and for films. Psyllion rubbed on the forehead arrests fluxes.

XCII. Some call the anagallis, acoron. There are two kinds of it: the male with a scarlet flower, and the female with a blue one; neither is more than a span in height, the stem being tender, and the leaves tiny, round and lying on the ground. They grow in gardens and on moist ground. The blue-flowered kind blossoms first. The juice of either kind, applied with honey, disperses film on the eyes, suffusions of blood from a blow, and reddish argema [e]; the results

[e] For *argema*, a small white ulcer, see list of diseases.

cruorem et argema rubens, magis cum Attico melle
inunctis. pupillas dilatat, et ideo hac inunguntur
ante quibus paracentesis fit. iumentorum quoque
oculis medentur. sucus caput purgat per nares
infusus, ita ut deinde vino colluatur. bibitur et
145 contra angues suci drachma in vino. mirum quod
feminam pecora vitant aut, si decepta similitudine—
flore enim tantum distant—degustavere, statim eam
quae asyla appellatur in remedium [1] quaerunt. a
nostris felis oculus [2] vocatur. praecipiunt aliqui
effossuris ante solis ortum, priusquam quicquam
aliud loquantur, salutare eam, sublatam exprimere,
ita praecipuas esse vires. de euphorbeae suco satis
dictum est. lippitudini, si tumor erit, absinthium
cum melle tritum, item [3] vettonicae farina conveniet.
146 XCIII. Aegilopas sanat herba eodem nomine quae
in hordeo nascitur, tritici folio, semine contrito cum
farina permixta inpositaque vel suco. exprimitur
hic e caule foliisque praegnantibus dempta spica et
in trimestri farina digeritur in pastillos.

---

[1] remedium (*i.e.* remediū) *Mayhoff* : remedia *Detlefsen,
codd.* : remedio *vulg.*
[2] felis oculus *Detlefsen, Mayhoff* : ferus oculus *vulg.* : felix
oculus *Urlichs* : feris oculis *codd.*
[3] item E *Detlefsen* : item cum *plerique codd. et Mayhoff, qui
lacunam post* cum *indicat, excidisse putat* vino. *Brakman
supplet* vetere mero.

---

[a] The subject of *colluatur* is apparently *sucus*. The subject
of passive *colluo* is normally the thing cleansed (nose), not the

are better if the ointment is made with Attic honey. It dilates the pupils, and so these are smeared with it before perforation for cataract. These plants also cure eye diseases in draught animals. The juice also clears the head if poured through the nostrils, but it [a] must be rinsed out afterwards with wine. A drachma dose of the juice is also taken in wine for snake bites. It is a wonderful thing that cattle avoid the female plant, or if deceived by the resemblance—for the only difference is in the flower—they have partaken of it, they at once seek as a remedy the plant called asyla. We Romans call it " cat's-eye ". Some instruct the diggers to say nothing until they have saluted it before sunrise, and then to gather it and extract the juice, for so they say its efficacy is at its greatest. About the juice of euphorbea [b] enough has been said. Ophthalmia, if there is swelling, will be benefited by wormwood beaten up with honey, and also by powdered [c] betony.

XCIII. Aegilops [d] is cured by the plant of the same name, which grows among barley and has a leaf like that of wheat; either the seed may be reduced to powder, mixed with flour and applied, or the juice may be used. This is extracted from the stem and juicy leaves after taking away the ears, and then it is worked into lozenges with the flour of three-month wheat.

thing rinsed away (juice) and possibly the subject has been left vague, e.g. *nasus* implied in *nares*. But see § 166.

[b] See § 78 of this book.

[c] The emendation of Mayhoff would mean : " and also powdered betony with wine."

[d] Aegilops the disease is a lacrimal fistula.

147 XCIV. Aliqui [1] et mandragora utebantur; postea
abdicatus est in hac curatione. epiphoris, quod
certum est, medetur et oculorum dolori radix tusa
cum rosaceo et vino. nam sucus multis oculorum
medicamentis miscetur. mandragoran alii circaeon
vocant. duo eius genera; candidus qui et mas, niger
qui femina existimatur, angustioribus quam lactucae
foliis, hirsutis et caulibus, radicibus binis ternisve
rufulis,[2] intus albis, carnosis tenerisque, paene
148 cubitalibus. ferunt mala abellanarum nucum magnitudine et in his semen ceu pirorum. hoc albo alii
arsena, alii morion, alii hippophlomon vocant. huius
folia alba, alterius [3] latiora ut lapathi sativae.
effossuri cavent contrarium ventum et tribus circulis
ante gladio circumscribunt, postea fodiunt ad
occasum spectantes. sucus fit et e malis et caule
deciso cacumine et e radice punctis aperta aut
decocta. utilis haec vel surculo. concisa quoque in
149 orbiculos servatur in vino. sucus non ubique in-

---

[1] aliqui *codd.* : antiqui *Mayhoff, qui* § 37, 53, 57, XX 52,
XXIII 97, 139, *alios locos confert.*

[2] rufulis *plerique codd., Detlefsen, Mayhoff*; nigris foris (*e
Dioscoride*) *Hermolaus Barbarus.*

[3] *Post* alterius *supplet* (*e Dioscoride*) foliis *Mayhoff* : quam
alterius *Hermolaus Barbarus.*

---

[a] Mayhoff's emendation would mean " of old," " in early
days."

[b] *Nam* here seems to be used in its Plinian sense, but the
ordinary meaning of " for " would not spoil the logic of the
passage.

[c] The *nigris foris,* "black outside," of Hermolaus Barbarus,
was suggested by Dioscorides IV. 75, μέλαιναι κατὰ τὴν ἐπιφά-

XCIV. Some [a] physicians used to employ the Mandrake for the eyes, etc. mandrake also; afterwards it was discarded as a medicine for the eyes. What is certain is that the pounded root, with rose oil and wine, cures fluxes and pain in the eyes. But [b] the juice is used as an ingredient in many eye remedies. Some give the name circaeon to the mandrake. There are two kinds of it: the white, which is also considered male, and the black, considered female. The leaves are narrower than those of lettuce, the stems hairy, and the roots, two or three in number, reddish,[c] white inside, fleshy and tender, and almost a cubit in length. They bear fruit of the size of filberts, and in these are seeds like the pips of pears. When the seed is white the plant is called by some arsen,[d] by others morion, and by others hippophlomos. The leaves of this mandrake are whitish, broader than those of the other,[e] and like those of cultivated lapathum. The diggers avoid facing the wind, first trace round the plant three circles with a sword, and then do their digging while facing the west. The juice can also be obtained from the fruit, from the stem, after cutting off the top, and from the root, which is opened by pricks or boiled down to a decoction. Even the shoot of its root can be used, and the root is also cut into round slices and kept in wine. The juice is not found

νειαν, ἔνδοθεν δὲ λευκαί. But even if *foris* can represent κατὰ τὴν ἐπιφάνειαν, *nigris foris* was most unlikely to be corrupted to *rufulis*. The word μέλας often means " of the colour of port wine," and *rufulus* is not very far away from that.

[d] "Male," Greek ἄρσην. Fée thinks that the *morion* was not the mandrake but *Atropa belladonna*.

[e] After *alterius* we can understand *foliis*. It is not necessary to insert it, nor to add *quam* before *alterius*.

venitur sed, ubi potest, circa vindemias quaeritur.
odor gravis ei, set[1] radicis et mali gravior ex albo.
mala matura in umbra siccantur. sucus ex his sole
densatur, item radicis tusae vel in vino nigro ad
tertias decoctae. folia servantur in muria, efficacius
150 albi.[2] rore tactorum[3] sucus pestis est. sic quoque
noxiae vires. gravedinem adferunt etiam olfactu,
quamquam mala in aliquis terris manduntur, nimio
tamen odore obmutescunt ignari, potu quidem
largiore etiam moriuntur. vis somnifica pro viribus
bibentium. media potio cyathi unius. bibitur et
contra serpentes et ante sectiones punctionesque, ne
sentiantur. ob haec satis est aliquis somnum odore
quaesisse. bibitur et pro helleboro duobus obolis in
mulso [4]—efficacius helleborum—ad vomitiones et ad
bilem nigram extrahendam.

[1] ei, set *Detlefsen post Hard. et cod. Dal.*; ei, ut et *Mayhoff*:
eius et *codd.*

[2] efficacius albi. rore *Urlichs et Detlefsen*: efficacius;
salsus rore *Mayhoff*: albus *non* albi *codd.*

[3] tactorum *Detlefsen*: tantum *Mayhoff, codd.*: *pro* rore
tantum *coni.* rorulenti *Urlichs.*

[4] *Sic distinxit Mayhoff.*

---

[a] Dioscorides, IV. 75 (Wellmann) has : ἔστι δὲ ἐνεργέστερος
τοῦ ὀποῦ ὁ χυλός. οὐκ ἐν παντὶ δὲ τόπῳ φέρουσιν ὀπὸν αἱ ῥίζαι·
ὑποδείκνυσι δὲ τὸ τοιοῦτον ἡ πεῖρα. Our two authorities differ
here; there seems nothing in Pliny to correspond to ἡ πεῖρα.

[b] What we call " red " wine.

[c] Urlich's emendation would give roughly the same sense;
Mayhoff's would mean : " more effectively in brine; juice
merely salted by the dew is deadly." Mayhoff compares *ros
salsus* (XXVII § 71), but the emendation is not happy. I think
that *rore . . . . est* is really a parenthesis. If so, *sic* is much
more natural.

[d] Possibly, " Its power to induce sleep depends upon the
resistance (reaction ?) of the patient."

everywhere, but where it can be found it is looked [a] for about vintage time. It has a strong smell, but stronger when the juice comes from the root or fruit of the white mandrake. The ripe fruit is dried in the shade. The fruit juice is thickened in the sun, and so is that of the root, which is crushed or boiled down to one third in dark [b] wine. The leaves are kept in brine, more effectively those of the white kind. The juice of leaves that have been touched by dew are deadly.[c] Even when kept in brine they retain harmful properties. The mere smell brings heaviness of the head and—although in certain countries the fruit is eaten—those who in ignorance smell too much are struck dumb, while too copious a draught even brings death. When the mandrake is used as a sleeping draught the quantity administered should be proportioned to the strength of the patient,[d] a moderate dose being one cyathus. It is also taken in drink for snake bite, and before surgical operations and punctures to produce anaesthesia. For this purpose some find it enough to put themselves to sleep by the smell.[e] A dose of two oboli of mandrake is also taken in honey wine instead of hellebore—but hellebore is more efficacious [f]—as an emetic and to purge away black bile.

---

[e] A clear indication, if one were needed, that the ancients used such anaesthetics, at the best very poor ones, as they possessed.
[f] The usual punctuation would give : " Hellebore is more efficacious as an emetic and purge of black bile." The punctuation of Mayhoff is neat, perhaps too neat for Pliny; but we must take into account a feature of Pliny's style not generally recognised—his habit of making parenthetic remarks. This habit sometimes causes misunderstandings, because a reader may easily fail to observe an instance.

151 XCV. Cicuta quoque venenum est, publica
Atheniensium poena invisa, ad multa tamen usus non
omittendi. semen habet noxium, caulis autem et
viridis estur a plerisque et in patinis. levis hic et
geniculatus ut calami, nigricans, altior saepe binis
cubitis, in cacuminibus ramosus, folia coriandri
teneriora, gravi odoratu,[1] semen aneso crassius, radix
concava, nullius usus. semini et foliis refrigeratoria
vis, sic et necat. incipiunt algere ab extremitatibus
152 corporis. remedio est, priusquam ad vitalia per-
veniat, vini natura excalfactoria. sed in vino pota
inremediabilis existit. sucus exprimitur foliis flori-
busque, tum enim maxime tempestivus est.[2] melior
semine trito expressus et sole densatus in pastillos.
necat sanguinem spissando—haec altera vis—et ideo
153 sic necatorum maculae in corporibus apparent. ad
dissolvenda medicamenta utuntur illo pro aqua.
fit ex eo et ad refrigerandum stomachum malagma.
praecipuus tamen est ad cohibendas epiphoras
aestivas oculorumque dolores sedandos circumlitus.[3]
miscetur collyriis, et alias [4] omnes rheumatismos cohibet. folia quoque tumorem omnem doloremque
154 et epiphoras sedant. Anaxilaus auctor est mammas
a virginitate inlitas semper staturas. quod certum

---

[1] gravi odoratu *plerique codd., Detlefsen* : gravia *Mayhoff,
qui* graviora *coni.*
[2] *Ab* est *usque ad* ideo *sic distinguit Mayhoff, qui* vis ei —
pro vis —et *scribit.*
[3] circumlitus E vulg., *Mayhoff* : circumlitu *Ianus, Detlefsen* : circumlitum *multi codd.*
[4] alias *Sillig, Detlefsen, Mayhoff* : alios *codd.*

XCV. Hemlock too is poisonous, a plant with a *Hemlock for* bad name because the Athenians made it their *the eyes, etc.* instrument of capital punishment, but its uses for many purposes must not be passed by. It has a poisonous seed, but the stem is eaten by many both as a salad and when cooked in a saucepan. This stem is smooth, and jointed like a reed, of a dark colour, often more than two cubits high, and branchy at the top; the leaves resemble those of coriander, but are more tender, and of a strong smell; the seed is coarser than that of anise, the root hollow and of no use. The seed and leaves have a chilling quality, and it is this that causes death; the body begins to grow cold at the extremities. The remedy lies in using the warming nature of wine before the vital parts are reached; but taken in wine hemlock is invariably fatal. A juice is extracted from the leaves and blossom, for the best time to do so is when the hemlock is in flower. A better juice is extracted from the crushed seed and thickened in the sun for making into lozenges. It causes death by thickening the blood—this is its other outstanding property —and for this reason spots are to be seen on the bodies of those who have been killed in this way. This juice is used instead of water as a solvent for drugs. There is also made from it a poultice to cool the stomach. Its chief use however is as a local application round the eyes to check summer fluxes and to allay pains in them. It forms an ingredient of eye salves, and it checks all catarrhs generally. The leaves also relieve every kind of swelling, pain or flux. Anaxilaus is responsible for the statement that if the breasts are rubbed with hemlock from adult maidenhood onwards they will always remain firm.

est, lac puerperarum mammis inposita extinguit
veneremque testibus circa pubertatem inlita.
remedia in [1] quibus bibenda censetur non equidem
praeceperim. vis maxima natae Susis Parthorum,
mox Laconicae, Creticae, Asiaticae, in Graecia vero
Megaricae, deinde Atticae.

155 XCVI. Cremnos agrios gremias tollit oculorum
inpositus, tumorem quoque polenta addita.

XCVII. Nascitur vulgo molybdaena, id est plumbago, etiam in arvo, folio lapathi, crassa, hispida.
hac commanducata si oculus subinde lingatur, plumbum, quod est genus vitii, ex oculo tollitur.

XCVIII. Capnos trunca,[2] quam pedes gallinacios
vocant, nascens in parietinis et saepibus, ramis
tenuissimis sparsisque, flore purpureo, folio [3] viridi,
suco caliginem discutit, itaque in medicamenta
oculorum additur.

156 XCIX. Similis et nomine et effectu sed alia est
capnos fruticosa, praetenera, foliis coriandri, cineracei coloris, flore purpureo. nascitur in hortis et

[1] remedia in *Mayhoff* : remedio *Detlefsen* : remedia *multi
codd.*
[2] trunca *Ianus, Detlefsen, Mayhoff* : truma *aut* truna *codd.* :
prima *vulg.*
[3] folio viridi *coni. Mayhoff* : viridis *Detlefsen, Mayhoff in
textu, codd.*

---

[a] Although there is no trace of it in the MSS, *radice* seems to
have fallen out either before or after *crassa*. The former
would give : " with a thick and hairy root," the latter :
" hairy and with a thick root."
[b] That is, rubbed lightly. But Pliny may mean that the
person giving the treatment should chew a wad of the plant,
pausing now and then to lick the patient's eye. One might
emend to *illinatur*, but it is very unlikely that so common a

What is certain is that an application of hemlock to the breasts of women in childbed dries up their milk, and to rub it on the testacles at the time of puberty acts as an antaphrodisiac. I should not like to give directions about remedies in which hemlock is recommended to be taken by the mouth. The most powerful hemlock grows at Susa in Parthia; the next in Laconia, Crete and Asia; in Greece however the strongest is found around Megara, after which comes that of Attica.

XCVI. An application of wild cremnos to the eyes removes rheum, and with the addition of pearl barley reduces swellings. *Other remedies for the eyes.*

XCVII. Molybdaena, that is plumbago, grows everywhere, even on cultivated land; it has a leaf like that of lapathum and is thick *a* and hairy. If the eye is licked *b* occasionally with this plant when chewed, there is removed the species of eye trouble called lead.

XCVIII. Capnos trunca,*c* the popular name of which is chicken's feet, growing among ruins and on wall-banks, has very slender branches which are far apart, a purple flower and green leaves; its juice disperses films, and so it is an ingredient of eye salves.

XCIX. Similar both in name and in its properties, though a different plant, is the bushy capnos, which is very delicate, and has the leaves of coriander, the colour of ashes, and a purple blossom. It grows in

medical term as this would be changed to anything so strange as *lingatur*. The MSS. read either this or *elingatur*, the *e*- coming from the final *-e* of *subinde*. For *plumbum* see list of diseases.

c " Lopped " or " maimed fumitory," in contrast with the *capnos fruticosa* of § 156.

segetibus hordeacis. claritatem facit inunctis oculis delacrimationemque ceu fumus, unde nomen.[a] eadem evolsas palpebras renasci probibet.

157 C. Acoron iridis folia habet, angustiora tantum et longiore pediculo, radices nigras minusque venosas, cetero et has similes iridis, gustu acres, odore non ingratas, ructu faciles. optumae Daspetiacae [1] e Galatia, mox Creticae, sed plurimae in Colchide iuxta Phasin amnem et ubicumque in aquosis. recentibus virus maius quam vetustis, Creticae candidiores Ponticis. siccantur, ut iris,[2] in umbra 158 digitalibus frustis. nec non inveniuntur qui oxymyrsinae radicem acoron vocant, ideoque quidam hanc acorion vocare malunt. vis ei ad calfaciendum extenuandumque efficax,[3] contra suffusiones et caligines oculorum, suco eiusdem poto contra serpentes.[b]

159 CI. Cotyledon parvula herba est in cauliculo tenero, pusillo folio,[4] pingui, concavo ut coxendices. nascitur in maritimis petrosisque viridis [5]; radice olivae modo rotunda. oculis medetur suco. est aliud genus eiusdem sordidis foliis, latioribus densioribusque circa radicem velut oculum cingentibus, asperrimi[c]

---

[1] Daspetiacae *Ianus, Detlefsen, Mayhoff*: Daspetiace V : Daspetice d : Daepetiace R : Despe ie E.

[2] ut iris *Mayhoff* : vere *Detlefsen* : utris *codd.*

[3] *Comma non post sed ante* efficax *ponit Mayhoff.*

[4] folio e *Dioscoride add. Hermolaus Barbarus.*

[5] viridis *Detlefsen, codd., vulg.* : umidis *Mayhoff.*

---

[a] The Greek for smoke is καπνός.

[b] Apparently not known. Pliny seems to have wrongly read some Greek word or words.

[c] The adjective *viridis* is nearly always used of a clean, fresh green. Cf. *vireo* and contrast *sordidis* a little lower down.

gardens and crops of barley. Used as ointment for
the eyes it improves the vision and, like smoke, produces tears, and to this fact it owes its name.[a] It
also prevents eyelashes that have been pulled out
from growing again.

C. Acoron has the leaves of the iris, only narrower *Acoron for*
and with a longer foot-stalk; it has dark roots and *the eyes, etc.*
less veined, though in other respects these too are
like those of the iris, pungent to the taste, with a not
unpleasant smell, and carminative. The best come
from † Daspetos † [b] in Galatia, then come Cretan roots,
but they are found most abundantly in Colchis near
the river Phasis and wherever there are watery
districts. Fresh roots have a stronger smell than
stale, and the Cretan are paler than those of Pontus.
They, like the iris, are dried in the shade in slices a
finger in length. There are to be found those who
give the name of acoron to the root of oxymyrsine, and
for this reason some prefer to call this plant acorion.
It has powerful properties as a calorific and discutient, is good for cataract and dimness of the eyes,
and its juice is taken internally for snake bites.

CI. The cotyledon is a tiny plant on a tender *Cotyledon for*
little stem, with a very small fleshy leaf, which is *the eyes.*
concave like the hip joint. It grows in maritime and
rocky places, fresh green [c] in colour, and with a root
that is oval like an olive. The juice is medicine
for the eyes. There is another kind of cotyledon
with dirty-green leaves, which are broader and closer
together than those of the other, spread round the
root as though it were an eye [d]; the taste is very

[d] Perhaps here a bud, with the sepals surrounding it. But
Littré has: " entourée comme l'oeil l'est de l'orbite."

gustus, longiore caule, sed pergracili. usus ad
eadem quae iridi.[1]

160 CII. aizoi duo genera: maius in fictilibus vasculis
seritur, quod aliqui buphthalmon appellant, alii
zoophthalmon, alii stergethron, quod amatoriis
conveniat, alii hypogeson, quoniam in subgrun-
diis fere nascitur, sunt qui ambrosiam potius vocant
et qui amerimnon, Italia sedum magnum aut
oculum aut digitillum. alterum minusculum, quod
erithales vocant, alii trithales, quia ter floreat, alii
erysithales, aliqui isoetes, Italia sedum, atque [2]
aizoum utrumque, quoniam vireat semper, aliqui
161 sempervivum. maius et cubiti altitudinem excedit,
crassitudine plus quam pollicari. folia in cacumine
linguae similia, carnosa, pinguia, larga suco, latitudine pollicari, alia in terram convexa, alia stantia,
ita ut ambitu effigiem imitentur oculi. quod minus
est in muris parietinisque et tegulis nascitur, fruticosum a radice et foliosum usque ad cacumen, foliis
angustis, mucronatis, sucosis, palmum alto caule.
radix inutilis.

162 CIII. Huic similis est quam Graeci andrachlen
agrian vocant, Italia inlecebram, pusillis latioribus
foliis et breviore cacumine. nascitur in petris et
colligitur cibi causa. omnium harum vis eadem re-

---

[1] iridi *Detlefsen, multi codd.* : sativi *Mayhoff, qui punctum
non ante sed post* aizoi *ponit.*
[2] atque *Detlefsen* : sed aeque *Mayhoff* : sed qui VRd : qui
E : alii *vulg.*

---

[a] Ox-eye.   [b] Animal-eye.
[c] Affection (although it means natural affection rather than
sexual love).
[d] Beneath the eaves (ὑπόγεισον).
[e] Immortal food.   [f] Care-free.

harsh, the stem longer than that of the other kind but very slender. It is used for the same purposes as the iris.

CII. Of the aizoüm there are two kinds, the *Aizoüm for* larger of which is planted in earthen pots, and is *the eyes.* sometimes called buphthalmos,[a] zoophthalmos,[b] stergethron [c] (because it is useful for love-philtres), hypogeson [d] (for it generally grows under eaves), although some prefer to call it ambrosia [e] or amerimnon [f]; Italians call it great sedum, or eye, or little finger. The other kind is rather small, and is called erithales,[g] trithales [h] (because it flowers three times), erysithales,[i] isoetes,[j] sedum by Italians, and both are called aizoüm, because they are always green, or sempervivum.[k] The greater aizoüm grows to even more than a cubit in height and is thicker than a thumb. At the point the leaves are like a tongue, fleshy, rich with copious juice, as broad as a thumb, some bent to the ground and others upright, so that the circle of them is like an eye in shape. The smaller aizoüm grows on walls, ruins, and roof-tiles; it is bushy from the root and leafy to the top, with narrow, pointed and juicy leaves, and a stem a span high. The root is not used.

CIII. Resembling this is a plant that the Greeks *Andrachle* call wild andrachle, the Italians inlecebra. It has *for the eyes,* very small leaves, but broader than those of *etc.* aizoüm, and the head is shorter It grows in rocky districts and is gathered for food. All these have the same properties; they are cooling and astrin-

---

[g] Luxuriant blossom.   [h] Thrice-blossoming.
[i] Reddish blossom.
[j] Possibly " equal all the year."
[k] Ever-flourishing.

163 frigerare et adstringere. medentur epiphoris folia
inposita vel sucus inunctis. purgat enim ulcera
oculorum expletque et ad cicatricem perducit, palpebras deglutinat. eaedem capitis doloribus medentur
suco vel folio temporibus inlitis, adversantur phalangiorum ictibus, aconito vero maius aizoum praecipue.
a scorpionibus quoque habentem id feriri negant.

164 medentur et aurium dolori, item sucus inunctus
hyoscyami modicus, item achilleae et centaurii
minoris et plantaginis, peucedani cum rosaceo et
meconio, acori sucus cum rosa. omnis autem strigili
calefactus infunditur, cotyledon etiam purulentis cum
medulla cervina calefacta, ebuli radicis tritae sucus
linteo colatus, mox in sole densatus et cum opus sit
rosaceo dilutus et calefactus. parotidas verbenaca,
item plantago sanat, item sideritis cum axungia
vetere.

165 CIV. Narium ozaenam emendat aristolochia cum
cypero.

CV. Dentibus remedio sunt panacis radix commanducata, praecipue chironiae, item sucus collutis, radix
hyoscyami ex aceto manducata, item polemoniae.
commanducatur et plantaginis radix, aut coluuntur in
aceto decoctae suco; et folia esse [1] utile,[2] vel si
sanguine gingivae putrescant. vel [3] semen eiusdem

166 apostemata et collectiones gingivarum sanat. et
aristolochia gingivas dentesque confirmat, verbenaca

[1] esse VRE, *Detlefsen, Mayhoff* : edere dT : sunt *vulg.*
[2] utile *Detlefsen, Mayhoff, multi codd.* : inutile E : utilia *vulg.*
[3] vel *ante* semen *in uncis Mayhoff.*

---

[a] There seems to be generally a difference between *inunguo*
and *inlino* : the former is to anoint or rub, as with oil, the latter
is to apply, but the distinction is not always observed. See
also p. 56.

gent. Fluxes of the eyes are cured by an application of the leaves or of the juice used as ointment. For it cleanses sores of the eyes, replaces lost tissue and makes them cicatrize; it unglues the eyelids when sticky. These plants also cure headaches if the temples are smeared *a* with the juice or leaves; they neutralize the bite of venomous spiders; for aconite, however, an especially good antidote is the greater aizoüm. It is also said that those who have this plant on their persons are not stung by scorpions. They also cure ear-ache, as does the application of a moderate amount of juice of henbane,*a* or of achillea, of the smaller centaury, of plantain, of peucedanum mixed with rose oil and poppy juice, and of acoron juice with rose leaves. But all these juices are warmed and injected with a strigil, cotyledon being good even for pus in the ears if warmed deer's marrow is added, or the juice of crushed root of ebulum strained through a cloth, then thickened in the sun and, when needed, diluted with rose oil and warmed. Vervain cures swollen parotid glands, as does the plantain, and sideritis with old axle-grease.

Cures for parotid glands.

CIV. Polypus in the nose is treated successfully by aristolochia with cyperus.

Polypus in the nose.

CV. For the teeth remedies are: chewed root of panaces, chewed root of chironia especially, the juice too if the teeth be rinsed with it, the root of henbane chewed with vinegar, and that of polemonia. The root of plantain also is chewed, or the teeth are rinsed with the juice of the decoction in vinegar. To eat the leaves also is useful, even if the gums are purulent; or the seed of the same plant heals abscesses and gatherings in the gums. Aristolochia too strengthens gums and teeth, as does

Remedies for the teeth.

253

cum radice commanducata et decoctae ex vino aut
aceto sucus collutus, item quinquefolii radicis
decoctae ad tertias in vino[1] aut aceto. prius quam
decoquatur aqua marina aut salsa lavatur. decoctum diu tenendum in ore. quidam cinere quinquefolii fricare malunt. et verbasci radix decoquitur in
vino ad colluendos dentes, et hysopo colluuntur et
peucedani suco cum meconio, vel radicum anagal-
lidis magis feminae suco ab altera nare quam doleat
infuso.

167 CVI. Erigeron a nostris vocatur senecio. hanc si
ferro circumscriptam effodiat aliquis tangatque ea
dentem et alternis ter despuat ac reponat in eundem
locum ita ut vivat herba, aiunt dentem eum postea
non doliturum. herba est trixaginis specie et
mollitia, cauliculis subrubicundis. nascitur in tegulis
et in muris. nomen hoc Graeci dederunt, quia vere
canescit. caput eius numerosa dividitur lanugine,
qualis est spinae, inter divisuras exeunte, quare
168 Callimachus eam acanthida appellavit, alii pappum.
nec deinde Graecis de ea constat. alii erucae foliis
esse dixerunt, alii roboris, sed minora multo, radice
alii supervacua, alii nervis utili, alii potu strangu-

---

[1] in vino *Mayhoff*: vino *codd.*

---

[a] However this sentence is punctuated, the grammar seems
to be imperfect. Were it not for the *vel* before *radicum* it
might be thought that the ablative absolute *suco infuso* referred
to preliminary treatment before rinsing the teeth with one of
the washes mentioned in the previous clause, but there is no
variant. Perhaps the *vel* means " The washes mentioned just
now may be used by themselves, *or* they may be preceded by
an injection of juice of anagallis root up the nostril further
away from the pain."

vervain chewed with its root, or the juice of a decoction in wine or vinegar used as a mouth-wash, and also that of the root of cinquefoil boiled down to one-third in wine or vinegar. Before it is boiled down it is washed in sea water or salt water, and the decoction should be kept in the mouth for a long time. Some prefer to use the ash of cinquefoil as a dentrifrice. The root of verbascum too is boiled down in wine to make a mouth-wash for the teeth, for which purpose also hyssop is employed and the juice of peucedanum with poppy juice; or the juice of anagallis roots, by preference of the female plant, is poured *a* into the nostril opposite to where pain is felt.

CVI. Erigeron is called by us Romans senecio. *Erigeron.* If a line is traced round it with an iron tool before it is dug up, and if one touches a painful tooth with the plant three times, spitting after each touch, and replaces it into its original ground so as to keep it alive, it is said that the tooth will never cause pain thereafter. This plant has the appearance and softness of trixago, with small, reddish stems. It grows on tiled roofs and on walls. Its name was given to it by the Greeks, because it is of a hoary colour in spring. Its head is divided by many pieces of down, like those of a thorn, that grow out from between the divisions, which is why Callimachus gave it the name of acanthis, and others pappus. Apart from this, however, the Greeks are not in agreement about this plant. Some have said that it has the leaves of rocket, others of the oak but much smaller; some that the root is useless, others that it is good for the sinews, others that it chokes if taken in drink. On the other

lante. e diverso quidam regio morbo cum vino
dederunt et contra omnia vesicae vitia, item cordis
et iocineris. extrahere renibus harenam dixere.
169 ischiadicis drachmam cum oxymelite ab ambulatione
propinavere, torminibus quoque et in passo utilissimam, praecordiis etiam cibo ex aceto eam praedi-
cantes serentesque in hortis. nec defuere qui et
alterum genus facerent nec quale esset demon-
strarent, contra serpentes in aqua bibendam eden-
damque comitialibus dantes. nos eam Romanis ex-
perimentis per usus digeremus. lanugo eius cum
croco et exiguo aquae frigidae trita inlinitur epiphoris,
tosta cum mica salis strumis.

170 CVII. Ephemeron folia habet lilii, sed minora;
caulem parem, florem caeruleum, semen supervacuum, radicem unam digitali crassitudine, dentibus
praecipuam concisam in aceto decoctamque ut
tepido colluantur. et ipsa etiam radix sistit, cavis
exesi [1] inprimitur. chelidoniae radix ex aceto trita
continetur ore, erosis veratrum nigrum inprimitur,
mobiles utrolibet decocto in aceto firmantur.

171 CVIII. Labrum Venerium vocant in flumine
nascentem. est ei vermiculus qui circa dentes
fricatur [2] aut cavis dentium cera includitur. cavendum ne avulsa herba terram tangat.

---

[1] carie exesis *coni. Mayhoff* (Appendix). sistit cariem, caris
exesi ⟨si⟩ imprimitur *coni. Warmington*.
[2] fricatur *Mayhoff, qui* XXII 121 *confert*: nectitur *Detlefsen*: ligatur *vulg.*: necatur *codd.*

hand some have given it with wine for jaundice, and as a cure for all complaints of the bladder, heart, and liver. They have said that it brings away gravel from the kidneys. They prescribed for sciatica a drachma with oxymel after a walk, this dose being also very useful in raisin wine for colic; they recommended it also as a salad with vinegar for the internal organs [a] generally, and they planted it in gardens. There have been some who distinguished a second variety, but without pointing out its qualities, prescribing it to be taken in water for snake bite, and to be eaten by epileptics. I myself shall treat of it only in so far as the Romans have found out by experiment how to use it. Its down, with saffron and a little cold water, is applied crushed to eye fluxes and, roasted with a grain of salt, to scrofulous sores.

CVII. Ephemeron has the leaves of a lily, but *Ephemeron* smaller, a stem of the same length, a blue flower, a *and Cheli-* seed of no value, and a single root of the thickness *donia.* of a thumb, a sovereign remedy for the teeth if it is cut up into pieces in vinegar, boiled down, and used warm as a mouth wash. And the root also by itself arrests decay if forced into the hollow of a decayed tooth. Root of chelidonia is crushed in vinegar and kept in the mouth, dark hellebore is plugged into decayed teeth, and loose teeth are strengthened by either of these boiled down in vinegar.

CVIII. A plant that grows in rivers they call the *Labrum* bath of Venus. In it is a worm which is rubbed *Venerium.* round the teeth or plugged with wax into the hollow of a tooth. Care must be taken that the plant does not touch the ground after being pulled up.

---

[a] See note on XXV. § 41.

172 CIX. Ranunculum vocamus quem Graeci batrachion. genera eius IIII : unum pinguioribus quam
coriandri foliis et ad latitudinem malvae accedenti-
bus, colore livido, caule alto gracili et radice alba.
nascitur in limitibus umidis et opacis. alterum folio-
sius, pluribus foliorum incisuris, altioribus [1] caulibus.
tertium minimum est, gravi odore, flore aureo.
173 quartum simile huic flore lacteo.[2] omnibus vis
caustica, si cruda folia inponantur, pusulasque ut
ignis faciunt. ideo ad lepras et psoras iis utuntur et
ad tollenda stigmata, causticisque omnibus miscent.
alopeciis inponunt celeriter removentes. radix in
dolore commanducata diutius rumpit dentes, eadem
174 sicca concisa sternutamentum est. nostri herbarii
strumum eam vocant, quoniam medetur strumis et
panis parte [3] in fumo suspensa, creduntque ea rursus
sata rebellare quae curaverint vitia,[4] quo scelere et
plantagine utuntur. oris ulcera intus sucus plantaginis emendat et folia radicesque commanducata,
vel si rheumatismo laboret os, ulcera faetoremque
quinquefolium, ulcera psyllium.
175 CX. Conposita quoque contra faetores, vel
maxime pudendum vitium, trademus. ergo folia
myrti et lentisci pari pondere, gallae Syriacae

---

[1] altioribus *coni. Warmington* : altius *codd.*

[2] lacteo (*e Dioscoride) Brotier, Littré, Detlefsen, Mayhoff* :
luteo *codd.*

[3] parte *vult delere Warmington, fortasse per dittographiam
ortum.*

[4] vitia in *Mayhoff.*

---

[a] " Employée en fumigation sur la partie malade " (Littré).
This is surely wrong, for the whole plant was not burnt, but
sometimes replanted. Perhaps the plant was smoked before
use, or perhaps the custom had a magical origin.

CIX. We call ranunculus a plant which the Greeks *Ranunculus for the teeth, etc.* call batrachion. There are four kinds of it: one with fatter leaves than those of coriander and nearly as broad as those of mallows, of a leaden colour, with a tall, graceful stem and a whitish root. It grows on moist and shaded cross-paths. The second is more leafy, with more indentations in the leaves, and with taller stems. The third is the smallest, with a strong smell and a golden flower. The fourth is like it, but the flower is of the colour of milk. All have a caustic property; if leaves are applied raw, they raise blisters as does fire. Accordingly they are used for leprous sores and itch, and to remove scars on the skin; they are ingredients of all caustic preparations. They are applied to mange, but are removed quickly. The root if chewed up for toothache too long breaks off the teeth, and the dried root chopped fine makes a snuff. Roman herbalists call it strumus, because it cures scrofula and superficial abscesses, if a piece of it is hung up in the smoke.[a] They believe that if it is replanted the maladies they have cured [b] break out again, a similar criminal use being made of the plantain. Sores inside the mouth are cured by juice of plantain, and also by the chewed-up leaves and roots, even if the mouth is suffering from a flux; sores and bad breath are removed by cinquefoil, sores by psyllium.

CX. I shall also give some prescriptions for *Offensive breath.* offensive breath, which is a very embarrassing complaint. For this purpose myrtle leaves are taken and an equal weight of leaves of lentisk with half the quantity of Syrian gall-nuts. This com-

The nearest instance I have found to *curare* in Pliny in the strict sense of " cure."

dimidium pondus simul terere et vino vetusto sparsa
mandere matutino ex usu est, vel hederae bacas cum
casia et murra pari pondere ex vino. naribus
utilissimum est dracontii semen contritum ex melle,
etiamsi carcinomata in iis sint. suggillata hysopo
emendantur, stigmata in facie mandragoras inlitus delet.

pound, when beaten up and sprinkled with old wine, may with benefit [a] be chewed in the morning, or one may be made of ivy berries, cassia and myrrh, in equal quantities, added to wine. If the nostrils are the seat of the trouble, even though a cancer-like growth is present, dracontium seed beaten up with honey is very useful. Bruises disappear under applications of hyssop, and scars on the face are removed by rubbing with mandrake.[b]

[a] Cf. XXVII § 81 *ex usu est fovere.*
[b] Possibly " by the use of mandrake ointment."

BOOK XXVI

LIBER XXVI

1 I. Sensit facies hominum et novos omnique aevo priore incognitos non Italiae modo verum etiam universae prope Europae morbos, tunc quoque non tota Italia nec per Illyricum Galliasve aut Hispanias magno opere vagatos, aut alibi quam Romae circaque, sine dolore quidem illos ac sine pernicie vitae, sed tanta foeditate ut quaecumque mors praeferenda esset.

2 II. Gravissimum ex his lichenas appellavere Graeco nomine, Latine, quoniam a mento fere oriebatur, ioculari primum lascivia, ut est procax multorum natura in alienis miseriis, mox et usurpato vocabulo mentagram, occupantem multis et totos [1] utique voltus, oculis tantum inmunibus, descendentem vero et in colla pectusque ac manus foedo cutis furfure.

[1] et totos *vulg.*, *Detlefsen* : et latius totos *Mayhoff* : *pro* latius *in codd. invenimus* intus V'RdTf, intuitus E *cod. Dal.*, intutus V². *Mayhoff* intentius *coni.* : *ego* intensius *malim*.

---

[a] *Lichen*, from the Greek λείχην, is in its medical sense the despair of the medical historian. Skin diseases are even today hard to diagnose; in ancient times it was still harder; hardest of all is it to understand now ancient diagnosis. *Lichen* included ringworm and many kinds of eczema, especially when

264

BOOK XXVI

I. The face of man has also been afflicted with new *New diseases.* diseases, unknown in past years not only to Italy but also to almost the whole of Europe, and even then they did not spread all over Italy, or through Illyricum, the Gaul̀s, and the Spains to any great extent, or in fact anywhere except in and around Rome. Though they are painless and without danger to life, yet they are so disfiguring that any kind of death would be preferable.

II. The most severe of these they called by a *Lichens.* Greek name lichens [a]; in Latin, because it generally began on the chin, it was called mentagra,[b] at first *Mentagra.* by way of a joke—so prone are many men to make a jest of the misfortunes of others—the name passing presently into common use. The disease seized in many cases [c] at least the whole of the face, with the eyes only unaffected, but passed down however also to the neck, chest and hands, covering the skin with a disfiguring, scaly eruption.

it resembled the botanical lichen in form. Here it may be some form of leprosy. See also list of diseases.

  [b] I.e. " chin gout," as *podagra* is " foot gout " and *chiragra* " hand gout." The joke, like most Roman jokes, is a feeble one.

  [c] Mayhoff's *latius* would mean that the disease spread from the chin. It seems unnecessary with *descendentem*. My *intensius* would mean that the disease became more violent as it spread from the chin. I believe that it could easily have been changed to *intus.*

3   III. Non fuerat haec lues apud maiores patresque
nostros, et primum Ti. Claudi Caesaris principatu
medio inrepsit in Italiam quodam Perusino equite
Romano quaestorio scriba, cum in Asia adparuisset,
inde contagionem eius inportante. nec sensere id
malum feminae aut servitia plebesque humilis aut
media, sed proceres veloci transitu osculi maxime,
foediore multorum qui perpeti medicinam tolera-
verant cicatrice quam morbo. causticis namque
curabatur, ni usque in ossa corpus exustum esset,
4 rebellante taedio. adveneruntque ex Aegypto
genetrice talium vitiorum medici hanc solam operam
adferentes magna sua praeda, siquidem certum est
Manilium Cornutum e praetoriis legatum Aqui-
tanicae provinciae HS CC elocasse in eo morbo
curandum sese. acciditque ¹ contra ² saepius ut nova
genera morborum gregatim sentirentur. quo mirabilius quid potest reperiri? aliqua gigni repente
vitia terrarum in parte certa membrisque hominum

¹ acciditque codd. et edd.: accidit quoque Mayhoff.
² contra ego transposui: om. V¹RT Detlefsen: post nova
posuit Mayhoff cum codd.V²dEr vulg.

ª Littré translates maxime by "surtout," "especially
through the quick contact of the kiss," which suggests that
kissing was more common among the nobles than elsewhere. I
think that the cursus verborum points to the translation : "but
the nobles through the momentary contact (speedy infection)
of a kiss suffered very much." This is rather obscure,
and perhaps vel, "even," has fallen out before veloci.
ᵇ The omission of contra in several MSS. shows that
the logic of the passage, which is certainly oddly
expressed, has been long misunderstood. The sequence
of thought here, as I understand the passage, is:

III. This plague was unknown to our fathers and
forefathers. It first made its way into Italy in the
middle of the principate of Tiberius Claudius Caesar,
when a Roman knight of Perusia, a quaestor's
secretary, introduced the infection from Asia Minor,
where he had taken up his duties. Women were
not liable to the disease, or slaves and the lower
and middle classes, but the nobles were very much
infected [a] through the momentary contact of a kiss.
The scar left on many who had been hardy enough
to endure the treatment was more unsightly than the
disease, for caustics were the method employed,
and the loathsome complaint broke out afresh unless
the flesh was burnt through right to the bones.
There arrived from Egypt, the parent of such diseases,
physicians who devoted all their attention to this
complaint only, to their very great profit, since it is
a fact that Manilius Cornutus, of praetorian rank and
legate of the province of Aquitania, laid out
two hundred thousand sesterces in getting himself
treated for that disease. On the other hand [b] it
has more usually happened that new kinds of
disease on their first appearance have been epidemic.
What can be found more marvellous than this, that
some diseases should arise suddenly in a special part
of the world, should attack special limbs of human

" Mentagra attacked a special class of people in Rome itself,
although it was a new disease to Italy; new diseases on their
first introduction usually attack whole masses indiscriminately.
How strange it is for a disease sometimes to pick as it were its
victims ! " It is hard for me to believe that *contra* is an
insertion of a scribe, or that *gregatim* can mean " among the
common people " (Lewis and Short), or in fact anything except
" whole masses at a time." See VIII. § 11 : *elephanti gregatim
semper ingrediuntur.*

certis vel aetatibus aut etiam fortunis, tamquam malo eligente, haec in pueris grassari, illa in adultis, haec proceres sentire, illa pauperes ?

5 IV. L. Paullo Q. Marcio censoribus primum in Italiam carbunculum venisse annalibus notatum est, peculiare Narbonensis provinciae malum, quo duo consulares obiere condentibus haec nobis eodem anno, Iulius Rufus atque Laecanius Bassus, ille medicorum inscientia sectus, hic vero † pollici laevae manus evulso acu ab semetipso tam parvo † ut vix cerni 6 posset. nascitur in occultissimis corporum partibus et plerumque sub lingua duritia rubens vari modo, sed capite nigricans, alias livida, in corpus intendens neque intumescens, sine dolore, sine pruritu, sine alio quam somni indicio, quo gravatos in triduo aufert; aliquando et horrorem adferens circaque pusulas

---

ᵃ The Pontifex Maximus compiled each year the official list of important events. These lists made up the *Annales*.

ᵇ 164 B.C.

ᶜ These men were consuls in A.D. 65 and 62 respectively.

ᵈ The words within daggers seem corrupt, although the general sense of the passage is clear. We expect a participle meaning " thrust in," not " plucked out," and there is no noun to go with *parvo* and *evulso*. There is no satisfactory restoration of the passage, which may possibly be, not corrupt, but badly written by Pliny himself. It may be that *punctu* (XXVIII § 198) has fallen out after *parvo* (the vulgate text has *vulnere* after it), but the difficulty of *evulso*

beings or special ages, or even people of a special position in life, (just as if a plague chose its victims), one children, another adults, one making the nobility especially liable, another the poor.

IV. It is noted in the Annals [a] that it was in the censorship [b] of Lucius Paullus and Quintus Marcius that there appeared for the first time in Italy the carbuncle, a disease peculiar to the province of *Carbuncles.* Gallia Narbonensis. There died of it in the same year as I compose my work two men of consular rank, Julius Rufus [c] and Laecanius Bassus,[c] the former through the ignorance of his physicians, who tried lancing; the latter, however, through his own tearing out with a needle from his left thumb a splinter (boil) so small that it could scarcely be seen.[d] The carbuncle forms in the most hidden parts of the body, and usually as a red hardness under the tongue, like a pimple but blackish at the top, occasionally of a leaden colour, spreading into the flesh but without swelling, pain, irritation, or any other symptom than sleep, overcome by which the patient is carried off in three days. Sometimes also the disease, bringing shivering, small pustules around the sore, and more rarely fever, has reached

remains. The MS. E has *evulsa* to agree with *acu*. After *acu* a word may have been lost, perhaps *aculeo* (splinter) or *furunculo* (boil). *Carbunculus* (when not anthrax) was a malignant pustule or ulcer. Celsus (V 28A) says that it should be cauterized, but does not mention cutting. "If *acus* does not mean 'head' here it is probably corrupt. There are two ways of transforming a simple boil into a general infection. One is to lance with a knife (Rufus), the other is to squeeze the head out with a dirty thumb (Bassus)." A.C.A.

parvas, rarius febrem, stomachum faucesque invasit, [1]
ocissime exanimans.

7 V. Diximus elephantiasim ante Pompei Magni
aetatem non accidisse in Italia, et ipsam a facie
saepius incipientem, in nare prima veluti lenticula,
mox inarescente [2] per totum corpus maculosa variis
coloribus et inaequali cute, alibi crassa, alibi tenui,
dura alibi ceu scabie aspera, ad postremum vero
nigrescente et ad ossa carnes adprimente, intumes-
8 centibus digitis in pedibus manibusque. Aegypti
peculiare hoc malum et, cum in reges incidisset,
populis funebre, quippe in balineis solia tempera-
bantur humano sanguine ad medicinam eam. et hic
quidem morbus celeriter in Italia restinctus est, sicut
et ille quem gemursam appellavere prisci inter
digitos pedum nascentem, etiam nomine oblitterato.
9 VI. Id ipsum mirabile, alios desinere in nobis,
alios durare, sicuti colum. Ti. Caesaris principatu
inrepsit id malum, nec quisquam id prior imperatore
ipso sensit, magna civitatis ambage, cum in edicto
eius excusantis valetudinem legeret nomen incog-

---

[1] faucesque invasit VR : paucisque E r : faucesque cum
invasit d(?) *vulg.*, *Detlefsen* : faucesque ut invasit *Mayhoff*,
*qui VIII 158, IX 122, 152, 153, XV 85, XVIII 115, XX 38,
XXX 63, XXXI 109, XXXIII 29, XXXVI 127 confert.*
[2] inarescente *Detlefsen cum codd.* : increscente *Ianus,
Mayhoff.*

---

[a] In spite of the vulgate *cum* before *invasit*, and of Mayhoff's
formidable list of parallel passages in support of *ut*, which he
substitutes for *cum*, I am inclined to believe that a new
sentence begins after *aufert*; in other words that two forms of
the disease are mentioned, one which kills by producing coma,
the other in which death is due to suffocation and choking.

the oesophagus and pharynx,[a] causing death very
quickly.

V. I have said that leprosy [b] did not occur in *Leprosy.*
Italy before the time of Pompeius Magnus, and that
though the plague usually begins on the face, a kind
of freckle on the tip of the nose, yet presently the
skin dries up [c] over all the body, covered with spots
of various colours, and uneven, in places thick, in
others thin, in others hard as with rough itch-scab,
finally however going black, and pressing the flesh
on to the bones, while the toes and fingers swell up.
This plague is native to Egypt. When kings were
attacked, it was a deadly thing for the inhabitants,
because the tubs in the baths used to be prepared with
warm human blood for its treatment. This disease
indeed quickly died out in Italy, as also did that
called by the ancients gemursa,[d] which appeared
between the toes, the very name being now obsolete.

VI. This itself is a wonderful fact, that some *Colum.*
diseases should disappear from among us while
others remain endemic, as for example colum.[e] It
was in the principate of Tiberius Caesar that this
malady made its way into Italy. Nobody suffered
from it before the Emperor himself, and the citizens
were greatly puzzled when they read in his edict,
in which he begged to be excused because of illness, a

Unfortunately there are no *similia* in the medical writings by
which the text might have been settled.

[b] See XX § 144 and list of diseases.

[c] With the reading *increscente*: "it increases over all the
body, the skin being, etc." I suggest "plague," to bring out
the force of the emphatic *ipsam*.

[d] We do not know what *gemursa* was, this being the only
place (except once in Festus) where the word occurs.

[e] An intestinal disease. See list of diseases.

nitum. quid hoc esse dicamus aut quas deorum
iras? parum enim erant homini certa morborum
genera, cum supra trecenta essent, nisi etiam nova
timerentur? neque ipsi autem homines pauciora sibi
10 opera sua negotia inportant. haec apud priscos
erant quae memoramus [1] remedia, medicinam ipsa
quodammodo rerum natura faciente, et diu fuere.
Hippocratis certe, qui primus medendi praecepta
clarissime condidit, referta herbarum mentione invenimus volumina. nec minus Diocli Carysti, qui
secundus aetate famaque extitit, item Praxagorae
11 et Chrysippi ac deinde Erasistrati Cei,[2] Herophilo
quidem, quamquam subtilioris sectae conditori, ante
omnes [3] . . . celebratam rationem eam, paulatim [4]
usu efficacissimo rerum omnium magistro, peculiariter utique medicinae, ad verba garrulitatemque
descendente.[5] sedere namque in scholis auditioni
operatos gratius erat quam ire per solitudines et
quaerere herbas alias aliis diebus anni.
12   VII. Durabat tamen antiquitas firma magnasque
confessae rei vindicabat reliquias, donec Asclepiades
aetate Magni Pompei orandi magister nec satis in
arte ea quaestuosus, ut ad alia quam forum [6] sagacis

---

[1] memoramus *Mayhoff cum codd.* : memoravimus *Urlichs,
Detlefsen.*
[2] Cei *Detlefsen, Mayhoff e Strabone (X v 6)* : Co *codd.*
[3] omnes *vulg.* : omnis *codd., Detlefsen, Mayhoff. Post*
omnes *excidit fortasse* scimus.
[4] eam, paulatim *codd.* : , iam paulatim *Mayhoff.*
[5] descendente *vulg.* : descendentem V[1] d t *Mayhoff.*
[6] quam forum *fere omnes codd.* : om. *vulg.*

---

[a] This emendation of the *Co* of the MSS. is certain, unless
Pliny has made one of his characteristic blunders.
[b] Or, " far-fetched doctrine."

name they had never heard before. What are we to
say that this means, what wrath of the gods? Were
the recognised kinds of human disease, more than
three hundred, too few, that they must be increased
by new ones also to add to man's fears? No fewer
either are the troubles which man brings upon himself by his own agency. These remedies that I *The old*
record were those used by the ancients, Nature in a *system of medicine.*
way making medicine herself, and their vogue was a
long one. Certainly the works of Hippocrates, who
was the first to put together, and that with great
distinction, rules for medical practice, we find full of
references to herbs, equally so the works of Diocles of
Carystus, who comes next after Hippocrates in time
and reputation, likewise those of Praxagoras and
Chrysippus, and then comes Erasistratus of Ceos *a*;
while Herophilus indeed, although the founder of
an over-subtle sect,*b* ⟨we know⟩ recommended
before all others this method of treatment.*c* But
little by little experience, the most efficient teacher
of all things, and in particular of medicine, degenerated into words and mere talk. For it was
more pleasant to sit in a lecture-room engaged in
listening, than to go out into the wilds and search
for the various plants at their proper season of the
year.

VII. However, the ancient system of medicine
remained unshaken, and claimed as its own considerable remains of its once acknowledged sphere,
until, in the time of Pompeius Magnus, one
Asclepiades, a professor of rhetoric, who found his *Asclepiades.*
gains in that profession too small, but had a brain

c These physicians flourished after Hippocrates, the last
two at Alexandria in the early part of the third century B.C.

PLINY : NATURAL HISTORY

ingenii, huc se repente convertit atque, ut necesse erat
homini qui nec id egisset nec remedia nosset oculis
usuque percipienda, torrenti ac meditata cotidie
oratione blandiens omnia abdicavit totamque medi-
13 cinam ad causas revocando coniecturae fecit, quinque
res maxume communium auxiliorum professus,
abstinentiam cibi, alias vini, fricationem corporis,
ambulationem, gestationes, quae cum unusquisque
semet ipsum sibi praestare posse intellegeret, faven-
tibus cunctis velut[1] essent vera quae facillima erant,
universum prope humanum genus circumegit in se
non alio modo quam si caelo demissus advenisset.

14   VIII. Trahebat praeterea mentes[2] artificio inani[3]
iam[4] vina promittendo aegris dandoque tempestive,
iam frigidam aquam, et quoniam causas morborum
scrutari prius Herophilus instituerat, vini rationem
inlustraverat Cleophantus apud priscos, ipse cognomi-
nari se frigida danda praeferens, ut auctor est M.
Varro.   alia quoque blandimenta excogitabat, iam

    [1] velut *Warmington* : ut *codd.*
    [2] mentes *plerique codd.*, *Mayhoff* : mentis V, *Detlefsen.*
    [3] inani *coni. Mayhoff, sed* alias *addit* : animos iam *Detlefsen* :
mirabili *vulg. et fortasse* d : animalia *plures codd.*, *Urlichs* :
aliae coniecturae sunt anili, animae, amabili.   *Vide notam.*
    [4] iam *coni. plures* : om. *codd.*

─────────────

    [a] It is supposed that Pliny here confuses Asclepiades the
physician with Asclepiades the rhetorician. See Clifford
Allbutt, *Greek Medicine at Rome*, p. 180.
    [b] With the MSS. reading: "were inclined to believe that
the easiest etc.," but *favere ut* = "to favour the belief that"
is dubious.
    [c] Mayhoff's *inani* is perhaps the least unlikely of the pro-
posed emendations of the *animalia* of the MSS. His *alias*,
however, with *iam* following will commend itself to few. The
vulgate *mirabili* gives excellent sense, but would not be

brilliant enough for success in other professions, suddenly abandoned rhetoric for medicine.[a] A man who neither had practised it nor knew anything of remedies that call for sharp eyes and personal experience, but could attract by his eloquent and daily-practised oratory, was forced to reject all simples, and reducing the whole of medicine to the discovery of causes, made it a matter of guess-work. He recognised especially five principles of general application: fasting from food, in other cases abstinence from wine, massage, walking, and the various kinds of carriage-rides. Since every man realised that he could provide these things for himself, and since all applauded[b] him as if the easiest things were also true, Asclepiades brought round to his view almost all the human race, just as if he had been sent as an apostle from heaven.

VIII. He used, moreover, to attract men's minds by the empty artifice[c] of promising the sick, now wine, which he administered as opportunity occurred, while now he would prescribe cold water; and since Herophilus had anticipated him in inquiring into the causes of diseases, and Cleophantus among the ancient physicians had brought to prominent notice the treatment by wine, he preferred, according to Marcus Varro, to win for himself the surname of " cold-water giver."[d] He devised also other attrac-

corrupted to *animalia*. Personally I thought for a time that *amabili* (" alluring ") might be right, and friends have suggested *anili* (" old woman's trick ") and *animae* (" psychological trick "). Perhaps *promittendo* is " by prescribing." See XXIV § 80.

[d] Asclepiades was actually nicknamed " wine-giver." See *Anonymus Londinensis* XXIV 30 Ἀσκληπιάδης ὁ οἰνοδώτης.

suspendendo lectulos quorum iactatu aut morbos
extenuaret aut somnos adliceret, iam balneas avidis-
sima hominum cupidine instituendo et alia multa dictu
grata atque iucunda, magna auctoritate nec minore
15 fama, cum occurrisset ignoto funeri, relato homine
ab rogo atque servato, ne quis levibus momentis
tantam conversionem factam existimet. id solum
possumus indignari, unum hominem e levissima gente
sine opibus ullis orsum vectigalis sui causa repente
leges salutis humano generi dedisse, quas tamen
16 postea abrogavere multi. Asclepiaden adiuvere
multa in antiquorum cura nimis anxia et rudia, ut
obruendi aegros veste sudoresque omni modo ciendi,
nunc corpora ad ignes torrendi solesve adsiduo
quaerendi, in urbe nimbosa, immo vero tota Italia
imperatrice,[1] tum primum pensili balinearum usu ad
infinitum blandiente. praeterea in quibusdam mor-
17 bis medendi cruciatus detraxit, ut in anginis, quas

---

[1] imperatrice *codd.*, *vulg.*: imbrium creatrice *Ianus*:
imitatrice *Detlefsen*: nimborum altrice *coni. Sillig*: imbrici-
trice *Mayhoff*: immo—imperatrice *uncis inclusit Urlichs.*

---

[a] Either revolution in medical practice or change in public
opinion. See § 13. *Levibus momentis* might mean " with slight
effects ".

[b] Urlichs is very likely right in putting within brackets the
words *immo . . . imperatrice.* It reads like a marginal comment that has crept into the text. None of the proposed
emendations of *imperatrice* are convincing, nor do they
explain how the supposed corruption has arisen. So I keep
the reading of all the MSS., which may have been written by
Pliny in one of his wilder flights of fancy: " Italy may rule
the world, but it cannot control the weather." Incidentally
the passage throws strange light on the climate of ancient
Italy, or indicates that even in Rome people grumbled at the
weather.

tive methods of treatment, such as suspended beds, so that by rocking them he could either relieve diseases or induce sleep; again, he organized a system of hydropathy, which appeals to man's greedy love of baths, and many other things pleasant and delightful to speak of, which won him a great professional reputation. His fame was no less great when, on meeting the funeral cortege of a man unknown to him, he had him removed from the pyre and saved his life. This incident I give lest any should think that it was on slight grounds that so violent a change *a* took place. One thing alone moves me to anger: that one man, of a very super-ficial race, beginning with no resources, in order to increase his income suddenly gave to the human race rules for health, which however have subsequently been generally discarded. The success of Asclepiades owed much to the many distressing and crude features of ancient medical treatment; for instance, it was the custom to bury patients under coverings, and to promote perspiration by every possible means, now to roast the body before a fire, or continually to make them seek sunshine in our rainy city, nay throughout rainy imperial *b* Italy: then for the first time were used hot-air baths, heated from below,*c* treatment of infinite attractiveness. Besides this he did away with the agonizing treatment em-ployed in certain diseases; for example in quinsy, which physicians used to treat by thrusting an

---

c Pliny says in IX, § 168, that the *pensiles balineae* were invented by one Sergius Orata. This kind of bath had a flooring suspended over the hypocaust. Asclepiades apparently prescribed a " Turkish bath " as a substitute for sunshine in cases where genial warmth was beneficial.

curabant in fauces organo demisso.   damnavit merito
et vomitiones tunc supra modum frequentes.   arguit
et medicamentorum potus stomacho inimicos, quod
est magna ex parte verum.   itaque nos in primis
quae sunt stomacho utilia signamus.

18   IX. Super omnia adiuvere eum magicae vanitates
in tantum evectae ut abrogare herbis fidem cunctis
possent: aethiopide herba amnes ac stagna siccari,
onothuridis [1] tactu clausa omnia aperiri, achaemenide
coniecta in aciem hostium trepidare agmina ac terga
verti, latacen dari solitam a Persarum rege legatis,
ut quocumque venissent omnium rerum copia
19   abundarent, ac multa similia. ubinam istae fuere,
cum Cimbri Teutonique terribili Marte ululárent, aut
cum Lucullus tot reges Magorum paucis legionibus
sterneret? curve Romaní duces primam semper in
bellis commerciorum habuere curam? cur Caesaris
miles ad Pharsaliam famem sensit, si abundantia
omnis contingere unius herbae felicitate poterat?
non satius fuit Aemilianum Scipionem Carthaginis
portas herba patefacere quam machinis claustra per
tot annos quatere? siccentur hodie meroide Pomp-
tinae paludes tantumque agri suburbanae reddatur
Italiae. nam quae apud eundem Democritum invenitur compositio medicamenti quo pulchri bonique

---

[1] onothuridis *Mayhoff*: chondridis *coni. Ianus*: condyendis
Urlichs: condiendis *plerique codd., Detlefsen.*

---

[a] Again I print Mayhoff's text without much confidence.
The *condiendis* of the MSS. is certainly wrong, and among the
magical herbs mentioned in Book XXIV none comes nearer
to it than this conjecture of Mayhoff.   One might accept
Jan's *chondridis* (cf. XXV, § 93) were that among the magical
herbs.   [b] Probably Pliny's use of *nam = sed*.
[c] Who has not been mentioned in any near context.

instrument into the throat. He rightly condemned emetics also, which were at that time employed unduly often. He disapproved also of administering draughts that are injurious to the stomach, a criticism which is to a great extent a sound one. That is why I always point out in the first place those remedies that are beneficial to the stomach.

IX. Above all Asclepiades was helped by Magian *Superstitions.* deceits, which prevailed to such a degree that they were strong enough to destroy confidence in all herbal remedies. It was believed that by the plant aethiopis rivers and pools are dried up; that by the touch of onothuris [a] all things shut are opened; that if achaemenis is thrown on the ranks of an enemy the lines turn their backs in panic; that latace was wont to be given by the Persian king to his envoys, so that wherever they went they might enjoy an abundant supply of everything, with much similar nonsense. Where then were these plants when the Cimbri and the Teutones raised their awful war yells, or when Lucullus with a few legions laid low so many kings of the Magi? Or why have Roman generals always made victualling a first care in their wars? Why did Caesar's soldiers at Pharsalia feel hunger, if abundant plenty could have been given them by the happy property of a single plant? Would it not have been better for Scipio Aemilianus to open the gates of Carthage by a plant than to shake the defences for so many years with battering-rams? Let the Pomptine marshes be drained today by the plant merois, and much land be recovered for Italy near Rome. But [b] as for the medical prescription found in the same Democritus, [c] to ensure the begetting of beautiful,

et fortunati gignantur liberi cui umquam Persarum
20 regi tales dedit? mirum esset profecto hucusque
provectam credulitatem antiquorum saluberrimis
ortam initiis, si in ulla re modum humana ingenia
novissent atque non hanc ipsam medicinam ab
Asclepiade repertam probaturi suo loco essemus
evectam ultra Magos etiam. haec est omni in re
animorum condicio, ut a necessariis orsa primo
cuncta pervenerint ad nimium. igitur demonstra-
tarum priore libro herbarum reliquos effectus
reddemus adicientes ut quasque ratio dictabit.

21   X. Sed in lichenis remediis atque tam foedo malo
plura undique acervabimus quamquam non paucis
iam demonstratis. medetur ergo plantago trita,
quinquefolium, radix albuci ex aceto, ficulni caules
aceto decocti, hibisci radix cum glutino et aceto acri
decocta ad quartas. defricant etiam pumice, ut
rumicis radix trita ex aceto inlinatur et flos visci cum
22 calce subactus. laudatur et tithymalli cum resina
decoctum, lichen vero herba omnibus his praefertur,
inde nomine invento. nascitur in saxis, folio uno ad
radicem lato, caule uno parvo, longis foliis dependentibus. haec delet et stigmata, teritur cum melle.
est aliud genus lichenis, petris totum adhaerens ut

---

^a XXIX, §§ 6 foll.
^b The glue-like juice of the mistletoe found chiefly in the
berry. For this sense of *flos* cf. Virgil, *Georgics*, IV. 39 :
*fucoque et floribus oras | explent, collectumque haec ipsa ad
munera gluten | et visco et Phrygiae servant pice lentius Idae.*

good and lucky children, did it ever give such offspring to any Persian king? It would certainly be wonderful that the credulity of our forefathers, though it arose from most sound beginnings, reached the height it did, if in any matter man's wit knew moderation, and I were not about to show,ª in the appropriate place, that this very system of medicine invented by Asclepiades has surpassed even Magian nonsense. It is without exception the nature of the human mind that what begins with necessities is finally carried to excess. I shall therefore go on to describe the omitted properties of the plants I dealt with in the preceding book, adding any other plants that my judgment will suggest.

X. But of lichen, which is so disfiguring a disease, *Lichen.* I shall amass from all sources a greater number of remedies, although not a few have been noticed already. Remedies, then, are pounded plaintain, cinquefoil, root of asphodel in vinegar, shoots of the fig-tree boiled down in vinegar, and the root of hibiscus with bee-glue and strong vinegar boiled down to one quarter. The affected part is also rubbed with pumice, as a preparation for the application of rumex root pounded in vinegar, or of mistletoe scum ᵇ kneaded with lime. A decoction too of tithymallus with resin is highly recommended; the plant lichen however is considered a better remedy than all these, a fact which has given the plant its name. It grows among rocks, has one broad leaf near the root, and one small stem with long leaves hanging down from it. This plant removes also marks of scars; it is pounded with honey. There is another kind of lichen, entirely clinging, as does moss, to rocks; this too is used by itself as a local applica-

muscus, qui et ipse inlinitur. hic et sanguinem sistit volneribus instillatus et collectiones inlitus. morbum quoque regium cum melle sanat ore inlito et lingua. qui ita curentur aqua salsa lavari iubentur, ungui oleo amygdalino, hortensiis abstinere. ad lichenas et thapsiae radice utuntur trita cum melle.

23 XI. Anginae argemonia medetur sumpta ex vino, hysopum cum fico decoctum et gargarizatum, peucedanum cum coagulo vituli marini aequis partibus, proserpinaca cum muria ex menis et oleo trita vel sub lingua habita. item sucus de quinquefolio potus cyathis tribus. hic et omnibus faucium vitiis medetur
24 gargarizatus, verbascum privatim tonsillis in aqua potum.

XII. strumis plantago, chelidonia cum melle et axungia, quinquefolium, radix persollatae item cum axungia—operitur folio suo inposita—item artemisia, radix mandragorae ex aqua. sideritis latifolia clavo sinistra manu circumfossa adalligatur, custodienda sanatis, ne rursus sata [1] herbariorum scelere, ut in quibusdam diximus, rebellet, quod et in his quos artemisia sanaverit praedici reperio, item in his
25 quos plantago. damasonium,[2] quae et alisma [3] voca-

---

[1] sata *Detlefsen cum aliquot codd.*: sata die E r: sata taedium *Mayhoff.*

[2] damasonium *Hermolaus Barbarus e Dioscoride, Mayhoff*: damasione VR *Ianus, Detlefsen.*

[3] alisma *Hermolaus Barbarus* : alcea *Caesarius, Detlefsen* : alcima *Ianus, Mayhoff* : caucalin *vulg.* : alcam, alcanam, alia nam, alia *codd.*

tion. It also stops bleeding if the juice is dropped into wounds, and applied locally it is good for gatherings. With honey also it cures jaundice, if the mouth and tongue are smeared with it. Patients undergoing this treatment are ordered to bathe in salt water, to be rubbed with almond oil, and to abstain from garden vegetables. To treat lichen is also used the root of thapsia pounded with honey.

XI. For the treatment of quinsy argemonia is *Quinsy.* taken in wine, hyssop is boiled down with figs and used as a gargle, peucedanum is used with rennet of the seal in equal parts, and proserpinaca pounded with sprats-brine and oil, or else held beneath the tongue. Cinquefoil juice also, in doses of three cyathi. This also used as gargle is good for all affections of the throat; verbascum taken in water is specific for the tonsils.

XII. For scrofulous sores are prescribed plantain, *Scrofula.* the great celandine with honey and axle-grease, cinquefoil, root of persollata also with axle-grease—the application is covered with the plant's leaves—artemisia also and the root of mandrake in water. Broad-leaved sideritis dug up with a nail in the left hand is attached as an amulet, but the healed patients must guard it, lest herbalists wickedly plant it again, as I have said in certain places,[a] and bring about a relapse,[b] a danger against which I find those also are warned who have been cured by artemisia, and those too cured by plantain. Damasonium,

---

[a] See XXI, § 144, and XXV, § 174.
[b] Elsewhere *rebellare* is used of the disease, so that Pliny has probably written carelessly. Mayhoff thinks that *taedium* (cf. XXVI, § 3, *rebellante taedio*) has fallen out after *sata*, where two MSS. have *die*. This may be right.

tur, sub solstitio collecta inponitur ex aqua caelesti,
folium tritum vel radix tusa cum axungia ita ut
inposita folio suo operiatur. sic et ad omnes cervicis
dolores tumoresque quacumque in parte.

26 XIII. Bellis in pratis nascitur, flore albo, aliquatenus rubente. hanc cum artemisia inlitam efficaciorem esse produnt.

XIV. Condurdum quoque herba solstitialis, flore
rubro, suspensa in collo conprimere dicitur strumas,
item verbenaca cum plantagine. digitorum vitiis
omnibus et privatim pterygiis quinquefolium
medetur.

27 XV. In pectoris vitiis vel gravissimum est tussis.
huic medetur panacis radix in vino dulci, sucus hyoscyami—etiam sanguinem excreantibus, nidor quoque accensi tussientibus—item scordotis mixto
nasturtio et resina cum melle tunsa arida—facit et
per se faciles excreationes—item centaurium maius
vel sanguinem reicientibus, cui vitio et plantaginis
28 sucus medetur, et vettonica obolis tribus in aqua
contra purulentas contraque cruentas exscreationes,
persollatae radix drachma ponderis cum pineis
nucleis undecim, peucedani sucus. pectoris doloribus acorum subvenit—et ideo [1] antidotis miscetur—

---

[1] ideo *Detlefsen, codd., vulg.* : idem *Mayhoff.*

---

[a] In deciding the right reading here we should take into
account Dioscorides III, 152 : ἄλισμα · οἱ δὲ δαμασώνιον
καλοῦσιν. Cf. XXV, 124.

[b] Is *folium* (singular) generic ? Perhaps : " so that the
application may be covered etc."

[c] In this context *antidota* may mean " cough mixtures,"
for *antidotum* in the sense of remedy is not without parallel.
Perhaps, however, the sweet-flag was put into antidotes for

which is also called alisma,[a] is gathered at the solstice
and applied in rainwater to the sores, the leaf being
crushed, or the root pounded, with axle-grease, but
the application must be covered with a leaf [b] from
the same plant. The same method is used for all
pains in the neck and for tumours in any part of
the body.

XIII. The daisy grows in meadows. It has a *Daisy.*
white flower, to a certain distance tinged with red.
It is held that an application of it is more efficacious
if artemisia is added.

XIV. Condurdum too is a plant blooming at the *Condurdum.*
summer solstice, having a red flower. Hung round
the neck it is said to arrest scrofula; the same is said
of vervain with plantain. All complaints of the
fingers and specifically whitlows are successfully
treated with cinquefoil.

XV. Of chest complaints quite the most distressing *Coughs.*
is cough. Remedies for it are: root of panaces taken
in sweet wine, juice of henbane (even when there is
spitting of blood; the fumes too of burning henbane
help the cough), scordotis also mixed with cress and
dry resin pounded with honey—even by itself it
makes expectoration easy—the greater centaury too,
even when there is spitting of blood, for which complaint the juice of the plantain also is a remedy,
three oboli of betony in water for spitting of pus or
blood, root of persollata in doses of one drachma
with eleven pine seeds, juice of peucedanum. For
pains in the chest acorum is a help, and for this
reason it is a component of antidotes,[c] a help too for

poisons in order to relieve chest pains. Mayhoff saw the
difficulty and conjectured *idem* for *ideo*; this, however,
makes the parenthesis pointless.

tussi daucum, item Scythica herba; eadem [1] omnibus
pectoris vitiis. tussi et purulenta excreantibus
obolis tribus in passi totidem, verbascum cuius est
29 flos aureus. huic tanta vis ut iumentis etiam non
tussientibus modo sed ilia quoque trahentibus
auxilietur potu, quod et de gentiana reperio. radix
caccaliae commanducata et in vino madefacta non
tussi tantum sed et faucibus prodest. hysopi quinque rami cum duobus rutae et ficis tribus decocti
thoracem purgant, tussim sedant.
30 XVI. Bechion tussilago dicitur. duo eius genera:
silvestris ubi nascitur subesse aquas credunt, et hoc
habent signum aquileges. folia sunt maiuscula
quam hederae quinque aut septem, subalbida a terra,
superne pallida, sine caule, sine flore, sine semine,
radice tenui. quidam eandem esse arcion et alio
nomine chamaeleucen putant. huius aridae cum
radice fumus per harundinem haustus et devoratus
veterem sanare dicitur tussim, sed in singulos
haustus passum gustandum est.
31 XVII. Altera a quibusdam salvia appellatur,
similis verbasco. conteritur et colata calfit atque ita
ad tussim laterisque dolores bibitur, contra scorpiones

---

[1] eadem *Sillig, Mayhoff* : ea demum *aliquot codd.* : ex V[1]R :
ea demum ex V[2].

---

[a] *Commanducata et in vino madefacta* is perhaps *hysteron
proteron.*
[b] *Thorax,* here " chest," often the whole torso.
[c] This chapter is structurally amorphous, and it is futile
to attempt to give it a regular structure, especially when we

cough are daucum and the Scythian herb. The last is helpful for all chest complaints. For cough and spitting of pus, the dose being three oboli in the same amount of raisin wine, the golden-flowered verbascum is a good remedy. The potency of this plant is so great that beasts of burden that are not only suffering from cough but also broken-winded, are relieved by a draught, and the same I find is true of gentian. The root of caccalia, soaked in wine and chewed,[a] is good not only for cough but also for the throat. A decoction of five sprays of hyssop, two of rue, and three figs, clears the chest [b] and soothes the cough.[c]

XVI. Bechion is also called tussilago. There are *Bechion.* two kinds of it. Wherever the wild kind grows it is believed that springs run under the surface, and the plant is considered a sign by the water-finders. The leaves are rather larger than those of ivy, numbering five or seven, whitish underneath and pale on the upper side. There is no stem, or flower, or seed, and the root is slender. Some think it is the same as arcion, and chamaeleuce under another name. The smoke of this plant, dried with the root and burnt, is said to cure, if inhaled deeply through a reed, an inveterate cough, but the patient must take a sip of raisin wine at each inhalation.

XVII. The second kind is called by some salvia, being like verbascum. Finely ground, strained and warmed, it is taken in drink for a cough and pains in the side; this prescription is also a remedy for

remember Pliny's fondness for parentheses. I have ventured on emendation and changes of punctuation only in the few cases where these seemed both necessary and certain.

eadem et dracones marinos efficax. contra serpentes
quoque ex oleo perungui ea prodest. hysopi fasci-
culus cum quadrante mellis decoquitur ad tussim,
lateris, pectoris dolores, verbascum cum ruta ex aqua,
vettonicae farina bibitur ex aqua calida.

32   XVIII. Stomachum conroborat scordotis suco, centaurium, gentiana ex aqua pota, plantago aut per se
in cibo sumpta aut cum lente alicaeve sorbitione.
vettonica alias gravis stomacho vitia tamen sanat pota
vel foliis conmanducata, item aristolochia pota,
agaricum manducatum siccum, ut ex intervallo
merum sorbeatur, nymphaea heraclia inlita, peucedani sucus. psyllion ardoribus inponitur, vel cotyledon trita cum polenta vel aizoum.

33   XIX. Molon scapo est striato, foliis mollibus,
parvis, radice quattuor digitorum in qua extrema alii
caput est. vocatur a quibusdam syron. ex vino
stomacho et ¹ dyspnoeae medetur, centaurium maius
ecligmate, plantago suco vel cibo, vettonicae tusae

---

¹ et om. Mayhoff, qui lacunam indicat.

ᵃ It is difficult to translate draco marinus, probably Tra-
chinus draco, the greater weever, that can inflict poisonous
wounds with its dorsal spines. " Sea snake " and " sea
serpent " are unsuitable for obvious reasons.

ᵇ For alica, groats·from wheat used to make a weak gruel,
see XXII, §§ 128, 129. The Romans used it in preference to
barley water.

ᶜ Ardores is a difficult, at least an ambiguous, term. It
occurs five times in Pliny, and except here always as the direct
object of the verb refrigerare; it is also always in the plural.
It could therefore mean : (1) superficial inflammation, (2)
feverishness, or (3) a feeling of being stifled by heat. In this
passage the verb inponitur makes (1) the most likely meaning.
The other passages are : ad refrigerandos in morbis corporum

scorpion stings and the poison of the sea dragon.[a] An embrocation also of the plant and oil is good for snake bites. For cough, pains in the side and in the chest, a decoction is made of a bunch of hyssop and a quarter of a pound of honey, and verbascum with rue is taken in water, or powdered betony in hot water.

XVIII. The stomach is strengthened by the juice *Stomach* of scordotis, by centaury, by gentian taken in water, *complaints.* by plantain, either taken by itself in food or mixed with lentils or alica[b] gruel. Although betony in general lies heavy on the stomach, yet taken in drink, or if the leaves are chewed, it cures its troubles; aristolochia also may be taken in drink or dry agaric chewed, neat wine being drunk after a while, and nymphaea heraclia or juice of peucedanum may be applied locally. Psyllion is applied to inflammations,[c] or pounded cotyledon with pearl-barley, or aizoüm.

XIX. Molon has a striated stalk, soft small leaves, *Molon, etc.* and a root four fingers long, at the end of which is a head like that of garlic. Some give it the name of syron. In wine it cures stomach troubles[d] and difficulty of breathing, as do the greater centaury in an electuary, plantain, its juice or as food, pounded betony, in the proportion of one pound to half an

ardores (XIV, 99); *ad refrigerandos ardores* (XX, 217); *ardores refrigerando* (of hydromel in a light diet, XXII, 110); *ardores refrigerat* (XXIV, 132). In XXII, 110 at any rate the sense of " feverishness " is the most appropriate.

[d] Mayhoff supposes that there is a lacuna after *stomacho*, probably because of the strange conjunction of complaints. But the whole of this sentence is strange, with scarcely any form at all, order and structure being queer.

pondo libra, mellis Attici semuncia ex aqua calida
cotidie bibentibus, aristolochia vel agaricum obolis
34 ternis ex aqua calida aut lacte asini potum. cissanthemos ad orthopnoeas bibitur, item hysopum et
asthmaticis, peucedani sucus in iocineris doloribus et
pectoris laterisque, si febres non sint. sanguinem
quoque expuentibus subvenit agaricum victoriati
pondere tritum et in mulsi quinque cyathis datum.
35 idem et amomon facit. iocineri privatim teucria
bibitur recens drachmis quattuor in poscae hemina,
vettonicae drachma una in aquae calidae cyathis
tribus, ad cordis vitia in frigidae cyathis duobus.
quinquefolii sucus iocineris et pulmonis vitiis san-
guinemque reicientibus et cuicumque vitio sanguinis
intus occurrit. iocineri anagallides mire prosunt.
capnon herbam qui edere bilem per urinam reddunt,
acoron iocineri medetur, thoraci et praecordiis
daucum.
36 XX. Ephedra ab aliis anabasis vocata nascitur
ventoso fere tractu scandens arborem et ex ramis
propendens, folio nullo, cirris numerosa qui sint
iunci geniculati, radice pallida. datur ex vino nigro
austero trita ad tussim, suspiria, tormina et sorbi-

---

* This probably means that a decoction or infusion is made,
as is often the case when a solid thing " *bibitur*."
b The adverb *intus* is difficult. Literally the clause seems
to mean " fights any blood complaint within," or " advances
to the inside against any blood complaint." This
might mean that impure blood in the internal organs
was purified, or that trouble in the constitution of
the blood anywhere was rectified. Pliny is rather loose
in placing his adverbs and adverbial phràses, so that we
cannot be sure whether *intus* goes more closely with *vitio
sanguinis* or with *occurrit*. Grammatically the latter
would be more correct, but personally I feel that the

ounce of Attic honey and taken daily in hot water,
and aristolochia or agaric in doses of three oboli taken
in hot water or ass's milk.   Cissanthemus is given
in drink [a] for orthopnoea, for that and for asthma
hyssop, while for pains in the liver, chest, and side,
if there is no fever, the juice of peucedanum.   For
spitting of blood also agaric is of help; a victoriatus
by weight is pounded and given in five cyathi of
honey wine.   For this complaint amomum is equally
good.   For liver complaints fresh teucria is specific,
taken in the proportion of four drachmae to one
hemina of vinegar and water, or betony, one drachma
to three cyathi of hot water: the same amount of
betony, in two cyathi of cold water, is given for heart
affections.   The juice of cinquefoil is a remedy for
affections of the liver and lungs, for spitting of blood,
and for all internal blood impurities.[b]   Both kinds of
anagallis are wonderfully good for liver complaints.
Those who have eaten the plant called capnos (smoke)
pass bile in their urine.   Acoron is a cure for liver
diseases, and daucum for those of the chest and
hypochondria.[c]

XX. Ephedra, called by some anabasis, grows *Ephedra.*
generally in wind-swept regions, climbs trees and
hangs down from their branches.   It has no leaves,
but numerous rush-like, jointed tufts, and a pale
root.   For cough, asthma and colic it is given
pounded in a dark-red, dry wine; and it may be made

former is right here.   See my note on XXIII, 163 (vol. VI,
p. 524 note *b*).   Littré translates as though *intus* were not
there, although it appears in his text.
  [c] This part of Pliny is so confused, and remedies and
diseases are so jumbled together, that a marginal analysis
becomes difficult.   The chief complaints considered are those
of the digestive organs.

tione facta in quam vinum addi convenit. item
gentiana madefacta pridie contrita denarii pondere
in vini cyathis tribus.

37 XXI. Geum radiculas tenues habet nigras, bene
olentes. medetur non modo pectoris doloribus aut
lateris sed et cruditates discutit iucundo sapore.
verbenaca vero omnibus visceribus medetur, lateri-
38 bus, pulmonibus, iocineribus, thoraci; peculiariter
autem pulmonibus et quos ab his phthisis temptet
radix herbae consiliginis, quam nuper inventam
diximus. suum quidem et pecoris omnis remedium
praesens est pulmonum vitio vel traiecta tantum in
auricula. bibi debet ex aqua haberique in ore adsidue sub lingua. superficies eius herbae an sit in
aliquo usu adhuc incertum est. renibus prodest
plantaginis cibus, vettonicae potus, agaricum potum
ut in tussi.

39 XXII. Tripolion in maritimis nascitur saxis ubi
alludit unda, neque in mari neque in sicco, folio isatis
crassiore, caule palmum alto, in mucrone diviso,
radice alba, odorata, crassa, calidi gustus. datur
hepaticis in farre cocta. haec herba eadem videtur
quibusdam quae polium de qua suo loco diximus.

XXIII. Gromphaena, alternis viridibus roseisque
per caulem foliis in posca sanguinem reicientibus
40 medetur, XXIV. iocineri autem herba malundrum,

---

a See Book XXV, § 86.
b See Book XXI, §§ 44, 145–147.

into a gruel, to which wine should be added. Another remedy is gentian, thoroughly pounded after being steeped the day before, the dose being a denarius by weight in three cyathi of wine.

XXI. Geum has little roots, slender, blackish and *Geum.* with a pleasant smell. It not only is a cure for pains in the chest or side, but also dispels indigestion, having besides a pleasant taste. Vervain however is a cure for troubles of all the internal organs—sides, lungs, liver and chest. But especially good for the lungs, and for those attacked by pulmonary tuberculosis, is the root of the plant consiligo, which I have said was but recently discovered.[a] It is a sovereign remedy indeed for lung trouble in pigs and in all cattle, even though it is merely placed across the ear-lap. It ought to be drunk in water and held continuously in the mouth under the tongue. Whether the part of this plant above ground is of any use is not yet agreed. The kidneys are benefited by plantain taken as food, by betony taken in drink, and by agaric taken in drink as is prescribed for cough.

XXII. Tripolion is found on coastal rocks washed by *Tripolion.* the waves, but neither in the sea nor on dry ground; the leaf is that of isatis only thicker, the stem a span high and divided at the end, and the root white, thick, with a strong smell and a hot taste. Cooked in emmer wheat it is prescribed for patients with liver complaint. This plant is thought by some to be the same as polium, about which I have spoken [b] in its proper place.

XXIII. Gromphaena, which has its leaves alter- *Gromphaena* nately green and rose-colour along the stem, taken *and other plants.* in vinegar and water cures spitting of blood; XXIV. and the plant malundrum cures troubles of the liver;

PLINY : NATURAL HISTORY

nascens in segete ac pratis, flore albo odorata. eius
cauliculus conteritur ex vino vetere. XXV. item
herba calcetum e vinaceis contrita inponitur. faciles
praestat vomitiones radix vettonicae, hellebori modo
quattuor drachmis in passo aut mulso, hysopum tritum
cum melle, utilius praesumpto nasturtio aut irione,
molemonium denarii pondere. et sillybi [1] lacteus
sucus qui densatur in cummim sumitur cum melle
supra dicto pondere praecipueque bilem trahit.

41 rursus sistunt vomitionem cuminum silvestre, vettonicae farina, sumuntur ex aqua. abstergent
fastidia cruditatesque digerunt daucum, vettonicae
farina ex aqua mulsa, plantago decocta caulium
modo. singultus hemionion sedat, item aristolochia, suspiria clymenus. pleuriticis et peripleumonicis centaurium maius, item hysopum bibitur,
pleuriticis peucedani sucus.

42 XXVI. Halus [2] autem, quam Galli sil [3] vocant,
Veneti cotoneam medetur lateri, item renibus con-
volsisque et ruptis. similis est cunilae bubulae,
cacuminibus thymo, dulcis et sitim sedans, radicis
alibi albae, alibi nigrae.

XXVII. Eosdem effectus in lateris doloribus habet
chamaerops myrteis circa caules geminos foliis,
capitibus Graeculae rosae, ex vino pota. ischiadicos
dolores et spinae levat agaricum potum ut in tussi,

---

[1] sillybi *Mayhoff, qui sic distinguit* : sillybus *Detlefsen, qui
cum* molemonium *coniungit* : *varia codd.*
[2] Halus *Detlefsen, codd.* : alus *coni. Mayhoff.*
[3] sil *Schneider, Sillig, Detlefsen* : sic *codd.*

---

a Or, " little stalk."

it grows among the corn and in meadows, with a strong scent and a white flower. Its young shoot [a] is beaten up in old wine.

XXV. The plant calcetum likewise is crushed with grape-skins and applied locally. Betony root acts as a gentle emetic, administered as is hellebore, the dose being four drachmae taken in raisin wine or in honey wine. The same is true of hyssop beaten up with honey, the result being better if cress or irio is taken first. Another cure is molemonium in doses of one denarius by weight. The milky juice of sillybum also, which thickens into a gum, is taken with honey, the dose being as above, and is excellent for carrying off bile. On the other hand, vomiting is arrested by wild cummin, or by powdered betony, both taken in water. Distaste for food is banished and indigestion dispelled by daucum, by powdered betony in hydromel, and by plantain boiled down as are greens. Hemionion relieves hiccoughs, as also does aristolochia, and clymenus relieves asthma. For pleurisy and pneumonia the greater centaury, and likewise hyssop, are taken in drink, and for pleurisy is taken juice of peucedanum.

XXVI. Halus also, which the Gauls call sil and the Veneti cotonea, cures pain in the side, as well as kidney troubles, sprains and ruptures. It is like ox-cunila, and the tops are like those of thyme. It is sweet and allays thirst. Its roots are in some districts light, in others dark.

XXVII. The same good effect on pain in the sides is given by chamaerops, taken in wine, a plant with myrtle-like leaves around its twin stems, and with heads like those of a Greek rose. Agaric, taken in drink as for cough, relieves sciatica and pains in the

item stoechadis aut vettonicae farina ex aqua mulsa.

43 XXVIII. Plurimum tamen homini negotii alvus exhibet, cuius causa maior pars mortalium vivit. alias enim cibos non transmittit, alias non continet, alias non capit, alias non conficit, eoque mores venere ut homo maxime cibo pereat. pessimum corporum vas instat ut creditor et saepius die appellat. huius gratia praecipue avaritia expetit, huic luxuria condit, huic navigatur ad Phasim, huic profundi vada exquiruntur. et nemo vilitatem eius aestimat consummationis foeditate. ergo numerosissima est circa hanc medi-

44 cinae opera. sistit eam scordotis recens drachma cum vino trita vel decocta potu, polemonia quae et dysintericis ex vino datur, verbasci radix pota ex aqua duorum digitorum magnitudine, nymphaeae heracliae semen cum vino potum radix superior e xiphio drachmae pondere ex aceto, semen planta-ginis in vino tritum vel ipsa ex aceto cocta aut alica ex suco eius sumpta, item cum lenticula cocta vel aridae farina inspersa potioni cum papavere tosto et trito, vel sucus infusus aut potus, vettonica in vino ferro calefacto. eadem coeliacis in vino austero datur, his et hiberis inponitur uti dictum est.

---

a The other verbs in this sentence are intelligible, but the difference between *non continet* and *non capit* is hard to grasp. I suggest, with some diffidence, that the former refers to vomiting, and the latter to the " full feeling " that rejects even the greatest delicacy. Professor Andrews however suggests diarrhoea and regurgitation.

spine, as does powdered stoechas or betony, taken
in hydromel.

XXVIII. The greatest part however of man's *Diseases of*
trouble is caused by the belly, the gratification of *the digestive*
which is the life's work of the majority of mankind. *organs.*
For at one time it does not allow food to pass, at another
it will not retain it, at another it does not take *ª* it, at
another it does not digest it; and so much have our
customs degenerated that it is chiefly through his
food that a man dies. This, the most troublesome
organ in the body, presses as does a creditor, making
its demands several times a day. It is for the belly's
sake especially that avarice is so acquisitive; for its
sake luxury uses spices, voyages are made to the
Phasis, and the bottom of the ocean is explored.
Nobody, again, is led to consider how base an organ
it is by the foulness of its completed work. Therefore the tasks of medicine concerned with the belly
are very numerous. Looseness of the bowels is
checked by a drachma dose of fresh scordotis beaten
up with wine, or by the same quantity taken in a
decoction, by polemonia in wine, which is also given
for dysentery, by root of verbascum in doses of two
fingers' size taken in water, the seed of nymphaea
heraclia taken with wine, the upper root of xiphium,
the dose being a drachma by weight, taken in
vinegar, the seed of plantain beaten up in wine,
plantain itself boiled in vinegar, or groats taken in
plantain juice, also the plant boiled with lentils, or
the plant dried, powdered and sprinkled in drink
with parched and pounded poppies, juice of plantain
injected or drunk, or betony in wine made warm
with hot iron. Betony is also administered in a
dry wine for coeliac affections, for which hiberis also

45 tenesmo radix nymphaeae heracliae e vino bibitur,
psyllium in aqua, acori radicis decoctum. aizoi sucus
alvum sistit et dysinterias et taenias rotundas pellit.
symphyti radix pota in vino alvum et dysinteriam
sistit, idem dauci. aizoum foliis contritis ex vino
torminibus resistit, alcimae siccae farina torminibus
pota cum vino.

46 XXIX. Astragalus folia habet longa incisuris multis
obliquis, circa radicem caules tres, aut quattuor
foliorum plenos, florem hyacinthi, radices villosas,
inplicatas, rubras, praeduras. nascitur in petrosis,
apricis et isdem nivalibus, sicut Pheneo Arcadiae.
vis ei ad spissanda corpora. alvum sistit radix in
vino pota, quo fit ut moveat urinam repercusso
liquore, sicut pleraque quae alvum sistunt. sanat et
dysintericos in vino rubro tusa, difficile autem tunditur. eadem gingivarum suppurationi utilissima est
fotu. colligitur exitu autumni, cum folia amisit,
siccatur in umbra.

47 XXX. Et ladano sistitur alvus utroque, quod in
segetibus nascitur contuso et cribrato ; bibitur ex
aqua mulsa item nobili e vino. ledon appellatur
herba ex qua fit in Cypro barbis caprarum adhae-
rescens. nobilius in Arabia. fit iam [1] et in Syria

---

[1] *Mayhoff ita distinguit* : nobilius in Arabia fit, iam.

---

[a] Book XXV, § 88.
[b] It is noticeable how Pliny carelessly repeats himself in
this chapter. In the last sentence *torminibus* occurs twice ; in
each of the two preceding sentences occurs the phrase *alvum
sistit*.
[c] *Rubrum vinum*, a light red wine ; *nigrum vinum*, a wine of
the colour of port.

is applied locally in the way I have described.[a] For tenesmus the root of nymphaea heraclia is taken in wine, psyllium in water, or a decoction of root of acoron. The juice of aizoüm checks looseness of the bowels and dysentery, and expels round worms. Root of symphytum taken in wine checks looseness of the bowels and dysentery, as does the root of daucum. Leaves of aizoüm thoroughly beaten up in wine arrest griping pains, as does dried alcima powdered and taken with wine.[b]

XXIX. Astragalus has long leaves with many *Astragalus.* slanting incisions, around the root three or four stems covered with leaves, blossom like that of the hyacinthus, and roots that are hairy, matted, red and very hard. It grows on stony ground that is exposed to sunshine and also to falls of snow, like the ground around Pheneus in Arcadia. Its property is to brace the body. Its root, taken in wine, checks looseness of the bowels, a result of which is that it is diuretic by forcing back their fluid, as most things do that check looseness. It cures dysentery also when ground in light-red[c] wine, but it is ground only with difficulty. Fomentation with the same plant is very good for gum-boils. It is gathered at the end of autumn, when it has lost its leaves, and is dried in the shade.

XXX. Looseness of the bowels is also checked by *Ladanum.* both kinds of ladanum; the one that grows in corn-fields must be first crushed and passed through a sieve. It is taken in hydromel, or in wine of a good vintage. The name of ledon is given to a plant from which in Cyprus is made the ladanum that clings to the beards of goats; a finer sort is prepared in Arabia. Today a kind is also found in Syria and in Africa, called

PLINY : NATURAL HISTORY

atque Africa, quod toxicum vocant. nervos enim in
arcu circumdatos lanis trahunt adhaerescente roscida
48 lanugine. plura de eo diximus inter unguenta.
hoc gravissimum odore est durissimumque tactu.
plurimum enim terrae colligit, cum probetur maxime
purum, odoratum, molle, viride, resinosum. natura
ei molliendi, siccandi, concoquendi, somnum ad-
liciendi. capillum fluentem cohibet nigritiamque
custodit, auribus cum hydromelite aut rosaceo infunditur, furfures cutis et manantia ulcera sale addito
sanat, tussim veterem cum storace sumptum, efficacissimum ad ructus.

49   XXXI. Alvum sistit et chondris sive pseudodictamnum. hypocisthis, orobothron quibusdam dicta,
malo granato inmaturo similis, nascitur ut diximus,
sub cistho, unde nomen. haec arefacta in umbra
sistit alvum ex vino nigro austero utraque. duo enim
genera eius, candida et rufa. usus in suco, spissat,
siccat, et rufa magis stomachi rheumatismos emendat,
pota tribus obolis sanguinis excreationes cum amylo,
dysinterias pota et infusa, item verbenaca ex aqua
data aut carentibus febri ex vino Aminneo, coch-
learibus quinque additis in cyathos tres vini.

---

    a The word τόξον means " bow."
    b See Book XII, §§ 73 foll.
    c Book XXIV, § 81.
    d The word " hypocisthis " in Greek means " under the
cisthus."
    e Et has often to be translated " or." Sometimes the sense
shows that " or " is the obvious translation, the difference

toxicum. For they surround with pieces of wool strings
fastened across a bow,[a] and drag it over the plant;
to this wool adhere the dew-like tufts of ladanum.
I have said more about the plant in my section on
unguents.[b] This ladanum has a very strong smell
and is very hard to the touch. In fact a great deal
of earth sticks to it, while the most valued kind is
clean, scented, soft, green and resinous. Its nature
is to soften, to dry, to mature abscesses, and to induce
sleep. It prevents the hair from falling off, and
preserves its dark colour. It is poured into the
ears with hydromel or rose-oil. With the addition
of salt it cures scurf on the skin and running sores,
and chronic cough when taken with storax; it is also
a very effective carminative.

XXXI. Looseness of the bowels is checked too by *Other diges-*
chondris, also called pseudodictamnum. Hypocisthis, *tive remedies.*
called by some orobothron, which is like an unripe
pomegranate, grows as I have said[c] under the
cisthus, and from this fact derives its name.[d] Either
kind of hypocisthis (there are two; the white and the
red), dried in the shade and taken in dark-red, dry
wine, checks looseness of the bowels. The part used
is the juice, which braces and dries, and it is the red
kind that arrests better stomach catarrhs, spitting of
blood when three oboli are taken with starch in
drink, and dysentery when taken in drink or[e]
injected; similarly vervain given in water, or in
Aminnean wine if there is no fever, the dose
being five spoonfuls added to three cyathi of
wine.

between the two languages being idiomatic; at other times
(as here) there is a real ambiguity, and nobody can decide
whether *et* is equivalent to " and " or " or."

50   XXXII. Laver quoque nascens in rivis condita et
cocta torminibus medetur, XXXIII. potamogiton
vero ex vino disintericis etiam et coeliacis, similis
betae foliis, minor tantum hirsutiorque, paulum
semper eminens extra aquam. usus in foliis :
refrigerant, spissant, peculiariter cruribus vitiosis
utilia et contra ulcerum nomas cum melle vel aceto.
51 Castor hanc aliter noverat, tenui folio velut equinis
saetis, thyrso longo et levi, in aquosis nascentem.
radice sanabat strumas et duritias. potamogiton
adversatur crocodilis, itaque secum habent eam qui
venantur eos. alvum sistit et achillea. eosdem
effectus praestat et statice, septem caulibus veluti
rosae capita sustinens.

52   XXXIV. Ceratia uno folio, radice nodosa et
magna, in cibo coeliacis et dysintericis medetur.
leontopodion alii leuceoron, alii dorypetron, alii
thorybethron vocant, cuius radix alvum sistit purgat-
que bilem, in aquam mulsam addito pondere
denariorum duorum. nascitur in campestri et
gracili solo. semen eius potum lymphatica somnia
facere dicitur. lagopus sistit alvum e vino pota aut
53 in febri ex aqua. eadem inguini adalligatur in
tumore. nascitur in segetibus. multi super omnia
laudant ad deploratos dysintericos quinquefolium

ª Bostock and Riley have : " neutralizes the effects of the
bite of the crocodile," a translation which fits in with the
usual sense of *adversari* in Pliny, and, absurd as it sounds,
may be right. Perhaps the plant was used as an amulet.
    ᵇ Not that it would be taken with that object. Cf. § 57.

XXXII. Laver also, which grows in streams, when preserved and boiled cures gripings, XXXIII. potamogiton, however, taken in wine, cures dysentery as well and coeliac affections. The latter is a plant with leaves like those of beet, only it is a smaller and more hairy plant, never rising more than a little above the surface of the water. Only the leaves are used, which have a cooling and bracing quality, being especially useful for bad legs, and, with honey or vinegar, for corroding ulcers. The plant known to Castor under this name was different; it had slender leaves like horse-hair, a long, smooth stem, and grew in marshy districts. With its root Castor used to cure scrofulous sores and indurations. The crocodile has an antipathy [a] to potamogiton, so that crocodile hunters carry some of it on their persons. Achillea too checks looseness of the bowels. Statice also has the same properties, a plant that bears seven heads, like the heads of a rose, upon seven stems.

XXXIV. Ceratia, a plant with one leaf, and a large, knotted root, taken in food cures sufferers from coeliac disease and dysentery. Leontopodium, called by some leuceoron, by others dorypetron, by others thorybethron, is a plant the root of which, in doses of two denarii by weight added to hydromel, checks looseness of the bowels and carries off bile. It grows on flat land with a thin soil. Its seed, taken in drink, is said to cause nightmares.[b] Lagopus taken in wine, or in water if there is fever, checks looseness of the bowels. It is also attached to the groin when there is swelling there. It grows in cornfields. Many recommend above all else for desperate cases of dysentery doses of a decoction

decoctis in lacte radicibus potis, et aristolochiam
victoriati pondere in cyathis vini tribus. quae ex
supra dictis calida sumentur, haec candente ferro
temperari aptius erit. e diverso purgat alvum sucus
54 centaurii minoris drachma in hemina aquae cum
exiguo salis et aceti bilemque detrahit, maiore
tormina discutiuntur. vettonica alvum solvit drachmis quattuor in hydromelitis cyathis novem, item
euphorbeum vel agaricum drachmis duabus cum sale
modico potum ex aqua aut in mulso obolis tribus.
solvit et cyclaminos ex aqua pota aut balanis subditis,
item chamaecissi balanus. hysopi manipulus decoctus ad tertias cum sale et pituitas trahit [1] vel
tritus in oxymelite et sale, pellitque ventris animalia.
pituitam et bilem detrahit peucedani radix.
55 XXXV. Alvum purgant anagallides ex aqua mulsa,
item epithymum, qui est flos e thymo satureiae
simili. differentia, quod hic herbaceus est, alterius
thymi albus; quidam hippopheon vocant. stomacho
minus utilis vomitiones movet, sed tormina et inflationes discutit. sumitur et ecligmate ad pectoris
56 vitia cum melle et aliquando iride. alvum solvit a
quattuor drachmis ad sex cum melle et exiguo salis
atque aceti. quidam aliter epithymum tradunt sine
radice nasci, capite tenui [2] similitudine pallioli,
rubens, siccari in umbra, bibi ex aqua acetabuli parte
dimidia, detrahere pituitam bilemque, alvo leniter

---

[1] *Post* trahit d(?) *et vulg.* inlitus *addunt.*
[2] capite tenui *coni. Mayhoff sed in textu* tenue *cum Har-
duino* : tenuis *Detlefsen* : tenui *codd.*

---

[a] In this chapter, as in most prescriptions given by Pliny,
although the dosage is often given, the frequency of the doses is
omitted, as is the length of the treatment. These important
points are often left to chance or common sense.

in milk of the roots of cinquefoil, or aristolochia,
a victoriatus by weight in three cyathi of wine.
When the prescriptions mentioned above are to be
taken warm, it will be found best to heat them
with red-hot iron. On the other hand a drachma
of the juice of the lesser centaury taken in a hemina
of water with a little salt and vinegar purges the
bowels and carries off bile; *a* the greater centaury
dispels griping pains. Betony acts as an aperient,
four drachmae being added to nine cyathi of hydromel;
so also euphorbeum or agaric, in doses of two
drachmae with a little salt, taken in water or in three
oboli of honey wine. Cyclamen too is an aperient,
either taken in water or used as a suppository; the
same in its action is a suppository of chamaecissos.
A handful of hyssop, boiled down to one third with
salt, or pounded in oxymel and salt, both carries off
phlegm and expels worms from the intestines. Root
of peucedanum carries off both phlegm and bile.

XXXV. Both kinds of anagallis, taken in hydromel,
are purgative, as is also epithymum, which is the
blossom of the thyme like satureia. The only difference is that this has a grass-green flower, the other
thyme a white one. Some call it hippopheos. Less
beneficial to the stomach, it causes vomitings, but
dispels colic and flatulence. As an electuary it is
also taken with honey, and sometimes with iris, for
chest troubles. From four to six drachmae with
honey and a little salt and vinegar move the bowels.
Others give a different account of epithymum: that
it grows without a root, has a small head like a little
hood, is red in colour and is dried in the shade, and a
dose of half an acetabulum, taken in water, carries
off phlegm and bile, acting as a gentle aperient.

57 soluta. XXXVI. et nymphaea in vino austero solvit et pycnocomon, erucae foliis crassioribus et acrioribus, radice rotunda lutei coloris terram olente, caule quadriangulo, modico, tenui, flore ocimi. invenitur in saxosis locis. radix eius in aqua mulsa ✶ II pondere et alvum et bilem et pituitam exinanit. semen somnia tumultuosa facit una drachma in vino potum. et capnos [1] trunca [2] detrahit bilem.

58 XXXVII. Polypodi, quam nostri filiculam vocant, similis filicis, radix in usu, pilosa, coloris intus herbacei, crassitudine digiti minimi, acetabulis cavernosa ceu polyporum cirri, subdulcis, in petris nascens aut sub arboribus vetustis. exprimitur sucus aqua madefactae, et ipsa minute concisa inspergitur oleri vel betae vel malvae vel salsamento aut cum pulticula coquitur ad alvum vel in febri leniter solvendam. detrahit bilem et pituitam, stomachum offendit. aridae farina indita naribus polypum consumit. florem et semen non fert.

[1] et capnos Vd, *Mayhoff* : et carnos E r : discutit panos *Detlefsen*.
[2] trunca *Ianus, Mayhoff* : struma d : strumam V *Detlefsen* : tru E r *unde Mayhoff* esu *coni. XX 178 collato* : per urinam *coni. Sillig.*

---

[a] Dioscorides has δριμέα (IV. 174).
[b] Perhaps deliberately induced for diagnostic purposes as by the cult of Aesculapius. The next sentence is corrupt in

XXXVI. Nymphaea too in a dry wine loosens the bowels, as also does pycnocomon, which has leaves like rocket, but thicker and more acrid,[a] a round root of a yellow colour and an earthy smell, a quadrangular stem, of moderate length and slender, and the blossom of basil. It is found on stony ground. Its root, taken in hydromel in doses of two denarii by weight, thoroughly purges the bowels of bile and phlegm. A drachma of the seed, taken in wine, causes wild dreams.[b] Capnos trunca also carries away bile.

XXXVII. Of polypodium, a plant called by *Polypodium.* Romans filicula, being like a fern (*filix*), the root is medicinal, hairy, grass-green inside, as thick as the little finger, with indented edges so as to look like a polypus's arms, of a sweetish taste, and to be found [c] in stony soils or under old trees. The juice is extracted from the root soaked in water, and chopped up fine the root itself is sprinkled on cabbage, beet, mallows and pickled fish, or else boiled with gruel to make a gentle aperient usable even in fever. It brings away bile and phlegm, although injurious to the stomach. Dried and reduced to powder it eats away polypus if pushed up the nostrils. There is no flower and no seed.[c]

the MSS. with no convincing emendation. I have followed Mayhoff without confidence, believing that there is a lacuna after *facit*: " although the seed causes nightmares yet ⟨it has beneficial effects on the bowels⟩."

[c] In both these places there is a kind of confusion between the root and the plant. It is the leaves that are indented. Only the root was used medicinally, as we see from *radix in usu,* and all the chapter applies to it except the phrases *acetabulis . . . cirri* and *in petris . . . vetustis* and the sentence *florem et semen non fert.* Although, however, the style is faulty, yet the sense is quite clear.

59   XXXVIII. Scamonium quoque dissolutione[1] stomachi[2] bilem detrahit, alvum solvit, praeterquam si
adiciantur aloes drachmae duae obolis eius duobus.
est autem sucus herbae ab radice ramosae pinguibus
foliis, triangulis, albis, radice crassa, madida, nausiosa.
60 nascitur pingui et albo solo.   radix circa canis ortum
excavatur, ut in ipsam confluat sucus qui sole siccatus
digeritur in pastillos.   siccatur et ipsa vel cortex.
laudatur natione Colophonium, Mysium, Prienense,
specie autem nitidum et quam simillimum taurino
glutini, fungosum tenuissimis fistulis, cito liquescens,
virus redolens, cumminosum, linguae tactu lactescens,
quam levissimum, cum diluatur albescens.   hoc
evenit et adulterino quod fit ervi farina et tithymalli
marini suco fere in Iudaea, quod etiam · strangulat
61 sumptum.   deprehenditur gustu, tithymallus enim
linguam excalefacit.   usus bimo, nec ante nec postea
utile, dedere et per se ex aqua vel[3] mulsa et sale
quaternis obolis, sed utilissime cum aloe ita ut incipiente purgatione mulsum bibatur.   fit et decoctum

---

[1] dissolutione *Detlefsen* : dissolutiones (*aut* -em) *multi codd.* :
non sine dissolutione *coni. Mayhoff* : *fortasse* cum dissolutione.
[2] stomachi] facit *addit Gelenii editio.*
[3] vel *multi codd., Detlefsen, Mayhoff, qui ex Dioscoride* pura
vel *coni*: vel *ante* ex aqua *trans. E. Wistrand* (*Eranos*, 1931.)

---

[a] The Latin of this sentence would be made more normal by
the addition of *non sine* or *cum* before *dissolutione.*   It would
be perhaps more " Plinian " if we kept the *dissolutionem* or
dissolutiones of the MSS. and added *facit* after *stomachi.*
Then from *bilem* to *solvit* would be a parenthesis characteristic
of Pliny, and the subordinate clause beginning with *praeterquam* would depend logically and grammatically on *dissolutionem stomachi facit.*

[b] Littré has : " On fait sécher aussi la plante même ou
l'écorce."

XXXVIII. It is by relaxing the stomach that *Scamonium.*
scamonium too brings away bile and loosens the
bowels, unless indeed to two oboli of it are added two
drachmae of aloes.[a] This is the juice of a plant
with many branches at the root, fleshy, three-cornered,
pale leaves, and a thick, wet, nauseating root. It
grows in rich, pale soil. Near the rising of the
Dogstar a hollow is made in this root, so that the
juice may collect in it automatically; this is dried
in the sun and worked into lozenges. The root itself
or the skin is also dried.[b] The kind most approved
grows in the regions of Colophon, Mysia and Priene.
This is shiny, as like as possible to bull glue,[c] spongy
with very fine cracks,[d] quickly melting,[e] with a poisonous smell, gummy, becoming like milk at a touch of
the tongue, extremely light, and turning white when
dissolved. This happens too with bastard scamonium, which is made, generally in Judaea, with flour of
bitter vetch and juice of sea spurge, and even chokes
those who take it. The bastard kind is detected by
the taste, for the genuine burns the tongue. It is
to be used when two years old, being of no use
either before or after. It has been prescribed by
itself in water or in hydromel and salt,[f] the dose
being four oboli, but most effectively with aloes,
though honey wine must be taken as soon as
purging begins. The root too is boiled down in
vinegar to the consistency of honey, the decoction

---

[c] For this see XXVIII, § 236.

[d] Dioscorides has (IV, 170) σήραγγας ἔχων λεπτάς, σπογγώδης.
Pliny may have mistaken the first word for σύριγγας.

[e] Or, "becoming flabby" (Professor A. C. Andrews).

[f] Wistrand's emendation is attractive: "either by itself or
in hydromel and salt."

PLINY : NATURAL HISTORY

radicis in aceto ad crassitudinem mellis, quo leprae
inlinuntur et caput inunguitur[1] in dolore cum oleo.

62 XXXIX. Tithymallum nostri herbam lactariam
vocant, alii lactucam caprinam, narrantque lacte eius
inscripto corpore, cum inaruerit, si cinis inspargatur,
apparere litteras, et ita quidam adulteras adloqui
maluere quam codicillis. genera eius multa: primus
cognominatur characias, qui et masculus existimatur, ramis digitali crassitudine, rubris, sucosis,
quinque aut sex, cubitali longitudine, a radice foliis

63 paene oleae, in cacuminibus coma iunci. nascitur in
asperis maritimis, legitur semen autumno cum coma,
siccatum sole tunditur et reponitur. sucus vero
incipiente pomorum lanugine defractis ramulis excipitur farina ervi aut ficis ut cum iis arescat. quinas
autem guttas singulis excipi satis est, traduntque
etiam totiens purgari hydropicos fico sumpta quot

64 guttas ea lactis exceperit. sucus cum colligitur, ne
attingat oculos cavendum est. fit et e foliis tunsis
priore minus efficax. fit et decoctum e ramis. est et
semen in usu cum melle decoctum ad catapotia
solvendae alvi gratia. semen et dentium cavis cera
includitur. coluuntur et radicis decocto e vino aut

---

[1] inunguitur d, *Mayhoff*: unguitur *plerique codd.*, *Detlefsen*.

---

[a] On *coma* see pp. 482, 483.
[b] Two sentences from Dioscorides IV, 164, are interesting.
They are : ὀπίζεται δὲ περὶ τὸν τρυγητόν, and : ἐν δὲ τῷ ὀπίζειν
οὐ δεῖ κατ᾽ ἄνεμον ἵστασθαι οὐδὲ τὰς χεῖρας προσάγειν τοῖς
ὀφθαλμοῖς.

310

being applied to leprous sores, and with oil it is used as an ointment for the head when there is headache.

XXXIX. Tithymallus is called " milky plant " by us Romans, sometimes " goat lettuce." It is said *Tithymallus.* that, if letters are traced on the body with its milk and then allowed to dry, on being sprinkled with ash the letters become visible. And it is by this means, rather than by a letter, that some lovers have preferred to address unfaithful wives. The kinds of it are many, the first being surnamed characias, which is also considered the male plant. It has five or six branches, a cubit long, as thick as a finger, red and juicy; the leaves at the root are very like those of the olive, and on the top of the stem is a head[a] like that of the rush. It grows on rough ground near the sea. The seed is gathered in autumn together with the head; after being left to get dry in the sun it is pounded and stored away; as to the juice, as soon as down begins to form on fruit,[b] twigs are broken off, and juice therefrom is caught on meal of bitter vetch or on figs and left to get dry with them. Five drops are enough to be caught on each fig, and it is reported that a dropsical patient on taking a fig has as many motions as the fig has caught drops of juice. When the juice is being collected care must be taken that it does not touch the eyes.[b] A juice is also extracted from pounded leaves, but one less efficacious than the former. A decoction too is made from the branches. The seed is also used, boiled down with honey, to make purgative pills. The seed is also inserted with wax into hollow teeth. A decoction too of the root in wine or oil is used as a mouth-wash. The juice is

oleo. inlinunt et lichenas suco, bibuntque eum ut
purget vomitione et alvo soluta, alias stomacho
65 inutilem. trahit pituitam sale addito in potu, bilem
aphronitro, si per alvum purgari libeat, in posca, si
vomitione, in passo aut aqua mulsa. media potio
tribus obolis datur. ficos a cibo sumpsisse melius est.
fauces urit leniter, est enim tam ferventis naturae ut
per se extra corpori inposita ¹ pusulas ignium modo
faciat et pro caustico in usu sit.
66 XL. Alterum genus tithymalli myrtiten vocant, alii
caryiten, foliis myrti acutis et pungentibus, sed
maioribus,² et ipsum in asperis nascens. colliguntur
comae eius hordeo turgescente siccataeque in umbra
diebus novem in sole inarescunt. fructus non pariter
maturescit, sed pars anno sequente, et nux vocatur.
67 inde cognomen Graeci dedere. demetitur cum ³
messium maturitate lavaturque, deinde siccatur et
datur cum papaveris nigri duabus partibus ita ut sit
totum acetabuli modus, minus hic vomitorius ⁴ quam
superior, ceteri item.⁵ aliqui sic et folium eius dedere,

---

¹ inposita *cod.* a, *Detlefsen* : inpositus *Mayhoff* : inpositum
plerique codd., vulg.
² maioribus *e Dioscoride* IV 164 (φύλλα . . . μείζω δὲ καὶ
στερεά) *Mayhoff* : mollioribus *codd., vulg., edd.*
³ cum *plerique codd., Mayhoff* : om. *cod.* a, *Detlefsen.*
⁴ vomitorius *C. F. W. Müller, Mayhoff* : vomitionibus
codd., vulg.
⁵ ceteri item *Mayhoff* : ceterum idem *Detlefsen* : (centum
a : idem V x a). *Fortasse* ceteri usus iidem, *ut Mayhoff coni.*

ᵃ Mayhoff's conjecture *inpositus (scil. sucus)* is what Pliny
ought to have written, but I think that he wrote the feminine
because he had *natura*, or perhaps *herba*, in mind. The better
attested reading *inpositum* can scarcely be right, as there is

applied locally for lichen; it is taken internally as a purge, being both an emetic and an aperient; apart from this it is bad for the stomach. Taken in drink with the addition of salt it brings away phlegm, but to bring away bile saltpetre must be added; if it is desired that the purging shall be by stool, the drink should be vinegar and water; if by vomiting, raisin wine or hydromel. A moderate draught is made up with three oboli. It is better taken on a fig, and after food. The juice burns the throat slightly; for it is of so heating a nature that, applied [a] externally by itself to the body, it raises blisters as fire does, and so it is sometimes used as a cautery.

XL. The second kind of tithymallus is called myrtites by some, and caryites by others, having leaves like those of the myrtle, pointed and prickly, but larger, and growing like the first kind in rough ground. Its heads are gathered when the barley is beginning to swell, dried in the shade for nine days and thoroughly dried in the sun. The fruit does not ripen all together, but a part in the following year. It is called the nut, and for this reason the Greeks have surnamed this tithymallus caryites.[b] It is gathered when the harvest is ready, washed, and then dried. It is given with twice the amount of black poppy,[c] the dose being one acetabulum altogether. It is a less violent emetic than the preceding, as are also the others. Some have given the leaf also in a similar dose, the nut however by itself in

Various kinds of tithymallus.

no neuter noun it could refer to, but *inpositū* might have been written by a scribe who was worried by *inposita.*

[b] The Greek word κάρυον means " a nut."

[c] Hort on Theophrastus IX, xi, 9, from which Pliny took his account, says that "μέλαινα must here mean ʻdark,ʼ i.e. red."

nucem vero ipsam in mulso aut passo vel cum sesima. trahit pituitam et bilem per alvum. oris ulcera sanat, ad nomas oris folium cum melle estur.

68 XLI. Tertium genus tithymalli paralium vocatur sive tithymallis folio rotundo, caule palmum alto, ramis rubentibus, semine albo, quod colligitur incipiente uva et siccatum teritur sumiturque acetabuli mensura ad purgationes.

69 XLII. Quartum genus helioscopion appellant, foliis porcillacae, ramulis stantibus a radice quattuor aut quinque rubentibus, semipedali altitudine, suci plenis. hoc circa oppida nascitur semine albo columbis gratissimo; nomen accepit, quoniam capita cum sole circumagit. trahit bilem per inferna in oxymelite dimidio acetabulo, ceteri usus qui characiae.

70 XLIII. Quintum cyparittian vocant propter foliorum similitudinem, caule gemino aut triplici, nascentem in campestribus. eadem vis quae helioscopio aut characiae.

XLIV. Sextum platyphyllon vocant, alii corymbiten, alii amygdaliten a similitudine. nec ullius latiora sunt folia. pisces necat, alvum solvit radice vel foliis vel suco in mulso aut aqua mulsa drachmis quattuor. detrahit privatim aquas.

---

a An adjective meaning : " by the sea."
b An adjective meaning : " looking at the sun." See *infra*.
c For *privatim* see note on XXIV, § 28.

honey wine or raisin wine, or with sesame. It
carries off phlegm and bile by stool. Sores in the
mouth it cures, but for corroding ulcers in the mouth
the leaf is eaten with honey.

XLI. The third kind of tithymallus is called
paralius [a] or tithymallis. It has a round leaf, a stem
a span high, reddish branches, and a white seed,
which is gathered when the grape begins to form,
and after being dried and pounded is taken in doses
of one acetabulum as a purgative.

XLII. The fourth kind of tithymallus is called
helioscopios.[b] It has the leaves of purslane, and four
or five small branches standing out from the root,
which are reddish, half a foot high and full of juice.
This kind grows around towns, and has a white seed
of which pigeons are very fond. The name helioscopios has been given to this plant because it moves
its heads round to follow the sun. Bile it carries
away by urine or stool when taken in doses of half
an acetabulum in oxymel. Its other uses are the
same as those of characias.

XLIII. The fifth kind is called cyparittias, because
its leaves are like those of cypress. It has a double
or triple stem, and grows in flat country. Its
properties are the same as those of helioscopios or
characias.

XLIV. The sixth kind is called by some platyphyllos, by others corymbites, and by others
amygdalites from its likeness to the almond tree.
Its leaves are broader than those of any other. It
kills fish. Root, leaves or juice are purgative if a
dose of four drachmae is taken in honey wine or
hydromel. It is specific [c] for carrying away morbid
fluids.

71 XLV. Septimum dendroides cognominant, alii cobion, alii leptophyllon, in petris nascens, comosissimum ex omnibus, maximis [1] cauliculis rubentibus, et semine copiosissimum, eiusdem effectus cuius characias.[2]

72 XLVI. Apios ischas sive raphanos agria, iuncos duos aut tres spargit in terra rubentes, foliis rutae. radix cepae, sed amplior, quare quidam raphanum silvestrem vocant. intus habet mammam candidam, extra cortices nigros. nascitur in montosis asperis, 73 aliquando et in herbosis. effoditur vere tusaque in fictili mergitur, deiectoque quod supernatat reliquus sucus purgat utraque parte sesquiobolo in aqua mulsa. sic et hydropicis datur acetabuli mensura. inspargitur et aridae radicis farina potioni. aiunt superiorem

---

[1] maximis *plerique codd., Detlefsen, Mayhoff*: maxime r a, *Mayhoff coni.* comosum [*corruptum in* comosissimum (comosumosum) *per dittographiam*] . . . . . maxime.
[2] characias] characian *coni. Mayhoff*: characia *aut* caracia *codd.*

---

[a] *Maximis* is perhaps a strange epithet to be applied to the diminutive *cauliculis.* It may mean that the minor stems are comparatively large, but the conjecture of Mayhoff is plausible, that Pliny wrote *comosum . . . maxime,* with no epithet

XLV. The seventh kind is surnamed dendroïdes, and is called by some cobios, and by others leptophyllos. It grows among rocks, and is the most thickly headed of all the kinds. It has very large,[a] reddish stems, and an abundance of seed. The properties are the same as those of characias.

XLVI. Apios ischas or raphanos agria spreads out *Apios ischas.* on the ground two or three rush-like stalks of a reddish colour with leaves like those of rue. The root is like that of an onion, but bigger, and this is the reason why some call it the wild radish. Inside it has a white pap, outside, dark skins. It grows in rough, hilly spots, sometimes also in grass land. Dug up in spring, it is pounded and immersed in an earthen vessel.[b] After throwing away what floats on the surface they use the juice that remains as a purge and emetic, the dose being an obolus and a half in hydromel. Prepared after this fashion a dose of an acetabulum is also given for dropsy. The dried root powdered is also sprinkled in a draught. They

going with *cauliculis* except the participle *rubentibus.* Dioscorides is not of much help; he says (IV, 164, 9): ὁ δὲ ἐν ταῖς πέτραις φυόμενος, δενδροειδὴς δὲ καλούμενος, ἀμφιλαφὴς ἄνωθεν καὶ πολύκομος, ὅπου μεστός, ὑπέρυθρος τοὺς κλάδους.

[b] Theophrastus does not help us in deciding the meaning of *mergitur* and *supernatat,* but Dioscorides is suggestive. His words are (IV, 175): ὁπίσαι δὲ βουληθεὶς κόπτε τὰς ῥίζας καὶ βαλὼν εἰς κρατηρίαν ὕδατος συντάραττε, καὶ τὸν ἐφιστάμενον ὁπὸν πτερῷ ἀναλέγων ξήραινε· τούτου τρία ἡμιωβόλια ποθέντα ἄνω καὶ κάτω καθαίρει. In Pliny we have "immersed in an earthen vessel," in Dioscorides "throw into a bowl of water and stir." In Pliny again the floating part is thrown away and the remainder used; in Dioscorides (unless, unnaturally, ξήραινε governs ῥίζας) it is collected, dried and used. Did Pliny follow a different account or did he read ἀποβαλὼν where now is read ἀναλέγων?

partem eius vomitione biles extrahere, inferiorem
per alvum †aqua†.[1]

74 XLVII. Tormina discutit quodcumque panaces,
vettonica praeterquam a cruditate, peucedani sucus et
inflationes, ructus gignens, item acori radix daucumve,
si lactucae modo sumatur. ladanum Cyprium potum
interaneorum vitiis occurrit, gentianae farina ex aqua
tepida fabae magnitudine, plantago mane sumpta
duabus lingulis et tertia papaveris in vini cyathis
quattuor non veteris. datur et in somnum euntibus
addito nitro vel polenta, si multo post cibum detur.
colo infunditur hemina suci vel in febri.

[1] †aqua† *codd.*: aquam *Ianus*: aeque *Detlefsen*: in aqua
Mayhoff, qui coni. (*e Dioscoride*) sed totam utraque.

---

[a] Dioscorides (IV, 175) has: ταύτης τὸ μὲν ἄνωθεν μέρος τῆς
ῥίζης ληφθὲν δι' ἐμέτων ἄγει χολὴν καὶ φλέγμα, τὸ δὲ πρὸς τῇ ῥίζῃ
κάτω καθαίρει, ὅλη δὲ ληφθεῖσα ἀμφοτέρας τὰς καθάρσεις κινεῖ.
The last clause has only *aqua* to correspond to it in the MSS.
of Pliny; hence Mayhoff's conjecture (for the MSS. *aqua*) *sed
totam utraque*. This suggestion implies that a scribe's eye
passed from *alvum* to *utr]aque*. This is the least unsatisfactory
solution yet proposed of this particular difficulty, but there are
other perplexing features of the chapter besides the one
mentioned here.

(1) κόπτε τὰς ῥίζας shows that *tusa* is *tusa radix*, but *nascitur*
in the sentence above refers to the plant. This change of
subject causes no difficulty, but the last sentence of Pliny,
corresponding to the first sentence in the section of
Dioscorides, contains an ambiguous and perplexing *eius*.
Does this refer to the plant or to the root? Littré translates
it "de la racine," but the words of Dioscorides, τὸ δὲ πρὸς τῇ
ῥίζῃ (*scil.* μέρος) κάτω καθαίρει, can only mean "the part near
the root purges by stool"; it cannot mean "the lower part
of the root purges by stool." Pliny translates as though it
were τὸ δὲ κάτω μέρος τῆς ῥίζης. The μὲν clause may mean
"the upper part of this root," although ταύτης is strangely
placed and could more naturally be translated: "Of this
plant the part above the root etc." Furthermore, it is odd to

318

say that the upper part of it brings away the biles by vomiting, the lower part by stool.[a]

XLVII. Colic is cured by any kind of panaces, by betony, except when the cause is indigestion, by the juice of peucedanum, which also, being carminative, dispels flatulence, by the root of acoron, or by daucum, if it is taken as a salad like lettuce. Cyprian ladanum, taken in drink, is good for intestinal complaints, as also is powdered gentian, of the size of a bean, taken in warm water, or plantain taken in the morning, the dose being two spoonfuls with one of poppy in four cyathi of wine which is not old. It is also given before going to sleep with the addition of soda or pearl barley, provided that it is long after the last meal. For colitis a hemina of the juice is injected, even when fever is present.

Digestive troubles continued.

speak of the upper part of the root and its lower part as acting differently; but it is natural enough for the upper part of the plant to act in one way and its lower part in another. Cf., however, § 79. May it be that a κάτω has been lost before πρὸς owing to the vicinity of κάτω before καθαίρει? μέρος, too, may have been originally before λημφθέν. This transposition of μέρος and omission of κάτω, if pre-Pliny, might well have caused him to misunderstand the passage. What I have said is mere speculation, and I have not thought it wise to alter the Latin text in any way. On the other hand, it is perhaps useful to point out, from an excellent example, the intricate nature of the problems that everywhere meet the translator of Pliny, who is often bewildered and reduced to guesses in which he can have little confidence.

(2) Dioscorides has φλοιὸν ἔχουσα (ρίζα) ἔξωθεν μέλανα, ἔνδοθεν δὲ λευκή: Pliny: (radix) intus habet mammam (Mayhoff suggests medullam) candidam, extra cortices nigros. A little later the Greek has χολὴν καὶ φλέγμα, the Latin biles (i.e. black and yellow). Pliny in fact seems to have had a Greek text very similar to that of Dioscorides but not verbally identical with it. So perhaps the difficulties dealt with above are even more complicated than they seem at first sight to be.

75 XLVIII. Agaricum potum obolis tribus in vini
veteris cyatho uno lieni medetur, e panace omnium
generum radix in mulso, sed teucria praecipue pota
arida et decocta quantum manus capiat in aceti
heminis tribus ad heminam.[1] inlinitur eadem ex
aceto aut, si tolerari non possit, ex fico vel aqua.
polemonia bibitur ex vino, vettonica drachma in
oxymelitis cyathis tribus, aristolochia ut contra ser-
76 pentes. argemonia septem diebus in cibo sumpta
lienem consumere dicitur, agaricum in aceto mulso
obolis duobus. nymphaeae heracliae radix in vino
pota et ipsa consumit. cissanthemus drachma bis
die sumpta in vini albi cyathis duobus per dies XL
lienem dicitur paulatim emittere per urinam. prodest et hysopum cum fico decoctum, lonchitidis radix
decocta priusquam semen demittat, peucedani quoque
77 radix et lieni et renibus. lien suco acori poto [2] con-
sumitur—praecordiis et ilibus utilissimae radices [3]—
clymeni semen potum diebus xxx pondere denarii
in vino albo, vettonicae farina ex melle et aceto scillite
pota, radix lonchitidis in aqua. teucrium inlinitur,
item scordium cum cera, agaricum cum farina e feno
Graeco.

---

[1] tribus ad heminam. *Sic dist. Mayhoff*: tribus. ad
flemina *Detlefsen.*
[2] lien suco acori poto *Mayhoff*: lien acori potu *Detlefsen*:
lienis acori (uco *om. ante* aco) V R d x : poto *vel* potu *codd.*
[3] utilissima radice *coni. Mayhoff, qui lacunam ante*
clymeni *in textu ponit.*

---

[a] *Ad flemina* is a clever emendation, but the chapter deals
with diseases of the spleen.

XLVIII. Agaric taken in drink, the dose being *Splenic troubles.* three oboli in one cyathus of old wine, is good for disorders of the spleen, as is the root in honey wine of all kinds of panaces, but best of all is teucria, dried and taken in drink by boiling down to one hemina [a] a handful of it with three heminae of vinegar. In vinegar it is also used as a liniment, or, if that cannot be borne, in figs or water. Polemonia is taken in wine, or a drachma of betony in three cyathi of oxymel, or aristolochia as used for snake bite. Argemonia, taken in food on seven consecutive days, is said to reduce the spleen, and so are two oboli of agaric in oxymel. It is reduced also by the root of nymphaea heraclia taken in wine or by itself. Cissanthemus, if a drachma is taken twice daily in two cyathi of white wine for forty days, is said to carry off the spleen gradually in the urine. Useful too is a decoction of hyssop with fig, or of the root of lonchitis before it sheds its seed, while a decoction of root of peucedanum is good for both spleen and kidneys. The spleen is reduced by the juice of acoron taken by the mouth—the roots are very useful for trouble of the hypochondria and groin [b]—by the seed of clymenus taken in drink for thirty days, the dose being a denarius by weight in white wine, by powdered betony taken in honey and squill vinegar, and by root of lonchitis in water. Teucrium [c] is used as liniment, likewise scordium with wax, or agaric with powdered fenugreek.

[b] It seems most natural to mend the grammar of this passage by making *praecordiis . . . radices* a parenthesis, a favourite trick of Pliny, and understanding *consumit* or *utile* before *clymeni.*

[c] Notice both forms, *teucria* and *teucrium*, in the same chapter.

78 XLIX. Vesicae malis contraque calculos, gravissimis cruciatibus, ut diximus, auxilio est polemonia ex vino pota, item agaricum, plantago foliis vel radice potis ex passo, vettonica ut in iocinere diximus, item ramiti pota atque inlita, eadem ad strangurias efficacissima. quidam ad calculos vettonicam et verbenacam et millefolium aequis portionibus ex aqua
79 pro singulari remedio bibere suadent. strangurias discuti et dictamno certum est, item quinquefolio decocto ad tertias in vino. hoc et enterocelicis dari atque inlini utilissimum est. xiphi quoque radix superior urinam ciet. infantibus enterocelicis [1] datur ex aqua et inlinitur; vesicae vitiis peucedani sucus, infantium ramiti et umbilicis eminentibus psyllion
80 inlinitur. urinam cient anagallides, acori radicis decoctum vel ipsa trita potaque, et omnia vesicae vitia,[2] calculos et herba et radix cotyledonis itemque genitalium inflammationem omnem pari pondere et
81 caulis et seminis et murrae. ebulum teneris cum foliis tritum ex vino potum calculos pellit, inpositum testes sanat. erigeron quoque cum farina turis et vino dulci testium inflammationes sanat. symphyti radix inlita enterocelas cohibet, genitalium nomas hypo-

---

[1] infantibus enterocelicis] *Sic dist. Mayhoff e Dioscoride* IV 20 : ἐντεροκηλικοῖς τε παιδίοις τὴν ἐπάνω ῥίζαν (*sc. τοῦ ξιφίου*) ἐν ποτῷ σὺν ὕδατι.
[2] *Ante* calculos *addunt* de **r a** : depellit *in textu Mayhoff* : demit *coni. Brakman.*

---

[a] See XXV, § 23.
[b] In XXVI, § 35, 1 drachma of betony in 3 cyathi of warm water is prescribed for the liver, but no mention is made there of bladder trouble.
[c] It is easier to supply from *cient* suitable verbs to govern *calculos* and *inflammationem*, than it is with Mayhoff to read

XLIX. For diseases of the bladder and for the cure Bladder
diseases of stone, which causes as we have said ^a the most severe torture, help is obtained from polemonia taken in wine, from agaric, from leaves or root of plantain taken in raisin wine, from betony as we prescribed it for the liver ^b; this last, taken in drink and used as liniment, is good for hernia and wonderfully effective for strangury. Some recommend betony, vervain and millefolium, in equal parts and taken in water, as a sovereign remedy for stone. It is certain that strangury is cured by dittany also, and by cinquefoil boiled down to one third in wine. The latter preparation is very useful to be taken, and to be used locally as a liniment, by sufferers from intestinal hernia. The upper part of the root of xiphium also is diuretic; it is given in water and applied locally as liniment for intestinal hernia in infants. For bladder troubles the juice of peucedanum is applied locally, and psyllion is so applied for hernia and umbilical rupture in infants. The two kinds of anagallis are diuretic, as is a decoction of root of acoron, or the root by itself pounded and taken in drink; these are good for all troubles of the bladder,^c for stone both cotyledon and its root, and also, for all inflammations of the genitals, equal parts by weight of the stem, of the seed, and of myrrh. Ebulum ground with its tender leaves and taken in wine expels stone, and applied locally cures complaints of the testicles. Erigeron too with powdered frankincense and sweet wine cures inflammation of the testicles. Root of symphytum used as liniment reduces intestinal hernia, and white hypocisthis is

depellit from the *de* of r a, for *depellit* does not suit the latter noun. Brakman's *demit* is attractive.

cisthis alba. artemisia quoque datur contra calculos
ex vino dulci et ad stranguriam, dolores vesicae sedat
ex vino radix nymphaeae heracliae.

82 L. Eadem vis crethmo ab Hippocrate admodum
laudatae.[1] est autem inter eas quae eduntur silves-
trium herbarum—hanc certe apud Callimachum
adponit rustica illa Hecale—speciesque elatae [2]
hortensiae. caulis unus palmum altus, semen
fervens, odoratum ceu libanotidis, rotundum; siccatum rumpitur, habet intus nucleum candidum, quem
aliqui cachrym vocant. folia pinguia albicant
vĕluti olivae, crassiora et salsa gustu, radices digiti
83 crassitudine tres aut quattuor. nascitur in maritimis
petrosis. estur cruda coctave [3] cum olere, odorati
saporis et iucundi; servatur etiam in muria praecipui
usus [4] ad strangurias folio vel caule vel radice ex vino.
colorem quoque corporis gratiorem facit, verum
largior inflationes.[5] alvum solvit decocto, urinam et
a renibus umorem trahit sicut alcimae [6] siccae farina

---

[1] laudatae *Hard.*, *Mayhoff*: laudato *Detlefsen*: laudata
codd. (*sc.* vis).

[2] elatae *codd.*, *Mayhoff*: elatinae *Urlichs, Detlefsen*: batis
Hermolaus Barbarus: althaeae *vel* malvae *coni. Mayhoff*.

[3] cruda coctave *Mayhoff*: crudum coctumve *codd.*

[4] praecipui usus *Gelenius, Detlefsen*: praecipue ei usus *Mayhoff*: praecipue usus (*aut* usque) *codd.*: vis ei ususque *coni.
Mayhoff*.

[5] inflationes] inflammationes *coni. Mayhoff*.

[6] alcimae *Ianus, Detlefsen, Mayhoff, cf.* § 45: varia *codd.*

---

[a] Elate was a term for the sprout-tips of the dwarf palm,
which was not cultivated. (A.C.A.)

[b] Or, " stony."

good for corroding ulcers of the genitals. Artemisia too in sweet wine is given for stone and for strangury; root of nymphaea heraclia in wine relieves pains of the bladder.

L. The same property is to be found in crethmos, a plant very highly praised by Hippocrates. It is also one of the wild plants that are eaten—at any rate in Callimachus the peasant Hecale puts it on the table—and a species of garden elate.[a] It has one stem a span high, and a hot seed, scented like that of libanotis, and round. When dried it bursts, and has inside a white kernel, which some call cachrys. The leaves are fleshy, and whitish like those of the olive only thicker, and salt to the taste; there are three or four roots, of the thickness of a finger. It grows in rocky [b] places by the sea. It is eaten, raw or boiled, with cabbage,[c] and has a pleasant, aromatic taste; it is also preserved in brine. It is especially useful for strangury, the leaves, stem, or root being taken in wine. The complexion also of the skin is improved by it, but too large a dose causes flatulence. A decoction relaxes the bowels, brings away urine and humours from the kidneys, as does the powder of dried alcima taken in wine,[d] and

[c] I have adopted Mayhoff's conjecture because (in this chapter at least) the form used is *crethmos* (fem.). *Cruda* might easily be taken for *crudum*, spelt *crudū*. The MSS. have *crudum coctumve* without variant, and were it not for *hanc* and *largior* one might take the neuters to be careless writing, for there was an alternative form *crethmum*.

[d] With the reading of Mayhoff: " taken in wine it relieves strangury more efficaciously if daucum is added." There is some uncertainty about the conjecture *alcimae* of Jan, accepted by both Detlefsen and Mayhoff, as it scarcely accounts for the confusion of the MSS., which have *alcme*, *almae*, *alme* and *alce*.

in[1] vino pota, stranguriam efficacius addito dauco.
lieni quoque utilis adversus serpentes bibitur, iumentis quoque in pituita aut stranguria, hordeo inspersa
succurrit.

84   LI. Anthyllion[2] est lenti simillima quae in vino
pota vesicas vitiis liberat, sanguinem sistit, altera
anthyllis chamaepityi[3] similis, flore purpureo, odore
gravi, radice intubi, vel magis medetur. . . .[4]

LII. Cepaea, similis porcilacae, nigriore radice, sed
inutili, nascens in litoribus harenosis, gustu amara.
in vino cum asparagi radice vesicae plurimum
prodest.

85   LIII. Eadem praestat hypericon (alii chamaepityn,
alii corissum appellant) oleraceo frutice, tenui, cubitali, rubente, folio rutae, odore acri, semine in siliqua

---

[1] in codd. r a Detlefsen : e codd. d x Mayhoff, qui post
farina comma ponit.

[2] Anthyllion vulg. e Dioscoride, Mayhoff : canthyllion VE
Detlefsen.   Postea quoque non anthyllis sed canthyllis codd.,
Detlefsen.

[3] chamaepityi Mayhoff (Dioscor. III 136 (ἀνθυλλίς) χαμαιπιτυΐ . . . ἔοικε . . . τὸ δ᾽ ἄνθος πορφυροῦν, βαρύοσμον ἰσχυρῶς,
ῥίζα ὥσπερ κιχορίου.

[4] Post medetur lacunam indicat Mayhoff : Detlefsen Vel
magis medetur ante cepaea ponit puncto anteposito. Dioscor.
III 136 ἡ δὲ τῇ χαμαιπιτυΐ ὁμοία . . . καὶ ἐπιληπτικῶν
βοήθημα σὺν ὀξυμέλιτι πινομένη, unde Mayhoff putat excidisse
fere comitialibus in oxymelite.

---

[a] It is easier to supply a verb (such as sanat) to govern
stranguriam than it is to emend to stranguriae with Mayhoff.

relieves strangury,[a] more efficaciously however if daucum is added. It is also good for the spleen, and is taken in drink for snake bites. Phlegm or strangury in draught animals also is relieved if crethmos is sprinkled over their barley.

LI. Anthyllion is very like the lentil, and taken in wine cures bladder troubles and arrests bleeding. A second plant,[b] anthyllis, is like chamaepitys, and has a purple flower, a heavy scent, and a root like that of endive. It is even better treatment ⟨taken in oxymel for epilepsy⟩.[c]

Anthyllion.

LII. Cepaea is like purslane, but has a darker root, which is of no value. It grows on sandy shores, and has a bitter taste. Taken in wine with root of asparagus it is very good indeed for the bladder.

Cepaea.

LIII. The same properties[d] are to be found in hypericon—some call it chamaepitys, others corissum—which has the stem[e] of a garden vegetable,[f] thin, reddish, and a cubit high. The leaves are like those of rue and have a pungent smell. The seed,

Hypericon.

---

[b] *Altera anthyllis* is strange after *anthyllion*. It may be a mere slip due to Pliny's carelessness, but the Latin may perhaps bear the sense I have given to it, with *herba* understood after *altera*.

[c] The sense of the missing words supplied by Mayhoff from Dioscorides. Professor Andrews thinks that Pliny, after saying that anthyllion is good for bladder and bleeding, goes on to say that anthyllis is even more effective. There is then no need to assume a lacuna.

[d] Or, "Also effective for bladder conditions is," i.e. *eādem* (*vesicā*). A.C.A.

[e] *Frutex* is usually "bush," "shrub." Here it means stem (= *caulis*), but it is not clear why Pliny has used this word rather than the other.

[f] So Littré (plante potagère) and Bostock and Riley. Perhaps "cabbage."

nigro maturescente cum hordeo. natura semini
spissandi, alvum sistit, urinam ciet, vesicae cum vino
bibitur.

86 LIV. Est aliud hypericon, quod aliqui caro[1]
appellant, folio tamaricis—et sub ea nascitur—sed
pinguioribus foliis et minus[2] rubentibus, odoratum,
palmo altius, suave, leniter acutum. vis semini
excalfactoria, et ideo inflammationem facit, sed
stomacho non inutile, praecipuum ad stranguriam, si
exulcerata non sit vesica. medetur et pleuriticis ex
87 vino potum, LV. vesicae autem callithrix trita
simul cum cumino et data ex vino albo. verbenaca
quoque cum foliis decocta ad tertias vel radix eius
e mulso calido calculos eicit, item perpressa, quae
Arreti et in Illyrico nascitur, in aqua decocta ex
tribus heminis ad unam pota, trifolium ex vino
sumptum et chrysanthemum, anthemis quoque
calculos eicit, parvis a radice foliis quinis, caulibus

[1] caro *codd.*, *Detlefsen* : corin e *Dioscoride Hermolaus Barbarus* : caron *vulg.*, *Mayhoff*.
[2] minus] minutis *Mayhoff* e *Dioscoride, qui scribit* (III 157)
φύλλον ἔχει παραπλήσιον τῷ τῆς ἐρείκης, μικρότερον δὲ καὶ
λιπαρώτερον καὶ ἐρυθρόν. *Fortasse* minoribus.

[a] Or " astringent," perhaps " thickening."
[b] It is tempting to emend to *minoribus* (rather than Mayhoff's *minutis*) so as to bring Pliny closer to Dioscorides, who has μικρότερον (φύλλον). On the other hand the MSS. give

which is black, is in a pod, and it ripens at the same
time as barley.   This seed is of a bracing [a] quality,
checks diarrhoea and promotes urine; it is taken
with wine for bladder troubles.

LIV. There is another hypericon, called by some
caro, having a leaf like that of the tamarisk—it grows
underneath it—but more fleshy and less red.[b]   It is
scented, more than a span high, with a sweet and
rather pungent [c] taste.   The seed is of a heating
nature and therefore causes inflammation, but it is
not injurious to the stomach; it is particularly good
for strangury, if the bladder is not ulcerated.   Taken
in wine it is also good for pleurisy, LV. as moreover
is callithrix for the bladder if beaten up with cummin
and administered in white wine.   Vervain too if
boiled down with the leaves to one third, or its root
in warm honey wine, expels stone from the bladder,
as does also perpressa, which grows near Arretium
and in Illyricum; it is taken in drink, boiled down
in water from three heminae to one.   Trefoil, taken
in wine, and chrysanthemum, have the same effect.
Stone is expelled also by anthemis, which has five
small leaves growing from the root, two long stems

no variant, and it is hard to see why a scribe should alter an
easy reading, whether *minoribus* or *minutis*, to *minus*.   It is
to be noted that Pliny has *pinguioribus . . . et minus rubentibus*, but Dioscorides μικρότερον δὲ καὶ λιπαρώτερον καὶ ἐρυθρόν.
If the Greek before Pliny (or his reader) had the adjectives in
Pliny's order, without connecting particles (λιπαρώτερον,
μικρότερον, ἐρυθρόν), it is just possible that they were taken
to mean "more fleshy and a little less red."   So, after long
hesitation, I have kept the MSS. reading.   Note that Pliny
read μυρίκης for ἐρείκης.

[c] *Acutus* when used of *sapores* seems to mean merely
"sharp"; *acer*, on the contrary, means not only pungent,
but salty and with a vinegary flavour.

329

longis duobus, flore roseo, radices tritae per se †cei
laver crudum.† [1]

88   LVI. Silaus nascitur glariosis et perennibus rivis,
cubitalis apii similitudine. coquitur ut olus acidum
magna utilitate vesicae, quae si scabiem sentiat,
panacis radice sanatur, aliter inutilis vesicis. calculos pellit malum erraticum radicis libra in vini congio
decocta ad dimidias—inde heminae sumuntur per
triduum, relicum ex vino [2]—et urtica marina et
daucum et plantaginis semen ex vino.

    LVII. Et herba Fulviana trita ex vino, et haec
nomen inventoris habet, nota tractantibus.[3]

89   LVIII. Urinas ciet scordion, testium tumores
sedat hyoscyamum, genitalibus medetur peucedani

---

[1] cei laver crudum VE : ceu *aliquot codd., Detlefsen.*
Mayhoff ante cei *lacunam indicat*; seu *vulg.*
   [2] vino *Mayhoff cum plerisque codd. : add.* conicio d :
cumcio *aliquot codd., Detlefsen, qui etiam* Pucino *coni.* XIV 60
coll.
   [3] tractantibus] *Usque ad* uno *ut Mayhoff distinguo.*

---

   [a] This is a *locus desperatus.* I have followed Mayhoff,
who marks a lacuna after *se.* The reading of V and E looks
like the ending of a word in *-ceum* or *-ceus,* but there is no
plant (except *chalceos*) the genitive of which would end in
-cei, and that *chalcei* is the right reading is most unlikely.
The reading *ceu* (adopted by Detlefsen) is specious; the word
being common in Pliny. The sense, " as it were raw laver,"
is odd, and so is the grammar, especially as laver is feminine,
for *radices* as it stands is very like a pendent nominative.
The vulgate *seu* is translated by Littré: " comme le laver
cru." But this would be *ceu.* (Laver was a water plant,
perhaps water cress. "Pliny may have intermingled drastic
purges with mild and suave foods." A.C.A.)
   [b] The word occurs here only. Its description is like the
account of *sion* in Dioscorides II 127, and *sion* = *laver,* which
has just been mentioned. The MSS. show no variants. It
may possibly be a " portmanteau " word (*si-lau*).

and a rose-coloured flower. The roots pounded by themselves . . .[a] laver, raw.

LVI. Silaus [b] grows in running streams with gravelly bottoms; a cubit high it resembles celery. It is boiled as is an acid vegetable, and is very good for the bladder, which if it suffers from *scabies* [c] is cured by the root of panaces, a plant otherwise injurious [d] to the bladder. Stone is expelled by the wild apple,[e] a pound of the root being boiled down to one half in a congius of wine—a hemina of it is taken daily for three days, the rest is taken in wine [f] —by sea-nettle, by daucum, and by the seed of plantain in wine.

LVII. The plant of Fulvius, beaten up with wine, is another remedy for stone. It is one of the plants named after the discoverer, and is well known to botanists.[g]

LVIII. Scordion is diuretic; hyoscyamus reduces swollen testicles; the genitals are effectively treated by juice of peucedanum, and by its seed in honey; *Scordion: various remedies.*

[e] A symptom of *scabies* of the bladder was urine containing scaly concretions.

[d] Perhaps here " useless."

[e] The commentators take this to be the same as the *malum terrae* of XXV § 95 = aristolochia.

[f] After *vino* some MSS. add *conicio* or *cumcio*. Some editors think that the addition conceals the name of a particular wine, but Mayhoff seems to be right in taking the words to be corruptions of *congio*, which might be, as he says, *prave iteratum.*

[g] Perhaps "those who treat the disease," i.e. physicians. *Tractare* is a very common word in the sense of " to deal with," but in the present context, with no expressed object, rather strange; it is stranger still that this seems to be the only mention of the plant. Hence Mayhoff's conjecture *nostratia.*

sucus, ex melle semen, stranguriae agaricum obolis
tribus in vini veteris cyatho uno, trifolii radix
drachmis duabus in vino, dauci una drachma vel
seminis. ischiadici semine et foliis erythrodani
tritis sanantur, panace poto et infricato, polemonia,
90 aristolochiae decocto folii. agarico quidem et nervus
qui platus appellatur et umerorum dolor sanatur
obolis tribus in vini veteris cyatho uno poto. quinquefolium ischiadicis et bibitur et inponitur, item
scamonia[1] decocta, et cum hordei farina. semen
hyperici utriusque bibitur ex vino. sedis vitia et
adtritus celerrime sanat plantago, condylomata
quinquefolium, sed ea in[2] callum iam[3] conversa[4]
cyclamini radix ex aceto. anagallidum caerulea
procidentiam sedis retro agit, e diverso rubens
91 proritat. cotyledon condylomata et haemorrhoidas
mire curat, testium tumores acori radix decocta in
vino tritaque inlita. intertrigines negat fieri Cato
absinthium Ponticum secum habentibus. alii adiciunt et puleium, quod ieiunus quis[5] legerit, si post
se alliget, inguinis dolores prohibet aut sedat coeptos.
92 LIX. Inguinalis, quam quidam argemonion
vocant, passim in vepribus nascens ut prosit in manu
tantum habenda est.

---

[1] scamonia] *Ante* decocta *vult addere* in aceto (*ex Dioscoride*)
Mayhoff. Ante cum *om. et vulg.*
[2] sed ea in *Detlefsen, Mayhoff* : sed eam VRE.
[3] callum iam *Detlefsen, Mayhoff* : calumniam *aut om. codd.*
[4] conversa *Detlefsen, Mayhoff* : conversam (-um) *codd.*
[5] quis *codd.* : qui *Gelenius. Ante* ieiunus *add.* si V² *Sillig.*
Detlefsen.

---

[a] The Achilles tendon.
[b] Mayhoff would add " in vinegar," suggested by a parallel
passage in Dioscorides. This addition would make more
natural the *et* before *cum.*

strangury by three-oboli doses of agaric in one
cyathus of old wine, by two-drachmae doses of root
of trefoil in wine, and by one-drachma doses of
daucum or of its seed. Sciatica is cured by pounded
seed and leaves of erythrodanus, by panaces taken in
drink and rubbed on the affected part, by polemonia,
and by a decoction of the leaves of aristolochia.
Agaric indeed cures both the tendon called "broad" [a]
and pain in the shoulders, the dose being three oboli
taken in one cyathus of old wine. For sciatica
cinquefoil is both taken in drink and applied, as is
also a decoction of scammony [b] with barley meal
added. The seed of either kind of hypericum is
taken in wine. Affections and chafings of the seat
are cured very quickly by plantain, condylomata by
cinquefoil; if however these have already become
callous, by cyclamen root in vinegar. The blue
anagallis pushes back prolapsus of the anus; the red
anagallis on the contrary makes it worse. Cotyledon
is wonderfully good treatment for condylomata and
for piles; so is, for swollen testicles, the application
of root of acoron, pounded and boiled down in
wine. Cato [c] says that those carrying on their persons
Pontic wormwood never suffer from chafing between
the thighs. Other authorities add pennyroyal to
the list of remedies; this, gathered by a fasting man
and tied behind him, prevents pains in the groin or
relieves those which have begun already.

LIX. Inguinalis (" groin-wort "), called by some *Inguinalis.*
argemonion, a plant growing anywhere in briar
patches, needs only to be held in the hand to be of
benefit.

See *R.R.* 159.

PLINY : NATURAL HISTORY

LX. Panos sanat panaces ex melle, plantago cum sale, quinquefolium, persollatae radix ut in strumis, item damasonium, verbascum cum sua radice tusum, vino aspersum folioque involutum et ita in cinere
93 calefactum ut inponatur calidum. experti adfirmavere plurimum referre, si virgo inponat nuda ieiuna ieiuno et manu supina tangens dicat: Negat Apollo pestem posse crescere cui nuda virgo restinguat, atque ita retrorsa manu ter dicat totiensque despuant ambo. medetur et radix mandragorae ex aqua, radicis scamoniae decoctum cum melle, sideritis cum adipe vetere contusa, marruvium cum axungia vetere, vel chrysippios cum ficis pinguibus. et haec ab inventore habet nomen.
94 LXI. Venerem in totum adimit, ut diximus, nymphaea Heraclia, eadem semel pota in XL dies, insomnia quoque veneris a ieiuno pota et in cibo sumpta. inlita quoque radix genitalibus inhibet non solum venerem sed et affluentiam geniturae. ob id corpus alere vocemque dicitur. adpetentiam veneris facit radix e xiphio superior data potui[1] in vino, item quam cremnon agrion appellant, ormenos agrios cum polenta contritus.

---

[1] potui *cod.* d, *Mayhoff*: potu *ceteri codd., Detlefsen.*

---

[a] See XXV § 75 and the note in which it is pointed out that Pliny differs (as the present passage clearly shows) from Dioscorides. In fact in the present section of XXVI the two are very unlike.
[b] Or, " or." The conjunction *et* often has to be translated in this way.

LX. Superficial abscess is cured by panaces in honey, plantain with salt, cinquefoil, root of persollata administered as for scrofula; also by damasonium and by verbascum, pounded with its root, sprinkled with wine, wrapped round with its leaves, and heated, thus prepared, on embers, so that it may be applied hot. Those with experience have assured us that it makes all the difference if, while the patient is fasting, the poultice is laid upon him by a maiden, herself fasting and naked, who must touch him with the back of her hand and say: "Apollo tells us that a plague cannot grow more fiery in a patient if a naked maiden quench the fire;" and with her hand so reversed she must repeat the formula three times, and both must spit on the ground three times. Other cures are mandrake root in water, a decoction of scammony root with honey, sideritis crushed with stale grease, marruvium with stale axle-grease, or chrysippios—another plant named after its discoverer—with plump figs.

Cures for superficial abscesses.

LXI. Nymphaea heraclia, as I have said,[a] takes away altogether sexual desire; a single draught of it does so for forty days; sexual dreams too are prevented if it is taken in drink on an empty stomach and [b] eaten with food. Applied to the genitals the root also checks not only desire but also excessive accumulation of semen. For this reason it is said to make flesh and to improve the voice. Sexual desire is excited by the upper part of xiphium root given in wine as a draught; also by the plant called cremnos agrios and by ormenos agrios crushed with pearl barley.

Nymphaea heraclia.

95 LXII. Sed inter pauca mirabilis est orchis herba
sive serapias, foliis porri, caule palmeo, flore purpureo, gemina radice testiculis simili, ita ut maior
sive, ut aliqui dicunt, tenuior [1] ex aqua pota excitet
libidinem, minor sive mollior e lacte caprino in-
hibeat. quidam folio scillae esse dicunt leviore ac
minore, caule spinoso. radices sanant oris ulcera,
thoracis pituitas, alvum sistunt ex vino potae.
96 concitatricem vim habet [2] satyrion. duo eius genera :
una longioribus foliis quam oleae, caule quattuor
digitorum, flore purpureo, radice gemina ad formam
hominis testium alternis annis intumescente ac
residente. altera satyrios orchis cognominatur et
†feminam [3] esse creditam.† distinguitur internodiis et ramosiore frutice, radice fascini. nascitur
fere iuxta mare. haec tumores et vitia partium

---

[1] tenuior *codd.*: durior *Caesarius*: plenior *ex Dioscoride*
coni. Mayhoff. *Vide notam.*

[2] habet *codd.*: habet et *Mayhoff.*

[3] feminam esse creditam *codd.*: feminam esse creditur
Detlefsen: femina esse credita est *Mayhoff, qui invenio*
excidisse coni.: feminam esse credunt *coni. Warmington.*
Fortasse femina esse creditur.

---

[a] All the MSS. have *tenuior*, a word that is scarcely a
contrast to *mollior*. Dioscorides says of one ὄρχις, not the one
equated with σεραπίας, (ἔχει) ῥίζαν βολβοειδῆ, ἐπιμήκη, διπλῆν,
στενήν, ὡς ἐλαίαν, τὴν μὲν ἄνω, τὴν δὲ κατωτέρω, καὶ τὴν μὲν
πλήρη, τὴν δὲ μαλακὴν καὶ ῥυσήν (III 126). There would be
much to be said for the conjectures *durior* and *plenior* were it
not that *tenuior*, the reading of all MSS., is far harder to
understand. Perhaps Pliny had a Greek text with στενή as
epithet of ἡ ἄνω ῥίζα. Pliny's words imply the existence of
differences in nomenclature.

[b] I have left the ungrammatical reading of the MSS.
unaltered, but obelized.

LXII. But very high on the list of wonders is the *Orchis.*
plant orchis, or serapias, which has the leaves of
leek, a stem a span high, and a purple flower.
The root has two tubers, like testicles, so that the
larger, or, as some put it, the thinner,[a] taken in
water excites desire; the smaller, or softer, taken in
goat's milk checks it. Some say that this orchis has
leaves like those of the squill, only smoother and
smaller, and a prickly stem. The roots cure sores
in the mouth and phlegm on the chest; taken in
wine they are constipating. Satyrion is a sexual *Satyrion.*
stimulant. There are two kinds of it: one with
longer leaves than those of the olive, a stem four
fingers high, purple blossom, and a double root
shaped like human testicles, which swells and sub-
sides again in alternate years. The other kind has
the further name of satyrios orchis, and is thought
to be female.[b] It is distinguished from the former
kind by the spaces between the joints, by its more
branchy, bushy shape[c]; also by its root's being like a
phallus.[d] The plant is generally found near the sea.

[c] Or, " by its stem's having many branches." The word
frutex sometimes = *caulis*, but here I think it means the
" skeleton " as it were of a small bush or shrub.

[d] To judge from Mayhoff's critical note the MS. E has
fascinis, the vulgate before Sillig *fascinis utili*, and the other
MSS. (*radice*) *fascini*. The meaning is surely that the root
is not, like the former kind, *ad formam hominis testium*, but
like a phallus. So the Latin *Thesaurus*. I think, however,
that the MSS. reading, retained without comment by both
Detlefsen and Mayhoff, can scarcely be quite right. Perhaps
we should add *simili*, which would explain the *fascinis utile* of
the vulgate, *fascini simili* being not very unlike *fascinis utili*.
It is strange that this account of satyrion should appear here,
just before the chapter (LXIII) in which that plant is
described. Commentators think that Pliny has been con-

earum cum polenta inlita sedat vel per se trita.
superioris radix in lacte ovis colonicae data nervos
intendit, eadem ex aqua remittit.

97 LXIII. Graeci satyrion foliis lilii rubris, minoribus
et tribus non amplius e terra exeuntibus tradunt,
caule levi, cubitali, nudo, radice gemina, cuius
inferior pars et maior mares gignat, superior ac minor
feminas. et aliud genus satyrii erythraicon appellant, semine viticis maiore, levi, duro, radicis cortice
rufo ; intus album includi sapore subdulce. fere[1] in
98 montuosis inveniri. venerem, etiam si omnino manu
teneatur radix, stimulari, adeo[2] si bibatur in vino
austero, arietibus quoque et hircis segnioribus in potu
dari, et a Sarmatia[3] equis ob adsiduum laborem
pigrioribus in coitu, quod vitium prosedamum vocant.
restinguit vim eius aqua mulsa aut lactuca sumpta.
99 in totum quidem Graeci, cum concitationem hanc
volunt significare, satyrion appellant, sic et cra-
taegin cognominantes et thelygonon et arrenogonon, quarum semen testium simile est. tithymalli quoque ramorum medullam habentes ad

[1] fere VRd, *Mayhoff* : fertur E, *Detlefsen*.
[2] adeo *codd.* : magis adeo *vulg.* : at eo magis *coni. Mayhoff.*
[3] Sarmatia *Ianus, Detlefsen, Mayhoff* : Sarmata *aut* Sarmat *codd.* : Sarmatis *vulg.*

---

fused by the fact that Greeks gave the name satyrion to all
plants supposed to be aphrodisiac. See § 99 : *in totum
quidem Graeci . . . testium simile est.* Indeed the whole of
§ 96, *concitatricem . . . remittit,* reads like a hasty after-
thought, and contains two ungrammatical phrases, if we can
trust our best MSS.

[a] The punctuation of the Latin text is that of Mayhoff; it
is based on the Greek of Dioscorides.

[b] The reading is very uncertain. We should certainly
expect the vulgate *a Sarmatis,* " by the Sarmatians," but *a*

This latter kind, if applied with pearl barley or by itself after being pounded, relieves swellings and affections of the privy parts. The root of the former kind, taken in the milk of a farm-yard sheep, causes erections; taken in water, however, it makes them subside.

LXIII. The Greeks speak of a satyrion that has leaves like those of the lily, but red, smaller, and springing from the ground not more than three in number, a smooth, bare stem a cubit high, and a double root, the lower, and larger, part favouring the conception of males, the upper, and smaller, the conception of females. Yet another kind of satyrion they call erythraicon, saying that its seed is like that of the vitex, but larger, smooth and hard; that the root is covered with a red rind, and contains [a] a white substance with a sweetish taste, and that the plant is generally found in hilly country. They tell us that sexual desire is aroused if the root is merely held in the hand, a stronger passion, however, if it is taken in a dry wine, that rams also and he-goats are given it in drink when they are too sluggish, and that it is given to stallions from Sarmatia [b] when they are too fatigued in copulation because of prolonged labour; this condition is called prosedamum. The effects of the plant can be neutralized by doses of hydromel or lettuce. The Greeks indeed always, when they wish to indicate this aphrodisiac nature of a plant, use the name satyrion, so applying it to crataegis, thelygonon, and arrenogonon, the seeds of which resemble testicles. Again, those carrying on their persons the pith of tithymallus branches are

Sarmatia, " from Sarmatia " (i.e. Sarmatian stallions), gives a good sense.

venerem proniores fieri dicuntur. prodigiosa sunt
quae circa hoc tradit Theophrastus, auctor alioqui
gravis, septuageno coitu durasse libidinem contactu
herbae cuiusdam cuius [1] nomen genusque non posuit.

100   LXIV. Sideritis adalligata varices minuit et sine
dolore praestat.[2] podagrae morbus rarior solebat
esse non modo patrum avorumque memoria, verum
etiam nostra, peregrinus et ipse, nam si Italiae fuisset
antiquitus, Latinum nomen invenisset. insanabilis
non est credendus, quippe quoniam et in multis
sponte desiit et in pluribus cura. medentur radices
panacis cum uva passa, sucus hyoscyami cum farina
vel semen, scordion ex aceto, hiberis uti dictum est,
verbenaca cum axungia trita, cyclamini radix, cuius

101 decoctum et pernionibus. podagras refrigerat radix
e xiphio, semen e psyllio, cicuta cum lithargyro aut
axungia, aizoum in primo impetu podagrae rubentis,
hoc est calidae. utrilibet vero convenit erigeron cum
axungia, plantaginis folia trita addito sale modico,
argemonia tusa ex melle. medetur et verbenaca
inlita, aut si pedes in aqua macerentur in qua decocta

102 sit, LXV. et lappago, similis anagallidi, nisi esset
ramosior ac pluribus foliis, gravis odoris. quae talis

---

[1] cuiusdam cuius *multi codd.* : cuius VE, *Mayhoff.*
[2] praestat] persanat f, *Hard.*

---

[a] See *H.P.* IX 18, 9.
[b] Book XXV § 88.
[c] The phrase *quae talis est* is generally taken to mean that
mollugo is the name of the *lappago* which is like *anagallis*.
But the Latin can scarcely mean that there are more than

said to become thereby more excited sexually. The remarks on this subject made by Theophrastus,[a] generally a weighty authority, are fabulous. He says that the lust to have intercourse seventy times in succession has been given by the touch of a certain plant whose name and kind he has not mentioned.

LXIV. Tied to the part as an amulet sideritis reduces varicose veins and does its work without pain. Gout was a rarer disease within the memory, *Cures for Gout.* not only of our fathers and grandfathers, but also of our own generation. It is also itself a foreign complaint; had it existed in Italy in early times it would have received a Latin name. It must not be considered incurable, for many cases have been cured without treatment, and yet more with it. Useful remedies are roots of panaces with raisins, juice of henbane with meal, or the seed of henbane, scordion in vinegar, hiberis as already prescribed,[b] vervain beaten up with axle-grease, and the root of cyclamen, a decoction of which is also good for chilblains. Cooling applications for gouty pains are made from xiphion root, psyllion seed, hemlock with litharge or axle-grease, and aizoüm for the first onset of red, that is hot, gout. Good for either kind however is erigeron with axle-grease, plantain leaves beaten up with a little salt added, and argemonia pounded with honey. Vervain too may be applied as a remedy—or the feet may be soaked in the water in which it has been boiled—LXV. or the lappago that is like anagallis, but more branchy and leafy, and with a strong smell. This kind of plant[c] is

one kind of *lappago*, and I feel certain that the hiatus of 76 letters after *gravis* in E once contained a description of a plant to which *talis* refers.

PLINY : NATURAL HISTORY

est mollugo vocatur; similis, sed asperioribus foliis,
asperugo. superioris et sucus p̄ X l in vini duobus
cyathis cotidie sumitur.

103 LXVI. Praecipue vero liberat eo malo phycos
thalassion, id est fucus marinus, lactucae similis, qui
conchyliis substernitur, non podagrae modo sed
omnibus articulorum morbis inpositus priusquam
arefiat.¹ tria autem genera eius: latum et alterum
longius, quadamtenus rubens, tertium crispis foliis,
quo in Creta vestes tingunt, omnia eiusdem usus.
104 Nicander ea et adversus serpentes in vino dedit.
salutare est et semen eius herbae quam psyllion
appellavimus madefactum aqua, admixtis in heminam
seminis resinae Colophoniae coclearibus duobus, turis
uno. laudantur et mandragorae folia cum polenta
tunsa. talis vero tumentibus limus aquaticus cum
oleo subactus mire prodest, articulis sucus ex centaurio minore, idem nervis utilissimus, item cen-
105 tauris. vettonica nervis discurrentibus per scapulas,
umeris, spinae, lumbis, pota ut in iocinere, articulis
quinquefolium inpositum, mandragorae folia cum
polenta vel radix recens tusa cum cucumere silvestri
vel decocta in aqua, digitorum in pedibus rimis
polypodii radix, articulis sucus hyoscyami cum

¹ arefiat VT *Ianus, Detlefsen, Mayhoff*: exarefiat d r *vulg.*

ᵃ Apparently *mollugo*, but the possibility of a hiatus makes
one uncertain.
ᵇ Or, with *exarefiat*, " quite dry."
ᶜ See Dioscorides IV 99: γίνεται τὸ μέν τι αὐτοῦ πλατύ, τὸ
δὲ ὑπόμηκες καὶ ὑποφοινικίζον, τὸ δὲ οὖλον (" curly "). Pliny's
latum and *longius*, therefore, may refer to the leaves and not
to the whole plant. See XIII §§ 135 foll.

342

called mollugo; like it, but with rougher leaves, is
asperugo. The juice of the former [a] is taken daily,
the dose being one denarius by weight in two cyathi
of wine.

LXVI. The sovereign remedy, however, for this
complaint is *phycos thalassion*, or seaweed, which is
like lettuce, and is used as a ground-colour for the
purple of the murex; it is sovereign, not for gout only,
but for all diseases of the joints, if applied before it
becomes dry.[b] There are moreover three kinds of it:
one is broad,[c] the second is rather long and inclining
to red, and the third, which has curly leaves, is used in
Crete to dye cloth. They have all the same medicinal uses. Nicander [d] gave these too in wine for
snake bite. A further remedy is the seed, soaked
in water, of the plant I have called [e] psyllion: one
hemina of such seed is compounded with two spoonfuls of Colophonian resin and one spoonful of frankincense. Another highly valued remedy is made from
leaves of mandrake pounded with pearl barley.
When however ankles swell, water-mud kneaded with
oil makes a wonderfully good plaster; for the joints
the juice of the smaller centaury is very beneficial, as
it is also for the sinews; beneficial too is centauris.
For the sinews running across the shoulder blades,
for the shoulders, for the backbone and the loins, a
good remedy is betony, taken as prescribed for the
liver [f]; for the joints an application of cinquefoil,
leaves of mandrake with pearl barley, or its root
pounded fresh with wild cucumber or boiled down in
water; for chaps on the toes the root of polypodium;
for the joints juice of henbane with axle-grease,

---

[d] *Theriaca* 845.   [e] Book XXV § 140.
[f] See XXVI § 35.

axungia, amomon suco decocto, item centunculus
decocta vel muscus recens ex aqua obligatus donec
inarescat, item lappae boariae radix e vino pota.
106 cyclaminos decocta in aqua perniunculos curat
omniaque alia frigoris vitia, perniunculos et cotyledon
cum axungia, folia ex batrachio, epithymi sucus.
clavos pedum extrahit ladanum cum castoreo,
verbenaca ex vino.

107 LXVII. Nunc peractis malis quae membratim
sentiuntur dicemus de iis quae totis corporibus
grassantur. remedia autem haec communia invenio: ante omnes[1] potandam[2] dodecatheum, de
qua diximus, deinde panacis omnium generum
radices, peculiariter longinquis morbis et semen
interaneorum vitiis, ad omnes vero dolores corporis
sucum e scordio, item vettonicae quae pota colorem
plumbeum corporis privatim emendat, gratiorem
reducit.

108 LXVIII. Geranion aliqui myrrin, alii myrtidan
appellant. similis est cicutae, minutioribus foliis et
caule brevior, rotunda, saporis et odoris iucundi.

---

[1] ante omnes codd., Detlefsen : aput auctores Mayhoff, qui
multa similia citat ex Plinio, et colon post invenio om.

[2] potandam Hard., cod. Dal., Detlefsen : potanda E,
Mayhoff : potam aut potu multi codd.

---

[a] There are a few peculiarities in this part of Pliny that
should be mentioned, although no explanation (except haste)
suggests itself. We have the formless structure of § 105, the
repetition of perniunculus, and its (apparently) sole use in
this section.

[b] With Mayhoff's reading : " I find in my authorities that
the following should be taken in drink." The deinde of the
next clause suggests that the MSS. reading ante omnes is
correct, and the gender of potandam is explained by the fact
that dodecatheum is a herba.

the decocted juice of amomum, a decoction too of
centunculus, or fresh moss soaked in water and
bound round the part until the water dries off, and
also root of lappa boaria taken in wine. Cyclamen
boiled down in water is a good remedy for chilblains
and for all other affections caused by cold; for
chilblains cotyledon too with axle-grease, leaves of
batrachion and the juice of epithymum. Corns are
extracted from the feet by ladanum mixed with
beaver-oil, and by vervain in wine.[a]

LXVII. Having now finished the complaints that
affect separate limbs I shall go on to describe those
that attack the whole body. Of remedies that are
generally useful I learn that the best is dodecatheum,
to be given in drink,[b] a plant I have already described[c]; next the roots of all kinds of panaces,
especially good for long illnesses, and the seed is used
for intestinal complaints; for general bodily pains
however juice of scordion and also of betony, which
taken in drink is specific[d] for removing a leaden
colour of the skin and restoring a more pleasing
complexion.

Remedies for diseases of the whole body.

LXVIII. Geranion is called by some myrris[e] and
by others myrtidas. It resembles hemlock, but
with smaller leaves and shorter in the stem, round,
and of a pleasant taste and smell. In this way

[c] See XXV § 28.
[d] For *privatim* see note on XXIV § 28.
[e] According to Dioscorides another plant; he says (IV 115):
ἔοικε κωνείῳ, ῥίζαν δὲ ἔχει ὑπομήκη, ἀπαλήν, περιφερῆ, εὐώδη,
ἡδεῖαν βρωθῆναι. "Round" is a strange word to apply to
the plant, and Urlichs would add (cf. the περιφερῆ of
Dioscorides) *radice* before *rotunda*. Others have emended to
rotundo (*sc. caule*). The leaves however are round.

nostri sic eam tradunt, Graeci foliis paulo candidioribus quam malvae, caulibus tenuibus, pilosis,
ramosam ex intervallis, binum palmorum, et in his
folia [1] inter quae in cacuminibus capitula sint gruum.
109 alterum genus foliis anemones, divisuris longioribus,
radice mali modo rotunda, dulci, reficientibus se ab
imbecillitate utilissima, et fere talis vera est.
bibitur contra phthisis drachma in cyathis vini tribus
bis die, item contra inflationes, et cruda idem praestat. sucus radicis auribus medetur, opisthotonis
semen drachmis quattuor cum pipere et murra
110 potum. phthisis sanat et plantaginis sucus, si bibatur, et ipsa decocta in cibo [2]; ex sale et oleo a somno
matutino refrigerat. eadem datur iis quos atrophos
vocant interpositis diebus, vettonica vero phthisicis
ecligmate cum melle, fabae magnitudine, agaricum
potum obolis duobus in passo, vel daucum cum centaurio maiore in vino. phagedaenis—quod nomen
sine modo esurientium est, et alias ulcerum—tithymalli medentur cum sesamis sumpti.
111   LXIX. Inter mala universi corporis vigiliae sunt
plerisque. harum remedio monstratur panaces,
clymenos, aristolochia odore et peruncto capite,

---

[1] folia VR : folius E *vulg.* : esse in his folia *coni. Mayhoff.*
[2] decocta in cibo;] *sic ex Dioscoride* (*Eup.* II 38) *dist.*
Mayhoff.

---

[a] Dioscorides (III 116) describes two kinds of γεράνιον.
Of the first he says φύλλον ὅμοιον ἀνεμώνῃ, ἐσχισμένον, μακρό
τερον δέ. This is Pliny's second kind, and *divisuris longioribus*
looks as though he mistranslated ἐσχισμένον, μακρότερον δέ,
unless we emend Pliny, and read *divisis, longioribus.* Of
Pliny's first kind, the second of Dioscorides; the latter says :
καυλία λεπτά, χνοώδη, δισπίθαμα, φύλλα μολόχῃ ἐμφερῆ καὶ ἐπ'

it is described by our Roman authorities; but Greeks *a* say that it has leaves a little lighter in colour than those of the mallow, thin stems, and downy, with branches at intervals and two spans long; on them are the leaves, among which on the tips of the stems are miniature heads of cranes. A second kind has leaves like those of anemone, which are marked with rather long incisions, and a round root like an apple, sweet, and very beneficial to convalescents. The last seems to be the true geranion. It is taken in drink for consumption twice a day in doses of one drachma in three cyathi of wine; the same prescription is good for flatulence, and eaten raw the plant has the same effect. The juice of the root is good for ear trouble; for opisthotonic tetanus four-drachmae doses of seed are taken in drink with pepper and myrrh. Consumption is cured too by drinking plantain juice, and by plantain itself boiled and taken as food. Eaten with salt and oil on waking from sleep in the morning it is very refreshing. It is also given every other day to those who we say are " wasting away," but to consumptives we give betony made up with honey into an electuary of the size of a bean, or agaric in raisin wine in two-oboli doses, or daucum with the greater centaury in wine. Cases of phagedaena, a word meaning bulimia as well as rodent ulcer, are treated by tithymallus with sesame.

LXIX. Of the maladies that affect the whole body sleeplessness is the most common. As remedies for it are recommended panaces, clymenos, aristolochia— by the smell or by bathing the head—aizoüm, that is

ἄκρων τῶν μασχαλῶν ἐξοχάς τινας ἀνανενευκυίας, ὡς γεράνων κεφαλάς.

aizoum sive sedum, si involutum panno nigro igno-
rantis pulvino subiciatur, et onothera sive onear, hila-
ritatem adferens in vino, amygdalae folio, flore
rosaceo, fruticosa, longa radice et, cum siccata est,
vinum olente. haec in potu data feras quoque miti-

112 gat. cruditates quae nausiam faciunt digerit vettonica, eadem pota a cena concoctionem facit, in oxymelitis cyathis tribus drachmae pondere et crapulam
discutit, item agaricum post cibum in aqua calida
potum. paralysin vettonica sanare dicitur, item
hiberis ut dictum est. eadem et torpentibus mem-
bris prodest, item argemonia omnia quae [1] secari
periclitentur discutiendo.

113   LXX. Comitiales sanantur [2] panacis [3] quam heraclion diximus radice [4] pota cum coagulo vituli marini
ita ut sint panacis tres partes. sanat et [5] plantago [6]
pota, vettonica in oxymelite [7] drachma vel agaricum [8]

---

[1] omnia quae R (?), *Gelenii editio Basileensis*; omnia quaeque VdE : omnia quaequae *Detlefsen* : omniaque, quae
Mayhoff, vulg.

[2] sanantur Vd *vulg.* : sanant *aliquot codd.*

[3] panacis *codd., vulg.* : panaces *Sillig, Detlefsen.*

[4] radice VRd *Sillig* : radices E.

[5] sanat et *ego transposui* ; *ante* archezostis *codd.*

[6] plantago *codd.* : plantagine *Mayhoff.*

[7] oxymelite *Gelenius* : oxymeliti *aut* oxymelitis *codd.*

[8] agaricum *Gelenius* : agaricon *Sillig* : agarico VRd :
agarici E r *vulg.*

---

[a] Or, " because taken in wine it dispels depression." Perhaps Pliny knew that depression was a common cause of
sleeplessness. In any case it is a strange phrase to be applied
to a cure for insomnia, although there can be no doubt about
the reading, for Theophrastus has (IX 19 § 1): ἡ δὲ τοῦ
ὀνοθήρα ῥίζα δοθεῖσα ἐν οἴνῳ πραότερον καὶ ἱλαρώτερον ποιεῖ τὸ

houseleek, wrapped in black cloth and placed under the pillow without the knowledge of the patient. Onothera also, that is onear, is soporific although exhilarating in wine,[a] having leaves like those of the almond tree, rose-coloured blossom, a bushy shape and a long root, which when dried smells of wine, and given in their drink soothes even wild beasts. Indigestion causing nausea is relieved by betony; it also if taken in drink after dinner promotes digestion; in doses of one drachma by weight in three cyathi of oxymel it also removes the after-effects of drink, as does agaric too taken in hot water after food. Betony is said to cure paralysis and so does hiberis as prescribed previously.[b] It is also good for numbness of the limbs; so also is argemonia, by removing all symptoms indicating that surgical treatment (i.e. venesection) may be necessary.[c]

LXX. Epilepsy is cured by the root of the panaces I have called heraclion[d] taken in drink with seal's rennet; three quarters of the mixture must be panaces. Other cures are plantain in drink, doses of one drachma of betony or three oboli of agaric in *Epilepsy.*

$\tilde{\eta}\theta o\varsigma$. The language of Dioscorides (IV 117) does not help much, although he mentions the soothing effect on wild beasts. It might be thought that not all the remedies given in this chapter are soporific. After *cruditates*, indeed, come some miscellaneous ones, but onothera is surely added (by the *et*) to the list of soporifics.

[b] See XXV § 88.

[c] I have kept the reading of R (queried as doubtful by Mayhoff) and of Gelenius because it avoids the dislocation of thought (violent even for Pliny) involved in the vulgate and accepted by Mayhoff. The use of argemonia is thus confined to the cure of paralysis, or partial paralysis.

[d] See XXV § 32.

obolis tribus, folia[1] quinquefolii ex aqua, archezostis, sed anno pota. sanat et baccaris radix arida
in pulverem contrita cyathis tribus cum coriandri
114 uno in aqua calida, et centunculus trita in aceto aut
melle aut in aqua calida, verbenaca ex vino pota,
hysopi bacae ternae contritae in aqua potae diebus
XVI, peucedanum cum coagulo vituli marini aequis
portionibus potum, quinquefolii contrita folia ex vino
pota diebus XXX, vettonicae farina p̄. X III cum aceti
scillitici[2] cyatho, mellis Attici uncia, scamonium
obolis duobus cum castorei drachmis quattuor.
115 LXXI. Febres frigidas leviores facit agaricum
potum in calida aqua, tertianas sideritis cum oleo,
item ladanum quod in segetibus nascitur contusum,
plantago ex aqua mulsa duabus horis ante accessionem pota binis drachmis vel sucus radicis madefactae vel tusae, vel ipsa radix trita in aqua ferro
calfacta. quidam ternas radices in tribus cyathis
116 aquae dedere. eadem in quartanis quaterna fece-
runt. buglosso inarescente, si quis medullam ex

---

[1] folia *codd.* : foliis *Mayhoff.*
[2] scillitici V²dEr *vulg.* : scillitis *Detlefsen* : scillini *Mayhoff,*
qui scillitae *coni.*

---

[a] The text here is in a very disturbed state, and the editors
are divided, Detlefsen adopting *sanat* followed by nomina-
tives and Mayhoff *sanantur* followed by ablatives. The
disturbance may have been caused by the accidental omission
of *sanat et* before *plantago* and its later re-insertion two lines
further on. The various readings of our MSS. were probably
due to conscious efforts to restore the grammar. Both Detlefsen
and Mayhoff adopt *oxymelitis*; but both *drachma* and *obolus*
are weights, not measures of capacity, and the sense requires
that the amount of betony and agaric should be given, not
the amount of oxymel in which they were taken. Professor
Andrews would keep the order of words in the MSS., com-

oxymel,[a] leaves of cinquefoil in water, and also
archezostis, but the last must be taken in drink for
a year. Other cures are dried root of baccar crushed
to powder and taken in hot water in doses of three
cyathi with one of coriander, pounded centunculus
in vinegar or honey or hot water,[b] vervain taken in
wine, three crushed berries of hyssop taken in water
for sixteen days, equal quantities of peucedanum
and seal's rennet taken in drink, crushed leaves of
cinquefoil taken in wine for thirty days, powdered
betony in doses of three denarii by weight with a
cyathus of squill vinegar and an ounce of Attic
honey,[c] scammony in doses [d] of two oboli with four
drachmae of beaver-oil.

LXXI. The chills of fever are relieved by agaric _Fevers._
taken in hot water, tertian fevers by sideritis with
oil, by crushed ladanum, a plant found in grain fields,
by plantain in hydromel taken in two-drachma doses
within two hours before a paroxysm, juice of its root
soaked or pounded, or by the root itself beaten up in
water [e] heated with hot iron. Some physicians
have prescribed doses of three roots in three cyathi
of water, changing three to four if the fever is
quartan. If one takes, when bugloss is withering,

menting that Pliny seems to say : " Yes, archezostis does cure,
but it takes a long time."

[b] It is often difficult to see whether in such phrases the
adverbial expression goes with the participle _tritus_ or not.
Here for instance the Bohn translators have " bruised in
vinegar." See note § 115.

[c] I take _uncia_ to be ablative with _cum_ understood, but as
far as the grammar is concerned, _mellis Attici uncia_ might
be a new remedy, with _uncia_ nominative.

[d] Littré translates as I do, but the Bohn translators think
that the numbers refer to the proportions of the prescription.

[e] Perhaps, " pounded root itself in water etc."

caule eximat dicatque ad quem liberandum febri
id faciat et alliget ei septem folia ante accessionem,
aiunt febri liberari, item vettonicae drachmam [1] in
aquae mulsae cyathis tribus vel agaricum, maxime
in iis febribus quae cum horrore veniant.   quinquefolii folia quidam terna tertianis dedere, quaterna
quartanis, plura ceteris, alii omnibus tres obolos cum
117   pipere ex aqua mulsa.   verbenaca quidem et iumentorum febribus in vino medetur, sed in tertianis a
tertio geniculo incisa, quartanis a quarto.   bibitur et
semen hyperici utriusque in quartanis et horroribus,
vettonicae farina, quae omnes horrores coercet,
item panaces adeo excalefactoria natura ut per
nivem ituris bibere id perunguique eo praecipiant.
et aristolochia perfrictionibus resistit.

118   LXXII. Phreneticos somnus sanat, qui continget [2]
peucedano ex aceto capiti infuso, anagallidum suco.
e diverso lethargicos excitare labor est ; hoc praestant
euphorbeum ex aceto naribus tactis, peucedani
sucus.   contra insanias vettonica bibitur.   carbunculos rumpit panaces, sanat vettonicae farina ex

---

[1] *Ante* drachmam *lacunam indicat Mayhoff, qui dari
supplendum esse putat.*
[2] continget *aliquot codd.*, *Detlefsen* : contingit E r *vulg.*,
Mayhoff.

---

[a] Mayhoff supposes that there is a lacuna before *drachmam* :
" *excidit* dari *vel aliud quid, unde pendeat drachmam.*"
Possibly *drachmam* is governed by *dedere* above. Both
eadem . . . facerent and *buglosso . . . liberari*—especially the
latter—look like later additions. Pliny, who was fond of
parentheses, may have added one or both of them as an after-
thought, overlooking the fact that so doing upset the syntax
of the passage.

the pith out of a stem and says that he does it to free
so and so from fever, attaching to the patient seven
leaves before a paroxysm begins, he is freed, it is
said, from the fever. Another remedy is betony in
doses of one drachma *a* in three cyathi of hydromel,
or agaric, especially in fevers attended with violent
shivers. Some have prescribed doses of three cinquefoil leaves for tertians, of four for quartans, and of
more for the other fevers; others prescribe for all
three oboli with pepper in hydromel. Vervain in
wine indeed is a remedy for fever even of beasts of
burden, but for tertians the plant must be cut at the
third joint, and for quartans at the fourth. For
quartans and feverish shivers is taken in drink the
seed of either kind of hypericum, powdered betony,
which checks all shiverings, and panaces also, which
is of such a heating nature that those about to
travel through snow are recommended to take it in
drink and to be rubbed with it. Violent chills *b* are
also checked by aristolochia.

LXXII. Phrenitis *c* is cured by sleep, which will be *Phrenitis.*
induced by pouring on the head an infusion of
peucedanum in vinegar, or the juice of either anagallis. On the other hand it is difficult to awaken
sufferers from lethargus *c*; this is done by touching
the nostrils with euphorbeum in vinegar, or with the
juice of peucedanum. For delirium *c* betony is
taken in drink. Carbuncles are made to burst by
panaces, and cured by powdered betony in water, or

b Either the chills of malarial fever, or perhaps the shiverings of a violent cold.
c *Phrenitis, lethargus,* and *insaniae* seem to be used in this
chapter of mild symptoms, and not of the severe diseases
often denoted by the terms.

aqua aut brassica cum ture, frequenti potu calidae,
vel e carbone in conspectu restincto favilla digito
sublata et inlita, vel plantago tusa, tithymallus
characites.[1]

119　LXXIII. Hydropicos sanat panaces, plantago in
cibo, cum prius panem siccum comederint sine potu,
vettonica drachmis duabus in duobus cyathis vini aut
mulsi, vel agaricum vel semen lonchitidis duabus
lingulis ex aqua potum, psyllion ex vino, anagallidum
sucus, cotyledonis radix e mulso, ebuli recentis radix
excussa tantum nec colluta, quod duo digiti conpre-
hendant, ex vini veteris caldi hemina, trifolii radix
drachmis duabus in vino, tithymallum platyphyllon
cognomine, semen hyperici quod caros appellatur,
120　acte, quam esse ebulum putant quidam, radice
contrita in vini cyathis tribus, si febris absit, vel
semine ex vino nigro, item verbenaca fasciculo
manus plenae in aqua decocta ad dimidias.　praecipue tamen chamaeactes sucus aptissimus creditur.
eruptiones pituitae emendant plantago, cyclamini
radix e melle, ebuli folia trita e vetere vino—inposita
etiam boam sanant, id est rubentes papulas—pruri-
ginem sucus strychni inlitus.

---

[1] characites *codd.*, *Detlefsen* : characias *Hard.*, *Mayhoff.*
Cf. §§ 62, 146.

---

[a] The *carbo* acts on the *carbunculus* by imitative magic.
[b] Or, " the crushed seed in dark (i.e. red) wine," *contrito*
being understood from *contrita* above.

by cabbage and frankincense with frequent draughts of hot water; or the ash from a burning coal [a] extinguished in the patient's presence may be picked up with a finger and applied. Other remedies are pounded plantain and tithymallus characites.

LXXIII. Remedies for dropsy are: panaces; *Dropsy.* plantain as food, after dry bread without any drink; two-drachma doses of betony in two cyathi of wine or honey wine; agaric, or lonchitis seed, two spoonfuls for a dose taken in water; psyllion in wine; juice of either anagallis; root of cotyledon in honey wine; root of fresh ebulum, shaken only and not washed, a two-finger pinch for a dose, taken in a hemina of old wine and hot water; root of trefoil in wine, two drachmae for a dose; the tithymallus called platyphyllon; seed of the hypericum known as caros; acte, which some identify with ebulum, the root, if there is no fever, being crushed in three cyathi of wine, or the seed [b] being taken in dark wine; vervain also, a good handful being boiled down in water to one half. The most efficacious remedy however is believed to be the juice of chamaeacte. An outbreak [c] of phlegm is relieved by plantain, by cyclamen root in honey, and by pounded leaves of ebulum in old wine. An application of the last cures boa [d] also, an eruption of red pimples, and the juice of strychnos applied as liniment cures itch.

[c] See list of diseases. Here perhaps nasal catarrh, but elsewhere (XXV § 61) pituitous eruptions on the body.

[d] The Latin *Thesaurus* gives a full list of references to boa, which was the name of more than one complaint. In Pliny it means some kind of eczema. The name was supposed to be connected with *bos*, because ox dung was used as a remedy. See XXVIII § 244.

355

121 LXXIV. Igni sacro medentur aizoum, folia trita
cicutae, mandragorae radix—secatur [1] in asses ut
cucumis, primumque super mustum suspenditur, mox
in fumo, dein tunditur [2]—e vino aut aceto. prodest
et vino myrteo fovere, mentae sextans, vivi sulpuris
uncia, ex aceto simul trita, fuligo ex aceto. ignis
sacri plura sunt genera, inter quae medium hominem
ambiens qui zoster vocatur et enecat,[3] si cinxit.
medetur plantago cum creta Cimolia et peristereos
per se, radix persollatae, aliis quae serpunt cotyledonis radix cum mulso, aizoum, sucus e linozosti ex
aceto.

122 LXXV. Radix polypodi inlita [4] luxatis medetur
doloremque et tumores tollunt semen psyllii, folia
plantaginis trita, sale modice addito, verbasci semen
ex vino decoctum tritum, cicuta cum axungia. folia

---

[1] secatur *Hard. ex cod. Murb.* : siccatur *codd.*

[2] tunditur (*aut tuditur*) *codd.* : teritur *coni. Mayhoff. Cf.
Theophrasti H.P.* IX ix 1 : τὴν δὲ ῥίζαν (τοῦ μανδραγόρου)
πρὸς ἐρυσίπελας ξυσθεῖσάν τε καὶ ὄξει δευθεῖσαν.

[3] et enecat E r. *Mayhoff, vulg.* : et necat *multi codd.* :
enecat *Ianus, Detlefsen.*

[4] radix polypodi inlita *cum priore sententia coniungit
Detlefsen.*

---

[a] Or, "are gourds."

[b] The emendation *teritur* is supported by Theophrastus
IX ix 1 : ῥίζαν . . . ξυσθεῖσαν " scraped "; but though he
and Pliny are very similar they are also in some respects
strangely unlike. Contrast for instance *secatur in asses ut
cucumis etc.* with τέμνουσι δὲ τροχίσκους ὥσπερ ῥαφανῖδος καὶ
ἐνείραντες ὑπὲρ γλεύκους ἐκρέμασαν ἐπὶ καπνῷ. Hort translates :
" they cut little balls of it, as of radishes, and making a string
of them hang them up in the smoke over must." Mayhoff
joins his *teritur* with *e vino aut aceto.* But as *teritur* has no
MS. authority, and the parenthesis gives a very Plinian

LXXIV. Erysipelas is treated with aizoüm, *Erysipelas.* pounded leaves of hemlock, and root of mandrake— it is cut into slices as is cucumber,[a] hung first over must, then in smoke, and finally pounded [b]—taken in wine or vinegar. It is beneficial too to foment with myrtle wine, or to use as an ointment two ounces of mint with one ounce of native sulphur beaten up together in vinegar, or soot mixed with vinegar. There are several kinds of erysipelas, among them one called zoster,[c] which goes round the patient's waist, and is fatal if the circle becomes quite complete. Remedies are: plantain with Cimolian chalk, peristereos by itself and the root of persollata; as remedies for the creeping forms can be used root of cotyledon with honey wine, aizoüm, and the juice of linozostis with vinegar.

LXXV. Root of polypodium made up into liniment is a remedy [d] for dislocations, and the pain and swelling are taken away by seed of psyllion, plantain leaves beaten up with a little salt, ground seed of verbascum boiled in wine, and hemlock with axle-grease.

character to the sentence, it seems unwise to resort to emendation. Mayhoff himself suggests that the text may be *tunditur, datur,* " is pounded and administered." It is difficult to discriminate between *tero, tundo, contero* in this connection, except that the first seems to denote less thorough and violent pounding. "Assume that the original text had *secatur* after *radix* and *siccatur* after *fumo.* Take *tunditur* with the following phrase. There is then no difficulty in translating." A. C. A.

[c] " The girdle," probably shingles. The Latin *erysipelas* is a much wider term than the English.

[d] The reading *medentur* is more strongly supported than *medetur.* Detlefsen, retaining *medentur,* took the words *radix polypodi inlita* as the end of the preceding sentence (§ 121). This change does not agree with Dioscorides.

ephemeri tuberibus tumoribusque inlinuntur quae
etiamtum discuti possunt.

123 LXXVI. Morbum regium in oculis praecipue
mirari est, tenuitatem etiam [1] densitatemque tuni-
cularum felle subeunte. Hippocrates a septimo die
in febri mortiferum signum esse dicit : nos scimus
vixisse aliquos etiam ab hac desperatione. fit vero
et citra febres expugnaturque centaurio maiore ut
diximus poto, vettonica, agarici obolis tribus ex vini
veteris cyatho, item verbenacae folia obolis tribus ex
124 vini calidi hemina quadriduo. sed celerrime quinquefolii sucus medetur tribus cyathis potus cum sale et
melle.[2] cyclamini radix drachmis tribus bibitur in
loco calido et a perfrictionibus tuto—sudores enim
felleos movet—folia tussilaginis ex aqua, semen
linozostis utriusque inspersum potioni vel cum
absinthio aut cicere decoctum, hysopi bacae cum aqua
potae, lichen herba, si, cum sumitur, cetero olere
abstineatur, polythrix in vino data, struthion in
mulso.

125 LXXVII. Passim et in quacumque parte sed
maxime incommoda nascuntur qui furunculi vocantur,
mortiferum aliquando malum consectis [3] corporibus.

---

[1] etiam VRT f, *Sillig, Mayhoff* : illam d (?) E *vulg.* : etiam
illam *Ianus, Detlefsen.*
[2] cum sale et melle V²Er *vulg., Detlefsen* : om. V¹RTf
Mayhoff.
[3] consectis VTfE *Detlefsen, Mayhoff* : confectis Rd(?) *vulg.*

---

[a] See e.g. *Aphorisms* IV 62.
[b] See XXV § 67.
[c] Mayhoff with many MSS. would omit "with salt and
honey," perhaps rightly, as Dioscorides has nothing to correspond.
[d] Or, "random" (A. C. A.). Or, "over a wide area" (of
the body).

The leaves of ephemeron are applied in the form of liniment to tumours and swellings that are still able to be dispersed.

LXXVI. The most striking symptom of jaundice *Jaundice.* is the effect upon the eyes; the bile penetrates even between the membranes, thin and close together as they are. Hippocrates [a] says that if jaundice supervenes from the seventh day of a fever it is a fatal symptom. I however know of recoveries even from this desperate condition. But cases of jaundice occur without fever, and can be overcome by the greater centaury, taken in drink as I have prescribed,[b] by betony, by three-oboli doses of agaric in a cyathus of old wine, and by three-oboli doses of vervain leaves taken for four days in a hemina of warmed wine. The quickest remedy however is juice of cinquefoil taken in doses of three cyathi with salt and honey.[c] Three-drachmae doses of root of cyclamen are taken in drink while the patient is in a warm place protected from chilly draughts—the medicine induces sweats full of gall—, and good is done by leaves of tussilago in water, by seed of linozostis of either kind sprinkled in drink or boiled down with wormwood or chick peas, by hyssop berries taken with water, by the herb lichen, the patient during the treatment abstaining from all other vegetables, by polythrix administered in wine, and by struthion in honey wine.

LXXVII. A common [d] complaint, affecting any *Boils.* part of the body, but especially an inconvenient part, is what are called boils, sometimes a fatal malady after surgical operations.[e] Pounded leaves of

[e] *Confectis* : " when the body is run down."

remedio sunt pycnocomi folia trita cum polenta, si
nondum caput fecerint.   discutiunt et folia ephedri
inlita.

126   LXXVIII. Fistulae quoque in omni parte serpunt
medicorum vitio male sectis corporibus.   auxilio est
centaurium minus collyriis cum melle decocto additis,
plantaginis sucus infusus, quinquefolium cum sale et
melle, ladanum cum castoreo, cotyledon cum medulla
cervina calefacta et inposita;   verbasci radicis
medulla collyrii tenuitate in fistulam additur vel
aristolochiae radix vel sucus tithymalli.

127   LXXIX. Collectiones inflammationesque sanant
argemoniae folia inlita, duritias et collectiones omnes
verbenaca vel quinquefolium decoctum in aceto,
verbasci folia vel radix, hysopum e vino inpositum,
acori radix decocto eius foventibus, aizoum, item
quae contusa sint duritiasque et in sinu [1] corporis [2]
illecebra.   omnia infixa corpori extrahunt folia
128 tussilaginis, daucum, semen leontopodii tritum in
aqua cum polenta.   suppurationibus inponuntur
pycnocomi folia trita cum polenta vel semen, item
orchis.   vitia quae sint in ossibus satyrii radice
inposita efficacissime sanari dicuntur, nomae et

---

[1] in sinu VdT *Detlefsen* : sinus E r *vulg.*, *Mayhoff.*

[2] corporis] *Cf.* § 141 sinus ulcerum.   *Urlichs del.* corporis
et ulcerum *scribit.*

---

[a] Literally " creep," from the shape of the fistula.   Littré
has " se creusent."

[b] The meaning of *collyriis* here is uncertain.   It might be
" salves " or " suppositories," but *additis,* and the common
occurrence of rectal fistulas, suggest the latter.   See too the
last sentence of this chapter.

[c] Prof. Andrews suggests: " supplemented by suppositories
made with boiled honey."   But cf. *in fistulam additur* below.

pycnocomon with pearl barley are a remedy if the
boil has not yet come to a head. Boils are also
dispersed by applications of leaves of ephedron.

LXXVIII. Fistulas also form [a] in any part of the *Fistulas.*
body through the careless use of the surgeon's knife.
The lesser centaury, if suppositories [b] made from it
are inserted with boiled honey,[c] is a help; so is
plantain juice poured into them, cinquefoil with salt
and honey, ladanum with beaver-oil, and cotyledon
with deer's marrow warmed and applied; the pith of
verbascum root, cut as slender as a suppository, is
inserted into the fistula, or there may be used root of
aristolochia or juice of tithymallus.

LXXIX. Gatherings and inflammations are cured *Suppura-*
by an application of argemonia leaves, all indurations [d] *tions and*
other com-
and gatherings by vervain, or by cinquefoil boiled *plaints.*
down in vinegar, by leaves or root of verbascum, by an
application of hyssop in wine, by fomenting with a
decoction of acoron root, and by aizoüm; for bruises,
indurations, and for pitted sores [e] in the flesh the
remedy is illecebra. All foreign bodies buried in the
flesh may be extracted by leaves of tussilago, by
daucum, or by seed of leontopodium beaten up in
water with pearl barley. To suppurations are applied
leaves, or seed, of pycnocomon beaten up with pearl
barley, likewise orchis. For affections of the bones a
very efficacious cure is said to be an application of

[d] Perhaps in this context " hard abscesses." Cf. Celsus V
25, 11: (*abscessus*) *rubet cum calore et paulo post etiam cum
duritia.*
[e] *In sinu,* "in the case of a (sore) hollow," is the harder,
and therefore perhaps the more likely reading. See (§ 141)
sinus ulcerum and (XXVII § 63) *explent sinus ulcerum. Sinus*
is the hollow or cavity formed by a deep ulcer. Perhaps ' sores
in a fold (*sinus*) of the body.'

collectiones omnes fuco maris, priusquam inarescat. et alcimae [1] radix collectiones discutit.

129 LXXX. Ambusta sanantur plantagine, arctio ita ut cicatrix fallat. folia eius in aqua decocta contrita inlinuntur, radices cyclamini cum aizoo, herba ipsa hyperici quod corissum appellavimus.

130 LXXXI. Nervis et articulis convenit plantago trita cum sale, argemonia tusa ex melle. peucedani suco perunguntur spastici, tetanici. nervorum duritiae aegilops suco, doloribus erigeron ex aceto inlinitur, epithymum. spasticis et opisthotonicis perungui semine hyperici, quod caros vocatur, itemque bibere prodest. phrynion dicitur etiam abscissos sanare nervos, si confestim inponatur trita vel mansa. spasticis, tremulis, opisthotonicis alcimae [2] radix bibitur ex aqua mulsa. sic et rigores excalfacit.

131 LXXXII. Sanguinis profluvia sistit herbae paeoniae semen rubrum—eadem et in radice vis— clymenus vero, sive ore sanguis reiciatur sive naribus, sive alvo fluat sive feminarum utero, item lysimachia pota vel inlita vel naribus indita, item plantaginis semen, quinquefolium potum et inlitum, cicutae semen in nares, si inde fluat, tritum ex aqua inditum,

---

[1] alcimae V f *Sillig*: alceae *Caesarius*: algmae RE: alginae d T.
[2] alcimae *Sillig, Detlefsen, Mayhoff*: alceae *Caesarius*: algmae V: alginae d T: algme *ceteri codd.*

---

[a] See § 85 of this book.
[b] There seems to be here a distinction between *trita* and *tusa*, which are sometimes strengthened into *contrita* and *contusa*. Perhaps the former points to breaking up into bits, and the latter merely to crushing. Any distinction is sometimes hard to observe in a translation.

satyrion root, and for corroding sores and gatherings of all kinds an application of sea-weed used while it is still wet. Root of alcima too disperses gatherings.

LXXX. Burns are healed by plantain, and by arctium so well that no scars are seen. A decoction in water of crushed arctium leaves is used as liniment for burns, and so are cyclamen roots with aizoüm, and the plant itself of the hypericum I have called [a] corissum. *Burns.*

LXXXI. Good for sinews and joints are plantain beaten up with salt and argemonia pounded [b] in honey. Juice of peucedanum is rubbed all over [c] those suffering from spasms or tetanus. For indurations of the sinews juice of aegilops is used as liniment, and for pains of the sinews erigeron (or epithymum) is so used in vinegar. Spasms and opisthotonic tetanus are benefited by thorough rubbing with seed of the hypericum known as caros, and this seed also benefits if taken in drink. Sinews even when severed are said to be healed by phrynion, beaten up or chewed, if it is applied immediately. Spasms, palsy, and opisthotonic tetanus are treated by root of alcima taken in hydromel. So taken it also warms rigors. *Sinews.*

LXXXII. Haemorrhage is checked by the red seed of the plant paeonia—the root also is styptic—but by clymenus when blood is discharged from the mouth or nostrils, or when it flows from the bowels or the uterus; by lysimachia too taken in drink, or applied as liniment, or inserted into the nostrils, also by plantain seed, by cinquefoil taken in drink and [d] applied, by hemlock seed beaten up in water and inserted into the nostrils should there be *Haemorrhage.*

[c] Or, " thoroughly on." [d] Perhaps " or ".

aizoum, astragali radix. sistit et ischaemon et
achillia.

132   LXXXIII. Equisaetum hippuris Graecis dicta et
in pratis vituperata nobis—est autem pilus terrae
equinae saetae similis—lienes cursorum extinguit
decocta fictili novo ad tertias quantum vas capiat et
per triduum heminis pota. unctis esculentis ex ante
diem unum interdicitur. Graecorum varia circa hanc
133 opinio : alii pinus foliis similem nigricantem eodem
nomine appellant, vim eius admirabilem tradentes,
sanguinis profluvia vel tacto tantum ea homine sisti,
alii hippurin, alii ephedron, alii anabasim vocant,
traduntque iuxta arbores nasci et scandentem eas
dependere comis iunceis multis nigris ut ex equorum
cauda, geniculatis ramulis, folia habere pauca, tenuia,
exigua, semen rotundum, simile coriandro, radice
134 lignosa, nasci in arbustis maxime. vis eius spissare
corpora. sucus sanguinem e naribus fluentem in-
clusus sistit, item alvum. medetur dysintericis in
vino dulci potus cyathis tribus, urinam ciet, tussim,
orthopnoeam sanat, item rupta et quae serpunt.
intestinis et vesicae folia bibuntur, enterocelen
cohibet. faciunt et aliam hippurim brevioribus et
mollioribus comis candidioribusque, perquam utilem
ischiadicis et vulneribus ex aceto inpositam propter

---

    [a] See XVIII § 259.
    [b] Perhaps " thin."
    [c] See Celsus II i, 10, *aquilo sanum corpus spissat.* Cf. p. 40,
note. Professor Andrews prefers : " to make the flesh more
compact." Dr. Spencer uses " brace " for the Celsus passage.
    [d] Perhaps *ex aceto* goes only with *vulneribus.* So Littré.
    [e] In this passage at least a distinction seems to be drawn
between *vulnus* and *plaga*, the former being a cut or thrust, and
the latter a blow that breaks the flesh. But the distinction is
not always strictly observed.

epistaxis, by aizoüm and by root of astragalus. Ischaemon too and achillia check bleeding.

LXXXIII. Equisaetum, called hippuris by the *Equisaetum.* Greeks, and found fault with by me when I discussed meadow land *a*—it is in fact " hair of the earth " resembling horse hair—reduces the spleen of runners if as much as the pot will hold is boiled down to one third in new earthenware, and taken in drink for three days in doses of one hemina. There must be abstinence from fatty foods for at least one day previously. The Greeks hold various views about this plant; some under the same name speak of a dark plant with leaves like those of the pine, assuring us that, so wonderful is its nature, its mere touch stanches a patient's bleeding; some call it hippuris, others ephedron, others anabasis. Their account is that it grows near trees, which it climbs, and hangs down in many dark, rush-like hairs as if from a horse's tail; that its little branches are jointed, and its leaves few, slender *b* and small; that the seed is round, resembling that of coriander, that its root is ligneous, and that it grows mostly in plantations. Its property is to brace *c* the body. Its juice, kept in the nostrils, checks haemorrhage therefrom, and it also checks looseness of the bowels. Taken in a sweet wine, in doses of three cyathi, it is good for dysentery, promotes passing of urine, and cures cough and orthopnoea, ruptures also and spreading sores. The leaves are taken in drink for complaints of the bowels and bladder; the plant itself reduces intestinal hernia. The Greeks recognise yet another hippuris, which has shorter, softer and paler hairs, making a very useful application in vinegar *d* for sciatica, and also for cuts,*e*

365

135 sistendum sanguinem. et nymphaea trita plagis
inponitur. peucedanum cum semine cupressi bibitur, si sanguis per os redditus est fluxitve ab infernis.
sideritis tantam vim habet ut quamvis recenti
gladiatoris vulneri inligata sanguinem claudat, quod
facit et ferulae cinis vel carbo, fungus vero etiam
efficacius, qui secundum radicem eius nascitur.

136 LXXXIV. per nares autem fluenti et cicutae semen
tritum ex aqua additumque efficax habetur, item
stephanomelis ex aqua. vettonicae farina e lacte
caprino pota sistit ex ubere fluentem, plantagoque
contusa. eiusdem sucus vomentibus sanguinem
datur. ad erraticum autem radix persollatae cum

137 axungia vetere inlita probatur. LXXXV. ruptis
convulsisque, ex alto deiectis centaurium maius,
gentianae radix trita vel decocta vel sucus, vettonica
et hoc amplius a vocis aut lateris contentionibus
panaces,[1] scordium, aristolochia pota, agaricum item [2]
contusis et eversis potum duobus obolis in mulsi
cyathis tribus aut, si febris sit, in aqua mulsa, verbascum cuius flos similis auro est, acori radix, aizoum
omne, sed maioris sucus efficacissime, item symphyti
ius [3] vel radicis decoctum, daucos cruda, erysithales

---

[1] sucus, vettonica et hoc . . . contentionibus panaces,
Diosc. coll. Mayhoff: sucus vettonicae, et hoc . . . contentionibus, panaces, *Detlefsen.*

[2] item *codd., Detlefsen* : idem *Mayhoff.*

[3] symphyti ius *Ianus coll.* xx 234 : symphyti ipsius *coni.
Mayhoff*: symphyticius d : symphitius V : symphyti E :
symphyti sucus *Sillig.*

---

[a] By *farina* apparently is meant dried betony ground to
powder. It might mean the ground seeds.

as it stanches the flow of blood. Nymphaea also *Lesions,* beaten up is applied to wounds from blows, and *ruptures, sprains.* peucedanum with cypress seed is taken in drink if blood is brought up through the mouth or flows from the lower passages. Sideritis has such a powerful effect that if bandaged to a gladiator's wound, however recent, it stops the bleeding, as does also the ash or cinders of fennel-giant, though more efficacious still is the fungus that grows about its root. LXXXIV. For epistaxis however hemlock seed also beaten up in water and inserted into the nostrils is held to be efficacious, and so is stephanomelis in water. Ground [a] betony taken in goat's milk checks haemorrhage from the breasts, as does crushed plantain. The juice of the latter is given to those who vomit blood. For sporadic bleeding [b] however is recommended an application of persollata root with stale axle-grease.

LXXXV. For ruptures, sprains, and falls from a height remedies are: the greater centaury, gentian root beaten up or boiled down, or its juice, betony, and especially when the lesion is caused by straining the voice or sides, panaces, scordium, aristolochia in drink, agaric also for bruises and falls, the dose being two oboli taken in three cyathi of honey wine or, if there is fever, in hydromel, the verbascum with the golden flower, root of acoron, all the kinds of aizoüm; the most efficacious preparation however being the juice [c] of the greater aizoüm, the broth too of symphytum or a decoction of the root, raw daucos, erysithales—the flower is yellow, the leaves

[b] Hardouin saw a reference in *erraticus sanguis* to the effects of erysipelas. It is more likely that some form of purpura is meant.

[c] For *sucus* and *ius* see note on XXIV § 146. Pliny may be translating different Greek words (χυλός, χυμός).

flore luteo, foliis acanthi e vino, item chamaerops et
in sorbitione irio vel plantago omnibus modis,
item. . . .

138   LXXXVI. Phthiriasi Sulla dictator consumptus est,
nascunturque in sanguine ipso hominis animalia
exesura corpus. resistitur [1] uvae taminiae suco aut
veratri cum oleo perunctis corporibus. taminia
quidem in aceto decocta etiam vestes eo taedio
liberat.

· 139   LXXXVII. Ulcera multorum sunt generum ac
multis modis curantur. panacis omnium generum
radix ex vino calido inlinitur manantibus. siccat
privatim quam chironiam diximus, cum melle trita
tubera aperit ulceribusque quae serpunt deploratis
auxilio est, cum aeris flore vino temperata omnibus
modis, vel semine vel flore vel radice. eadem cum
140 polenta vetustis volneribus prodest; heraclion quoque siderion, apollinaris, psyllium, tragacantha.
scordotis cum melle purgat. farina eius carnis
excrescentes per se inspersa consumit. polemonia
ulcera quae cacoethe vocant sanat; centaurium
maius inspersum vel inlitum, item minoris coma
decocta vel trita vetera quoque ulcera purgat et
persanat. folliculi clymeni recentibus plagis inponuntur. inlinitur autem gentiana ulceribus quae
serpunt radice tusa vel decocta in aqua ad mellis
crassitudinem vel suco, volneribus ex ea factum

---

[1] *Post* item *lacunam indicat Sillig, quem sequitur Mayhoff* :
modis, item phthiriasi qua Sulla dictator consumptus est—
nascunturque . . . corpus—resistitur *Detlefsen.*

---

[a] The text of Mayhoff (which I follow) is here smoother than
that of Detlefsen, but leaves one difficulty—the *que* after
nascuntur. One would rather expect *quo morbo nascuntur* or
the like. Perhaps there is another lacuna after *consumptus est.*

those of the acanthus—taken in wine, chamaerops also and irio in soup, or any preparation of plantain, likewise. . . .

LXXXVI. Sulla the dictator perished from *Phthiriasis.* phthiriasis; in the very blood of the patient creatures come to life that will eat up his flesh.[a] The disease is combated by rubbing the whole body with juice of the taminian grape, or with hellebore juice and oil. Taminian grapes indeed boiled down in vinegar remove this nuisance even from garments.

LXXXVII. Ulcers are of many kinds, and the *Ulcers.* methods of treatment are many. To running sores is applied in warmed wine the root of any kind of panaces. A specific for drying them is the herb I have called [b] chironia; beaten up with honey it opens hard swellings, and affords relief to desperate cases of spreading ulcers; it is diluted with wine and combined with flower of copper, and seed, flower or root may be used indiscriminately. This plant with pearl barley is also good for old wounds, so too is heraclion siderion, apollinaris, psyllium and traga-cantha. Scordotis with honey cleanses them; its powder consumes morbid excrescences of flesh, if sprinkled on them by itself. Polemonia heals ulcers that are called malignant; the greater centaury, whether sprinkled or applied as liniment, the tuft [c] also of the lesser centaury, boiled down or beaten up, cleanses and thoroughly heals even chronic ulcers. The seed pods of clymenus are applied to fresh wounds. From gentian too is made a liniment for spreading ulcers; the pounded root is boiled down in water to the consistency of honey or the juice may be used; from gentian is made a lycium

[b] See XXV § 32. [c] Or, " top."

141 lycium. lysimachia recentibus plagis medetur, plantago omnium generum ulceribus, peculiariter senum
et infantium. igni emollita melior et cum cerato
crassa ulcerum labra purgat, nomas sistit. tritam
suis foliis integere oportet. suppurationes, collectiones, sinus ulcerum chelidonia quoque siccantur,
volnera adeo ut etiam pro spodio utantur, eadem iam
142 desperatis cum axungia inponitur. dictamnum pota
sagittas pellit et alia tela extrahit inlita—bibitur ex
aquae cyatho foliorum obolo—proxime pseudodictamnum; utraque et suppurationes discutit.
aristolochia quoque putria ulcera exest, sordida
purgat cum melle vermesque extrahit, item clavos in
ulcere natos et infixa corpori omnia, praecipue sagit-
143 tas et ossa fracta cum resina, cava vero ulcera explet
per se et cum iride, recentia volnera ex aceto,
vetera ulcera verbenaca, quinquefolium cum sale et
melle. radices persollatae volneribus ferro inlatis
recentibus inponuntur, folia veteribus, cum axungia
utrumque, et suo folio operitur, damasonium [1] ut in
144 struma, folia verbasci ex aceto aut vino. peristereos

---

[1] veteribus; cum axungia utrimque et suo folio operitur
damasonium Mayhoff.

---

[a] For lycium see XXIV §§ 124 foll.
[b] The difference between plaga (πληγή) and volnus (τραῦμα)
seems here to be nil. Littré has plaie for both.
[c] Mayhoff's emendation here seems to give the sense :
" damasonium with axle-grease on both sides is covered over
with its own leaves." It is difficult to state with confidence
what is, or is not, possible in a passage so amorphous in style as
the present, but there can hardly be any objection to utrumque
in the sense of " either application," especially when the words
referred to (radices, folia) are of different genders, and each of

for wounds.[a] Lysimachia is good treatment for
fresh wounds,[b] and plantain for ulcers of all kinds,
especially for those of old men and babies. It is better
when softened by fire, and with wax-salve cleanses
the thickened lips of ulcers and arrests corrosive
sores. The pounded plant when applied should be
covered with its own leaves. Suppurations, gatherings and pitted ulcers are also dried up by chelidonia,
wounds are healed so well that it is even used instead
of spodium. It is also applied with axle-grease to
sores that are already despaired of. Dittany taken
in drink forces out arrows; an external application
causes to fall out other kinds of weapons—the dose
for a draught is an obolus of the leaves in a
cyathus of water—and bastard dittany is almost as
effective; both too disperse suppurations. Aristolochia also eats away festering ulcers, with honey
cleanses those that are foul, expels worms, the
callosities also that form in ulcers and all things
embedded in the flesh, especially with resin arrows
and bone splinters; but the pits of ulcers it fills
up by itself or with the addition of iris. For fresh
wounds it is used in vinegar; for chronic ulcers
vervain is used, or cinquefoil with salt and honey.
The roots of persollata are applied to fresh wounds
that have been inflicted by iron, and the leaves
to old wounds, axle-grease being added to both [c]
with a covering of the plant's leaves.[d] Other
applications are damasonium, used as for scrofula, and
the leaves of verbascum in vinegar or wine. Peris-

them is an *impositum*. So rather reluctantly I have not adopted
this brilliant attempt to restore the true text.

[d] Or, " with axle-grease as a base for either, and a pledget
of the plant's leaves " (A. C. A.).

ad omnia genera vel callosorum putrescentiumque
ulcerum facit. manantia nymphaeae heracliae radix
sanat, item cyclamini radix vel per se vel ex aceto vel
cum melle. eadem et contra steatomata efficax,
sicut ad ulcera manantia hysopum, item peucedanum,
et ad recentia volnera vis tanta est ut squamam
ossibus extrahat. praestant hoc et anagallides
cohibentque quas vocant nomas et rheumatismos,
utiles et recentibus plagis, sed praecipue senum corpori. cum cerato apostemata et ulcera taetra folia
145 mandragorae recentia, radix volnera cum melle aut
oleo, cicuta cum siligine mixta mero, aizoum herpetas quoque ac nomas ac putrescentia, sicut erigeron
verminosa, recentia autem volnera astragali radix et
vetera ulcera quae purgat hypocisthis utraque.
leontopodii semen tritum in aqua et cum polenta
inlitum spicula sagittarum extrahit, item pycnocomi
146 semen. tithymallus characites suco gangraenas,
phagedaenas, putria vel decocto ramorum cum
polenta et oleo, orchis radices hoc amplius et cacoethe
cum melle, siccae et recentes per se vulnera, onothera
efferantia sese ulcera sanat. Scythae vulnera[1]
Scythica curant. ad carcinomata argemonia ex
147 melle efficacissima est. ulceribus praesanatis aspho-
deli radix decocta ut diximus, trita cum polenta et

[1] vulnera *codd.* : ulcera *Mayhoff ex Theophrasto* (*H.P.*
IX 13, 2).

---

[a] From *herpetas* to *putrescentia* may be considered a parenthesis : " —herpes too, nomae and festering sores—." In
most of this chapter however the sentences are almost formless,
and resist efforts to make them conform to the normal.

[b] Mayhoff may be right in reading *ulcera* from Theophrastus.
As however the MSS. have *vulnera*, Pliny, rather loose in his
renderings of his Greek authorities, probably wrote it.

tereos is good for all kinds of ulcers, even when hard
and festering. Running ulcers are cured by root of
nymphaea heraclia, also by the root of cyclamen, by
itself, in vinegar, or with honey. This last is also excellent for fatty tumours, as is hyssop for running ulcers,
and peucedanum also, which when used for fresh
wounds is so powerful as to exfoliate bones. The two
kinds of anagallis also have this property, and check
fluxes and the sores called *nomae*, being useful for fresh
wounds, but especially for those on the flesh of the
aged. Abscesses and foul ulcers ⟨may be treated
with⟩ fresh leaves of mandrake and wax-salve,
wounds with its root and honey or oil, or with
hemlock added to wheat and neat wine. For
herpes also, nomae and festering ulcers,[a] aizoüm
may be used, as may erigeron for verminous sores, for
fresh wounds root of astragalus, and for chronic ulcers
either kind of hypocisthis, which cleanses them.
The seed of leontopodium, beaten up in water and
applied with pearl barley, extracts the heads of
arrows, as does also the seed of pycnocomon. The
juice of tithymallus characites heals gangrenes,
phagedaenic sores and purulent ulcers, as does a
decoction of the branches with pearl barley and oil;
the roots of orchis moreover with honey cure even
malignant sores, healing wounds without further
addition, and whether dry or freshly gathered.
Onothera heals ulcers that are becoming virulent.
The Scythians treat wounds[b] with scythice. For
carcinoma argemonia applied with honey is very
efficacious. For ulcers prematurely healed root of
asphodel, boiled down as I have said,[c] beaten up with
pearl barley and applied, is good; but apollinaris is

[c] See XXII § 70.

373

inlita, quibuscumque vero apollinaris, astragali radix
in pulverem trita umidis ulceribus prodest, item
callithrix decocta in aqua, privatim vero his quae
calciamento facta sint verbenaca, nec non et lysimachia contrita ac nymphaea arida infriata. polythrix inveteratis isdem utilior est.

148   LXXXVIII. Polycnemon cunilae bubulae similis
est, semine pulei, surculosa, multis geniculis, corymbo
odorato,[1] acri et dulci odore, ferro factis conmanducata inponitur, quinto die solvitur. ·symphyton ad
149 cicatricem celerrime perducit, item sideritis. haec
inponitur ex melle. verbasci semine ac foliis ex
vino decoctis ac tritis omnia infixa corpori extra-
huntur, item mandragorae foliis cum polenta,
cyclamini radicibus cum melle. trixaginis folia in
oleo contrita his maxime adhibentur ulceribus quae
serpunt, et alga in[2] melle trita, vettonica ad carcinomata et malandrias veteres addito sale.

150   LXXXIX. Verrucas tollit argemonia ex aceto
vel batrachii radix, quae et ungues scabros aufert,
linozostidis utriusque folia vel sucus inlitus. tithymalli omnes genera verrucarum omnia, item pterygia, varos tollunt. cicatrices cum elegantia ad
colorem reducit ladanum. artemisiam et elelis-
phacum alligatas qui habeat viator negatur lassitudinem sentire.

----

[1] odorato *Gelenius, Detlefsen* : odorata *codd.* : *in uncis
Mayhoff.*
[2] alga in *vulg. Detlefsen* : alcima in *Mayhoff* : algam in
VE.

----

[a] For *malandria* see list of diseases ; and XXIV § 44.

good for any kind of sore, and root of astragalus, beaten to powder, for ulcers that are running, and so is callithrix boiled down in water; specific however for sores caused by footwear is vervain, crushed lysimachia also, and dried nymphaea reduced to powder. But when these last have become chronic polythrix proves more useful.

LXXXVIII. Polycnemon is like ox cunila, and its seed resembles that of pennyroyal; it has a wood-like stem with many joints, and its clusters are scented, with a pungent but sweet smell. When chewed it is applied to cuts made by iron, but is taken off on the fifth day. Symphyton very quickly causes a scar to form, as also does sideritis, which is applied with honey. The seed and leaves of verbascum, boiled down in wine and beaten up, bring away everything embedded in the flesh, as do mandrake leaves with pearl barley, or cyclamen roots with honey. Trixago leaves crushed in oil are applied especially to spreading ulcers, as is also sea-weed beaten up in honey; betony, with the addition of salt, is used for carcinoma and chronic pustules [a] on the neck.

LXXXIX. Warts are removed by argemonia in *Warts.* vinegar, by root of batrachium, which also brings away scabrous nails, and by an application of the leaves or juice of either kind of linozostis. All kinds of tithymallus remove all kinds of warts, hangnails, and pimples [b] on the face. Ladanum smooths away scars and restores the colour. A traveller who has artemisia and [c] elelisphacus tied on him does not, they say, feel any fatigue.

[b] Or, "eruptions."

[c] Is *et* here equivalent to " or "? The plural (*alligatas*) seems against this.

151 XC. Muliebribus morbis medetur maxime in
universum paeoniae herbae semen nigrum ex aqua
mulsa. eadem et in radice vis. menses ciet panacis
semen cum absinthio, menses et sudores scordotis potu
et inlitu. vettonica drachma in vini cyathis tribus
bibitur contra omnia volvarum vitia aut quae a partu
fiunt. menses nimios sistit achillia inposita[1] et
152 decoctum eius insidentibus. mammis inponitur hyoscyami semen ex vino—locis radix in cataplasmate—
et[2] chelidonia. secundas morantes vel partus
emortuos radices panacis adpositae extrahunt. ipsum panaces e vino potum volvas purgat adpositum-
que cum melle. polemonia pota ex vino secundas
153 pellit, nidore corrigit volvas. centauri minoris sucus
potu fotuque menses ciet, item maioris radix in volvae doloribus isdem modis prodest, derasa vero et
adposita extrahit partus emortuos. plantago ad-
ponitur in lana in dolore volvae, in strangulatu bibitur.
sed praecipua dictamno vis est; menses ciet, partus
emortuos vel traversos eicit—bibitur ex aqua foliorum
obolo—adeo ad haec efficax ut ne in cubiculum
quidem praegnantium inferatur. nec potu tantum
sed et inlitu et suffitu valet. proxime pseudodic-

---

[1] inposita E *Detlefsen* : adposita V *Mayhoff*.
[2] et *Detlefsen* : mammis et *Mayhoff* : et mammis et *codd.*

---

[a] The word *et* here may mean either " and " or " or."
[b] The parenthesis removes the difficulty of this sentence.
[c] Littré has : " bonne pour l'hystérie," but I find it hard to
distinguish the phrase from *vulvas conversas corrigit* in XXIV
§ 22.
[d] The Latin *Thesaurus* gives many examples of *adponere* in
Pliny used of uterine applications, but it is hard to see how it
differs from *subdere* and *subiectus* in § 154. The Greek words
corresponding are πρόσθετον and προστίθημι.

XC. For diseases of women a very good general *Diseases of* remedy is the black seed, taken in hydromel, of the *women.* plant paeonia; its root also has the same property. An emmenagogue is seed of panaces with wormwood, and a sudorific emmenagogue is scordotis, taken internally or *a* applied locally. Betony in doses of one drachma to three cyathi of wine is taken for all uterine affections, and for those that result from child-birth. Excessive menstruation is checked by an application of achillia or *a* a sitz bath in a decoction of it. To the breasts is applied henbane seed in wine —but to the uterus henbane root in a plaster *b*—and also chelidonia. A pessary of panaces roots brings away retarded after-birth or the dead foetus. The uterus is purged by panaces, taken by itself in wine, and by a pessary of it with honey. Polemonia taken in wine forces out the after-birth, and the fumes of it when burnt correct the uterus.*c* Juice of the lesser centaury taken in drink or used as a fomentation is an emmenagogue, and the root of the greater centaury, used in the same ways, is good for uterine pains, while if it is scraped and applied as a pessary it brings away a dead foetus. Plantain is applied as a pessary *d* in wool for pain in the uterus; for hysterical suffocation it is taken in drink. But it is dittany that is of the greatest efficacy; it is an emmenagogue, and forces out the foetus when dead or lying transversely —an obolus of the leaves is taken in water—being so efficacious in these respects that it is not even introduced into the bedroom of pregnant women. Not only when taken in drink but also when used as embrocation or a fumigation it has medicinal power. Bastard dittany is very nearly as good, but for an emmenagogue it is boiled down with neat wine, the

tamnum, sed menses ciet cum mero decoctum denarii
154 pondere. plurimis tamen modis aristolochia prodest,
nam et menses et secundas ciet et emortuos partus
extrahit, murra et pipere additis pota vel subdita.
volvas quoque procidentes inhibet fotu vel suffitu vel
155 subiectu, maxime tenuis. strangulatum ab his
mensumque difficultatem agaricum obolis tribus in
vini veteris cyatho potum emendat, peristereos adposita in adipe suillo recenti, antirrhinon cum rosaceo
et melle. item adposita nymphaeae Thessalae radix
dolori medetur, in vino nigro pota profluvia inhibet ;
e diverso ciet cyclamini radix pota et adposita, et
156 vesicae insidentium decocto medetur. secundas pota
cissanthemos pellit, volvam sanat. e xiphio radix
superior menses ciet drachma ex aceto pota. peucedanum strangulatus volvae nidore ustum recreat,
menses albos [1] praecipue psyllion drachma in cyathis
tribus aquae, semen mandragorae potum volvam
purgat, menses ciet sucus adpositus et emortuos par-
157 tus. nimia rursus profluvia sistit semen cum vivo
sulphure, contra ea ciet batrachium potu vel cibo,
ardens alias, ut diximus, cruda, sed cocta commen-
datur sale et oleo et cumino. daucum et menses et
secundas potu facillime pellit, ladanum suffitu

---

[1] albos T *Detlefsen, Mayhoff* : albo Vd : alvos E : alvosque
vulg.

---

[a] Again, *et* may mean here " and."
[b] See XXV § 173.

dose being one denarius by weight. Very many however are the ways in which aristolochia does good, for it is an emmenagogue, hastens the after-birth, and brings away a dead foetus; myrrh and pepper being added it is taken in drink or used as a pessary. It also checks prolapsus of the uterus, whether used as fomentation, fumigation or pessary, especially the slender aristolochia. Hysterical suffocations and delayed menstruation are relieved by agaric taken in doses of three oboli to a cyathus of old wine, by a pessary of peristereos in fresh lard, and by antirrhinon with rose oil and honey. The root also of Thessalian nymphaea cures uterine pain when used as a pessary; taken in dark-red wine it checks excessive menstruation; on the contrary, root of cyclamen is an emmenagogue if taken in drink or [a] used as a pessary; a sitz bath in the decoction is a remedy for troubles of the bladder. Cissanthemos taken in drink forces out the after-birth and heals the uterus. The upper part of the root of xiphium is an emmenagogue, the dose being a drachma taken in vinegar. Peucedanum calms hysterical suffocations by its smell when burnt; leucorrhoea is purged especially by psyllion in doses of one drachma to three cyathi of water. Seed of mandrake taken in drink purges the uterus; a pessary of its juice is an emmenagogue and brings away a dead foetus. Excessive menstruation again is checked by mandrake seed with live sulphur; on the contrary, menstruation is promoted by batrachium, taken in drink or food, a plant which, though when raw it has, as I have said,[b] a burning taste, is made agreeable, when cooked, by salt, oil and cummin. Daucum in drink readily acts as an emmenagogue, and readily brings away the after-birth; fumigation

corrigit volvas, dolori earum exulceratisque inponitur. emortua scamonium pellit potum vel adposi-
158 tum. menses ciet hypericum utrumque adpositum, ante alia vero, ut Hippocrati videtur, crethmos e vino semine vel radicis cortice,[1] trahit et secundas, succurrit et strangulationibus ex aqua pota, item radix e geranio peculiariter secundis inflationibusque volvarum conveniens. purgat hippuris pota et adposita volvas, polygonus pota.[2] menses ciet et alcimae radix, folia plantaginis pellunt, item agari-
159 cum ex aqua mulsa. artemisia volvae medetur trita, ex oleo irino aut cum fico aut cum murra adposita. eiusdem radix pota in tantum purgat ut partus enectos extrahat. menses et secundas ciet ramorum decoctum insidentibus, item folia pota drachma. ad eadem omnia prosunt vel inposita
160 ventri imo cum farina hordeacia. acoron quoque utile est interioribus feminarum morbis et conyza utraque et crethmos. et anthyllides[3] duae vulvis utilissimae torminibusque et secundarum morae in vino potae. callithrix fotu locis medetur, albugines in capite tollit, capillos inficit oleo trita. geranion in

---

[1] radicis cortice *vet. Dal.*, *Mayhoff* : radice, cortice *aliquot codd.*, *Detlefsen* : radice corticis T E f.
[2] pota] *ita dist. Mayhoff ex Dioscoride.*
[3] anthyllides *Mayhoff*, *Hermolaum Barbarum secutus* : canthyllides V, *Detlefsen.*

---

[a] Cf. Dioscorides I 97 § 4 (of ladanum) : ὑποθυμιᾶται δὲ καὶ πρὸς δευτέρων ἐκβολάς. This sentence (not referred to by Mayhoff) has πρὸς δευτέρων ἐκβολάς for Pliny's 'corrigit volvas, a warning to editors who try to bring the two writers into too close agreement.
[b] Littré has " guérit l'hystérie." See however the note on § 152 of this book.
[c] See Littré's index (Vol. X) *sub voce.*

with ladanum *a* corrects the uterus,*b* and the plant is applied locally for pain there and ulceration. Scammony taken in drink or used as a pessary forces out a dead foetus. Either kind of hypericum, used as a pessary, acts as an emmenagogue; pre-eminently so, however, as Hippocrates believes, does crethmos,*c* the seed, or the skin of the root, being taken in wine; it also brings away the after-birth, and taken in water is helpful in hysterical suffocations, as is the root of geranion, which is specific for the after-birth and for inflation of the uterus. Hippuris, taken in drink and *d* applied as a pessary, purges the uterus, as does polygonus taken in drink. The root of alcima too is an emmenagogue, leaves of plantain a violent one, as is also agaric in hydromel. Artemisia beaten up is good for the uterus, applied as a pessary in iris oil or with fig or with myrrh.*e* Its root taken in drink purges the uterus so violently that it expels a dead foetus. A sitz bath of a decoction of the branches is an emmenagogue, and also hastens the after-birth; so too acts a drachma of the leaves taken in drink. For all the same purposes the leaves are also good when merely applied with barley meal to the base of the abdomen. Acoron too is beneficial for internal diseases of women, and so is either kind of conyza, and also crethmos. The two kinds of anthyllis, taken in wine, are very useful for uterine troubles, for griping pains there, and for delay of the after-birth. Callithrix used for fomentations is healing to the uterus, removes albugo on the head, and beaten up in oil *f* stains the

---

d Perhaps " or."
e Note both *ex* and *cum* in a single phrase.
f Here *oleo* seems equivalent to the usual *ex oleo*.

vino albo potum, hypocisthis in rubro profluvium
sistunt. hysopum suffocationes laxat. radix verbenacae pota ex aqua ad omnia in partu aut ex partu
161 mala praestantissima est. peucedano quidam miscent in vino nigro semen cupressi contritum. nam
semen psyllii defervefactum in aqua, cum intepuit,
epiphoras omnes uteri lenit. symphyton tritum
in vino nigro evocat menses. partus accelerat
scordotis pota drachma suci in aquae mulsae cyathis
IIII. dictamni folia praeclare dantur ex aqua. constat unius oboli pondere, vel si mortui sint in utero
infantes, protinus reddi sine vexatione puerperae.
similiter prodest pseudodictamnum, sed tardius,
cyclaminos adalligata, cissanthemos pota, item
vettonicae farina ex aqua mulsa.

162 XCI. Arsenogonon et thelygonon herbae sunt
habentes uvas floribus oleae similes, pallidiores [1]
tamen, semen album papaveris modo. thelygoni
potu feminam concipi narrant; arsenogonon ab ea
semine oleae, nec alio distat; huius potu mares
generari, si credimus. alii utramque ocimo similem
tradunt, arsenogoni autem semen geminum esse
testibus simile.

163 XCII. Mammarum vitiis aizoum quod digitillum
appellavimus unice medetur. erigeron ex passo
mammas uberiores facit, soncum cum farre coctum,[2]

[1] pallidiores d(?) *vulg.* : pallidioris Detlefsen, Mayhoff.
[2] soncum cum farre coctum *ego* : sonci cum farre cocti ius
Mayhoff : sonchum in farre coctum Detlefsen et codd.

---

[a] See XXV § 160.

hair. Geranion taken in a white wine, and hypocisthis taken in a red, check excessive menstruation.
Hyssop relieves hysteria. The root of vervain, taken
in water, is a sovereign remedy for all troubles at or
after child-birth. Some physicians prescribe peucedanum in dark-red wine mixed with crushed cypress
seed. But seed of psyllium, boiled in water and
taken while still warm, relieves all fluxes of the
uterus. Symphyton beaten up in dark-red wine
promotes menstruation. Scordotis taken in drink
hastens delivery, the dose being a drachma of the
juice in four cyathi of hydromel. Leaves of dittany
given in water are excellent for this purpose. It is
an established fact that a single obolus of them by
weight immediately brings away the foetus, even if
it is dead in the uterus, without any distress to the
lying-in woman. Good in a similar way is bastard
dittany, but slower, also cyclamen used as an amulet,
cissanthemos taken in drink, and powdered betony in
hydromel.

XCI. Arsenogonon and thelygonon are plants
bearing clusters like the flowers of the olive, but
paler, and a white seed like that of the poppy. It is
said that thelygonon, taken in drink, causes the
conception of a female; arsenogonon differs from it in
having a seed like that of the olive, but in no other
way; taken in drink this plant is said to cause the
generation of males, if we care to believe it. Some
hold that both plants are like basil, but that the seed
of arsenogonon is double, resembling testicles.

XCII. For affections of the breasts the aizoüm I
have called *a* digitillum is an outstanding remedy.
Erigeron in raisin wine makes the breasts richer in
milk, as does soncum boiled with emmer wheat; the

quae vero mastos vocatur inlita. pilos mammarum
partu nascentes,[1] testas in facie aliaque cutis vitia
emendat gentiana, nymphaea heraclia inlita, cyclamini radix maculas omnes. caccaliae grana mixta
cerae liquidae extendunt cutem in facie erugantque,
vitia omnia acori radix emendat.

164   XCIII. Capillum lycium suco[2] flavum facit,
denigrat hypericum quod et corissum vocatur, item
ophrys herba denticulato oleri similis, foliis duobus.
nigritiam dat et polemonia in oleo decocta. psilotrum nos quidem in muliebribus medicamentis tractamus, verum iam et viris est in usu. efficacissimum
autem habetur archezostis, item tithymalli, suco vel
in sole cum oleo inlito crebro vel evolsis pilis.
quadripedum scabiem sanat hysopum ex oleo, suum
anginas peculiariter sideritis. verum et reliqua
genera herbarum reddamus.

----

[1] nascentes *vet. Dal., Mayhoff* : nascentium *codd.*
[2] lycium suco *e Dioscoride* [(λύκιον) ξανθίζει δὲ καὶ τρίχας,
I 100 § 3] *Mayhoff* : lysimace VE : lysimachia *vulg.*

plant called mastos, however, is applied as liniment. The hairy affection appearing on the breasts at child-birth, brick-red spots on the face, and other skin troubles, are removed by gentian, or by an application of nymphaea heraclia, and all kinds of spots by root of cyclamen. The grains of caccalia, mixed with melted wax, smooth the face, taking away the wrinkles, and all facial troubles are removed by root of acoron.

XCIII. Lycium [a] juice dyes the hair flaxen; *Dyes and* hypericum, also called corissum, dyes it black, as does *depilatories.* ophrys, a plant like indented cabbage, but with only two leaves. Polemonia, too, boiled down in oil, imparts a black colour. Depilatories I myself indeed regard as a woman's cosmetic, but now today men also use them. But very efficacious is held to be archezostis, as also the tithymalli, the juice being applied frequently with oil either in the sun or when the hairs have been pulled out. Hyssop in oil heals the itch in quadrupeds, and sideritis is specific for the quinsy in swine. But I must go on to describe the remaining kinds of plants.

[a] See XXIV §§ 124 ff.

BOOK XXVII

LIBER XXVII

1 I. Crescit profecto apud me certe tractatu ipso
admiratio antiquitatis, quantoque maior copia herbarum dicenda restat, tanto magis adorare priscorum
in inveniendo curam, in tradendo benignitatem subit.
nec dubie superata hoc modo posset videri etiam
rerum naturae ipsius munificentia, si humani operis
2 esset inventio. nunc vero deorum fuisse eam apparet
aut certe divinam, etiam cum homo inveniret, ean-
demque omnium parentem et genuisse haec et
ostendisse, nullo vitae miraculo maiore si verum
fateri volumus. Scythicam herbam a Maeotis
paludibus, et euphorbeam e monte Atlante ultraque
Herculis columnas ex ipso rerum naturae defectu,
parte alia britannicam ex oceani insulis extra terras
positis, itemque aethiopidem ab exusto sideribus
3 axe, alias praeterea aliunde ultro citroque humanae
saluti in toto orbe portari, inmensa Romanae pacis
maiestate non homines modo diversis inter se terris
gentibusque verum etiam montes et excedentia in

ª *Scythicam herbam . . . portari* seems to be exclamatory.

BOOK XXVII

I. THE mere treatment of this subject undoubtedly The bounty
of Nature. increases the admiration that I at least feel for the men of old; the greater the number of plants waiting to be described, the more one is led to revere the careful research of the ancients and their kindness in passing on the results. Without a doubt even the bounteousness of Nature herself might seem to have been surpassed by them in this way if the discoveries had been the result of human endeavour. But as it is, it is clear that this bounteousness has been the work of the gods, or at least due to their inspiration, even when the actual discoverer was a man, and that the same Mother of all things both produced the herbs and made them known to us. This is the greatest miracle of life, if we care to admit the truth. To think that[a] the Scythian plant, for example, is brought from the marshes of Maeotis, euphorbea from Mount Atlas and from beyond the pillars of Hercules, where the works of Nature actually begin to fail; on another side britannica, from islands in the ocean lying beyond the mainland, aethiopis too from the clime scorched by the constellations of heaven, and other plants moreover passing hither and thither from all quarters throughout the whole world for the welfare of mankind, all owing to the boundless grandeur of the Roman Peace, which displays in turn not men only with their different lands and tribes, but also moun-

nubes iuga partusque eorum et herbas quoque in-
vicem ostentante. aeternum quaeso, deorum sit
munus istud! adeo Romanos velut alteram lucem
dedisse rebus humanis videntur.

4   II. Sed antiquorum curam diligentiamque quis
possit satis venerari? constat omnium venenorum
ocissimum esse aconitum et tactis quoque genitalibus
feminini sexus animalium eodem die inferre mortem.
hoc fuit venenum quo interemptas dormientes a
Calpurnio Bestia uxores M. Caelius[1] accusator obiecit.
hinc illa atrox peroratio eius in digitum. ortum
fabulae narravere e spumis Cerberi canis extrahente
ab inferis Hercule ideoque apud Heracleam Ponti-
5   cam, ubi monstratur is ad inferos aditus, gigni. hoc
quoque tamen in usus humanae salutis vertere
scorpionum ictibus adversari experiendo datum in
vino calido. ea est natura ut hominem occidat nisi
invenerit quod in homine perimat. cum eo solo
conluctatur, †veluti[2] praesentius[3] invento.† sola haec
pugna est, cum venenum in visceribus reperit,[4]

    [1] Caelius *Ruhnken ad Vell. Pat. II 68, Mayhoff*: Caecilius
codd., Detlefsen.
    [2] veluti] velum V[1].
    [3] praesentius V[2] *vulg., Detlefsen*: parte intus *multi codd.*:
pari intus *Hermolaus Barbarus.*
    [4] sola . . . reperit *in uncis I. Müller, Mayhoff.*

    [a] Detlefsen and Mayhoff agree in reading *eum eo solo con-
luctatur, veluti praesentius invento.* Mayhoff adds " *invento =
quam inventum.*" After J. Müller, Mayhoff brackets *sola . . .
reperit,* which certainly looks like a marginal explanation of the
preceding sentence added to the text by a subsequent scribe.
Sola haec pugna est corresponds to *cum eo solo conluctatur,*
and *reperit* to *invento.* We should therefore expect in the
first sentence something to correspond to *venenum* and to *in
visceribus.* It might be *veneno* for the first and *intus* for
the second. The whole would be *veneno praesenti intus invento,* " the quick-acting poison found inside." In XVI 51

tains, and peaks soaring into the clouds, their offspring and also their plants. May this gift of the gods last, I pray, for ever! So truly do they seem to have given to the human race the Romans as it were a second Sun.

II. But who could revere enough the diligent *Aconite.* research of the ancients? It is established that of all poisons the quickest to act is aconite, and that death occurs on the same day if the genitals of a female creature are but touched by it. This was the poison that Marcus Caelius accused Calpurnius Bestia of using to kill his wives in their sleep. Hence the damning peroration of the prosecutor's speech accusing the defendant's finger. Fable has it that aconite sprang out of the foam of the dog Cerberus when Hercules dragged him from the underworld, and that this is why it grows around Heraclea in Pontus, where is pointed out the entrance to the underworld used by Hercules. Yet even aconite the ancients have turned to the benefit of human health, by finding out by experience that administered in warm wine it neutralizes the stings of scorpions. It is its nature to kill a human being unless in that being it finds something else to destroy. Against this alone it struggles, †regarding it as more pressing than the find.† [This is the only fight, when the aconite discovers a poison in the viscera.]*a* What a marvel!

occurs *praesentis veneni.* The reading of Hermolaus Barbarus is brilliant, but if it is the original how did *praesentius* arise? I leave the text and translation within daggers, as I consider my own suggestion too conjectural. The sense, however, of the text of Hermolaus Barbarus is excellent: "as though it had found inside a foe to match it." Professor Andrews thinks that the text is sound, with the sense: "as though it had found something more urgent, and so fights solely with this."

mirumque, exitialia per se ambo cum sint, duo venena
6 in homine conmoriuntur ut homo supersit. immo
vero etiam ferarum remedia antiqui prodiderunt
demonstrando quomodo venenata quoque ipsa sana-
rentur. torpescunt scorpiones aconiti tactu stupent-
que pallentes et vinci se confitentur. auxiliatur his
helleborum album tactu resolvente, ceditque aconitum duobus malis, suo et omnium. quae si quis
ulla forte ab homine excogitari potuisse credit,
7 ingrate deorum munera intellegit. tangunt carnes
aconito necantque gustatu earum pantheras, nisi
hoc fieret, repleturas illos situs. ob id quidam
pardalianches appellavere. at illas statim liberari
morte excrementorum hominis gustu demonstratum.
quod certe casu repertum quis dubitet et quotiens
fiat etiam nunc ut novum nasci, quoniam feris ratio et
8 usus inter se tradi non possit? hic ergo casus,
hic est ille qui plurima in vita invenit deus, hoc habet
nomen per quem intellegitur eadem et parens rerum
omnium et magistra,[1] utraque coniectura pari, sive
ista cotidie feras invenire sive semper scire iudicemus.
pudendumque rursus omnia animalia quae sint salu-
9 taria ipsis nosse praeter hominem. sed maiores

[1] hoc habet . . . magistra *in parenthesi Mayhoff.*

---

[a] Perhaps " poisoned."
[b] After *carnes* Mayhoff would supply *Hyrcani,* and the
name of a people seems omitted (because of *illos situs* at the
end of the sentence).

Although by themselves both are deadly, yet the two poisons in a human being perish together so that the human survives. Moreover even remedies used by wild beasts have been handed down by the ancients, who have shown how venomous *a* creatures also by themselves obtain healing. Scorpions, touched by aconite, become numbed, and are pale and stupefied, acknowledging their defeat. They find a help in white hellebore, its touch dispelling the torpor; the aconite yields to two evil foes, one peculiar to itself and one common to all creatures. If anyone believes that these discoveries could, by any chance, have been made by a man, he shows himself ungrateful for the gods' gifts. They touch *b* flesh with aconite, and kill panthers by a mere taste of it, otherwise panthers would overrun the regions where they are found. For this reason some have called aconite pardalianches, that is panther-strangler. But it has been proved that panthers are at once saved from this death by tasting human excrement; surely nobody doubts that this remedy has been found by Chance, and that on every occasion it is even today a new find, since wild animals have neither reason nor experience for results to be passed from one to another. This Chance therefore, this is that great deity who has made most of the discoveries that enrich our life, this is the name of him by whom is meant she who is at once the Mother and the Mistress of all creation. Either guess is equally likely, whether we judge that wild animals make these discoveries every day or that they possess a never-failing instinct. Again it is shameful that all animals except man know what is health-giving for themselves. Our ancestors however advertised the

oculorum quoque medicamentis aconitum misceri saluberrime promulgavere aperta professione malum quidem nullum [1] esse sine aliquo bono. fas ergo nobis erit qui nulla diximus venena monstrare quale sit aconitum, vel deprehendendi gratia. folia habet cyclamini aut cucumeris non plura quattuor, ab radice, leniter hirsuta, radicem modicam cammaro similem marino, quare quidam cammaron appellavere, alii thelyphonon, ex qua diximus causa. cauda [2] radicis incurvatur paulum scorpionum modo, quare et scorpion aliqui vocavere. nec defuere qui myoctonon appellare mallent, quoniam procul et e longinquo 10 odore mures necat. nascitur in nudis cautibus quas aconas nominant, et ideo aconitum aliqui dixere, nullo iuxta ne pulvere quidem nutriente. hanc aliqui rationem nominis adtulere, alii, quoniam vis eadem esset in morte quae cotibus in ferri acie deterenda, statimque admota velocitas sentiretur.

11 III. Aethiopis folia habet phlomo similia, magna ac multa et hirsuta ab radice, caulem quadriangulum,

---

[1] malum quidem nullum d(?) *vulg.*, *Detlefsen* : ne malum quidem ullum *Mayhoff*.

[2] cauda V, *Mayhoff* : arida E : cauda arida *Detlefsen* : radix *sine* cauda radicis d, *vulg.*, *fortasse recte*.

---

[a] There is perhaps little to choose between the two readings. Mayhoff's *ne* is quite as likely as the vulgate text.

[b] I.e. " mouse-killer."

[c] I.e. κόνις dust and α privative.

[d] A whetstone is in Greek ἀκόνη.

[e] It is interesting to compare Pliny's account of aconite with Dioscorides IV 76 (Wellmann). In the latter is given the effect of aconite on scorpions with its antidote in the touch of white hellebore. The preceding sentence is : ῥίζα ὁμοία σκορπίου οὐρᾷ, στίλβουσα ἀλαβαστροειδῶς. For this last Pliny has only :

view that aconite is also a very health-giving ingredient of preparations for the eyes, openly declaring their belief that no evil[a] at all is without some admixture of good. It will therefore be right for me, who have described no poisons, to point out the nature of aconite, if only for the purpose of detecting it. It has leaves like those of cyclamen or of cucumber, not more than four, rising from the root and slightly hairy, and a root of moderate size, like a crayfish (*cammarus*), whence some have called it *cammaron*, and others *thelyphonon*, for the reason I have given already. The end of the root curves up a little like a scorpion's tail, whence some have called it also scorpion. There have been some who would prefer to call it *myoctonos*,[b] since at a distance, even a long distance, its smell kills rats and mice. The plant grows on bare crags which are called *aconae*, and for that reason some have given it the name of aconite, there being nothing near, not even dust,[c] to give it nourishment. This then is the reason for its name given by some; others have thought it was so named because it had the same power to cause rapid death as whetstones[d] had to give an edge to an iron blade; no sooner was the stone applied than its rapid action was noticeable.[e]

III. Aethiopis has leaves like those of phlomos, *Aethiopis.* large, numerous and hairy, growing from the root. The stem is quadrangular, rough, like that of arction

---

cauda radicis incurvatur paulum scorpionum modo. The phrase *cauda radicis* is peculiar, and suggests that Pliny had a Greek text before him in which ῥίζα and οὐρά (or some case of it) were side by side. There is nothing in Dioscorides corresponding to *arida*, which appears to have arisen from its partial likeness to *cauda*.

scabrum, similem arctio, multis concavum alis,
semen ervo simile, candidum, geminum, radices
numerosas, longas, plenas, molles, glutinosas gustu.
siccae nigrescunt indurescuntque ut cornua videri
12 possint. praeter Aethiopiam nascuntur et in Ida
monte Troadis et in Messenia. colliguntur autumno,
siccantur in sole aliquot diebus ne situm sentiant.
medentur volvis potae in vino albo, ischiadicis,
pleuriticis, faucibus scabris decoctae potui dantur, sed
quae ex Aethiopia venit eximie atque illico prodest.
13 IV. Ageraton ferulacea est, duorum palmorum
altitudine, origano similis, flore bullis aureis. huius
ustae nidor urinam ciet volvasque purgat, tanto magis
insidentibus. causa nominis [non haec, sed]¹ quoniam
diutissime non marcescit.
14 V. Aloe scillae similitudinem habet, maior et
pinguioribus foliis, ex obliquo striata—caulis eius
tener est, rubens medius, non dissimilis antherici,
radice una ceu palo in terram demissa ²—gravis
odore, gustu amara. laudatissima ex India adfertur,
sed nascitur et in Asia, non tamen ea utuntur nisi

---

¹ non haec sed *in uncis ponunt Pintianus, Sillig, Mayhoff.*
² *Hic* ipsa *add. Mayhoff.*

ᵃ "With numerous axillary concavities" (Bostock and
Riley), "offrant de nombreux goussets" (Littré). Dioscorides has : καυλὸν τετράγωνον . . . μασχάλας ἀνιέντα πολλάς
(IV. § 104).
ᵇ ῥίζας . . . πολλάς, μακράς, παχείας, γενομένῳ κολλώδεις
(Dioscorides).
ᶜ Strictly the subject of *nascuntur* is *radices*.
ᵈ *Scabris* is rather difficult. Bostock and Riley translate
"eruptions of the throat," and Littré has (vaguely) "les
maux de gorge." Perhaps it is a loose term, like our "sore
throat."

and hollowed by many axils.[a] The seed is like that of
vetch, white and geminate; the roots are numerous,
long, fleshy, soft, and gluey to the taste.[b] When
dry these become black and hard, so that they might
be taken for horns. This plant[c] grows not only in
Aethiopia, but also on Mount Ida in the Troad and
in Messenia. The roots are gathered in autumn and
dried in the sun for some days to prevent their
growing mouldy. Taken in white wine they are a
remedy for uterine troubles, and a decoction is given
by the mouth for sciatica, pleurisy and rough[d]
throats. The Aethiopian kind, however, gives the
greatest, and immediate, relief.

IV. Ageraton resembles fennel-giant, is two spans *Ageraton.*
high and like origanum, and the flowers are golden
knobs. The fumes when the plant is burnt are
diuretic and purge the uterus: used in a sitz bath
the plant does this more effectively. The reason
for the name is [not this but][e] because it lasts for a
long time without fading.[f]

V. The aloe bears a resemblance to the squill, *Aloe.*
but it is larger, and has more fleshy leaves, and with
slanting streaks. Its stem is tender, red in the
centre, and not unlike anthericus; the root is single,
as it were a stake sunk into the ground.[g] It has
an oppressive smell, and a bitter taste. The most
valued kind is imported from India, but it also grows
in the province of Asia. This kind is used only for

[e] Bracketed by some, but may be an allusion to a supposed
derivation from ἄγειν, or from *agere* "to drive" (i.e. "purge").
[f] In Greek the plant is ἀγήρατον, "not growing old."
[g] Mayhoff puts a full stop at *striata* and a semicolon at
demissa, adding *ipsa*. Dioscorides (III 22) has ὅλη. The
parenthesis, however, is after the manner of Pliny.

ad volnera, mirifice enim conglutinat recentibus
foliis[1] vel suco. ob id in turbinibus cadorum eam
15 serunt ut aizoum maius. quidam et caulem ante
maturitatem seminis incidunt suci gratia, aliqui et
folia. invenitur et per se lacrima adhaerens. ergo
pavimentandum ubi sata sit censent, ut lacrima non
absorbeatur. fuere qui traderent in Iudaea super
Hierosolymam metallicam eius naturam, sed nulla
magis inproba est, neque alia nigrior est aut umidior.
16 erit ergo optima pinguis ac nitida, rufi coloris,
friabilis et iocineris modo coacta, facile liquescens,
inprobanda nigra et dura, harenosa quaeque gustu
intellegitur cummi adulterata et acacia. natura eius
spissare, densare et leniter calfacere; usus multi,[2]
sed principalis alvum solvere, cum paene sola medicamentorum quae id praestant confirmet etiam sto-
17 machum, adeo non infestet ulla vi contraria. bibitur
drachma, ad stomachi vero dissolutionem in duobus
cyathis aquae tepidae vel frigidae coclearis mensura
bis terve in die ex intervallis, ut res exigit, purgationis autem causa plurimum tribus drachmis,
efficacior, si pota ea sumatur cibus. capillum
fluentem continet cum vino austero capite contra

---

[1] recentibus foliis] *in codd. post* volnera. *Transponenda*
esse coni. Mayhoff, qui in textu conglutinant suco *scribit.*
[2] multi *Mayhoff* : multis V E *Detlefsen* : multis et d T.

---

[a] Mayhoff suggests, but does not adopt, the transposition,
which certainly eases the construction. See critical note [1].
[b] Mayhoff suggests *ne* for *non*. Prof. Andrews takes this
clause as consecutive.
[c] I.e. the borders of the Dead Sea. Pliny refers to asphalt
or bitumen. At this point Pliny turns from the plant to the
preparations from it.

wounds, the freshly gathered leaves,[a] or the juice, having a wonderful power of uniting. For this reason it is planted in conical jars, as is the greater aizoüm. Some, before the seed ripens, make an incision in the stem to get the juice; some do so in the leaves as well. Drops too form spontaneously on it, and adhere. Some therefore recommend that the ground where the aloe has been planted should be beaten down hard, so as to prevent [b] absorption. Some have reported that in Judaea beyond[c] Jerusalem can be found mineral aloes. This however is the most inferior kind of all, and no other is darker or more moist. So the best aloes will be fatty and shiny, of a ruddy [d] colour, friable, compact like liver,[e] and easily melted. The kind to be rejected is dark and hard, gritty, and adulterated with gum and acacia, the adulteration being easily detected by the taste. The nature of an aloe is bracing, astringent,[f] and gently warming. There are many uses for it, but the chief is to relax the bowels, for it is almost the only laxative that is also a stomach tonic, no ill effects whatever resulting from its use. A drachma is taken in drink, but for fluxes of the stomach a spoonful in two cyathi of warm or cold water is taken twice or three times a day at intervals, as circumstances require; but for purging the bowels the maximum dose is three drachmae, which is more effective if food is taken after the draught. With a dry wine it prevents the hair from falling out, the

[d] Dioscorides III 22, has ὑπόξανθον.

[e] Dioscorides has εὔθρυπτον καὶ ἡπατίζουσαν.

[f] Spissare and densare are difficult words. Dioscorides has : δύναμιν δ᾽ ἔχει στυπτικήν, ξηραντικήν, πυκνωτικὴν τῶν σωμάτων.

pilum peruncto. dolorem capitis sedat temporibus
et fronti inposita ex aceto et rosaceo dilutiorque in-
18 fusa. oculorum vitia omnia sanari ea convenit, privatim prurigines et scabiem genarum, item insignita
ac livida inlita cum melle, maxime Pontico, tonsillas,
gingivas et omnia oris ulcera, sanguinis excreationes,
si modicae sint, drachma ex aqua, si minus, ex aceto
pota. volnerum quoque sanguinem et undecumque
19 fluentem sistit per se vel ex aceto. alias etiam
est volneribus utilissima ad cicatricem perducens.
eadem inspergitur exulceratis genitalibus virorum,
condylomatis rimisque sedis, alias ex vino, alias ex
passo, alias sicca per se, ut exigat mitiganda curatio
aut coercenda. haemorrhoidum quoque abun-
20 dantiam leniter sistit. dysinteriae infunditur et, si
difficilius concoquantur cibi, bibitur a cena modico
intervallo, et in regio morbo tribus obolis ex aqua,
devorantur et pilulae cum mellis decocto aut resina
terebinthina ad purganda interiora. digitorum
pterygia tollit, oculorum medicamentis lavatur ut
quod sit harenosissimum subsidat, aut torretur in
testa pinnaque subinde versatur ut possit aequaliter
torreri.
21   VI. Alcea folia habet similia verbenacae quae
aristereon cognominatur, caules tres aut quattuor
foliorum plenos, florem rosae, radices albas cum
plurumum sex, cubitales, obliquas. nascitur in
400

head being thoroughly rubbed in the contrary way to the hair. It relieves headache if it is applied in vinegar and rose oil to the temples and forehead, or a more dilute solution may be poured over them. All eye troubles, it is agreed, are cured by the aloe, but it is specific for itch and scaliness of the eyelids; [a] it is also good, applied with honey, especially with Pontic honey, for marks and bruises; for diseased tonsils or gums, for all sores in the mouth, and for spitting of blood, the dose is a drachma, taken in water if the spitting is not excessive, and in vinegar if it is. Haemorrhage due to wounds also, or to any other cause, it arrests if used by itself or in vinegar. In other ways too it is very useful for wounds, as it promotes cicatrization. It is also sprinkled on ulcerated male genitals, condylomata and chaps of the anus, sometimes in wine, in raisin wine, or else dry by itself, according as the treatment may need mild measures or coercive. It also gently arrests excessive bleeding from haemorrhoids. For dysentery it is injected, and for indigestion it is taken in drink shortly after the evening meal. For jaundice the dose is three oboli in water; for internal purgings pills also are swallowed made up with boiled honey or turpentine resin. It removes hangnails; for eye preparations it is washed, to let the most gritty parts settle, or else it is roasted in an earthen vessel and occasionally stirred with a feather so that the roasting may be even throughout.

VI. Alcea has leaves like those of the vervain *Alcea.* called aristereon, three or four stems covered with leaves, flowers like a rose, and white roots, six at most, a cubit long, and slanting. It grows in a soil

---

[a] Professor Andrews thinks "cheeks."

pingui solo nec sicco. usus radicis ex vino vel aqua dysintericis, alvo citae, ruptis, convulsis.

22 VII. Alypon cauliculus est molli capite, non dissimile betae, acre gustatu ac lentum mordensque vehementer et accendens. alvum solvit in aqua mulsa addito sale modico. minima potio duarum drachmarum, media quattuor, maxima sex, †ea purgationi quibus†[1] datur e gallinaceo iure.[2]

23 VIII. Alsine, quam quidam myosoton appellant, nascitur in lucis, unde et alsine dicta est. incipit a media hieme, arescit aestate media. cum prorepit, musculorum aures imitatur foliis. sed aliam docebimus esse quae iustius myosotis vocetur. haec eadem erat quae helxine, nisi minor minusque hirsuta esset. nascitur in hortis et maxime in parietibus. cum teritur, odorem cucumeris reddit. usus

24 eius ad collectiones inflammationesque et in eadem[3] omnia in quae[4] helxine,[5] sed infirmius. epiphoris

---

[1] ea purgationi quibus *Jo. Müller* : eximia purgatione quibus *Mayhoff* : ea purgatio quibusdam *vet. Dal., Littré. Fortasse* purgationi a quibusdam.

[2] iure *Hermolaus Barbarus, edd.*: fere d E r : ffere R : fferre V : *malit* datur in iure e gallinaceo vetere *Mayhoff.*

[3] et in eadem (ni E) V R E : emendat d T : item eadem *Mayhoff.*

[4] in quae *ego* : quae *codd. et edd.*

[5] helxine *Hermolaus Barbarus* : helxines *Mayhoff* : *varia codd.*

---

[a] It is difficult to suggest a restoration of this sentence, but the general sense, I think, is that when used as a purge and not as a laxative alypon should be administered in chicken broth. Dioscorides tells us that the bowels might be injured by the use of alypon, and in § 95 we learn that chicken broth was used to mitigate such harmful effects. The various readings show that the text is corrupt. It is very strange that *iure*, the practically

which is rich but not dry. The root is used in wine or water for dysentery, diarrhoea, ruptures and sprains.

VII. Alypon is a small sprout with a soft head, and *Alypon.* not unlike beet, sharp to the taste and viscous, very pungent and burning. In hydromel with a little salt added it loosens the bowels. The smallest dose is two drachmae, a moderate one four, the maximum being six. When given as a purge it is taken in chicken broth.[a]

VIII. Alsine, which some call myosoton, is found *Alsine.* in groves; hence its name.[b] It begins to grow just after midwinter, and withers at midsummer. When it puts forth its leaves, they are like the ears of little mice. However, I shall describe another plant,[c] to which more properly would be given the name myosotis. Alsine would be just the same as helxine, were it not that it is smaller and less hairy. It grows in gardens and especially on walls.[d] When being bruised it smells like cucumber. It is used for gatherings and inflammations, and for all purposes for which helxine is employed, but with less efficacy.

---

certain emendation of Hermolaus Barbarus, should appear in no extant MS.; the variants give some support to Mayhoff's suggestion *vetere*. It may be that *ea* arose from a misplaced *a*, that Io. Müller's *purgationi* is right, and that *quibusdam* (*datur* follows) should replace *quibus*. I print between daggers, as no emendation is very convincing. Dioscorides' account of ἄλυπον is different from this chapter, and affords little or no help.

[b] From the Greek ἄλσος (grove).

[c] See § 105.

[d] Pliny says in the first sentence that it grows in groves. He has expressed himself carelessly, but the first *habitat* is displaced in order to explain the name alsine, but the plant commonly grows in all the places named.

peculiariter inponitur, item verendis ulceribusque
cum farina hordeacia. sucus eius auribus infunditur.
25 IX. Androsaces herba est alba, amara, sine foliis,
folliculos in cirris habens et in his semen. nascitur
in maritimis Syriae maxime. datur hydropicis
drachmis duabus tusa aut decocta in aqua vel aceto
vel vino. vehementer enim urinas ciet. datur et
podagricis inliniturque. idem effectus et seminis.
26 X. Androsaemon sive, ut alii appellavere, ascyron
non absimile est hyperico, de qua diximus, cauliculis
maioribus densioribusque et magis rubentibus. folia
alba rutae figura, semen papaveris nigri. comae
tritae sanguineo suco manant. odor eis resinosus.
gignitur in vineis, fere medio autumno effoditur
27 suspenditurque. usus ad purgandam alvum tusae
cum semine potaeque matutino vel a cena duabus
drachmis in aqua mulsa vel vino vel aqua pura,
potionis totius sextario. trahit bilem, prodest
ischiadi maxime, sed postera die capparis radicem
resinae permixtam devorare oportet drachmae
pondere, iterumque quadridui intervallo eadem
facere, a purgatione autem ipsa robustiores vinum
bibere, infirmiores aquam. inponitur et podagris et
ambustis et volneribus cohibens sanguinem.
28 XI. Ambrosia vagi nominis et circa alias herbas
fluctuati unam habet certam, densam, ramosam,

---

[a] See XXVI § 85.

[b] It seems uncertain whether this sentence applies to both
the preceding remarks or only to the latter. Littré, followed
by Bostock and Riley, make the *sed* clause apply only to
sciatica.   On the other hand, *a purgatione ipsa* would, I think,
suggest that the clause *trahit bilem* is also included. Dioscorides is of no help here.

[c] E.g. in XXV 160 it = aizoüm maius, and in XXV 74 it =
artemisia.

Especially is it applied to eye fluxes, and with barley meal to sore genitals and ulcers. Its juice is poured into the ears.

IX. Androsaces is a whitish plant, bitter, leafless, *Androsaces.* with seed pods in hairy tufts. It grows especially along the sea coast of Syria. For dropsy are prescribed two-drachma doses of the plant pounded or boiled down in water, vinegar, or wine, for it is a powerful diuretic. It is also prescribed for dropsy and applied locally. The seed too has the same properties.

X. Androsaemon, or, as others have called it, *Androsae-* ascyron, is not unlike hypericum, about which I have *mon.* already spoken,[a] but the stalks are larger, closer together, and redder. Its leaves are pale and shaped like those of rue; the seed resembles that of the dark poppy. The stalk tops when crushed give out a juice of the colour of blood. Their smell is resinous. It grows in vineyards; about the middle of autumn it is dug and hung up. When used as a purge it is pounded with the seed and taken early in the morning or after dinner, the dose being two drachmae in hydromel, wine, or plain water, and the whole draught a sextarius. It brings away bile, and is excellent for sciatica, but[b] on the following day should be swallowed a drachma of caper root well mixed with resin. This dose should be repeated after an interval of four days. After the actual purging wine should be drunk by the stronger patients and water by the weaker. The plant is applied also to gouty limbs, to burns, and, as it stanches blood, to wounds.

XI. Ambrosia, an indeterminate name loosely *Ambrosia.* given to other[c] plants, is the primary name of one in particular, which is branchy and close set,

405

tenuem, trium fere palmorum, tertia parte radice
breviore, foliis rutae circa imum caulem. in ramulis
semen est uvis dependentibus, odore vinoso qua de
causa botrys a quibusdam vocatur, ab aliis artemisia.
coronantur illa Cappadoces. usus eius ad ea quae
discuti opus sit.

29   XII. Anonim quidam ononida malunt vocare ramosam, similem feno Graeco, nisi fruticosior hirsutiorque
esset, odore iucunda, post ver [1] spinosa. estur
etiam muria condita, recens vero margines ulcerum
erodit. radix decoquitur in posca dolori dentium.
eadem cum melle pota calculos pellit. comitialibus
datur in oxymelite decocta ad dimidias.

30   XIII. Anagyros, quam aliqui acopon vocant, fruticosa est, gravis odore, flore oleris, semen in corniculis
non brevibus gignit, simile renibus, quod durescit per
messes. folia collectionibus inponuntur difficulterque
parientibus adalligantur ita ut a partu statim
auferantur. quod si emortuus haereat et secundae
mensesque morentur, drachma bibuntur in passo folia.
sic et suspiriosis dantur, et in vino vetere ad phalangiorum morsus. radix discutiendis concoquendisque
adhibetur, semen commanducatum vomitiones facit.

31   XIV. Anonymos non inveniendo nomen invenit.
adfertur e Scythia, celebrata Hicesio non parvae

---

[1] ver R d *vulg.*, *Mayhoff*: vero V *Detlefsen*.

---

[a] Dioscorides (III 114) has no such epithet for the plant as
a whole, but says that the root is λεπτή, διοπίθαμος. The
similarity of διοπίθαμος and τρισπίθαμος probably caused the
error.

[b] The word in Greek means " grape-cluster."

slender,[a] about three spans high, with a root one span less, and with leaves around the bottom of the stem resembling those of rue. The seed is on the twigs, hanging down in clusters, and has a vinous smell; and so the plant is called botrys [b] by some, although others call it artemisia. The Cappadocians use it for chaplets. In medicine it is used as a discutient.

XII. Anonis, which some prefer to call ononis, *Anonis.* is branchy, and like fenugreek, except that it is more bushy and more hairy. It has an agreeable smell, and becomes prickly after spring. Preserved in brine it is also used as food, while the fresh plant cauterizes the edges of ulcers. The root is boiled down in vinegar and water for tooth-ache, and taken in drink with honey it also expels stone from the bladder. For epilepsy it is given in oxymel boiled down to one half.

XIII. Anagyros, which some call acopon, is bushy, *Anagyros.* with a strong smell and a flower like that of cabbage. The seed grows in little horn-like pods of some length; it is kidney-shaped and becomes hard during the harvests. The leaves are placed on gatherings, and tied as an amulet on women in difficult labour, care being taken to remove them immediately after delivery. But if a dead foetus does not come away, or if the after-birth or menstruation is retarded, the leaves are taken in raisin-wine, a dose being a drachma. Similar doses are given for asthma, and in old wine the leaves are given for the bites of poisonous spiders. The root is employed to disperse or mature boils; the seed chewed acts as an emetic.

XIV. Anonymus has found a name by not finding *Anonymus.* one. It is imported from Scythia. Hicesius, a

auctoritatis medico, item Aristogitoni, in volneribus
praeclara, ex aqua tusa inposita, pota vero mammis
praecordiisve percussis, item sanguinem excreantibus.
putavere et bibendam volneratis. fabulosa arbitror
quae adiciuntur, recente ea si uratur ferrum aut aes
feruminari.

32   XV. Aparinen aliqui omphalocarpon, alii philanthropon vocant, ramosam, hirsutam, quinis senisve
in orbem circa ramos foliis per intervalla. semen
rotundum, durum, concavum, subdulce. nascitur in
frumentario agro aut hortis pratisve, asperitate etiam
vestium tenaci. efficax contra serpentes semine poto
ex vino drachma et contra phalangia. sanguinis
abundantiam ex volneribus reprimunt folia inposita,
sucus auribus infunditur.

33   XVI. Arction aliqui potius arcturum vocant.
similis est verbasco foliis, nisi quod hirsutiora sunt,
caule longo, molli, semine cumini. nascitur in
petrosis, radice tenera, alba dulcique. decoquitur in
vino ad dentium dolorem ita ut contineatur ore.[1]
decoctum bibitur propter ischiada et stranguriam.
ex vino ambustis inponitur et pernionibus. foventur
eadem cum radice semine trito in vino.

34   XVII. Asplenon sunt qui hemionion vocant, foliis
trientalibus multis, radice limosa, cavernosa sicut

----

[1] ita ut contineatur ore *vulg.*: ut ore ita contineatur *Mayhoff*: ita *sine* ut *codd.*

----

[a] *Praecordia* is a difficult word. It may mean : (1) the
diaphragm, or the region just above it; (2) the two hypochondria; (3) the chest; (4) viscera generally. Here (2), the
usual meaning, is perhaps to be preferred to (1).
[b] Dioscorides III 90 : ὑπόκοιλον ἐκ μέσου ὡς ὀμφαλός.
[c] The reading seems to be settled by § 108 of this book :
decoctum . . . medetur ita, ut contineatur ore.

physician of no small authority, spread its fame, as did Aristogiton; it is excellent for wounds if applied pounded in water; taken however in drink it is equally good for blows on the breasts or on the hypochondria,[a] likewise for spitting of blood. Some authorities have held that wounded patients should take it in drink. The further statement I think fabulous, that if burnt fresh it acts as solder for iron or copper.

XV. Aparine, called by some omphalocarpos, by others philanthropos, is branchy, hairy, and with five or six leaves arranged at intervals in a circle around the branches. The seed is round, hard, hollowed,[b] and rather sweet. It grows in cornfields, or gardens, or meadows, and is so prickly as even to cling to the clothes. The seed, taken in drachma doses in wine, is efficacious against the bite of serpents and poisonous spiders. The leaves, applied locally, check excessive bleeding from wounds. The juice is poured into the ears. *Aparine.*

XVI. Arction, which some prefer to call arcturus, has leaves like those of verbascum, except that they are more hairy. The stem is long and soft, and the seed like that of cummin. It grows on rocky soils, and has a tender root, whitish and sweet. A decoction of it in wine is given for tooth-ache, but it must be retained in the mouth.[c] The decoction is drunk for sciatica and strangury. In wine the root[d] is applied to burns and chilblains, which are also fomented with the seed pounded in wine with the root. *Arction.*

XVII. Asplenon, called by some hemionion, has many leaves four inches long, a slimy root, pitted as is *Asplenon.*

[d] It is necessary to put a full stop at *stranguriam* and to understand *herba* or *radix* as the subject of *inponitur*.

filicis, candida, hirsuta, nec caulem nec florem nec
semen habet. nascitur in petris parietibusque opacis, umidis, laudatissima in Creta. huius foliorum
in aceto decocto per dies xxx poto lienem absumi
aiunt, et illinuntur autem eadem. sedant et singultus.
feminis non danda, quoniam sterilitatem facit.

35 XVIII. Asclepias folia hederae habet, ramos
longos, radices numerosas, tenues, odoratas, floris
virus grave, semen securiclatum.[1] nascitur in montibus. radices torminibus medentur et contra serpentium ictus non solum potu, sed etiam inlitu.

36 XIX. Aster ab aliquis bubonion appellatur, quoniam inguinum praesentaneum remedium est.
cauliculus foliis oblongis duobus aut tribus, in cacumine capitula stellae modo radiata. bibitur et
adversus serpentes. sed ad inguinum medicinam
sinistra manu decerpi iubent et iuxta cinctus alligari.
prodest et coxendicis dolori adalligata.

37 XX. Ascyron et ascyroides similia sunt inter se et
hyperico, sed maiores habet ramos quod ascyroides
vocatur, ferulaceos, †omnia†[2] rubentes, capitulis
parvis, luteis. semen in caliculis pusillum, nigrum,
resinosum. comae tritae velut cruentant, qua de

---

[1] securiclatum V. *Detlefsen, Mayhoff*: securidacae *Hermolaus Barbarus*. Cf. XVIII, § 155.
[2] omnia *codd.*: omnino *vulg.*: coma *Mayhoff*.

---

[a] Dioscorides (III 134), says it is the leaves that are
ἐντετμημένα and ἄνωθεν χλωρά.
[b] Dioscorides has ἡμέρας τεσσαράκοντα.
[c] The Greek βουβών means " groin."
[d] I have left the *omnia* of the MSS. within daggers, as the
coma of Mayhoff does not convince me. Dioscorides says
(III 155) that it is the καρπός of ascyron that stains red, and of

a fern's, whitish and hairy.[a]   There is no stem, flower
or seed. It grows on rocks and on shaded, damp walls,
the most approved kind in Crete. A decoction of
its leaves in vinegar, taken as a draught for thirty
days,[b] is said to reduce the spleen, the leaves being
also applied locally. They relieve too hiccoughs.
This plant, as it causes barrenness, must not be given
to women.

XVIII. Asclepias has leaves like those of ivy, long *Asclepias.*
branches, numerous roots that are slender and
scented, stinking flowers, and a hatchet-shaped seed.
It grows on hills. The roots cure colic and are
used for snake bite; they are not only taken in drink
but also applied locally.

XIX. Aster is called by some bubonion, because *Aster.*
it is a sovereign remedy for affections of the groin.[c]
Its stem has two or three oblong leaves, and on the
top are little heads with rays like stars.   In drink it is
also taken for snake bites.   But as medicine for the
groin it is enjoined to be plucked with the left
hand, and to be tied as an amulet next the girdle.
As an amulet it is also good for sciatica.

XX. Ascyron and ascyroides are like one another *Ascyron.*
and also like hypericon, but what is called ascyroides
has larger branches, which are like fennel-giant,
red[d] . . . and with small yellow heads. The seed, in
little cups, is very small, black, and resinous. The
hairy tufts when crushed cause stains like blood, and

androsaemon (III 156) he says : πεφοινιγμένος τὰ ῥαβδία. So
possibly some word meaning " altogether " may be right.
Professor Andrews writes : " It looks as if he were being more
specific than Dioscorides, localising the staining substance in
the filament, the hair-like part of the stamen that supports
the anther."

causa quidam hanc androsaemon vocavere. usus
seminis ad ischiadicos poti duabus drachmis in
hydromelitis sextario. alvum solvit, bilem detrahit.
inlinitur et ambustis.

38   XXI. Aphaca tenuia admodum folia habet et [1]
pusilla. altior lenticula et [2] siliquas maiores fert in
quibus terna aut quaterna semina sunt nigriora et
minora lenticula. nascitur in arvis. natura ad
spissandum efficacior quam lenti, reliquos usus
eosdem habet. stomachi alvique fluctiones sistit
semen decoctum.

39   XXII. Alcibium qualis esset herba non repperi
apud auctores, sed radicem eius et folia trita ad
serpentis morsum inponi et bibi, folia quantum manus
capiat trita cum vini meri cyathis tribus aut radicem
drachmarum trium pondere cum vini eadem mensura.

40   XXIII. Alectoros lophos, quae apud nos crista
dicitur, folia habet similia gallinacei cristae plura,
caulem tenuem, semen nigrum in siliquis. utilis
tussientibus cocta cum faba fresa, melle addito et
caligini oculorum. solidum semen coicitur in oculum, nec turbat, sed in se caliginem contrahit, mutat
colorem et ex nigro albicare incipit et intumescit ac
per se exit.

41   XXIV. Alum nos vocamus, Graeci symphyton
petraeum simile cunilae bubulae, foliis parvis, ramis

---

[1] et *post* habet *coni. Mayhoff.*
[2] et VRd *Mayhoff* : est Er *vulg., Detlefsen.*

---

[a] I.e. " man's blood."
[b] A difficult sentence; perhaps Mayhoff's punctuation and
conjecture (he adds *et* before *pusilla*) are the best solution.
Pusilla might be taken with the next sentence, to explain the
abrupt introduction of the lentil : " Though small it is yet
taller than the lentil," but Dioscorides (II, 148) has merely :

therefore some have called the plant androsaemon.[a]
Two-drachmae doses of the seed, taken in a sextarius of hydromel, are used for sciatica. It loosens
the bowels, brings away bile, and is applied to burns.

XXI. Aphaca has very slender and tiny [b] leaves. *Aphaca.*
Taller than the lentil it also bears larger pods, in
which are three or four seeds, darker and smaller
than those of the lentil. It grows in cultivated fields,
and has bracing [c] qualities more powerful than those
of the lentil, its other uses being the same. A decoction of the seed checks fluxes of the stomach and
bowels.

XXII. In my authorities I have found no descrip- *Alcibium.*
tion of alcibium, but only that its pounded root and
leaves are applied locally, and taken in drink, for
snake bite; a handful of the pounded leaves with
three cyathi of neat wine, or three drachmae by
weight of the root with the same measure of wine.

XXIII. Alectoros lophos, which we Romans call *Alectoros*
" comb " (*crista*), has several leaves like a cock's comb, *lophos.*
a slender stem, and black seed in pods. Boiled with
ground beans it is useful for cough, and with the
addition of honey for film on the eyes. The seed is
cast whole into the eye; it does no harm but
attracts the film to itself. Changing colour it begins
to turn from black to white, swells, and works out by
itself.

XXIV. We Romans call alum what the Greeks call *Alum.*
symphyton petraeum. It is like ox cunila, with
small leaves and three or four branches growing from

φακοῦ ὑψηλότερος, λεπτόφυλλος. The Greek suggests that
pusilla may be an addition (either by Pliny himself or by a
scribe) to explain *tenuia*, but Pliny may have had before him
a different Greek text.
   [c] Or " astringent."

tribus aut quattuor a radice, cacuminibus thymi, surculosum, odoratum, gustu dulce, salivam ciens, radice longa rutila. nascitur in petris ideo petraeum cognominatum, utilissimum lateribus, renibus, torminibus, pectori, pulmonibus, sanguinem reicientibus, faucibus asperis. bibitur radix trita et in vino
42 decocta, et aliquando superlinitur. quin et commanducata sitim sedat praecipueque pulmonem refrigerat. luxatis quoque inponitur et contusis, lenit interanea. alvum sistit cocta in cinere detractisque folliculis trita cum piperis granis novem et ex aqua pota. volneribus sanandis tanta praestantia est ut carnes quoque, dum cocuntur, conglutinet addita, unde et Graeci nomen inposuere. ossibus quoque fractis medetur, XXV. alga rufa scorpionum ictibus.
43 XXVI. Actaea gravi foliorum odore, caulibus asperis geniculatis, semine nigro ut hederae, bacis mollibus, nascitur in opacis et asperis aquosisque. datur acetabulo pleno interioribus feminarum morbis.
44 XXVII. Ampelos agria vocatur herba foliis duris cineracei coloris, qualem in satis diximus, viticulis longis, callosis, rubentibus, qualiter flos quem Iovis flammam appellamus. in uvolis [1] fert semen simile Punici mali acinis. radix eius decocta in aquae cyathis ternis, additis vini Coi cyathis duobus, alvum solvit leniter ideoque hydropicis datur. uvolae vitia cutis in facie mulierum emendant. ischiadicos quo-

---

[1] uvolis *Ianus e Dioscoride* : *varia codd.*

---

[a] I.e. " coalescing," " grown together."
[b] See XXIII § 19. The word *satis* is strange, as *sata* includes all cultivated plants and trees, and the reference accordingly seems vague. Perhaps Pliny means that this *wild* vine is described in his account of *cultivated* vines.

the root, which have tips like those of thyme; a ligneous plant, scented, sweet to the taste, promoting saliva, and with a long, red root. It grows on rocks (hence its surname *petraeum*, " rocky ") and is very useful for affections of the sides and kidneys, for colic, chest, lungs, spitting of blood, and sore throat. The root is pounded and taken in drink or boiled down in wine; sometimes too this is used as embrocation. Moreover, chewed it allays thirst, and is especially cooling to the lungs. It is also applied to dislocations and bruises, and it soothes the intestines. Cooked in hot ashes, pounded, after removal of the pods, with nine peppercorns and taken in water, it is binding to the bowels. So excellent is it for healing wounds that, added even to pieces of meat that are being boiled, it binds them together. Hence its Greek name symphyton.[a] It is also good for broken bones.

XXV. Red seaweed for scorpion stings. *Alga rufa.*

XXVI. Actaea has leaves with an offensive smell, *Actaea.* rough and jointed stems, black seed like that of ivy, and soft berries. It grows on shaded, rough, watery ground. In doses of a full acetabulum it is given for internal diseases of women.

XXVII. Ampelos agria is a name given to a plant *Ampelos* with hard leaves of an ashy colour, as I have described *agria.* in my account of cultivated trees.[b] It has long, hard-skinned twigs, of a red colour like the blossom we call flame of Jupiter. It bears in little clusters seed like pomegranate pips. Its root, boiled down in three cyathi of water with the addition of two cyathi of Coan wine, is a gentle aperient, and therefore is given to dropsical patients. The clusters remove the spots on women's faces. Sciatica too is

que uti hac herba prodest tusa cum foliis et inlita cum
suco suo.

45 XXVIII. Absinthii genera plura sunt : Santonicum
appellatur e Galliae civitate, Ponticum e Ponto, ubi
pecora pinguescunt illo et ob id sine felle reperiuntur,
neque aliud praestantius,multoque Italicum[1] amarius,
sed medulla Pontici dulcis. de usu eius convenit,
herbae facillimae atque inter paucas utilissimae,
praeterea sacris populi Romani celebratae peculiariter, siquidem Latinarum feriis quadrigae certant in
Capitolio victorque absinthium bibit, credo, sanitatem
praemio dari honorifice arbitratis maioribus.   sto-
46 machum corroborat, et ob hoc sapor eius in vina
transfertur, ut diximus. bibitur et decoctum aqua
ac postea nocte et die refrigeratum sub divo,[2]
†decoctis sex drachmis foliorum cum ramis suis in
caelestis aquae sextarii tribus, oportet et salem addi.
vetustissimum usu est†.[3] bibitur et madefacti dilutum, ita enim appelletur hoc genus.   diluti ratio ut,
quisquis fuerit modus aquae, tegatur per triduum.

---

[1] Italicum d *Hard.*, *Mayhoff* : Italico VRE *Detlefsen*.
[2] divo E *vulg.*, *Detlefsen* : diu V¹Rd *Ianus*, *Mayhoff*.
[3] †decoctis . . . usu est†] *Sic Detlefsen post Urlichs* :
decoci VI drachmis foliorum cum ramis suis in caelestis aquae
sextariis III oportet, nec non salem addi vetustissimi usus est
Mayhoff : *in codd.* decocti *aut* decoctis, nec (*pro* et) vetus-
tissime *aut* vetus sine usu est.

---

[a] See XIV § 109.
[b] I have kept Detlefsen's text within daggers because no
proposed emendation is quite satisfactory. The negative *nec*
is probably genuine, but seems to require *sine usu* afterwards,
leaving *vetus* without grammatical connection unless a full
stop is put at *addi*. It is just possible to make sense of the
MSS. reading if we do this and also accept the attractive *decoci*
of Mayhoff : " six drachmae . . . ought to be boiled down

relieved by this plant ground up with the leaves and applied with its own juice.

XXVIII. There are several kinds of wormwood. *Absinthium.* The Santonic comes from the state of the Santoni in Gaul, the Pontic from Pontus, where cattle fatten on it, and so are found to be without gall; there is no finer wormwood than this, the Italian being far more bitter, but the pith of Pontic wormwood is sweet. About its use there is general agreement, for it is a plant very easily found, and one of the most useful, being moreover especially honoured at the religious rites of the Roman people, seeing that at the Latin festival there is a race for four-horse chariots on the Capitoline Hill, the winner of which takes a draught of wormwood, our ancestors thinking, I believe, that health was a very grand prize to give. It strengthens the stomach and for this reason it is used, as I have said,[a] to give a flavour to wines. A decoction in water, which is afterwards cooled in the open for a day and a night, is also taken; six drachmae of the leaves with their branches are boiled down in three sextarii of rain water; salt too should be added. When very old it can still be used.[b] There is also administered an infusion of wormwood in water; for this preparation should be styled "infusion," and an essential of the infusion is that, whatever quantity[c] of water is used, for three days the preparation should be wholly enclosed. Pounded wormwood is rarely

without the addition of salt. When old the decoction cannot be used." Perhaps the *nec* looks to the occasions (§ 48) when we are told that salt *is* added. Mayhoff's emendations give us : "six drachmae . . . should be boiled down, and to add salt is a very old usage."

[c] Perhaps " kind."

47 tritum raro in usu est, sicut et sucus expressi. exprimitur autem, cum primum semen turgescit,
madefactum aqua triduo recens aut siccum septem
diebus, dein coctum in aeneo vaso ad tertias decem
heminis in aquae sextariis XLV iterumque per-
colatum, herba electa,[1] coquitur ad crassitudinem
mellis, qualiter ex minore centaurio quaeritur sucus.
sed hic [absinthii][2] inutilis stomacho capitique est,
48 cum sit ille decoctus[3] saluberrimus. namque adstringit stomachum bilemque detrahit, urinam ciet,
alvum emollit et in dolore sanat, ventris animalia
pellit, malaciam stomachi et inflationes discutit
cum sile et nardo Gallico, aceti exiguo addito. fastidia
absterget, concoctiones adiuvat, cruditates detrahit
cum ruta et pipere et sale. antiqui purgationis
causa dabant cum marinae aquae veteris sextario
seminis sex drachmas cum tribus salis, mellis cyatho.
49 efficacius purgat duplicato sale. diligenter autem
teri debet propter difficultatem. quidam et in
polenta dedere supra dictum pondus, addito puleio,
alii pueris folia[4] in fico sicca, ut amaritudinem fal-
lerent. thoracem purgat cum iride sumptum. in
regio morbo crudum bibitur cum apio aut adianto.
adversus inflationes calidum paulatim sorbetur ex

---

[1] herba electa *Mayhoff*: herbae lecta V : herba elisa
Urlichs, Detlefsen: herba lente *vulg.*: *fortasse* eiecta.

[2] absinthii] *In uncis Dal., Mayhoff.*

[3] decoctus *cod. Dal., vulg., Mayhoff*: decocti T *Detlefsen*:
decoctis *codd.*

[4] folia] *In uncis Hard., Mayhoff.*

---

[a] Literally " the juice of the squeezed wormwood."

employed; rarely too the extracted[a] juice. It is extracted, however, as soon as the seed begins to swell, the plant[b] being soaked in water for three days when fresh and for seven when dried; it is then boiled down to one third in a bronze vessel, ten heminae to forty-five sextarii of water; and after being strained to remove the solid pieces it is boiled down again to the thickness of honey, just like juice obtained from the lesser centaury. But this juice is injurious to the stomach and head, while the decoction I mentioned is very wholesome. For it is astringent to the stomach, and with sil, Gallic nard and a little vinegar, brings away bile, promotes urine, soothes the bowels, curing them when in pain, drives out worms from the belly, and removes nausea and flatulence. With rue, pepper and salt, it takes away the distaste for food, and aids digestion, bringing away undigested food. As a purge, the old custom was to give six drachmae of the seed, three of salt, and a cyathus of honey, in a sextarius of sea water kept for a time, the purge being more efficacious if the amount of salt is doubled. The pounding however must be carefully done, as it is a difficult task. Some have also given the aforesaid weight in pearl barley with the addition of pennyroyal; some the leaves in a dried fig to children, so that the bitter taste is not noticed. Taken with iris it purges the thorax. For jaundice it is taken raw in drink with celery or adiantum. For flatulence it is slowly sipped hot in water; for the liver it is taken with

---

[b] Littré and the Bohn translators say the seed. This is possible with their reading *lente coquitur*, but scarcely so with *herba electa*, which I think must mean that the plant, and not the seed only, is used for the decoction.

aqua, iocineris causa cum Gallico nardo, lienis cum
50 aceto aut pulte aut fico sumitur. adversatur fungis
ex aceto, item visco, cicutae ex vino et muris aranei
morsibus, draconi marino, scorpionibus. oculorum
claritati multum confert. epiphoris cum passo inponitur, suggillatis cum melle. aures decocti [1]
eius vapor suffitu sanat aut, si manent sanie, cum
melle tritum. urinam ac menses cient tres quat-
tuorve ramuli cum Gallici nardi radice una, cyathis
aquae sex, menses privatim cum melle sumptum
51 et in vellere adpositum. anginae subvenit cum melle
et nitro. epinyctidas ex aqua sanat, volnera recentia
prius quam aqua tangantur inpositum, praeterea
capitis ulcera. peculiariter ilibus inponitur cum
52 Cypria cera aut cum fico. sanat et pruritus. non est
dandum in febri. nausias maris arcet in naviga-
tionibus potum, inguinum tumorem in ventrali habi-
tum. somnos adlicit olfactum aut inscio sub capite
positum. vestibus insertum tineas arcet. culices ex
oleo perunctis abigit et fumo, si uratur. atramentum
librarium ex diluto eius temperatum litteras a musculis [2] tuetur. capillum denigrat absinthii cinis un-
guento rosaceoque permixtus.
53   XXIX. Est et absinthium marinum, quod quidam
seriphum vocant, probatissimum in Taposiri Aegypti.
huius ramum Isiaci praeferre sollemne habent.

---

[1] decocti *Mayhoff*: decoctae *multi codd.*, *Detlefsen* :
decocte R d.
   [2] musculis d(?) *Hermolaus Barbarus e Dioscoride* : muscis
plerique codd., *vulg.*

---

   [a] See XXVI § 31.
   [b] Or " and."
   [c] The *ilia* are the upper abdomen from the ribs to the pubes;
the *inguen* is the lower abdomen on either side of the pubes.

Gallic nard; for the spleen, with vinegar, pottage or fig. In vinegar it is an antidote to poisonous fungi, as also to mistletoe; in wine, to hemlock, the poison of the shrew mouse, sea weever [a] and scorpions. It is a great aid to clear vision. With raisin wine it is applied to eye fluxes, and with honey to bruises. Ear trouble is cured by fumigation with the steam of the decoction, or when bloody pus exudes, by pounded wormwood with honey. Three or four twigs, with one root of Gallic nard and six cyathi of water, are diuretic and an emmenagogue; it is specific for faulty menstruation if taken with honey or [b] applied as a pessary in wool. With honey and soda it is helpful for quinsy. In water it cures night rashes. Recent wounds it heals if applied before they have been touched with water; it cures, moreover, sores on the head. With Cyprian wax or with fig it makes an exceptionally good application for affections of the flanks.[c] It also cures pruritus, but must not be given to feverish patients. Taken in drink on sea voyages it prevents nausea; worn under a belly-band, swellings of the groin.[c] It induces sleep if inhaled through the nose or placed secretly under the sufferer's head. Put into clothes it keeps away moth. Rubbing the body all over with it in oil drives away gnats, as does the smoke of it when burnt. Writing ink mixed with the infusion protects the writing from mice. Ashes of wormwood mixed with ointment and rose-oil stain the hair black.

XXIX. There is also a sea wormwood, called by some seriphum, the most approved growing at Taposiris in Egypt. At the ceremonies of Isis the priests carry a branch of it ritually before them.

angustius priore minusque amarum, stomacho ini-
micum, alvum mollit pellitque animalia interaneorum. bibitur cum oleo et sale aut in farinae tri-
mestris sorbitione dilutum.[a] coquitur quantum manus
capiat in aquae sextario ad dimidias.

54 XXX. Balloten alio nomine porrum nigrum Graeci
vocant, herbam fruticosam angulosis caulibus nigris,
hirsutis foliis vestientibus, maioribus quam porri et
nigrioribus, graveolentibus.[b] vis eius efficax adversus
canis morsus ex sale foliis tritis inpositae, item ad
condylomata coctis cinere in folio oleris.[d] purgat et
sordida ulcera cum melle.

55 XXXI. Botrys fruticosa herba est luteis ramulis.
semen circa totos nascitur, folia cichorio similia.
invenitur in torrentium ripis, medetur orthopnoicis.
hoc Cappadoces ambrosiam vocant, alii artemisiam.

XXXII. Brabilla[e] spissandi[f] vim habet cotonei mali
modo, nec amplius de ea tradunt auctores.

56 XXXIII. Bryon[g] marinum herba sine dubitatione
est lactucae foliis similis, rugosa velut contracta, sine
caule ab una radice exeuntibus foliis. nascitur in
scopulis maxime testisque terra conprehensis. prae-

---

[a] That this is the meaning of *dilutum* seems to be likely from
the phrase in Dioscorides (III 23) σὺν ῥοφήματι φακῆς καθε-
ψηθεῖσα.

[b] Dioscorides has (III 103): καυλοὺς ἀνίησι τετραγώνους.

[c] Dioscorides (*loc. cit.*) δυσώδη.

[d] It is uncertain whether *in folio oleris* goes with *coctis* or with
impositae (understood). There is nothing in Dioscorides to
correspond.

[e] Sometimes spelt *brabyla*.

[f] Or, " bracing," or, " thickening."

[g] Not mere seaweed, as Theophrastus (*H.P.* IV vi 6) seems
to suggest.

Narrower than the former, and less bitter, it is
injurious to the stomach, but softens the bowels and
expels intestinal worms. It is taken in drink with
oil and salt, or infused [a] into gruel of three-month
wheat. A handful is boiled down in a sextarius of
water to one-half.

XXX. Ballote has a second name, black leek, given   *Ballote.*
to it by the Greeks. It is a bushy plant, with quad-
rangulate,[b] dark stems, covered with hairy leaves,
larger and darker than those of leek, and with an
offensive smell.[c] It proves an effective antidote to
dog-bites, the pounded leaves being laid with salt
on the wound; cooked also in hot ashes and wrapped
in a cabbage leaf[d] they are applied to condylomata.
With honey the plant also cleanses foul ulcers.

XXXI. Botrys is a bushy plant with yellow twigs.   *Botrys.*
Seed grows all round them, and the leaves are like
those of chicory. It is found on the banks of
torrents, and is used as treatment for orthopnoea.
The Cappadocians call it ambrosia, others artemisia.

XXXII. Brabilla [e] has an astringent [f] property like   *Brabilla.*
the quince; apart from this my authorities tell me
nothing about it.

XXXIII. Sea bryon is without doubt a plant [g]; it   *Bryon*
has leaves like those of lettuce, wrinkled, and as it   *marinum.*
were crumpled.[h] It has no stem, the leaves growing
out of a single root. It grows more especially upon
rocks and on shells sunk in the ground.[i] Its special

---

[h] See Theophrastus *loc. cit.*: ῥυτιδωδέστερον καὶ ὥσπερ
συνεσπασμένον.

[i] See Theophrastus *loc. cit.*: ἐπὶ τῶν λίθων . . . πρὸς τῇ γῇ
καὶ τῶν ὀστράκων, and Dioscorides (IV 98): φύεται ἐπὶ λίθων
καὶ ὀστράκων παρὰ θαλάσσῃ. Is Pliny's *terra conprehensis* a
mistranslation?

cipua siccandi spissandique vis ei et collectiones
inflammationesque omnes inhibendi, praecipue podagrae et quicquid refrigerari opus sit.

57   XXXIV. Bupleuri semen ad ictus serpentium dari
reperio foverique plagas decocta ea herba adiectis
foliis mori aut origani.

   XXXV. Catanancen Thessalam herbam qualis sit
describi a nobis supervacuum est, cum sit usus eius
ad amatoria tantum. illud non ab re est dixisse ad
detegendas magicas vanitates, electam ad hunc usum
coniectura, quoniam arescens contraheret se ad
speciem unguium milvi exanimati. eadem ex causa
et cemos silebitur nobis.

58   XXXVI. Calyx duorum generum est. una similis
aro nascitur in arationibus, colligitur antequam
inarescat, usus eosdem habet quos aris.[1] bibitur
quoque radix huius ad exinaniendas alvos mensesque
mulierum, item caules cum foliis in leguminibus
59 decocti sanant tenesmon. XXXVII. alterum genus
eius quidam anchusam vocant, alii rhinocliam.[2]
folia[3] lactucae longiora, plumosa, radice rubra, quae
ignes sacros cum flore polentae sanat inposita, iocineris autem vitia in vino albo pota.

60   XXXVIII. Circaea trychno sativo similis est, flore
nigro pusillo, parvo semine milii nascente in quibusdam corniculis, radice semipedali, triplici fere aut
quadruplici, alba, odorata, gustus calidi. nascitur in

---

[1] aris *Hard.* : ars *aut* hars *codd.* : *post* ars *in codd.* a, *unde* at
coni. Mayhoff : om. *Detlefsen.*
[2] rhinocliam *Ianus e Plinii indice* : onocliam *Sillig e*
Dioscoride : *varia codd.*
[3] folia d E *vulg., Mayhoff* : folio VR *Detlefsen, qui* longiore
et plumoso *coni.*

---

[a] Or, " to thicken."

properties are to dry, astringency,[a] and to reduce all gatherings and inflammations, in particular those of gout, and whenever there is need of cooling applications.

XXXIV. The seed of bupleuron I find is given for *Bupleuron.* snake bite, and that wounds are fomented with a decoction of this plant to which has been added leaves of mulberry or of origanum.

XXXV. Catanance, a Thessalian plant, it would be *Catanance.* a waste of time for me to describe, since it is used only for love-potions. One thing it is quite pertinent to say in order to show up the fraud of sorcery: the plant was chosen for this purpose through an inference[b] because as it withers it crumples up into the shape of the claws of a dead kite.[c] For the same reason I shall say nothing about cemos.

XXXVI. There are two kinds of calyx. One is *Calyx.* like arum, and grows on ploughed land. It is gathered before it withers, and has the same uses as aris. Its root is also taken in drink as a powerful aperient and emmenagogue, while its stalks, boiled down with the leaves in pulse, cures tenesmus.

XXXVII. The other kind of it is called by some anchusa, by others rhinoclia, having leaves like those of lettuce, but longer and downy, and a red root. This applied with the finest pearl barley cures erysipelas, and, taken in white wine, liver complaints.

XXXVIII. Circaea is like cultivated trychnos, *Circaea.* having a tiny, dark flower, small seed like that of millet forming in a sort of little horn, a six-inch root, generally triple or quadruple, whitish, scented, and with a hot taste. It grows on sunny rocks. An

---

[b] *Coniectura* is an interpretation of a diviner.
[c] By imitative magic it hooks its victim.

apricis saxis. diluitur in vino bibiturque ad dolorem
vulvae et vitia. macerari oportet in sextariis tribus
quadrantem radicis tusae nocte et die[1]; trahit
eadem potio et[2] secundas. semine lac minuit[3] in
vino aut mulsa aqua poto.

61 XXXIX. Cirsion cauliculus est tener duum cubitorum, triangulo similis, foliis spinosis circumdatus.
spinae molles sunt. folia bovis linguae similia,
minora, subcandida, in cacumine capitula purpurea
quae solvuntur in lanugines. hanc herbam radicemve
eius adalligatam dolores varicum sanare tradunt.

62 XL. Crataegonon spicae tritici simile est, multis
calamis ex una radice emicantibus multorumque
geniculorum, in opacis, semine milii, vehementer
aspero gustu, quod si bibant ex vino ante cenam
tribus obolis in cyathis aquae totidem mulier ac vir
ante conceptum diebus XL, virilis sexus partum
futurum aiunt. et alia est crataegonos quae thely-
63 gonos vocatur. differentia intellegitur lenitate gustus. sunt qui florem crataegoni bibentes mulierum
intra XL diem concipere tradant. eaedem sanant
ulcera vetera nigra cum melle, explent sinus ulcerum
et atropha carnosiora faciunt, purulenta expurgant,
panos discutiunt, podagras collectionesque omnes

---

[1] nocte et die *plures codd.*, *Mayhoff*: noctem et diem E
Detlefsen.
[2] potio et *codd.*, *Detlefsen*: potione *Mayhoff.*
[3] minuit *in uncis ponit Mayhoff, Dioscoridem secutus.*

---

[a] Dioscorides (III 119) has γάλα κατασπᾷ, and therefore
Mayhoff brackets *minuit.* Perhaps Pliny thought that
κατασπᾷ means " keeps (draws) away from the breasts."
[b] A " soft prickle " may sound strange, but is quite intelligible. Perhaps here " spine " might be better.

infusion of it in wine is taken for uterine pains and
affections. Three ounces of the pounded root should
be steeped for a night and a day in three sextarii of
wine. The same draught also brings away the after-
birth. The seed taken in wine or hydromel reduces [a]
the supply of milk.

XXXIX. Cirsion is a tender, little sprout, two cubits *Cirsion.*
high, triangular, and surrounded by prickly leaves,
the prickles [b] being soft. The leaves are like those of
bugloss, but smaller, and whitish. At the tip are
small, purple heads, which fall off as down.[c] It is
said that this plant, or its root, used as an amulet,
cures the pain of varicose veins.

XL. Crataegonon is like an ear of wheat, with many *Crataegonon.*
reed-like shoots, full of joints, springing from a single
root. It is found in shaded places. The seed is
like that of millet, with a very sharp taste. If three
oboli of it in three cyathi of water are taken in wine
before supper by the woman, and also by the man,
for forty days before conception [d] takes place, the
child they say will be of the male sex. There is
another crataegonos, which is called thelygonos; it is
distinguished from the other by its mild taste.
There are some who maintain that women who take
the flower of crataegonos in drink conceive within
forty days. These plants with honey also heal
chronic black ulcers, fill up the pits of ulcers, add
flesh to atrophied parts, thoroughly cleanse purulent
sores, disperse superficial abscesses, and soothe gout
and every kind of gathering, in particular those on

[c] Littré : " qui tombent en duvet "; so the Bohn translators. Perhaps better : " which break up (turn) into down."
[d] Littré takes *ante* to be an adverb and *conceptum* a participle : " l'enfant, même conçu depuis quarante jours."

leniunt, peculiariter mammarum. Theophrastus arboris genus intellegi voluit crataegon [1] sive crataegona, quam Itali aquifolium vocant.

64 XLI. Crocodileon chamaeleonis herbae nigrae figuram habet, radice longa aequaliter crassa, odoris asperi. nascitur in sabuletis. pota sanguinem per nares pellit copiosum crassumque; item [2] lienes consumere dicitur.

65 XLII. Cynosorchim aliqui orchim vocant, foliis oleae, mollibus, ternis per semipedem longitudinis in terra stratis, radice bulbosa, oblonga, duplici ordine, superiore quae durior est, inferiore quae mollior. eduntur ut bulbi coctae, in vineis fere inventae. ex his radicibus si maiorem edant viri, mares generari dicunt, si minorem feminae, alterum sexum. in Thessalia molliorem in lacte caprino viri bibunt ad stimulandos coitus, duriorem vero ad inhibendos. adversantur altera alteri.

66 XLIII. Chrysolachanum in pineto lactucae simile nascitur. sanat nervos incisos, si confestim inponatur. et alibi genus chrysolachani traditur, flore aureo, foliis oleris. coctum estur ut olus molle. haec herba adalligata morbum regium habentibus ita ut spectari ab his possit sanare id malum traditur.

---

[1] crataegon *Hard. e Theophrasto, Mayhoff*: crataegonon *Detlefsen cum multis codd.*

[2] item *Urlichs, Detlefsen*: ita et *Mayhoff*: ita *aut* ida *codd.*

---

[a] See Theophrastus, *H.P.* III 15, 6. The tree described there is a type of thorn, perhaps *Crataegus Heldreichii*. But *aquifolium* is our holly. A mistake apparently of Pliny.

[b] The *ita* of the MSS. may be right, but it generally refers to some more elaborate preparation than the single word *pota.*

the breasts. By crataegos or crataegon Theophrastus [a] would have us understand the tree which in Italy is called aquifolium.

XLI. Crocodileon is like black chamaeleon in shape, with a long root uniformly thick, and a pungent smell. It grows in sandy places. Taken in drink it causes copious epistaxis of thick blood; it is also [b] said to reduce the spleen. *Crocodileon.*

XLII. Cynosorchis, called by some orchis, has leaves like olive leaves, soft, three [c] in number and lying on the ground to the length of half a foot. The root is bulbous, longish, and in two parts, the upper being harder and the lower softer. Found generally in vineyards these are boiled and eaten as are bulbs. If men eat the larger of these roots, male children are said to be conceived, but female if the smaller is eaten by women. In Thessaly men take in goat's milk the softer root as an aphrodisiac, but the harder as an antaphrodisiac. The one part neutralizes the other. *Cynosorchis.*

XLIII. Chrysolachanum, growing in pine woods, is like lettuce. If applied at once it heals cut sinews. Elsewhere too is said to grow a kind of chrysolachanum with a golden flower and leaves like those of cabbage. It is eaten boiled as a soft [d] vegetable. This plant, tied on as an amulet so that the patient can look at it, is said to cure jaundice. I know that *Chrysolachanum and other plants.*

---

[c] Parts of the description are not in Dioscorides (III 126), but the two authorities in this chapter are remarkably alike, though with startling differences. *E.g.*, Dioscorides has: προσιστορεῖται δ' ἔτι καὶ τὰς ἐν Θεσσαλία γυναῖκας τὸν μὲν ἀπαλὸν κ.τ.λ., where Pliny has *viri*.

[d] So Littré. The Bohn translators say " laxative "; but I can find only one instance of *mollis* in (almost) that sense, being used however as an epithet of *alvus*, *i.e.*, " relaxed bowels."

67 de chrysolachano nec satis dici scio nec plura reperio,
namque et hoc vitio laboravere proximi utique herbarii nostri, quod ipsis notas veluti vulgares strictim
et nominibus tantum indicavere, tamquam coagulo
terrae alvum sisti, stranguriam dissolvi, si bibatur ex

68 aqua aut vino, XLIV. cuculli [1] folia trita cum aceto
serpentium ictibus et scorpionum mederi. quidam
hanc alio nomine strumum appellant, alii Graece
strychnum, acinos habet nigros. ex his cyathus suci
cum mulsi duobus medetur lumbis, item capitis dolori
cum rosaceo infusus, ipsa strumae [2] inlita.

69 XLV. Peculiaris est Alpinis maxime fluminibus
conferva appellata a conferuminando, spongea
aquarum dulcium verius quam muscus aut herba,
villosae densitatis atque fistulosae. curatum ea scio
omnibus fere ossibus confractis prolapsum ex arbore
alta putatorem, circumdata universo corpori, aquam
suam adspergentibus quotiens inaresceret, raroque
nec nisi deficientem herbam mutationis causa resol-
ventibus, convaluisse vix credibili celeritate.

70 XLVI. Cocco Cnidio color cocci, magnitudo grano
piperis maior, vis ardens. itaque in pane devoratur
ne adurat gulam transitu. vis praesentanea contra
cicutam, sistit alvum.

---

[1] cuculli *coni. Detlefsen, quem sequitur Mayhoff*: aliae
coniecturae sunt cucubali *et* cacubali : cuculi *aut* culiculi *codd.*
[2] strumae *Ianus, Mayhoff*: struma *codd., Detlefsen.*

---

[a] Or, " arrests diarrhoea," " binds the bowels."
[b] Literally, " cures strangury."

this account of chrysolachanum is inadequate, yet I find no more detail given, for a further fault of which our modern herbalists, at least, are guilty is that they have described but briefly, and even by a mere name, plants well known to themselves just as if these were generally familiar. They say, for instance, that coagulum terrae (earth rennet) is constipating [a] and diuretic [b] if taken in water or wine, and that (XLIV) the pounded leaves of cucullus with vinegar cure the bites of serpents and the stings of scorpions. Some give this plant another name, strumus, others the Greek name of strychnus. It has black berries; a cyathus of juice from these, with two of honey wine, is good treatment for lumbago, as also for headache if used with rose oil for bathing the brow, while for scrofulous sores the plant itself is applied locally.

XLV. Conferva is peculiar to running streams, *Conferva.* Alpine in particular, so named from *conferuminare*, to solder together. It is more like a fresh-water sponge than a moss or vascular plant, being a hairy, dense, and porous mass. To my knowledge a man who, pruning a very high tree, fell and broke nearly all his bones, was treated with this plant. His entire body was enveloped in it; whenever it dried it was sprinkled with its native water but rarely taken off, only in fact for renewals when the plant lost its strength. The patient recovered in an almost incredibly short time.

XLVI. The Cnidian grain has the colour of kermes- *Coccus* red, and in size is larger than a peppercorn. Its *Cnidius.* heating properties are so great that it is swallowed in bread, lest it should scorch the throat in its passage. A sovereign remedy for hemlock poisoning, it also checks looseness of the bowels.

71   XLVII. Dipsacos folia habet lactucae bullasque spinosas in dorsi medio, caulem duum cubitorum isdem spinis horridum, genicula eius binis foliis amplectentibus concavo alarum sinu in quo subsistit ros salsus. in cacumine capitula sunt echinata spinis. nascitur in aquosis. sanat rimas sedis, item fistulas decocta in vino radice usque dum sit crassitudo cerae, ut possit in fistulas collyrium mitti, item verrucas omnium generum. quidam et alarum quas supra diximus sucum inlinunt his.

72   XLVIII. Dryopteris felicis similis in arboribus nascitur, tenui foliorum subdulcium incisura, radice hirsuta. vis ei caustica est, ideo et psilotrum est radix tusa, inlinitur enim usque dum sudores evocet iterum et tertium ita ne sudor abluatur.

73   XLIX. Drabe phono[1] similis herba est cauliculis tenuibus cubitalibus, circumdatis utrimque foliis pollicari amplitudine qualia oxymyrsines, sed candidioribus mollioribusque, flore candido sabuci. edunt cauliculos decoctos, semine vero eius pro pipere utuntur.

74   L. Elatine folia habet casiae,[2] pusilla, pilosa, rotunda, semipedalibus ramulis quinis senisque a radice statim foliosis. nascitur in segete, acerba gustu et ideo oculorum fluctionibus efficax foliis cum polenta tritis et inpositis, subdito linteolo. eadem

---

[1] drabe phono *Detlefsen coll. indice Pl. et XXI § 95* : draeffono VRE : draphono d : dryophonon *Caesarius.*
[2] casiae *codd.* : helxinae e *Dioscoride Hermolaus Barbarus.*

XLVII. Dipsacos has leaves like those of lettuce, *Dipsacus.* with prickly knobs on the middle of their backs. The stem, two cubits long and rough with the same prickles, has joints enfolded by pairs of leaves, forming hollow axils in which collects a salt, dewy fluid. On the top of the stem are little heads, which bristle with prickles. The plant grows on watery ground. A decoction of the root in wine heals chaps of the anus; fistulas as well, but the decoction must be reduced to the consistency of wax, so that a suppository may be inserted into the fistula. It also removes warts of all kinds, for which purpose some apply the juice that is found in the axils which I mentioned above.

XLVIII. Dryopteris, which is like fern, grows on *Dryopteris.* trees; it has sweetish leaves with a slight indentation and a hairy root. It has caustic properties, so that its crushed root is also used as a depilatory, for it is rubbed on until the skin sweats, and then again and a third time without washing the sweat away.[a]

XLIX. Drabe is a similar plant to phonos, with *Drabe.* slender stalks a cubit high surrounded on either side by leaves the size of a thumb, similar to those of oxymyrsine, but whiter and softer. The blossom is white and like that of the elder. The stalks are eaten boiled, but its seed is used instead of pepper.

L. Elatine has leaves like those of cassia, very *Elatine.* small, shaggy and round, with five or six little branches, half a foot long, which are covered with leaves right from the root. The plant grows among the corn, is harsh to the taste and therefore good for fluxes of the eyes; the leaves are pounded with pearl barley and applied, a napkin being placed under-

[a] Or, "so that the sweating may not be interrupted."

cum lini semine cocta sorbitionis usu dysinteria
liberat.

75 LI. Empetros, quam nostri calcifragam vocant,
nascitur in montibus maritimis, fere in saxo. quae
propius mari fuit salsa est potaque trahit bilem ac
pituitas, quae longius magisque terrena amarior
sentitur. trahit aquam, sumitur autem in iure
aliquo aut in hydromelite, vetustate vires perdit,
recens urinas ciet decoctum in aqua vel tritum
calculosque frangit. qui fidem promisso huic quaerunt, adfirmant lapillos qui subfervefiant una rumpi.

76 LII. Epicactis ab aliis elleborine vocatur, parva
herba, exiguis foliis, iocineris vitiis utilissima et contra
venena pota.

LIII. Epimedion caulis est non magnus hederae
foliis denis atque duodenis, numquam florens, radice
tenui, nigra, gravi odore ac[1] . . . in umidis nascitur.
et huic spissandi refrigerandique natura, feminis
cavenda. folia in vino trita virginum mammas
cohibent.

77 LIV. Enneaphyllon longa folia novena habet
causticae naturae. inponitur lana circumdatum ne
urat latius, continuo enim pusulas excitat, lumborum
doloribus et coxendicum utilissimum.

78 LV. Filicis duo genera. nec florem habent nec
semen. pterim vocant Graeci, alii blachnon, cuius ex

---

[1] ac VdT : hac R : om. E Sillig, Detlefsen : lacunam
indicat Mayhoff e Diosc. IV 19 (ῥίζαι . . . γευσαμένῳ μωραί).

---

[a] Littré : " entre deux linges."
[b] Littré : " prise en potage."
[c] Of dropsy ?
[d] This seems to be the force of atque, but Dioscorides has
only ἤ.

neath.[a] The plant boiled with linseed makes a gruel [b] that cures dysentery.

LI. Empetros, called calcifraga by us Romans, *Empetros.* is found on coastal mountains, generally on a rock. When it has grown near the sea it is salt, and taken in drink brings away bile and phlegms; when farther off and in deeper soil it tastes more bitter. It brings away fluid,[c] and is taken in broth of some kind or in hydromel. When stale it loses its potency, but when fresh and boiled down in water or beaten up it is diuretic and breaks up stone in the bladder. Those who seek to win belief in this assurance assert that pebbles boiled with it are broken up.

LII. Epicactis, called by some elleborine, is a *Epicactis.* small plant with tiny leaves; taken in drink it is very useful for liver complaints and to counteract poisons.

LIII. Epimedion is a stem, not large, with ten or *Epimedion.* even [d] twelve leaves like ivy leaves. It never flowers, has a slender, blackish, evil-smelling root, and . . .[e] This plant, which grows in damp soils, is one of those with bracing and cooling properties, and should be avoided by women. Its leaves, beaten up in wine, check the growth of maidens' breasts.

LIV. Enneaphyllon has nine long leaves, and is of *Enneaphyl-* a caustic nature. When applied it is wrapped up in *lon.* wool, lest it cauterize too far,[f] for it raises blisters immediately. It is very good for the pains of lumbago and sciatica.

LV. Ferns are of two kinds, neither having blossom *Filix.* or seed. Some Greeks call pteris, others blachnon, the kind from the sole root of which shoot out several

---

[e] Mayhoff would fill up the lacuna by *gustu languido*, " an insipid taste," from Dioscorides.
[f] Perhaps, " too deeply."

una radice conplures exeunt filices bina etiam cubita
excedentes longitudine, non graves odore. hanc
marem existimant. alterum genus thelypterim
Graeci vocant, alii nymphaeam pterim, est autem
singularis atque non fruticosa, brevior molliorque et
79 densior, foliis ad radicem canaliculata. utriusque
radice sues pinguescunt, folia utriusque lateribus
pinnata, unde nomen Graeci inposuere. radices
utriusque longae in oblicum, nigrae, praecipue cum
inaruere. siccari autem eas sole oportet. nascuntur
ubique, sed maxime frigido solo. effodi debent
vergiliis occidentibus. usus radicis in trimatu tantum, neque ante nec postea. pellunt interaneorum
animalia, ex his taenias cum melle, cetera ex vino
dulci triduo potae, utraque stomacho inutilissima.
alvum solvit primo bilem trahens, mox aquam, melius
80 taenias cum scamonii pari pondere. radix eius
pondere duum obolorum ex aqua post unius diei
abstinentiam bibitur, melle praegustato, contra
rheumatismos. neutra danda mulieribus, quoniam
gravidis abortum, ceteris sterilitatem facit. farina
earum ulceribus taetris inspergitur, iumentorum quoque in cervicibus. folia cimicem necant, serpentem
non recipiunt, ideo substerni utile est in locis sus-
pectis, usta etiam fugant nidore. fecere medici

---

[a] Dioscorides (IV 184) has ὑποδυσώδη, " rather rank."
[b] The Greek πτερόν means " feather."
[c] Both Detlefsen and Mayhoff omit the comma after
praegustato. To do so improves the run of the sentence :
" taking honey beforehand to prevent fluxes." But it leaves
unmentioned the ailment for which this particular treatment

other ferns exceeding even two cubits in length,
with a not unpleasant smell.[a] This is considered
male. The other kind the Greeks call thelypteris,
some nymphaea pteris. It has only one stem, and
is not bushy, but shorter, softer and more compact
than the other, and channelled with leaves at the
root. The root of both kinds fattens pigs. In
both kinds the leaves are pinnate on either side,
whence the Greeks have named them " pteris." [b]
The roots of both are long, slanting, and blackish,
especially when they have lost moisture ; they should,
however, be dried in the sun. Ferns grow everywhere, but especially in a cold soil. They ought to
be dug up at the setting of the Pleiades. The root
must be used only at the end of three years, neither
earlier nor later. Ferns expel intestinal worms, tapeworms when taken with honey, but for other worms
they must be taken in sweet wine on three consecutive
days ; both kinds are very injurious to the stomach.
Fern opens the bowels, bringing away first bile,
then fluid, tapeworms better with an equal weight of
scammony. To treat catarrhal fluxes two oboli by
weight of the root are taken in water after fasting
for one day, with a taste of honey beforehand.[c]
Neither fern should be given to women, since either
causes a miscarriage when they are pregnant, and
barrenness when they are not. Reduced to powder
they are sprinkled over foul ulcers as well as on the
necks of draught animals. The leaves kill lice and will
not harbour snakes, so that it is well to spread them in
suspected places ; by the smell too when burnt they
drive away these creatures. Among ferns also

was a remedy ; it is naturally, in spite of the order of words,
rheumatismi.

huius quoque herbae discrimen, optima Macedonica
est, secunda Cassiopica.

81   LVI. Femur bubulum appellatur herba nervis et
ipsa utilis recens in aceto ac sale trita.

LVII. Galeopsis aut, ut alii, galeobdolon vel galion
caulem et folia habet urticae leviora et quae gravem
odorem trita reddant, flore purpureo. nascitur circa
saepes ac semitas ubique. folia caulesque duritias et
carcinomata sanant ex aceto trita et inposita, item
strumas, panos, parotidas discutiunt. ex usu est
et decoctae suco fovere. putrescentia quoque et
gangraenas sanat cum sale.

82   LVIII. Glaux antiquitus eugalacton vocabatur,
cytiso et lenticulae foliis similis; aversa candidiora.
rami in terram serpunt quini seni admodum tenues a
radice. flosculi purpurei exeunt.[1] invenitur iuxta
mare. coquitur in sorbitione similaginis ad exci-
tandam ubertatem lactis. eam qui[2] hauserint balineis
uti convenit.

83   LIX. Glaucion in Syria et Parthia nascitur, humilis
herba densis foliis fere papaveris, minoribus tamen
sordidioribusque, odoris taetri, gustus amari cum
adstrictione. granum habet crocei coloris. hoc in
olla fictili luto circumlita in clibanis calfaciunt, deinde
exempto sucum exprimunt eiusdem nominis. usus
et suci et foliorum, si terantur, adversus epiphoras

---

[1] exeunt] *Ut Mayhoff hic distinguo.*
[2] qui *codd., Detlefsen, Mayhoff* : quae *vet. Dal., Sillig* : *Mayhoff coni.* cumque.

---

[a] A town in Corcyra.
[b] *Et ipsa* might mean " even by itself," " without further
addition." The translation takes it to be : " itself also."
[c] Note this meaning of *ex usu est.* See XXV § 175.
[d] The *qui* is strange, and may be an early mistake for *quae.*

physicians have their preference; the Macedonian is
the best, the next best comes from Cassiope.[a]

LVI. Femur bubulum (" ox thigh ") is the name *Femur*
given to a plant which, applied fresh and beaten up in *bubulum.*
vinegar and salt, is one of the remedies [b] beneficial
for the sinews.

LVII. Galeopsis, called by some galeobdolon or *Galeopsis.*
galion, has stem and leaves like those of the nettle,
but smoother, and giving off when beaten up an
offensive smell; the flower is purple. It grows along
hedges and lanes everywhere. Its leaves and stalks,
beaten up in vinegar and applied, cure indurations
and malignant growths, dispersing scrofulous sores,
superficial abscesses and parotid swellings. It is also
beneficial [c] to use the juice of a decoction as a fomentation. With the addition of salt moreover it heals
festering sores and gangrenes.

LVIII. Glaux, called of old eugalacton, has leaves *Glaux.*
like those of cytisus and the lentil; they are whiter
underneath. The branches, five or six in number,
extremely slender and springing from the root,
lie along the ground; on them form small, purple
blossoms. It is found near the sea, and is boiled in
similago porridge to stimulate a rich supply of milk;
those who [d] have drunk a dose should proceed to a
bath.

LIX. Glaucion grows in Syria and Parthia, a low *Glaucion.*
plant, with tightly packed leaves, rather like those of
the poppy but smaller and dirtier looking; it has
a foul smell and a bitter, astringent taste. The seed,
of a saffron colour, is put into a pot luted with fuller's
clay and heated in an oven. Then it is taken out,
and a juice of the same name is extracted from it.
Both the juice and beaten-up leaves are used for the

quae universo impetu cadant. hinc temperatur
collyrium quod medici dia glauciu vocant. lactis
quoque ubertas intermissa restituitur. sumitur
huius rei causa ex aqua.

84   LX. Glycyside, quam aliqui paeoniam aut pentorobon vocant, caulem habet duum palmorum,[1] comi-
tantibus duobus aut tribus, subrutilum, cute lauri,
folia qualia isatis, pinguiora rotundioraque et minora,
semen in siliquis, aliud grano rubente, aliud nigro.
85 duo autem genera sunt: femina existimatur cuius
radicibus ceu balani longiores circiter octo aut sex
adhaerent. mas plures non habet, quoniam una
radice nixus est palmi altitudine, candida, quae
gustu adstringit. feminae folia murram redolent et
densiora sunt. nascuntur in silvis. tradunt nocte
effodiendas, quoniam interdiu periculosum sit pico
Martio inpetum in oculos faciente; radix vero cum
effodiatur, periculum esse ne sedes procidat, magna
vanitate ad ostentationem rei fictum arbitror. usus
86 in his diversus. rubra grana rubentes menses sistunt
xv fere pota in vino nigro. nigra grana vulvis
medentur ex passo aut vino totidem pota. radix
omnes ventris dolores sedat in vino alvumque purgat,
sanat opisthotonum, morbum regium, renes, vesicam,
arteriam autem et stomachum decocta in vino,
alvumque sistit. estur etiam in alimentis,[2] sed in

[1] palmorum *plerique codd. (sic Dioscorides), Mayhoff*: cubitorum Er, *vulg., Detlefsen.*
[2] in alimentis *Ianus, Mayhoff, cod. Murbacensis*: contra
malum mentis RE *vulg., Detlefsen.*

---

[a] Some old editions have *universae uno impetu cadunt*, " all
together, at one rush."
[b] The Greek διὰ γλαυκίου, " made from glaucion."
[c] See Book X § 40.

fluxes that fall in streams from the whole eye.[a]
There is made from it a salve called by physicians
diaglauciu.[b] It also restores a rich supply of milk if
this fails. When taken for this purpose, water is the
medium.

LX. Glycyside, called by some paeonia or pentoro- *Glycyside.*
bon, has a stem two spans high; two or three others
go with it. This stem is reddish, with bark like that
of bay; the leaves resemble those of isatis, only
more fleshy, rounder, and smaller. The seed is in
pods, with some grains red, some black. There are
however two kinds of the plant. The one to the roots
of which are attached about six or eight rather long
bulbs like acorns is regarded as female. The male has
no more bulbs, since it is supported only by a single
root, a span deep, white, and astringent to the taste.
The leaves of the female smell of myrrh, and are closer
together. The plants grow in woods. It is said that
they should be dug up by night, because to do so in
the daytime is dangerous, for the woodpecker called
" bird of Mars " [c] assaults the eyes. That there is a
danger, however, of prolapsus of the anus when a
root is being dug up, I hold to be a very fraudulent
lie, calculated to exaggerate the real facts. These
plants are of manifold use. The red grains check red
menstrual discharge, about fifteen being taken in
dark-red wine. The black grains are healing to the
uterus, the same number being taken in raisin or
ordinary wine. The root in wine relieves all pains of
the belly, opens the bowels, cures opisthotonic
tetanus, jaundice, and complaints of the kidneys and
bladder; for the trachea and the stomach however a
decoction in wine is used, which also acts astringently
on the bowels. It is eaten too as a food, but as a

441

87 medendo quattuor drachmae satis sunt. grana nigra
auxiliantur et suppressionibus nocturnis in vino pota
quo dictum est numero, stomachicis vero et rosionibus
et esse eam et inlinere prodest. suppurationes quoque discutiuntur, recentes nigro semine, veteres
rubro. utrumque auxiliatur a serpente percussis et
pueris contra calculos incipiente [1] stranguria.

88   LXI. Gnaphalium aliqui chamaezelon vocant,
cuius foliis albis mollibusque pro tomento utuntur,
sane et similia sunt. datur in vino austero ad
dysinteriam, ventris solutiones mensesque mulierum
sistit. infunditur autem tenesmo. inlinitur et
putrescentibus ulcerum.

89   LXII. Gallidragam vocat Xenocrates leucacantho
similem, palustrem et spinosam, caule ferulaceo alto,
cui summo capite inhaereat simile ovo. in hoc
crescente aestate vermiculos nasci tradit quos pyxide
conditos adalligari cum pane bracchio ab ea parte
qua dens doleat, mireque ilico dolorem tolli. valere
non diutius anno et ita si terram non adtigerint.

90   LXIII. Holcus in saxis nascitur siccis. aristas
habet in cacumine, tenui culmo, quale hordeum
restibile. haec circa caput alligata vel circa lacertum
educit e corpore aristas. quidam ob id aristida
vocant.

LXIV. Hyoseris intubo similis, sed minor et tactu
asperior, volneribus contusa praeclare medetur.

---

[1] incipiente *codd.* : incipientes *Mayhoff, qui confert Diosc.
III 140* ἀρχὰς λιθιάσεως παραιτοῦνται.

---

[a] The emendation of Mayhoff, though easy and ingenious,
is not necessary, for the passage in Dioscorides is rather
vague and makes no mention of strangury.

medicine four drachmae are enough. The black
grains, taken in wine to the number mentioned, also
prevent nightmares, while for stomach ache and for
gnawing colic it is beneficial both to eat them and to
apply them locally. Suppurations too are dispersed,
recent by the black seed and old by the red. Both
kinds are good for snake bites, and to cure stone in
children when strangury is beginning.[a]

LXI. Gnaphalium is called by some chamaezelon; *Gnaphalium.*
its pale, soft leaves are used as flock; the two
indeed are similar. It is given in a dry wine for
dysentery, arrests fluxes of the belly and excessive
menstruation, is injected for tenesmus and applied to
festering ulcers.

LXII. Xenocrates calls gallidraga a prickly marsh- *Gallidraga.*
plant like leucacanthus, with a tall stem like fennel-
giant, on the top of which is perched an egg-shaped
ball. In this, he says, as summer advances, are
bred maggots, which are kept in a box and attached
with bread, as an amulet, to the arm on the same side
as an aching tooth, and the pain disappears at
once in a wonderful manner. These maggots, he
says, retain their potency for not more than a year,
and then only if they have not touched the ground.

LXIII. Holcus grows on dry rocks. The plant is *Holcus.*
like barley that has grown again after cutting, with
ears at the top of a slender straw. Tied round the
head or round the arm this plant [b] draws ears
(*aristas*) from the flesh, for which reason some call
it aristis.

LXIV. Hyoseris is like endive, but smaller and *Hyoseris.*
rougher to the touch; crushed it is a splendid remedy
for wounds.

[b] *Haec* might be *arista.*

443

91 LXV. Holosteon sine duritia est herba ex adverso appellata a Graecis, sicut fel dulce, radice tenui [1] usque in capillamenti speciem, longitudine quattuor digitorum, ceu gramen foliis angustis, adstringens gustu. nascitur in collibus terrenis. usus eius ad vulsa, rupta in vino potae. et volnera quoque conglutinat, nam et carnes, dum coquuntur, addita.

92 LXVI. Hippophaeston nascitur in spinis ex quibus fiunt aënae fulloniae, sine cauliculo, sine flore, capitulis tantum inanibus et foliis parvis multis, herbacei coloris, radiculas habens [2] albas, molles. sucus earum exprimitur aestate ad solvendam alvum tribus obolis, maxime in comitialibus morbis et tremulis, hydropicis, contra vertigines, orthopnoeas, paralysis incipientes.

93 LXVII. Hypoglossa folia habet figura silvestris myrti, concava,[3] spinosa et in his ceu linguas folia parva exeuntia e [4] foliis. capitis dolores corona ex his inposita minuit.

LXVIII. Hypecoön in segetibus nascitur foliis rutae. natura eius eadem quae papaveris suco.

---

[1] radice tenui *ego, qui Hermolai Barbari* tenui radice *inverto* : radice tenuis *Mayhoff* : tenuis *codd.*, *Detlefsen*. *Dioscorides* (IV 11) ῥίζαν δὲ σφόδρα λεπτὴν ὡς τρίχα.

[2] habens *vulg. Detlefsen* : om. *codd.* : radiculae albae *Mayhoff*.

[3] concava *codd.*, *vulg.* : coma *e Dioscoride Mayhoff, qui etiam* comantia *coni.*

[4] folia parva exeuntia e foliis *coni. Mayhoff* : folio parvo exeunte de foliis *codd.*, *Detlefsen, Mayhoff in textu.*

---

[a] A strange phrase, which should mean : "grows among etc." See now additional note, p. 483.

[b] The sense is the same whichever reading is adopted.

LXV. Holosteon (all-bone) is a plant with nothing *Holosteon.*
hard about it, the name being an antiphrasis coined
by the Greeks, just as they call gall sweet. Its root
is so slender as to look like hair. Four fingers long,
the plant has narrow leaves like grass and an astringent taste, growing on hills with deep soil. Taken in
wine for sprains and ruptures it also closes wounds,
for it even fastens together pieces of meat when
boiled with them.

LXVI. Hippophaeston is to be found [a] among the *Hippo-*
thorns out of which fullers' pots are made up, having *phaestum.*
no stem, no blossom, but only little, hollow heads and
many small leaves of the colour of grass. Its little
roots are whitish and soft.[b] Their juice is extracted in
summer; the dose to open the bowels is three oboli,
being used especially in epilepsy, palsy, dropsy, and
to treat giddiness, orthopnoea, and incipient paralysis.

LXVII. Hypoglossa has leaves shaped like those of *Hypoglossa.*
wild myrtle, concave, prickly, and on them as it
were tongues, small leaves growing out of the leaves
proper. A chaplet made from these and placed on
the head relieves headache.[c]

LXVIII. Hypecoön grows in cornfields and has *Hypecoön.*
leaves like those of rue. Its properties are those of
poppy juice.

[c] Dioscorides has (IV 129): θαμνίσκος ἐστὶ μυρσίνη ἀγρίᾳ
καὶ λεπτῇ ἔχων τὰ φύλλα ὅμοια, κόμην δὲ ἀκανθώδη καὶ ἐπ᾽
ἄκρου οἱονεὶ γλωττίδας, παραφύσεις μικρὰς παρὰ τοῖς φύλλοις.
δοκεῖ δὲ ἡ κόμη περίαμμα εἶναι χρήσιμον κεφαλαλγοῦσι. The
reason why Mayhoff emended *concava* to *coma* is clear, but
the Greek and the Latin, although very much alike, have some
differences, the greatest perhaps being Pliny's *corona* where
the Greek has κόμη. The Latin *coma*, and also κόμη, are
difficult words, and there is no English word that will serve
as a translation on every occasion. Some remarks on them
will be found on pp. 482–483.

445

LXIX. Idaeae herbae folia sunt quae oxymyrsines. adhaerent iis velut pampini, in quibus flos. ipsa alvum mensesque et omnem abundantiam sanguinis sistit. spissandi cohibendique naturam habet.[1]

94 LXX. Isopyron aliqui phaselion vocant, quoniam folium quod est aneso simile in passeoli pampinos torquetur. capitula sunt in summo caule tenuia, plena seminis melanthi, contra tussim et cetera pectoris vitia cum melle aut aqua mulsa, item iocineri utilissima.[2]

95 LXXI. Lathyris folia habet multa lactucae similia, tenuiora, germina multa, in quibus semen tuniculis continetur ut capparis, quae cum inaruere, eximuntur grana piperis magnitudine, candida, dulcia, facilia purgatu. haec vicena in aqua pura aut mulsa pota hydropicos sanant. trahunt et bilem. qui vehementius purgari volunt cum folliculis ipsis sumunt ea, nam stomachum laedunt, itaque inventum est ut cum pisce aut iure gallinacei sumerentur.

96 LXXII. Leontopetalon alii rapadion vocant, folio brassicae, caule semipedali. alae plures,[3] semen in

---

[1] habet *vulg. Mayhoff emendat* : sanguinis sistit spissandi cohibendique natura.

[2] utilissima d(?) *vulg., Detlefsen* : utilissimo VRE : utilissimi *Mayhoff*.

[3] plures *Sillig* : mirae *Detlefsen* : numerosae *Mayhoff*: nures E : nure VR.

---

[a] Or, " without addition."
[b] Or, " styptic."

LXIX. The plant of Ida has leaves like those of *Idaea herba.*
oxymyrsine, and to them adhere as it were tendrils,
which bear the blossom. The plant itself [a] checks
looseness of the bowels, menstruation, and all excessive bleeding, as it has astringent [b] and repressive
properties.

LXX. Isopyron is called by some phaselion, *Isopyron.*
because its leaf, which resembles that of anise, twists
itself into the shape of the tendrils of the passeolus.[c]
At the top of the stem grow little heads, slender,[d]
full of seed like that of melanthium, and very
efficacious, when taken with honey or hydromel, for
cough, other chest complaints, and also those of the
liver.

LXXI. Lathyris has many leaves like those of *Lathyris.*
lettuce, but slighter, and many buds, in which the
seed is enclosed in envelopes as is that of the caper.
When the buds are dry,[e] the seeds, of the size of a
peppercorn, are taken out; they are white, sweet,
and easily shelled. Twenty of them in fresh water
or hydromel cure dropsy, and also draw away bile.
Those who wish for a more violent purge take the
pods themselves with the seeds, but[f] since they
injure the stomach the plan has been devised of
taking them with fish or chicken broth.

LXXII. Leontopetalon, called by some rapadion, *Leonto-*
has leaves like cabbage leaves and a stem half a foot *petalon.*
long. There are several side branches, and at the

---

[c] *Phaseolus* and *passeolus* are different forms of the same
name.
[d] Perhaps " slender " should be omitted, as *tenuia* may
merely strengthen the diminutive.
[e] Or, " have withered."
[f] A clear instance of *nam* = but.

cacumine in siliquis ciceris modo, radix rapo [1]
similis, grandis, nigra. nascitur in arvis. radix
adversatur omnibus [2] serpentium generibus ex vino
pota, nec alia res celerius proficit. datur et ischiadicis.

97 LXXIII. Lycapsos longioribus quam lactucae foliis
crassioribusque, caule longo, hirsutis [3] adgnatis multis,
cubitalibus, flore parvo, purpureo. nascitur in
campestribus. inlinitur cum farina hordeacea igni
sacro, sudores in febribus movet suco aquae calidae
admixto.

98 LXXIV. Inter omnes herbas lithospermo nihil est
mirabilius. aliqui exonychon vocant, alii Dios pyron,
alii Heracleus. herba quincuncialis fere, foliis duplo
maioribus quam rutae, ramulis surculosis, crassitudine
iunci. gerit iuxta folia singulas veluti barbulas et
in earum cacuminibus lapillos candore et rotunditate
margaritarum, magnitudine ciceris, duritia vero
lapidea. ipsi qua pediculis adhaereant cavernulas
99 habent et intus semen. nascitur et in Italia, sed
laudatissimum in Creta, nec quicquam inter herbas
maiore equidem miraculo aspexi. tantus est decor
velut aurificum arte alternis inter folia candicantibus
margaritis, tam exquisita difficultas lapidis ex herba
nascentis. iacere atque humi serpere auctores
tradunt ; ego volsam, non haerentem vidi. his

[1] rapo r *Gelenius, Mayhoff* : rapa E : napo *aliquot codd.,
Detlefsen.*
[2] omnibus *Mayhoff* : omnium *codd., Detlefsen. Ego coni.*
omnium serpentium ictibus.
[3] caule longo, hirsutis *ego* : caulem longum hirsutum habet
Detlefsen : cauli longo hirsutis *Mayhoff* : caulem longum hirsutis *codd.*

[a] Dioscorides (III 96) : μασχάλας πλείστας ἐφ᾽ ὧν ἄκρων
λοβοὶ ὅμοιοι ἐρεβίνθοις. Hence my rendering of *alae.*

ends, in pods like those of chick-peas,[a] is the seed. The root is like a turnip, large and blackish. It grows on cultivated ground. Taken in wine the root neutralises the poison of serpents of every kind,[b] and no other remedy acts more quickly. It is also given to sufferers from sciatica.

LXXIII. Lycapsos has longer and coarser leaves *Lycapsus.* than those of lettuce, a long stem, with many subsidiary others, hairy and a cubit long, and a small, purple flower. It grows in flat, meadowy land. With barley meal it makes a local application for erysipelas. The juice with hot water added promotes perspiration in fevers.

LXXIV. Among all plants nothing is more wonderful than lithospermum, called by some exonychon, *Lithospermon.* by others " Juppiter's corn," and by others " corn of Hercules." The plant is about five inches high, with leaves twice as big as those of rue, and ligneous little branches of the thickness of a rush. Near the leaves it grows as it were little beards, which are single, and on their tops little stones, white and round as pearls, as big as a chick-pea but as hard as a stone. Where they are attached to pedicels these jewels have little holes, in which is the seed. The plant grows indeed in Italy, but the most highly valued in Crete, and I have never seen anything among plants that filled me with greater wonder. So charming the adornment that one might think that the jeweller's art had arranged gleaming white pearls symmetrically among the leaves ; so elegantly solved is the problem of causing a gem to grow from a plant ! The authorities say that it lies and spreads over the ground ; *I* have seen it only when gathered, not when so growing. It is

[b] My conjecture: " of the bites of all serpents."

lapillis drachmae pondere potis in vino albo calculos
frangi pellique constat et stranguriam discuti.
neque in alia herbarum fides est certior,[1] ad quam
medicinam nata sit, est autem [2] eius species ut etiam
sine auctore visu statim nosci possit.

100   LXXV. Lapis vulgaris iuxta flumina fert muscum
siccum, canum. hic fricatur altero lapide addita
hominis saliva, illo lapide tangitur inpetigo. qui
tangit dicit:

φεύγετε κανθαρίδες, λύκος ἄγριος αἷμα διώκει.

101   LXXVI. Limeum herba appellatur a Gallis qua
sagittas in venatu tingunt medicamento, quod
venenum cervarium vocant. ex hac in tres modios
salivati additur quantum in unam sagittam addi solet,
ita offa demittitur boum faucibus in morbis. alligari
postea ad praesepia oportet, donec purgentur—
insanire enim solent—si sudor insequitur, aqua
frigida perfundi.

102   LXXVII. Leuce mercurialis [3] similis nomen ex
causa accepit, per medium folium candida linea
transcurrente, quare mesoleucion quidam vocant.
sucus eius fistulas sanat, ipsa contrita carcinomata.
fortassis eadem sit quae leucas appellatur, contra
marina omnia venena efficax. speciem eius auctores

---

[1] certior Mayhoff : aequa Detlefsen : visu statim codd.
[2] est autem vulg., Detlefsen : talis autem Mayhoff : autem
VRE.
[3] Mercurialis codd., Ianus, Detlefsen : Mercuriali vulg.,
Mayhoff.

---

[a] For cantheris see Book XVIII § 152.
[b] Mayhoff thinks that tritici, or some such word, is understood with salivati. But this is not necessary.

indisputable that a drachma by weight of these jewels taken in white wine breaks up and brings away stone, and cures strangury. There is no other plant the medicinal property of which can be recognised with greater confidence; its very appearance is such that at once by a glance, even without being told, people can become aware of this property.

LXXV. On ordinary stones near rivers grows a dry, hoary moss. One of them is rubbed with another one smeared with human spittle; with the latter stone is touched eczema, and he who touches says:

" Begone, cantharides,[a] for a savage wolf seeks
    your blood."

LXXVI. Limeum is the name given by the Gauls *Limeum.* to a plant that they use to make a drug, called by them deer poison, with which when hunting they poison their arrows. As much of the plant as is usually used for one arrow is mixed with three bushels of saliva stimulant,[b] and when cattle are sick this mash is forced down their throats. Afterwards they must be tied to their stalls until they are purged— for they usually go wild—and if sweating ensues cold water should be poured over them.

LXXVII. Leuce, a plant like mercurialis, has a *Leuce.* reason for the name it bears, because a white line runs down the middle of the leaves, which is why some call it mesoleucion.[c] Its juice heals fistulas; crushed, the plant itself cures malignant ulcers. Perhaps it is the same as the plant called leucas, which is a remedy for the poison of all sea creatures. My authorities do not report its appearance; they

c " White down the middle."

non tradunt, nec aliud quam silvestrem latioribus
foliis esse, efficaciorem hanc [1] semine acriore.

103 LXXVIII. Leucographis qualis esset scriptum non
repperi, quod eo magis miror, quoniam utilis proditur
sanguinem excreantibus tribus obolis cum croco,
item coeliacis, trita ex aqua et adposita profluvio
feminarum, oculorum quoque medicamentis et ex-
plendis ulceribus quae fiant in teneris partibus.

104 LXXIX. Medion folia habet seridis [2] sativae, caulem
tripedalem et in eo florem grandem, purpureum,
rotundum, semine minuto, radicem semipedalem.
in saxis opacis nascitur. radix drachmis duabus cum
melle menses feminarum sistit ecligmate per aliquot
dies sumpto. semen quoque in vino contra abundantiam feminarum datur.

105 LXXX. Myosota sive myosotis, levis herba caulibus
pluribus ab una radice, aliquatenus rubentibus, concavis, ab imo foliis angustis, oblongis, dorso acuto,
nigris, per intervalla adsidue geminatis, tenuibus
cauliculis ex alis prodeuntibus, flore caeruleo. radix
digitali crassitudine multis capillamentis fimbriata.
vis ei †septica† [3] et exulceratrix, ideoque aegilopas

---

[1] hanc *codd.*, *Mayhoff* : ac *Urlichs, Detlefsen.*
[2] seridis *e Diosc. (IV 18) Hermolaus Barbarus, Detlefsen* :
iridis *Mayhoff* : hiridis E.
[3] septica *codd.* : *ego* smectica *coni.* : caustica *coll.* § 112
Warmington.

---

[a] With Mayhoff's reading, "iris."
[b] Dioscorides on the contrary says (IV 18): ἄγει ἔμμηνα.
[c] Mayhoff for *levis* suggests *tenuis*, "slender."
[d] Mayhoff punctuates *concavis ab imo*, and suggests that
ab imo should be transposed to come after *rubentibus.*
[e] Littré translates this puzzling sentence thus : "La
qualité de cette racine est septique et exulcérante; ainsi
guérit-elle aegilops." But how can a "septic and ulcerating"
application cure a lacrimal fistula? Something or other must

only say that the wild plant has the broader leaves, that this is the more efficacious, and has the more pungent seed.

LXXVIII. A description of leucographis I have *Leuco-*
nowhere found in writing. I am the more surprised *graphis.*
at this because in three-oboli doses with saffron it is
considered useful for haemoptysis, and also for the
coeliac disease; beaten up in water and applied as a
pessary for excessive menstruation; useful too as
an ingredient of eye salves, and for filling up ulcers
that form on tender parts of the body.

LXXIX. Medion has leaves like those of cultivated *Medion.*
seris *a*; the stem is three feet long, on which is a
large, purple, round flower, bearing tiny seeds; the
root is half a foot long. The plant grows on shaded
rocks. The root checks excessive menstruation,
two-drachma doses, with honey, being taken in the
form of an electuary for a few successive days. For
the same purpose the seed too is given in wine.*b*

LXXX. Myosota or myosotis is a smooth *c* plant *Myosota.*
with several stems growing from one root, these being
red to a certain extent and hollow; narrow leaves grow
at the bottom,*d* longish, with a spine along the back,
dark, carefully arranged in pairs at regular intervals.
There are slender stalks growing from the axils, and
the blossom is blue. The root, of the thickness of a
finger, is fringed with many filaments like hairs.
It has †septic and ulcerating† properties,*e* and so

be wrong. Unfortunately Dioscorides (II 183) is of no help
here, for although he mentions the cure, he says nothing about
the properties of the root: ἡ δὲ ῥίζα καταπλασθεῖσα αἰγιλώπια
ἰᾶται.

I suggest that *exulceratrix* means, not " ulcerating," but
" clearing away ulcers," just as *exulcerare corpus* in XXIII
§ 22 means "free the flesh from sores." Cf. *tussim exasperant*

sanat. tradunt Aegypti, mensis quem Thoti vocant die xxviii fere in Augustum mensém incurrente si quis huius herbae suco inungatur mane priusquam loquatur, non lippiturum eo anno.

106 LXXXI. Myagros herba ferulacea est foliis similis rubiae, tripedania. semen oleosum, quod et fit ex eo. medetur oris ulceribus perunctis hoc suco.

LXXXII. Herba quae vocatur nyma, tribus foliis longis intubaceis, inlita cicatrices ad colorem reducit.

107 LXXXIII. Natrix vocatur herba cuius radix evulsa virus hirci redolet. hac in Piceno feminis abigunt quos mira persuasione Fatuos vocant, ego species lymphantium hoc modo animorum esse crediderim quae tali medicamento iuventur.

108 LXXXIV. Odontitis inter feni genera est, cauliculis densis ab eadem radice, geniculatis, triangulis, nigris. in geniculis folia parva habet, longiora tamen quam polygonum, semen in alis hordeo simile, florem

---

(XXIII § 97), " takes away roughness from a cough." Then *septica* may be a mistake, either of Pliny or of a scribe, for *smectica*. In XXX § 29 *septica* is actually found as a variant of the correct reading *smectica* (*vi*). The translation would then be : " the root is cleansing, and clears away sores, and so it heals lacrimal fistulas." So also *exulcerat* in § 112.

An old reading *stiptica* (i.e., *styptica*, " styptic ") is mentioned by Dalecamp, and may be right. At any rate it shows that the passage puzzled the old commentators. As Detlefsen and Mayhoff agree in their text, and as Littré raises no doubts, I have left text and translation within daggers.

Professor Andrews thinks that the text is correct, referring to the drastic treatment of eye-fistulas in early times.

[a] *I.e.*, for the next twelve months.

heals lacrimal fistulas. The Egyptians say that if, on
the twenty-eighth day of the month they call thoti
(a day generally falling in our August), you rub
yourself over in the morning with the juice of this
plant before speaking to anyone, you will not in that
year [a] suffer from ophthalmia.

LXXXI. Myagros is a plant like fennel-giant, with *Myagros.*
leaves like those of madder; it is three feet high.
The seed is oily, and from it is extracted an oil. This
juice, used as liniment, is good treatment for an ulcerated mouth.

LXXXII. The plant called nyma, with its three *Nyma.*
long leaves like those of endive, makes a liniment
that restores the colour of a skin disfigured by scars.

LXXXIII. Natrix is the name of a plant the root of *Natrix.*
which, when pulled up, gives out the foul smell of he-
goats. In Picenum they use this plant to drive away
from women what are, with a strange credulity, called
Fatui.[b] I myself should believe that it is the hallu-
cination of minds delirious in this way that is helped
by such a drug.[c]

LXXXIV. Odontitis is classed as a hay with close- *Odontitis.*
set stalks growing from the same root, jointed,
triangular and dark. At the joints it has small leaves,
longer however than those of polygonum, seed like
barley in the axils, and a tiny, bright red flower. It

[b] *Fatui*, " clowns," were kept by some Romans. Here it
means " night-demons," referring to some kind of nightmare.
The Delphin editor has : *qui viros aggredi existimati sunt, ii
Fauni, qui mulieres, Fatui dici consueverunt.*
[c] I take *species* to mean " visions." Literally, " those
who need such a remedy are the visions of minds suffering
from such hallucinations." Professor Andrews thinks that
this cannot be so, as it is the *species* that are said to be
" relieved ", according to my construe.

purpureum, pusillum. nascitur in pratis. decoctum
cauliculorum eius in vino austero quantum manus
capiat dentium dolori medetur ita ut contineatur ore.

109   LXXXV. Othonna in Syria nascitur, similis erucae,
perforatis crebro foliis, flore croci,[1] quare quidam
anemonem vocaverunt. sucus eius oculorum medicamentis convenit. mordet enim leniter et calfacit
adstringitque siccando ; purgat cicatrices et nubeculas
et quicquid obstet. quidam tradunt lavari atque ita
siccatam digeri in pastillos.

110   LXXXVI. Onosma longa folia habet fere ad tres
digitos, in terra iacentia, ad similitudinem anchusae,[2]
sine caule, sine flore, sine semine. praegnas, si edit
eam aut supergradiatur, abortum facere dicitur.

LXXXVII. Onopradon si comederunt, asini crepi-
tus reddere dicuntur. trahit urinas et menses, alvum
sistit, suppurationes et collectiones discutit.

111   LXXXVIII. Osyris ramulos fert nigros, tenues,
lentos, et in his folia nigra ceu lini semenque in
ramulis nigrum initio, dein colore mutato rubescens.
smegmata mulieribus faciunt ex his. radicum decoctum potu sanat arquatos. eaedem priusquam
maturescat semen concisae et sole siccatae alvum
sistunt. post maturitatem vero collectae et in sorbitione decoctae rheumatismis ventris medentur et per
se tritae ex aqua caelesti bibuntur.

[1] croci e *Dioscoridae vulg.* : cocci VRdf *Detlefsen.*
[2] *Post* anchusae *in codd.* incisis (VdE) *aut* incissis (R) :
incisa *vulg.* : *ego delevi* (*ex* anchusae *ortum* ?). anchusae . . .
similis sive caule, sive flore, sive semine. *Mayhoff.*

grows in meadows. A decoction of its stalks, a handful in a dry wine, is a cure for toothache, but it must be kept in the mouth.

LXXXV. Othonna grows in Syria. It is like *Othonna.* eruca, has leaves full of holes and a saffron flower. This is why some have called it anemone. Its juice is a suitable ingredient of eye salves, for it is slightly biting, warming, and astringent, because of its drying nature; it clears away scars, films and all obstructions. Some say that it is washed, and then, after drying, worked up into lozenges.

LXXXVI. Onosma has long leaves up to about *Onosma.* three fingers in length, lying on the ground like those of anchusa. It has no stem, no blossom and no seed.[a] If a woman with child should eat it or step over it, she is said to miscarry.

LXXXVII. Asses are said, if they have eaten *Onopradon.* onopradon, to break wind. It is diuretic and an emmenagogue, checks looseness of the bowels, and disperses suppurations and gatherings.

LXXXVIII. Osyris bears dark twigs, slender and *Osyris.* pliant, on which are dark leaves like those of flax. The seed on the twigs is black to begin with, and then the colour changes to red. From them are made cosmetics for women. A decoction of the roots taken by the mouth cures jaundice. These roots also, if cut off before the seed ripens and dried in the sun, check looseness of the bowels; but, if dug up after the ripening and boiled down in gruel, they are good treatment for catarrhs of the belly, and by themselves they are beaten up and taken in rain water.

---

[a] Dioscorides III 131 : ἐπὶ γῆς κατεστρωμένα ἐμφερέστατα τῆς ἀγχούσης. ἔστι δὲ ἄκαυλος καὶ ἄκαρπος καὶ ἀνανθής. So there is no need to alter, with Mayhoff, *sine* to *sive*.

112 LXXXIX. Oxys folia terna habet. datur ad
stomachum dissolutum. edunt et qui enterocelen
habent.

XC. Polyanthemum, quam quidam batrachion
appellant, caustica vi exulcerat cicatrices et ad
colorem reducit, eademque vitiligines concorporat.

113 XCI. Polygonum Graeci vocant quam nos san-
guinariam. non attollitur a terra, foliis rutae,
similis graminis. sucus eius infusus naribus sup-
primit sanguinem et potus cum vino cuiuslibet partis
profluvium excreationesque cruentas inhibet. qui
plura genera polygoni faciunt hanc marem intellegi
volunt appellarique a multitudine seminis aut densi-
tate fruticis, alii polygonaton a frequentia geniculorum, alii thalattiada, alii carcinothron, alii clema,
multi myrtopetalum. nec non inveniuntur qui hanc
feminam esse dicant, marem autem maiorem minusque nigram et geniculis densiorem, semine sub
114 omnibus foliis turgescentem.[1] quocumque haec
modo se habent, vis earum est spissare ac refrigerare.
semine alvum solvunt, largius sumpto urinam cient,
rheumatismos cohibent, qui si non fuere, non prosunt.
stomachi fervori folia inponuntur, vesicae dolori
inlinuntur et ignibus sacris. sucus et auribus purulentis instillatur et oculorum dolori. per se dabatur

[1] turgescentem *codd., vulg., Detlefsen* : turgescente *Mayhoff
Dal. secutus.*

---

[a] The Delphin editor says : *reddit reliquo corpori parem.* On
exulcerat see page 453, note.
[b] Mayhoff suggests that *similis graminis* should come after
terra : " resembles grass in not rising from the ground."
[c] The name means " having much seed."
[d] Or, " brace." Dioscorides IV 4 : δύναμιν δὲ ἔχει στυπτικὴν
καὶ ψυκτικήν.

LXXXIX. Oxys has three leaves. It is given for a *Oxys.* relaxed stomach, and is also eaten by sufferers from intestinal hernia.

XC. Polyanthemum, called by some batrachion, *Polyanthe-* with its caustic property clears away scars and brings *mum.* back a healthy colour.[a] It also effaces psoriasis.

XCI. Polygonum is the name given by the Greeks *Polygonum,* to the plant we Romans call sanguinaria. It does not *four kinds.* rise from the ground, has leaves like those of rue, and resembles grass.[b] Its juice poured into the nostrils checks epistaxis, and taken with wine stays haemorrhage in any part of the body and the spitting of blood. Those who hold that there are several kinds of polygonum would have this to be considered the male plant, and to be so named because of the great number of its seeds,[c] or from its being a shrub with close-packed branches. Some call it polygonaton from its many joints, others thalattias or carcino-thron or clema, many myrtopetalum. There are also to be found some who say that this kind is the female, and that the male is larger, less dark, with the joints closer together, and swelling with seed under all the leaves. However this may be, the pro-perty of these plants is to be astringent[d] and to cool. Their seed relaxes the bowels, and taken in larger doses is diuretic; it checks catarrhs, and if these have not occurred it is of no use.[e] The leaves are applied to a heated stomach, and also used to make liniment for a painful bladder and for erysipelas. The juice is also dropped into purulent ears and painful eyes. It used also to be given by itself in

[e] *I.e.*, the seed checks catarrhs, but is not a preventive. There is nothing of this in Dioscorides, who has merely: ἁρμόζει τοῖς κατὰ κοιλίαν ῥεύμασι.

et in febribus ante accessiones duobus cyathis in tertianis quartanisque praecipue, item cholericis, 115 dysintericis et in solutione stomachi. tertium genus orion vocant in montibus nascens, harundini tenerae simile, uno caule, densis geniculis et in se infarctis, foliis autem piceae, radicis supervacuae, inefficacius 116 quam superiora, peculiare ischiadicis. quartum genus silvestre appellatur, paene arboris modo frutex, radice lignosa, stirpe cedri rubicunda, ramis sparti binum palmorum, nigris geniculorum ternis quaternisque articulis. huic quoque spissandi natura, sapor mali cotonei. decoquitur in aqua ad tertias aut aridi farina inspergitur et oris ulceribus et adtritis partibus. propter gingivarum vero vitia ipsa com-117 manducatur. nomas sistit omniaque quae serpunt aut difficilem cicatricem habent, privatim vero sanat a nive facta ulcera. herbarii et ad anginas utuntur illa et in capitis dolore coronam ex ea inponunt et contra epiphoras collo circumdant. in tertianis quidam[1] sinistra manu evulsam adalligant, adeo contra profluvia sanguinis, nec ullam magis aridam quam polygonum servant.

118 XCII. Pancratium aliqui scillam pusillam appellare malunt, foliis albi lilii longioribus crassioribusque, radice bulbi magni, colore rufo. alvum solvit suco cum farina ervi sumpto, ulcera purgat. hydropicis, splenicis cum melle datur. alii decocunt eam donec

---

[1] quidam *codd. multi*: quidem V *vulg., Mayhoff.*

---

[a] Dioscorides IV 5 : γόνατα συνεχῆ ἔχον ἐγκείμενα ἀλλήλοις ὥσπερ σάλπιγγος.
[b] Or " only."
[c] Possibly, " bracing."
[d] Or, with *quidem*, " indeed."

doses of two cyathi, before the paroxysms of agues, especially tertian and quartan, also for cholera, dysentery and a relaxed stomach. The third kind, called orion, grows on mountains and is like a tender reed. It has one stem with knots close together and fitted one into another,[a] leaves resembling those of the pitch pine, and a root of no medicinal use. This kind is less efficacious than those already mentioned, and used especially[b] for sciatica. The fourth kind is called wild polygonum, a shrub that is almost a tree; it has a ligneous root, a red trunk like that of the cedar, branches like those of spartum, two spans long, and with three or four dark, knotted joints. This kind too is of an astringent[c] nature, and tastes like a quince. It is boiled down in water to one third, or dried and powdered for sprinkling on ulcerations of the mouth and excoriated bruises, but for sore gums the plant itself is chewed. It arrests corrosive ulcers, and all those that spread or are slow to heal; for frost-bite however it is specific. Herbalists also use it for quinsy; for headache they make a chaplet of it which they place on the head; while to cure eye fluxes they put one round the neck. For tertian ague some[d] pluck it with the left hand and attach it as an amulet, and for haemorrhage also. There is no other plant that they keep in a dry state more than they do polygonum.

XCII. Pancratium some prefer to call "little *Pancratium.* squill." It has leaves resembling those of the white lily, but longer and thicker, and a root like a large, red bulb. Its juice taken with vetch flour relaxes the bowels and cleans[e] ulcers. With honey it is given for dropsy and affections of the spleen. Others

[e] Or, "clears up."

461

aqua dulcis fiat, eaque effusa radicem terentes digerunt in pastillos sole siccatos et postea utuntur ad
capitis ulcera et cetera quae repurganda sint, item ad
tussim quantum tribus digitis adprehenderint in vino
dantes, et ad lateris dolores aut peripleumonicis
ecligmate. dant et propter ischiada in vino bibendam
et propter tormina mensesque ciendos.

119 XCIII. Peplis, quam aliqui sycen, alii meconion,
alii mecona aphrode vocant, ex una radice tenui
fruticat foliis rutae paulo latioribus, semine sub foliis
rotundo, minore quam candidi papaveris.[1] inter
vites fere colligitur messibus siccaturque cum fructu
suo subiectis in quae excidat. hoc poto alvus solvitur,
bilis ac pituita detrahitur. media potio est acetabuli
mensura in aquae mulsae heminis tribus. et cibis
inspergitur obsoniisque ad molliendam alvum.

120 XCIV. Periclymenon fruticat et ipsa ex intervallo
duo folia habens subcandida, mollia. in cacumine
autem semen inter folia durum et quod difficile
vellatur. nascitur in arvis ac saepibus circumvolvens
se adminiculis quibuscumque. semen eius in umbra

---

[1] minore quam candidi papaveris *Hermolaus Barbarus* :
minor candido papavere *Detlefsen post Urlichs* : semen est
sub foliis, rotundum, minus candido papavere *Mayhoff* :
minus d *vulg.* : minos VR : papaver VR : papaveris d(?)*vulg.*

---

[a] Dioscorides IV 14 : θαμνίσκος . . . ἔχων ἐκ διαστήματος
φυλλάρια περιειληφότα αὐτόν, ὑπόλευκα, κισσοειδῆ καὶ παρὰ τὰ
φύλλα ἐκβλαστήσεις, ἐφ' ὧν καρπὸς κισσῷ παραπλήσιος, οἱονεὶ
ἐπικείμενος τῷ φύλλῳ, σκληρὸς καὶ δυσαπόσπαστος. "*Periclymenon fruticat* seems to mean 'Periclymenon forms a
shrub.' This fits honeysuckle, *Lonicera etrusca*, to which the
name is usually referred. Pliny is inclined to treat any plant
name as feminine, regardless of what it is, probably with *herba*
in his mind. *Ipsa* therefore means 'this plant.' As I study

boil it down until the water becomes sweet, pour this off, pound the root, and work it into lozenges, which they dry in the sun and use afterwards for sores on the head and all other ailments that call for a detergent. Moreover, they give in wine a three-finger pinch for cough, and an electuary made of it for pleurisy or pneumonia. They also give it to be taken in wine for sciatica, for colic, and as an emmenagogue.

XCIII. Peplis, called by some syce, by others *Peplis.* meconion or mecon aphrodes, grows into a shrub from one slender root, and has leaves like those of rue but a little broader. Under the leaves is a round seed, smaller than that of the white poppy. It is generally gathered among vines at harvest time, and is dried with its seed after a vessel has been placed beneath to catch this. Taken in drink it relaxes the bowels, bringing away bile and phlegm. A moderate dose is an acetabulum in three heminae of hydromel. It is sprinkled over foods and relishes to loosen the bowels.

XCIV. Periclymenon too is a plant which grows *Pericly-* into a shrub, having after an interval two leaves *menon.* which are whitish and soft. And at the top among the leaves is a seed which is hard, and difficult to pluck.[a] The plant grows in cultivated fields and in hedges, climbing round supports of any kind. Its seed is dried in the shade, pounded, and worked up

this passage, it seems to me that Pliny in condensing probably omitted a description of the flower-head after *fruticat.* There is one odd feature of the genus *Lonicera.* Quite a few of the species have a flower growing on an axillary bracted peduncle. A little below the flower-head (*ex intervallo*) there are two pairs of these bracts, so conjoined that each seems to be a single leaf. This is a fairly distinctive feature, one likely to be noted for purposes of recognition." (A.C.A.)

siccatum tunditur et in pastillos digeritur. hi resoluti
dantur in vini albi cyathis ternis tricenis diebus ad
lienem, eumque urina cruentata aut per alvum
absumit, quod intellegitur a decimo statim die.
urinam cient et folia decocta, quae et orthopnoicis
prosunt. partum quoque adiuvant secundasque
pellunt pota simili modo.

121 XCV. Pelecinon in segetibus diximus nasci, fruticosam cauliculis, foliis ciceris. semen in siliquis fert
corniculorum modo aduncis ternis quaternisve, quale
git novimus, amarum, stomacho utile. additur in
antidota.

XCVI. Polygala palmi altitudinem inplet, in caule
summo foliis lenticulae, gustu adstricto, quae pota
lactis abundantiam facit.

122 XCVII. Poterion aut, ut alii vocant, phrynion vel
neuras large fruticat, spinis retorrida, lanugine spissa,
foliis parvis, rotundis, ramulis longis, mollibus, lentis,
tenuibus, flore longo, herbacei coloris, seminis nullius
usus sed gustu acuto et odorato. invenitur in aquosis
123 collibus. radices habet duas aut tres binum cubitorum in altitudinem, nervosas, candidas, firmas.
circumfoditur autumno et praeciso frutice[1] radix[2]
dat sucum radix gummis similem. mira vulneribus
sanandis traditur praecipueque nervis vel praecisis
inlita. decoctum quoque eius cum melle potum
dissolutiones nervorum et infirmitates et incisuras
iuvat.

[1] praeciso frutice *codd.*: praecisa radice *Mayhoff.*
[2] radix *del. Detlefsen.*

---

[a] See Book XVIII § 155.
[b] What is the force of *novimus*? " Like git as we know it,"
i.e. in the form of imported seed. (A.C.A.)
[c] Polygala = much milk.

into lozenges. These, dissolved in three cyathi of white wine, are given for thirty days to cure splenic affections, the spleen being reduced either by blood in the urine or through the bowels, as is plain immediately from the tenth day. The boiled leaves too are diuretic, and also beneficial to asthmatics; they aid delivery and bring away the after-birth if taken in drink in a similar way.

XCV. Pelecinos I have said [a] grows in cornfields. *Pelecinos.* It makes a bushy plant with its stalks, and has leaves like those of the chick-pea. It bears seed, like git seed as we know it,[b] in three or four pods curved like little horns. This seed is bitter, a good stomachic, and an ingredient of antidotes.

XCVI. Polygala is a full span in height, with *Polygala.* leaves, like those of lentil, on the top of the stem, and with an astringent taste. Taken in drink it promotes an abundant supply of milk.[c]

XCVII. Poterion, or as some call it, phrynion *Poterion.* or neuras, is a spreading shrub, shrivelled and prickly, with thick down, small round leaves, long branches that are soft, flexible and slender, and a long flower of a grass-green colour. The seed is not used in medicine, but has a sharp, aromatic taste. The plant is found on moist hills. It has two or three roots, two cubits in depth, sinewy, white and firm. It is dug up in autumn, and when the shrub has been cut away,[d] the root yields a juice like gum. An application of the root is said to be a wonderful healer of wounds, especially of sinews even when they have been severed. A decoction of the root also, taken with honey, is good for relaxed, weak, or cut sinews.

---

[d] There seems no need for Mayhoff's correction. When the top was cut off the root would " bleed."

124 XCVIII. Phalangitis a quibusdam phalangion vocatur, ab aliis leucanthemum vel, ut in quibusdam exemplaribus invenio, leucacantha. ramuli sunt ei numquam pauciores duobus in diversa tendentes, flos candidus, lilio rubro similis, semen nigrum, latum,[1] ad lenticulae dimidiae figuram, multo tenuius,[2] radice tenui, herbacei coloris. huius folio vel flore vel semine auxiliantur contra scorpionum phalangiorumque et serpentium ictus, item contra tormina.

125 XCIX. Phyteuma quale sit describere supervacuum habeo, cum sit usus eius tantum ad amatoria.

C. Phyllon a Graecis vocatur herba in saxosis montibus. femina magis herbacei coloris, caule tenui, radice parva. semen papaveris[3] rotundo simile. haec sui sexus facit partus, mares autem mas,[4] semine tantum differens quod est incipientis olivae. utrumque bibitur in vino.

126 CI. Phelandrion nascitur in palustribus folio apii. bibitur semen eius propter calculos et vesicae incommoda.

CII. Phaleris thyrsum habet longum, tenuem ceu calamum, in summo florem inclinatum, semen simile sesamae. et hoc calculos frangit potum ex vino vel aceto vel cum melle et lacte, idem et vitia vesicae sanat.

[1] semen nigrum latum, *Mayhoff* : semine nigro lato, *codd.*
[2] tenuius *Mayhoff* : tenuis *codd.*
[3] papaveris *ego* : papaveri *codd.*
[4] mas *Brotier* : a *codd.*

---

[a] Dioscorides III 108 : σπέρμα δὲ πλατύ, μέλαν, ὥσπερ φακοῦ ἥμισυ, ἰσχνότερον μέντοι πολλῷ. The Greek decides the readings of the Latin, and also explains the apparent inconsistency between *latum* and *tenuius*.

XCVIII. Phalangitis is called by some phalangion, *Phalangitis.*
by others leucanthemum, or, as I find in some copies,
leucacantha. It has little branches, never fewer
than two, which grow in opposite directions; white
flowers like the red lily in shape, a black, broad seed,
of the shape of half a lentil, but much thinner,[a] and a
slender root of a grass-green colour. The leaves,
flowers or seed of this plant are of help for the
treatment of wounds inflicted by scorpions, poisonous spiders, and serpents; they are also good for
griping colic.

XCIX. To describe phyteuma is in my opinion a *Phyteuma.*
waste of time, because it is used only for love-
philtres.

C. Phyllon is the name given by the Greeks to a *Phyllon.*
plant that grows on rocky heights. The female
is more grass-green in colour than the male, with a
slender stem and a small root. The seed is like the
round seed of a poppy. This kind causes births of its
own sex, the male those of males, differing from the
female merely in its seed, which resembles that of
the olive when it is just beginning to form. Both
kinds are taken in wine.

CI. Phelandrion grows in marshy places, and has *Phelandrion.*
leaves resembling celery. Its seed is taken in drink
for [b] stone and troubles of the bladder.

CII. Phaleris has a stalk which is long and slender *Phaleris.*
as a reed; at the top is a drooping flower; the seed
resembles sesame seed, and is one of the remedies
that break up stone in the bladder, being taken in
wine, vinegar, or with honey and milk; it also cures
complaints of the bladder.

[b] It seems impossible to distinguish in such phrases, *propter,
contra, ad, adversus.*

CIII. Polyrrhizon folia habet myrti, radices multas. hae tusae dantur e vino contra serpentes, prosunt et quadripedibus.

127 CIV. Proserpinaca herba vulgaris est, eximii adversus scorpiones remedii. eadem contrita, addita muria et oleo e menis,[1] anginam eximie curari tradunt, praeterea et in quantalibet lassitudine recreari defessos, etiam cum obmutuerint, si subiciatur linguae; si devoretur, vomitionem sequi salutarem.

128 CV. Rhecoma adfertur ex his quae supra Pontum sunt regionibus. radix costo nigro similis, minor et rufior paulo, sine odore, calfaciens gustu et adstringens. eadem trita vini colorem reddit ad crocum inclinantem. inlita collectiones inflammationesque sedat, vulnera sanat, epiphoras oculorum sedat ex passo, insignita cum melle et alia liventia ex aceto.

129 farina eius inspergitur contra cacoethe et sanguinem reicientibus drachmae pondere in aqua, dysintericis etiam et coeliacis, si febri careant, in vino, sin aliter, ex aqua. facilius teritur nocte antecedente madefacta. datur et decoctum eius bibendum duplici mensura ad rupta, convolsa, contusis, ex sublimi

130 devolutis. si pectoris sint dolores, additur piperis aliquid et murrae, si dissolutio stomachi, ex frigida aqua sumitur, sic et in tussi vetere ac purulentis excreationibus, item hepaticis, splenicis, ischiadicis, ad[2] renium vitia, suspiria, orthopnoeas. arteriae

---

[1] et oleo e menis *hoc ordine codd.*: e menis et oleo *Mayhoff.*
[2] ad *codd.*: at *Mayhoff, qui post* ischiadicis *punctum, post* orthopnoeas *comma ponit.*

---

[a] Mayhoff's reading : " oil and sprats-brine."

CIII. Polyrrhizon has leaves like those of myrtle, *Polyrrhizon.* and many roots These are pounded and given in wine for snake bite. They are also of benefit when quadrupeds are bitten.

CIV. Proserpinaca is a common plant, and an *Proser-* excellent remedy for scorpion stings. It also, they *pinaca.* say, when thoroughly crushed and with the addition of brine and sprats-oil,[a] makes an excellent remedy for quinsy; moreover, however tired one may be, even so weary as to lose one's voice, to put it under the tongue is said to dispel the fatigue; also that to swallow it results in healthful vomiting.

CV. Rhecoma is imported from the regions beyond *Rhecoma.* Pontus. The root resembles dark costus, but is smaller and a little redder, without smell but with a hot, astringent taste. When pounded it also is of a wine-like colour, but inclining to saffron. Used as liniment it reduces gatherings and inflammations, and heals wounds; in raisin wine it relieves eye-fluxes; with honey it removes dark bruises, and in vinegar other livid marks. Powdered it is sprinkled over malignant sores; for spitting of blood a drachma by weight is taken in water; for dysentery too and coeliac disease, should no fever be present, it is given in wine, but where there is fever, in water. It is easier to pound if it is steeped the night before. Its decoction too is given, to be drunk in double doses, for ruptures, sprains, bruises, and tumbles from a height. Should there be pains in the chest, a little quantity of pepper and myrrh is added; should the stomach be relaxed, it is taken in cold water; so also for chronic cough and spitting of pus, like-wise for liver complaints, spleen complaints, sciatica, kidney troubles, asthma, and orthopnoea. Rough-

scabritias sanat ex passo tribus obolis potis trita aut
decoctum eius. lichenas quoque ex aceto inposita
purgat. bibitur contra inflationes et perfrictiones,
febres frigidas, singultus, tormina, herpetas, capitis
gravitates, melancholicas vertigines, lassitudinum
dolores et convolsiones.

131   CVI. Circa Ariminum nota est herba quam rese-
dam vocant. discutit collectiones inflammationesque
omnes. qui curant ea addunt haec verba:

> Reseda, morbis reseda,
> scisne, scisne quis hic pullus egerit radices?
> nec caput nec pedes habeat.

haec ter dicunt totiensque despuunt.

CVII. Stoechas in insulis tantum eiusdem nominis
gignitur, odorata herba coma hysopi, amara gustu.
menses ciet potu, pectoris dolores levat. antidotis
quoque miscetur.

132   CVIII. Solanum Graeci στρυχνόν vocant, ut tradit
Cornelius Celsus. huic vis reprimendi refrigerandique.

133   CIX. Smyrnion caulem habet apii, folia latiora et
maxime circa stolones multos quorum a sinu exiliunt,
pinguia et ad terram infracta, odore medicato cum
quadam acrimonia iucundo, colore in luteum langue-

---

^a A pun on the noun and the verb.
^b Dioscorides says thyme, III 26 : ὁμοίαν ἔχουσα θύμῳ κόμην,
but ὕσσωπος occurs a few words later. See also the note on
coma, p. 482.
^c See Book II 33. In Book VI 6, 2 Celsus speaks of *medi-
camenta reprimentia*.
^d Perhaps " parsley."

ness of the trachea is cured by three-oboli doses of it pounded and taken in raisin wine, or by its decoction. Lichen also is cleared away by an application of the root in vinegar. It is taken in drink for flatulence, chills, feverish shivers, hiccough, colic, herpes, heaviness of the head, bilious giddiness, tired pains, and sprains.

CVI. Around Ariminum is well known the plant *Reseda.* called reseda. It disperses all gatherings and inflammations. Those who use it in treatment add these words:

> Reseda, allay [a] diseases;
> Dost know, dost know, what chick here uprooted
>   thee?
> May he have neither head nor feet.

They say these words three times, and spit three times on the ground.

CVII. Stoechas grows only in the islands of the *Stoechas.* same name, a fragrant plant with the foliage of hyssop [b] and a bitter taste. Taken in drink it is an emmenagogue, and relieves pains in the chest. It is also an ingredient of antidotes.

CVIII. Solanum according to Cornelius Celsus [c] is *Solanum.* called στρυχνόν by the Greeks. It has repressive and cooling properties.

CIX. Smyrnion has a stem like that of celery,[d] and *Smyrnion.* rather broad leaves, which grow mostly about its many shoots, from the curve of which they spring; they are juicy,[e] bending towards the ground, and with a drug-like smell not unpleasing with a sort of sharpness. The colour shades off to yellow; the heads

---

[e] Dioscorides for *pinguia* has ὑπολίπαρα.

scente, capitibus caulium orbiculatis ut apii, semine
rotundo nigroque[1]; arescit incipiente aestate. radix
quoque odorata gustu acri mordet, sucosa, mollis.
cortex eius foris niger, intus pallidus. odor murrae
134 habet qualitatem, unde et nomen. nascitur et in
saxosis collibus et in terrenis. usus eius calfacere,
extenuare. urinam et menses cient folia et radix
et semen, alvum sistit radix, collectiones et suppurationes non veteres item duritias discutit inlita.
prodest et contra phalangia ac serpentes admixto
cachry aut polio aut melissophyllo in vino pota, sed
particulatim, quoniam universitate vomitionem
movet: qua de causa aliquando cum ruta datur.
135 medetur tussi et orthopnoeae semen vel radix, item
thoracis aut lienis aut renium aut vesicae vitiis,
radix autem ruptis, convolsis. partus quoque adiuvat
et secundas pellit. datur et ischiadicis cum crethmo
in vino. sudores ciet et ructus, ideo inflationem
stomachi discutit, vulnera ad cicatricem perducit.
136 exprimitur et sucus radici utilis feminis et thoracis
praecordiorumque desideriis, calfacit enim et concoquit et purgat. semen peculiariter hydropicis datur
potu, quibus et sucus inlinitur. et ad malagmata[2]
cortice arido et ad obsonia utuntur cum mulso et
oleo et garo, maxime in elixis carnibus. sinon
concoctiones facit sapore simillima piperi. eadem in
dolore stomachi efficax.

---

[1] nigroque *Mayhoff* : nigro quod *Basileensis editio, Detlefsen* : nigro qui *codd.*

[2] ad malagmata *ego* : in malagmate *Mayhoff* : malagmate
aut malagmata *sine praepositione codd.*

---

[a] *E.g.* a cough, catarrh or induration.
[b] Professor Andrews thinks that there is a lacuna after
arido.

of the stems are umbellate, as are those of celery; the seed is round and black. It withers at the beginning of summer. The root too has a smell, and a sharp, biting taste, being soft and full of juice. Its skin is dark on the outside, but the inside is pale. The smell has the character of myrrh, whence too the plant gets its name. It grows on rocky hills, and also on those with plenty of earth. It is used for warming and for reducing.[a] Leaves, root, and seed are diuretic and emmenagogues. The root binds the bowels, and an application of it disperses gatherings and suppurations, if not chronic, as well as indurations; mixed with cachry, polium, or melissophyllum, it is also taken in wine to counteract the poison of spiders and serpents, but only a little at a time, for if taken all at once it acts as an emetic, and so is sometimes given with rue. Seed or root is a remedy for cough and orthopnoea, also for affections of thorax, spleen, kidneys or bladder, and the root is for ruptures and sprains; it also facilitates delivery and brings away the after-birth. In wine with crethmos it is also given for sciatica. It promotes sweating and belching, and therefore dispels flatulence of the stomach. It causes wounds to cicatrize. There is also extracted from the root a juice useful for female ailments, and for affections of the thorax and of the hypochondria, for it is warming, digestive and cleansing. The seed is given in drink, especially for dropsy, for which the juice also is used as liniment. The dried skin is used in plasters, and also as a side-dish [b] with honey wine, oil and garum, especially when the meat is boiled.

Sinon tastes very like pepper and aids digestion. *Sinon.* It also is very good for pain in the stomach.

137 CX. Telephion porcilacae similis est et caule et
foliis. rami a radice septeni octonique fruticant
foliis crassis, carnosis. nascitur in cultis et maxime
inter vites. inlinitur lentigini et, cum inaruit,
deteritur. inlinitur et vitiligini ternis fere mensibus,
senis horis noctis aut diei,[1] postea farina hordeacia
inlinatur. medetur et vulneribus et fistulis.

138 CXI. Trichomanes adianto simile est, exilius modo
nigriusque, foliis lenticulae densis, parvis,[2] adversis
inter se. decoctum eius strangurias sanat in vino
albo potum addito cumino rustico. esum[3] cohibet
capillos fluentes, aut si effluxerint, reparat, alopecias-
que densat tritum et in oleo inlitum. sternumenta
quoque gustatu movet.

CXII. Thalictrum folia coriandri habet pinguiora
paulo, caulem papaveris. nascitur ubique, praecipue
in campestribus. medentur ulceribus folia cum
melle.

139 CXIII. Thlaspi duorum generum est: angustis
foliis digitali latitudine et longitudine in terram versis,
in cacumine divisis, cauliculo semipedali, non sine
ramis, peltarum specie semine incluso lenticulae
effigie, nisi quod infringitur, unde nomen. flos albi-
cat. nascitur in semitis et saepibus. semen asperi
gustus bilem et pituitam utrimque extrahit, modus

[1] *Hic* et ut *add. Mayhoff* : aut VRd[1].
[2] parvis *e Theophrasto* (VII 14. 1) *Mayhoff* : amaris *codd.*
[3] esum *Ianus* : lienem *Mayhoff coll. Diosc.* : iesum *codd.*

[a] With Mayhoff's addition of *lienem*, " and also splenic
disease."
[b] See list of diseases.
[c] Dioscorides IV 97 : φύλλα . . . λιπαρώτερα.
[d] See Dioscorides II 156 : οἰονεὶ ἐντεθλασμένον. *Peltae* were

CX. Telephion resembles purslane in both stem *Telephion.* and leaves. Seven or eight branches from the root make a bushy plant with coarse, fleshy leaves. It grows on cultivated ground, especially among vines. It is used as liniment for freckles and rubbed off when dry; it makes liniment also for psoriasis, to be applied for about three months, six hours each night or day; afterwards barley meal should be applied. It is also good treatment for wounds and fistulas.

CXI. Trichomanes resembles adiantum, but is *Tricho-* thinner and darker; the leaves are like those of *manes.* the lentil, closely set, small, and opposite one another. The decoction, taken in white wine, with wild cummin added, cures strangury.[a] Eaten as food it prevents hair falling off, or if it has already done so, restores it. Beaten up and applied in oil it makes a thick growth when there is mange.[b] Sneezing too is provoked by the taste.

CXII. Thalictrum has coriander-like leaves, but a *Thalictrum.* little more fleshy,[c] and the stem of a poppy. It grows everywhere, but particularly in flat, meadowy country. The leaves with honey are good treatment for ulcers.

CXIII. Thlaspi is of two kinds. One has narrow *Thlaspi.* leaves, a finger in breadth and length, turned towards the ground, and divided at the tip. The stem is half a foot long, not without branches, and with seed enclosed in shield-like pods and shaped like a lentil, except that—hence comes the name—it is indented.[d] The blossom is white, and the plant grows in lanes and in hedges. The seed has a sharp taste and brings away bile and phlegm by both vomit and

crescent-shaped shields. Either half of pepper-wort seed-pod is so shaped.

sumendi acetabuli mensura. prodest et ischiadicis
infusum donec sanguinem trahat. menses quoque
140 ciet, sed partus necat. alterum thlaspi aliqui Persicon napy vocant, latis foliis, radicibus magnis, et
ipsum utile ischiadicorum infusioni. prodest et
inguinibus utraque. praecipitur ut qui colligat dicat
sumere se contra inguina et contra omnes collectiones
et contra vulnera, una manu tollat.

141 CXIV. Trachinia herba qualis sit non traditur.
credo falsum et promissum Democriti portentosum
esse, adalligatam triduo absumere lienes.

CXV. Tragonis sive tragion nascitur in Cretae
tantum insulae maritimis, iunipiro similis et semine
et folio et ramis. sucus eius lacteus in cummim
spissatus vel semen in potione spicula e corpore eicit.
tunditur recens et cum vino inlinitur aut siccae farina
cum melle. eadem lactis abundantiam facit mam-
misque unice medetur.

142 CXVI. Est et alia herba tragos quam aliqui
scorpion vocant, semipedem alta, fruticosa, sine
foliis, pusillis racemis rubentibus grani tritici, acuto
cacumine, et ipsa in maritimis nascens. huius
racemorum[1] x aut xii cacumina trita ex vino pota
coeliacis, dysintericis, sanguinem excreantibus mensumque abundantiae auxiliantur.

---

[1] racemorum e Diosc. Mayhoff : ramorum codd., Detlefsen.

---

[a] I.e. like an enema.
[b] Probably a mistake of Pliny's. Dioscorides (II 156) has
only ἄγει δὲ καὶ αἷμα. Mayhoff would change donec to potione,
but the ποθὲν after αἷμα is, according to Wellmann, a part of
the next clause.
[c] " Persian mustard."
[d] Mayhoff's emendation racemorum for the ramorum of the
MSS. is confirmed by Dioscorides IV 51 : ἐπὶ δὲ τῶν κλάδων

stools. The measure of a dose is an acetabulum. Injections [a] are good for sciatica, if continued until they draw blood.[b] It is also an emmenagogue but kills the foetus. The other thlaspi is called by some Persicon napy; [c] it has broad leaves and large roots, while the plant itself is useful to make an injection for sciatica. Both kinds are good for affections of the groin. The picker is recommended to say that he is taking it as a remedy for the groin, all kinds of gatherings, and wounds. He should lift it with one hand.

CXIV. We are not told the nature of the plant *Trachinia.* trachinia. I think it untrue, and the assurance of Democritus fantastic, that used as an amulet it consumes the spleen in three days.

CXV. Tragonis, or tragion, grows only on the *Tragonis.* shores of the island of Crete, and resembles juniper in seed, leaf and branches. Its milky juice, hardened into gum, or its seed taken in drink, brings away sharp points embedded in the flesh. For use as liniment it is beaten up when fresh and applied with wine, or it is dried, powdered, and applied with honey. It also promotes abundance of milk, and is a specific for ailments of the breasts.

CXVI. There is also another plant, tragos, called *Tragos.* by some scorpion, half a foot high, bushy, without leaves, and bearing tiny red clusters with wheat-like seeds, and pointed at the extremity. This plant too grows in coastal districts. Ten or twelve extremities of clusters,[d] pounded and taken in wine, are good for coeliac affections, dysentery, spitting of blood, and excessive menstruation.

πρόσκεινται οἰονεὶ ῥᾶγες μικραί, πυρραί, κατὰ μέγεθος πυροῦ, ὀξεῖαι ἐπ᾽ ἄκρου . . . τούτου ὁ καρπός, ὡς ῥᾶγες δέκα, σὺν οἴνῳ ποθεῖαι κοιλιακοὺς καὶ ῥοϊκὰς ὠφελοῦσι.

CXVII. Est et tragopogon quem alii comen vocant, caule parvo, foliis croci, radice longa dulci, super caulem calice lato nigro. nascitur in asperis manditurque, sine usu.

143 CXVIII. Et de herbis quidem memoria digna hactenus accepimus aut comperimus. in fine earum admonere non ab re iudicamus alias aliis virium aetates esse. longissimo tempore durat elaterium, ut diximus, chamaeleon niger XL annis, centaurium non ultra XII, peucedanum et aristolochia ad VI, vitis silvestris anno, in umbra si serventur. et animalium quidem exterorum nullum aliud radices a nobis dictas adtingit excepta sphondyle quae omnes persequitur. genus id serpentis est.

144 CXIX. Ne illud quidem dubitatur, omnium radicum vim effectusque minui, si fructus prius ematurescant, item seminum ante radice propter sucum incisa, resolvitur autem omnium vis consuetudine, et desinunt prodesse, cum opus est, quae cottidie in usu fuere aeque quam nocere. omnes vero herbae vehementiores effectu viribusque sunt in frigidis et in aquilonis, item siccis.

145 CXX. Sunt et gentium differentiae non mediocres, sicut accipimus de taeniis lumbricisque, inesse Aegypti, Arabiae, Syriae, Ciliciae populis, e diverso Threciae, Phrygiae omnino non innasci. minus id mirum quam quod in confinio Atticae et Boeotiae Thebanis

---

[a] See Book XX § 5.

[b] This phrase is probably an interpolation, a marginal note added to the text.

[c] Or " seed."

CXVII. There is also tragopogon, called by some *Tragopogon.* *come*, with a small stem, leaves like those of saffron, a long, sweet root, and at the top of the stem a broad, dark calyx. It grows on rugged soils, and is eaten but never used in medicine.

CXVIII. Such is all that I have been told or dis- *Age and* covered worth recording about plants. At the close, *plants.* I think it not out of place to add a warning that their properties vary with their age. As I have said,[a] elaterium lasts longest, dark chamaeleon forty years, centaury not more than twelve, peucedanum and aristolochia up to six, and the wild vine one year— that is, if they are kept in the shade. And of external animals indeed none attack the roots that I have mentioned except the sphondyle, a kind of creeping thing,[b] which infests them all.

CXIX. There is no doubt either that the potency *Drugs and* and efficacy of all roots are lessened if the fruit[c] *habit.* ripens before they are dug, and it is the same with seeds if the root has been cut previously for the sake of the juice. The properties moreover of all plants are weakened by habit, and they cease to be beneficial when needed if they have been in daily use; similarly with harmful plants. All plants however have greater efficacy and potency when they grow in cold regions subject to north-east winds, and likewise those that grow in dry.

CXX. There are also considerable differences between races. I have heard for instance about tapeworms and maw-worms, that they infest the peoples of Egypt, Arabia, Syria and Cilicia, while on the contrary they are never found at all among those of Thrace and Phrygia. This is less remarkable than their being found among the Thebans, but not among

innascuntur, cum absint Atheniensibus. quae con-
146 templatio aufert nos ad ipsorum animalium naturas
ingenitasque his vel certiores morborum omnium
medicinas. rursus enim cum rerum[1] parens nullum
animal ad hoc tantum ut pasceretur aut alia satiaret
nasci voluit, artesque salutares inseruit et visceribus,
quippe cum surdis etiam rebus insereret, tum vero
illa animae auxilia praestantissima ex alia anima
esse voluit contemplatione ante cuncta mirabili.

[1] rursus enim cum rerum *Mayhoff* : rursus enim eam rem
tractabimus, quandoquidem natura omnium rerum *Detlefsen* :
rursus enim eam rem (ea re d T) *codd.*

the Athenians, although Attica and Boeotia are adjoining territories. That thought brings me to the nature of animals themselves, and to the remedies for all diseases, of even greater reliability, that are implanted in them at birth. For again, the Mother of all creation both willed that no animal should be born merely to eat or to satisfy the appetites of others, implanting also healthful medicines in their vitals, because she was implanting them even in unconscious things, and she also willed that those outstanding aids to life should come from another life, a thought beyond all else most wonderful.

ADDITIONAL NOTES

The word *coma* in Pliny, like κόμη in Greek, is sometimes perplexing when it is used, not literally, but of a part of a plant or tree. This is especially true when the word *folium* occurs in the immediate context.

When used in its strict sense *coma* is the hair of the head, and so can be coupled with *barba*. We should expect, therefore, to find it used figuratively of anything that grows at the top of a plant or tree, such as the tuft of a bulrush; see Pliny XXVI § 62 *in cacuminibus coma iunci*. In several passages, however, *coma* seems to be foliage generally, while *folium* is used of a single leaf. Examples are :

XII § 113. *folium proximum tuberi, perpetua coma.*
XVI § 84. *neque his autem quae semper retinent comas eadem folia durant.*
XIX § 102. *schistam hieme cum coma sua relinquunt, vere folia detrahunt.*

In Dioscorides IV § 129 there is a distinct contrast between φύλλα and κόμη, which leads Mayhoff in the parallel passage of Pliny (XXVII § 93) to substitute *coma* for the *concava* of the MSS. Here Mayhoff suggests, without adopting it, *comantia*, citing as a parallel XIII § 59, *semper comantibus foliis*. Here, however, the addition of *semper* makes a difference. Leaves can be *semper comantia*, " evergreen," but one could hardly say that the leaves are " like those of wild myrtle, *comantia, spinosa.*" The passage of Dioscorides reads : μυρσίνη ἀγρία . . . ἔχων τὰ φύλλα ὅμοια, κόμην δὲ ἀκανθώδη κ.τ.λ. Here there seems to be a real difference between the two words, nor can κόμη be a filament, as that could hardly be ἀκανθώδης.

There remain those passages where *comae* means " hair-like filaments," the clearest being XXVI § 133 : *dependere comis iunceis multis, nigris, ut ex equorum cauda.* Two dubious instances near the beginning of Book XXVII call for special notice. In § 26 we have : *comae tritae sanguineo suco*

ADDITIONAL NOTES

manant, the corresponding words in Dioscorides being (III 156) πεφοινιγμένος τὰ ῥαβδία; in § 37 : *comae tritae velut cruentant*, the Greek being (III 155) ἄνθη . . . ἐν τῷ παρατριβῆναι οἱονεὶ αἱμάσσοντα τοὺς δακτύλους.

Apparently Pliny here may be localizing the staining substance. He seems to put it in the filament, the hair-like part of the stamen that supports the anther.

Summing up we may say that *coma* means :

(1) everything except the bare skeleton of stem (trunk) and branches, *i.e.* foliage and its appendages;
(2) a tuft;
(3) any hair-like part of a plant.

ADDITIONAL NOTE ON XXIV § 166

It is obvious from the phrases *pulchros bonosque* of this section and *pulchri bonique et fortunati* of XXVI § 19, both of which profess to report Democritus, that Pliny had before him some case of καλὸς κἀγαθός, and that it, or some variant of it, gives the general sense here. Why the text has been corrupted, as it obviously has, is a puzzle, for the meaning is both clear and easy. The reading of Detlefsen and Mayhoff, with *bonis*, is hard to translate, implying that the parents must be *boni*. I have printed (within daggers) the vulgate text, which is that of the MS. X. Perhaps the *excellentis* of the MS. d is right, and the original was merely *excellentis animi et formae* with *partum* (Mayhoff suggests *excellentem* for *excellentes*) understood. *Bonos* or *bonis* may be later insertions.

Alternatively, *formae* may be a corruption of *formosos* or *fortunatos*. Improbable as this is, it is less improbable than the actual corruptions which occurred in a phrase so plain and so simple.

ADDITIONAL NOTE ON XXVII § 92

The *hippophaeston* is usually a thistle of uncertain identity used by fullers. But in XVI 244 it is a species of *Cuscuta* parasitic on the *spina fullonia*, which is the teasel, *Dipsacus fullonum*. In XXVII 92 it is again this parasitic *Cuscuta*, and the *spinae* are the teasel. In XXIV 111 Pliny says specifically that the fullers' pots are filled (*inplentur*) with this *spina*. Hence the only trouble in XXVII 92 is the word *fiunt*, which perhaps should be amended to *inplentur*.

INDEX OF PLANTS

(Further revised by A. C. Andrews)

Problems incidental to the identification of plants mentioned by Pliny have already been discussed (Vol. VI, Introd., pp. xvi–xviii).

The identifications of such early editors of the *Natural History* as Hardouin (1713), Fée (1826), Bostock and Riley (1855), and Littré (1855) are unreliable, since data on the actual flora of Italy and Greece were then inexact; and there has been no systematic, comprehensive approach to the problem in the succeeding century. Many of the plants mentioned by Pliny are discussed also by Dioscorides; but the more recent editions of Dioscorides, such as those of Berendes (1902) and Gunther (1934), mostly list the identifications of such early scholars as Sprengel, Fraas, and Daubeny. As for Theophrastus, only in the case of Sir William Thiselton-Dyer's index of plants in the LCL edition of his *Enquiry into Plants* by Sir Arthur Hort is consideration given to the scientific enumeration of the native plants of Greece by E. de Halácsy in his *Conspectus florae Graecae* (1901–1904, supplements 1908 and 1912) and special research prosecuted by De Candolle, Hanbury, Yule, Schweinfurth, Bretzl, and others. Halácsy's work has been refined by M. Rikli and E. Rübel in their article, " Über Flora und Vegetation von Kreta und Griechenland " (*Vierteljahrsschrift der naturforschenden Gesellschaft in Zürich*, 68 [1923], pp. 103–227), and there is also available Rikli's general survey of the Mediterranean flora, *Das Pflanzenkleid der Mittelmeerländer* (1943 and 1946). As for Italy, we now have Adriano Fiori's comprehensive survey, *Nuova flora analitica d'Italia* (1923–1929), and Eugenio Baroni's briefer compendium, *Guida botanica d'Italia* (1932). Problems relative to cultivated plants have been considerably clarified by the work of Elisabeth Schiemann (*Die Entstehung*

485

INDEX OF PLANTS

der Kulturpflanzen, 1932) and Karl and Franz Bertsch (*Geschichte unserer Kulturpflanzen*, 2nd ed., 1949). The new edition of the *Greek-English Lexicon* of Liddell and Scott draws upon most of these sources and is very helpful in those instances in which Pliny cites Greek plant names.

Nevertheless, identification of Pliny's plant names is still often difficult and sometimes impossible. It is necessary frequently to qualify the identification by " probably," " possibly," or " perhaps," or simply to say " unknown." Pliny's practice of citing several secondary names for a plant, adopted from certain of the pharmaceutical sources he consulted, involves much overlapping. In the index, the identification is regularly coupled with the primary name, and with this the secondary names are equated.

INDEX OF PLANTS

201, XXIX 46, XXXIII 146. In XVI 66–67 acer album or Gallicum is the sycamore maple, *Acer pseudoplatanus*; a. crassivenium is perhaps the common maple, *A. campestre*; a. pavonaceum = opulus; a. rubens = zygia; and a. campestre and a. montanum = glinon.

Achaemenis, perhaps a variety of ancient milkwort, *Euphorbia antiquorum*, XXIV 161, XXVI 18.

Achilleos (also achillea and achillia), Achilles' woundwort, *Achillea tomentosa*, *A. millefolium*, *A. ptarmica*, and *A. magna*, XXV 42, 164, XXVI 51, 131, 151.

Achne pyros, mezerlon, *Daphne mezereum*, XIII 114.

Achynops, rib grass, a plantain, *Plantago lanceolata* (? κύνοψ Theophrastus VII 7, 3), XXI 89, 101 (emended).

Acinos, perhaps wild basil, *Ocimum basilicum*, or (Littré) acinos, *Thymus acinos*, XXI 174.

Aconitum, wolf's bane, *Aconitum anthora*, VI 4, VIII 100, XX 50, 132, XXII 18, XXIII 43, 92, 135, XXV 163, XXVII 4–10, XXVIII 161, XXIX 74, 105.

Acopon(-os)=anagyros, XXVII 30.

Acorna, a thistle, perhaps welted thistle, *Cnicus acarna*, XXI 94, 95.

Acoron (-um), yellow flag iris, *Iris pseudacorus*, or sweet flag, *Acorus calamus*, XIV 111, XXV 157, 164, XXVI 28, 35, 45, 74, 77, 80, 91, 127, 137, 160, 163. In XXV 144 prob-

ably a mistake for corchoron; in XV 27 = chamaemyrsine; in XXV 158 = root of oxymyrsine.

Actaea, baneberry, *Actaea spicata*, XXVII 43.

Acte, usually the elder, *Sambucus nigra*, identified in XXVI 120 with ebulum, usually the dwarf elder, *S. ebulus*.

Adamantis, unknown, XXIV 162.

Adiantum, black maidenhair, *Adiantum capillus Veneris*, or maidenhair spleenwort, *Asplenium trichomanes*, XXI 100, XXII 62–65, XXVII 49, 138, XXVIII 163.

Adipsos, (1) a kind of date, XII 103; (2) = glycyrrhiza, XXII 26.

Ador (adoreum), emmer wheat, *Triticum dicoccum*, XVIII 14, 81, 163, 166, 191.

Aegilops in XVI 22 and 33, Turkey oak, *Quercus cerris*, elsewhere the grass *Aegilops ovata*, XVIII 155, XXI 103, XXV 146, XXVI 130.

Aegoceras, fenugreek, *Trigonella foenum graecum*, XXIV 184.

Aegolethron, rosebay, chiefly common azalea, *Rhododendron ponticum*, XXI 74.

Aera, darnel, *Lolium temulentum*, XVIII 155, 156, XXI 129 (emend.), XXII 125, XXIV 100.

Aeschynomene, sensitive plant, *Mimosa asperata*, XXIV 167.

Aesculus, chestnut oak, *Quercus sessiliflora*, XII 3, XVI 11, 17, 19, 20, 25, 37, 106, 127, 219, XVII 151.

Aethalium, a kind of grape, XIV 74.

Aethiopis, perhaps silver sage,

487

INDEX OF PLANTS

INDEX OF PLANTS

Altercum or altercangenum = hyoscyamos, XXV 35.

Althaea, marsh mallow, *Althaea officinalis*, XX 129, 222, 229.

Alum, a term applied to several different plants, in Pliny usually a type of comfrey, Symphytum, esp. *S. officinale*, XIX 116, XXVII 31. See also Halus.

Alypon, globe daisy, *Globularia alypum*, XXVII 22.

Alysson, madwort, *Asperugo procumbens*, or madder, *Rubia peregrina*, XXIV 95.

Amaracus, sweet marjoram, *Majorana hortensis*, XIII 5, 13, 14, 18, XXI 37, 59, 61, 67, 163, 176. In XXI 176 a secondary name for pellitory, *Parietaria officinalis*.

Amarantus, cockscomb, *Celosia cristata*, or amaranth, *Amaranthus caudatus*, XXI 47, 68.

Ambrosia = aizoüm maius, XXV 160; = artemisia, XXV 74, XXVII 28, 55; a kind of grape, XXVII 40.

Ambubaia = intubus erraticus, wild chicory, *Cichorium* sp., XX 73.

Amerimnon, house-leek, *Sempervivum tectorum*, XXV 160.

Ami, has been identified as bishop's weed, *Carum copticum* (*Ammi copticum*), and picktooth, *Ammi visnaga*, XX 163, 264.

Amomis a substitute for amomum, XII 49.

Amomum, a product probably of one or more of the usual cardamom substitutes, such as *Amomum subulatum*, *A. cardamomum*, and *A. krevanh*, XII 48, 50, XIII 15, 16, 18, XIV 107, XVI 134, XXVI 34, 105, XXXVII 204.

Ampelodesmos, esparto, *Lygeum spartum*, XVII 209.

Ampeloprason, wild leek, *Allium ampeloprasum*, XXIV 136.

Ampelos agria, probably black bryony, *Tamus communis*, XXVII 44. In XXIII 19 = labrusca.

Ampelos leuce = vitis alba, XXIII 21.

Amygdala, almond, *Prunus amygdalus*, XII 25, 36, 37, 56, 125, XIII 8, 19, 60, 66, XV 26, 42, 89, 109, 114, XVI 83, 86, 103, 109, 117, XVII 11, 63, 88, 131, 135, 237, 248, 252, XXIII 85, 144–145, XXIV 22, XXVI 111, XXVIII 254. Amygdala amara, vars. *amara* and Webii (XV 252); a. dulcis, var. *sativa* (*ibid.*); a. putamine fragili, var. *fragilis* (XV 90).

Amygdalites = platyphyllos, XXVI 70.

Anabasis = ephedra, XXVI 36; = equisaetum, XXVII 133.

Anacampseros, perhaps *Sedum anacampseros*, XXIV 167.

Anagallis, pimpernel, *Anagallis arvensis*, incl. subsp. *phoenicea* and *caerulea*, XXV 144, 166, XXVI 35, 55, 80, 90, 102, 118, 119, 144.

Anagyros, stinking bean-trefoil, *Anagyris foetida*, XXVII 30.

Anarrinon, *v.l.* for pararinon *aut sim.*, XXV 129.

Anchusa, alkanet, *Anchusa officinalis*, XIII 7, 9, 10, XXI 85, 99, 121, XXII 48, 50, XXVII 59, 110, XXVIII 151, XXXII 85, XXXVII 48. In XXII 51 a secondary name for onochilon. The type also

489

INDEX OF PLANTS

called rhinoclia (XXVII 59) is dyer's bugloss, *Alkanna tinctoria*.

Andrachle (andrachne), (1) andrachne, *Arbutus andrachne*, XIII 120, XVI 80, XVII 234; (2) purslane, *Portulaca oleracea*, XIII 120, XXV 162.

Androsaces, sea-navel, *Acetabularia mediterranea*, or white coralline, *Corallina officinalis*, XXVII 25.

Androsaemon, perfoliate St. John's wort, *Hypericum perfoliatum*, XXVII 26, 37.

Anemone, usually poppy anemone, *Anemone coronaria*, XXI 64, 65, 99, 164, XXV 102, 151, XXVI 109; = othonna, XXVII 109. The wild form is *A. blanda* in Greece and *A. apennina* in Italy.

Anesum, anise, *Pimpinella anisum*, XIX 167, XX 185–195, 249, 253, 264, XXVII 94, XXVIII 100, XXX 115.

Anetum, dill, *Anethum graveolens*, XIII 123, XIX 62, 117, 119, 123, 124, 167, 170, 186, 188, XX 21, 87, 110, 191, 196, 260, XXII 77, XXVIII 97, 208, XXIX 47, 70, 80, 121, XXXI 119, XXXII 94, 101.

Angemon, Avens, Geum urbanum, but in XXIV 6 = Lappa canaria.

Anicetum = anesum, XX 186.

Anonis (see also Ononis), restharrow, *Ononis antiquorum*, XXI 91, 98, XXVII 29.

Anonymos, "nameless plant," XXVII 31.

Anthalium, earth-almond, *Cyperus esculentus*, XXI 88, 175.

Anthedon, Oriental thorn, *Crataegus orientalis*, XV 84.

Anthemis, wild chamomile, *Matricaria chamomilla*, also *Anthemis chia*, XXI 99, 103, XXVI 87. Other species of *Anthemis* may be referred to in XXII 53.

Anthericus, stalk of asphodel, XXI 109, XXII 67, XXVII 14.

Anthophoros = smilax, XXIV 83.

Anthyllis, herb ivy, *Ajuga iva*, XXVI 84, 160.

Anthyllium, Cretan pitch-plant, *Cressa cretica*, XXI 175, XXVI 84.

Anthyllum = anthyllium, XXI 175.

Anticyricon, the second type of sesamoides, *s.v.*, XXII 133.

Antirrhinum, snapdragon, *Antirrhinum orontium*, XXV 129, XXVI 155.

Antiscorodon, Cyprian garlic, a form of *Allium sativum*, XIX 112.

Aparine, bedstraw, *Galium aparine*, XXVII 32.

Aphaca, tare, *Vicia sativa*, XXI 89, 99, 100, 105, XXVII 38.

Apharce, hybrid arbutus, *Arbutus hybrida*, XIII 121.

Aphron = mecon aphrodes (1), XX 207.

Apiaca brassica, "celery" cabbage, from its crisped leaves, Savoy cabbage, *Brassica oleracea sabauda*, XIX 136.

Apiana, a kind of grape, XIV 81.

Apiastrum, balm, *Melissa officinalis*, XX 116, XXI 53; in XXI 70 perhaps *Selinum palustre*. The poisonous type mentioned in XX 116 is perhaps a *Ranunculus*.

Apios ischas, a spurge, *Euphorbia apios*, XXVI 72.

INDEX OF PLANTS

491

INDEX OF PLANTS

INDEX OF PLANTS

and *A. microcarpus*, XXI 108, XXII 31, 67–72, 73, XXVI 147.

Asplenon, scale fern, *Asplenium ceterach*, XXVII 34.

Astaphis = staphis, XXIII 17.

Aster, Italian aster, *Aster amellus*, XXVII 36.

Astercum, wall-pellitory, *Parietaria officinalis*, XXII 43.

Astragalus, Spanish tragacanth, *Astragalus baeticus*, XXVI 46, 131, 145, 147.

Asyla = felis oculus, unknown, XXV 145.

Ateramon, see Teramon.

Atinia, loose-flowering elm, *Ulmus effusa*, XVI 72, 108, XVII 200, 208.

Attractylis, distaff-thistle, *Carthamus lanatus*, XXI 95; = cnecos, XXI 90, 184.

Atriplex, orache, *Atriplex hortense*, XIX 99, 117, 119, 120, 123, 170, 181, XX 219. The wild form (XIX 117, XX 219–221) is perhaps *Atriplex nitens* or *Chenopodium album*.

Auleticon, a kind of reed, XVI 169.

Avena, oats, *Avena sativa*, IV 95, VI 188, XVII 56, XVIII 61, 143, 149–150, 205, XXI 129, XXII 137, 161, XXIX 143, XXX 38, 75. See also Bromos.

Babbia, a kind of olive, XV 15.

Baccar, hazelwort, *Asarum europaeum*, XXI 29, 30, 132, 133, 135, XXVI 113.

Baccaris (XII 45, XXI 29) = baccar.

Bacchica, a kind of ivy, XVI 147.

Balanitis, chestnut, *Castanea vesca*, XV 93.

Balanos, normally a term for an acorn, in XII 121, XIII 8, 12, 13, 15, XXII 149 rather the fruit of the Egyptian balsam, *Balanites aegyptiaca*, or perhaps the behen-nut, *Moringa oleifera*, in XIII 61 the tree. Balanos Sardianos and Dios balanos (XV 92) are the chestnut, *Castanea vesca*.

Balis, perhaps the squirting cucumber, *Momordica elaterium*, XXV 14.

Balisca, a kind of grape-vine, XIV 30.

Ballote = porrum nigrum, black horehound, *Ballota nigra*, XXVII 54.

Balsamodes, a type of cassia, XII 97.

Balsamum, balsam of Mecca, *Commiphora opobalsamum*, XII 111–123, XII 8, 11, 13, 15, XV 30, XVI 111–123, 135, XXIII 92.

Bananica, a kind of grape-vine, XIV 37.

Barba Iovis, silver-leaved woolblade, *Anthyllis barba Jovis*, XVI 76.

Basilicon (caryon), walnut, *Juglans regia* XV 87.

Batis hortensis, samphire or sea fennel, *Crithmum maritimum*, and batis marina, sea-kale, *Crambe maritima*, XXI 86. See also XXI 174.

Batrachion, celandine, *Ranunculus* sp., XXVI 106, 150, 157; = ranunculus, XXV 172; = polyanthemum, XXVII 112.

Bdellium, vine-palm, *Borassus flabelliformis*, XII 35. Pliny is vague in this passage, and apparently uses bdellium of both tree and gum.

493

INDEX OF PLANTS

Bechion, colt's foot, *Tussilago farfara*, XXVI 30. The second type, also called salvia (XXVI 31), is perhaps *Verbascum lychnitis*.

Bellio, yellow ox-eye daisy, *Chrysanthemum segetum*, XXI 49.

Bellis, white daisy, *Bellis perennis*, XXVI 26.

Beta, beet, *Beta vulgaris*, XIX 86, 98, 113, 117, 118, 119, 122, 132–136, 181, 182, XX 69–72, 220, XXII 61, 143, 144, XXIV 150, XXV 44, 48, XXVI 50, 58, XXVII 22, XXVIII 209, 214, XXIX 40. Beta candida is probably *Beta cicla*, XIX 132, XX 69. Beta silvestris is *B. maritima*, XX 72.

Betulla, birch, *Betula alba*, XVI 74, 176, 209.

Bimammia, a kind of grape-vine, XIV 41.

Blachnon (blechnon), male fern, *Aspidium filix mas*, XXVII 78.

Blattaria, moth mullein, *Verbascum blattaria*, XXV 108.

Blechon, pennyroyal, *Mentha pulegium*, XX 156.

Blitum, primarily blite, *Amaranthus blitum*, secondarily *A. retroflexus*, *Blitum Bonus-Henricus*, and *Euxolus viridis*, XIX 99, 117, 119, XX 252.

Boletus, mushroom, usually *Agaricus caesarius*, but probably also *Boletus edulis*, XVI 31, XXII 92, XXIII 116, XXIX 103.

Bombycia, a kind of reed, XVI 169.

Botane hiera = verbenaca, XXV 105.

Botrys, usually denotes a grape cluster, but = artemisia, XXV 74, XXVII 28, 55.

Brabilla, probably the sloe, *Prunus spinosa*, or the bullace, *P. insititia*, XXVII 55.

Brace, perhaps spelt, *Triticum spelta*, otherwise a soft emmer, *T. dicoccum*, XVIII 62.

Brassica, cabbage, *Brassica oleracea*, XIX 135, 136, 137, 143, 167, 176, XX 78–96, 127, XXII 151, XXIV 158, XXV 120, XXVI 118, XXVII 96, XXVIII 81, XXIX 106, XXX 24, 30. Brassica selinas, or " celery " cabbage, is Savoy cabbage, *Brassica oleracea sabauda*, XX 79. The wild form (*e.g.*, XX 92) is generally *Brassica cretica*. Brassica marina in XX 96 is perhaps *Convolvulus soldanella*.

Brathy, savin, *Juniperus sabina*, and odorous cedar, *J. foetidissima*, XXIV 102.

Bratus, a tree resembling the cypress, XII 78.

Britannica, grainless dock, *Rumex aquaticus*, XXV 20, 99, XXVII 2.

Brochos or brochon = fruit (gum) of bdellium, XII 35.

Bromos, oats, *Avena sativa*, XVIII 93, XXII 161.

Brya, tamarisk, *Tamarix africana* and *orientalis*, XIII 116, XXIV 69.

Bryon, green laver, *Ulva lactuca*, XII 108, 132, XIII 2, 137, XXIII 137, XXVII 56, XXXII 110. In XXIV 27 = sphagnos (1).

Bryonia, bryony. (1) the black type is white bryony, *Bryonia alba*, (2) the white type, common bryony, *B. dioica*,

494

INDEX OF PLANTS

or perhaps Cretan bryony, *B. cretica*. See XXIII 21–28 with many alternative names to each.

Bubonion = aster, XXVII 36.

Buceras, fenugreek, *Trigonella foenum-graecum*, XXI 37, XXIV 184.

Bucolicon, a kind of panaces, XXV 31.

Buconiates, a kind of grape, XIV 39.

Buglossos, Italian alkanet, *Anchusa italica*, XXV 81, XXVI 116.

Bulapathon, patience dock, *Rumex patientia*, XX 235.

Bulbine (or bolbine), star of Bethlehem, *Ornithogalum umbellatum*, XIX 95, XX 107.

Bulbus (or bolbos), the bulb of any small, onion-like plant (XIX 60, 93), or of the reed, *Arundo donax* (XVII 144), or the plant itself (XVII 87, XIX 95, XX 102), or *Pancratium maritimum* (XIX 32), but most of all the tassel-hyacinth, *Leopoldia comosa*. See XVIII 34, XIX 93, 97, 99, 109, 121, 134, XX 102–106, 107, XXI 107, XXIII 62, XXV 131, XXVIII 192, 197, XXIX 44, XXX 73.

Bumastus, a kind of grape, XIV 15, 42.

Bumelia, an ash, *Fraxinus excelsior*, XVI 63.

Bunias, French turnip, *Brassica napus*, XX 21.

Bunion, cited as a term for a kind of navew, actually probably *Bunium pumilum* or *B. bulbocastanum*, XX 21.

Buphthalmus. In XXV 82 the yellow daisy, *Chrysanthemum coronarium*; in XXV 160 a type of house-leek, probably *Sempervivum arboreum*.

Bupleuron, of uncertain identity, *Ammi majus*, *Bupleurum rigidum*, and *B. baldluse* suggested, but dubious, XXII 77, XXVII 57.

Buprestis, hare's ear, *Bupleurum protractum*, XXII 78.

Buselinum, Cretan alexanders, *Smyrnium perfoliatum*, XX 118.

Buxus, box-tree, *Buxus sempervirens*, VI 79, XI 46 (*emend.* Detlef.), XVI 70, 71, 73, 80, 92, 120, 121, 172, 183, 204, 212, 221, 226, 227, 230, 231, XVII 163, XXI 83, XXIII 28, XXX 97, XXXIV 133, XXXV 77.

Caccalia = leontice, *Mercurialis tomentosa*, XXV 135, XXVI 29, 163.

Cachla (*v.l.*) = buphthalmus, XXV 82.

Cactos, cardoon, *Cynara cardunculus*, XXI 97.

Cadytas, a dodder, *Cuscuta filiformis*, XVI 244.

Caerefolium, chervil, *Anthriscus cerefolium*, XIX 170.

Caesapon, a kind of wild lettuce, *Lactuca*, XX 59.

Calabrix, perhaps buckthorn, *Rhamnus infectorius*, XVII 75. Fournier proposes the oxyacanth, *Crataegus oxyacanthus*.

Calamus, (1) reed, *Arundo donax*, V 44, VI 166, XII 104–106, XIII 8, 9, 10, 11, 12, 13, 15, 18, 73, XIV 92, 107, 112, XV 30, XVI 80, 157, 159, XVII 102, 107, 114, 168, XXIX 56, XXX 104, XXXII 141; (2) as a foreign plant, sweet flag, *Acorus calamus*, V

INDEX OF PLANTS

44, XII 22, 104, XIII 8, 11, 18, 73; (3) calamus Laconicus is perhaps reed canary-grass, *Phalaris arundinacea*, XVI 166.

Calcetum, *v.l.* for chalcetum, *s.v.*, XXVI 40.

Calchas = buphthalmus, XXV 82.

Calcifraga, perhaps hartstongue, *Asplenium scolopendrium*, or smooth sea-heath, *Frankenia hirsuta*, and powdery sea-heath, *F. pulverulenta*, XXVII 75.

Calicia, a plant supposed to make water freeze, unknown, XXIV 156. See p. 110, note *a*.

Callion = vesicaria, XXI 177.

Callithrix, maidenhair spleenwort, *Asplenium trichomanes*, XXV 132, 135, XXVI 87, 147, 160.

Callitrichon = adiantum, XXII 62.

Caltha, perhaps marigold, *Calendula officinalis*, XXI 28.

Calventina, a kind of grapevine, XIV 38.

Calyx (calsa in MSS.), (1) perhaps monk's-hood, *Arum arisarum*, XXVII 58; (2) = anchusa, alkanet, *Anchusa officinalis*, XXVII 59.

Camararium, climbing gourd, *Cucurbita longior*, XIX 70.

Cammaron = aconitum, XXVII 9.

Cancamum, an Arabian gum, from *Balsamodendron Katuf*, XII 98.

Cannabis, hemp, *Cannabis sativa*, XIX 29, 63, 173, XX 259, XXV 65. Cannabis silvestris is a species of marsh mallow, *Althaea cannabina*, XX 259.

Cantabrica, Cantabrian bindweed, *Convolvulus cantabrica*, XXV 85, 101.

Canthareos, a kind of grapevine, XIV 75.

Canthyllion, *v.l.* for anthyllion, XXVI 84.

Canthyllis, *v.l.* for anthyllis, *s.v.*, XXVI 160.

Capnos, a kind of grape, XIV 39.

Capnos fruticosa, XXV 156, fumitory, *Fumaria officinalis* (Littré), and capnos trunca, XXV 155, XXVI 57, *Corydalis digitata* (Littré). In XXVI 35 merely capnos. Both are fumitories. See note on XXV 155. Dioscorides gives only one kind (IV 109).

Capparis (cappari), caper, *Capparis spinosa*, XIII 127, XV 15, 117, XIX 163, XX 165–167, XXIV 97, 121, XXVII 27, 95, XXVIII 242, XXIX 80.

Caprificus, the male fig-tree or caprifig, *Ficus carica*, XI 40, 118, XII 35, XIV 134, XV 79, 80, XVI 95, 114, 227, XVII 225, 242, 254, 256, XXIII 126–130, XXXIV 133.

Carbonica, a kind of grape-vine, XIV 43.

Carcinothron = polygonus, knotgrass, *Polygonum aviculare*, XXVII 113.

Cardamomum, cardamom, esp. *Elettaria cardamomum*, XII 50, XIII 8, 12, XV 30.

Cardamum, garden cress, *Lepidium sativum*, XIX 118.

Carduus, (1) a thistle-like growth, XII 72; (2) a generic term for thistles, XVIII 153, XXI 91, 94, 96; (3) the golden thistle, *Scolymus hispanicus*, XX 262; (4) the cardoon, *Cynara cardunculus*, wild or

INDEX OF PLANTS

cultivated, XIX 55, 152–153, XX 262.

Careum, caraway, *Carum carui*, XIX 164.

Caro(s) = hypericon, XXVI 86, 119, 130.

Carphos = fenum Graecum, XXIV 184.

Carpinus, hornbeam, *Carpinus betulus*, XVI 67, 73, 74, 75, 193, 206, 226, 230, XVII 201, XXVIII 191.

Carpophyllon, kind of laurel, XV 131.

Caryites, a kind of tithymalus, XXVI 66.

Caryon = iuglans, XV 87.

Caryophyllon, dried flower-bud of clove-tree, *Eugenia caryophyllata*, XII 30.

Casia (cassia), cassia, the bark of various species of *Cinnamomum*, perhaps especially *C. iners, C. zeylanicum*, and *C. tamala*, X 4, XII 82, 85, 95–98, 99, XIII 10, 11, 13, 18, XIV 107, XVI 136, XXI 70, XXV 175, XXIX 55, XXXVII 204. As a term for a native European plant, probably common marjoram, *Origanum vulgare*, as in XII 98, XVI 136, XXI 70, XXVII 74. In XXI 53 a term for cneorum.

Casignete = hestiateris, XXIV 165.

Cassiopica filix, "fern of Cassiope," unknown, XXVII 80.

Castanea, chestnut-tree, *Castanea vesca*, XIII 110, XV 28, 92, 93, 112, 114, XVI 20, 74, 76, 98, 138, 206, 212, XVII 59, 122, 136, 147–150, XXIII 150.

Catanance, a vetch, *Ornithopus compressus*, XXVII 57.

Caucalis, of uncertain identity,

perhaps *Tordylium apulum, T. officinale, Caucalis grandifolia*, or *Pimpinella saxifraga*, XXI 89, XXII 83, XXVI 25 (*v.l.*).

Caulis, in Pliny generally synonymous with brassica, as a term for a particular type, kale, *Brassica oleracea acephala*, XIX 54, 57, 136, 139.

Caulodes, kale, *Brassica oleracea acephala*, XX 79.

Cedrelate, Greek juniper, *Juniperus excelsa*, XIII 53, XXIV 17.

Cedrosis = vitis alba, XXIII 21.

Cedrus, chiefly prickly juniper, *Juniperus oxycedrus*, XII 125, XIII 2, 52, 53, 100, XIV 112, 122, XV 28, XVI 62, 73, 80, 90, 91, 137, 186, 187, 197, 203, 207, 212, 213, 216, XVII 236, XXIV 17–20, 54, XXVIII 118, XXXI 98, XXXII 76, 135, XXXIV 177. In XIII 52 the Phoenician type of cedrus is the Phoenician cedar, *Juniperus phoenicea*, and the Syrian type is the Syrian cedar, *J. excelsa*. Cedrus magna = cedrelate, XXIV 17.

Cedrys, juniper, *Juniperus communis*, XIII 53.

Celthis, nettle-tree, *Celtis australis*, XIII 104.

Cemos, of uncertain identity, perhaps *Plantago cretica, Micropus erectus, Evox pygmea*, or everlasting, *Gnaphalium leontopodium*, XVII 57.

Centauris, a kind of centaury, *Erythraea centaurium*, XXV 69, XXVI 166.

Centaurium, centaury, (1) maius, *Centaurea salonitana* or *C. cen-*

INDEX OF PLANTS

taurium, XIX 186, XX 52, XXV 66, 100, 142, XXVI 27, 33, 41, 54, 110, 123, 137, 140, 153; (2) minus, *Gentiana centaurium*, XXV 68, 142, 164, XXVI 54, 104, 126, 140, 153, 185, XXVII 47. See also XIX 186, XX 52, XXV 33, XXVI 32, XXVII 143.

Centigranium triticum, hundred-grain wheat, XVIII 95.

Centum capita, eryngo, *Eryngium campestre*, XXII 20.

Centunculus = clematis, XXIV 138. See also XXVI 105, 114.

Cepa (caepa), onion, *Allium cepa*, II 10, XIII 133, XIX 99–107, 111, 115, 117, 121, XX 39–43, XXIII 147, 148, XXV 26, 53, XXIX 108, 133, 134, XXX 30, XXXVI 179. The Ascalonian onion (cepa Ascalonia) (XIX 101), often identified as the shallot, *Allium ascalonicum*, is actually a form of the onion.

Cepaea, an orpine, *Sedum cepaea*, XXVI 84.

Cerais, a type of wild radish, *Raphanus raphanistrum*, XIX 82.

Cerasus, cherry-tree, more especially the sweet cherry, *Prunus avium*, and the sour cherry, *P. cerasus*, but also the mahaleb, *P. mahaleb*, and the bog cherry, *P. padus*, XII 14, XIII 66, 105, XV 57, 101, 102, 104, 105, 109, 111, 113, XVI 74, 104, 124, 125, 126, 138, 181, 183, 210, 219, XVII 65, 88, 99, 110, 135, 234, 260, XVIII 232, XXIII 141, XXIV 106, XXXVII 42.

Ceratia, carob-tree, *Ceratonia siliqua*, XXVI 52.

Ceratitis, horned poppy, *Glaucium flavum*, XX 206.

Ceraunion, a truffle, probably *Tuber aestivum*, XIX 36.

Cerinthe, wax-flower, *Cerinthe major*, XXI 70.

Ceronia, carob-tree, *Ceratonia siliqua*, XIII 59.

Cerrus, Turkey oak, *Quercus cerris*, XVI 17, 19, 20, 25, 218, 230, XXIV 13, XXX 92.

Cestros, betony, *Betonica officinalis*, XXV 84.

Chalceos, yellow fish thistle, *Carlina corymbosa*, XXI 94.

Chalcetum, unknown, perhaps *Valeriana locusta*, XXVI 40.

Chamaeacte, dwarf elder, *Sambucus ebulus*, XXIV 51, XXVI 120.

Chamaecerasus, dwarf cherry-tree, *Prunus prostrata*, XV 104.

Chamaecissos, (1) ground-ivy, *Glecoma hederacea*, XVI 152, XXIV 82, 135, XXVI 54; (2), sowbread, *Cyclamen europaeum*, XXV 116.

Chamaecyparissos, "ground-cypress," lavender cotton, *Santolina chamaecyparissus*, XXIV 136.

Chamaedaphne, "dwarf laurel," periwinkle, *Vinca herbacea*, or double-tongue, *Ruscus hypophyllum*, XV 131, XXI 68, 172, XXIV 132.

Chamaedrys, wall-germander, *Teucrium chamaedrys*, XIV 112, XXIV 130.

Chamaeleon, (1) pine-thistle, *Atractylis gummifera*; (2) the black type probably *Cardopatium corymbosum*, XXI 94, XXII 45–47, 85, 157, XXIII 75, XXVII 64, 143, XXVIII 115, 162, XXX 30.

498

INDEX OF PLANTS

499

INDEX OF PLANTS

perhaps *C. scammonia*.
Clematis Aegyptia, periwinkle, *Vinca minor*, XXIV
141.

Clematitis (clematis MSS.), a kind of aristolochia, probably *Aristolochia clematitis*, XXV
95.

Cleonicon, *v.l.* for cleopiceton = clinopodion, XXIV 137.

Cleopiceton = clinopodion, XXIV 137.

Clinopodion, wild basil, *Calamintha clinopodium*, XXIV
137.

Clymenus, (1) honeysuckle, *Lonicera etrusca* and *caprifolium*, XXV 70; (2) some species of *Lathyrus*, ibid.

Cnecos, cultivated, safflower, *Carthamus tinctorius*; wild, the same or perhaps *Carthamus leucocaulos* or blessed thistle, *Cnicus benedictus*, XXI 94, 184. In XXI 90 one of the two wild types is *Carthamus lanatus*.

Cneorum, widow-wail, *Daphne gnidium*, XXI 53, 55; in XIII 114 perhaps mezerlon, *Daphne mezereum*.

Cnestor, mezerlon, *Daphne mezereum*, XIII 114.

Cnidinum, oil from stinging nettle, *Urtica urens*, XV 31.

Coagulum terrae, probably bedstraw, *Galium verum*, XXVII
67.

Cobios = dendroides, XXVI 71.

Coccolobis, a kind of grape-vine, XIV 30.

Coccus Cnidius, berry of the shrub eneorum, *Daphne gnidium*, XXVII 70.

Coccygia, a kind of sumach, perhaps wig-tree, *Rhus cotinus*, XIII 121. *Coccus gnid-*

ius and *Daphne gnidium* have also been suggested.

Coeca or coix, doum-palm, *Hyphaene thebaica*, XIII 47.

Colocasia, taro, *Colocasia antiquorum*, XXI 174; in XXI
87 apparently erroneously applied to the Indian lotus, *Nelumbo nucifera*.

Colocynthis, colocynth, *Citrullus colocynthis*, XX 14–17.

Columbina, a kind of grape-vine, XIV 40.

Comacum, perhaps spice-nutmeg, *Myristica fragrans*, or ailanthus, *Ailanthus malabarica*, XII 135, XIII 18.

Comaros, Greek for arbute-tree, *Arbutus unedo*, wrongly taken by Pliny to be the fruit, XV
99.

Combretum, perhaps a species of immortelle, *Helichrysum*, XXI 30, 133.

Come = tragopogon, XXI 89, XXVII 142.

Commagene, an unknown plant, XXIX 55.

Condrion = condrille = chondrille, gum succory, *Chondrilla juncea*, XXII 91.

Condurdum, perhaps a soapwort, cow basil, *Saponaria vaccaria*, XXVI 26.

Conferva, probably some species of *Conferva*, a water-plant, XXVII 69.

Conseminea, a kind of grape-vine, XIV 36.

Consiligo, a species of hellebore, probably green hellebore, *Helleborus viridis*, XXV 86, XXVI 38.

Convolvulus, hedge bind-weed, *Convolvulus sepium*, XVII
264, XXI 23.

Conyza, (1) viscous elecampane,

INDEX OF PLANTS

INDEX OF PLANTS

INDEX OF PLANTS

with the orchis satyrios of XXVI 96.

Cynozolon, black type of chamaeleon, *Cardopatium corymbosum*, XXII 47.

Cyparittias, a type of spurge, perhaps *Euphorbia aleppica*, XXVI 70.

Cyperus (or cypirus), basically a term for *Cyperus* sp., the exact species unidentifiable without descriptive details, extended sometimes to similar plants, as in XXI 107, 111, 115 to gladiolus, corn-flag, *Gladiolus segetum*. See XII 42, 43, XIII 13, 18, XVII 95, 209, XXI 88, 107, 111, 115, 116, 117, 118, XXII 40, XXV 165.

Cypira, perhaps curcuma, *Curcuma longa*, the source of turmeric, XXI 117.

Cypros (-us), henna plant, *Lawsonia inermis*, XII 30, 108, 109, 121, XIII 9, 11, 12, 13, 18, XXIII 90, XXIV 74, XXIX 106, XXX 21, 110, 126, XXXV 195.

Cytisus, tree-medick, *Medicago arborea*, XII 20, XIII 130–134, XVI 92, 186, 204, XVII 52, 239, XVIII 145, 148, 165, XXI 70, XXVII 82.

Dactylus, (1) dog's-tooth grass, *Cynodon dactylon*, XXIV 182; (2) a kind of grape, XIV 15.

Damasonion = alisma, XXV 124, XXVI 25, 92, 143.

Danae, a type of laurel, XV 131.

Daphnidis, a type of cassia, XII 98.

Daphnoides, (1) mezerlon, *Daphne mezereum*, XV 132, XXIII 158; (2) an Egyptian type of clematis, XXIV 141.

Daucos (-um), a generic term applied to several plants, including the wild carrot (*Daucus carota* subsp. *carota*), various species of *Athamanta*, *Malabaila aurea*, and *Bupleurum fruticosum*. See XIV 111, XIX 89, XXV 110, 112, 119, 134, XXVI 28, 35, 41, 45, 74, 83, 88, 89, 110, 128, 137, 157, XXXII 101. In XXV 110–112 four kinds are mentioned, but can be reduced to two or at most three.

Dendroides, a kind of spurge, wolf's milk, *Euphorbia dendroides*, XXVI 71.

Dialeucon, a kind of saffron, *Crocus sativus*, XXI 33.

Diaxylos = aspalathos (1), XXIV 112.

Dictamnos, in XX 156 a secondary name for a wild type of pennyroyal, *Mentha pulegium*.

Dictamnum, dittany, *Amaracus dictamnus*, VIII 97, XIV 111, XXV 92–94, 101, XXVI 79, 142, 153, 161.

Dicte = dictamnum, XXIV 164.

Digitellum, house-leek, *Sempervivum arboreum*, XVIII 159, XXV 160, XXVI 163.

Dionysonymphas = hestiateris, XXIV 165.

Dios balanum, chestnut, *Castanea vesca*, XV 93.

Diospyron, usually the fruit of the false lote-tree, *Diospyrus ebenum*, but in XXVII 98 = lithospermon.

Dipsacos, teasel, *Dipsacus fullonum*, XXVII 71.

Dodecatheon, probably common primrose, *Primula acaulis*, XXV 28, XXVI 107.

INDEX OF PLANTS

INDEX OF PLANTS

INDEX OF PLANTS

Erysimon = irio, XVIII 96, XXII 158.

Erysisceptrum = aspalathos (1), XII 110. Mentioned also in XXIX 56.

Erysithales, in XXVI 137 perhaps *Cnicus erysithales*; in XXV 160 an emend. for erithales, *s.v.*

Erythraicon, a kind of satyrion, fritillary, *Fritillaria graeca*, XXVI 97.

Erythranus, red-berried ivy, *Hedera helix*, XVI 147, XXIV 82.

Erythrocomus, a type of pomegranate-tree, *Punica granatum*, XIII 113.

Erythrodanum, madder, *Rubia tinctorum*, XXIV 94, XXVI 89.

Erythron = dorycnion, XXI 179.

Escaria, a kind of grape, XIV 42.

Etesiaca, a kind of grape-vine, XIV 36.

Euclea, euclia or euplia, unknown, possibly Pliny has mistaken Greek εὔκλεια (glory) for a plant, XXV 130.

Eugalacton = glaux, XXVII 82.

Eugenia, a kind of grape-vine, XIV 25, 46.

Euonymos, spindle-tree, *Euonymus europaeus*, XIII 118.

Eupatoria, agrimony, *Agrimonia eupatoria*, XXV 65, XXX 121.

Eupetalon, spurge laurel, *Daphne mezereum*, XV 132.

Euphorbea (-ia), ancient milkwort, *Euphorbia antiquorum*, V 16, XXV 77, 143, 145, XXVI 54, 118, XXVII 2. A North African species of milkwort, *E. resinifera*, V 16,

XXV 77. Euphorbeaum is the juice. See also Spina.

Euphrosynum = buglossos, XXV 81.

Euplia, unknown. See Euclea.

Euripice, unknown reed, XXI 119.

Euthalon, *v.l.* for eupetalon, *s.v.*

Eutheriston, "easily harvested," a variety of balsam-tree, *Commiphora opobalsamum*, XII 114.

Euzomon, rocket, *Eurica sativa*, XX 126.

Exacum, type of centaurium, XXV 68.

Exedum, unknown, possibly tanner's sumach, *Rhus coriaria*, XXIV 175.

Exonychon, gromwell, *Lithospermum officinale*, XXVII 98.

Faba, field bean, *Faba vulgaris*, IV 97, XI 14, XII 23, 126, XIII 54, 105, 107, XIV 43, XVI 123, XVII 55, 56, 72, 240, XVIII 10, 50, 51, 57, 58, 59, 60, 62, 95, 101, 117–122, 126, 143, 155, 157, 164, 181, 184, 185, 187, 191, 193, 198, 205, 228, 241, 245, 253, 257, 259, 304, 305, 307, XIX 40, 118, 133, 157, XX 53, 56, 89, 203, 211, XXI 70, XXII 91, 140–141, XXIV 22, XXV 46, XXVII 40, XXIX 63, XXX 67, XXXIII 109, XXXVI 133. The wild faba of Mauretania (XVIII 121) is probably *F. pliniana*, and the type which grew on islands in the North Sea (ibid.) is *Pisum maritimum*. Faba Aegyptia, Indian lotus, *Nelumbo nucifera*, XVIII 121. Faba Graeca, the fruit of the nettle-

INDEX OF PLANTS

509

INDEX OF PLANTS

third type, unnamed (ibid.), is the mango, *Mangifera indica*; the Idaean ficus of the Troad (XV 68) is perhaps the snow-pear, *Pyrus nivalis*, or the amelanchier, *Amelanchier vulgaris*; and the ficus Aegyptia is the carob-tree, *Ceratonia siliqua* (XIII 59) and sycamore-fig, *Ficus sycamorus* (XIII 56). The ficus described as a seaweed (XIII 138) is perhaps an alcyonidian polyp.

Filix = felix, fern.

Flamma Iovis, possibly *Agrostemma coronaria*, XXVII 44.

Flammeum = phlox, XXI 64.

Flos Iovis, Jove's flower, *Agrostemma flos Jovis*, XXI 59, 67.

Forensis, a kind of grape, XIV 42.

Fraga, strawberry, *Fragaria vesca*, XV 98, XXI 86, XXV 109.

Fraxinus, ash-tree, usually *Fraxinus excelsior* and F. oxyphylla, XI 77, XIII 117, XV 67, XVI 62–64, 69, 74, 83, 106, 210, 219, 228, 229, 230, XVII 67, 78, 81, 151, 200, XVIII 240, XXII 95, XXIV 46, XXV 71, XXIX 94. Fraxinus = ornus, XVI 63.

Frumentum, in Pliny's time, usually a generic term for grain, occasionally for wheat, II 211, VII 64, 191, XVI 49, 176, XVII 14, 40, 46, XVIII 14, 16, 48, 49, 51, 52, 56, 58, 59, 60, 61, 62, 65, 67, 69, 70, 71, 79, 81, 88, 91, 93, 96, 97, 101, 117, 126, 140–157, 163, 164, 166, 170, 188, 191, 192, 196, 198, 223, 259, 296, 298, 301–308, 322, 341, XIX 79, XXI 98, XXIV 158, XXVIII 28, XXXII 35, XXXVII 201.

Frutex coriarius = rhus (1), XXIV 91.

Frutex sanguineus, cornel, *Cornus sanguinea*, XVI 74, 176.

Fucus marinus. See Phycos.

Fungus, mushroom, tree-fungus, usually *Agaricus*, XIII 139, XVI 33, 85, 208, XIX 38, 63, XX 25, 47, 86, 94, 132, 236, XXI 126, 184, XXII 31, 96–100, 108, XXIII 43, 65, 115, 159, 162, XXV 103, 131, XXVI 135, XXVII 50, XXIX 103, XXXI 119, XXXII 44, XXXVI 138.

Gabalium, Arabian aromatic shrub, unknown, XII 99.

Galbanum, galbanum, a gum resin obtained from galbanum giant fennel, *Ferula galbaniflua*, XI 16, XII 121, 126, XIII 9, XV 8, XIX 180, XXIV 12, 21, 22, XXXI 121.

Galeobdolon, brownworth, *Scrophularia peregrina*, or red dead nettle, *Lamium purpureum*, XXVII 81.

Galeopsis = galeobdolon, *ibid.*

Galion = galeobdolon, *ibid.*

Gallidraga, hairy teasel, *Dipsacus pilosus*, XXVII 89.

Gelotophyllis, Indian hemp, *Cannabis sativa*, XXIV 164.

Genista, greenweed, *Genista tinctoria* or *pilosa*, XVI 74, 176, XVII 136, XVIII 240, XXI 51, 72, 82, XXIV 65. The genista used for making nets (XIX 15) is Spanish broom, *Spartium junceum*.

Gentiana, various species of gentian, *Gentiana*, including G. *lutea* and G. *purpurea*, XIV

INDEX OF PLANTS

111, XXV 71, 100, 142, XXVI 29, 32, 36, 74, 137, 140, 163, XXXII 54.

Geranion, crane's bill, *Geranium* sp., XIX 36, XXVI 108, 158, 160. In XXVI 108 the first type is probably round-leafed crane's bill, *G. rotundifolium*, or perhaps a species of heron's bill, such as *Erodium malachoides*, and the second is probably tuberous crane's bill, *G. tuberosum*.

Gethyon (getion, getium, gethyum), long onion, a variant of *Allium cepa*, XIX 100, 105, 107, 117, 118, 121, 181, 183.

Geum, avens, *Geum sativum*, XXVI 37.

Gingidion, seka-kul, *Malabaila seka-kul*, XX 33.

Git, Roman coriander, *Nigella sativa*, XIX 168, XX 182–184, XXVII 121. See Melanthion.

Gladiolus, corn-flag, *Gladiolus segetum*, XXI 65, 107, 108, 111, 115. In XXI 111 Pliny speaks of another gladiolus = cypiros.

Glans, acorn, as in XXIV 7; but glans faginea, beechnut, as in XXIV 14.

Glastum, greenweed, *Genista tinctoria*, or woad, *Isatis tinctoria*, XXII 2.

Glaucion, greater celandine, *Chelidonium glaucium*, or red celandine, *Glaucium corniculatum*, XXVII 83. In XX 206 it is the horned poppy, *Glaucium flavum*.

Glaux = eugalacton, wartcress, *Coronopus procumbens*, and sea milkwort, *Glaux maritima*, proposed, but neither fits, XXVII 82.

Glinon, a kind of maple, *Acer creticum*, XVI 67.

Glycyrrhiza, liquorice, *Glycyrrhiza glabra* and *echinata*, XI 284, XXII 24, XXVIII 97. In XXI 91 an error for cnecos, *s.v.*

Glycyside, peony, *Paeonia officinalis*, XXV 29, XXVII 84–87.

Gnaphalion, cotton-weed, *Diotis maritima*, XXVII 88.

Gossipion, cotton-tree, *Gossypium arboreum*. See Appendix p. 546 (XIX 15), also Gossypinus and Arbor lanigera.

Gossypinus = gossipion, XII 39.

Gramen, grass, particularly dog's tooth grass, *Cynodon dactylon*, XVII 89, XVIII 259, XIX 98, XXII 8, XXIV 178–183, XXVII 113.

Granatum, pomegranate, *Punica granatum*, XIII 9, 10, 112, XV 115, XVI 84, 86, XX 149, XXVI 49.

Gromphaena, perhaps a kind of amaranth, *Amaranthus tricolor*, XXVI 40.

Gynaecanthe = vitis nigra, XXIII 27.

Habrotonum, southernwood, *Artemisia arborescens*, XIII 12, XIV 105, XIX 100, XX 68, XXI 37, 59, 60, 61, 160–162, 168, 170.

Hadrobolon, black gum of tree bdellium, XII 35.

Hadrosphaerum, type of nardus, XII 44.

Haemodorum, broom-rape, *Orobanche cruenta* or *caryophyllacea*, XIX 176.

Halicacabum (-os, -us), (1) = vesicaria, XXI 177; (2)

INDEX OF PLANTS

strawberry tomato, *Physalis alkekengi*, XXI 180, 182, XXII 112. In XXI 180 it is a sleepy nightshade, also called moly and morion.

Halimon, sea orache, *Atriplex halimus*, XVII 239, XXII 73.

Haliphloeos, sea-bark oak, *Quercus pseudosuber*, XVI 24.

Halmyris, sea fennel, *Crambe maritima*, XIX 142.

Halus, comfrey, *Symphytum officinale*, XXVI 42. See also Alum.

Harundo, reed, the genus *Arundo*, VII 21, 206; VIII 96, IX 56, X 9, 84, XI 14, 32, XII 32, 124, XIII 122, XVI 90, 92, 125, 126, 156–173, 174, 262, 267, XVIII 46, 122, 240, 341, XIX 92, XX 56, XXIII 28, 68, XXIV 85–87, 150, XXV 93, XXVI 30, XXVIII 230, XXIX 108, XXX 88, 101, XXXI 44, 83, XXXV 46. The Indian harundo of XVI 162, 163 is the bamboo, *Bambusa arundinacea*; that of XXV 46 is one or more species of indigo-plant, *Indigofera*.

Hastula regia = asphodelus, XXI 109.

Hebenus, wood of false lote-tree, *Diospyros ebenum*, when the tree is native, otherwise ebony, *D. melanoxylon*, VI 197, XII 17–20, XVI 186, 204, 212, 213, 214, XXIV 89.

Hedera, ivy, *Hedera helix*, VIII 98, XII 47, 74, XV 100, 115, XVI 9, 79, 85, 86, 88, 90, 92, 144–153, 155, 207, 208, 243, XVII 96, 101, 239, XVIII 245, XXI 52, 55, 78, 177, XXII 75, XXIII 21, XXIV

75–80, 82, 83, 98, XXV 70, 89, 95, 114, 116, 175, XXVI 30, XXVII 35, 43, 76, XXVIII 79, 130, 219, XXXI 44.

Hedyosmum, water mint, *Mentha aquatica*, XIX 160, XXXV 181.

Hedypnois, ox-tongue, *Helminthia echioides*, XX 75.

Helenium, generic term for a number of similar plants; in XIV 108, elecampane, *Inula helenium*; in XXI 59, 159, probably *Thymus incana*, but perhaps *Teucrium marum*; applied also to calamint, *Calamintha incana*; identity uncertain in XV 30, XXVIII 117.

Heleoselinum (helioselinum), wild celery, *Apium graveolens*, XIX 124, XX 117.

Helia, kale, *Brassica oleracea acephala*, XX 79.

Helianthes, laudanum plant, *Cistus laurifolius*, XXIV 165.

Heliocallis = helianthes, XXIV 165.

Heliochrysus, cassidony, *Helichrysum stoechas*, or annual tansy, *Tanacetum annuum*, XXI 65, 66, 168.

Helion, dwarf elder, *Sambucus ebulus*, XXIV 51.

Helioscopios, sun-spurge, *Euphorbia helioscopia*, XXII 57, XXVI 69.

Helioscopium, a kind of heliotropium, XXII 57; a kind of tithymalus, XXVI 69.

Heliotropium, heliotrope, (1) *Heliotropium villosum*; (2) (helioscopium) *H. europaeum*; (3) (tricoccum) turnsole, *Chrozophora tinctoria*, II 109, XII 100, XVIII 252, XIX

INDEX OF PLANTS

100, 178, XX 7, XXI 46, 100, XXII 57–61, XXV 39, XXXVII 83, 165.

Helix, ivy, *Hedera helix*, XVI 145, 148. In XVI 177 a kind of willow.

Helleborum (-os), hellebore, the white, probably *Veratrum album*, and the black, some species of *Helleborus*, such as *H. niger*, *H. cyclophyllus*, *H. orientalis*, or *H. officinalis*, XIV 110, XXI 134, XXII 133, XXIV 22, 65, XXV 47–61, 122, 150, XXVI 40, XXVII 6, XXVIII 140, XXIX 110, XXXI 63, XXXII 31, 79.

Helvennaca, a kind of grape-vine, XIV 32, 84.

Helvia, a kind of grape-vine, XIV 46.

Helvola, a kind of grape, XIV 29.

Helxine, VIII 101, XXI 94, 96, XXII 41, 42, XXV 92 (*v.l.*), XXVII 23, XXVIII 220, XXX 77.

(1) A thistle, *Atractylis gummifera*, XXI 94.

(2) sea-side knotweed, *Polygonum maritimum*, XII 41.

(3) pellitory, *Parietaria officinalis*, VIII 101.

(4) *Convolvulus arvensis* in Diosc. 4.39 W., and possibly in some passages in Pliny.

Hemeris, usually the gall-oak, *Quercus infectoria*, XVI 22, 26.

Hemerocalles, Martagon lily, *Lilium martagon*, XXI 59, 158.

Hemionion, scale fern, *Asplenium ceterach*, XXV 45, XXVI 41, XXVII 34.

Heptapleuron = plantago, XXV 80.

Heracleon = origanum heracleoticum, XXV 32; hera-

cleon (ion) siderion, Cretan fig-wort, *Scrophularia lucida*, XXV 34, XXVI 140; = nymphaea, XXV 75.

Heracleus pyros = lithospermon, XXVII 98.

Heraclion, wild purslane, *Euphorbia peplis*, XX 207; a type of panaces, XXVI 113.

Heraclium, see origanum, XX 177–180.

Herba Fulviana, unidentified, XXVI 88.

Herba lactaria = tithymalus, XXVI 62.

Herba lanaria, probably = radicula, *s.v.*, XXIV 168. Cf. XIX 48, XXV 52.

Herba Sabina = brathy, XXIV 102. See also XXIX 103.

Herba Scythica. See Scythica.

Hermupoa = linozostis, XXV 38.

Heroum = asphodelus, XXII 67.

Hesperis, night-scented stock, *Matthiola tristis*, and dame's violet, *Hesperis matronalis*, XXI 39.

Hestiateris, areca nut, from areca-palm, *Areca catechu*, XXIV 165.

Hexastichas, a type of myrtle, perhaps *Myrtus angustifolia boetica*, XV 122.

Hiberis. See Iberis.

Hibiscum (-us), marsh-mallow, *Althaea officinalis*, XIX 89, XX 29, XXVI 21.

Hieracion, hawkweed, the large type *Urospermum picroides*, the small type *Hymenonema graecum*, XX 60.

Hippace, in XXV 83 a Scythian herb; usually mare's milk cheese, as in XI 284, XXVIII 131, 204.

INDEX OF PLANTS

INDEX OF PLANTS

INDEX OF PLANTS

INDEX OF PLANTS

Labrum Venerium, XXV 171, is an unidentified river-plant.

Labrusca, wild vine, *Vitis labrusca*, XII 48, 132, XIV 37, 98, XVI 154, 208, XVII 213, XXIII 8, 17, 19, XXVII 143.

Laburnum, laburnum, *Cytisus laburnum*, XVI 76, XVII 174.

Lactoris, a milky plant, unknown, perhaps = herba lactaria XXIV 168.

Lactuca, lettuce, *Lactuca sativa*. Wild lettuce is probably generally acrid lettuce, *L. virosa*, as in VIII 99, XIX 126; but Pliny classifies as wild lettuce several other plants, e.g., caesapon (XX 59), q.v., isatis (ibid.), q.v., a plant used by wool dyers (ibid.), which is woad, *Isatis tinctoria*, and hieracion (XX 60), q.v. Lactuca caprina (XIX 128, XX 58, XXVI 62) is probably *Euphorbia helioscorpia*. See VIII 99, IX 128, XIX 117, 120, 122, 125–128, 130, 131, 132, 134, 154, 168, 177, 183, 185, 186, 199, XX 58–68, 199, XXII 88, XXV 28, 71, 147, XXVI 74, 98, 103, XXVII 56, 59, 66, 71, 95, 97, XXXII 101, 111.

Lactuca caprina = tithymalus, XXVI 62. See also XIX 128, XX 58.

Lacuturris, a kind of cabbage or kale, XIX 141.

Lada, a type of cassia, XII 97.

Ladanum, perhaps *Galeopsis ladanum*, a hemp nettle, sometimes the resin (collected by goats' beards) of the plant leda, XII 73–76, XIII 18, XXVI 47, 74, 106, 115, 126, 150, 157, XXVIII 163, XXXVII 204.

Lagine, secondary name for clematis, XXIV 139.

Lagopus, in part field clover, *Trifolium arvense*, and hare's foot clover, *T. lagopus*, XXVI 52.

Lamium, dead-nettle, *Lamium album*, *purpureum*, or *maculatum*, XXI 93, XXII 37–38, 43.

Lapathum, dock and sorrel, species of *Rumex*, XIX 46, 98, 123, 170, 184, XX 59, 231–235, XXI 125, XXV 84, 148, 155, XXXII 131.

Lappa, bur, *Arctium lappa*, XVIII 153, XXI 104, XXIV 176, XXV 81, 104, XXVI 105. Lappa in XXI 104 is probably the clotbur, *Xanthium strumarium*, or bedstraw, *Gallium sparine*. Lappa boaria, perhaps *Lappa canina*, XXVI 105. Lappa canaria, perhaps *Lappa canaria*, XXIV 176.

Lappago, a sort of bur, XXVI 102.

Lapsana, hoary mustard, *Hirschfeldia incana*, XIX 144, XX 96.

Larix, larch-tree, *Larix communis*, XIII 100, XVI 24, 30, 32, 43, 45, 46, 48, 49, 58, 73, 80, 91, 95, 100, 125, 127, 186, 187, 190, 195, 200, 204, 212, 218, 219, 222, 245, XXIV 28, 32, 136, XXVIII 195.

Laser or laserpicium, the resinous juice of silphium, *s.v.*, XVI 143, XVII 259, XVIII 308, XIX 38–48, XX 34, 56, 80, 90, 141, XXII 101–106, XXXI 120.

Latace, a magic herb, XXVI 18.

Lathyris, chickling vetch, *Lathyrus sativus*, XXVII 95.

INDEX OF PLANTS

INDEX OF PLANTS

INDEX OF PLANTS

XXVIII 61, 79, XXX 52, 55, 90, 107, XXXI 99, XXXIV 127, XXXVII 202. In XIII 114 it means the seed of the thymelaea.

Lithospermon, gromwell, *Lithospermum officinale*, XXVII 98.

Lolium, darnel, *Lolium temulentum*, XVIII 153, XXII 160.

Lonchitis, wood-fern, *Aspidium linguum*, or holly-fern, *A. lonchitis*, XXV 137, XXVI 76, 119.

Lotometra, a meal made from the seeds of the white lotus, *Nymphaea lotus*, and the blue lotus, *N. caerulea*, XXII 56.

Lotos: (1) As a term for a tree, probably originally denoted the Jew thorn, *Zizyphus lotus*, later extended to the nettle-tree, *Celtis australis*, and even to the clove-tree of India, *Eugenia caryophyllata* (XII 30); Jew thorn and nettle-tree confused in XIII 104–106; Jew thorn mentioned in XIV 101 (shrub); nettle-tree mentioned or described in XIV 101 (tree), XV 101 (bore berries), XVI 235, 236, XVII 5 (grew at Rome), XXIV 6 (grew in Syria), XV 116 (grew in Egypt and Mesopotamia), XIII 61, XVI 172 (wood used for flutes), XVI 186, 204, 212 (wood described). (2) The herb lotos is usually a trefoil, perhaps especially *Trifolium fragiferum* (XIII 107, XIV 101, XXI 34, 99, 103, XXIV 6), but sometimes the trefoil *Lotus corniculatus* (XXI 34, XXII 55). (3) The Egyptian lotos in Pliny (XIII 107–110, XXII 56, XXIV 6) is the white lotus, *Nymphaea lotus*, and the blue lotus, *N. caerulea*, although elsewhere it is sometimes the Indian lotus, *Nelumbo nucifera*. (4) The lotos used as an ingredient in an unguent (XIII 18) is of uncertain identity.

Lupinus, lupin, especially *Lupinus hirsutus*, *L. albus*, and *L. termis*, XII 38, XIII 141, XV 30, XVII 54, 55, 56, 260, 266, XVIII 47, 50, 57, 59, 125, 133–136, 163, 185, 187, 198, 252, 257, 304, XX 20, XXII 154–157, XXIII 75, 94, XXXII 87, XXXV 102.

Lupus salictarius, perhaps hop, *Humulus lupulus*, XXI 86.

Lutum, weld, dyer's weed, *Reseda luteola*, XXXIII 87, 91.

Lycapsos, viper's herb, *Echium italicum*, XXVII 97.

Lychnis, rose-campion, *Lychnis coronaria*, XXI 18, 67, 171, XXV 68; lychnis agria = antirrhinum, XXV 129.

Lychnitis, the third type of phlomis, *s.v.*, XXV 121.

Lycium, a juice obtained from the buck-thorn, *Rhamnus lycioides*, XII 31, XXII 25 (*emend.*), XXIII 109, XXIV 124–126, XXVI 164. See also Pyxacanthus chironius.

Lygos = vitex, XXIV 59.

Lynx, unknown plant, XXXVII 34.

Lyron = alisma, XXV 124.

Lysimachia, purple loosestrife, *Lythrum salicaria*, XXV 72, 100, XXVI 131, 141, 147, 164.

Macir, red bark of the root of an Indian tree, probably *Holarrhena antidysenterica*, XII 32.

INDEX OF PLANTS

INDEX OF PLANTS

Marmaritis = aglaophotis, XXIV 160.

Maron, Mt. Sipylos marjoram, *Amaracus* Sipyleus, XII 111, XIII 13, 18.

Marrubium (marruvium), horehound, *Marrubium vulgare* and *M. peregrinum*, XIV 105, XX 118, 241–244, XXII 41, XXV 43, XXVI 93. Marrubium nigrum is black horehound, *Ballota nigra*, XX 244.

Massaris, a product of the flower clusters of the labrusca, XII 133, XXIII 2, 9.

Mastiche, mastich, *Pistacia lentiscus*, XII 72, XXIV 42, XXXVII 51.

Mastos, unknown, XXVI 163.

Mecon (1) usually a generic term for poppy, *Papaver*, especially *P. somniferum*; (2) in XX 209 = tithymalus. Mecon aphrodes (1) usually the frothy "poppy," *Silene venosa*, as in XX 207; in XXVII 119 small purple spurge, *Euphorbia peplis*, confused with a poppy because of its juice. Sometimes called heraclion.

Meconion = peplis, XXVII 119; = a product of the mecon, XXIII 43, 61, 80, XXV 143.

Meconis, probably acrid lettuce, *Lactuca virosa*, XIX 126, XX 67.

Medica, lucerne, *Medicago sativa*, XVIII 144–148; in XIV 108 probably elecampane, *Inula helenium*.

Medion, perhaps a bellflower, such as *Campanula lingulata*, or perhaps *Convolvulus althaeoides*, XXVII 104.

Melamphyllum = paederos, XXII 76.

Melampodion, black type of helleborum, XXV 47.

Melancranis, bog-rush, *Schoenus nigricans*, XXI 112.

Melanion, perhaps by error for melanthion, otherwise a transcription of μέλαν ἰον, in that case the violet, *Viola odorata*, XXI 65.

Melanthion (-um), Roman coriander, *Nigella saliva*, XX 182, XXIII 67, XXVIII 188, 217, XXXI 84, XXXIII 85, XXXV 185; = anthemis, XXII 53.

Melaspermon = melanthion, XX 182.

Melilotos, an aromatic fenugreek, *Trigonella graeca*, XIII 13, XV 30, XXI 39, 53, 63, 70, 151, XXII 123, 142, XXIII 85, XXIX 37.

Melimelum, often a type of quince, but in XV 51, 59, XXIII 104 a type of apple, *Malus domestica*.

Melissophyllum, balm, *Melissa officinalis*, XX 116, XXI 53, 70, 82, 149–150, XXVII 134. See also Apiastrum.

Melittaena = melissophyllum, XXI 149.

Melopepo, perhaps the melon, *Cucumis melo*, XIX 67.

Melothron (melotrum), bryony, *Brynia cretica*, XXI 53, XXIII 21.

Memaecylon, fruit of the strawberry-tree, *Arbutus unedo* XV 99.

Menta, usually water mint, *Mentha aquatica*, sometimes such similar species as *Satureia calamintha*, XIX 100, 159, 176, 177, XX 44, 80, 147–

wort, *Plumbago europaea*,
XXV 155.

Morion, (1) white type of mandragoras, perhaps *Atropa belladonna*, XXV 148, (2) sleepy
nightshade, *Withania som-
nifera*, XXI 180, XXV 148.

Morus, mulberry-tree, *Morus
nigra* and *M. alba*, XIII 56,
XV 52, 96, 97, 101, 109, 113,
116, XVI 28, 74, 83, 102, 119,
182, 186, 207, 210, 218, 227,
XVII 124, 136, XVIII 253,
XXI 183, XXIV 120, 122,
XXVII 57, XXX 23, XXXIV
133. But morum denotes
either a mulberry or a blackberry (*e.g.*, XV 97, XXIV
117). The Egyptian morus
(XXIII 134–136) is the sycamore, *Ficus sycamorus*.

Muralis, pellitory, *Parietaria
officinalis*, XXI 176.

Murra (sometimes myrra),
myrrh or the tree that produces it, *Balsamodendron
myrrha*, VI 174, XII 33, 51,
66–71, 81, XIII 8, 10, 12, 15,
16, 17, 18 XIV 91, 92, 93, 107,
134, XIX 162, 187, 188, XX
164, 212, 249, 251, XXI 38,
131, XXIII 109, 136, 139,
XXIV 22, 86, 164, 166, 179,
XXV 41, 175, XXVI 81, 109,
154, 159, XXVII 85, 130, 133,
XXVIII 118, 120, 174, 175,
179, 214, 245, XXIX 41, 46,
115, 137, XXX 24, 87, 88, 93,
105, 116, 140, 145, XXXI 100,
XXXII 101, XXXIV 153,
XXXV 181.

Muscus, generic term for moss,
esp. sphagnum, X 96, XIX
24, XXVI 22, 105, XXVII
69, 100.

Musteum, quince, *Cydonia vulgaris*, XV 38.

Mycanthus, a kind of wild
asparagus, perhaps *Asparagus
acutifolius*, XIX 151.

Myagros, ball-mustard, *Neslia
paniculata*, or camelina, *Cam-
aelina sativa*, XXVII 106.

Myoctonos = aconitum, XXVII
9.

Myophonon, wolf's bane, *Aconitum anthora*, or perhaps
Alyssum sativum, XXI 54.

Myosota or myosotis, mad-
wort, *Asperugo procumbens*,
XXVII 23, 105.

Myosotan = alsine, XXVII 23.

Myrice, tamarisk, *Tamarix tet-
randra* or *T. articulata*, XIII
116, XXIV 64; = erica,
XXIV 67.

Myriophyllon, water-milfoil,
Myriophyllum spicatum,
XXIV 152.

Myrobalanum, behen-nut and
the tree, *Moringa oleifera*.
Oil of ben is extracted from
the fruit, XII 100–103, XIII
18, XXIII 98.

Myrra = myrris, XXIV 154;
= murra, VI 174.

Myrris, sweet cicely, *Myrrhis
odorata*, XXIV 154; = geranion or myrtidas, XXVI 108.

Myrriza = myrris, XXIV 154.

Myrsineum = feniculum silvestre, wild fennel, XX 255.

Myrtidanum, an excrescence
on the stem of the myrtle,
XIV 104, XV 118, XXIII 164.

Myrtidas (perhaps better mer-
tryx, cf. Diosc. 3.116 W.) =
geranion, XXVI 108.

Myrtites, a type of spurge, perhaps *Euphorbia myrsinites*,
XXVI 66–67.

Myrtopetalum (-s), a kind of
polygonus, XXVII 113.

Myrtus, myrtle-tree, *Myrtus*

INDEX OF PLANTS

communis, XII 3, 29, 76, 112, 115, 121, XIII 9, 10, 18, 52, 105, 114, XIV 104, XV 27, 34, 101, 109, 118–126, XVI 74, 79, 90, 92, 112, 121, 137, 234, XVII 62, 88, 95, 96, 123, 124, 257, XX 158, XXI 69, XXII 139, 144, XXIII 87, 159–166, XXIV 6, 165, XXV 159–166, 175, XXVI 42, 66, 121, XXVII 93, 126, XXVIII 81, 137, 194, 207, 209, 260, XXIX 106, 108, XXX 56, 58, 68, 105, 140, XXXII 30, XXXIII 110, XXXIV 133, XXXV 116, 160. Myrtus candida, var. *leucocarpa*, XV 122, XXIII 159; m, nostras, var. *romana*, XV 122; m. Tarentina, var. *Tarentina*, XV 122; XVII 62; m. silvestris butcher's broom, *Ruscus aculeatus*, XV 27, 122, XXIII 165.

Myxa, sebesten, *Cordia myxa*, XIII 51, XV 45, 97, XVII 75, XXII 120.

Napus, navew, *Brassica napa*, XIV 106, XVIII 50, 131–132, 192, 314, XIX 62, 75–77, 85, 100, 117, 177, 179, 183, XX 21, XXI 109, XXIII 52, XXIV 153, XXVII 96 (*v.l.*).

Napy, mustard, *Brassica nigra* and *Sinapis alba*, XIX 171; napy Persicum = alterum thlaspi, XXVII 140.

Narcissus, principally pheasant's eye narcissus, *Narcissus poeticus*, but also autumn narcissus, *N. serotinus*, Italian narcissus, *N. italicus*, and polyanthus narcissus, *N. tazetta*, XIII 6, XV 30, XVIII 244, XXI 25, 64, 128–129, XXIII 94, XXVIII 72.

Narcissus = lilium purpureum, XXI 25.

Nardus, (1) as an import, the rootstock of spikenard, *Nardostachys Jatamansi*; (2) nardus Celticus or "Celtic nard" (XIV 107) and nardus Gallicus or "Gallic nard" (XII 45, XIII 18, XIV 106, XV 30, XXI 135, XXVII 48, 49) are French spikenard, *Valeriana celtica*; (3) nardus rusticus, also called baccaris (XII 45, XXI 30, 135), is hazelwort, *Asarum europaeum*, as is nardus silvestris (XIV 106). See also XII 42–46, 47, 129, XIII 10, 15, 18, XIV 106, 107, XV 30, XVI 135, 214, XXI 11, 29, 129, 135, XXIII 97, XXIV 21, XXVII 48–50, XXVIII 164, 178, 226, 256, XXIX 135. References to nardi folia (*e.g.*, XII 42, 129, XXI 11) may involve confusion with malobathrum.

Narthecia, ferula, *Ferula communis*, XIII 123.

Narthex, ferula, *Ferula communis*, XIII 123.

Nasturtium, garden cress, *Lepidium sativum*, XIX 117, 123, 154, 155, 181, 185, 186, XX 127–130, 134, 251, XXII 84, 158, XXIV 27, 186, XXV 87, XXVI 27, 40, XXVIII 130, 197, XXIX 48. The second type in XX 127 is *Roripa* sp.

Natrix, goat-root, *Ononis natrix*, XXVII 107.

Nectaria, probably elecampane, *Inula helenium*, XIV 108.

Nepenthes, opium poppy, *Papaver somniferum*, XXI 159, XXV 12.

525

INDEX OF PLANTS

INDEX OF PLANTS

bright, *Euphrasia odontites*, XXVII 108.

Oenanthe, (1) in XXI 65, 167 drop-wort, *Spiraea filipendula*; (2) apparently a product obtained from the flower clusters of the labrusca in XII 132, 133, XIII 18, XXIII 2, 8–9, 18, 80, 91.

Oenobreches (ὀνοβρυχίς in Diosc.), sainfoin, *Onobrychis viciaefolid*, XXIV 155.

Oetum, unknown, perhaps earth nut, *Arachis hypogaea*, XXI 88.

Oistos, arrowhead, *Sagitta sagittifolia*, XXI 111 (*emend.*).

Olea, olive-tree, *Olea europaea*, II 108, 226, III 41, VI 131, VIII 204, XI 18, XII 3, 35, 40, 77, 130, XIII 67, 141, XIV 7, XV 1–8, 11, 19, 34, 78, 134, 135, XVI 19, 79, 87–91, 104, 127, 128, 131, 176, 183, 186, 206, 212, 219, 222, 230, 234, 239, 240, 241, XVII 11, 17, 30, 31, 47, 53, 81, 93, 96, 97, 103, 112, 113, 119, 125, 126, 127, 128, 129, 130, 133, 137, 174, 200, 223, 228, 229, 230, 232, 233, 237, 241, 242, 243, 257, 262, 263, XVIII 162, 188, 240, 243, 254, 266, 287, 288, 329, 337, XIX 48, XXI 51, 57, XXII 73, XXIII 69–75, 96, 97, XXVI 96, 162, XXVII 65, XXXIV 1, 133, XXXV 160. The Arabian olea (XII 77) is the white mangrove, *Avicennia officinalis*, also described, but not named, in XII 37. The olea of India (XII 26) is *Olea cuspidate*.

Oleaginea, a kind of grape, XIV 38.

Oleaster, oleaster, *Olea oleaster*, V 3, VIII 101, XII 26, XIII 114, XV 19, 24, XVI 70, 74, 199, 206, 212, 219, 230, 240, 244, XVII 129, 242, XXIII 72, 76–78, 129, 242, XXIV 50, XXXIV 133.

Oleastrum, a kind of buxus, XVI 70.

Oliva, olive-berry, *Olea europaea*. VIII 204, XI, 18, 46 (*emend.* Detlef.), XII 26, 67, 130, XIII 32, 54, 63, 139, 141, XV 4–6, 9–17, 18, 20, 34, 68, 96, 101, 104, 109, 111–113, 115, XVI 28, 108, 121, 234, XVII 229, 230, 237, 241, XVIII 38, 254, 273, 320, 329, XIX 79, XXI 71, XXIII 73, XXVI 82, XXXVII 161, 184, 188. The oliva of India (XII 26) is *Olea cuspidata*.

Olus, originally a generic term for potherbs, in Pliny usually specifically the cabbage, *Brassica oleracea*, XVII 177, 240, XVIII 165, 188, XIX 79, 133, 134, 136–144, 177, 179, 180, 188, XX 33, XXII 74, 77, 80, 82, XXIV 1, 139, XXVI 58, 83, 88, 164, XXVII 54, 66, XXVIII 171, XXIX 80, XXXI 115, XXXII 94, XXXV 189.

Olus maritimum, sea orach, *Atriplex halimus*, XXII 73–74, XXXII 94. Cf. olus marinum, XXIX 79.

Olusatrum, alexanders, *Smyrnium olusatrum*, XII 67, XIX 162, 164, 187, XX 117, XXII 79.

Olyra, two-grained wheat, *Triticum dicoccum*, XVIII 62, 75, 92, XXII 121; in XVIII 75 wrongly equated with oryza; in XVIII 81 mentioned as oryza.

527

INDEX OF PLANTS

Omphalocarpos = aparine, XXVII 32.

Onear = onothera, XXVI 111.

Onitis, sweet winter marjoram, *Origanum heracleoticum*, XX 175. In XX 177 = heraclium heracleoticum.

Onochelis, onochilis in XXI 100, XXII 51, probably identical with onochilon.

Onochilon, bugloss, *Echium diffusum*, called also anchusa, archebion, enchrysa, onochelis, rhexia, XXII 51.

Ononis (see also Anonis), restharrow, *Ononis antiquorum*, XXVII 29.

Onopordon or onopradon, a thistle, perhaps the cotton thistle, *Onopordon acanthium*, XXVII 110.

Onopyxos, a thistle, *Onopordon illyricum*, XXI 94.

Onosma, stone bugloss, *Onosma echioides*, XXVII 110.

Onothera, oleander, *Nerium oleander*, XXVI 111, 146.

Onothuris, oleander, *Nerium oleander*, XXIV 167, XXVI 18.

Ophiostaphyle, probably the caper, *Capparis spinosa*, XIII 127. Elsewhere, also bryony, *Bryonia dioica*.

Ophiusa, a magical plant, XXIV 163.

Ophrys, ivy-blade, *Ophrys ovata* or *bifolia*, XXVI 164.

Opition, earth-nut, *Bunium ferulaceum* (in Greece, but not in Italy), XIX 95.

Opobalsamum, balsam of Mecca, the juice of the balsam-tree, *Commiphora opobalsamum*, XIII 18.

Opulus, a kind of maple, *Acer opulus*, XIV 12, XVI 73, 206, 231, XVII 201.

Orchis, (1) generic term for orchis, *Orchis* sp., many species of which grow in the Mediterranean region, XXVI 95, 96, 128, 146, XXVII 65, (2) a kind of olive, XV 3, 13, 20, 21.

Oreoselinum, perhaps wild parsley, *Petroselinum sativum*, XIX 124, XX 117.

Orestion, probably elecampane, *Inula helenium*, XIV 108.

Origanum, (1) white type is sweet winter marjoram, *Origanum heracleoticum*, (2) black type is probably common marjoram, *O. vulgare*, (3) origanum heracleoticum is *O. heracleoticum*, VIII 98, X 195, XII 89, 91, XIV 105, XIX 100, 117, 118, 121, 165, 184, 186, XX 55, 128, 156, 170, 175, XXI 53, 55, 56, XXII 46, XXIV 1, XXV 32, 68, XXVII 13, 57, XXVIII 152, 156, XXXI 98, 101.

Orion, a kind of polygonus, perhaps *Equisetum pallidum*, XXVII 115.

Orminos or orminus, wild asparagus, perhaps especially *Asparagus acutifolius*, XIX 151, XX 110, XXVI 94 (ormenos agrios).

Ornithogala, star of Bethlehem, *Ornithogalum* sp., especially *O. umbellatum*, XXI 102.

Ornus, mountain ash, *Fraxinus ornus*, XVI 74, XVII 201.

Orobanche, probably a species of *Orobanche*, perhaps *O. caryophyllacea*, XVIII 155, XXII 162. In Theophrastus, usually dodder, *Cuscuta europaea*.

Orobothron = hypocisthis, XXVI 49.

INDEX OF PLANTS

Orsinus, perhaps a mistake for ὀρεινός, XXI 67.

Orthocissos, ivy, *Hedera helix*, XVI 152.

Ortyx = stelephuros, XXI 101.

Oryza, rice, *Oryza sativa*, XV 28, XVIII 71, 75, 93, XXVIII 110. In XVIII 81 probably an error for olyra.

Osiritis, Egyptian name for cynocephalia, XXX 18.

Ostrys (or ostrya), hop horn-beam, *Ostrya carpinifolia*, XIII 117.

Osyris, poet's cassia, *Osyris alba*, XXVII 111.

Othonna, perhaps the greater celandine, *Chelidonium majus*, XXVII 109.

Oxalis, sour dock, *Rumex acetosa*, XX 231.

Oxycedrus, prickly cedar, *Juniperus oxycedrus*, XIII 52.

Oxylapathon, sharp-pointed dock, *Rumex crispus*, XX 231, 233.

Oxymyrsine, butcher's broom, *Ruscus aculeatus*, XXIII 88, 158, 165, XXV 158, XXVII 73, 93. In XV 27, 122, and XXIII 88 = chamaemyrsine.

Oxys, (1) wood-sorrel, *Oxalis acetosella*, XXVII 112; (2) a form of the great sea-rush, *Juncus acutus*, XXI 112.

Oxyschoenos, great sea-rush, *Juncus acutus*, XXI 112.

Oxytriphyllon, a type of trifolium with pointed leaf, probably a species of trefoil, *Trifolium*, XXI 54.

Padus, Gallic term for picea, III 122.

Paederos, (1) = caerefolium, *Anthriscus cerefolium*, XIX 170; (2) = melamphyllum,

a type of acanthus, *Acanthus mollis*, XXII 76.

Paeonia, peony, *Paeonia* sp., XXV 29, XXVI 131, 151, XXVII 84. Paeonia mascula is perhaps the male peony, *P. corallina*, and p. femina perhaps the female peony, *P. officinalis*, XXVII 85.

Pala, the banana or plantain-tree, *Musa paradisiaca*, XII 24.

Paliurus, Christ's thorn; when the habitat is Africa (XIII 111, XXIV 115), *Zizyphus spina Christi*; when the habitat is southern Europe (XVI 98, 121), *Paliurus aculeatus*.

Pallacana, horn onion, a variant of *Allium cepa*, XIX 105.

Palma, palm, chiefly the date-palm, *Phoenix dactylifera*, sometimes the dwarf-palm, *Chamaerops humilis*, V 73, VI 131, 161, 205, VII 29, XII 19, 40, 103 (= elate), 108, 134, XIII 26–30, 62, 69, 90, 111, 119, 125, 138, XIV 102, 107, XV 67, 109, 113, 115, 116, XVI 79, 80, 90, 109, 112, 119, 125, 126, 135, 211, 223, 231, 240, XVII 31, 58, 60, 65, 228, 244, 245, 261, XVIII 188, XIX 31, XXIII 52, 97, 98, 99, 111, XXIV 29, 165, XXVIII 118, 255, XXX 55. Palma denotes the behen-nut tree, *Moringa oleifera*, in XXIII 98. Palma as a seaweed (XIII 138) is *Callophyllis laciniata*.

Panacea = cunila bubula, XX 169.

Panaces (panax), "all-heal," sometimes galbanum plant, *Ferula galbaniflua*, at other times = ligusticum; in XII

INDEX OF PLANTS

121 a kind of pastinaca. XII 127, XIII 12, 14, 18, XIV 111, XV 30, XIX, 187, XX 169, 178, XXIII 16, XXIV 97, XXV 30–33, 42, 99, 131, 134, 142, 165, XXVI 27, 74, 75, 88, 89, 92, 100, 107, 111, 117, 118, 119, 137, 139, 151, 152, XXVIII 258, XXXII 30, 133. The type called chironium (XXV 32, 99) is elecampane, *Inula helenium*. The type called Heracleon (XXV 32), Heraclion (XXVI 113), or Heraclia (XXV 42) is *Origanum heracleoticum*. Cunila bubula was sometimes called panax (XIX 165).

Pancration (·um), (1) = cichorium, XX 74; (2) *Pancratium maritimum*, XXVII 118.

Panicum, Italian millet, *Setaria italica*, XVIII 49, 50, 52–54, 60, 61, 91, 96, 99, 101, 107, 111, 116, 153, 160, 163, 182, 185, 192, 198, 250, 297, 314, XX 241, XXII 131.

Papaver, generic term for poppy, *Papaver* sp., including *P. somniferum*, *P. rhocas*, *P. hybridum*, and *P. argemone*, XIII 98, 107, XVII 56, XVIII 53, 59, 122, 205, 229, XIX 21, 167–169, XX 20, 61, 188, 198–209, XXI 70, 165, XXII 123, XXIII 119, 128, XXV 35, 66, 76, 90, 102, 131, XXVI 44, 67, 74, XXVII 26, 83, 119, 125, 138, XXIX 43, XXX 53, 59, 71, XXXII 77, XXXVII 71.

Pappus = erigeron, XXV 168.

Papyrus, papyrus, *Cyperus papyrus*, V 44, VI 82, 205, VII 206, XIII 68–89, 128, XV 117, XVI 157, 178, XVIII 108, XXII 48, XXIV 88, XXVIII

61, 168, XXIX 43, XXXIII 94, XXXIV 112.

Paralium, (1) horned poppy. *Glaucium flavum*, XX 206; (2) sea spurge, *Euphorbia paralias*, XX 209; (3) sun spurge, *Euphorbia helioscopia*, XXVI 68.

Pararinon or parananrhinon = antirrhinum, wild lion's-mouth, *Antirrhinum orontium*, XXV 129.

Pardalianches = aconitum, VIII 99, XX 50, XXVII 7.

Parthenis = artemisia, XXV 73.

Parthenium (parthenion), a term for a variety of similar plants, including (1) pellitory, *Parietaria officinalis* (XXI 176, XXII 43, 44), (2) seaside knotweed, *Polygonum maritimum* (XXI 89, XXII 41), and (3) annual mercury, *Mercurialis annua* (XXV 38). See also XXI 176.

Passiolus (phasiolus, phaseolus), probably usually the black-eyed cowpea, *Dolichos melanophthalmus*, sometimes perhaps other similar legumes, XII 26, XVIII 58, 125, 186, 198, 202, 314, XXIV 65.

Pastinaca, a generic term for the carrot, *Daucus carota*, and carrot-like plants, including *Althaea officinalis*, *Athamanta cretensis*, *A. cervaria*, *Seseli ammoides*, and *Malabaila aurea*, the identity in some instances very uncertain, XIX 62, 88, 90, 92, XX 29, 30, XXI 86, 167, XXV 89, 112.

Pecten Veneris, shepherd's needle, *Scandix pecten-veneris*, XXIV 175.

Pedes gallinacii = capnos trunca, XXV 155.

INDEX OF PLANTS

Pelasgum, spurge laurel, *Daphne mezereum*, XV 132.

Pelecinus, axe-weed, *Securigera coronilla*, XVIII 155, XXVII 121.

Pentapetes, pentaphyllon = quinquefolium, XXV 109.

Pentorobon = paenoia, XXV 29, XXVII 84.

Peplis, small purple spurge, *Euphorbia peplis*, XX 210–215, XXVII 119.

Pepo, perhaps the water-melon, *Citrullus vulgaris*, XIX 65, XX 11–12.

Peraticum, gum of the tree bdellium, XII 35.

Perdicium, (1) pellitory, *Parietaria officinalis*, XXI 176, XXII 43; (2) seaside, knotweed, *Polygonum maritimum*, XXI 102, XXII 41; (3) uncertain, XIX 100, XXVIII 219.

Pericarpum, a bulb, XXV 131.

Periclymenon, honeysuckle, *Lonicera*, perhaps *L. etrusca* or *L. caprifolium*, XXVII 120.

Perisson = dorycnion, XXI 179.

Peristereos, vervain, *Verbena officinalis*, XXV 126, 134, 143, XXVI 121, 144, 155; = hierabotane, XXV 105.

Perpressa = baccar, XXI 132, XXVI 87.

Persea, a sacred tree of Egypt and Persia, *Mimusops Schimperi*, XIII 60, 63, XV 45.

Persicon napy, " Persian mustard," perhaps *Lunaria annua*, XXVII 140. Cf. Thlaspi.

Persicum (caryon) = iuglans, XV 87.

Persicus, peach tree, *Amygdalus persica*, XII 14, XIII 60, XV 39–45, 48, 109, 110, 111,

114, 115, XVI 111, 138, XVII 136, 151, XXIII 132.

Persolata or personata, probably common bur-dock, *Arctium lappa*, XXV 104, 113, XXVI 24, 28, 92, 113, 121, 136, 143.

Persoluta, Egyptian plant used for chaplets, XXI 184.

Petellium, water avens, *Geum rivale*, proposed by Sprengel, but flowers of wrong colour, possibly a species of *Cyclamen*, XXI 49.

Petroselinum, parsley, *Petroselinum sativum*, XX 118, XXVIII 197, XXXII 101.

Peuce, (1) generic term for firs and pines, XI 118; (2) a kind of grape, XIV 75.

Peucedanum, sulphur-wort, *Peucedanum officinale*, XXV 117, 118, 139, 143, 164, 166, XXVI 23, 28, 33, 34, 41, 54, 74, 76, 79, 89, 114, 118, 130, 135, 144, 156, 161, XXVII 143, XXXII 28, 33.

Pezica, a mushroom, perhaps *Morchella esculenta* or *Lycoperdon bovista*, XIX 38.

Phalangion or phalangitis, Greek alplily, *Lloydia graeca*, XVIII 156, XXVII 124.

Phalaris, perhaps canary grass, *Phalaris canariensis*, but more likely *P. nodosa*, XXVII 126.

Pharnaceon, great centaury, *Centaurea centaurium*, XXV 33.

Phascos = sphagnos, XXIV 27.

Phaselion = isopyron, XXVII 94.

Phaseolus and phasiolus, see Passiolus.

Phasganion = xiphium, cornflag, *Gladiolus segetum*, XXV 137, 138.

Phaunus, probably actually a

INDEX OF PLANTS

533

INDEX OF PLANTS

Polyanthemum, a crowfoot, *Ranunculus polyanthemus*, XXVII 112.

Polycnemon, field basil, *Zizyphora capitata*, or perhaps the wild basil, *Calamintha clinopodium*, XXVI 148.

Polygala, a milkwort, *Polygala venulosa*, XXVII 121.

Polygonaton, perhaps Solomon's seal, *Convellaria polygonatum*, XXVII 113. In XXII 40 a secondary name for leucacantha, milk-thistle, *Silybum marianum*.

Polygonoides, a kind of clematis, XXIV 141.

Polygonon (-os, -us), knotgrass, *Polygonum aviculare*, XXV 158, XXVII 108, 113–117. The description of the third type in XXVII 115 fits marestail, *Hippurus vulgaris*, but the name does not.

Polypodium, polypody, *Polypodium vulgare*, XVI 244, XXVI 58, 80, 105, 122, XXIX 80.

Polyrrhizon, (1) black hellebore, *Helleborus niger*, XXV 51; (2) = plistolochia, XXV 96, 98; (3) in XXVII 126 uncertain.

Polythrix = polytrichon, XXV 132, XXVI 124, 147.

Polytrichon = adiantum, XXII 62.

Populus, poplar, *Populus* sp., II 108, XI 16, XII 3, 132, XIII 58, 141, XIV 10, XV 67, XVI 77, 85–87, 91, 92, 97, 108, 119, 126, 133, 173, 176, 209, 223, XVII 68, 78, 90, 143, 151, 200, 242, XVIII 240, 266, 360, XXIV 47, 135, XXXV 160, XXXVII 31. The white type is the abele, *P. alba*, and the

black is the black poplar, *P. nigra*, XVI 85.

Porcillaca, purslane, *Portulaca oleracea*, XIII 120, XIX 167, XXIII 143, XXVI 69, 84, XXVII 137, XXX 111. The type called peplis (XX 210) is small purple spurge, *Euphorbia peplis*.

Porphyritis, a type of fig, XV 71.

Porrum, leek, *Allium porrum*, XIII 132, XVIII 71, XIX 107, 108–110, 118, 120, 177, 181, 183, 185, XX 44–49, XXI 109, XXII 105, 159, XXIV 136, XXV 137, XXVII 54, XXVIII 65, 108, 173, 176, 199, 233, 241, 248, XXIX 47, 123, 136, XXXI 117, 129, XXXII 94, 124, XXXIV 118, XXXVII 109, 113. Porrum nigrum = ballote, XXVII 54.

Posia (or posea), a kind of olive, XV 4, 13, 17, 20, 21.

Potamaugis = thalassaegle, a narcotic plant of India, XXIV 164.

Potamogiton, (1) waterplantain ottelia, *Ottelia alismoides*, XXVI 50; XXXII 53; (2) perhaps marestail, *Hippuris vulgaris*, XXVI 51; (3) in other authors commonly pondweed, *Potamogeton natans*.

Poterion, goat's thorn, *Astragalus creticus* or *poterium*, XXV 123, XXVII 122.

Poterion aureum = radicula, XXIV 96.

Pothos, the asphodel, especially *Asphodelus ramosus*, XXI 67.

Praecia, a kind of grape-vine, XIV 29.

Praecox, peach, *Amygdalus persica*, XVI 103.

Prasion, (1) white horehound,

534

INDEX OF PLANTS

INDEX OF PLANTS

INDEX OF PLANTS

INDEX OF PLANTS

131) and r. mustelina (XX 132) are mountain rue, *Ruta montana*.

Sabellicum, a kind of cabbage, XIX 141.

Sabina, usually savin, *Juniperus sabina*, X 157, XVI 79, XVII 98, XXIV 102. The first type in XXIV 102 is *J. foetidissima*.

Sabucus or sambucus, elder-tree, *Sambucus nigra*, XV 64, 100, 115, XVI 74, 83, 103, 122, 179, 180, 183, 187, 209, 231, XVII 68, 151, 174, XXIV 51, XXVII 73.

Saccharon, tabaschir, produced principally by the spiny bamboo, *Bambusa arundinacea*, and the berry bamboo, *Melocanna bambusoides*, XII 32.

Sacopenium, of uncertain identity, not the same plant as sagopemon, XII 126, XIX 40, 167, XX 197, XXVIII 177.

Sagapemon, the juice of *Ferula persica*, XX 197.

Sagitta, arrowhead, *Sagitta sagittifolia*, XXI 111.

Sagittarium, a kind of reed, XVI 166.

Salicastrum, a plant growing in willow-beds, perhaps the melothron of Theophrastus, bryony, *Bryonia cretica*, XXIII 20.

Saliunca, probably French spikenard, *Valeriana celtica*, XXI 40, 43, 44, 144.

Salix, willow, various species of *Salix*, II 108, XI 14, XIV 110, XVI 77, 87, 90, 97, 110, 133, 173–177, 201, 209, XVII 28, 68, 95, 99, 109, 136, 141–143, 147, 201, 209, XVIII 99, 240, 267, XXIV 56, 58, XXV 72,

XXXI 44. In XVI 177 salix nigra is *S. amplexicaulis*; s. candida is the white willow, *S. alba*; s. Gallica is *S. amygdalina*, s. graeca, also called s. vitellina, is *S. vitellina*; and s. purpurea or viminalis is the purple willow, S. purpurea.

Salvia, (1) = elelisphacus, XXII 147; (2) secondary name for a type of bechion, perhaps *Verbascum lychnitis*, XXVI 31.

Samolus, perhaps brook-weed, *Samolus Valerandi*; some think pasque-flower, *Anemone pulsatilla*, XXIV 104.

Sampsuchum, sweet marjoram, *Majorana hortensis*, XIII 10, XV 29, 30, XX 177, XXI 61, 163.

Sanguinaria = polygonus, XXVII 113.

Sarcocolla, a Persian tree, *Penaea sarcocolla*, XIII 67, XXIV 128.

Saripha, an Egyptian water-plant, perhaps *Cyperus auricomus*, XIII 128.

Satureia, usually summer savory, *Satureia hortensis*, XIX 107, 165. See also XXVI 55.

Satyrion (-ios). Four types described in XXVI 96–98: (1) man orchis, *Acera anthropophora*; (2) if not a species of *Orchis*, probably seaside crosswort, *Crucianella maritima*; (3) a Greek type of uncertain identity; and (4) fritillary, *Fritillaria graeca*, mentioned also in XXVI 128 and XXVIII 119. Modern nomenclature indicates term was applied also to *Himantoglossum hircinum*, *Serapias cordigera*, and *Phallus im-*

INDEX OF PLANTS

pudicus. In XXV 98 = aristolochia polyrrhizos.

Saurion, cited as a term for mustard as a result of careless reading of Diosc. 2. 156 W. on Θλάσπι, or his source, XIX 171.

Saxifragum = adiantum, XXII 64.

Scammonia, scammony, *Convolvulus scammonia*, XIV 110, XXV 54, XXVI 59, 90, 93, 114, 157, XXVII 79. Scammonia tenuis = lagine, XXIV 139.

Scandix, wild chervil, *Scandix pecten-veneris*, XXI 89, XXII 80–81.

Scandula, perhaps spelt, *Triticum spelta*, otherwise emmer, *T. dicoccum*, XVIII 62.

Scapula, a kind of grape-vine, XIV 34.

Sceptrum = aspalathos (1), XII 110.

Schista cepa, a kind of onion, XIX 101.

Scilla, sea onion or squill, *Urginea maritima*, XIV 106, XV 63, XVII 87, XVIII 244, XIX 93, 96, 99, 101, 121, XX 97–101, XXI 106, 108, XXIII 59, XXIV 44, XXV 26, 115, XXVI 95, 114, XXVII 14, XXX 23, 52, XXXII 101, 135; scilla pusilla (XXVII 118), *Pancratium maritimum*; scilla Epimenidu (XIX 93), *Ornithogalum pyrenaicum*.

Scirpula (*v.l.*), a kind of grapevine, XIV 81.

Scirpus, a bulrush, VII 206, XIII 76, XVI 178.

Scolymus, golden thistle, *Scolymus hispanicus*, XX 262, XXI 94–96, XXII 86–87.

Scopa regia, probably *Cheno-*

podium scoparia, XXI 28, XXV 44.

Scordastum, an unknown tree, XII 36.

Scordion, germander, *Teucrium scordium*, XXV 63, XXVI 77, 89, 100, 107, 137.

Scordotis = scordion, XXV 63, 100, 127, XXVI 27, 32, 44, 140, 151.

Scorpio, a term applied to several different plants, of uncertain identity, in some instances apparently *Aconitum anthora*, *Asparagus acutifolius*, *Scorpiurus sulcata*, scorpion furze, *Genista acanthoclada*, and scorpion root, *Doronicum cordatum*. Two types described in XXII 39; a secondary name for tragos, XIII 116, XXVII 142; a secondary name for thelyphonon, XXV 122; a secondary name for aconitum, XXVII 9; a type of cucumis, XX 8; a spinous plant, XXI 91, 93.

Scorpiuron = tricoccum, XXII 60.

Scripula, a kind of grape, XIV 81.

Scythica or scythice = glycyrrhiza, XXV 82, XXVI 28, 146, XXVII 2.

Secale, rye, *Secale cereale*, XVIII 141. In XVIII 140 a kind of fenugreek.

Securiclata, axeweed, *Securigera coronilla*, XVIII 155.

Sedum, house-leek, the usual type *Sempervivum tectorum*, the large type *S. arboreum*, XVIII 159, XIX 179, XXV 160, XXVI 111. See Aizoüm.

Selago, fir clubmoss, *Lycopodium selago*, XXIV 103.

INDEX OF PLANTS

Selinas, a type of cabbage with crisp leaves like celery, XX 79.

Semen, emmer, *Triticum dicoccum*, XVIII 82, 102, 112, 184, 198.

Semnion = theobrotion, XXIV 162.

Senecio = erigeron, XXV 167.

Serapias = orchis, XXVI 95.

Serichatum, Arabian aromatic shrub, unknown, XII 99, XIII 18.

Sericum, a type of tuber (1), *s.v.*, XV 47.

Seriphum, sea wormwood, *Artemisia maritima*, XXVII 53, XXXII 100.

Seris, the cultivated form endive, *Cichorium endivia*, the wild form chicory, especially *C. intybus*, XX 73, 76, XXVII 104.

Serpyllum (serpullum), creeping thyme, *Thymus serpyllum*, XIV 105, XVI 244, XIX 100, 172, 176, XX 138, 173, 176, 245, 264, XXI 59, XXIV 137, XXX 148.

Serrata = chamaedrys, XXIV 130.

Serratula = vettonica, XXV 84.

Sertula campana, Latin name for melilotus, *Trigonella graeca*, XXI 53.

Sesama (sesima, sesamon), sesame, *Sesame indicum*, VI 161, XIII 11, 12, 118, XV 25, 28, 30, XVIII 49, 53, 58, 60, 96, 98, 99, 304, XXII 132, 158, XXIII 95, XXVI 67, 110, XXVII 126, XXVIII 103, 130, 168. Wild sesamon = cici, XV 25.

Sesamoides. Two kinds mentioned in XXII 133 (see also XXV 52): (1) perhaps purple rock-cress, *Aubrieta deltoidea*, *Astragalus sesameus*, or *Reseda canescens*; (2) perhaps *Reseda mediterranea* or *alba*, *Helleborus cyclophyllus*, or herb terrible, *Daphne tartonraira*.

Seseli, small hartwort, *Tordylium officinale*, VIII 112, XX 238, XXV 92.

Setania, (1) medlar, *Mespilus germanica*, XV 84, XXIII 141; (2) the " annual " onion, a small, sweet form of *Allium cepa*, XIX 101.

Setanion, (1) a spring wheat, club wheat, *Triticum compactum*, or perhaps common wheat, *T. vulgare*, XVIII 70; (2) an " annual " type of bulb, unidentified, XIX 95.

Sibi = cici, XV 25.

Sicelicon = psyllion, XXV 140.

Siderion, epithet of heracleon, *s.v.*

Sideritis, perhaps usually *Stachys heraclea*, perhaps sometimes *Sideritis romana*, VIII 101, XXV 42, 100, 142, 164, XXVI 24, 93, 100, 115, 135, 148, 164. In XXII 41 *Polygonum maritimum* and in XXII 43 *Parietaria officinalis*. Dioscorides (IV 33–36) mentions four kinds, including Ἡρακλεία and Ἀχίλλειος, but the identification of some is doubtful.

Sil = seseli, XII 128, XX 36, XXII 79, XXIV 177, XXVII 48. A secondary name for halus, XXVI 42 (*emend.*).

Silaus, a water plant similar to celery, unidentified, XXVI 88.

Siler, brookwillow, *Salix vitellina*; broad-leaved spindle-tree, *Evonymus latifolius*, also

INDEX OF PLANTS

proposed, XVI 77 and XXIV 73.

Sili, castor-oil tree, *Ricinus communis*, XV 25.

Silicia, fenugreek, *Trigonella foenum graecum*, XVIII 140, 165, 166, XXIV 184.

Siligo, probably usually common wheat, *Triticum vulgare*, or club wheat, *T. compactum*, XVIII 61, 76, 81, 85, 86, 87, 88–91, 93, 106, 164, 184, 198, 205, 298, XXII 119, XXVI 145, XXVIII 8.

Siliqua, carob, *Ceratonia siliqua*, XIII 59, XIV 103, XV 95, 117, XVII 136, XXIII 151.

Siliquastrum = piperitis, XIX 187, 188, XX 174.

Sillybum (syllibum), milk thistle, *Silybum marianum*, XXII 85, XXVI 40.

Silphium, an extinct species of the asafoetida-producing group, similar in appearance to *Narthex asa foetida* and closely related to *Scorodosma foetida*. If a reference in Pliny is contemporary, not historical, it is to asafoetida, obtained from *Scorodosma foetida* and similar plants. See XIX 38–46, XX 104, XXII 100–106, XXIV 93.

Sinapi, white mustard, *Brassica alba*, and black mustard, *B. niger*, XII 28, XVI 167, XVIII 128, XIX 117, 119, 133, 138, 170, 181, 186, 133, 138, 170, 171, 181, 186, XX 25, 129, 236–241, XXI 71, 155, XXVIII 165, 219, 220, XXIX 108.

Sinon, stone-parsley, *Sison amomum*, XXVII 136.

Sion (sium), probably water speedwell, *Veronica anagallis*, or perhaps broad-leaved water-parsnip, *Sium latifolium*, XXII 84 (emend.), XXVI 88. In other authors, it also denotes water cress, *Nasturtium officinale*.

Siser, the parsnip, *Peucedanum sativum*, XIX 62, 90–92, XX 34.

Sisymbrium, bergamot mint, *Mentha aquatica*, XIX 172, 176, XX 247, XXI 59, XXV 94. The first type in XX 247 is water cress, *Nasturtium officinale*.

Sisyrinchion, Barbary nut, *Iris sisyrinchium*, XIX 95.

Sisyrum = erica, XI 42.

Sium. See Sion.

Smilax (or milax), a term for several plants of twining character, including bindweed, especially hedge bindweed, *Convolvulus sepium* (XVI 153, XXI 52, XXIV 82). A second possibility is *Smilax aspera*. The cultivated smilax of Diosc. 2.146 W. is the black-eyed cowpea, *Dolichos melanophthalmus*. In XVI 51 milax is a term for the yew, and in XVI 19 a variety of holm-oak, *Quercus ilex* var. *integerrima*. The smilax called anthophoros (XXIV 83) is rough bindweed, *Smilax aspera*.

Smyrnium (or smyrnion, also zmyrnium and zmyrnion), (1) usually Cretan alexanders, *Smyrnium perfoliatum*, XIX 187, XX 186, XXVII 133–136; (2) sometimes common alexanders, *S. olusatrum*, XIX 162, 188.

Solanum = strychnon, XXVII 132.

541

INDEX OF PLANTS

Somphos = cucurbita silvestris, XX 13.

Sonchos (-cus, soncum), sow-thistle, *Sonchus Nymani* and *S. oleraceus*, XXII 88–90, XXVI 163.

Sopina, a kind of grape-vine, XIV 36.

Sorbus, service-tree, *Sorbus domestica*, XIII 58, XIV 103, XV 43, 61, 62, 84, 85, 114, XVI 74, 92, 183, 226, 228, XVII 64, 67, 75, 136, 221, 242, 253, XIX 92, XXI 72, XXIII 141, XXIV 129, XXVIII 132, XXXIII 117, *Sorbus torminalis* in XV 85.

Spalax, possibly meadow saffron, *Colchicum parnassicum*, XIX 99.

Sparganion, flowering rush, *Butomus umbellatus*, and bur-weed, *Sparganium* sp., XXV 109.

Spartum (-on), esparto, *Stipa tenacissima*, XI 18, XIII 73, XVII 29, XIX 26–31, XXIV 65, XXVIII 46, 49, XXXV 137, XXXVII 203.

Spathe, a term for the so-called cabbage of the dwarf-palm, *Chamaerops humilis* (XVI 112), erroneously given by Pliny for the palm itself (XXIII 99), and even confused with the silver fir (XII 134).

Sphacos, a sage, *Salvia calycina* or *S. officinalis*, XXII 146.

Sphagnos, (1) Tree-moss, *Usnea barbata*, XII 108, XXIV 27; (2) = aspalathos (1), XXIV 112.

Spica, the mass of fibres surrounding the upper end of the rootstock of spikenard, *Nardostachys Jatamansi*, XII 43, XIII 18.

Spina, (1) generically, a term for a thorn-bush (XV 57, 101, XVI 244, XVII 62, XVIII 360, XXI 68); (2) the Egyptian spina (XIII 66) is the acacia, *Acacia* sp., the white type (spina candida or alba) being *A. albida* and the black type (spina nigra) *A. arabica* (XIII 63, XXIV 109); (3) the usual Arabian spina (XXIV 107) is *Acacia arabica*; (4) the spina sitiens of the Arabian desert (XIII 139) is *Acacia tortilis*; (5) the spina regia (XIII 129) is probably *Acacia albida*; (6) the spina alba of Europe (XIII 115, XV 117, XXI 68, XXIV 108) is probably the oxyacanth, *Crataegus oxyacanthus*; (7) the spina that grew with the service-tree and the birch in Gaul (XVI 75) is probably also the oxyacanth; (8) spina alba in XXIV 108 and XXVIII 185 is perhaps the pine-thistle, *Atractylis gummifera*; (9) spina silvestris in XVII 75 = calabrix, i.e., buckthorn, *Rhamnus infectorius*, but in XXIV 111 = aspalathos (1), i.e., camel's thorn, *Alhagi maurorum*; (10) spina appendix (XXIV 114) is the barberry, *Berberis vulgaris*; (11) the spina of India producing lycium = pyxacanthus chironius, i.e., the buckthorn, *Rhamnus lycioides* (X 100, 205, XII 30–31, XXIV 125; cf. XXIV 124); (12) spina candida in XII 110 and XXIV 111 = aspalathos (1); (13) the spinae growing in Aria (XII 33–34) are *Balsamodendron Mukul* and asafoe-

INDEX OF PLANTS

tida, *Scorodosma foetidum*;
(14) the spina growing in
Gedrosia (XII 34) is ancient
milkwort, *Euphorbia antiquorum*; (15) the spina of India
with translucent, ebony-like
wood (XII 21) is of uncertain
identity; and (16) the spina
fullonia (XVI 244; cf. XXIV
111, XXVII 92) is the teasel,
Dipsacus fullonum.

Spinea, a kind of grape-vine,
XIV 34.

Spionia, a kind of grape-vine,
XIV 34.

Spiraea, (1) drop-wort, *Spiraea
filipendula*; (2) meadow-
sweet, *Spiraea ulmaria*, XXI
53.

Splenion = hemionion, XXV
45.

Spondylium, bear's foot, *Herac-
leum spondylium*, XII 128,
XXIV 22, 25.

Stachys, in XXIV 136 perhaps
downy woundwort, *Stachys
germanica*.

Stacte, a type of murra, XII 68,
XIII 17.

Stagonitis, galbanum giant fennel, *Ferula galbaniflua*, and
the resin obtained from it,
XII 126.

Staphis, a type of larkspur,
Delphinium staphis agria,
XXIII 17.

Staphyle = vitis alba, XXIII
21.

Staphylinus, the cultivated
carrot, *Daucus carota*, XIX
88, XX 30, 32, 33, XXV 112,
XXVIII 232.

Staphylodendron, bladder-nut,
Staphylea pinnata, XVI 69.

Statice, perhaps common thrift,
Armeria vulgaris, XXVI 51.

Stelephuros (also called ortyx

and plantago), a plantain,
probably *Plantago lagopus*,
XXI 101.

Stelis, mistletoe, *Viscum album*,
XVI 245.

Stephanitis, a kind of grape-
vine, XIV 42.

Stephanomelis, perhaps goose
grass, *Potentilla anserina*,
XXVI 136.

Stephanon Alexandri, spurge
laurel, *Daphne mezereum*, XV
132.

Stergethron, house-leek, *Sempervivum arboreum*, XXV 160.

Stobrus, a tree imported from
Carmania for fumigation, unidentified, XII 79.

Stoebe = pheos, XXI 91, XXII
28.

Stoechas, French lavender, *Lav-
andula stoechas*, XIV 111,
XXVI 42, XXVII 131.

Storax (styrax), officinal storax,
a resinous gum, or the tree
producing it, *Storax officinalis*,
X 195, XII 81, 98, 124, 125,
XIII 18, XV 26, XXIV 24,
XXVI 48.

Storbon, the resin of ladanum,
s.v., XII 74.

Strangias, a kind of wheat,
XVIII 64.

Stratiotes, the great duck-weed,
Pistia stratiotes (a tropical
plant), XXIV 169.

Streptis, a kind of grape, XIV 39.

Strumus, (1) = ranunculus,
XXV 174; (2) = strychnos,
XXVII 68.

Strutheum, quince, *Cydonia vulgaris*, XIII 11, XV 38, 48, 58,
XXI 142, XXIII 91, 103.

Struthion = radicula, *s.v.*, XIX
48, XXIV 96, XXVI 124.

Strychnos, basically and generally a term for the night-

543

INDEX OF PLANTS

Andropogon schoenanthus, XXI 120.

Teucria = teucrion, XXIV 130, XXV 99, XXVI 35, 75.

Teucrion, in XXIV 130, germander, *Teucrium chamaedrys*, in XXV 45 and XXVI 77, spleen wort, *Teucrium flavum*. See XXVII 77.

Teuthalis, a *v.l.* for thalattias, XXVII 113.

Teutrion = polium, XXI 44.

Thalasaegle = potamaugis, XXIV 164.

Thalattias = polygonum, XXVII 113. So Detlefsen and Mayhoff, but the MSS. have halattas, alattas and balattas.

Thalictrum, meadow-rue, either *Thalictrum flavum* or *T. minus*, XXVII 138.

Thapsi, *v.l.* for thlaspi, XIX 171.

Thapsia, a poisonous shrub, drias plant, *Thapsia garganica*, XIII 124–126, XIX 173, XXVI 22.

Tharrupia, a kind of grape, XIV 39.

Thasia, a kind of laurel, *Laurus nobilis*, XV 130.

Theangelis, an intoxicating herb, unknown, XXIV 164.

Thelygonon, (1) perennial mercury, *Mercurialis perennis*, or *Mercurialis tomentosa*, XXVI 162; (2) = satyrion, XXVI 99.

Thelygonos = crataegonos, XXVII 62. See also XXVI 99.

Thelyphonon = scorpio, XXV 122; = aconitum, XXVII 4, 9.

Thelypteris, bracken, *Pteris aquilina*, XXVII 78.

Theobrotion, probably ancient milk-wort, *Euphorbia antiquorum*, XXIV 162, 166.

Theriaca, a kind of grape-vine, XIV 117.

Therionarca (theronarca), probably oleander, *Nerium oleander*, see XXIV 163 and XXV 113.

Thesium, holewort, *Corydalis densiflora*, XXI 107, XXII 66.

Thlaspi, a kind of cress, variously identified with (1) pepperwort, *Lepidium campestre*; (2) shepherd's purse, *Capsella bursa pastoris*; (3) *Cochlearia draba*, and (4) *Lunaria annua*, XXVII 139. In XIX 171 Pliny cites thlaspi as a secondary name for mustard through careless reading of Diosc. 2. 156 W. or his source, and his reference in XXVII 140 to a second type of thlaspi, also called " Persian mustard," is another garbling of the same account.

Thorybethron = leontopodion, XXVI 52.

Thryallis, a secondary name for the third type of phlomis, *s.v.*, XXI 101, XXV 121.

Thryselinum, perhaps a kind of sion, XXV 141.

Thya = thyon, thyine-wood tree, *Callitris quadrivalvis*, XIII 100. See also Citrus.

Thymbra, savory, *Satureia hortensis*, XIX 165.

Thymbraeum = sisymbrium silvestre, XX 247.

Thymelaea, mezerlon, *Daphne mezereum*, XIII 114.

Thymum, (1) garden thyme, *Thymus vulgaris*; (2) Cretan thyme, *Thymbra capitata*, XI

545

INDEX OF PLANTS

Triticum, used in three senses, depending on context, (1) wheat generically, (2) naked wheat generically, and (3) poulard, *Triticum turgidum*, in particular, XVII 72, XVIII 48, 49, 50, 56, 61–70, 76, 79, 81, 82, 85, 89, 94, 97, 98, 102, 104, 106, 116, 155, 164, 165, 166, 184, 189, 191, 198, 202, 298, 299, 304, 305, 307, XIX 17, XX 20, XXI 127, XXII 119, 120, 121, 124, 136, 161, XXIII 23, XXIV 135, XXVII 62, XXXIII 108.

Trixago, germander, *Teucrium chamaedrys*, XXIV 130, XXV 167, XXVI 149.

Trychnos = strychnos, XX 141, XXI 89, 177, XXVII 60.

Trygonis = pastinaca, IX 155.

Tuber, (1) probably a form of the common jujube, *Zizyphus vulgaris*, XII 113, XV 47, XVI 103, XVII 75; (2) truffle, chiefly the black truffle, *Tuber cibarium*, XIX 33–37, 63.

Tuber terrae, a species of *Cyclamen*, XXV 115.

Tus, as a term for a tree, the frankincense-tree, *Boswellia Carteri*, XII 55–57, 67, 76, 81, XVI 136, XIX 187.

Tus terrae = chamaepitys, XXIV 29.

Tussilago, colt's foot, *Tussilago farfara*, XXVI 30, 124, 128, XXXI 44.

Ulex, a shrub like rosemary, XXXIII 76.

Ulmus, elm, *Ulmus sp.*, XI 14, XIII 55, 58, 67, XIV 12, XV 57, XVI 72, 74, 87, 92, 97, 108, 123, 125, 132, 176, 181, 193, 210, 218, 219, 228–230, XVII 65, 76, 77, 90, 116, 124, 200, 201, 210, 252, XVIII 240, 243, 266, 286, XXI 98, XXIV 48. Ulmus atinia, *U. levis*, XVI 72, 108, XVII 200; u. Gallica, *U. levis*, XVI 72; u. Campestris or nostras, common elm, *U. campestris*, ibid.; u. montana or silvestris, Scotch elm, *U. montana*, ibid.

Ulophonon, black type of chamaeleon, *Cardopatium corymbosum*, XXII 47.

Ulpicum, Cyprian garlic, a form of *Allium sativum*, XIX 112.

Ulva, sedge, *Ulva conferva*, XVI 4, XVII 55, 209, XXI 111.

Uncialis, a kind of grape, XIV 42.

Unedo, strawberry-tree, *Arbutus unedo*, XII 15, 37, 67, XIII 120, XV 96, 98, XVI 80, 126, XXIII 151. See Arbutus.

Urceolaris, wall pellitory, *Parietaria officinalis*, XXII 43.

Urtica, the nettle, chiefly the stinging nettle, *Urtica urens*, and the large nettle, *U. dioica*, but also *U. pilulifera*, *U. membranacea*, *U. rupestris*, and *U. atrovirens*, X 163, XVI 91, XXI 92–93 (various kinds), XXII 31–38, XXIV 172, XXVII 81, XXIX 68, XXX 52, 78, 90, XXXII 102, 135; *U. urens*, XV 31. The urtica marina (IX 146, XXVI 88, XXXI 96, XXXII 102, 135, 146) is not a plant, but the sea-nettle.

Uva taminia, the fruit of the tamnus, XXIII 17, 19, XXVI 138, XXVIII 152, 161, XXIX 94, XXX 82.

Vaccinium, whortleberry, *Vaccinium myrtillus*, XVI 77.

547

INDEX OF PLANTS

INDEX OF PLANTS

APPENDIX

Plants described or indicated, but not named.

XII 37: white mangrove, *Avicennia officinalis*.

XII 39; tamarind, *Tamarindus indica*. Also XII 40.

XII 47 (plant in Thrace similar to Indian nard): *Valeriana Dioscoridis*.

XIII 65: *Mimosa asperata* (called aeschynomene in XXIV 167).

XIII 129: a species of dodder, perhaps *Cuscuta filiformis*. Cf. cadytas, XVI 244.

XIII 138: (1) (a leaf like leek) Ligurian grass-wrack, *Posidonia oceanica*; (2) (foliage of bay and thyme) a madrepore.

XVI 221: teak, *Tectona grandis*.

XVI 221: calamander-wood, *Diospyros quaesita*.

XIX 15 (thread made from apples and gourds): cotton-tree, *Gossypium arboreum*, usually called gossipion.

LIST OF DISEASES AND AFFECTIONS MENTIONED BY PLINY

To equate modern diseases with the names used by ancient physicians is a task full of uncertainty. In some cases indeed there is no difficulty; a disease may have such distinctive symptoms, and be so unlike any other, that its description in Celsus or Galen points clearly to one, and only one, diagnosis, examples being intermittent malarial fevers and the common cold. Pneumonia again in both Greek and Latin writings is usually easy to detect (although there is some chance of confusion with acute bronchitis), and so are also dropsy and pleurisy. Often, however, we can do no more than divide into groups: (1) diseases and (2) the ancient names of diseases, and then identify a group from one with a group from the other. Many quite different diseases are so alike symptomatically that identification can be established, even today, only by a microscopic examination conducted with a technique quite unknown to the ancients. Great care is needed with eye diseases and skin diseases, both of which were far more common in earlier days than they are with us, for dust was everywhere and disinfecting cleansing was practically unknown. The principle of grouping is nearly always the safest one to adopt; to attempt more is hazardous. For example, we have on the one hand *collectio*, *furunculus*, *panus*, *vomica* and *tumor*; on the other we have " boil," " abscess," " gathering " and " carbuncle." The group of complaints covered by the Latin terms is nearly, if not quite, the same as that covered by the English, but any attempt to make more specific identification is attended with much uncertainty; perhaps *panus* is the only one we can isolate more completely.

551

LIST OF DISEASES

More important for our appreciation of antiquity than the identification of specific diseases is to ascertain which, if any, modern diseases were unknown in the Hellenistic age. Here the evidence, especially that relating to infectious fevers, is most disappointing. These fevers are endemic in the modern world, and figure largely in treatises on pathology. But the old medical writers—"Hippocrates," Celsus, Galen and the many compilers who succeeded Galen—do not describe, or give treatment for, small-pox, chicken-pox, measles, scarlatina, typhoid or even influenza. The most that can be said is that in isolated clinical histories or in chance aphoristic remarks one or other of them may be referred to; the evidence is strongest for diphtheria. Moreover, in the pseudo-Aristotelian *Problems* (VII 8) it is said that consumption, ophthalmia and the itch are infectious, but that fevers are not. It is difficult to believe that a people who knew that consumption is infectious would have called scarlatina non-infectious if it had been endemic among them.

The Romans borrowed many names of diseases from the Greeks. Usually, of course, the Latin word refers to the same disease as does the Greek, especially in the works of medical writers. But care must be exercised; λέπρα, for instance, seems to be much narrower than *lepra*.

Celsus is by far the most trustworthy authority to follow in identifying the diseases mentioned by Pliny, for both were Romans, both (probably) laymen and nearly contemporaries.

Aegilops.—A lacrimal fistula at the angle near the nose.

Albugo.—An unknown kind of white ulcer on the eye. In XXVI § 160 used of a head ulcer. The word occurs only in the Vulgate Bible and in Pliny.

Alopecia.—A disease in which the hair fell out. Meaning literally "fox mange," it is translated "mange" in the text. It is perhaps unsafe to limit it to the modern alopecia. Celsus (VI 4) has a brief ac-count of it, saying that it occurred in the hair and beard. He distinguishes it from ὄφίασις, probably ring-worm, for this had a winding shape, whereas *alopecia* "*sub qualibet figura dilatatur.*"

Amphemerinos.—Quotidian malaria.

Angina.—An acute swelling in the neck, generally quinsy. A loose term like our "sore throat." Sometimes possibly diphtheria.

LIST OF DISEASES

Apostema.—Greek for abscess.

Argema.—A small white ulcer, partly on the cornea, partly on the sclerotic coat of the eye.

Articularius morbus.—This in XXII 34 is joined to *podagricus*, and so means probably not gout but arthritis.

Asthma.—Apparently only XXVI 34. See also XXV 82.

Atrophus.—"Wasting away," of all such conditions, of which phthisis is one.

Boa.—"A disease when the body is red with pimples," XXIV 53. See also XXVI 120. An exanthem not certainly identified. Shingles is localised. It cannot be, as Hardouin thought, measles, because that disease seems to have been first described by Rhazes.

Cachecta.—A patient who is in a very bad state of health; sometimes a "consumptive" patient is meant.

Cacoethes.—A Greek adjective applied to sores that are very difficult or impossible to cure; "malignant" is the nearest, but not quite exact, equivalent.

Calculus.—Stone or gravel in the bladder.

Caligo.—Dimness of the eyes, hard to distinguish from *nubecula* (film) and *caligatio* (mistiness).

Carbunculus.—In XXVI 5, 6 seems certainly to be anthrax, and Pliny's description resembles that of Celsus V 28, 1. The word was, however, used of minor affections; for example, *carbunculus oculi* is a stye, and it is often used of a bad abscess.

Carcinoma.—Superficial malignant disease, severe forms of which are called *cacoethe.* It seems impossible to distinguish, at least in Pliny, *carcinoma* from *ulcera cacoethe, phagedaena* and *gangraena.*

Cardiacus.—The adjective refers to either disease or patient. Sometimes a simple ailment, heartburn, is referred to, at other times a serious complaint, said by W. G. Spencer on Celsus III 19 to be a kind of syncope. In fact the reference may be to any ailment supposed to be connected with the heart.

Cephalaea.—Aretaeus (III 2) calls this a severe, chronic headache, and says that there are ἰδέαι μυρίαι. Persistent neuralgia, except when it means malarial headache, must be the complaint referred to.

Cerium.—Described by W. G. Spencer on Celsus V 28, 13 as a follicular abscess among hair. Its appearance—κηρίον means "honeycomb"—enables us to distinguish it from *panus* ; it was also often more severe.

Chiragra.—Gout or gouty pains in the hands. But see *podagra.*

Cholera.—Perhaps never Asiatic cholera, but *cholera nostras* and possibly certain types of dysentery and severe diarrhoea. The word is derived from χολή, "bile."

Clavus.—Wart, corn or callus.

Coeliacus morbus.—W. G. Spencer on Celsus IV 19, 1 (last note) says that the author appears to be de-

scribing pyloric spasm and intestinal atony. Cf. Aretaeus IV 7.

Collectio.—The most general term for a boil or abscess, a " gathering."

Colostratio.—Disease of babies caused by the first milk.

Colum.—Colitis, or inflammation of the colon.

Comitialis morbus.—Epilepsy and sometimes other fits.

Condyloma.—A small tumour in the anus due to inflammation. See Celsus VI 18, 8.

Convulsa.—Sprains.

Cotidiana. — Quotidian ague, malaria with fever occurring every day.

Destillatio.—A "running" cold in the head. Sometimes internal catarrh.

Duritia.—An induration, from whatever cause, in any part of the body.

Dysinteria.—Usually dysentery, but probably also severe diarrhoea, however caused.

Dyspnoea.—Difficulty of breathing, however caused.

Elephantiasis.—The usual name of leprosy. See XXVI 7 and 8, where it is said to have quickly died out in Italy.

Enterocele.—Hernia.

Epinyctis.—Either (1) a sore on the eye-lid or (2) an eruption caused by fleas or bugs.

Epiphora.—Running from the eyes as the result of some ailment.

Eruptio.—A bursting out of morbid matter, either through the skin or sometimes in other ways.

Extuberatio.—A fleshy excrescence, perhaps not morbid.

The word apparently occurs only in XXXI 104.

Febris.—Feverishness, or else one of the recognised types of malaria.

Fistula.—Practically synonymous with the modern term.

Flemina.—A severe congestion of blood around the ankles. It is neuter plural.

Fluctio and *fluxus.*—There seems to be little if any difference in the meaning of these words —any flow, but usually a morbid one. Pliny prefers *fluctio.*

Formicatio.—An irritating wart. See Celsus V 28, 14.

Furfur.—Scurf (anywhere).

Furunculus.—A boil, said by Celsus (V 28, 8) not to be dangerous, whereas Pliny (XXVI 125) says that it is sometimes *mortiferum malum.*

Gangraena.—Gangrene, hard to distinguish from *phagedaena* and *ulcera serpentia.*

Gemursa.—A disease the seat of which was between the toes. It is said by Pliny (XXVI 8) to have died out quickly in Italy. See Littré's note.

Glaucoma.—Opaqueness of the crystalline lens.

Gravedo.—The usual term for the common cold.

Gremia.—Rheum.

Hepaticus.—A sufferer from any liver complaint.

Herpes.—A spreading eruption on the skin.

Hydrocelicus.—A sufferer from hydrocele.

Hydropisis.—Dropsy.

Hypochysis.—Cataract.

Ictericus.—A sufferer from jaundice.

Ignis sacer.—Erysipelas. Per-

LIST OF DISEASES

haps also some form of eczema or lupus. Also = shingles.

Ileus.—Severe colic. Possibly appendicitis was included under this term.

Impetigo.—The Romans used this term of various kinds of eczema. Celsus (V 28, 17) mentions four, the last being incurable.

Impetus.—Inflammation or an inflamed swelling; Pliny has *impetus oculorum.* With the genitive of a word meaning a specific disease it denotes an attack of it.

Intertrigo.—Chafing, especially between the legs.

Ischias.—Sciatica.

Laterum dolor.—" Severe pain in the side," nearly always pleurisy.

Lentigo.—Freckles.

Leprae.—Seems to be used of any scaly disease of the skin; Pliny gives cures. There was a kind regarded as incurable, but this is not mentioned by Pliny, who has forty-six references, all to cures.

Lethargus (*lethargia*).—In Hippocrates probably the comatose form of pernicious malaria, but later perhaps also prolonged coma of any kind.

Lichen.—This is said by Pliny (XXVI 2–4) to be a new disease to Italy, usually beginning on the chin. Hence the name *mentagra* (chin disease). Littré diagnoses it as leprosy, but Pliny says (XXVI § 1) *sine dolore quidem illos, ac sine pernicie vitae.* This statement, as Pliny puts it, applies also to *carbunculus* and *elephantiasis,* but Pliny's own account of these diseases is quite inconsistent with *sine pernicie.* So Pliny's remark is carelessly inaccurate, or applies only to *lichenes.*

Lippitudo.—Inflammation of the eye, generally ophthalmia.

Luxata.—Dislocations.

Malandria.—Pustules on the neck.

Melancholicus.—One suffering from melancholia, which included malarial cachexia and many melancholic conditions, even mere nervousness. In fact it included any disease supposed to be caused by " black bile " (μέλαινα χολή).

Mentagra.—In XXVI 2 called a lichen beginning on the chin. See *lichen.*

Nome (pl. *nomae*).—A spreading ulcer, much the same as *ulcus serpens.*

Nubecula.—A cloudy film on the eye, sometimes cataract.

Nyctalops.—One afflicted with night blindness.

Opisthotonus.—The form of tetanus in which the body curves backwards.

Orthopnoea.—Serious asthma, when the patient cannot breathe unless upright.

Panus.—Spencer in a note on Celsus V 18, 19 calls this a " superficial abscess in a hair follicle." It occurred chiefly on the scalp, on the groin and under the arm.

Paronychia (-*um*).—Whitlow.

Parotis.—A swelling of the glands by the ears. Some authorities think that it may have included mumps, which is described in Hippocrates, *Epidemics* 1.

555

LIST OF DISEASES

Perfrictio.—Sometimes a severe chill.

Peripleumonicus.—A sufferer from pneumonia.

Pernio.—Chilblain.

Pestilentia.—Plague; a term as vague as the English, but usually bubonic.

Phagedaena.—Gangrene, hard to distinguish from *gangraena.* In XXVI 100 an abnormal diseased appetite.

Phlegmon.—Inflammation beneath the skin.

Phreniticus.—Properly a sufferer from *phrenitis* or *phrenesis*, pernicious malaria accompanied by raving. It also refers to the symptom when not caused by malaria, for in post-Hippocratic medical works it often seems equivalent to "brain fever." Perhaps sometimes meningitis.

Phthiriasis.—Phthiriasis, skin disease caused by lice.

Phthisis.—Pulmonary consumption.

Pituita.—Excessive mucus, in any part of the body.

Pleuriticus.—A sufferer from pleurisy.

Plumbum in XXV 155, points to the leaden bluish colour of certain eye diseases. Serenus XIV 33: *si vero horrendum ducent glaucomata plumbum.*

Podagra.—Gout or gouty pains in the foot. Sometimes perhaps the result of lead poisoning. See Spencer's *Celsus* I 464. Pliny (XXVI 100) says that the disease was on the increase in his day. The word (often with *chiragra*) refers sometimes to pains caused by senile degeneration.

Porrigo.—Dandruff or scurf (on hairy parts).

Prurigo and *pruritus.*—Itch; the words can scarcely be discriminated, although perhaps *pruritus* tends to be used of the symptom, *prurigo* of the infection.

Psora.—Several skin diseases are included under this term among which are itch and perhaps leprosy.

Pterygium.—An inflammatory swelling at the inner angle of the lower eyelid; another name for it is *unguis*. It also means a whitlow.

Pusula.—Pustule or blister.

Quartana.—Quartan ague, or malaria occurring after intervals of two days. It was reckoned the mildest form of the disease.

Ramex.—Hernia.

Regius morbus.—Jaundice.

Rhagades.—Chaps.

Rheumatismus.—Catarrh, whether of the nose, throat or stomach.

Rosio.—Gnawing pain in the chest or bowels.

Rupta.—Torn muscles etc.

Scabies.—Not our scabies, which is caused by the itch mite, but described by Celsus (V 28, 16) as a hardening of the skin, which grows ruddy and bursts into pustules with itching ulceration. It includes many types of eczema. *Scabies* of the bladder, a disease of which the symptom was scaly concretions in the urine.

Scabritia.—Diseased roughness of fingers, nails, eyes, etc.

Scelotyrbe.—Lameness of the knee or ankle.

556

LIST OF DISEASES

Siriasis.—Probably some form of sunstroke.

Spasma.—Cramp.

Splenicus.—Suffering from enlarged or diseased spleen. Enlargement of the spleen is a common after-effect of repeated attacks of malaria.

Stegna.—See note on XXIII 120.

Stomacace.—Scurvy of the mouth.

Stomachicus.—It is doubtful whether this means "one with stomach trouble" or "one with disease of the oesophagus." It is a word not much used by medical writers, but Caelius Aurelianus has a section on disease of the oesophagus. Although the Romans distinguished (Celsus IV 1) stomach from oesophagus (*stomachus* can mean either), they appear to have described under the same name their morbid conditions. In English "stomach," at least in popular speech, is equally vague.

Stranguria.—Strangury.

Struma.—A scrofulous sore.

Suffusio.—Usually cataract.

Suspiriosus.—Asthmatic. Apparently a popular word, as it is rarely found in the medical writers.

Syntecticus.—One wasting away, from whatever cause.

Tertiana.—Tertian ague, malaria with an onset every other day.

Testa.—A brick-coloured spot on the face. See XXVI 163 and XXVIII 185.

Tetanus.—Tetanus. See Celsus IV 6, 1 with Spencer's notes on *opisthotonus* and *emprosthotonus*.

Tormina (neut. pl.).—A general word for colic. It also sometimes means strangury.

Tremulus.—One with morbid tremors, palsied. See XX 85 *paralyticis et tremulis*.

Tuber.—A hard tumour.

Tumor.—Any morbid swelling.

Tussis.—A cough—the complaint rather than the act.

Tympanicus.—One afflicted with tympanites, a kind of dropsy, which makes the belly swell.

Ulcus.—A favourite word with Pliny, usually used in the plural. *Ulcera manantia* are "running" sores, and *ulcera putrescentia* (*serpentia*) include gangrene and superficial malignant diseases.

Unguis.—Another name for *pterygium*, an inflammatory swelling at the inner angle of the lower eyelid.

Varix.—Varicose vein.

Varus.—A pimple on the face.

Verruca.—Wart, a less wide term than *clavus*.

Vertigo.—Vertigo, usually giddiness caused by illness.

Vitiligo.—This includes more than one kind of psoriasis. The Romans distinguished the dull white, the dark, and the bright white. Sometimes perhaps leprosy.

Vomica.—Abscess; any gathering of pus, but apparently larger than *furunculus*. It was sometimes internal, but *panus* was superficial.

Zoster.—This ("girdle disease") was herpes round the waist, possibly shingles. Pliny calls it a form of erysipelas (*ignis sacer*), XXVI 121.

INDEX OF NAMES

559

INDEX OF NAMES

INDEX OF NAMES

INDEX OF NAMES

561